Securities World

Jurisdictional comparisons   **Third Edition**

General Editor: Willem J L Calkoen
NautaDutilh NV

THE EUROPEAN LAWYER
REFERENCE

General Editor
Willem J L Calkoen

Publisher
Mark Wyatt

International Director
Michele O'Sullivan

Commercial Manager
Katie Burrington

Publishing Services Director
Ben Martin

Publishing and Production Manager
Emily Kyriacou

Sub Editor
Lisa Naylor

Production Editor
Caroline Byrne

Design and Production
Dawn McGovern

Published by
The European Lawyer Publications Ltd
Futurelex Ltd
23-24 Smithfield Street
London EC1A 9LF
T: +44 20 7332 2582
F: +44 20 7332 2599
www.europeanlawyer.co.uk

Printed in the UK by CPI William Clowes Beccles NR34 7TL
ISBN: 978-1-908239-01-3
© Futurelex Limited 2011

Contents

Foreword Willem J L Calkoen   NautaDutilh NV   v

European Union Petra Zijp, Larissa Silverentand, Willem Verschuur & Elvira de Jong   vii
NautaDutilh

Australia Robert Hanley   Mallesons Stephen Jaques   1

Belgium Benoît Feron & Marie-Laure De Leener   NautaDutilh NV   23

British Virgin Islands Jacqueline Daley-Aspinall & Ross Munro   55
Harney Westwood & Riegels

Bulgaria Svetlina Kortenska   Borislav Boyanov & Co   73

Canada Alfred L J Page, David R Surat & Andrew M Bunston   93
Borden Ladner Gervais

England & Wales Robert Boyle & Mark Slade   Macfarlanes   113

Finland Paula Linna, Elisa Heinonen & Essi Rimali   Roschier   147

France Antoine Maffei & Guillaume Touttée   De Pardieu Brocas Maffei   171

Germany Dr. Wolfgang Groß & Dr. Thomas Paul   Hengeler Mueller   193

Ireland Stephen Hegarty   Arthur Cox   219

Italy Marcello Gioscia & Gianluigi Pugliese   Ughi e Nunziante   251

Japan Kunihiko Morishita   Anderson Mori & Tomotsune   269

Luxembourg François Warken & Laurence van Zuylen   Arendt & Medernach   293

Netherlands Arjan J J Pors, Fleur S M van Tilburg, Lotte van de Loo &   309
Pim Heemskerk   NautaDutilh NV

Portugal Ricardo Andrade Amaro & Diana Ribeiro Duarte   Morais Leitão,   329
Galvão Teles, Soares da Silva & Associados

Russia Alexey Andrusenko, Tatyana Boyko, Nikita Gurin, Daria Izotova, Julia
Kulyamina, Elena Kuznetsova, Valentin Osipov, Alexander Rudyakov, Nadezhda   355
Rybinskaya, Irina Skidan, Alexey Vasilyev & Uliana Volina   Egorov Puginsky
Afanasiev & Partners

South Korea Je Won Lee & Mark B Rolfson   Lee & Ko   383

Spain Javier Ybáñez & José Luis Palao   J&A Garrigues   407

Sweden Ola Åhman, Mattias Friberg & Malin Karvonen   Roschier   433

Switzerland Martin Lanz, Lorenzo Olgiati & Philippe Borens   Schellenberg Wittmer   455

USA John B Meade & Jake S Tyshow   Davis Polk & Wardwell   473

Contacts   495

Foreword

Willem J L Calkoen, NautaDutilh NV

Directors of issuers, investor relationship directors and enterprise risk directors work together with their financial advisers, accountants, lawyers, representatives of financial institutions, supervisors and governments to create trust in the securities market. At the same time, they all try to work on establishing cost effectiveness and efficiency to lower the cost of capital. While it is true that balance must be found between the creation and maintenance of trust on the one hand and cost effectiveness on the other, in the end it is trust that is the most important, because the point of capital markets is that the public is prepared to invest money in the activities of entrepreneurs, with the hope of success. The more trust that exists, the higher and more consistent the listed prices will be. We all know that trust must be built up carefully over many years, but its fragility is such that it can be shattered with one event. Modern history has known crises, of which one of the largest took place in September 2008.

Since then, stock exchanges have played an important role in the revival of economies. First by debt capital bonds guaranteed by governments, then in 2009 companies raised the capital they could not borrow from banks using rights issues and in 2010 they raised clean equity and initial public offerings started up again. The stock exchanges of the BRIC countries (Brazil, Russia, India and China) are gradually becoming more important, while the Western stock exchanges are being used increasingly by BRIC corporations. For the convergence that is taking place it is useful to understand the differences. Regulations are being relaxed slightly and there are more special arrangements for smaller start-ups and special acquisition companies. At the same time the thresholds for exemptions for approaching high net worth individuals for capital are being raised.

Unsolicited public tender offers are an important phenomenon that stimulates the market. Several countries have legal defence mechanisms. Now even the British Financial Services Authority, in the aftermath of Kraft's acquisition of icon Cadbury, is proposing higher thresholds for tender offerors.

The first edition of *Securities World* appeared in 2005 after the Internet bubble burst. The second edition appeared after the implementation of many European directives in 2007 and now I am proud to present this third edition after the financial crisis. The idea of *Securities World* is to have a jurisdictional comparison of the key questions: how does one get a listing on the stock exchange and how does one take over a listed company.

Our aim has been to achieve a high quality of content, so that *Securities World* will be seen as an essential reference work in our field. We have had some very favourable comments from stock exchanges around the world that are very happy with this book.

To meet the all-important content quality objective, it was a condition *sine qua non* to attract as contributors colleagues who are among the recognised leaders in the field of securities and takeover law from each jurisdiction. I am very grateful to them for all their unstinting work.

Without the efforts of the European Lawyer we would not have completed the book. I am very grateful to the team at FutureLex Ltd. I am also grateful to Anke Antonissen (of NautaDutilh Rotterdam) who managed the extensive correspondence with our contributors with skill, good humour and patience.

If you as reader have any comments, I would be very grateful to hear from you. Future editions of this work will obviously benefit from your thoughts and suggestions.

Willem J L Calkoen, NautaDutilh
General Editor
Rotterdam, 2011

European Union

NautaDutilh Petra Zijp, Larissa Silverentand,
Willem Verschuur & Elvira de Jong

* Authors' note – the law in this chapter is up to date as of July 2010. More recent developments will be included in the next edition.

1. INTRODUCTION

As a result of the financial crisis, the European Union is currently working on substantial reforms in the financial sector, which will be implemented over the next few years. An overview of the causes of the financial crisis and the actions that have been contemplated was provided in the report of the high-level group on financial supervision in the European Union chaired by Jacques de Larosière in Brussels 25 February 2009 (the De Larosière Report), which will form the starting point of this contribution. The full report can be found on the Europa Web site. Furthermore, this contribution aims to provide an overview of the amendments to existing directives and regulations and new recent directives and regulations, including an overview of legislation which is currently being prepared.

2. THE DE LAROSIÈRE REPORT

The De Larosière Group was set up in 2008 as a result of the financial turmoil, to make recommendations to the Commission on strengthening European supervisory arrangements covering the financial sector, with the objective of establishing a more efficient, integrated and sustainable European system of supervision and also to reinforce the cooperation between European supervisors and their international counterparts.

More specifically, the De Larosière Group was requested to examine the following:

- how the supervision of European financial institutions and markets would best be organised to ensure the prudential soundness of institutions, the orderly functioning of markets and thereby the protection of depositors, policy-holders and investors;
- how to strengthen European cooperation on financial stability oversight, early warning mechanisms and crisis management, including the management of cross-border and cross sectoral risks; and
- how supervisors in the EU's competent authorities should cooperate with other major jurisdictions to help safeguard financial stability on a global level.

The study resulted in 31 recommendations published in the De Larosière Report. The recommendations can be subdivided into:
(i) recommendations regarding the correction of regulatory weaknesses;

(ii) recommendations with a view to the European system of financial supervision; and

(iii) recommendations on how the European Union should contribute to global financial stability. A few of the more important recommendations will be discussed below.

Even though the Basel II Framework (Basel Committee on Banking Supervision, International Convergence of Capital Measurement and Capital Standards, a revised framework, June 2004) entered into force on 1 January 2008, the De Larosière Group was of the opinion that it needs fundamental revision, as this framework seems to have been too based on economic data from the recent past and good liquidity conditions. The De Larosière Group promotes, among other things, the gradual increase of minimal capital requirements, a reduction of pro-cyclicality, stricter rules for off-balance sheet items, tightened norms on liquidity management and strengthened rules for bank's internal control and risk management.

Also, the De Larosière Group considers it important to look into the activities of the 'parallel banking system'. The parallel banking system consists of market parties that are not actually banks, but do perform certain tasks that are traditionally performed by banks. The system encompasses investment banks, hedge funds, other funds, various off-balance sheet items and mortgage brokers in some jurisdictions. Jointly these players on the financial markets potentially have a systemic impact and such institutions can be vulnerable when liquidity evaporates, as these market players generally do not have a deposit base.

It has been proposed by several parties that the European Central Bank (ECB) could play a major role in macro-prudential supervision and micro-prudential supervision. For several reasons the De Larosière Group supports an extended role for the ECB on macro-prudential oversight, but it does not support any role for the ECB for micro-prudential supervision. The ECB forms the centre of the European System of Central Banks and is therefore well placed to perform the task of macro-prudential supervision, which includes making recommendations on macro-economic policy, issuing risk warnings, comparing observations on macro-economic and prudential developments and giving direction to these issues. Together with a newly to-be-established body, the European Systemic Risk Council (ESRC), the ECB should set up an effective risk warning system. Among other things, the ESRC will prioritise and issue macro-prudential risk warnings with a mandatory follow up. Micro-prudential supervision should be reorganised according to the De Larosière Group. It proposes to set up a politically independent European System of Financial Supervisors that operates parallel to the national supervisors, which will continue to carry out the day-to-day-supervision. According to the De Larosière Group, three new financial supervisors should be introduced that replace the currently existing ones. The Committee of European Banking Supervisors should be replaced by the European Banking Authority (EBA); the Committee of European Insurance and Occupational Pensions Supervisors should be replaced by the European Insurance and Occupational Pensions Authority (EIOPA); and the Committee of European Securities Regulators should be replaced by the European Securities and Markets Authority (ESMA). As described above, these supervisory authorities will be working in tandem with the European System of Financial Supervisors, both facilitating micro-economic prudential supervision. In addition, colleges of supervisors should be set up to monitor all major cross-border institutions. Proposals for the introduction of these authorities have already been adopted by the Commission and are currently being read for the first time by the Parliament.

Furthermore, the De Larosière Group recommends stronger regulation of credit rating agencies, more transparency and unity of accounting principles, the equipment of supervisors with sufficient supervisory powers and sufficiently deterrent sanctions, simplification and central clearing of certain derivatives, more common rules on investment funds, the limitation of compensation schemes in the financial sector, more solid internal risk management systems and a better crisis management structure on an EU level. A few of those recommendations have already been translated into various forms of regulation and will be discussed in further detail below.

The De Larosière Group also issued recommendations relating to global financial stability. As the De Larosière Group states, global economic and financial integration has by now reached a level where no country or region can any longer insulate itself from developments elsewhere in the world. There is a need for a coordinated, global policy response not only in the area of financial regulation and supervision, but also in the macro-economic and crisis management field. A start in addressing the weaknesses of the existing financial architecture was made at the G20 summit in Washington on 15 November 2008, whereby agreement was reached on an action plan for the months and years to come. An important aspect of this reform is regulatory consistency. The De Larosière Group considers the Basel Committee and the Financial Stability Forum (the latter in a strengthened form) well placed to promote the convergence of international financial regulation. Another important step is that the cooperation between (national) supervisors should be enhanced.

The report does not address the current discussion on whether the financial sector in the European Union should be rearranged, ie, whether banks and other financial institutions should be subdivided into high-risk departments and low-risk departments. However, the De Larosière Group does recommend introducing appropriate capital requirements for banks owning or operating hedge funds or being otherwise engaged in significant proprietary trading.

3.   RECENT DEVELOPMENTS (AS AT JULY 2010)

The overview below provides short descriptions of both amendments to existing legislation and new legislation, some of which were introduced further to the De Larosière Report.

Prospectus Directive

On 24 September 2009, the Commission published a proposal for the review of the Prospectus Directive (Commission Proposal). The context of the Commission Proposal was formed by: (i) the striving of the Commission for a reduction of administrative burdens on companies within the EU; and (ii) Article 31 of the Prospectus Directive (2003/71/EC), which requires the Commission to assess the application of the Prospectus Directive five years after its entry into force and to present, where appropriate, proposals for its review.

The overarching goal of the Commission Proposal is to simplify and improve the application of the Prospectus Directive, increasing its efficiency and enhancing the EU's international competitiveness, bearing in mind the importance of enhancing the level of investor protection envisaged in the Prospectus Directive and ensuring that the information provided is sufficient and adequate to cover the needs of retail investors, particularly in the context of the financial market turbulence that started in 2007.

After months of discussion on the Commission Proposal between the Commission, the Council and the Parliament, a Directive which will amend the current Prospectus Directive was adopted on 17 June 2010 (Amending Directive). Member states of the European Union are expected to have implemented this Amending Directive by March or April 2012.

A specific part of the Commission Proposal which caused significant debate, was the proposal to remove the current limit of 2,500 words for the summary of the prospectus and for the summary to include 'key information', which enables investors to make comparisons between different products and to make an informed investment decision. The reason for the debate was that the risk of prospectus liability would increase significantly after this amendment. Whereas the current rules provide that civil liability arises if the summary, when read together with the other parts of the prospectus, is misleading, the Commission Proposal stated that civil liability would arise if the summary did not provide key information enabling investors to take informed investment decisions and to compare the securities with other investment products. In the end the current word limit of 2,500 was not removed and no civil liability can be incurred solely on the basis of the summary. After the implementation of the Amending Directive, civil liability can only be incurred if the summary is misleading, inaccurate or inconsistent with the other parts of the prospectus or if it does not provide, when read together with the other parts of the prospectus, key information in order to aid investors when considering investing in such securities. The Amending Directive empowers the Commission to adopt delegated acts wherein the required content of the summary will be described in further detail.

Another important amendment following from the Amending Directive will be that the threshold for 'wholesale' securities shall be set at EUR 100,000 instead of EUR 50,000. This means that while issues of securities with a denomination of EUR 50,000 or more are currently exempted from the obligation to publish a prospectus, from the date of the implementation of the Amending Directive, only issues of securities with a denomination of EUR 100,000 or more are exempted from the requirement to publish a prospectus. In the recital to the Amending Directive, it is explained that the current threshold of EUR 50,000 no longer reflects the distinction between retail investors and professional investors in terms of investor capacity, since it appears that even retail investors have recently made investments of more than EUR 50,000 in one single transaction. On the other hand, the Amending Directive broadens the exemption for offers addressed to natural or legal persons, other than qualified investors, from 100 to 150 persons per member state.

The Commission Proposal also contained a recommendation to extend the validity period of the prospectus from 12 months to 24 months in order to decrease the time and costs that are associated with drafting a prospectus. The Commission reasoned that the prospectus can be kept up to date by way of supplements. In the end this recommendation was not included in the Amending Directive, as the Parliament considered investor protection better secured where investors are not required to consult both a prospectus and various supplements. Related to this topic is the question of what information should be included in the final terms relating to a specific issue and what information should be published by way of a supplement. The Amending Directive clarifies this by stating that final terms shall only contain information that relates to the securities note. Examples of such information are the *International Securities Identification Number,* the issue price, the maturity, the coupon, the exercise date and the redemption price and other terms not known at the time of drawing up the prospectus.

Regarding so-called 'retail cascades', whereby the issuer sells its securities to an investment bank that in turn sells them to retail distributors who sell the securities to their clients, the Amending Directive states that in principle, a valid prospectus drawn up by the issuer or the person responsible for drawing up the prospectus and available to the public at the time of the final placement of securities through financial intermediaries, or in any subsequent sales of securities, should provide sufficient information for investors to make investment decisions. Therefore, financial intermediaries should be entitled to rely on a valid and duly supplemented prospectus if the person responsible for drawing up the prospectus consents to its use by written agreement, whereby conditions may be attached to the consent. Should the person responsible for drawing up the prospectus withhold its consent, the financial intermediary is required to publish its own prospectus.

Another amendment following from the Amending Directive will be a proportionate disclosure regime for offers of shares to existing shareholders who can either subscribe for those shares or sell the right to subscribe for those shares; offers by small and medium sized enterprises; offers by issuers with reduced market capitalisation; and offers of non-equity securities by credit institutions. The newly to-be-established European Securities and Markets Authority will issue guidelines in this respect that will ensure a consistent approach by the competent authorities.

Furthermore, the Amending Directive will make it easier to issue securities to employees, align the Prospectus Directive with certain other directives, prescribe rules on the publication of the prospectus by electronic means and clarify when a supplement should be prepared and when a right of withdrawal exists should such supplement be published.

4. MIFID
General
The Markets in Financial Instruments Directive, or MiFID (2004/39/EC), is the successor to the Investment Services Directive (ISD), which was adopted in 1993. The ISD introduced the European passport for investment firms, which allowed these firms to offer their services in each of the countries of the European Union based upon a licence obtained in their home country. However, as a result of the fact that the ISD was implemented in different manners across the different member states of the EU, investment firms were confronted with local differences when offering their services in the European Union. MiFID was introduced in order to produce an effective 'single passport' regime allowing investment firms and regulated markets to operate across Europe under a common set of rules which enhances the protection of European investors.

The MiFID has been developed in accordance with the Lamfalussy legislative process. This process was introduced in 2001 in order to accelerate the development of new European legislation in the field of financial services. According to the Lamfalussy process, the level 1 measures – MiFID – consist of a framework directive which sets forth the central principles. These principles are worked out in more detail in the level 2 measures. With respect to the MiFID, the principles set forth in the MiFID are further elaborated upon in an Implementation Directive (Directive 2006/73/EC) and an Implementation Regulation (Regulation 1287/2006). These implementing measures add technical detail to the framework provided by MiFID. Both the MiFID and the Implementation Directive had to be implemented in the national laws of the EU member states. The Implementation Regulation did not need to be implemented – it is directly applicable in each EU member state.

Future developments
The Commission was scheduled to review the MiFID during 2010. In preparation for the review, the Committee for European Securities Regulators (CESR) intended to provide technical advice on the review of the MiFID to the Commission in relation to certain areas of the MiFID where CESR has identified a need for improvement. In the first half of 2010, CESR published six consultation papers on its technical advice to the Commission. These consultation papers cover the following topics:
- investor protection and intermediaries;
- transaction reporting;
- equity markets;
- client categorisation;
- standardisation and exchange trading of over-the-counter (OTC) derivatives; and
- transaction reporting and extension of the scope of transaction reporting obligations.

Below we will describe some of the most important amendments to MiFID as set out in the consultation papers of CESR.

4.1 Investor protection and intermediaries

CESR proposes to introduce a requirement to record the telephone conversations and electronic communications of investment firms which receive and transmit orders, execute orders on behalf of a client and deal on its own account. In order to ensure that all conversations and communications can be recorded, employees of investment firms should only be allowed to provide these investments services on equipment belonging to the investment firm. In the recording requirements no differentiation should be made between the different types of financial instruments. Pursuant to the proposal of CESR, it is not necessary for the recording requirement to be applied when investment firms provide portfolio management services or investment advice.

In addition, CESR proposes to oblige regulated markets, multilateral trading facilities (MTFs) and systemic internalisers to produce quarterly reports on the execution quality of liquid shares, including information on prices, costs, volumes, likelihood of execution and speed.

Furthermore, CESR proposes a more graduated risk-based approach to the distinction between complex and non-complex financial instruments. For instance, shares in an investment firm admitted to trading on a regulated market would no longer automatically qualify as non-complex pursuant to CESR's proposals. This is relevant in the context of the appropriateness test, as this test is generally not required in relation to non-complex financial instruments.

Also, CESR seeks to amend the definition of investment advice by clarifying that a recommendation through a distribution channel will qualify as investment advice. The background of this amendment is that the Internet is increasingly used for providing investment advice.

4.2 Equity markets

The main topics addressed in CESR's consultation paper on equity markets relate to improving pre-trade and post-trade transparency for organised markets. In relation to pre-trade transparency CESR seeks to move from a principle based approach to a more rule based approach. Furthermore, CESR proposes to apply transparency obligations to equity-like instruments admitted to trading on a regulated market, including depository receipts, exchange-traded funds or commodities and certificates.

4.3 Transaction reporting

CESR's consultation paper on transaction reporting deals among other things with a number of issues in relation to client identification. For example, CESR proposes to make it mandatory for the competent authorities to collect client identification for all counterparties.

4.4 Client categorisation

With respect to the client categorisation regime, CESR proposes a number of amendments to Annex II.1(1) to MiFID. Firstly, in order to strengthen investor protection it proposes to narrow the range of regulated entities which qualify as clients which can be considered to be professionals. Secondly, CESR proposes to clarify that local authorities do not qualify as public bodies that manage public debts, and as such do not qualify as clients which are considered to be professionals.

Furthermore, CESR states that it believes that some issues with respect to client categorisation should be discussed further:

- Whether investment firms should use tests to assess the knowledge and experience of clients more widely than is currently the case, before such clients could be considered to be professionals.
- Whether the client categorisation rules should be changed with respect to complex products.
- Whether clarification is necessary of the standards which apply to investment firms when dealing with eligible counterparties.

4.5 Standardisation and exchange trading of OTC derivatives

With respect to derivatives which are traded over-the-counter, CESR intends to investigate what measures can be taken in order to provide for further standardisation. CESR is of the opinion that firms should retain flexibility with respect to certain aspects such as standard valuation, payment structures and payment dates. However, CESR believes that a greater standardisation of OTC derivatives might deliver efficiency benefits, for example, by using electronic confirmation systems.

Also, CESR states that it believes that trading of derivatives on organised markets could deliver a number of benefits, such as a higher level of transparency, enhancing liquidity, ensuring efficiency and risk reductions and providing easy access for market participants. CESR wishes to further discuss with market participations what incentives would be required to promote the trading of derivatives on an organised market.

4.6 Transaction reporting and extension of the scope of transaction reporting obligations

The Commission proposed to regulate the clearing of OTC derivatives and to introduce a type of obligation to report OTC derivatives trades to trade repositories. In this respect a distinction should be made between transaction reporting and position reporting. Transaction reporting entails that individual transactions should be reported. Position reporting focuses on the economic exposure of an investor. CESR has identified two possible options for a reporting regime: (i) establish a single reporting regime for both transaction and position reporting on OTC derivatives, based on reporting through trade repositories; or (ii) define a new position reporting regime through trade repositories and allow MiFID transaction reporting through trade repositories. The latter option is currently favoured by CESR.

In addition, CESR proposes to extend the transaction reporting obligations of Article 25 of the MiFID to financial instruments that are admitted to trading only on multilateral trading facilities and to OTC derivatives.

Next steps
Once CESR's consultation on the amendments to the MiFID, including the proposals described above, has been concluded, CESR will provide its advice to the Commission.

Capital Requirements Directive II
On 7 December 2009, a directive amending the Capital Requirements Directive (which comprises Directive 2006/48/EC and Directive 2006/49/EC), commonly referred to as the Capital Requirements Directive II (2009/111/EC) entered into force. The main changes introduced by this Directive relate to capital requirements in respect of large exposures held by banks, cross-border banking groups (including the introduction of colleges of supervisors), the assessment of hybrid capital instruments and risk management of securitisations. National legislation necessary to comply with the Directive must be adopted by 31 October 2010 and applied from 31 December 2010.

Capital Requirements Directive III
Apart from the Capital Requirements Directive II, as described above, other amendments are in the pipeline, which are known as the Capital Requirements Directive III. The proposed amendments, adopted by the Commission in July 2009 include higher capital requirements for re-securitisation positions to reflect the higher risks entailed by such complex products; upgraded standards for securitisation exposures; strengthened capital requirements for the trading book that better reflect the potential losses from adverse market movements under stressed conditions; and rules requiring the adoption of sound remuneration policies that do not encourage or reward excessive risk-taking. The proposed principles on remuneration are not intended to prescribe the amount and form of remuneration and are flexible as to the size and internal organisation of credit institutions and investment firms and the nature, scope and complexity of their activities. Under the proposal, the deadline for the entry into force of the requisite national legislation is 31 December 2010.

Furthermore, the Basel Committee published for consultation a set of proposals with the goal of promoting a more resilient banking sector. The key areas covered by these proposals are: (i) the quality, consistency and transparency of the capital base; (ii) counterparty credit risk exposures arising from derivatives, repos and securities financing; (iii) operational risk; (iv) leverage; and (v) the mitigation of pro-cyclicality. The Basel Committee intends to develop an integrated and fully calibrated set of standards based on these proposals by the end of 2010.

Solvency II Directive
The Solvency II Directive (2009/139/EC), which was adopted on 10 November 2009, sets new solvency requirements for insurance and

reinsurance companies. It recasts 14 existing insurance directives into a single legal text and it intends to reflect the latest developments in prudential supervision, actuarial science and risk management, and to allow for updates in the future. The Solvency II Directive consists of three pillars, being: (i) the quantitative capital requirements; (ii) the own risk and solvency assessment and supervisory review process; and (iii) reporting obligations and disclosure. The implementation deadline for most of the provisions of the Solvency II Directive is 31 October 2012.

Financial Sector Acquisitions Directive

The Financial Sector Acquisitions Directive, which amends the Recast Consolidated Banking Directive, MIFID and several insurance directives, aims to establish harmonised procedural rules and evaluation criteria for the prudential assessment of mergers and acquisitions in the banking, securities and insurance sectors (2007/44/EC). The implementation date of this Directive was 21 March 2009. The Directive states that a party that intends to acquire or increase a holding in a 'regulated financial undertaking' is under the obligation to notify the holding as it transgresses certain thresholds. By making the notification, an assessment procedure will be initiated which imposes a strict time frame for the assessment of the acquisition by the competent authority. In addition, the Financial Sector Acquisitions Directive introduces limitative prudential criteria for such assessment.

Deposit Guarantee Schemes Directive

On 11 March 2009, the Parliament and the Council adopted a Directive (2009/14/EC) which amends Directive 94/14/EC on deposit-guarantee schemes as regards the covering level and the payout delay, as they were of the opinion that the current deposit-guarantee scheme has proved not to be adequate. As the title suggests, the main purposes of this Directive are to increase the coverage level of the deposit-guarantee scheme, to EUR 50,000 by 30 June 2009 and to EUR 100,000 by 31 December 2009, and to shorten the payout delay, from three months with a possible delay of six months to 20 working days which period can only be extended after approval by the competent authorities. Furthermore, where the payout is triggered by a determination of the competent authorities, the decision period, which is currently 21 working days, will be limited to five working days. Member states were required to implement these rules in their respective jurisdictions by 30 June 2009.

Credit Rating Agencies Regulation

On 16 September 2009, the Parliament and the European Council adopted a new regulation on credit rating agencies, the Credit Rating Agencies Regulation (1060/2009) (CRA Regulation), which entered into force on 7 December 2009. Subject to certain exceptions, the CRA Regulation is directly applicable in all member states. The CRA Regulation applies to credit ratings that are issued by credit rating agencies registered in the EU and are disclosed publicly or distributed by subscription.

From 7 December 2010, where a prospectus published under the Prospectus Directive and the Prospectus Regulation refers to a credit rating, the issuer, offeror or party requesting admission to trading on a regulated market must ensure that the prospectus specifies whether the rating has been issued by a credit rating agency established in the EU and registered in accordance with the CRA Regulation.

In addition, as from that same date, credit institutions, investment firms, insurance undertakings, assurance undertakings, reinsurance undertakings, undertakings for collective investment in transferable securities (UCITS) and institutions for occupational retirement provision may use credit ratings for regulatory purposes only if they are:

- issued by a credit rating agency established in the EU and registered in accordance with the CRA Regulation; or
- issued in a non-EU country and endorsed by a credit rating agency established in the EU and registered in accordance with the CRA Regulation (such an endorsement may only be given if certain criteria are met).

Also, conflicts of interest have been identified as a key area of concern within the credit rating business. The CRA Regulation requires credit rating agencies to comply with various measures aimed at the avoidance of conflicts of interest, or at least the adequate management of those that are unavoidable.

Another important objective of the CRA Regulation is to improve the methodologies used by credit rating agencies. By September 2010, CESR should have issued guidance on common standards for the assessment of whether credit rating methodologies meet these requirements.

Credit rating agencies are required to submit their application for registration no earlier than 7 June 2010 and agencies already operating in the EU before this date must apply by 7 September 2010 and must adopt all necessary measures to comply with the CRA Regulation by that date.

Payment Services Directive

The Payment Services Directive (2007/64/EC), which entered into force on 25 December 2007, aims to establish a modern and coherent framework for payment services across the EU. The directive lays down rules in two areas: (i) a licensing regime for payment service providers; and (ii) conduct of business requirements for payment service providers (including obligations to provide information).

The deadline for implementation of the directive in national law was 1 November 2009.

Under the Payment Services Directive, it is prohibited to conduct the business of payment service provider without a licence from the relevant national regulator. Payment services include services in relation to:

- the placement of cash on, and withdrawal cash from, a payment account;
- the execution of various types of payment transactions, such as credit

transfers and automatic direct debits;
- the issuance and/or acquisition of payment instruments; and
- money transfers.

A payment service provider that has obtained a licence will be allowed to provide such services in the whole of the EEA on the basis of a 'European passport'. If payment services are provided by a credit institution, a separate licence is not required. Credit institutions may provide payment services pursuant to their banking licence, provided that this licence allows them to provide such services.

The conduct of business requirements apply to both credit institutions and licensed payment institutions. Most notable are the provisions on the maximum period for the execution of payment transactions and the maximum period for value dating.

The directive is supplementary to the initiative of the European banking sector to create a Single Euro Payment Area (SEPA). In this context, European banks have drawn up standards and have been developing the technical infrastructure to make electronic payments across the euro zone – eg, by credit card, debit card, bank transfer or direct debit – as easy as payments within one country. A first step was taken in January 2008, with the introduction of the SEPA credit transfer. On 2 November 2009, the European Payments Council (EPC), the decision-making and coordination body of the European Banking industry in relation to payments, launched the SEPA Business-to-Business Direct Debit Scheme. It is anticipated that SEPA will become fully operational in the course of 2010.

Electronic Money Institutions Directive

The new Electronic Money Institutions Directive (2009/110/EC), which entered into force on 30 October 2009, repeals the original Electronic Money Directive and updates the regime applicable to electronic money institutions in a number of ways. Its aims are to provide a clear legal framework designed to strengthen the internal market while ensuring an adequate level of prudential supervision, remove unnecessary or disproportionate barriers to market entry and ensure greater consistency with the Payment Services Directive.

Important changes include:
- the minimum amount of initial capital that electronic money institutions must hold has been lowered from EUR 1 million to EUR 350,000;
- new rules on the calculation of own-funds have been introduced; and
- the exclusivity principle has been abolished, thereby making it easier for electronic money institutions to engage in other business activities.

The Electronic Money Institutions Directive must have been implemented into national law no later than 30 April 2010.

Market Abuse Directive

The Commission held a public hearing on the review of the Market Abuse Directive (2003/6/EC) on 2 July 2010 in Brussels. The conference brought together senior policymakers, regulators, industry experts and academics, whereby four panels discussed the main issues in the ongoing review of the Market Abuse Directive. Following this conference, a consultation document was published by the Commission on 25 June 2010. In short, the following key objectives are thereby pursued:

- to increase market integrity and investor protection by extending the scope and modernising the legislative framework where necessary;
- to strengthen effective enforcement;
- to increase cost-effectiveness by reducing national discretions and introducing more harmonised standards;
- to improve the transparency, supervisory oversight, safety and integrity of the derivatives markets; and
- to increase the coordination of action among national regulators and reduce the risk of regulatory arbitrage.

Transparency Directive

On 27 May 2010, the Commission published a report on the operation of the Transparency Directive (2004/109/EC), accompanied by a consultation document, which is the basis for a public consultation on possible ways forward to modernise the transparency regime for listed companies. At the same time, the Commission has published a staff working document, which analyses in detail the impact of the Directive and the issues emerging from its application. In its consultation document, the Commission specifically asks for opinions regarding the attractiveness of regulated markets for small listed companies, the transparency on corporate ownership and diverging implantations of the Transparency Directive. The consultation period lasts until 23 August 2010, following which a proposal for amendments can be expected.

Alternative Investment Fund Managers Directive

On 30 April 2009, the Commission published a proposal for a directive on managers of alternative investment funds. The proposed directive provides for far-reaching changes to the supervision of managers of non-UCITS funds. The funds covered by the directive include not only hedge funds and private equity funds, but also real estate funds, equity funds and funds of funds, among others. The proposed directive refers to all these types of funds as alternative investment funds (AIFs).

At present, only UCITS are subject to specific harmonised rules at EEA level. Other types of investment funds are, in most cases, regulated solely (if at all) at national level. The proposed directive will change this situation by introducing extensive harmonised rules for managers of AIFs. The subjects covered by these rules include the following:

- an obligation for all AIF managers operating in the EEA to obtain authorisation from the competent authority of their home member state for the marketing and management of the relevant AIF(s);
- a 'European passport' system for AIF managers;
- conduct of business obligations and capital requirements for AIF

managers;
- the valuation of the assets required by the AIF and of the AIF's shares or units;
- the appointment, tasks and liability of a depositary;
- the delegation by the AIF managers of their functions;
- disclosure requirements (eg notification of controlling influence in companies);
- leverage limits; and
- third country issues (ie issues concerning non-EEA countries).

Since its publication in April 2009, the proposed directive has been the subject of considerable criticism and fierce debate because of its significant implications for AIF managers, AIFs and investors globally. The Commission, Parliament and the Council are currently working towards a common position and common text. If political consensus is reached, the directive could come into force in 2012.

Australia

Mallesons Stephen Jaques Robert Hanley

1. GENERAL DESCRIPTION OF THE CAPITAL MARKETS
The Australian capital market provides for domestic and foreign capital
in the form of ordinary equity, debt and other securities. The primary
stock exchange in Australia is the Australian Securities Exchange which is
operated by ASX Limited (ASX). This was formed by the amalgamation of
six independent stock exchanges that formerly operated in the state capital
cities and the Sydney Futures Exchange.

2. REGULATORY STRUCTURE
2.1 Regulatory Framework
The Corporations Act 2001 (Cwlth) (CA) provides a general framework of
combined legislation for prudential supervision and conduct supervision.
The CA and regulations pursuant to the CA govern the offering of securities,
supervision of financial institutions (banks, insurers, collective investment
schemes etc.), the provision of services by financial institutions (eg,
securities brokers or portfolio managers) and public takeover bids.
Listed entities must comply with the ASX Listing Rules ('Listing Rules') and
various regulatory guides, information releases and class orders issued by the
corporate regulator, the Australian Securities and Investments Commission
(ASIC), as well as the CA.

2.2 Financial Services Licencing Requirements
All persons carrying on a financial services business in Australia are required
to have an Australian financial services licence (AFS licence) or have the
benefit of an exemption from this requirement.

AFS licences are issued by ASIC on satisfaction of the relevant licensing
application criteria. Licence applications can require quite extensive proofs
in support. Licence holders have an extensive range of obligations imposed
on them.

Breaches of the AFS licence regime can lead to criminal sanctions and
the possibility that unlicensed Australian counterparties can rescind
transactions.

Under the CA and its regulations:
* a financial service provider may be deemed to carry on a financial
  services business in Australia even though it has no physical presence in
  Australia; and
* there are general licensing exemptions for a financial service provider
  only dealing with institutional Australian counterparties (eg, Australian

banks, financial services licence holders, insurers and fund managers), these will generally only apply to services provided from outside of Australia.

Lenders are generally not covered by this licensing system, but most other types of financial services are covered (eg, deposit taking, foreign exchange contracts, derivatives, custody, managed investments, stock broking, insurance and superannuation). This also includes wholesale over-the-counter treasury and derivative trading, potentially even by entities who would consider themselves end-users of these products.

Foreign companies which may be affected by the AFS licence regime include those which:

- enter into spot, swap, repo, option or forward transactions in currency, commodities, metals, rates and indexes with persons in Australia through either the over-the-counter markets or through automated dealing systems;
- issue securities, shares, stocks, deposits, debentures, bonds, managed investment products or insurance to persons in Australia;
- effect secondary market trades in securities, shares, stocks, debentures, bonds or managed investment products as an agent or trustee of a person in Australia;
- whilst acting as an agent or trustee of a third person, enter into secondary market trades in securities, shares, stocks, debentures, bonds or managed investment products with counterparties who are persons in Australia;
- provide giro post or other electronic non-cash payment facilities to persons in Australia; or
- hold securities, shares, stocks, debentures, bonds, managed investment products, or interests in such products, on trust for persons in Australia.

Exemptions may be available to foreign financial service providers. These can include:

- transactions arranged or effected by an AFS licensee;
- certain products or services offered to Australian wholesale clients by financial services providers who are regulated by certain approved foreign regulators, such as the US Securities and Exchange Commission (SEC), the UK Financial Services Authority (FSA), the Monetary Authority of Singapore or the Securities and Futures Commission in Hong Kong, and who comply with other applicable conditions so as to qualify for this relief;
- certain foreign service providers who are not otherwise carrying on business in Australia and who only provide limited financial services to Australian wholesale or professional investor clients from outside Australia; and
- supplementary services to an Australian client in relation to a product issued and acquired outside Australia.

The exact scope of these exemptions is technical and complex. Much depends on the individual circumstances of the relevant financial services provider.

The Australian financial services regime differentiates between retail and wholesale clients. There are significant additional disclosure and conduct requirements where financial services are provided to retail clients.

In addition, persons who operate financial markets in Australia must obtain an Australian market licence or fall within an exemption from this requirement. In certain circumstances, this market licensing regime may affect foreign companies that operate markets in financial products in which Australian persons are participants.

3.   OFFERING OF SECURITIES OR HAVING SECURITIES ADMITTED TO TRADING ON A REGULATED MARKET

3.1   Australian Securities Law Regulation

Issues of securities in Australia are regulated by the CA, while the administration and enforcement of the CA is vested in ASIC. The provisions of the CA relating to offers of securities apply to offers of securities that are received in Australia, regardless of where any resulting issue, sale or transfer occurs. They do not have extra-territorial application, so do not apply to offers of securities received outside Australia.

3.2   Other requirements

A person must not offer or invite applications for the issue, sale or purchase of shares, debentures or other securities in Australia (including an offer or invitation which is received by a person in Australia), unless a prospectus or other disclosure document complying with CA requirements has been lodged with ASIC, unless an exemption applies.

3.3   Exemptions

The exemptions to the prospectus regime are based on types of issuers or investors. Of most relevance to the domestic capital markets in Australia is that the requirement to issue a prospectus or other disclosure document does not apply where the relevant securities are issued for a consideration of at least A$500,000 per offeree. There is also no requirement for a prospectus where the investor is either a:

- Sophisticated Investor – Certified as having net assets of at least A$2.5 million or gross income for each of the last two financial years of at least A$250,000; or
- Professional Investor – Professional Investors are defined in the CA and include an AFS licensee , certain bodies regulated by the APRA, a person who has or controls at least A$10 million (including any amount held by an associate or under a trust and/or a superannuation fund that the person manages), a listed entity, or a related body corporate of a listed entity.

In addition, a prospectus is not required for offers of securities issued by an Australian bank or a registered life insurance company or by Australian governments and certain semi-government authorities.

4. SUPERVISORY AUTHORITIES
4.1 Australian Prudential Regulation Authority (APRA)

APRA is the prudential regulator of the Australian financial services industry. It oversees banks, credit unions, building societies, general insurance and reinsurance companies, life insurance, friendly societies and most members of the superannuation industry.

The chief task of APRA is to ensure that organisations in the Australian financial services industry manage their risk appropriately so that they are able to meet their financial commitments as they fall due and so that the stability of the financial system is not threatened. APRA focuses on prudential supervision which includes creating and enforcing standards in the industry, advising the Commonwealth Government regarding regulatory policy and protecting the stability of the financial system from being threatened by ill-advised or fraudulent behaviour by financial services companies.

APRA's regulatory approach is risk-based; targeting limited resources to where they are required most and consulting with industry as appropriate. Its goal is to be 'in line with best international practice' and regulate the financial sector in a consistent and efficient manner. Under the Australian Prudential Regulation Authority Act 1998 (Cth) (APRA Act). APRA's supervision of bodies in the financial sector is required to 'balance the objectives of financial safety and efficiency, competition, contestability and competitive neutrality'.

4.2 ASIC
Regulatory role

ASIC regulates consumer protection in the financial sector and seeks to build confidence in financial sector companies specifically, and in the system as a whole. ASIC has responsibility for managed investment schemes and consumer protection issues relating to all financial services providers (including APRA-regulated entities such as banks). One of ASIC's chief roles is to protect consumers in the financial system against unfair practices and misleading or deceptive conduct.

The CA provides a single licensing system for financial service providers who carry on a financial services business. It also made ASIC the regulator of all financial service providers in Australia.

5. OFFERING DOCUMENTATION OR PROSPECTUS REQUIREMENTS
5.1 'Reasonable investor' test

The CA specifies that a prospectus must contain all the information investors and their professional advisers would reasonably require to make an informed assessment of:
(a) the assets and liabilities, financial position and performance, profits and losses, and prospects of the company; and
(b) the rights and liabilities attaching to the shares.

Information must be disclosed only:
(a) to the extent to which it is reasonable for investors and their professional advisers to expect to find the information in the prospectus; and
(b) if a relevant person actually knows it or ought reasonably to have obtained the information.

Information cannot be withheld from the prospectus because it is confidential.

5.2 Specific disclosure requirements
Specific disclosure requirements include:
(a) the terms and conditions of the offer;
(b) the interests held by directors, proposed directors, underwriters, promoters and advisers during the last two years;
(c) the payments and benefits to directors or proposed directors to induce them to become directors of the company;
(d) the payments and benefits to directors, proposed directors, underwriters, promoters and advisers in relation to the offer;
(e) statements that consents have been obtained from persons who have provided reports or statements which are included in the prospectus or on which statements in the prospectus are based;
(f) that an application for listing has been made or will be made within seven days; and
(g) the date of the prospectus and expiry date of the offer.

5.3 'Clear, concise and effective' requirement
The information in a prospectus must be worded and presented in a clear, concise and effective manner. ASIC may issue a stop order if it is satisfied the prospectus does not meet this standard. Disclosure should:
• be as short as possible and not contain extraneous information;
• highlight key information and organise information in a logical way;
• use navigation aids and consider the typeface and layout;
• focus on the needs of different audiences;
• consider incorporating technical and detailed financial information by reference;
• use plain language and avoid jargon; and
• use a range of communication tools.

5.4 Materiality
Usually, the company's accountant provides a letter advising on an appropriate level of materiality to be used for the due diligence process. A specially formed due diligence committee comprising representatives of the company and its advisers then adopts qualitative and quantitative materiality guidelines for the due diligence process.

5.4.1 Qualitative materiality
The need for a qualitative materiality assessment arises from the judgment

requirement in the general disclosure test in the CA.

The general test for qualitative materiality will be to assess whether there is a substantial likelihood that a reasonable investor would consider that the matter would influence the investment decision.

For this test, it is important at an early stage of the due diligence process that all those involved understand who is likely to be the 'typical' reasonable investor for the offer.

5.4.2 Quantitative materiality

A quantitative materiality assessment may be undertaken in respect of financial matters in addition to, but not in substitution for, the qualitative assessment. Accounting standards provide that information is material if its omission, misstatement or non-disclosure has the potential, individually or collectively, to:

- influence the economic decisions of users taken on the basis of the financial reports; or
- affect the discharge of accountability by the management or governing body of an entity.

Materiality is assessed using the following quantitative methodology:

- an amount equal to or more than 10 per cent of an appropriate base amount should be presumed to be material unless there is evidence or a convincing argument to the contrary; and
- an amount equal to or less than 5 per cent of an appropriate base amount ought to be presumed to be immaterial unless there is evidence or a convincing argument to the contrary.

The level between 5 per cent and 10 per cent of an appropriate base amount is considered to be a subjective area. These guidelines are indicative only and the qualitative test referred to above is an overriding requirement.

5.5 Prospects, forecasts and forward looking statements

The CA does not require the provision of a financial forecast. However, the requirement to disclose information about a company's prospects often translates into the provision of a financial forecast prepared by the directors in the form of a profit and loss and cash flow statement for one or more future financial periods. Particular care must be taken in relation to the preparation of statements about future matters, such as profit forecasts.

ASIC has indicated that the general test for whether to include prospective financial information is whether it is relevant to its audience and whether it is reliable.

The key issue for those involved in preparing the prospectus is whether there are reasonable grounds for making the financial forecast. The CA provides that a person is taken to make a misleading statement about a future matter if they do not have reasonable grounds for making the statement.

The forecast period should be based on the financial year of an issuer to allow comparison with results of previous periods. Forecasts are usually for a period of one to two years.

ASIC requires any financial forecast to be accompanied by details of any underlying assumptions, the length of the forecast period, the risks of not achieving the forecast and an explanation of how the forecast was calculated (including the reasons for any departures from accounting or industry standards). A sensitivity analysis is also normally expected showing the impact of changes on the key assumptions.

It is market practice for an investigating accountant to be commissioned to give an opinion on the assumptions underlying the forecast. This is often in the form of a 'negative assurance', that is a confirmation that nothing has come to the attention of the accountant to suggest that the assumptions underlying the forecast are unreasonable.

In circumstances where there are no reasonable grounds for making a financial forecast, the prospectus should still contain a general narrative disclosure about the prospects of the company, including an explanation as to why a financial forecast would not be reliable.

5.6 Accountants' report
The prospectus will include an accountants' report on the historical financial information for, and prospects of, the company. The accountants also report on the directors' forecasts. The historical financial information is presented in a pro forma basis derived from audited and unaudited consolidated financial statements and accounting records.

6. LISTING
6.1 General listing requirements for securities
A company seeking to list must satisfy the Listing Rules requirements relating to size, profitability and shareholder spread (see paragraph 6.2 below). The company must also ensure that its structure and constitution are consistent with the Listing Rules. The Listing Rules not only bind listed entities contractually, but also can be enforced under the CA.

A listing application must be made to ASX within seven days, and the shares must be quoted within three months of the date of the prospectus. ASX has discretion as to whether to list a company. Issues it may take into account include the terms of any asset-management services contracts, the existence of pre-emptive rights or change of control provisions, board appointment rights and other 'unusual' arrangements for a listed entity.

Depending on the circumstances, a company may seek waivers of particular Listing Rules. This is at the discretion of ASX and may be granted subject to conditions, which must be complied with for the waiver to be effective. In deciding whether to grant a waiver ASX takes into account the policy surrounding the Listing Rules.

6.2 Additional listing requirements for shares
A company seeking to float must satisfy ASX's Listing Rules relating to size, profitability and shareholder spread. The listing criteria differ depending on the basis for the company's listing application, namely:

- the Profits Test (aggregate operating profits of A$1 million for the last three financial years, and A$400,000 in last 12 months), with the main business activity of the company being the same for the last three years; or
- the Assets Test for non-investment companies (net tangible assets of A$2 million, after offer costs, or market capitalisation of A$10 million) with working capital of A$1.5 million, and certain limits on cash assets; or
- the Assets Test for investment companies (net tangible assets of A$15 million, after offer costs).

In each case, ASX will require the company to provide three full years of audited financial accounts (with audit reports).

6.3 ASX approval and pre-quotation conditions

ASX will initially give a conditional approval of an application for listing. ASX will identify certain requirements to be fulfilled for listing and quotation to proceed. These must be satisfied shortly before the scheduled listing date, and usually include:

(a) providing undertakings and indemnities to ASX regarding compliance with the Listing Rules, and consequences of quotation;

(b) signing up to the ASX online agreement, which enables access to ASX's electronic disclosure lodgement platform and making announcements to ASX; and

(c) providing pre-quotation disclosure to ASX, which includes:
    (i) a distribution analysis of shareholder allocations, which should indicate that the company has satisfied ASX's shareholder 'spread' requirements (for example 500 shareholders with at least A$2,000 worth of shares each);
    (ii) a list of the top 20 shareholders;
    (iii) details of any voluntary or mandatory shareholder restriction/ lockup arrangements (eg, for founding shareholders); and
    (iv) if not included in the prospectus, a description of the company's corporate governance arrangements indicating whether or not those arrangements comply with the ASX Corporate Governance Council's 'Corporate Governance Principles and Recommendations' (ASX Recommendations).

6.4 Corporate structure and share capital

There are specific requirements relating to corporate structure and share capital which must be met before listing. For example:

(a) A company must be a public company in order to offer its shares to the public and seek listing. A non-public company must convert to a public company, and adopt a public company constitution consistent with the CA, Listing Rules and approved by ASX. Both of these steps require shareholder approval.

(b) The share capital of the company may need to be restructured so that after listing:
    (i) there will be an appropriate number of shares on issue;

(ii) there is only one class of ordinary shares on issue (unless ASX approves another class or the additional class is partly paid shares which would be in the same class as ordinary shares if fully paid); and

(iii) the minimum issue price per share is achieved.

7.   CONTINUING OBLIGATIONS

7.1   Continuous disclosure

Once listed, the company is subject to the continuous disclosure regime in the Listing Rules and CA.

The company must disclose to ASX any information regarding the company that a reasonable person would consider to have a material effect on the price or value of its shares as the company becomes aware of the information. This includes disclosures required to correct or prevent a false market in the shares (whether as a result of market speculation, press comment or otherwise) and information regarding capital, options, change of office location or registers and changes of directors. There are limited carve-outs available (for example, for incomplete, confidential or trade secret information). The civil penalties for non-compliance with the continuous disclosure requirements have increased and ASIC has been given powers to fine entities who have not complied with the requirements.

Most listed entities adopt rigorous monitoring and reporting systems to enable price-sensitive information to be identified and disclosed in a timely fashion. The company must also appoint a communications officer.

7.2   Periodic disclosure and financial reporting

The CA and the ASX Listing Rules set out the requirements for periodic reporting, including content requirements for full-year and half-year financial reports, directors' reports, and the auditor's report. Reports must be given to ASIC and ASX.

A listed company must provide or make available to shareholders either a hard or electronic copy of a full or concise annual report (at each shareholder's election) in respect of each financial year. The annual report must include a remuneration report and a corporate governance statement disclosing the extent to which the company has followed the ASX Recommendations during the reporting period and, if not, why not.

The financial statements must give a true and fair view of the financial position and performance of the company or consolidated group. Importantly, there are also requirements to identify the senior ranks of the executive team and disclose details of their remuneration package, including share plan entitlements and other performance incentive components.

8.   CORPORATE GOVERNANCE

8.1   Sources

Companies and trusts, particularly those listed on ASX, are subject to a large range of corporate governance requirements and guidelines in Australia. These arise from various sources including:

- the CA;
- the ASX Listing Rules;
- the ASX Corporate Governance Council's 'Corporate Governance Principles and Recommendations' (ASX Recommendations);
- prudential standards issued by APRA for regulated financial and superannuation institutions, including banks, building societies and insurers; and
- other industry standards which are adopted voluntarily, often in line with those adopted in the United States (US) and United Kingdom (UK).

The Australian market has high expectations of corporate governance compliance, with most major corporations and other entities aiming to comply with governance requirements, recommendations and standards.

8.2 The board of directors

Most listed entities in Australia have boards of directors which comprise more non-executive, independent directors than executive non-independent directors. It is rare in Australia for the chairperson of a listed entity to hold an executive position with the entity. The ASX Recommendations make various recommendations regarding director selection, appointment and independence of directors and also the role of the chairman. From the start of a listed entity's financial year on or after 1 January 2011, it should also have a diversity policy addressing gender diversity on the board, in senior management and throughout the entity.

Generally, directors may delegate any of their powers to another director, a committee of directors, an employee of the company or any other person. Large boards will often operate through board committees. Consistent with the ASX Recommendations, larger listed entities tend to establish board committees to address oversight of audit, risk, compliance, nomination and remuneration issues.

8.3 Directors' duties

Directors' duties in Australia are prescribed by legislation, in particular the CA, and an extensive body of case law (common law). As fiduciaries, directors owe stringent duties:

- of honesty;
- to exercise care and diligence;
- to act in good faith in the best interests of the company and for a proper purpose;
- not to improperly use their position or company information; and
- to disclose their material personal interests and avoid conflicts of interest.

Directors have duties regarding financial and other reporting and disclosure and can be liable under various laws including for breaches of fund raising, anti-money laundering, environmental, trade practices, privacy, and occupational health and safety laws. If the company they manage is in financial distress, there are duties and issues that the directors must address with particular care and consideration.

Some defences are available to directors including under the business judgment rule in certain circumstances, for reliance in good faith after making an independent assessment and for appropriate delegation. Directors can be granted indemnities from companies (subject to certain constraints) and companies often take out D&O (directors' and officers') insurance to cover directors' liabilities. Breaches of directors' duties carry a range of fines or terms of imprisonment or both.

8.4   Disclosure obligations
8.4.1 Financial and other reporting
All listed entities must prepare and lodge an annual audited financial report and an audited or audit-reviewed half-year financial report. Shareholders are entitled to receive either a hard copy of those reports or a notice of where they can view an electronic copy, depending on the election made by the shareholder. These reports must comply with Australian accounting standards and also, in the case of many major corporations whose securities are listed in the US or the UK, with the accounting standards for those jurisdictions. All directors (executive and non-executive) are responsible for the entity's financial reports being accurate and complying with accounting standards. The CA requires that the Chief Executive Officer and the Chief Financial Officer of a listed entity sign-off on the reports to the rest of the board of directors.

Listed entities must describe their corporate governance practices in detail in their annual reports. They must report on whether they comply with the ASX Recommendations and, if not, why not.

Unlisted companies and registered schemes must also prepare annual financial reports and directors' reports each financial year. There is an exception for small proprietary companies unless they have been controlled by a foreign company for all or part of the year. 'Disclosing entities' must also comply with half-yearly financial reporting obligations.

8.4.2 Continuous disclosure
Listed entities and the responsible entities of listed schemes must fully disclose price-sensitive information to the market (via announcements made to ASX) as soon as they become aware of the information. There are limited carve-outs available (eg, for information that is incomplete and remains confidential). The civil penalties for non-compliance with the continuous disclosure requirements are significant and ASIC has been given powers to fine entities which have not complied with the requirements. Most listed entities adopt rigorous monitoring and reporting systems to enable price-sensitive information to be identified and disclosed in a timely fashion.

Unlisted 'disclosing entities' must provide similar information to ASIC.

9.   MARKET ABUSE
9.1   Insider trading
The CA includes insider trading prohibitions which apply to all persons. If a person has inside information (as defined in paragraph 9.2 below) relating to

a company it is illegal to:

(a) deal in or procure another person to deal in (that is, apply for, acquire or dispose of) that company's securities or options over a company's securities or enter into an agreement to do so; or

(b) directly or indirectly communicate, or cause to be communicated, that information to any other person if the person knows, or ought reasonably to know, that the other person would or would be likely to use the information to engage in the activities specified in the paragraph above.

It does not matter how or in what capacity a person becomes aware of the inside information, nor does the inside information have to be obtained from the company.

Breach of the insider trading laws may result in civil as well as criminal penalties.

9.2 What is inside information?

'Inside information' is information relating to a listed company which is not generally available but, if it were generally available, it would be likely to have a material effect on the price or value of the company's securities. Inside information can include matters of speculation or supposition and matters relating to intentions or likely intentions of a person.

Information is regarded as being likely to have a material effect if it would, or would be likely to, influence persons who commonly invest in securities or other traded financial products in deciding whether or not to deal in the company's securities.

9.3 Market manipulation

The CA contains prohibitions on market manipulation:

* carrying out a transaction or causing a transaction to be carried out, in financial products, which creates or maintains an artificial price for the product;

* creating a false or misleading appearance of active trading in financial products, which secures the price of such financial products at an artificial level;

* engaging in conduct in relation to a financial product or service which is misleading or deceptive or likely to mislead or deceive; and

* disseminating information which gives or is likely to give a false or misleading signal as to the supply of, demand for or price of financial instruments while the person disseminating the information knows or should reasonably know that the information is incorrect or misleading.

Breach of these prohibitions may result in civil as well as criminal penalties.

10. MUTUAL OR INVESTMENT FUNDS

10.1 Background on trusts

Businesses in Australia may be carried on through a trust as well as by a company. A trustee owns the assets of the business and carries on the trading activities on behalf of the beneficiaries of the trust. The trustee may be an individual or a corporation.

The type of interest which the beneficiaries have in the profits and assets of the business may vary. Traditionally, trusts have been divided into fixed trusts, unit trusts and discretionary trusts. Most large trusts provide for the beneficiaries to hold units in them, with the entitlements being similar to those attaching to shares in a company (although there are important differences). Trusts may be private or public. Public trusts can be listed on ASX.

10.2 Managed investment schemes

A managed investment scheme is a common trust structure which allows people to pool funds for a common purpose in order to make a profit. The contributors to the fund have no day-to-day control of the scheme. The trustee for the scheme, called the responsible entity, requires an AFS licence. If the scheme has more than 20 members, the scheme must (in most cases) be registered with ASIC. There are additional compliance and disclosure obligations for a registered scheme, as well as increased liability for the responsible entity and its officers.

10.3 Mutual recognition of managed investment schemes

Australia has entered into mutual recognition arrangements with New Zealand, the US, Hong Kong and Singapore. The terms of the arrangements vary but the Australian government has indicated that it proposes to maximise mutual recognition and develop a framework to promote investment between jurisdictions subject to the integrity of the markets and protection of investors.

Foreign schemes regulated by certain authorities (the UK FSA; the US SEC, Federal Reserve, Office of Comptroller of the Currency and Commodity Futures Trading Commission; the Monetary Authority of Singapore; the HK Securities and Futures Commission; and the German BaFin) may be able to take advantage of ASIC 'passport relief' from AFS licence requirements regarding providing financial services to wholesale clients in Australia.

ASIC has also enabled interests in certain foreign schemes to be offered to retail clients in Australia without Australian registration. This applies to foreign schemes authorised in a foreign jurisdiction recognised by ASIC and which satisfy the applicable conditions.

11. NOTIFICATION OBLIGATIONS

The CA requires that a person notify a listed entity and the ASX of a 'relevant interest' in 5 per cent of the voting securities of the listed entity (a 'substantial holding') within two business days of becoming aware of the interest. The concept of relevant interest is defined very broadly and (subject to certain exceptions) essentially picks up all shares over which a person has influence – in terms of the voting or acquisition or disposal of those shares. This obligation to give notification also applies to any 1 per cent change in a substantial holding and on ceasing to hold 5 per cent.

The notification obligation also applies to interests of an 'associate' of the notifying person (disclosure is required to be made on an aggregate basis of the interests of the person making disclosure and the interests of their associates). The associate concept is broad and will include a company within the same corporate group, and a person with whom an arrangement exists for influencing a listed entity's affairs. In the context of a takeover, it may include a person with whom the bidder has an agreement to sell an asset of the target after completion of the takeover.

A substantial holding notice must include details of the identity of the substantial holder and its associates, and the nature of its interest in the listed entity (including any agreement under which the interest was acquired). In particular, the identity of those that control the substantial shareholder must be disclosed. The information must be given in the prescribed form and be accompanied by certain documents.

If a takeover bid is made in respect of a listed entity, the disclosure obligations are more onerous. In such circumstances, the bidder is deemed to have a substantial holding in the listed entity and is required to lodge a substantial holding notice with ASX (even if a 'nil' holding notice need only be lodged). The initial notice (and any notice for a 1 per cent change in the substantial holding) during a takeover bid must be lodged with the target and the ASX by the next business day (rather than the usual two business days requirement).

11.1 Equity derivatives

The Australian Takeovers Panel ('Panel') is the primary adjudication body for takeovers in Australia. The Panel has issued a Guidance Note on disclosure of positions taken in equity derivatives. The Panel requires disclosure of equity derivative contracts in circumstances where there is a 'control transaction'. The Panel defines 'control transaction' as a transaction which affects or is likely to affect control or potential control of a company, or the acquisition or proposed acquisition of a 'substantial interest' in a company.

Where there is a control transaction, the Panel may make a declaration of 'unacceptable circumstances' and consequent orders where there is non-disclosure of long equity derivative positions.

In the event of a control transaction, the Panel requires disclosure of positions taken in equity derivatives by 'takers' who have a combined long and physical position exceeding 5 per cent of the underlying stock – ie, derivative positions which, alone or when aggregated with holdings of physical securities, relate to 5 per cent or more of a listed Australian company's voting securities (or listed Australian registered scheme's voting interests) need to be disclosed to the market or any changes by more than a notional 1 per cent above that level.

Takers must meet the timetable for disclosure set out above in relation to disclosure of substantial holdings. Importantly, disclosure needs to be given as and when incremental exposure under the derivative is agreed to between the parties, not merely when the total desired exposure is contracted and the final swap confirmation is signed. The Panel has made it clear that it will not normally take account of whether the equity derivative is hedged.

11.2 Reporting of short positions

As part of the short selling disclosure regime introduced by the Australian government in response to the global financial crisis, all short sellers of ASX listed securities must report their short positions to ASIC within three days of the creation of the short position. A short position arises where the quantity of the securities which a person has is less than the quantity of the securities which the person has an obligation to deliver. Each person must assess their own short position and separately report it to ASIC if it exceeds the reporting threshold. A short position need not be reported if both the following apply:

*   the value of the position is A$100,000 or less; and
*   the position is 0.01 per cent or less of the total quoted securities in that class.

12. PUBLIC TAKE-OVERS

12.1 Prohibition on acquiring relevant interests

Unlike the UK and many European countries, there is no 'mandatory offer' obligation in Australia. Instead, there is a 'takeovers prohibition' in Chapter 6 of the CA which applies in relation to the acquisition of relevant interests in issued voting shares in all Australian listed companies, listed managed investment schemes and unlisted companies with more than 50 members.

Under this prohibition, a person must not obtain a 'relevant interest' (including indirect interests) in issued voting shares of a company or a voting interest in a scheme that results in a person having 'voting power' of more than 20 per cent, except through one of the permitted exceptions (for example, a takeover bid, a scheme of arrangement with target security holder approval or making a permitted 'creeping' acquisition). When calculating whether a person has a relevant interest or not, the interests of any associates are aggregated and added to that person's interest.

The prohibition is relevant where, because of a transaction, a person's voting power in the company increases:

*   from 20 per cent or below to more than 20 per cent; or
*   from a starting point that is between 20 per cent and 90 per cent.

12.2 Type of takeover bid

12.2.1 Off-market bids

Off-market bids are made by written offers to a target's shareholders.

Off-market bids are the more common form of takeover bid due to their flexibility. Off-market bids may be conditional, be either full or partial bids, and the consideration offered may be cash, securities or a combination.

An offer under an off-market takeover bid cannot be withdrawn without the written consent of ASIC. This is seldom given.

An uncontested off-market bid will usually take a minimum period of three months from announcement to completion. If the bid is contested by the target company or another bidder, the period for the takeover bid may be substantially longer.

12.2.2 Market bids
Market bids are undertaken by on-market acquisitions on the ASX by the bidder at a stated price. Market bids must be unconditional, in cash, and be a full bid for all shares in a class. There are very few market bids.

12.3 Regulation and filings
The principal legislation and regulations regulating takeovers in Australia are the:
* CA;
* ASX Listing Rules;
* Foreign Acquisitions and Takeovers Act 1975 (Cth) (FATA); and
* Competition and Consumer Law 2010 (CCA).

Other legislation applies to specific industry sectors such as the media, insurance and banking.

For a takeover bid, the key documents to be filed are the bidder's statement, the offer document (if the bidder's statement does not set out all of the terms of the offer) and the target's statement. These documents and other notices dealing with extensions, price increases and the waiver of conditions need to be filed with ASIC and ASX.

12.4 The regulators
The main regulatory bodies are ASIC and the Panel. ASIC supervises the operation of the CA and has wide powers to investigate, amongst other things, the conduct and share trading activities of parties involved in a takeover. Through its regional offices in each state of Australia, ASIC also reviews most of the documents issued by parties involved in a takeover.

The Panel is a non-judicial body comprised of representatives of industry and the legal and accounting professions. During a takeover bid the Panel may, on the application of the bidder, the target, ASIC or any other person whose interests are affected by the relevant circumstances, make a declaration of 'unacceptable circumstances' and consequent orders.

ASX may become involved in a takeover if it is concerned that its rules are not being complied with by the parties involved in the takeover. The principal concern of ASX is to ensure that there is an informed market in shares in the target company.

If the offeror is a foreign company for the purposes of the FATA, in most circumstances the acquisition must be approved by the Treasurer of Australia acting on the advice of the Foreign Investment Review Board (please refer to section 13 for more details of Australia's foreign investment regime).

The Australian Competition and Consumer Commission (ACCC) administers the CCA and may be involved in the takeover if competition issues are likely to arise.

Specific industry bodies such as the Australian Broadcasting Authority, APRA and the Reserve Bank of Australia may also become involved.

12.5   Information to be disclosed

Prior to the transaction, if the target or the bidder is a listed entity, the ASX Listing Rules require a listed entity to disclose immediately to ASX any information having a material effect on the price of its securities. This obligation will not apply to confidential and incomplete merger proposals unless there is an indication of specific market speculation.

The key documents in a takeover are the bidder's statement, the offer document and the target's statement.

12.5.1 Bidder's statement

The bidder's statement must contain certain information prescribed by the CA, such as the identity of the bidder and its intentions for the target, and otherwise must include all information material to the target shareholders' decision whether or not to accept the offer. If the bid consideration includes shares in the bidder, the bidder's statement must include a prospectus level of disclosure in respect of the bidder.

12.5.2 Offer document

The offer document contains the terms of the offer, specifying the consideration, the length of the offer period, and the conditions, if any, to which the offer is subject.

The CA permits the variation of offers under an off-market bid by increasing the amount and type of consideration or by extending the offer period. If the variation increases the consideration offered, every person whose shares were acquired before the variation is entitled to receive the increased consideration. If cash is offered as an alternative to shares, an offeree who has accepted an offer may elect to accept cash in lieu of the other consideration.

12.5.3 Target's statement

The target's statement must contain all information that the target's shareholders would require to make an informed decision on whether to accept the bid. It must include a recommendation from each target director as to whether or not to accept the bid. The CA requires, in certain circumstances, that the target's statement includes an expert's report on whether the takeover offer is fair and reasonable. In practice an expert's report is usually included, even if it is not required under the CA.

12.5.4 Hostile takeovers

There is no requirement under Australian law for a target's directors to provide due diligence to a bidder. Nor is there any requirement to cooperate with a potential bidder, though this must be balanced against the target's directors' general obligation to act in the best interests of the company. It should be noted however, that the Panel has indicated that it will closely scrutinise a decision by a target to deny access to due diligence to rival bidders where one of the bidders includes existing management.

12.6 Conditions to the offer

There are restrictions on the conditions that may be included in takeover offers.

An offer under a market bid must be unconditional. An offer under an off-market bid may be conditional though certain conditions are prohibited.

The prohibited conditions are those which:

- are discriminatory, in that they may result in the bidder acquiring securities from some but not all of the persons who accept the offer;
- provide that the offer terminates upon the bidder receiving acceptances for a maximum number or percentage of shares (however, a partial takeover – for a proportion of each offeree's holdings – is not prohibited);
- provide for approval of a benefit given to an officer of the target in connection with a loss of office; and
- depend on the opinion or belief, or an event within the sole control of the bidder or an associate.

Cash acquisitions that are conditional on financing are not prohibited as such. However, the CA prohibits a person from publicly proposing a takeover bid if the person is reckless as to whether it will be able to perform on the bid if a substantial proportion of the offers are accepted. Highly conditional financing arrangements may lead to a finding that the bidder is reckless as to performing its bid obligations, and may also lead to a declaration of 'unacceptable circumstances' and consequent orders by the Panel.

12.7 Notification requirements in respect of entitlements to shares during offer period

As discussed, a bidder must notify ASX of all changes in its voting power in the target company on a daily basis. The initial notice must be served by 9:30am on the trading day after the service of the bidder's statement on the target. During the period of the takeover bid, any change in entitlement must be notified to ASX by 9:30am on the next trading day.

12.8 Tax and stamp duty

Capital gains tax will generally be payable by the target's Australian resident members on disposal of their units or shares. However, rollover relief may be available if the disposal is for shares or units in the bidder or its ultimate parent entity, and the acquirer acquires at least 80 per cent of voting shares or units in the target.

Capital gains tax will not generally be payable by the target's members who are not residents of Australia if they hold less than 10 per cent of the target or if the majority of the value of the target is not attributable (directly or indirectly) to taxable Australian property (including mining interests).

Stamp duty is not payable on transfers of securities if the securities are quoted on ASX or a recognised stock exchange. However, stamp duty will be payable by the purchaser on acquisitions of unlisted marketable securities in certain Australian jurisdictions.

12.9 Schemes of arrangement

An acquisition of shares in an Australian company that would otherwise contravene the 20 per cent prohibition is exempt from that prohibition if it results from a compromise or arrangement approved by the court under Part 5.1 of the CA.

Using a scheme of arrangement can be an attractive alternative structure to a takeover bid. It requires the support of the target so it can only be used for an agreed bid. Schemes are flexible transaction structures and multiple schemes can be combined in a transaction for multiple purposes. For instance, an 'acquisition' scheme can be combined with a 'demerger' scheme – this allows a business to be divided into different parts which can then be transferred to purchasers that are interested in each of those parts. Schemes are particularly appropriate for complex transactions.

A Part 5.1 compromise or arrangement must have been agreed to at a meeting of the relevant class of shareholders convened by order of the court by a resolution passed by a majority in number of those shareholders present and voting (in person or by proxy) representing 75 per cent of the votes cast on the resolution and must then be approved by the court.

The court may not approve a Part 5.1 compromise or arrangement unless:

- it is satisfied that the compromise or arrangement has not been proposed for the purpose of enabling any person to avoid Chapter 6 of the CA; or
- there is produced to the court a statement in writing by ASIC stating that ASIC has no objection to the compromise or arrangement.

Schemes of arrangement are a court-controlled process. An originating process must be filed with a court to convene the scheme of arrangement meeting and an interlocutory process for the court to subsequently approve the scheme. The scheme booklet and notice for the shareholders' meeting to approve the scheme must be lodged with ASIC for review prior to being lodged with the court.

13. FOREIGN INVESTMENT CONTROLS

13.1 Framework

Foreign investment in Australia is regulated principally under federal legislation, including the FATA, and by the federal government's Foreign Investment Policy ('Policy').

The Policy has no legislative force, but adherence to its requirements is achieved in practice by a number of means, including by refusal to grant necessary ministerial or other approvals under other federal legislation and by the prospect of ongoing resistance from the federal government to the relevant investor, including the likelihood that future applications under the FATA might be refused.

The Federal Treasurer is ultimately responsible for all decisions relating to foreign investment and to the administration of the Policy. The Treasurer is advised and assisted by the Foreign Investment Review Board (FIRB), which administers the FATA in accordance with the Policy.

The test applied by the Treasurer in determining whether to provide a 'statement of no objection' to a proposal is whether it is contrary to the national interest. Proposals normally receive no objection unless they are judged contrary to the national interest or they otherwise warrant special consideration on a case-by-case basis.

The purpose of the regime is to empower the Treasurer to make orders in respect of proposals that ultimately are considered by the Treasurer to be contrary to the national interest. That is the test against which all proposals are assessed. In considering whether the national interest test is met, the Treasurer may impose conditions upon the statement of no objection which the Treasurer considers necessary to protect the national interest.

13.2 Notification requirements
Under the FATA and the Policy, certain proposed investments by foreign persons should be notified and a 'statement of no objection' obtained. These include:
(a) acquisitions of 15 per cent or more in an Australian corporation (with gross assets of A$231 million or more) – the 15 per cent may be of actual shares, voting power, potential voting power or rights to shares.
(b) acquisitions of 15 per cent or more in an existing Australian business (where the gross assets of the business are valued at A$231 million or more).
(c) takeovers of offshore companies with Australian assets where the gross Australian assets of the company are valued at A$231 million or more, and make up less than 50 per cent of the company's global assets. (Where the Australian assets comprise more than 50 per cent of the total assets the threshold is applied to the target's total assets not just the Australian assets).
(d) acquisitions of interests in Australian urban land. (An interest in land may be legal or equitable, under a lease or licence, financing and profit sharing arrangements, or an interest in an urban land corporation or trust). Some exemptions apply under FATA and its Regulations.
(e) proposals by foreign government related entities to establish new businesses of any size.
(f) portfolio investments in the media sector of 5 per cent or more.
There are also special rules applying to acquisitions in the following sectors: banking; civil aviation; telecommunication; airports and airlines; shipping; media; and resource sectors.

13.3 Foreign government interests
Direct investments by foreign governments or related entities and any acquisition of an interest in Australian urban land are notifiable irrespective of their size. 'Direct' in this context essentially means that the investment is by the foreign government or the related entity. It does not mean 'in Australia' and is intended to capture offshore investments with underlying Australian interests.

Where an interest of less than 10 per cent is acquired (and without any control elements) it will not be considered to be a direct investment for the purposes of the Policy and notice is not required. Where there is any control element acquired, or the investment can be used to influence the target, or if the interest is acquired as preliminary to a takeover bid, notification must be made under the Policy irrespective of the percentage interest acquired.

In examining proposed investments by foreign governments and their agencies or related entities, the Australian government will typically have regard to the following six issues:

(a) an investor's operations are independent from the relevant foreign government;

(b) an investor is subject to and adheres to the law and observes common standards of business behaviour;

(c) an investment may hinder competition or lead to undue concentration or control in the industry or sectors concerned;

(d) an investment may impact on Australian government revenue or other policies;

(e) an investment may impact on Australia's national security; and

(f) an investment may impact on the operations and directions of an Australian business, as well as its contribution to the Australian economy and broader community.

13.4 Sensitive sectors

In addition to the FIRB regime, additional restrictions may apply to acquisitions in sensitive sectors, which include:

(a) urban land (other than developed commercial real estate);

(b) media sector;

(c) banking and financial sector;

(d) aviation and airports;

(e) shipping;

(f) entities subject to specific legislation such as Telstra and Qantas Airways Limited; and

(g) entities that are Australian icons, regardless of the industry sector.

13.5 US investors

The acquisitions by US investors of interests in Australian businesses valued below the relevant threshold are exempt from the need to obtain approval. The following thresholds apply for the calendar year 2011:

(a) A$231 million (indexed annually) for acquisitions of substantial interests in prescribed sensitive sectors or by an entity controlled by a US government;

(b) A$231 million (indexed annually) for offshore takeovers involving prescribed sensitive sectors or an entity controlled by a US government, where the Australian assets or businesses of the target company comprise less than 50 per cent of its global assets; and

(c) A$1005 million (indexed annually) in any other case.

(It is important to note that a non-US incorporated subsidiary of a US enterprise, including one incorporated in Australia, does not benefit from the higher thresholds.)

Under the Australia-United States Free Trade Agreement (AUSFTA), the prescribed sensitive sectors are:

(a) media;
(b) telecommunications;
(c) transport, including airports, port facilities, rail infrastructure, international and domestic aviation and shipping services provided either within, or to and from, Australia;
(d) the supply of training or human resources or the development, manufacture or supply of military goods, equipment or technology to the Australian Defence Force or other defence forces;
(e) the manufacture or supply of goods, equipment or technology able to be used for a military purpose;
(d) the development, manufacture or supply of, or provision of services relating to, encryption and security technologies and communications systems; and
(e) the extraction of (or holding of rights to extract) uranium or plutonium or the operation of nuclear facilities.

The acquisition of interests in Australian urban land (other than developed commercial property are also sensitive and the usual land thresholds apply. For developed commercial property, however, the threshold for 2011 (indexed annually) is A$1005 million.

13.6 FIRB timing

Under FATA, the Treasurer has a period of 30 days in which to make a decision on an application and a further 10 days to notify of the decision made. If further time is required, an interim order may be made extending the time for consideration by up to 90 days. However, applications involving foreign government investment generally take longer to process (up to 60 days) and it is not uncommon to see the FIRB request a notice be withdrawn to allow for further consideration of the application.

Belgium

NautaDutilh NV Benoît Feron and Marie-Laure De Leener

1. GENERAL DESCRIPTION OF THE CAPITAL MARKETS
NYSE Euronext is the European regulated market of the NYSE Euronext Group, the leading equities marketplace in the world. NYSE Euronext, the holding company created by the combination of NYSE Group, Inc. and Euronext N.V. (created from the merger of the Amsterdam, Brussels, Lisbon and Paris exchanges in 2000), was launched on 4 April 2007. As of 31 December 2010, around 1,200 companies were listed on NYSE Euronext, representing a total global market value of approximately EUR 2.2 trillion. NYSE Euronext regulated market is split up in three market segments based on market capitalisation, distinguishing Segment A (market capitalisation of more than EUR 1 billion), Segment B (between EUR 150 million and EUR 1 billion) and Segment C (less than EUR 150 million).

The decreasing number of new listings for all markets of NYSE Euronext (Euronext, Alternext and Free Market (*Marché Libre/Vrije Markt*)) that had been witnessed since 2006 bounced back in 2010: 142 in 2006, 140 in 2007, 78 in 2008, 42 in 2009 and 81 in 2010. Moreover, the modality of listing tended to change, direct listings replacing the traditional initial public offering (IPO).

2. REGULATORY STRUCTURE
The Act of 16 June 2006, transposing Directive 2003/71/EC on the prospectus to be published when securities are offered to the public or admitted to trading (the Prospectus Directive), regulates the public offering of securities in Belgium and the admission to trading of securities on a Belgian regulated market as well as the prospectus and the communications with a promotional character regarding the public offering of securities for a total amount of no less than EUR 2,500,000 or the admission to trading of securities taking place on the territory of one or more member states of the European Economic Area (EEA) (with the exception of Belgium) when Belgium is the member state of origin.

Article 3(1) of the Act provides the definition of a 'public offering' of securities. It means a communication to persons in any form and by any means, presenting sufficient information on the terms of the offer and the securities to be offered, so as to enable an investor to decide to purchase or subscribe to these securities, and which is made by the person authorised to emit or sell the securities or on their account.

According to Article 3(2) of the Act, an offering of securities shall not qualify as public in the following cases:

- the offering is directed exclusively at professional investors;
- the offering is directed at less than 100 persons, other than professional investors, per member state of the EEA;
- the offering requires a minimum investment of EUR 50,000 per investor and per separate offer;
- the offering has a nominal value per unit of at least EUR 50,000 or
- the total amount of the offering is less than EUR 100,000.

These criteria shall be soon amended in order to comply with the recently adopted changes to the Prospectus Directive.

A public offering of securities in Belgium and the admission to trading of securities on a Belgian regulated market require beforehand the publication of a prospectus by the issuer. This prospectus has to be approved by the Banking, Finance and Insurance Commission (*Commissie voor het Bank-, Financie- en Assurantiewezen* or CBFA) within 10 days of the presentation of a complete file by the issuer.

3.   REGISTRATION OF THE ISSUER AND OF SECURITIES

There is no need for a foreign company offering securities in Belgium to be locally registered or licensed or to have any formal local presence or agent to accept legal process. In the event of a public offering, however, a foreign issuer must appoint a financial intermediary to act as its paying agent for Belgian investors, and the CBFA shall require and ensure that the Belgian public receives the same financial information provided abroad (particularly in the issuer's home country).

Pursuant to Article 88 of the Company Code, any issuer offering its securities in Belgium to the public without a subsidiary or branch in Belgium must file its instrument of incorporation and articles of association with the clerk of the Brussels Commercial Court and register with the company registry of the Crossroads Bank for Enterprises.

Securities were until recently in either bearer or registered form. However, pursuant to the Act of 14 December 2005 on the abolishment of bearer securities, it is no longer possible for companies to issue shares or other securities in bearer form and only the issue of registered or dematerialised securities remains possible. This prohibition does not affect eg, debt securities issued abroad or otherwise governed by foreign law.

On 1 January 2008, bearer securities admitted to trading on a regulated market (and most other bearer securities) were automatically converted into dematerialised (book-entry) form, provided they were held in a securities account in Belgium on that date. Listed companies were required to amend their articles of association in order to allow the issuance of dematerialised shares and to make the relevant arrangements with the legally recognised settlement institution, Euroclear Belgium. On that date the physical delivery in Belgium of bearer securities: (i) held in a Belgian securities account (excluding those automatically converted as referred to above); (ii) issued abroad; (iii) governed by a foreign law; or (iv) issued by a foreign issuer, became prohibited. The holders of bearer securities that were not automatically converted on 1 January 2008 have the following options: (i) to deposit their securities into a securities account after which they will be automatically converted into dematerialised securities provided that the issuer's articles of association allow this; (ii) to request the issuer to convert their securities into registered securities; or (iii) to keep their bearer securities until they are automatically converted.

All bearer securities not converted by 31 December 2013 will be automatically converted into dematerialised securities or, if the articles of association do not allow this, into registered securities.

Special powers have been granted to company's board of directors to amend the articles of association in order to bring them in line with the Acts. Ordinarily this would require the convening of a general shareholders' meeting.

An Omnibus Act of 25 April 2007 on miscellaneous tax law-related matters has clarified the rules applicable to bearer securities issued by undertakings for collective investment.

4. SUPERVISORY AUTHORITIES

Supervision of the Belgian financial markets is governed by the Act of 2 August 2002 on the supervision of the financial sector and financial services. This Act has reorganised the separation of powers between the CBFA, on one hand, and the stock exchange authorities, on the other. According to the Act, NYSE Euronext is responsible for issuing, supervising and enforcing its internal rules, which are contractual in nature and binding on market participants. The CBFA oversees compliance with all general rules of public policy and is responsible for ensuring respect by listed companies of obligations regarding the provision of financial information and the transparency of their shareholder structure and, in general, for supervising the secondary markets. NYSE Euronext is therefore in charge of setting the rules for admitting securities to its own markets, while the CBFA is responsible for approving the admission prospectus. In this respect, the CBFA can also veto an admission to trading of securities if such an admission would undermine investor protection.

These rules have been deeply amended. The Act of 2 July 2010 puts in place a new institutional structure for the supervision of financial institutions and financial markets in Belgium based on the 'Twin Peaks' model.

This Act follows the trend established in several other eurozone countries towards bringing together the micro- and the macro-components of prudential supervision. The first stage of the reorganisation of the Belgian supervisory structure will be the creation of the Systemic Risk Committee, consisting of the management committees of the National Bank of Belgium (NBB) and the CBFA. This committee will oversee the gradual consolidation of the NBB and the CBFA teams involved in prudential supervision, and will also facilitate the development of new tools for such supervision. Once the reorganisation is complete – several implementing decrees were to be taken by 31 March 2011 – the NBB will be responsible for all prudential supervision in Belgium. The post-reform CBFA will be in charge of the supervision of financial markets (including the supervision of listed companies and of financial products, services and intermediaries), and will be given increased powers as regards consumer protection and financial information. At this occasion, and as from 1 April 2011, the CBFA will be renamed Financial Services and Markets Authority (FSMA).

This second stage of the reform will be effective as from 1 April 2011 according to the Royal Decree of 3 March 2011.

5. OFFERING DOCUMENTATION

The Act of 16 June 2006 or the legislation of the member state where the offering or admission is taking place (Belgium being the member state of origin) requires the publication of a prospectus for a public offering of securities (for a total amount of at least EUR 2,500,000) and for the admission to trading of securities on one or more regulated market as described in the Prospectus Directive for the so-called harmonised operations.

The prospectus must firstly be approved by the CBFA before being published. The CBFA must ensure that the prospectus complies with the applicable regulations and contains all necessary information, depending on the characteristics and nature of the offering, to enable the public to make a properly informed assessment of the proposed investment. The minimum information to be included in a prospectus is set out in the Commission Regulation (EC) No 809/2004 of 29 April 2004 implementing the Prospectus Directive as regards information contained in prospectuses as well as the format, incorporation by reference and publication of such prospectuses and dissemination of advertisements. The CBFA may not give any appreciation on the opportunity or the quality of the operation nor on the situation of the issuer.

The prospectus must also mention the identity and capacity of those persons responsible for it and a statement by the latter that, to the best of their knowledge, the information contained in the prospectus is in accordance with the facts and that there are no omissions likely to affect the content of the prospectus. These persons are traditionally directors of the issuer. As noted above, advisers can also be held liable for misleading information in a prospectus, but such cases are rare.

A prospectus is traditionally drafted by the bidder, with the assistance of its bank, legal counsels to the bank and the bidder, and its auditors. All of these parties usually take part in meetings organised with the CBFA prior to submission of a draft prospectus and during the examination process. There is no statutory requirement to perform due diligence before an offering of securities, but it is now common practice to do so. Banks may be held liable if the prospectus contains misleading information and for failure to perform due diligence.

The prospectus should be drafted in French or in Dutch or in a language of the international financial markets accepted by the CBFA. If the offer is taking place totally or partially in Belgium, the summary of the prospectus must be established or translated into French or Dutch.

The prospectus may consist of a single document or may be composed of several separate documents. In the latter case, the information required is divided into:
- a registration document containing information on the issuer;
- a securities note relating to the securities offered to the public or admitted to trading; and
- a summary (reference document, base prospectus or final terms of the offer).

The issuer can also incorporate certain information in the prospectus by reference.

When examining the prospectus, the CBFA will have to respect the time limits set forth in the Prospectus Directive (10 days for approval) (if the information provided is complete). Once approved, the prospectus will be valid for 12 months following publication, provided, however, it is duly updated (eg, mention of a new fact, correction of an error). If the issuer's home member state is Belgium, the prospectus will qualify for the European passport if it contains a summary translated into the language(s) required by the host member state(s). At the issuer's request, the CBFA will address the notification referred to in the Prospectus Directive to the competent authorities of the host member state(s). A prospectus approved by the competent authority of another member state will also be valid within the framework of a public offering on the Belgian territory or an admission to trading on a Belgian regulated market, provided the other member state is the issuer's home country and the CBFA has received the notification referred to in the Prospectus Directive from the competent authorities, along with a translation into Dutch and French.

6. DISTRIBUTION SYSTEM

Securities offerings are traditionally distributed by commercial or merchant banks or, for smaller offerings, by stockbrokerage companies (investment firms). Depending on the size of the transaction, a large consortium of banks may be involved (with lead managers, global coordinators, book-runners, co-managers, selling agents, etc). In any case, all of these parties must be registered as credit institutions or investment firms and be familiar with securities distribution methods (underwriting versus best efforts, book-building, green-shoe, etc). Bankers' fees are in line with international practice and depend on the banks' commitments.

The distribution process usually takes between 10 and 20 days from approval of the prospectus by the CBFA. Anyone wishing to publicly offer securities must inform the CBFA in advance. Moreover, any form of advertisement regarding the transaction must be submitted to the CBFA for prior approval.

7. LISTING
7.1 Listing requirements
Pursuant to Rule B.3.3 of Euronext Brussels' Rule Book, in order to be admitted to trading on Euronext Brussels, issuers must meet the following

main requirements: audited financial statements drawn up in accordance with IAS for at least three financial years must be made available and the free float must represent at least 25 per cent of the issuer' share capital (publicly held shares must represent a least EUR 5 million).

For debt securities, the loan may not be less than EUR 200,000, except in the case of tap issues where the amount of the loan is not fixed or if Euronext Brussels is satisfied there will be a sufficient market. Euronext Brussels may require that debt securities be rated by a designated financial rating agency.

7.2 Review process

Simultaneously with the filing of a draft prospectus (if any) with the CBFA, an application must be submitted to Euronext Brussels, including *inter alia* the issuer's articles of association, the draft prospectus, a written commitment from a financial intermediary to act as paying agent, the issuer's annual accounts for the last three financial years prepared in accordance with IAS, a description of the business sectors in which the issuer operates and expects to operate, a financial forecast for at least the coming three years, an overview of the issuer's technical and human resources, copies of any liquidity agreements, etc. The applicant must designate a sponsor, the listing agent (normally an investment bank), who will advise the applicant, liaise with Euronext and the CBFA and coordinate other advisers.

Traditionally, the filing of a prospectus with the CBFA (for approval) and of an application with Euronext Brussels are preceded by informal contacts between the CBFA and Euronext Brussels, on the one hand, and the issuer, its sponsor and counsel, on the other. Additional meetings with the supervisory authorities may take place during the examination process.

Euronext Brussels and the applicant jointly agree on a timetable for the listing process. Euronext Brussels then rules on the application for listing as soon as possible and, in any event, always within the regulatory time limits (ie, within 90 days from receipt of all required documentation and information for a first admission and 30 days in all other cases). Euronext publishes the date on which the admission of the relevant securities to listing on Eurolist shall become effective, as well as the particulars for the trading of such securities. The offering may not start as long as the prospectus (if any) has not been approved and distributed.

The rules for Alternext are less stringent than those applicable to regulated markets, with listing requirements adapted to small and mid-cap companies and ongoing requirements sized to meet their needs.

The Act of 2 August 2002 provides for a system of appeal against decisions by Euronext Brussels and the CBFA in certain matters. Decisions by Euronext Brussels not to admit certain securities to trading and decisions of the CBFA not to approve a prospectus submitted by an issuer may now be brought before the Brussels Court of Appeals.

7.3 Listing costs

Euronext admission fees range from EUR 10,000 to EUR 3 million, based on the issuer's market capitalisation at the time of the IPO. Centralisation fees amount to 0.3 per cent of the capital raised. Annual fees range from EUR 3,000 to EUR 20,000, depending on the number of securities admitted to trading.

7.4 Primary market practices

With a view to promoting the integrity of the markets, the Primary Market Practices Decree of 17 May 2007 has clarified certain market practices in connection with initial public offerings of financial instruments carried out in accordance with the Act of 16 June 2006.

A number of measures have been introduced with a view to safeguarding the fair treatment of retail investors, including: (i) the conditions for the offering must be identical for retail and institutional investors, in particular with respect to pricing; and (ii) in any offering not limited to a particular group of investors, at least 10 per cent of the financial instruments must be allocated to retail investors, unless an exemption has been granted by the CBFA. Secondly, the over-allotment and green-shoe options may not exceed 15 per cent of the amount actually subscribed for in the offering, unless an exemption has been granted by the CBFA. On the other hand, save for certain exceptions, any party that has acquired financial instruments in the year preceding the first listing of these instruments, except as part of a public offering, at a price below the offer price is subject to a one-year lock-up, effective as from the listing of the financial instruments.

Without prejudice to the provisions on marketing materials in the Act of 16 June 2006, information disclosed in connection with a public offering may not be inaccurate or misleading, even by omission.

In the event of disclosure of the subscription level, such disclosure may only refer to subscriptions at a price equal to or greater than the offering price. In addition, certain information must be provided by the issuer or the offeror to the CBFA.

8.   ONGOING COMPLIANCE REQUIREMENTS

8.1   Sources of obligations

Continuing requirements for both listed and unlisted companies are set forth in various sources, such as the Belgian Company Code and the new pieces of legislation resulting from the implementation of Directive 2004/109 of 15 December 2004 (the Transparency Directive)The financial reporting provisions in the Transparency Directive have been implemented by means of the Decree of 14 November 2007 on information requirements. The decree entered into force on 1 January 2008 and replaced the Royal Decree of 31 March 2003 on the obligations of issuers of financial instruments admitted to trading on a Belgian regulated market. These disclosure rules apply to Belgian companies whose shares are listed on Euronext or, with certain variations, Alternext Brussels. They do not apply to Belgian companies whose shares are listed on the Free Market of NYSE Euronext Brussels. An exemption system is available to third-country (non-EU) issuers which are subject to equivalent disclosure rules in their home country. All practical details can be found in the CBFA Circular FMI/2007_02 (Obligations applying to issuers listed on a regulated market).

8.2 Obligations of listed companies relating to periodic information

The annual announcement (*communiqué annuel/jaarlijkse communiqué*) on the listed company's activities and financial position has become optional. If a company, however, chooses to publish such an announcement, it must be published during the period between the drawing up of the financial statements and the publication of the annual financial report. It should be communicated to the CBFA and to Euronext as well as to the media through a press release mentioning the Web site of the company on which the report will be available (and kept for at least five years).

The annual announcement contains figures exclusively on the performance, comments on the evolution of the business, the performance and the position of the company as well as any specific indication having had an impact on those elements during the period under review, the anticipated development of the company for the current financial year and finally an indication on whether the financial statements have, or have not, been audited by the auditor and, as the case may be, indicate the state of progress of the audit work.

The annual financial report must be published no later than four months after the close of the financial year. Once again communication to the media will take place through a press release mentioning the Web site on which the report will be available (and kept for at least five years). This press release must clearly indicate: (i) that the information is regulated information: (ii) the identity of the issuer: (iii) the time and date of the communication of the information to the media; and (iv) as the case may be, that the issuer has placed an embargo on the information. The CBFA and Euronext will be informed at the latest on the day that the information is made available to the public and the securities holders.

The annual financial report must contain the following items:
- the audited financial statements (statutory and consolidated);
- the management report containing information with respect to the company's strategy and business, a discussion and analysis of financial conditions and the results of operations, corporate governance disclosures, a list of material contracts the company has entered into during the past year, the auditor's report, etc;
- a statement made by the persons responsible within the company (whose names and functions shall be clearly indicated) certifying that to their knowledge: (i) the financial statements prepared in accordance with the applicable set of accounting standards give a true and fair view of the assets, liabilities, financial position and profit or loss of the issuer and the undertakings included in the consolidation; and (ii) the management report includes a fair review of the development and performance of the business and the position of the issuer and the undertakings included in the consolidation, together with a description of the principal risks and uncertainties that they face;

- the report of the auditor;
- the corporate governance statement (see below).

Half-year reporting requirements have been increased. A financial report is now required and must be published within two months (four months if the company is listed on Alternext) after the end of the first six-month period of the financial year. The publication requirements are the same as described above for the optional annual announcement. This report contains amongst others a condensed set of financial statements, an interim management report and indications on the status of the external audit.

Interim management statements are now mandatory twice a year and should be published within the period starting 10 weeks after the beginning of the concerned six-month period and ending six weeks before the end of the considered six-month period. They can however be replaced by quarterly financial reports published at the latest two months after the end of the first and third quarters. The interim statement contains an explanation of the material events and transactions that have taken place during the considered period and their impact on the financial position of the company and a general description of the financial position and performance of the company during the considered period. As far as the quarterly financial report is concerned, its content is identical to that of the half-yearly financial report. The publication requirements are once again identical.

Since 1 January 2005, Belgian issuers listed on the Euronext regulated market have been required to draw up their annual, half-yearly and quarterly financial reports in accordance with IAS/IFRS. Issuers subject to the legislation of an EU member state or issuers governed by the legislation of a non-EU country can prepare their financial statements in accordance with the accounting standards applicable in their home country. However, the CBFA may request such issuers to submit, within 15 days, a declaration from their auditor or the financial supervisory authority of their home country indicating that the financial data in the issuer's annual, half-yearly and quarterly reports have been prepared in accordance with the applicable accounting standards.

According to Euronext's Rule Book, the issuer's annual consolidated financial reports must be audited by its accountants in accordance with the standards of the International Federation of Accountants or national GAAP. The half-yearly financial reports for the first six months of the financial year must be subjected to a limited review by the issuer's auditors. The report on this limited review shall be published along with the half-yearly report.

Additional reporting requirements apply with respect to mechanisms liable to frustrate takeover bids (including golden parachutes).

8.3 Other disclosure and governance obligations

Aside from the obligation to provide periodic information, a company admitted to trading on a Belgian regulated market must immediately disclose price-sensitive information. Occasional information must be disclosed through press agencies whether or not in combination with the company's Web site (under conditions) or Euronext's Web site or the financial media, and simultaneously transmitted to Euronext and the CBFA (which may order a halt on trading). Companies that wish to postpone disclosure, particularly of occasional information, must apply to the CBFA.

According to the Corporate Governance Code, any company admitted to trading on a regulated market should draw up a charter describing its corporate governance policy. This charter must be posted on the Web site of the company and should include a description of the company's governance structure and policies on matters such as its structure, the terms of reference of the board of directors and its committees as well as related-party transactions, remuneration and insider trading, and market manipulation. This charter must be regularly updated. The company is also required to disclose in its annual report information regarding its board's activity and top-level remuneration.

The Company Code also provides that under certain circumstances the board of directors of any commercial company must draft special reports for shareholders, such as in the event of a capital increase due to a contribution in kind, the restriction or suppression of shareholders' pre-emptive right in the event of a capital increase due to a contribution in cash, a change in the company's corporate purpose, any changes to the rights attached to the company's shares, issuance of convertible bonds or warrants, a merger, etc.

The Company Code also sets forth procedures for dealing with conflicts of interest. If a director has a direct or indirect financial conflict with a decision to be taken by the board, that director must inform the other directors accordingly. As long as the company is not a public company and its articles of association do not provide otherwise, the director may vote on the decision. If the company is listed and if the decision is likely to result in a financial advantage to one or more major shareholders, the board must appoint three independent directors and an expert to draft a report on the decision and its financial implications for the company and its shareholders, on the basis of which the board shall take its decision. A new procedure, directed in particular at intra-group transactions, was recently introduced to extend the scope of application of the conflict-of-interest rules and strengthen the criteria used to assess the 'independence' of directors.

Companies admitted to trading on a Belgian regulated market must post on their Web site at least the following information: occasional information (in the form of a press release), any changes to the company's shareholder structure, annual information in brochure form, annual and half-yearly financial reports, quarterly reports (if published), the company's articles of association, information needed by the holders of financial instruments in order to exercise their rights, information concerning rights attached to the holding of financial instruments, the financial service offered, the financial year, etc.

9. CORPORATE GOVERNANCE

Principles of corporate governance for all companies admitted to trading on a Belgian regulated market are set forth in the Company Code and the Corporate Governance Code which was adopted in 2004 by the CBFA, Euronext Brussels and the Federation of Belgian Enterprises (FEB-VBO).

The Company Code reflects the 'one-tier' board model. All Belgian limited companies (*sociétés anonymes/naamloze vennootschappen*) must appoint a board of directors (*conseil d'administration/raad van bestuur*) responsible for managing the company. The board is entrusted with general managerial authority and may take legal action on the company's behalf. Members of the board of directors are accountable to the company's shareholders for the performance of their duties and may be removed from office by the latter at any time. The board is led by a chairperson (*président/voorzitter*) and is composed of both executive and non-executive directors, including independent non-executive directors (*administrateurs indépendants/ onafhankelijke bestuurders*).

The board may delegate the day-to-day management of the company to one of its members (the *administrateur délégué/gedelegeerd bestuurder* or CEO) or to a management committee (*comité de direction/directiecomité*). Both of these are responsible for running the company on a day-to-day basis, implementing internal controls, preparing the company's financial statements and all information necessary for the board to perform its duties properly, presenting to the board a balanced and comprehensible assessment of the company's financial situation, etc. Persons entrusted with daily managerial authority are accountable to the board for the performance of their duties and may be removed from office by the latter at any time.

The Corporate Governance Code requires a clear division of authority within a company between the board of directors and those responsible for running the company's business. The chairman of the board and the chief executive officer should not be the same person. The division of authority between the chairman of the board and the CEO should be clearly established, set out in writing and approved by the board.

According to the Chapter 5 of the Corporate Governance Code, all companies admitted to trading on a Belgian regulated market must set up specialised committees to analyse specific issues and advise the board, in particular an audit committee, composed exclusively of outside directors, a nomination committee and a remuneration committee.

9.1 Revision of the corporate governance code for listed companies

In early 2008, the Corporate Governance Committee decided to review the Corporate Governance Code in order to consider developments in international practice and amendments to the corporate governance codes of other countries and the outcome of the public consultation on the 2004 Code conducted between October and November 2007. This consultation took on board the results of three years' experience, in particular with regard to the Code's effectiveness, structure and scope, the 'comply or explain' approach and disclosure by the company in its annual accounts of actions taken to implement the Code. Based on this review and further consultations, an amended Code – the 2009 Code – was adopted and published on 12 March 2009. The 2009 Code applies to reporting years starting on or after 1 January 2009, with the exception of the provisions on executive remuneration, which apply to contractual arrangements entering into force after 1 July 2009. The most important changes under the 2009 Code relate to the separation of the positions of board chairman and CEO, the role of the company secretary, corporate social responsibility, the evaluation of the board, the respective roles of the board and the company's executive management with regard to disclosure, fair and responsible remuneration and finally the dialogue with shareholders and investors.

9.2 Corporate governance code for non-listed companies
On 23 June 2009, the Buysse Code II was presented to the public, replacing the 2005 Buysse Code. The Buysse Code II contains recommendations on corporate governance for Belgian companies other than listed companies as defined in the Company Code.

As the debate surrounding corporate governance originated in the need to protect investors, its principles initially appeared to be irrelevant for unlisted companies. However, to the extent corporate governance involves rendering a company's management structure and decision-making processes more efficient, transparent and objective, unlisted enterprises can also benefit from these principles.

Unlike listed companies, which are subject to the comply-or-explain principle, non-listed companies can decide for themselves the extent to which they wish to follow the recommendations in the Buysse Code II and the degree of transparency they wish to apply in this regard. The Buysse Code II recommends that each company adopt a corporate governance statement and, if it is required to publish an annual report, to include the statement therein. The Code also recommends mentioning the most important corporate governance-related events in the annual report. The recommendations in the Buysse Code II are much more detailed than those in the 2005 version.

The new elements of the Buysse Code II relate to corporate social responsibility, the establishment of an advisory committee, risk identification and risk management, the role of the board of directors, the performance of senior management, the remuneration of directors and senior management and finally shareholder engagement.

9.3 Audit committee
The Act of 17 December 2008 on the establishment of an audit committee in listed companies and financial institutions implements Directive 2006/43 of 17 May 2006 on statutory audits of annual accounts and consolidated accounts in three key areas: (i) the mandatory establishment of an audit committee in listed companies and regulated financial institutions; (ii) the new definition of 'independent director'; and (iii) the appointment and removal of auditors.

The main provisions of the Act have been incorporated into the Company Code and entered into force on 8 January 2009. The rules with respect to the duties and responsibilities of the audit committee applied as from the first financial year opening after publication of the Act in the Belgian State Gazette (ie, after 29 December 2008). In most cases this was the financial year starting on 1 January 2009.

Previously, there was no statutory obligation to set up an audit committee. The Corporate Governance Code recommended that every listed company establish an audit committee and contained guidelines and recommendations with respect to the duties, composition and functioning of such a committee. However, the provisions of this code are soft law. Since the entry into force of the Act of 17 December 2008, all companies listed on a regulated market in Belgium (ie, Euronext Brussels) as well as all Belgian credit institutions, insurance companies, investment companies and collective investment undertakings must set up an audit committee. Other companies may do so on a voluntary basis.

The audit committee must monitor: (i) the financial reporting process; (ii) the effectiveness of the company's internal control and risk-management systems; (iii) internal audits, if any, and their efficiency; (iv) statutory audits of the company's annual and consolidated accounts and the follow up of any questions asked, or recommendations made, by the auditor; and (v) the auditor's independence, in particular the provision of additional services by the auditor to the company. The audit committee may be entrusted with additional duties, if necessary, and must report to the board of directors on the above matters.

The audit committee must be composed solely of non-executive directors. In addition, at least one member of the audit committee must be an independent director and must have expertise in accounting and/or auditing matters. The board's annual report must demonstrate that the above conditions are fulfilled.

The establishment of an audit committee is not mandatory for listed companies and regulated financial institutions that meet at least two of the following three criteria: (i) the company has less than 250 employees on average during the financial year; (ii) the company's balance sheet total does not exceed EUR 43 million; (iii) the company's net annual turnover does not exceed EUR 50 million.

If the company does not set up an audit committee, the board of directors is responsible for carrying out the audit committee's statutory duties, provided: (i) the board has at least one independent director; and (ii) if the board is chaired by an executive member, this member does not act as chair when the board performs the duties of the audit committee. If these two conditions cannot be met, the company must set up an audit committee.

9.4 Remuneration committee

Under the Act of 6 April 2010 on corporate governance and remuneration in listed companies, companies whose shares are admitted to trading on a regulated market are, subject to certain limited exceptions, obliged to set up a remuneration committee within the board of directors.

All the members of the remuneration committee must be non-executive directors, and the majority must be independent (the relevant criteria are specified in the Company Code). Expertise in the area of compensation policy is a prerequisite. The remuneration committee will be responsible for,

among other things:
- formulating proposals concerning the company's remuneration policy and its application in individual cases (for executive directors, members of the management committee and persons in charge of day-to-day management);
- preparing the remuneration report;
- commenting on the remuneration report at the annual general meeting.

9.5 Corporate governance statements

Pursuant to Directive 2006/46 of 14 June 2006 on annual accounts, member states must require companies whose securities are admitted to trading on a regulated market to include a corporate governance statement in their annual report. These provisions have been implemented trough the Act of 6 April 2010 mentioned above.

Belgium has chosen to limit the scope of the corporate governance statement required for companies whose securities other than shares are admitted to trading on a regulated market unless the shares of this company are traded in a multilateral trading facility.

The statement which must be set out in a separate section of the company's annual report, must contain, among other things, the following information:
- a reference to: (i) the corporate governance code to which the company is subject; and/or (ii) the corporate governance code which the company may have voluntarily decided to apply; and/or (iii) all relevant information about the corporate governance practices applied beyond the requirements under national law;
- to the extent that a company departs from a corporate governance code referred to under (i) or (ii), an explanation by the company as to which parts of the code it departs from, and the reasons for doing so;
- a description of the main features of the company's internal control and risk management systems in relation to the financial reporting process;
- the operation of the shareholder meeting and its key powers, and a description of shareholders' rights and how they can be exercised as well as the structure of the shareholding of the company according to the notifications of substantial shareholdings received;
- the composition and operation of the administrative, management and supervisory bodies and their committees.

10. INSIDER TRADING AND MARKET ABUSE

10.1 Insider trading

Articles 25 and 40 of the Act of 2 August 2002 on the supervision of the financial sector and financial services provide that insider trading is a crime.

In order to be considered privileged, information must not be public and must: (i) be sufficiently precise; (ii) relate to one or more issuers of securities or to one or more classes of securities; and (iii) be such that its publication would likely have a material effect on the price of the securities or their derivatives.

An insider is a anyone in possession of 'privileged information' who knows or should be aware of the privileged nature of such information in its capacity as: (i) a member of management or of a controlling body of the issuer or of a company closely related to the issuer; (ii) a holder of the securities in question; or (iii) due to access to such information through their work, profession or function. Insiders may also be anyone who comes into possession of privileged information through criminal activities, any natural person who takes part in the decision to enter into a transaction or to pass an order on behalf of a legal entity, or any other person knowingly in possession of information that it knows or should know is privileged and which originates, directly or indirectly, from any of the persons mentioned above.

Anyone in possession of privileged information must refrain:

- from using such information in order to acquire or sell, directly or indirectly, for its own account of for a third party, any of the securities concerned;
- on the basis of this information, from recommending that a third party, directly or indirectly, acquire or sell any securities to which the information pertains;
- from disclosing it to any third party, except in the ordinary course of business or in the exercise of their profession or function.

The applicable criminal sanctions include a prison term ranging from three months to one year and fines from EUR 50 to EUR 10,000, capped at three times the capital gain derived from the insider trading. The CBFA can also impose administrative fines up to EUR 2,500,000. The criminal sanctions are applicable to financial instruments admitted to trading on Euronext, the Free Market and Alternext (all organised by NYSE Euronext Brussels). The administrative fines, however, only apply to the Euronext and Alternext markets.

There are nevertheless safe harbours to protect transactions such as buy-back programmes and stabilisation of financial instruments (subject to the fulfilment of several conditions). The literature is divided as to whether buying before the launch of a takeover bid constitutes insider trading if performed by the bidder who has already decided to launch a bid. It is advisable to notify this kind of transaction to the CBFA.

Notwithstanding the fact that Directive 2003/125 on the fair presentation of investment recommendations and the disclosure of conflicts of interests has direct effect in Belgium, a specific set of rules has been enacted which entails, amongst others that:

- any recommendation must disclose clearly and prominently the identity of the person responsible for its production, in particular the name and the job title of the individual who prepared the recommendation and the name of the legal person responsible for its production.
- reasonable care should be taken to ensure that the facts are clearly distinguished from interpretations and opinions and that all sources are reliable and clearly indicated.

ECJ rules on implementation of insider trading prohibition
In the *Spector Photo Group* case, the Brussels Court of Appeal referred several questions to the European Court of Justice (ECJ) on the interpretation of Article 2(1) of Directive 2003/6 of 28 January 2003 on market abuse.

One of the questions referred to the ECJ was whether it is sufficient, for a transaction to be classed as prohibited insider trading, that a primary insider in possession of inside information trades on the market in financial instruments to which that information relates or whether it is necessary, in addition, to establish that that person has 'used' that information in full knowledge. Unlike Article 2(1) of the directive, Article 25 of the Act of 2 August 2002 (which implements Article 2(1)) does not explicitly refer to the use of the inside information.

In its decision of 23 December 2009, the ECJ held that the fact that a primary insider in possession of inside information acquires or disposes of, or tries to acquire or dispose of, for its own account or for the account of a third party, either directly or indirectly, the financial instruments to which that information relates implies that that person has 'used that information' within the meaning of the directive. This presumption is without prejudice to the rights of the defence and can be rebutted. According to the ECJ, the question of whether the insider has infringed the prohibition on insider trading must be analysed in the light of the directive's purpose, which is to protect the integrity of the financial markets and to enhance investor confidence, which is based, in particular, on the assurance that investors will be placed on an equal footing and protected from the misuse of inside information.

Based on this decision of the ECJ, the Brussels Court of Appeal judged on 7 December 2010 that neither Spector nor its investor relations manager had committed insider dealing and decided to revoke the administrative sanction imposed by the CBFA.

10.2 Market abuse
The royal decree of 5 March 2006 transposed into Belgian law Directive 2003/124 of 22 December 2003 on the definition and public disclosure of inside information and the definition of market manipulation (market abuse) and Directive 2004/72 of 29 April 2004 on accepted market practices, the definition of inside information in relation to commodities derivatives, the drawing-up of lists of insiders, and the notification of managerial and suspicious transactions. The royal decree clarifies certain provisions of the Act of 2 August 2002, provides guidance on conduct liable to amount to market abuse, and introduces measures intended to prevent such abuse. These provisions entered into force on 10 May 2006.

The preventive elements in the decree relate to the identity of any person with access to inside information, the notification of transactions in financial instruments by persons entrusted with managerial authority within an issuer, and intermediaries' obligation to report any suspicious transactions. These obligations are applicable to financial instruments admitted to trading on Euronext and Alternext.

Issuers whose financial instruments are admitted to trading on a Belgian regulated market or which are in the process of being admitted to such a market must provide a list of all persons working for them (whether under an employment contract or otherwise) who have access, on a regular or incidental basis, to inside information directly or indirectly concerning the issuer. This list must mention the identity of any person with access to such inside information, the reason for including that person on the list, and the date on which that person received access to the inside information and on which the list was created and updated. The royal decree also requires that persons on these lists be made aware of their statutory and regulatory obligations and the sanctions that can be imposed for abuse or improper disclosure of inside information.

Persons entrusted with managerial authority (ie, members of the issuer's administrative, management or supervisory bodies or senior executives who are not members of the foregoing bodies but who have regular access to inside information relating directly or indirectly to the issuer and the power to take managerial decisions affecting the future development of the issuer's business and business prospects) and, if relevant, any persons closely associated with them (ie, the spouse or any partner of that person considered under national law to be a spousal equivalent, dependent children, other relatives who have shared the same household as that person for at least one year on the date of the transaction or any legal entity, trust or partnership for which any of the foregoing persons exercise managerial responsibility or which is directly or indirectly controlled by such a person or which has been set up for the benefit of such a person or whose economic interests are substantially equivalent to those of such a person) must henceforth notify the CBFA of transactions performed for their own account involving shares of the issuer or any derivatives or other financial instruments related to these shares.

Notification must be made within five working days following the transaction, although a deferral is possible as long as the total value of the transactions completed during the current calendar year does not exceed EUR 5,000. Once this threshold is attained, all previously completed (but undeclared) transactions must be reported within five working days from the date of the last transaction. If the total value of the transactions is below EUR 5,000 for the current calendar year, the transactions in question must be reported before 31 January of the following year. The CBFA has established a model document (Form B – Reporting of Insider Transactions) to ensure that the notification meets the requirements set forth in the royal decree. Notifications are posted on the CBFA's Web site.

10.3 Short selling
Since June 2008, regulatory authorities throughout the world have taken action to ban or restrict the short selling of securities of financial institutions in an attempt to protect financial institutions against steep declines in their share prices, which would undermine confidence in those institutions and hamper their efforts to raise capital.

On 19 September 2008, the CBFA issued a ban on the naked (ie, uncovered) short selling of financial instruments with voting rights issued by financial institutions listed on Euronext Brussels (shares and derivatives (including futures) of the following financial institutions: Dexia SA, Fortis NV/SA, KBC Group NV, KBC Ancora NV and ING Group NV). This and related measures were introduced in light of the exceptional market circumstances and after consultation with the foreign supervisory authorities responsible for overseeing Euronext. The measures are intended to ensure the integrity and smooth operation of the markets. They are, in particular, aimed at preventing the execution of transactions which give or are likely to give false or misleading signals regarding the supply of, demand for or price of financial instruments, within the meaning of the Act of 2 August 2002. The ban was confirmed in the Decree of 23 September 2008 regarding anti-short selling measures, initially for a period of three months.

Following several extensions, the ban has been extended for an indefinite period under a Royal Decree of 22 September 2009. Under this last decree, ING Group NV was removed from the list of issuers whose securities are covered.

Pursuant to the ban, all short selling orders relating to the abovementioned financial instruments that result in postponed settlement/delivery must be 100 per cent covered by the financial instruments that form the object of such orders. Any individual or entity holding a net short position which represents a financial stake of more than 0.25 per cent of the share capital of a financial institution listed on Euronext Brussels is required to disclose its position to the CBFA and the market by any appropriate means, no later than the day following that on which the position came into existence (D+1). Financial institutions are also required to refrain from lending securities issued by financial institutions listed on Euronext Brussels, except to cover transactions entered into before 22 September 2008. The ban covers transactions entered into either for the trader's own account or on behalf of third parties, with the exception of transactions entered into by financial intermediaries acting in their capacity as market makers, liquidity providers (as defined in Euronext's Rule Book) or counterparties with respect to block trades.

The CBFA announced enforcement actions in the event of non-compliance with the above measures and published FAQs on the technical issues they raise.

11. MUTUAL FUNDS
11.1 Regulatory framework
The UCITS III Directive was transposed into Belgian law by the Act of 20 July 2004 on certain forms of undertakings for collective investment in transferable securities (UCITS). The Act of 4 December 1990 on financial transactions and the financial markets and its implementing decrees, however, still govern certain aspects of UCITS whose units are publicly offered for sale or subscription in Belgium or listed on a Belgian stock exchange.

Before commencing operations in Belgium, all UCITS must register with the CBFA. UCITS remain subject to continuous supervision by the CBFA or, if they are listed on Euronext, by the latter.

Only investment funds whose units are intended to be publicly offered in Belgium must take the form of an UCITS. These funds are subject to specific registration and information requirements. There are no statutory or regulatory constraints for a private offering of units in Belgium.

Foreign UCITS must appoint a financial intermediary established in Belgium responsible for circulating all information directed at Belgian investors and acting as the fund's Belgian paying agent. This intermediary must be approved by the CBFA and ensure the circulation in Belgium of the information published in the home state in at least one of Belgium's official languages.

An UCITS prospectus on the public offering or marketing of units in Belgium must be submitted in advance to the CBFA for approval. In addition, the net asset value per share must be published in at least one Belgian newspaper each day subscription or repurchase of the shares is possible and at least twice per month. The annual and semi-annual reports, translated into at least one of Belgium's official languages, must be made available to the public at the UCITS' agents for subscription and repurchase orders. Foreign UCITS must ensure that Belgian unit-holders are provided with the same information as holders in the home country.

On 13 July 2009, a new, recast UCITS directive was adopted – UCITS IV – which will repeal and replace the original UCITS Directive (as amended) with effect from 1 July 2011. The deadline for implementing the UCITS IV Directive in national law is 30 June 2011.

The UCITS IV Directive contains the following changes:

* notification procedure: the cross-border registration process will be simplified and accelerated by the introduction of an electronic regulator-to-regulator procedure;
* mergers and master-feeder structures: cross-border mergers between UCITS will become easier and master-feeder structures will be permitted;
* key investor information: the simplified prospectus will be replaced by a more user-friendly key investor information document (KII);
* supervision: more generally, cooperation between national supervisors will be further improved;
* management company passport: the introduction of the management company passport will allow for the cross-border management of UCITS. This will enable a UCITS to be administered and managed by a management company authorised and supervised in a member state other than its home member state.

Level-2 implementing measures of the UCITS IV Directive have been adopted by the European Commission on 1 July 2010 (with effect from 1 July 2011) under the form of two regulations, regarding: (i) key investor information; and (ii) notification procedure and supervisory co-operation, and two directives regarding: (i) UCITS mergers and master-feeder structures; and (ii) rules for the conduct of UCITS management companies. In this connection, the Commission has requested and received advice from CESR on various subjects, including the management company passport and the format and content of the key investor information document.

11.2 Investment powers
Article 7 of the Act of 20 July 2004 provides for nine investment classes, adding one class to the eight pre-existing ones listed in Article 122 of the Act of 4 December 1990 (effective until 14 February 2007). All UCITS established under Belgian law must select one of the following investment classes:
• investments that comply with the UCITS Directive;
• securities and cash;
• commodities, options and forwards on commodities;
• options and forwards on securities, foreign currency or stock exchange indices;
• real estate;
• high-risk capital;
• receivables owned by third parties and assigned to the vehicle by agreement;
• another class of investments approved by royal decree; and
• securities issued by unlisted companies (added by the 2004 Act).
  Only vehicles whose investment policy meets the requirements of the UCITS Directive will be able to market their shares or units across the European Union.

11.3 Alternative Investment Funds
In addition, as a result of the adoption by the European Parliament on 11 November 2010 of the Directive on Alternative Investment Fund Managers (AIFM), Belgian legislation will have to be adapted by the beginning of 2013. There is currently no draft legislation ready.

11.4 Private pricafs
A private pricaf (*private equity société d'investissement à capital fixe/private equity beleggingsvennootschap met vast kapitaal*) is a closed-end collective investment vehicle for private investors which is aimed at the private equity market. Changes introduced by the Decree of 23 May 2007 on the private pricaf – including a reduced minimum investment requirement per investor and the elimination of withholding tax on dividends paid to foreign investors – have made this a more attractive investment vehicle.
The key rules applicable to a private pricaf are:
• it must take the form of a public limited liability company (*société anonyme/naamloze vennootschap*), a limited partnership (*société en commandite simple/gewone commanditaire vennootschap*) or a limited partnership with shares (*société en commandite par actions/commanditaire vennootschap op aandelen*) and is subject to the provisions of the Company Code;
• its purpose must be to invest in unlisted financial instruments issued by mainly small and midsized companies and growth companies (through either venture capital or buyout transactions) but it can also invest in

secured or unsecured loans to unlisted companies (eg, mezzanine loans);
- before commencing its activities, a private pricaf must request registration in the list of such entities maintained by the Belgian Federal Government Service for Finance, which will notify the CBFA of each registration. Both bodies have limited supervisory powers with respect to private pricaf ;
- a private pricaf's term of existence may not exceed 12 years (but, if so desired by the investors, all or part of its assets may be contributed to a new private pricaf);
- a private pricaf must have at least six non-affiliated shareholders, or less if certain categories of investors, such as other UCITS, hold at least 30 per cent of the pricaf's voting rights and none of the other investors controls the pricaf. The minimum investment per shareholder is EUR 50,000 (this used to be EUR 250,000);
- investments made through a private pricaf are tax neutral as compared to direct investments. Tax neutrality is effected through: (i) a fixed tax base; (ii) an exemption for capital gains realised by corporate shareholders in the pricaf; (iii) the dividends-received deduction; and (iv) a tax credit for corporate shareholders for withholding tax paid by the pricaf.

11.5 New REIT (*sicafi/vastgoedbevak*) Royal Decree
A new REIT Royal Decree of 7 December 2010, which replaces Royal Decrees of 10 April 1995 and 21 June 2006, represents a significant overhaul of the existing rules. Some of the most relevant changes include:
- the extension of favourable tax treatment to REIT subsidiaries;
- the easing of restrictions on access to capital markets;
- the introduction of the ability to offer an optional stock dividend;
- the introduction of new rules on the calculation of distributable profits;
- the easing of restrictions on the participation by REITs in public private partnerships;
- the introduction of new restrictions on investments held through non-wholly owned subsidiaries;
- the introduction of new requirements regarding the debt-to-assets ratio; and
- the easing of restrictions on the issuance of REIT shares as consideration for the acquisition of property.

12. SECURITIES INSTITUTIONS
12.1 Regulatory framework
The provision of investment services in Belgium is regulated by the Act of 6 April 1995 on the secondary markets and the status and supervision of investment firms, financial intermediaries and investment advisers and by the Act of 2 August 2002 and the Royal Decree of 20 December 1995 on foreign investment firms.

Investment firms are subject to supervision by the CBFA, which may request information on the financial status of firms subject to its supervision, their transactions, the manner in which they are organised and the way in which they conduct business. The CBFA may carry out spot inspections and inspect and copy, at the investment firm's premises, any information in the firm's possession. The CBFA also has powers to suspend investment firms. Upon entry into force of the reform explained in chapter 4, the control over investments firms will be transferred to the NBB.

Belgium has implemented Directive 2004/39 of 21 April 2004 on markets in financial instruments by two Royal Decrees of 27 April 2007 and 3 June 2007. MiFID's main aim is to improve the functioning of the European internal market for investment services while at the same time protecting investors. MiFID as well as the two Royal Decrees came into effect on 1 November 2007. Together with the implementing directive and the implementing regulation issued by the European Commission (both of which add technical detail to the framework provided by the main directive), MiFID has introduced significant changes to the regulation of investment firms and financial markets in the European Union.

The key changes introduced by these Decrees are the following:

- Belgian law used to recognise four categories of investment firms: (i) stock brokerage companies (*sociétés de bourse/beursvennootschappen*); (ii) asset management companies (*sociétés de gestion de fortune/ vennootschappen voor vermogensbeheer*); (iii) companies for the placement of orders in financial instruments (*sociétés de placement d'ordres en instruments financiers/vennootschappen voor plaatsing van orders in financiële instrumenten*); and (iv) financial instrument brokerage companies (*sociétés de courtage en instruments financiers/vennootschappen voor makelarij in financiële instrumenten*). Under the new decrees, only two categories of investment firms are recognised, stock brokerage companies and asset management companies. This means that it is no longer possible to obtain a separate, more limited licence as a company for the placement of orders in financial instruments or a financial instrument brokerage company;
- stock brokerage companies may also be licensed to operate multilateral trading facilities;
- rendering investment advice is now classified as an investment service and companies rendering such advice on a regular basis must therefore be duly authorised to do so;
- although investment firms were already subject to general conduct of business and organisational obligations, the rules have become stricter and more detailed. The new rules concern, among other things the principle 'know your customer', the conflicts of interest and the provision of information to clients both before and in the course of providing investment services.

Investment firms established in Belgium must participate in a self-financed collective scheme that aims to reimburse or indemnify certain categories of investors who do not conduct financial activities in the event of default by such a firm and, if necessary, to enable action to be taken to prevent such an event of default.

12.2 Special arrangements for foreign entities

Investment firms authorised in other EU member states may provide investment services in Belgium through a branch or in the context of freedom of establishment. Such firms are carefully overseen by the financial supervisory authority in their home country.

Investment firms authorised in a non-EU member state that effectively provide investment services in their home country may render such services in Belgium without being established or licensed in this country, but only to certain institutional investors such as the Belgian government, regions and communities, the European Central Bank, the National Bank of Belgium, the Belgian Securities Regulation Fund, Belgian and foreign credit institutions, and Belgian and foreign investment firms. Such firms need not register with the CBFA but must identify themselves to the CBFA in advance, indicating the investment services they intend to provide and the categories of investors they intend to target.

13. NOTIFICATION OBLIGATIONS
13.1 Notification of substantial shareholdings

The provisions in the Transparency Directive on the disclosure of major holdings in listed companies have been implemented through the Act of 2 May 2007 on transparency.

The Act of 2 May 2007 applies to all issuers whose securities are admitted to trading on a regulated market within the EU, regardless of whether their registered office is located in Belgium. The specific rules that apply, however, depend on whether Belgium is the home or the host member state.

The legislation on the disclosure of large shareholdings in listed companies and the regulation of public takeover bids requires that any person acquiring or disposing of voting securities issued by a Belgian company admitted to trading on a regulated market in an EU member state, so that this person's percentage of voting rights in that company exceeds or falls below 5, 10, 15, 20 per cent etc, must indicate to the CBFA and the company as soon as possible and in any case no later than four trading days from the first trading day following the date on which the holder of the significant shareholding learns, or should have learned, of the acquisition or disposal the number of securities held. The notification obligation is also triggered if a threshold is reached or crossed: (i) as a result of a corporate event changing the breakdown of voting rights (eg an increase in the issuer's share capital or the cancellation of redeemed shares); or (ii) as a result of the conclusion, amendment or termination of an agreement providing for concerted action in respect of the exercise of voting rights. Notwithstanding the above, the company's articles of association may provide thresholds of 1, 2, 3, 4 and 7.5 per cent (under the former legislation, the articles of association could not provide for a minimum notification threshold of less than 3 per cent).

The notification must contain the information prescribed in the Act. A standard form of notification is available on the CBFA's Web site. It may be drafted in French, Dutch or English. It may be sent by electronic means.

The issuer must make the notification public within three trading days by providing it to the press and making it available on its Web site. The CBFA's Web site contains a practical guide to the new transparency rules, including the statutory deadlines for notification (CBFA_2008_16 of 9 December 2009).

Under the Decree of 21 August 2008 on Multilateral Trading Facilities (MTFs), some of the above rules have been adapted for companies listed on Alternext, the Free Market (*Marché Libre/Vrije Markt*), Easynext and the Trading Facility (all being MTFs organised by Euronext Brussels). The most noteworthy difference is that the notification thresholds for Alternext have been set at 25, 30, 50, 75 and 95 per cent.

Any listed company notified by a shareholder of the acquisition or disposal of a substantial shareholding of its securities must make such notification public the following day and include a mention to this effect in its annual accounts. The CBFA may, at the request of such a company, grant an exemption in exceptional circumstances if publication could be seriously detrimental to the company (provided the exemption does not mislead the public).

The Decree of 14 February 2008 on major shareholdings sets out details regarding the practical application of the disclosure obligations.

13.2 Notification of substantial holdings in a credit institution

The Act of 31 July 2009 implements Directive 2007/44 on Financial Sector Acquisitions in Belgian law.

The Act amends the existing notification thresholds for the notification of a decision to acquire or increase a 'qualifying holding' in regulated financial undertakings (credit institutions, investment firms or UCITS management companies, or insurance or reinsurance undertakings), sets out clear notification and decision-making processes for the CBFA and introduces prudential criteria to assess proposed acquisitions or increases. The Act amends existing legislation on the status and supervision of credit institutions, investment firms, insurance and reinsurance undertakings and certain forms of collective investment undertakings.

According to the new harmonised rules, any natural or legal person or any such persons acting in concert that has taken a decision to acquire, directly or indirectly, a qualifying holding (a direct or indirect holding in a regulated undertaking which represents 10 per cent or more of the capital or voting rights of the regulated undertaking or which renders it possible for the proposed acquirer to exercise a significant influence over the management of the regulated undertaking) in a regulated undertaking or to further increase, directly or indirectly, a qualifying holding, as a result of which the proportion of voting rights or capital held by that person or persons in the regulated undertaking would reach or exceed 20, 30 or 50 per cent or the regulated undertaking would become its subsidiary, must notify its decision to the CBFA in advance.

The Act sets out clear rules and timeframes for the notification and assessment of the proposed acquisition. The acquirer must notify the CBFA of the proposed acquisition in writing indicating the size of the holding and providing any information necessary for the CBFA to carry out its assessment (the information required will be published on the CBFA's Web site). The CBFA must acknowledge in writing receipt of the acquirer's notification within two working days following receipt of the notification and the relevant information. The CBFA has a maximum of 60 working days as from the date of the aforementioned acknowledgement of receipt to assess the proposed acquisition. During the assessment period, the CBFA may, request in writing any information necessary to complete its assessment. If the CBFA opposes the proposed acquisition (with reasonable grounds), it shall notify the proposed acquirer in writing of its decision within two working days and in any event before expiry of the assessment period. The acquirer may request the CBFA to make the reasons for its objection available to the public. If the CBFA does not object in writing to the proposed acquisition within the assessment period, the acquisition shall be deemed approved.

Under the new rules, the CBFA shall, in order to ensure the sound and prudent management of regulated undertakings in which acquisitions are proposed, and having regard to the acquirer's likely influence on the undertaking in question, weigh the suitability of the acquirer and the financial soundness of the proposed acquisition against several criteria:

*   the reputation and the financial soundness of the acquirer;
*   the reputation and experience of any person who will conduct the business of the regulated undertaking as a result of the acquisition;
*   whether the regulated undertaking will be able to comply and continue to comply with the prudential requirements based on its status as a regulated undertaking after completion of the acquisition;
*   whether there are reasonable grounds to suspect that, in connection with the acquisition, money laundering or terrorist financing is being or has been committed or attempted or that the acquisition could increase the risk thereof.

On 18 December 2008, CERS, CEBS and CEIOPS published joint guidelines for the prudential assessment of acquisitions and increases in holdings that are subject to Directive 2007/44. On 18 November 2009, the CBFA issued a communication to parties proposing to acquire or increase a qualifying holding containing all information necessary for the smooth functioning of the assessment procedure and attaching the various forms to be used and a circular directed at the regulated financial undertakings covered by the Act concerning – among other things – the obligation of such undertakings to notify the CBFA upon becoming aware that a holding in their capital has been or will be acquired, increased, decreased or disposed of, causing the thresholds of 10, 20, 30 or 50 to be crossed (in an upward or downward direction). Such undertakings must also notify the CBFA annually of the identity of any parties holding a qualifying holding in their capital.

14. PUBLIC TAKEOVERS
14.1 Supervision
Takeover bids are now governed by the Act of 1 April 2007 on public takeover bids implementing Directive 2004/25 of 21 April 2004 on takeover

bids (the Takeover Directive). The Act is supplemented by two Royal Decrees of 27 April 2007, one on takeover bids and one on squeeze-outs. The Royal Decree on takeover bids governs both voluntary and mandatory public takeover bids.

Public takeover bids are supervised by the CBFA, which may grant exemptions from the takeover rules and impose penalties for their violation. Non-compliance with the CBFA's orders can give rise to administrative sanctions. The Act of 1 April 2007 reinforces the exclusive competence of the Brussels Court of Appeals for judicial proceedings related to takeover bids.

14.2 The takeover process
A public takeover bid can only be launched after publication of an offer document (prospectus). Before such date it is prohibited to announce the takeover bid. The prospectus can only be published after its approval by the CBFA, once the legal conditions for the takeover bid are satisfied. If the prospectus is approved by another supervisory authority in accordance with the Takeover Directive, the CBFA will have to recognise this offer document in order to permit use in Belgium.

Voluntary takeover bid
The rules on voluntary takeover bids, apply to all public takeover bids on securities, which are not mandatory (ie, because of acquisition of more than 30 per cent). Securities include not only shares, convertible bonds, warrants, stock options and bonds, but any rights which are transferable on the market, including real estate certificates, futures, forward rate agreements, equity swaps and derivatives.

The offeror who intends to launch a public takeover bid must prior to any public announcement inform the CBFA of its intention. The communication contains all information which establishes that the conditions for a takeover bid have been complied with. All advertisements or other announcements in relation to the public takeover bid from an offeror, the offeree company or their intermediaries must prior to publication be approved by the CBFA.

Put up or shut up
In the event that a person as a result of declarations creates in the market the impression that it intends to launch a public takeover bid, the CBFA can request that they formally take a position. In general, this will be the result of statements in the press or in private to an analyst. The CBFA specifies a time, not longer than 10 banking days, in which the position must be rendered public. In the event that the concerned person confirms its intentions, they will have to launch a takeover bid. If it denies or does not take a position in time, they will be prohibited from launching a takeover bid during a period of six months.

This prohibition applies equally to persons acting in concert with them. It no longer applies when important changes occur in the circumstances of the offeree company or in the shareholding of the concerned persons.

Mandatory takeover bid

Any person which, either individually or in concert, becomes holder of more than 30 per cent of the voting securities in the target company shall, by way of a mandatory bid, offer the other shareholders the possibility to dispose of their voting securities. The obligation to initiate a bid does not follow from mere possession, but rather from the acquisition of securities whereby a threshold of 30 per cent of the voting securities in the target company is exceeded. Belgian law already provided for such an obligation but it was triggered by the acquisition of control at a price over the market price of the relevant securities.

On the other hand, the acquisition of control over a legal person or similar construction that itself holds more than 30 per cent of the voting securities in the target company shall in certain circumstances be assimilated with directly exceeding the threshold.

Exceptions to the obligation to make a mandatory public takeover bid applies in a number of situations where the 30 per cent threshold has been exceeded, eg: (i) in the case of an acquisition resulting from a voluntary public takeover bid; (ii) where a third party already controls, or holds a larger stake in, the target company; (iii) in the case of intra-group transfers of securities; and (iv) under certain conditions, where the ownership of voting rights in excess of the threshold is temporary.

Procedure
Notification of the intention to launch a public takeover bid

The offeror must notify the CBFA of its intention to launch a takeover bid by registered mail during working hours. Simultaneously it should communicate a draft of prospectus for approval by the CBFA. Furthermore, the notification of its intention should contain the offer price and the conditions of the offer, and the information which establishes that the legal requirements for a public takeover bid are satisfied. A draft announcement should also be included. Finally, if the offeror has control over the offeree company, it must also join the report of the independent expert on the value of the securities. The notification of the intention to launch a bid is published by the CBFA at the latest next banking day following receipt by the CBFA. The CBFA also informs the market authority, the board of the offeree company and the offeror of the publication. The offeree company will verify whether the prospectus is complete and not misleading, and inform the CBFA of any shortcomings within five banking days.

Approval and publication of the prospectus

The CBFA will examine the prospectus to determine whether it contains all information which is required. The CBFA must within 10 banking days decide on the approval of the prospectus or indicate that the filed information is not complete in order to take a decision. If the CBFA fails to react in time, the offeror can formally request the CBFA to take a decision. If the CBFA fails to take a decision within 10 banking days from such request, the approval is deemed refused. Appeal against this refusal is possible with the Brussels Court of Appeal.

Opinion of the board of the offeree company

The board of the offeree company must prepare a report in which it:
(i) comments on the prospectus and in particular further explains the
implications of the bid taking into account the interest of the offeree
company, the securities holders, the creditors and the employees and on
employment, and gives its understanding of the strategic plans of the bidder
for the offeree company and its presumed implications for its results, and
employment and establishments as described in the offer document; (ii)
mentions the number of voting securities and securities entitling to such
securities are held by the directors and the persons which they represent
in reality (this refers to reference shareholders nominating directors) and
whether these persons intend to tender their securities; (iii) defines the
transfer restrictions and indicates whether the board will agree with the
transfer if such restrictions apply to the takeover bid; and (iv) describes the
right of specific persons to acquire securities under the transfer restrictions.

The directors and the persons whom they represent must act in
accordance with the information they have disclosed with respect to their
intentions whether to tender their securities; if they change their intentions,
they should inform the board, which will publish this in a supplement to
the opinion of the board. In the event that the board of directors of the
offeree company decides to oppose the transfer of securities in the takeover
bid in accordance with an applicable approval requirement or to request the
application of rights of first refusal, the holders of securities are entitled to
tender their securities under the condition subsequent of the indication of
an alternative acquirer of the securities within five days from the end of the
acceptance period (in accordance with the provisions of Articles 511 and 512
of the Company Code).

The report should be notified to the CBFA within five banking days
following the approval of the prospectus by the CBFA. The report can only
be made public after approval by the CBFA. The CBFA decides within five
banking days. The CBFA may require that additional information is included
in the report if such is necessary for the protection of the interests of the
securities holders. The report by the offeree company should preferably be
published simultaneously with the prospectus as an annex to it. If this is not
possible because it is only ready after publication of the prospectus, it will be
published afterwards in the same manner as the prospectus was published.

Employee information and consultation

In the event of a takeover bid on voting securities or securities entitling
to such securities, the offeree company and the offeror should inform the
employee representatives or, when no representatives have been appointed,
the employees of the bid. The board of the offeree company must likewise
inform the representatives of the employees of its opinion on the bid. In
the event that the works' council, in companies which have elected such
council, expresses an opinion on the bid and the consequences of the
bid on employment, this opinion should be attached to the report of the
offeree company if it is communicated in time to the board of the offeree

company. The works' council may invite the offeror to explain its intentions with respect to its industrial and financial policy and the strategic plans with respect to the offeree company and the possible implications for employment and the establishments of the offeree company.

Acceptance period
The acceptance period for the bid must be defined in the prospectus. It may not be shorter than two weeks and not longer than 10 weeks. It may start at the earliest five banking days after approval of the prospectus or following approval of the report of the offeree company if such date is earlier. In the event of a shareholders meeting of the offeree company is called to decide on the bid and in particular on an action to frustrate the bid, the acceptance period will be prolonged until two weeks after such shareholders' meeting. Furthermore, the acceptance period will be prolonged if the offeror or persons acting in concert with the latter acquire or undertake to acquire securities outside the bid at a price which is higher than the offer price – in which case the offer price will by law be increased to such higher price – to permit the securities holders to have five banking days after publication of the increase of the offer price, to accept the offer. The holders of securities which tender their securities are entitled to come back on their decision at any time during the acceptance period. This right should be mentioned in the prospectus.

Publication of results
The results of the bid are published within five banking days after the end of the acceptance period. Within the same time, the offeror must communicate whether the conditions to the bid are satisfied (or whether they are waived). The price must be paid within 10 banking days after publication of the results. The bid must be reopened if the offeror together with the persons acting in concert with the latter, if any, hold at least 90 per cent of the voting rights, if the offeror requests within three months after the acceptance period to cancel the admission to trading to a regulated market or an assimilated market, or if the offeror, during the acceptance period, undertook to acquire securities at a higher price than the offer price (and the acceptance period was not prolonged because of this undertaking). The acceptance period of this new bid will start within 10 banking days after publication of the results, and may not be shorter than five nor longer than 15 banking days.

Squeeze-outs
The key changes to the squeeze-out rules brought about by the Decrees of 27 April 2007 include the following:
*   shares held by the target company may be taken into account when assessing whether a party holds 95 per cent or more of the voting rights of a listed company. This percentage gives such a party the right to require the holders of the remaining voting rights to sell it their securities;

- the decree sets out a list of parties who cannot serve as an independent expert for the purposes of rendering a fairness opinion. The list includes the offeror's and the target company's auditors; and
- an expert must always ascertain whether it has a conflict of interest.

Sell-outs

The Decree of 27 April 2007 on takeovers has introduced a sell-out right (also called reverse squeeze-out) allowing minority shareholders to require an offeror that holds at least 95 per cent of the voting securities after a public takeover bid to buy their remaining shares, subject to certain conditions. The sell-out right must be exercised within a period of three months after the end of the acceptance period. Following a mandatory bid, the consideration offered in the bid will generally be deemed to be a fair price for the purposes of the sell-out. Following a voluntary bid, the consideration provided for in that bid will generally be deemed a fair price if shares representing at least 90 per cent of the company's capital were acquired through the bid.

14.3 Financing obligations

The price offered can be composed of cash or securities, or both. However, if the offeror controls the offeree company, one or more independent experts must render a fairness opinion on the value of the securities which the bidder offers to purchase and, in the event of an exchange bid, on the securities offered as consideration. The fairness opinion must be published as an annex to the offer document.

The price of a voluntary bid is set freely by the offeror and the control of the CBFA over the price is limited to ensuring that it is such that the bid is likely to succeed. On the contrary, the price of a mandatory bid is set by the Decree of 27 April 2007 on takeover bids, which provides that it must be at least equal to the higher of: (i) the highest price paid for the securities subject to the bid by the offeror (or persons acting in concert with it) during 12 months preceding the bid announcement; and (ii) the weighted average market price of such securities during the 30 calendar days preceding the event triggering the obligation to launch the mandatory bid. In addition, the CBFA may impose conditions or adjustments if the price of a mandatory bid as set above is not appropriate.

14.4 Defences

Belgium has opted out of the provisions of the Takeover Directive aimed at restricting the use of defensive measures. Companies may, however, voluntarily include such restrictions in their articles of association. If the offeror itself has defensive measures in place, companies with such restrictions may nevertheless apply defensive measures similar to those of the offeror (the 'reciprocity rule').

Two sets of measures aiming at reducing the possibilities to oppose a takeover bid have been implemented:

- the board of directors of the target company may not take any action (other than seeking alternative bids) which may result in the frustration of the bid without the prior consent of the general meeting of shareholders; and

- all specific rights of the shareholders are 'frozen' during the period of the bid (including at any shareholders' meeting convened to adopt defensives measures) and during the first general meeting of shareholders after such period if the offeror holds more than 75 per cent of the voting rights. During these periods, the restrictions on the transfer of securities or on voting rights and the extraordinary right of shareholders concerning the appointment or removal of board members shall not be enforceable towards the offeror. Moreover, any multiple vote securities shall only carry one vote.

15. FOREIGN INVESTMENT CONTROLS

In principle, without prejudice to labour or competition law, the acquisition of securities in a company does not necessitate compliance with any specific formalities. However, the Ministry of Economic Affairs and the Ministry of Finance must be informed in advance of any operation resulting in the acquisition of more than one-third of the share capital in a company conducting a business in Belgium whose net asset value is at least equal to EUR 2.5 million. In addition, a limited liability company that acquires or disposes of a certain number of securities in another company so that its shareholding exceeds or falls below 10 per cent of the shares or voting rights of that company must notify the company, by registered mail, of such acquisition or disposal. Such a notification is not mandatory if notification of a substantial shareholding in a listed company has been made.

All exchange control regulations were abolished in 1991. All transfers of funds into and out of Belgium are therefore free from regulation, provided anti-money laundering rules are met. Moreover, foreign investors do not need any specific authorisations or to make any particular filings before investing in Belgium.

British Virgin Islands

Harney Westwood & Riegels
Jacqueline Daley-Aspinall & Ross Munro

1. GENERAL DESCRIPTION OF THE CAPITAL MARKETS

While the British Virgin Islands (BVI) is recognised as a leading offshore centre with more than 800,000 registered companies (with quite a few of those being publicly listed on stock exchanges in jurisdictions such as the United Kingdom, the United States of America and Norway) the territory has opted not to create its own stock exchange. Instead, it has elected to be a jurisdiction whose legislation is such that companies formed here are adaptable and therefore may easily be used as listing vehicles.

1.1 Number of companies listed
Not applicable.

1.2 Total volume and market value
Not applicable.

1.3 Issue activity
Not applicable.

1.4 Takeover activity
Not applicable.

1.5 Hostile takeover attempts
Not applicable.

2. REGULATORY STRUCTURE
2.1 General
Traditionally, the BVI has taken the approach of having 'light but effective' regulation. Licensing requirements have been in existence for companies operating in the territory whose business includes banking, insurance, company management, acting as a registered agent or registered office or owning real property in the BVI.

Licensing requirements have also existed for companies acting as investment funds whether their activities were carried out in the BVI or elsewhere. These investment funds were principally regulated under the Mutual Funds Act 1996 (MFA).

The 'light' approach to regulation has, however, undergone substantial changes in the last five years and the jurisdiction has introduced various

pieces of legislation aimed at augmenting the regulatory framework.
To this end, on 23 April 2010 the Securities and Investment Business Act
(SIBA) was passed. Among other things, SIBA effectively repealed the MFA
and replaced it as the applicable legislation guiding companies engaged in
investment business.

On 17 May 2010 a large portion of SIBA became effective but it is very
important to note that Part II of SIBA, which for the first time under BVI
law would restrict and regulate public issues of securities in a non-mutual
funds context, was not brought into force and is intended not to come into
force until a future date. Additionally, SIBA makes reference to a number of
pieces of subsidiary legislation such as the Investment Business Regulations,
the Public Funds Code, the Mutual Funds Regulations, the Public Issuers
Code and the Market Abuse Regulations, of which only the Mutual Funds
Regulations and the Public Funds Code have been enacted at the time of
writing.

2.2 Regulation of the offering of new securities

Prior to SIBA, outside the scope of companies engaged in investment
business, there was no BVI legislation regulating the offering of new
securities.

Part II of SIBA, when it comes into force, will provide that no securities
may be offered to the 'public in the BVI' by or on behalf of any 'issuer'
(which is defined as any person by whom security is, or is to be, issued)
unless (i) the offer is contained in a registered prospectus and (ii) the offer
complies with the requirements of a not-yet finalised Public Issuers Code.

2.3 Public offering

SIBA provides that an offer to any person in the BVI is capable of being a
public offer. There is, at present, no distinction made between a 'private' and
a 'public' offering based on the number of recipients of the offer, but this or
a similar distinction is likely to be made in subsidiary legislation before Part
II of SIBA comes into force.

2.4 Private offering

See above.

2.5 Differences between local and foreign companies

No distinction is currently made under SIBA with respect to whether the
issuer is registered in the BVI or elsewhere. It is possible, however, that the
ancillary legislation will draw a distinction.

2.6 Admission to trading on a regulated market

Not applicable.

2.7 Financial promotion

Not applicable.

2.8 Rule books
Not applicable.

3. REGISTRATION OF THE ISSUER AND SECURITIES
3.1 Registration requirements
There is no requirement for an issuer to be a BVI-registered company and there is no mechanism for the 'registration' of securities. Part B, schedule 2 of SIBA expressly excludes the issuing of shares, debentures or instruments giving entitlement to shares or debentures from the list of activities for which a licence is required. An issuer would therefore not need to be licensed under SIBA merely for issuing shares, unless they were carrying on some other activity for which a licence is required.

Part II of SIBA, when it comes into force, does require any offer of securities to 'the public in the BVI' to be 'registered' in that it must be in the form of a prospectus, which must be filed with the Financial Services Commission (FSC).

3.2 Other requirements
Not applicable.

3.3 Nature of securities
Securities are defined both under SIBA and the BVI Business Companies Act (BCA), which is the BVI's corporate statute, to mean shares or debt obligations of any kind, options, warrants or a right to acquire a share or debt obligation or any interests or rights specified in the forthcoming Public Issuers Code.

Part B, schedule 2 of SIBA expressly excludes the issuing of shares, debentures or instruments giving entitlement to shares or debentures from the list of activities for which a licence is required. An issuer would therefore not need to be licensed under SIBA merely for issuing shares, unless they were carrying on some other activity for which a licence is required.

Part II of SIBA, if and when it comes into force, does require any offer of securities to 'the public in the BVI' to be 'registered' in that it must be in the form of a prospectus, which must be filed with the Financial Services Commission (FSC).

4. SUPERVISORY AUTHORITIES
The FSC, established under section 3 of the Financial Services Commission Act 2001 of the BVI, serves as the regulatory authority for all financial services business operating in and from within the BVI.

4.1 Conduct: prudential, cooperation, self-regulation of stock exchange
Not applicable.

4.2 New listings measures in connection with the credit crisis
Not applicable.

5. OFFERING DOCUMENTATION OR PROSPECTUS REQUIREMENTS

5.1 Nature and statutory requirements of the offering document or disclosure document

As stated above, under Part II of SIBA (if and when it comes into force), any offer of securities to the public in the BVI must be contained in a prospectus. The prospectus must be submitted to the FSC for registration and must be dated and in writing. The date for the prospectus must be no later than the date of the application to the FSC to register the prospectus.

5.2 Exemptions

Unless an offer is not deemed to constitute an offer of securities to the public in the BVI, the offer must be contained in a prospectus.

An offer will not be seen as made to the public: (i) if it is made to certain specified persons such as the government of the BVI, a person having a close connection to the issuer or if the offer is made to a 'qualified investor' as the term is defined in schedule 4 of SIBA; (ii) unless the minimum purchase price payable for the securities under the offer has been paid before the shares are issued or the amount is equal to or exceeds the amount specified in the Public Issuers Code; or (iii) if the offer is exempted pursuant to the provisions of the Public Issuers Code.

5.3 Preparation of the offering document, general contents

In terms of content, the prospectus must provide the full and accurate disclosure of all such information as investors would reasonably require and expect to find for the purpose of making an informed investment decision, and must include certain other matters as specified in the forthcoming Public Issuers Code.

SIBA provides that the Public Issuers Code, when it comes into force, may impose specific requirements in relation to, among other things, the form of the prospectus, the documents to be attached and the manner in which it may be distributed among other matters.

As the legislation is not yet in force no practical examples of the contents of the prospectus exist. Presumably the issuer and its legal counsel would prepare the prospectus.

5.4 Due diligence

SIBA is silent on the requirements for this.

5.5 Responsibility

SIBA does not directly address who is responsible for the contents of the prospectus.

Section 33 of SIBA, however, provides that the BVI court may, on the application of a subscriber who acquired securities in reliance of the prospectus and who suffered loss or damage as a result, make a compensation order against the issuer, its directors or any person named as agreeing to become a director, a guarantor of information contained in the prospectus, any person who accepts or is stated in the prospectus as accepting responsibility for the prospectus, a promoter of the offer (including its directors at the time the prospectus is distributed) or any other person who has authorised the contents of the prospectus.

5.6 Disclaimer/selling restrictions
There is no prohibition in SIBA with respect to including disclaimers or selling restrictions in the prospectus.

5.7 Recognition of prospectuses by other exchanges
Not applicable.

5.8 Supplementary prospectuses
Section 29 of SIBA allows an issuer to apply to the FSC to register a supplementary prospectus during the period commencing on the registration of the prospectus and ending with the closure of the offer to which the prospectus relates. Such a supplementary prospectus would set out amendments to a prospectus that had previously been registered.

5.9 Issuing of bonds
Bonds are not dealt with separately under SIBA, but would be classed as a 'security'.

6. DISTRIBUTION SYSTEMS
As the requirements under SIBA relating to the public issue of securities are new and not yet in force, there is no precedent for how such offers are distributed.

6.1 Normal structure of a distribution group
No precedent established.

6.2 Methods of distribution
SIBA provides that the Regulatory Code may provide for or restrict the issue, form and content of advertisements, brochures or similar documents, but the Regulatory Code currently fails to include such provisions.

6.3 Underwriting
No precedent established.

6.4 Fees and commission
No precedent established.

6.5 Stabilisation
No precedent established.

6.6 Involvement of a distributor in the preparation of the offering document
No precedent established.

6.7 Timing of distribution process
No precedent established.

6.8 Rules on distribution to the public
SIBA expressly prohibits a person licensed under the legislation from issuing
or causing or permitting the issue of any advertisement, brochure or similar
documents or the making of any statement, promise or forecast which
the licensee knows is false or misleading or which contains an incorrect
statement of fact.

7. PUBLICITY
Not applicable.

8. LISTING
8.1 Special listing requirements, admission criteria
Not applicable.

8.2 Mechanics of the review process
Not applicable.

8.3 Prospectus obligation, due diligence, exemption
Not applicable.

8.4 Appeal procedure in the event of a prospectus refusal
Not applicable.

8.5 Authority of the Exchange
Not applicable.

8.6 Sponsor
Not applicable.

8.7 Special arrangements for smaller companies such as Alternext, AIM or SPACs
Not applicable.

8.8 Costs of various types
Not applicable.

9. SANCTIONS AND DISPUTES
9.1 Disciplinary and administrative sanctions
Not applicable.

9.2 Civil actions
Where a subscriber acquires securities in reliance on a prospectus and
suffers loss or damage by reason of any untrue or misleading statement in
the prospectus or the omission of any matter required to be included in

the prospectus, the court may make a compensation order in favour of the subscriber under SIBA. Such an order would be made against an issuer of securities or any person involved with the issue such as a guarantor for the issue, a promoter of the offer or a person who accepts responsibility for the prospectus, unless the person avails themselves of the exceptions provided by SIBA under which no compensation order would be awarded.

Also, common law claims against a company are non-exhaustive and the list might include fraud, misrepresentation, negligent misrepresentation, misstatement and deception, among others.

9.3 Criminal penalties
Under SIBA, a person who commits the offence of insider dealing is liable on summary conviction to a fine not exceeding $50,000 or imprisonment for a term not exceeding three years or both. A person who commits the said offence who is convicted on indictment faces a fine not exceeding $100,000 or imprisonment for a term not exceeding five years or both.

SIBA also provides that a person who commits the offence of market manipulation or misleading statements is liable on summary conviction to a fine not exceeding $40,000 or imprisonment for a term not exceeding three years or both. A person who commits the said offence who is convicted on indictment faces a fine not exceeding $100,000 or imprisonment for a term not exceeding five years or both.

10. CONTINUING OBLIGATIONS
10.1 Disclosure and transparency rule
Not applicable.

10.2 Information
Not applicable.

10.3 Listing rules
Not applicable.

10.4 Obligations regarding proxy solicitation
Not applicable.

10.5 Continuing requirements of reporting and notification of substantial shareholdings or a substantial transaction
No person with a significant interest in a person holding a licence under SIBA may dispose of any part of their interest without the prior approval of the FSC.

10.6 Clearing
Not applicable.

10.7 Requirements for unlisted issuers
Not applicable.

11. CORPORATE GOVERNANCE

11.1 Law and/or Code

The relevant legislation would be the BCA although SIBA does contain certain additional provisions relating to companies licensed thereunder. The principles of common law also apply.

11.2 Management structure

The BCA provides for the business and affairs of a company to be managed by, or under the direction or supervision of, the directors of the company. The BCA therefore gives the directors the powers necessary to manage the company. It should be noted, however, that provisions made in the BCA for the role and powers of the directors may be effectively modified or restricted by the company's memorandum and articles.

11.3 Obligations to publish information on the Internet

Not applicable.

11.4 Responsibility of inside/outside directors

BVI law does not make any distinction.

Instead, the BCA provides that all directors between executive and non-executive directors, must act honestly and in good faith in the best interests of the company. In addition, a director is required to exercise their powers for a proper purpose and must act in accordance with the company's memorandum and articles and the BCA.

When performing their duties or exercising their powers, a director shall exercise the care, diligence and skill that a reasonable director would exercise in the same circumstances.

The statute effectively codifies existing common law principles.

The BCA does, however, contain provisions that permit a director of a wholly owned subsidiary to act in the interests of its holding company even if not in the best interests of the subsidiary. In addition, where the subsidiary is not wholly owned but all shareholders (save for the holding company) agree, the director may similarly act in the interests of the holding company. Finally, in the context of a joint venture, a director may act in the interests of a shareholder or shareholders even if not in the best interests of the company. The above only applies if expressly stated in the memorandum and articles of association of the company.

11.5 Committees

Subject to the memorandum and articles of association of the company, the directors may designate one or more committees each consisting of one or more directors. The committees may exercise any of the powers of the directors delegated to them and may in turn delegate such powers to a sub-committee.

Not all powers of the directors may be delegated to a committee of directors, however, and section 110 of the BCA lists the powers which are excluded.

11.6 Obligation to ask for consent of a shareholders' meeting

Shareholder consent must be requested in relation to a merger or consolidation (except where a subsidiary is merging or consolidating with its parent), a sale of more than 50 per cent in value of the company's assets (unless the sale is exempted under the company's memorandum and articles of association) and amendments of the company's memorandum and articles of association. Shareholder consent must also be sought if required under the company's memorandum and articles of association or under an order obtained from the BVI court. It should be noted, however, that directors cannot resolve to amend the memoradum and articles of association of a public issuer under schedule 6 of SIBA.

Note that there is no requirement to hold an annual general meeting and resolutions of shareholders generally may be passed either at a meeting or by written consent.

11.7 Depth of information – proxy solicitation
Not applicable.

11.8 Appointment/dismissal of directors
A BVI company is required by the BCA to have a registered agent and a registered office in the BVI. The registered agent is responsible for the appointment of the first director(s) of the company. Subsequent directors are to be appointed by the resolution of members (unless the memorandum and articles of association provide otherwise), or by the directors if permitted by the memorandum and articles of association, for the term as may be specified in the resolution. The directors may also fill a vacancy on the board unless the memorandum and articles of association of the company provide otherwise.

Note, however, that no person may be appointed a director unless they have consented in writing to act. The BCA also stipulates that certain persons, such as an undischarged bankrupt or a person under 18 years of age are disqualified from being able to act.

Where a company is licensed under SIBA then no director may be appointed without the prior written approval of the FSC.

A director may be removed from office by a resolution of members (unless the memorandum and articles of association provide otherwise) or by the directors where expressly permitted by the memorandum and articles of association.

11.9 Income and options for directors
Subject to a company's memorandum and articles of association, the directors of the company may fix the emoluments of directors in respect of any services rendered to the company. There are no restrictions on the form that such emoluments must take.

11.10 Earnings guidance
Not applicable.

11.11 Management discussion and analysis (MD&A)
Not applicable.

11.12 Directors' liability
A director's liability arises both under statute and the common law.

Generally speaking, no director of a company will be liable for any debt, obligation or default of the company, unless such a liability is specifically provided in the BCA or in any other enactment, and except to the extent that they are liable for their own acts or conduct.

Note, however, that a director who vacates office remains liable under the provisions of the BCA in respect of any acts or omissions or decisions made whilst they were a director for which they would have been liable.

12. MARKET ABUSE
12.1 Insider trading
SIBA has introduced criminal offences for individuals based in the BVI who conduct insider 'dealing'. Insider dealing occurs, in summary, where an insider, ie, a person in receipt of 'inside information', deals in price-affected securities (or encourages another person to deal, or discloses the inside information to another person otherwise than in the course of their employment.

12.2 Market manipulation
SIBA also introduced criminal offences for individuals based in the BVI who carry on market manipulation or make misleading statements. A person will commit an offence, in summary, where they make a statement, promise or forecast which they know to be misleading, dishonestly conceal any material facts or recklessly make misleading, false or deceptive statements, honestly or otherwise.

12.3 Miscellaneous
Not applicable.

13. MUTUAL OR INVESTMENT FUNDS
13.1 Introduction to these two categories
SIBA requires all investment funds falling within its definition of 'fund' to be recognised or registered with the FSC. SIBA restricts the definition of 'mutual fund' to open-ended funds that entitle investors to demand redemption of their fund interests immediately or within a period of notice. Accordingly only such funds are regulated under SIBA. Closed-ended funds are not subject to specific regulation although BVI-established managers and other BVI-established functionaries of closed-ended funds will in many circumstances require a licence under SIBA.

SIBA introduces a wide-ranging licensing regime which requires any person carrying on 'investment business' in or from within the BVI to hold a licence. The activities constituting investment business include acting as an investment manager, administrator, investment advisor or custodian with respect to a wide variety of financial instruments. It includes most functionaries of open- and closed-ended funds but the precise outcome depends on the services provided and the structure of the fund. It is important to note, however, that non-BVI functionaries of a BVI fund carrying on business from outside the BVI will not generally need to hold a licence under SIBA.

13.2 Investment companies, open-ended, close-ended
Sponsors and fund managers considering setting up investment funds in the BVI may choose from the following range of possible vehicles:
* BVI business company;
* limited partnership; and
* unit trust.

The vast majority of BVI investment funds are established as companies limited by shares under the BVI Business Companies Act 2004, or as limited partnerships formed under the Partnership Act 1996.

13.3 Categories of fund
The three categories of regulated fund are as follows:
* **private fund**: restricted to either: having no more than 50 investors; or only making an invitation to subscribe for or purchase fund interests on a private basis;
* **professional fund:** may only issue fund interests to 'professional investors' and the initial investment for all investors, other than exempt investors (as defined), may not be less than $100,000 or equivalent in another currency; and
* **public fund:** greater regulation is imposed as there are no restrictions on investors or minimum investment.

Private funds and public funds must be recognised or registered under SIBA before they commence business whereas professional funds may commence business for a period of up to 21 days without being recognised, provided that they otherwise comply with the requirements of SIBA as if they were recognised and that an application is submitted to the FSC within 14 days.

A professional investor is a person either: whose ordinary business involves the acquisition or disposal of property of the same kind as the property or a substantial part of the property of the fund; or who has signed a declaration that they, whether individually or jointly with their spouse, have net worth in excess of $1 million and that they consent to be being treated as a professional investor.

Closed-ended funds are not regulated in the British Virgin Islands.

13.4 Licence requirements
Fund documentation
Public funds: Public funds may not make an invitation to the public to subscribe for or purchase fund interests unless the offer is contained in a

prospectus which has been approved by the fund's governing body and the prospectus has been registered (ie, approved) by the FSC. The prospectus is required to provide full and accurate disclosure of all information as investors would reasonably require and expect to find for the purpose of making an informed investment decision. Additional minimum disclosure requirements for a prospectus are contained in the Public Funds Code.

Private/professional funds: A private or professional fund must submit a copy of its proposed offering document to the FSC upon application for recognition or provide an explanation as to why no offering document is to be issued. The prescribed investment warning must be included in a prominent place within an offering document (or if no offering document is issued, provided to each investor or potential investor in a separate document) but otherwise SIBA does not prescribe what should be included within the offering document. Copies of offering documents issued to investors or potential investors must be filed with the FSC. The constitutional documents of private and professional funds must contain prescribed statements referring to their status as private and professional funds respectively.

13.5 Directors/authorised representative
SIBA requires that every fund established as a company have at least two directors. Corporate directors are permitted for private and professional funds, provided that at least one director is an individual, but are not permitted for public funds. There are no requirements for local directors. Each fund must appoint an authorised representative. The authorised representative itself must be a person located in the BVI holding a certificate from the FSC authorising it to act in such capacity.

13.6 Functionaries/service providers
All functionaries of funds regulated under SIBA must satisfy the FSC's 'fit and proper' criteria. Functionaries of a public fund require the prior approval of the FSC. Every public fund must have a manager, administrator and custodian and each must be independent or functionally independent of the fund and each other.

Private and professional funds must generally have a manager, administrator and custodian although an exemption from the requirement to appoint a manager and/or custodian is available upon application to the FSC.

The FSC has confirmed that functionaries of funds established and located in the BVI or any of the following countries may be recognised and accepted by the FSC for the purposes of acting as a functionary of a BVI fund :

Argentina, Australia, Bahamas, Bermuda, Belgium, Brazil, Canada, Cayman Islands, Chile, China, Denmark, Finland, France, Germany, Gibraltar, Greece, Guernsey, Hong Kong, Ireland, Isle of Man, Italy, Japan, Jersey, Luxembourg, Malta, Mexico, Netherlands, Netherland Antilles, New Zealand, Norway, Panama, Portugal, Singapore, Spain, South Africa, Sweden,

Switzerland, United Kingdom and United States of America.

The FSC has also stated that it may accept a functionary from outside the BVI and the above countries if it is satisfied that the country has a system for the effective regulation of investment business, including funds.

13.7 Restrictions on strategy, leverage or valuation

There are no restrictions on the strategy a fund may pursue, provided it is not otherwise in breach of the laws of the BVI. There are no limits on leverage taken by the funds. There are currently no rules imposed on funds as to how they value their assets. However, a Public Funds Code (which was to come into force on 31 March 2011) applies to registered public funds and imposes additional disclosure and governance requirements on public funds (including provisions relating to valuation policy and disclosure).

13.8 Continuing requirements
13.8.1 Financial statements and audit

Public funds: Financial statements for each financial year must be prepared which comply with the international reporting standards (IFRS), US, UK or Canadian generally accepted accounting principles (GAAP) or other such accounting standards as may be approved by the FSC on a case-by-case basis. The financial statements must be audited by an auditor approved by the FSC. There is no local sign off.

Private and professional funds: Financial statements for each financial year must be prepared in accordance with one of the prescribed financial standards (UK, US or Canadian GAAP or IFRS) or internationally recognised and generally accepted accounting standards equivalent to such standards. The financial statements must be audited by an auditor meeting certain prescribed criteria unless the fund is exempted from the audit requirement by the FSC (no local sign off). The above provisions are not applicable to financial years commencing prior to 17 May 2010.

Annual return

All funds regulated under SIBA must submit a return to the FSC no later than 30 June in each year in respect of the calendar year ending on 31 December of the previous year. The return contains basic prudential and governance information and summary financial information. The return does not require any information on the identity of investors or the specific investments within the fund's portfolio. Such information is confidential to the FSC and may only be publicly disclosed on an aggregated basis.

Anti-money laundering (AML)

All BVI funds, managers and administrators must comply with the Anti-Money Laundering Regulations 2008, and the Anti-money Laundering and Terrorist Financing Code of Practice 2008. However, BVI funds commonly outsource the majority of their obligations under such legislation to their

administrators who are then required to comply with the AML laws of their
home jurisdiction.

Ongoing requirements
Regulated funds are subject to a reasonable number of requirements to
notify the FSC either before or after the occurrence of certain events such as
the appointment and resignation of directors and functionaries and changes
to documents.

13.9 Custodians
Not applicable.

13.10 Undertakings for Collective Investment in Transferable Securities (UCITS)
Not applicable.

13.11 Non-UCITS funds
See above.

13.12 Hedge funds
See above.

13.13 Marketing and distribution requirements
See above.

13.14 Manager
A licence may be granted by the FSC to a person proposing to carry on
business in or from within the BVI as the functionary of funds if the FSC is
satisfied that, *inter alia*:
• the applicant, its directors and senior officers and significant
  shareholders satisfy the FSC's fit and proper criteria; and
• the organisation, management and financial resources of the applicant
  are adequate for the carrying on of the relevant investment business.
   A holder of a licence under SIBA must comply with the requirements of
the act and, upon it becoming applicable to SIBA licensees, relevant sections
of the Regulatory Code 2009.

14. SECURITIES INSTITUTIONS
14.1 Market executive undertaking
Not applicable.

14.2 Securities clearing house
Not applicable.

14.3 Central securities depository
Not applicable.

14.4 Investment services providers (ISP)
Not applicable.

15. NOTIFICATION OBLIGATIONS
15.1 Notification of major shareholding
Not applicable.

16. PUBLIC TAKEOVERS
There is no takeover code or similar document providing guidance on the process to effect a takeover under BVI law. The applicable rules when a BVI-registered company is faced with a 'takeover offer' are, therefore, dictated by the common law and the relevant sections of the BCA that pertain to the usual mechanisms for the acquisition of shares, such as the provisions relating to a sale, transfer, merger, consolidation or scheme of arrangement.

Where a company is licensed under SIBA then a person holding a significant interest in the licensee may only dispose of all or part of same with the prior approval of the FSC.

16.1 Applicable laws and regulations or regulatory framework
Not applicable.

16.2 Competent authorities
Not applicable.

16.3 Dealing with disclosures and stake building
Not applicable.

16.4 Types of takeover bids
Not applicable.

16.5 Procedural aspects
Not applicable.

16.6 Nature and value of consideration offered
Not applicable.

16.7 Timetable and variations
Not applicable.

16.8 Strategy
Not applicable.

16.9 Irrevocable
Not applicable.

16.10 Share dealings, buying shares
Not applicable.

16.11   First announcement
Not applicable.

16.12   Drafting of offer documents
Not applicable.

16.13   Further announcements
Not applicable.

16.14   Responsibility
Not applicable.

16.15   Despatch
Not applicable.

16.16   Due diligence in advance of a takeover bid
Not applicable.

16.17   Conditions to the offer
Not applicable.

16.18   Financing
Not applicable.

16.19   For cash/for shares/mixed
Not applicable.

16.20   Inducement
Not applicable.

16.21   Defence mechanisms
Not applicable.

16.22   Nature of listed securities
Not applicable.

16.23   Squeeze-out
The BCA provides that shareholders holding: (i) 90 per cent of the votes of the outstanding shares entitled to a vote; and (ii) 90 per cent of the votes of the outstanding shares of each class of shares entitled to a vote as a class, may direct the company in writing to redeem the shares of the minority shareholders and upon receipt of the instruction the company must redeem those shares.

No other 'squeeze-out' mechanism is set out under BVI law but provisions may be built into the company's memorandum and articles of association.

16.24 Schemes of arrangement

The BCA provides for schemes of arrangement wherein the BVI court may order that a meeting be summoned in the manner directed by the court upon an application made by, among others, the company, a creditor, a member or a voluntary liquidator.

If persons representing 75 per cent of the members or class of members present and voting at such a meeting agree to an arrangement, then if the same is sanctioned by the court, it will bind all members and the company. Arrangement is defined in the context of a scheme of arrangement to include a reorganisation of the company's share capital.

An order made by the court with respect to the arrangement has no effect, however, until the order is filed with the BVI Registrar of Corporate Affairs.

A copy of any such order must, however, be annexed to every copy of the company's memorandum and articles of association after the order has been made.

It should be noted that the BCA also provides for a plan of arrangement, in which an 'arrangement' means a merger or consolidation, a reorganisation or reconstruction, a sale or issue of shares, debt obligations or securities in the company in exchange for shares, debt obligations or securities in another company, the separation of two or more businesses, an amendment to the memorandum and articles of association or a dissolution. The process to effect a plan of arrangement also involves the making of an application to the BVI court.

17. FOREIGN INVESTMENT CONTROLS
17.1 Foreign investments
Not applicable.

17.2 Exemptions
Not applicable.

17.3 Exemptions of notification or prior authorisation
Not applicable.

17.4 Notification in order to establish a balance of payments
Not applicable.

Bulgaria

Borislav Boyanov & Co Svetlina Kortenska

1. GENERAL DESCRIPTION OF THE CAPITAL MARKETS
1.1 Number of companies listed
There are 467 listed companies in Bulgaria as of July 2010.

1.2 Total volume and market value
The overall market capitalisation of the Bulgarian Stock Exchange (BSE) as of 20 July 2010 was of circa EUR 5.25 billion.

The total volume of lots traded during 2009 was 615,355,722.

The total turnover of the BSE in 2009 was circa EUR 800 million (47 per cent less than 2008).

1.3 Issue activity
The BSE reported the listing of 555 issues of financial instruments (ie, not only securities). The new issuers listed for the first time in 2009 were 37 (53 per cent less compared to 2008). There were no initial public offerings (IPOs) completed through the BSE.

1.4 Takeover activity
With few exceptions related to the disclosed acquisition of majority stakes in listed companies off the floor of the BSE, there were no stock exchange takeovers completed during 2009.

1.5 Hostile takeover attempts
No hostile attempts were reported for the year 2009.

2. REGULATORY STRUCTURE
2.1 General
The legal framework of the financial services market encompasses the following key acts:
* the Public Offering of Securities Act (POSA);
* the Markets in Financial Instruments Act (MIFIA);
* the Law against Market Abuse with Financial Instruments (LAMAFI);
as well as a large number of other acts and secondary legislation.

The POSA regulates: (i) public offering of and the trade in securities; (ii) investment and management companies; (iii) the Central Depository of Securities (CDS); and (iv) listed companies.

The MIFIA regulates the financial markets and the market participants, the activities of investment intermediaries, the systematic internalisers and

Multilateral Trading Facilities, and the financial supervision on trade in financial instruments.

Following implementation of Directive 2004/39/EC of the Parliament and the Council of 21 April 2004 (MiFID), Bulgarian law defined in addition to securities and related securities markets, a number of other financial instruments which became subject to more stringent financial regulation and supervision.

Namely, the market and trading rules set out therein apply to:
- securities; and
- instruments other than securities: (i) money-market instruments; (ii) units in collective investment undertakings; (iii) derivative instruments meeting the MiFID and Regulation EC 1287/2006 of the EC requirements.

The capital markets regulator is the Financial Supervision Commission (FSC).

The only regulated market licensed by the FSC is the BSE. The rules and regulations adopted by the BSE board of directors provide for market self-regulation.

2.2 Regulation of the offering of new securities
New issues of securities in private companies, if not publicly offered, are not regulated and may be privately placed without particular restrictions unless the statutes and the general provisions of the Commerce Act otherwise provide.

The public offering of new securities is provided for in the POSA and subject to the regulatory requirements set out below.

Public offering
Pursuant to the definition of the POSA, a public offering shall be 'the provision of information on offering of securities to 100 or more persons or to an unlimited number of persons, in whatever form and by whatever means, containing sufficient data on the terms of the offering and the securities offered, in a manner allowing investors to decide on the subscription or purchase of securities'.

Subject to certain exemptions, a public offering of securities triggers disclosure and regulatory requirements, such as:
- approval (confirmation) by the FSC of a prospectus or 'passporting' of a prospectus approved in another EU member state;
- requirement for registration of the issuer in the FSC and CDS;
- requirement for publication of a notification about the offering and, in case of an IPO, filing of a notification with the FSC about the results of the offering; and
- ongoing disclosure of periodic and material information.

The POSA prospectus requirements are subject to the same exemptions as those set out in Directive 2003/71/EC of the European Parliament and the Council (Prospectus Directive) (see section 5.2).

Private offering
A private offering is any offering of securities which does not qualify as a
public offering.

2.3 Differences between local and foreign companies
Bulgarian law is not discriminative, although depending on whether the
foreign company is registered, licensed and/or has a prospectus published
within the EU or in a non-EU country, different approval procedures apply.

EU companies may benefit from the prospectus published in their home
jurisdictions. Following the 'passporting' of the prospectus, the securities of
the EU issuer will be admitted for offering to investors in Bulgaria.

Securities issued by non-EU issuers, not offered publicly or traded on the
regulated market in another EU member state, will be admitted to public trade in
Bulgaria following the approval and publication of a prospectus and registration
with the FSC, unless there is a bilateral international agreement providing for the
recognition of prospectuses issued in the contracting country.

2.4 Admission to trading on a regulated market
The admission of securities to trading is made pursuant to the Listing Rules
of the BSE (section 8).

2.5 Financial promotion
The form and content of marketing and financial promotion materials is in
line with the new MiFID requirements.

2.6 Rule books
The rules and regulations of the BSE are available on the BSE's Internet site at
www.bse-sofia.bg.

3. REGISTRATION OF THE ISSUER AND SECURITIES
3.1 Registration requirements
The issuers of publicly offered securities, public companies and securities'
issues are to be registered by the FSC.

The issuer would need to obtain first either a confirmed or 'passported'
prospectus or to get an exemption from the prospectus requirements.
The securities that are to be registered, need to be de-materialised,
freely transferable, fully paid in and issued in compliance with all legal
requirements.

3.2 Other requirements
Depending on the type of securities as well as other circumstances,
such as reorganisation, liquidation or insolvency, there are specific rules
and provisions, supplementing or amending the general registration
requirements.

3.3 Nature of securities
Securities are defined in the POSA as transferable rights, registered in

accounts at the CDS or in foreign depository institutions (dematerialised securities), or documents incorporating transferable rights (paper form securities), which may be traded on the capital market, such as:

- shares or equivalent securities;
- bonds and other debt instruments;
- other securities which entitle their holder to the right to acquire or sell such securities or which result in a monetary payment, determined on the basis of securities, currency exchanges, interest rates or yield, commodities or other indices or ratios as well as debt securities

Though physical securities fall within the definition of 'securities' under the POSA these cannot be listed on the regulated market and are not traded at the BSE.

4. SUPERVISORY AUTHORITIES
4.1 Conduct: prudential, cooperation, self-regulation stock exchange
The overall supervisory function of the regulated market and market participants is exercised by the FSC.

The rules and regulation of the BSE govern the supervision exercised by the BSE on its members; the treatment of conflicts of interest; prevention of market manipulation and insider trading; the procedure for conduct of examinations; and for imposition of sanctions, arbitration and reconciliation procedures.

4.2 New listings measures in connection with the credit crisis
The BSE announced as anti-crisis measures the application of a more flexible policy in terms of fees and various incentive measures, including governmental support, listing of companies subject to privatisation, etc.

5. OFFERING DOCUMENTATION OR PROSPECTUS REQUIREMENTS
5.1 Nature and statutory requirements of the offering document or disclosure document
The issuers of securities must disclose full complete and accurate information that would allow investors to make informed investment decisions. In line with the Prospectus Directive, the law prohibits the public offering of securities or admission to trade without publication of an approved prospectus, unless a prospectus exemption is applicable (section 5.2).

A basic prospectus may be approved for certain non-equity securities issued periodically or continuously.

The prospectuses should comply with POSA, the secondary legislation (ordinances) of FSC and the relevant EU regulations, like Commission Regulation (EC) No 809/2004 implementing Directive 2003/71/EC.

5.2 Exemptions
No prospectus will be required, if:
- securities are offered to: (i) qualified investors; or (ii) less than 100 persons in Bulgaria or another EU member state;

- the minimum consideration is equivalent to EUR 50,000 per investor for each separate offering;
- the nominal value per unit of the offered securities is at least the equivalent of EUR 50,000;
- the total value of the offered securities is less than the equivalent of EUR 100,000 per annum.

5.3 Preparation of the offering document, general contents
The prospectus should contain the minimum mandatory information on the financial standing, the assets and liabilities, the financial results, the prospects for development of the issuer and the persons guaranteeing the securities, as well as on the rights attached to the securities.

The prospectus can be organised as one single document or in three separate documents, namely: a registration document with information on the issuer; a document on the securities; and a summary.

5.4 Due diligence
Given the liability involved such due diligence is a must despite the absence of express rules on the process.

5.5 Responsibility
The prospectus should be signed by the issuer (the offeror or the person requesting admission to trade), as well as by the guarantor for the securities, who declare that the prospectus meets the requirements of the law.

The managers of the issuer and the offeror are jointly and severally liable for untrue, misleading or incomplete data.

The auditor is liable for the damage caused as a result of untruthfulness of the audited financial statements.

5.6 Disclaimer/selling restrictions
There is no standard disclaimer or selling restrictions wording or special guidance in this respect.

5.7 Recognition of prospectuses by other exchanges
The FSC is entitled to recognise the prospectus, published in conformity with the laws of the jurisdiction where it has been confirmed, if such possibility is provided for in an agreement to which Bulgaria is a party.

5.8 Supplementary prospectuses
The issuer and the offeror of securities are required to supplement the prospectus:
- prior to FSC prospectus confirmation: within three days of becoming aware of a circumstance which requires changes in the prospectus.
- after the confirmation of a prospectus until the final date of the offering or the commencement of trade: not later than one business day from becoming aware of a material new circumstance, serious mistake or error in the information contained in the prospectus.

5.9 Issuing of bonds

Different provisions apply depending on the bond issuer and the purpose and type of bond issues. The most common types of bonds are corporate bonds, mortgage bonds issued by banks under the Mortgage Bonds Act, municipal bonds issued by the municipalities under the Municipal Debt Act, compensatory instruments as defined in the Transactions with Compensatory Instruments Act, domestic T-bills (short term and long term), Eurobonds, etc.

In the case of public offering of corporate bonds the following undertakings will be required: (i) a confirmation of the prospectus; (ii) registration of the issuer and the bond issue with the FSC; (iii) registration with the CDS; and (iv) listing of the bonds at the BSE.

For initial offering of bonds the issuer should enter into an agreement with a bondholders' trustee. The trustee is a mandatory figure for secured bonds. It may also be appointed in case of unsecured bonds at the discretion of the issuer.

A bondholder trustee can only be a Bulgarian bank or a licensed or 'passported' branch of a foreign bank.

Special rules exist with respect to the issue of municipal or governmental bonds.

6. DISTRIBUTION SYSTEMS

6.1 Normal structure of a distribution group

There are no special provisions of the law setting out standards for structuring a distribution group. The simplest possible structure would normally encompass the appointment of an investment intermediary as underwriter or distributor.

6.2 Methods of distribution

The law does not provide for definitions of specific methods of distribution.

6.3 Underwriting

The law does not provide for specific rules in relation to the underwriting of issues other than those generally applicable to the activities of investment intermediaries. However, an underwriter would be restricted from assuming other conflicting roles.

6.4 Fees and commission

Distributors' commissions and fees are contractually agreed.

6.5 Stabilisation

The law and the rules and regulations of the BSE allow for the undertaking of certain transactions (which would otherwise fall within the scope of prohibited manipulative transactions) for the purposes of stabilisation of the price of the securities traded.

6.6 Involvement of a distributor in the preparation of the offering document

An investment intermediary may be and is normally assigned the preparation of the offering documents.

6.7 Timing of distribution process

Unless certain statutory terms are applicable to an offering (for example, in the case of a takeover bid or an IPO) the timing of the distribution is a matter of planning and contractual arrangement between the issuer and the investment intermediary.

6.8 Rules on distribution to the public

There are special national (non-harmonised) rules in relation to the distribution of undertakings for collective investments in transferable securities (UCITS). For other types of offering and distribution, the requirements as to the activities of the investment intermediaries would apply.

7. PUBLICITY

Publicity is provided through the BSE Bulletin, the issuers' Web site or though the mass media.

8. LISTING
8.1 Special listing requirements, admission criteria

Segment A (official equities market) – the securities must have been traded on the official market Segment B for at least one year or on the unofficial market for at least two years; the issuer shall have completed at least five financial years; at least 25 per cent shall be held by minority shareholders or the total value of minority shareholdings is at least BGN 20 million (circa EUR 10 million); the average turnover for the last six months shall be not less than BGN 1 million (circa EUR 500,000); the average monthly number of transactions shall be not less than 500; the issuer shall have realised profit for at least three out of five financial years and shall be committed to apply the National Code for Corporate Governance (NCCG).

Lower thresholds apply for segment B of the official market.

For the official bonds market: the time left to maturity of the bond shall be not less than one year and the issue shall not be subject to a time limit; the non-depreciated value of the principal is not less than the equivalent of BGN 5 million (circa EUR 2.5 million); the number of bonds is at least 5,000.

Logically, other criteria (predominantly less stringent than those applicable to the official market) apply to the other market segments. Special rules are also provided depending on the type of instruments traded.

8.2 Mechanics of the review process

The issuer shall file an application before the BSE accompanied by 17 supporting documents. The applications are reviewed by the Board of Directors (BD). The issues of subscription rights are admitted to trade by an order of the Director of Trading.

The BD may refuse listing on the grounds set out in the Listing Rules of the BSE.

The refusal must be reasoned and accompanied by a refund of the admission fee. The refusal is subject to appeal before the Arbitration Court of the BSE.

8.3 Prospectus obligation, due diligence, exemption

Please refer to question 5.

8.4 Appeal procedure in the event of a prospectus refusal

A prospectus is subject to approval (confirmation) or refusal by the FSC, not the BSE.

The FSC may refuse to confirm a prospectus if it does not comply with the law or if the interests of the investors is affected.

The decision of the FSC is subject to administrative appeal.

8.5 Authority of the exchange

The following bodies are in charge of the operation of the exchange:

- BD and the Chief Executive Officer;
- Chief Operating Officer;
- Director of Trading; and
- Surveillance Directorate.

The main activity is split between the Trading Directorate and the Surveillance Directorate.

The effective authority lies on the BSE BD which is entitled to manage and represent the BSE.

8.6 Sponsor

Not applicable.

8.7 Special arrangements for smaller companies such as Alternext, AIM or SPACs

There is no alternative market, though lower admission requirements apply for certain securities traded at the unofficial market of the BSE.

8.8 Costs of various types

The costs related to the listing on the BSE are set out in its tariffs and are as follows:

- fees for admission to trade and for maintenance of the registration. These vary depending on the type of issue and are calculated as a percentage of the market value, subject to a specified cap;
- fees for membership of the BSE (applies to the associated members only);
- fees for trade and announcement of transactions concluded outside the regulated market, which depend on the value of transactions;
- fees for dissemination of stock exchange information and use of trade marks;
- other fees pursuant to the rules.

9. SANCTIONS AND DISPUTES
9.1 Disciplinary and administrative sanctions
Sanctions for violation of the various laws on trading in securities and market rules may be imposed by the FSC or the BD of the BSE.

See also section 12.3.

9.2 Civil actions
See section 12.3.

9.3 Criminal penalties
See section 12.3.

10. CONTINUING OBLIGATIONS
10.1 Disclosure and transparency rule
The Transparency Directive (Directive 2004/109/EC) has been implemented in Bulgaria along with the Prospectus Directive and MIFID.

Accordingly, the Commission Regulation (EC) 1287/2006 implementing Directive 2004/39/EC of the European Parliament and of the Council as regards recordkeeping obligations for investment firms, transaction reporting, market transparency, admission of financial instruments to trading, and defined terms for the purposes of that Directive (Regulation (EC) 1287/2006) applies directly in Bulgaria.

10.2 Information
BSE is required to announce uninterrupted information on the bid and sell prices of the securities admitted to trade as well as on the orders made.

The BSE ensures access to its systems and mechanisms on disclosure and announcement of information to the brokers who are obliged to publish their quotes when acting as systematic internalisers.

The BSE publishes the time, price and volume of trades in shares.

The content and scope of the information subject to disclosure by the market as well as the terms for postponed announcement are set out in Regulation (EC) 1287/2006.

The investment intermediaries are required to notify the FSC as soon as possible, but not later than the following day, about the entry into transactions in financial instruments traded at the BSE.

Transactions outside the regulated market are announced publicly with details on the type, issue, number and unit price of the traded instruments, the currency, the date and time of conclusion, with indication that these were made off the floor of the exchange. The announcement is made by publication at the BSE and on the Internet site of the broker or by other generally accessible manner.

10.3 Listing Rules
Please see question 8 above.

10.4 Obligations regarding proxy solicitation
Please see question 11.7 below.

10.5 Continuing requirements of reporting and notification of substantial shareholdings or substantial transactions
Please see question 15 below.

10.6 Clearing
Currently the CDS does not provide clearing services.

10.7 Requirements for unlisted issuers
There are no special rules with respect to unlisted issuers.

11. CORPORATE GOVERNANCE
11.1 Law and/or Code
The corporate governance of listed companies is regulated by the POSA and in NCCG to which the BSE adhered in October 2001.

11.2 Management structure
The general meeting of the shareholders (GM) is the supreme managing body in a listed company.

The company may implement either:
- a one-tier management system, consisting of a BD of three to nine members; or
- a two-tier management system, comprising of a supervisory board (SB), appointed by the GM, and management board (MB), appointed by the SB.

The POSA requires that at least one-third of the SB or BD members are independent as defined in the POSA.

In addition to this, each listed company is required to appoint a director for relations with the investors, responsible for communicating with the FSC and the public.

11.3 Obligations to publish information on the Internet
Listed companies and other issuers of securities are required to disclose to the public, including by way of publication on the corporate Internet site:
- regulated information as required under the POSA and the Ordinances thereunder;
- periodic information on their activities such as quarterly reports and financial statements and the audited annual financial statements; and
- other important information.

11.4 Responsibility of inside/outside directors
The independent members should not be:
- employees of the listed company;
- shareholders holding, whether directly or through connected persons, at least 25 per cent of the votes in the GM, or shareholders who are

connected with the company;
- persons who are in a sustained business relationship with the company;
- members of MB/SB/BD, procurists or employees of the entities under the above; or
- persons connected with another member of the MB/SB/BD.

The members of the board are obliged to perform their duties with due care and diligence and to show loyalty to the company by placing its interest before their own, avoiding conflicts of interest, and by not disclosing inside information even after resignation.

11.5 Committees
These are recommended in the NCCG but not required by law.

11.6 Obligation to ask for consent from a shareholders' meeting
Certain related and interested parties' transactions as well as large scale transactions (of values exceeding the thresholds set out in the law) are subject to prior approval by the GM.

11.7 Depth of information – proxy solicitation
At least 30 days before the GM, the listed company is required to provide to the shareholders a convocation notice, containing the agenda and the specified materials under each item of the agenda, along with a form of proxy on which the shareholder may indicate approval or disapproval of each proposal expected to be presented and voted on at the meeting by a proxy holder.

Copies of the notice for the convocation of the meeting (together with all materials) and the form of proxy must be filed with the FSC and the BSE upon announcement of the notice in the Commercial Registry. The same shall be also made available on the company's Web site. The FSC reviews the notice and the materials and may, depending on the circumstances, intervene and prohibit the voting of certain resolutions.

The proposal for representation of a shareholder or shareholders with more than 5 per cent of the shares ('proxy solicitation') needs to be published in one central daily newspaper or sent to each shareholder to whom it refers with at least the minimum mandatory content set out in the law in relation to the agenda and proposed GM resolutions.

11.8 Appointment/dismissal of directors

One-tier management system
The GM appoints and dismisses the members of the BD in accordance with the law and the statutes. The grounds for dismissal are set out in the management agreements.

Two-tier management system
The SB is elected by the GM and in its turn appoints and dismisses the MB members.

11.9 Income and options for directors

The remuneration and options of the board members are determined by the GM. The members are required to deposit a guarantee for their management equal to at least the triple amount of their gross remuneration as board members. The company will be entitled to retain the guarantee upon decision of the GM to cover damages caused to it.

11.10 Earnings guidance

Pursuant to the NCCG it is recommended that the remuneration of the members of the BD consists of two parts: permanent remuneration and additional benefits. The company may provide as additional remuneration to the members of the boards shares, options or other appropriate instruments.

11.11 Management discussion and analysis (MD&A)

Bulgarian law provides for certain rules in relation to management presentations, management accounts or management reports.

11.12 Directors' liability

Civil liability

All members of the boards are jointly liable for any damage caused to the company as a result of a fault when performing their duties and obligations. Civil claims can be filed by: (i) a special representative of the company appointed by the GM and; (ii) any shareholder/shareholders possessing at least 5 per cent of the company's capital.

Criminal liability

This is a personal liability for committing major breaches of the established public rules of conduct, which are declared punishable under the Bulgarian Penal Code. The major offences are prosecuted *ex officio*, even if there is no complaint from the company.

Administrative liability

This is personal liability for breaching the administrative rules in the country, normally involving the imposition of fines.

Special liability in case of market abuse

Please see section 12.3 below. The members of the managing bodies as well as the investment intermediary who has signed the prospectus, are jointly and severally liable for damages due to untrue, misleading or incomplete information.

12. MARKET ABUSE

LAMAFI transposes the Market Abuse Directive and sets out the framework on prevention of market abuse by insiders in listed companies.

12.1 Insider trading

Trading on the basis of inside information is prohibited.

Inside information is any precise information still undisclosed to the public (though subject to public disclosure) and to the market and the regulatory authorities, which refers directly or indirectly to issuers of financial instruments or to the financial instruments themselves, if its disclosure, may materially influence the price of the financial instruments or related derivatives.

Generally, price sensitive inside information is any information which:

- sets out facts and circumstances which have occurred or may be reasonably expected to occur in the future and are sufficiently precise in order to make conclusions on their possible effect on the price of the financial instruments; and
- which is customarily used by investors in order to decide on an investment in a particular instrument.

Non-exhaustive lists of facts and circumstances which may be considered to be price sensitive information are set out in a special ordinance of the FSC. It is subject to mandatory disclosure, unless disclosure is reasonably postponed in conformity with the provisions of the ordinance.

Certain persons are considered by law to be insiders and are prohibited from trading in securities on the basis of inside information held or acquired as a result of:

- membership of the management or controlling body of the issuer;
- shareholding or voting rights in the GM;
- access to the information due to professional obligations; or
- illegal acquisition of inside information.

The same prohibitions are also applicable to the natural persons related to the insiders, when such natural person participates in the adoption of decisions for entry into transactions on the account of a legal person.

Finally, the prohibitions also apply to any other person who is not otherwise an insider if they hold information which qualifies as inside information and are aware or should be aware that it is falling within the scope of inside information.

The company is required to maintain a list of insiders. The entries are kept for a period of at least five years. The FSC may request a copy of the list at any time.

12.2 Market manipulation

The following transactions may qualify as manipulative, and are prohibited under the LAMAFI:

- conduct by a person, or two or more persons acting together, to secure a dominant position over the supply of or demand for financial instruments, which has the effect of fixing, directly or indirectly, purchase or sales prices or creating other unfair trading conditions;
- the conclusion of transactions in financial instruments upon closing of the regulated market which results in misleading the investors acting on the basis of the closing prices;
- expression of opinions about financial instruments or their issuer

through the media, including the Internet while having previously taken positions on those financial instruments and profiting subsequently from the impact of those opinions on the prices of the instruments, without simultaneously having disclosed that conflict of interest; and

• other actions and transactions by which market manipulation is committed.

12.3 Miscellaneous

Although insider trading and market manipulation are prohibited, the transactions concluded in breach of those prohibitions will be valid. The liable persons will be subject to administrative fines only. There is no criminal liability for insider trading or market manipulation.

13. MUTUAL OR INVESTMENT FUNDS
13.1 Introduction to these two categories

Investment companies (open ended and close-ended)
Investment companies are joint stock companies with a minimum capital of BGN 500,000 (circa EUR 250,000), licensed by the FSC for public fundraising for the purpose of investing in securities or other liquid financial instruments. Any other joint stock company which raises funds publicly and whose investments in securities represent more than 50 per cent of their balance sheet assets for the last six months is also considered an investment company.

Investment companies are prohibited to enter into commercial transactions and are restricted with respect to the financial instruments in which they can invest.

Investment companies may be open-ended or close-ended. All capital contributions in both companies must be made in cash.

Mutual (contractual) funds
The mutual fund does not have legal personality. It is a segregated block of assets collected for the purposes of collective investment in securities or other liquid financial assets and cash, raised by public offering of units on the basis of risk sharing. Mutual funds are only open-ended. The net value of assets of the mutual fund cannot be less than BGN 500,000 (circa EUR 250,000). The fund is managed by a fund manager and licensed by FSC.

13.2 Investment companies, open-ended, close-ended
The capital of the open-ended company is always equal to the net value of its assets. The registered capital is the one with which the company was founded.

The close-ended investment company needs to have its capital at any time not less than BGN 500,000 (EUR 250,000) and shall maintain a structure in conformity with a special ordinance of the FSC.

13.3 Licence requirements
For licensing purposes the investment company has to present the

following (in addition to its constitutive documents and the data on capital contributions):

- data on the members of the management and controlling bodies and the representatives of the company, including their professional qualification and experience;
- contract with the fund manager and contract for depositary services with a bank-depositary;
- identification and other data of the persons holding 10 per cent or more of the shares or with a controlling interest in the company;
- rules on evaluation of the portfolio and determination of the net value of assets;
- the prospectus of the open-ended investment company;
- rules on risk management and other data set out in a special ordinance of the FSC.

The fund manager applying for a permit for organising and managing a mutual fund completes a standard form application to which it attaches various documents required by law, like the rules of the mutual fund, the resolution of the competent corporate body for organising the fund, rules on evaluation of the portfolio and determination of the net value of assets, the contract for depositary services with a bank-depositary, the prospectus, etc.

The FSC issues decisions on the licensing of an investment company or the issuance of a permit to raise a fund and on the approval of the prospectus within three months from the submission of all documents.

13.4 Continuing requirements
The public offering of shares and units may commence only following publication of the approved prospectus. It is subject to regular update.

13.5 Custodians
Custodian services may be provided only by financial institutions meeting the special requirements set out in the POSA and MIFIA.

13.6 Undertakings for Collective Investments in Transferable Securities (UCITS)
The units in collective investment schemes (CIS) are defined as financial instruments containing entitlement of their owners to the assets of the scheme.

Such CISs under Bulgarian law are open-ended investment companies and mutual funds. Units of foreign CISs are offered following 'passporting' of the prospectus in conformity with the UCITS Directive and the *Committee of European Securities Regulators* (CESR) Guidelines Ref CESR/06-120 b (CESR Guidelines).

13.7 Non-UCITS funds
Currently, Bulgarian law does not regulate funds other than those referred to above.

13.8 Hedge funds
The law does not provide for special rules applicable to hedge funds.

13.9 Marketing and distribution requirements

No advertisements related to the public offering of units can be disseminated unless a copy of it is delivered to the FSC.

The advertisements and publications should necessarily include information about the location(s) where the prospectus and the constitutive acts are accessible to the public, warnings that the value of units or income may decrease, that the investments are not guaranteed and that future yield is not related to past results.

There are also rules in relation to telephone calls, meetings with investors, verbal announcements and communications, presentation of the results of the activity in advertisements and publications.

13.10   Manager

The activities of an open-ended investment company and a mutual fund are managed only by a licensed managing company (fund manager) on the basis of a management contract.

A close-ended investment company may be managed by a managing company on the basis of a contract or by corporate management bodies. If the activities of the close-ended company are undertaken by corporate bodies a contract shall be entered into with a person qualified for investment consultations under the MIFIA.

14.   SECURITIES INSTITUTIONS
14.1 Market executive undertaking

Not applicable.

14.2 Securities clearing house

The CDS is intended to act as the clearing house in charge of both the clearing and the settlement of securities in Bulgaria, though currently it only provides for settlement of securities.

14.3 Central securities depository

The organisation and the activity of the CDS is governed by POSA, the Ordinance on the CDS and the Rules of the CDS, adopted by its BD.

The CDS maintains two types of accounts: deposit accounts and securities accounts. The securities accounts of a member of the CDS are separated from the securities accounts of its clients. Transactions in securities are registered and settled through the CDS system.

T-Bills issued by the Bulgarian state are recorded in a special registry of the Bulgarian National Bank.

14.4 Investment services providers (ISP)

Transactions in financial instruments as a business is a regulated activity of entities licensed for that purpose by the FSC. Except where certain persons and entities are exempt from the regulation of the MIFIA, only the following persons/entities are entitled to provide investment services and undertake investment activities:

- persons who are holders of an investment brokerage licence issued by the FSC;
- licensed banks;
- licensed local branches of foreign investment firms or banks; or
- investment firms or banks of EU member states which have been 'passported' to operate in Bulgaria on a cross-border basis or on the basis of the freedom to provide services, or through a local branch.

The investment services defined in MIFIA follow the list provided in Annex I to MiFID.

15. NOTIFICATION OBLIGATIONS
15.1 Notification of major shareholding
Subject to few exceptions, any shareholder who acquires (directly or indirectly) 5 per cent or more (if divisible by five) of the voting rights in the GM of a listed company is obliged to notify the company, the FSC and the BSE and to disclose the persons directly or indirectly controlling it.

16. PUBLIC TAKEOVERS
16.1 Applicable laws and regulations or regulatory framework
The POSA provides for the main legal framework in relation to public takeovers. Details on the terms and conditions for registration and publication of mandatory and voluntary takeover bids as well as on the content of the bid and the determination of the price are given in:
- ordinance No 13/2003 of the FSC on the takeover bid for purchase of exchange of shares, as amended and supplemented;
- ordinance No 41/2008 on the Requirements to the Content of the Reasoning of the Price of the Shares in a Listed Company, including to the Application of the Valuation Methods in case of Reorganisation, Joint Venture Contract and Takeover Bid.

16.2 Competent authorities
The FSC is competent to clear for publication the takeover bids following their registration and publication.

16.3 Dealing with disclosures and stake building
Please see question 15.1.

There are no other rules in relation to stake building, except for the so-called 'creeping minority limitations'. Shareholders with either more than 50 per cent or more than 66.67 per cent of the voting rights in a company shall not be allowed to acquire during the year shares, representing more than 3 per cent of the total number of the voting shares of the company, without having registered the takeover bid with the FSC.

16.4 Types of takeover bids
Bulgarian law provides for two types of takeover bids:
- mandatory takeover bids – for acquisition (directly or indirectly) of voting rights above the thresholds of 50 per cent and 66.67 per cent of

the voting rights in the GM; and
- voluntary takeover bids – when passing over the threshold of 90 per cent of all voting right shares or where a shareholder with at least 5 per cent of the voting rights wants to acquire at least one-third of the voting rights in a company. *See also 16.3.

16.5 Procedural aspects

A mandatory takeover bid shall be registered at the FSC within 14 days of the takeover event.

The takeover bidder may publish the bid if the FSC does not issue a prohibition on the publication.

If the FSC does not issue a decision prohibiting the takeover bid, it is considered cleared for publication.

A competitive takeover bid may also be registered and in such a case both bidders will be given additional time to improve their offers.

The takeover bid has certain mandatory content required by POSA.

A copy of the filed bid is sent to the BSE and to the management of the company and its employees with a warning that it has not yet been cleared by the FSC. Within seven days from filing, the management of the company submits to the FSC and gives to the employees or their representatives an opinion on the bid.

Following the expiration of the term for prohibition by the FSC (if the FSC has failed to expressly clear it), the takeover bid, together with the management opinion of it, is published in two central newspapers.

16.6 Nature and value of consideration offered

The takeover bid should contain an invitation to all other shareholders to sell their shares against: (i) cash consideration; or (ii) shares issued by the offeror for the purpose. In the second case, a cash alternative for the exchange shares is required.

The offered acquisition price or exchange value in the case of mandatory takeover bids cannot be lower than the higher of: (i) the fair price per share as stated in the reasoning of the offer; and (ii) the average weighted market price of the company's shares during the last three months before submission of the takeover bid; or (iii) if such market price cannot be determined (if the shares do not have a market price) the highest price per share paid by the bidder during the six months preceding the registration of the bid. If the share price cannot be determined as set out in the preceding sentence, it is determined as the higher between the latest issue value and the latest price paid by the bidder.

16.7 Timetable and variations

Amendment and variations to the bids are permitted subject to certain requirements until acceptance of the takeover bid by the offerees. Each change is subject to registration prior to publication. The term for acceptance cannot be shorter than 28 days and longer than 70 days from the date of publication of the takeover bid, except in the case of a competitive takeover bid. In such a case the term of the first takeover bid is extended until expiration of the competitive takeover bid.

16.8 Strategy
The strategy for development of the company accompanies the registration of the takeover bid. If the takeover bidder intends to de-list the company it will need to announce this in the takeover bid.

16.9 Irrevocable
Mandatory takeover bids are irrevocable following their publication (subject to certain exceptions).

16.10 Share dealings, buying shares
The takeover bid is accepted by express statement and depositing of the share certificates with an investment intermediary or at the CDS. The acceptance may be withdrawn until the expiration of the term for acceptance. The transaction is considered completed at the time of expiration of the acceptance term. The payment of the consideration is made within seven days from completion of the transfer. The title passes with the registration of the transfer at the CDS.

Following the expiration of the acceptance term the offeror publishes the result and notifies the FSC.

16.11 First announcement
Please see section 16.5 on the procedural aspects.

16.12 Drafting of offer documents
The drafting of the offer documents is to be entrusted to an investment intermediary.

16.13 Further announcements
Please see section 16.5 on the procedural aspects in relation to the filing and clearance of competitive takeover bids.

16.14 Responsibility
The offeror and the investment intermediary are jointly and severally liable for the damage caused by untrue, misleading or incomplete data in the takeover bid.

16.15 Despatch
The offeror is obliged to complete the takeover bid through a licensed investment intermediary using the possibilities for remote acceptance of the takeover bid though the CDS.

16.16 Due diligence in advance of a takeover bid
Given the mandatory content of the takeover bid and the rules on reasoning of the consideration the due diligence process is a must, although not expressly required under the law.

16.17   Conditions to the offer
Conditions to the offer cannot contradict the provisions on the mandatory content of the takeover bid prescribed by the law.

16.18   Financing
A takeover bid may be made only for secure and proven possibility for full payment/exchange of the shares.

16.19   For cash/for shares/mixed
Please see 16.6. Mixed consideration is not excluded.

16.20   Inducement
Inducement under Bulgarian law is restricted.

16.21   Defence mechanisms
The investors can get a defence through: (i) negative opinion by the management of the company; (ii) possibility to organise and register a competitive takeover bid; and (iii) power of FSC to prohibit the takeover bid publication.

16.22   Nature of listed securities
Please see question 3.3 above

16.23   Squeeze-out
The squeeze-out right may be exercised by the acquirer of more than 95 per cent of the voting rights in the company as a result of a takeover bid. The squeeze-out right may be exercised within a period of three months from the completion of the takeover bid.

16.24   Schemes of arrangement
No special regulation.

17.   FOREIGN INVESTMENT CONTROLS
17.1 Foreign investments
There are no restrictions for foreign investments in the Bulgarian capital market.

17.2 Exemptions
Not applicable.

17.3 Exemptions of notification or prior authorisation
Not applicable.

17.4 Notification in order to establish a balance of payments
Banks and investment intermediaries are required to maintain registries for transactions between local and foreign persons of value exceeding the equivalent of BGN 100,000 (circa EUR 50,000), subject to receipt of standard statistical declarations filed in the BNB.

Canada

Borden Ladner Gervais LLP
Alfred L J Page, David R Surat & Andrew M Bunston

1.   GENERAL DESCRIPTION OF THE CAPITAL MARKETS
1.1   Numbers of companies listed
There are more than 3,600 listed companies in Canada. The Toronto Stock Exchange (the TSX), the senior equity market, had 1,516 listings and the TSX-Venture Exchange (the TSX-V), the principal junior equity market, had 2,154 listings as of 31 December 2010.

1.2   Total volume and market value
TSX issuers had an aggregate quoted market value of C$2.2 trillion, and TSX-V issuers C$71.5 billion as of 31 December 2010. Trading volume for 2010 was 104.6 billion shares (C$1.39 trillion) on the TSX and 67.3 billion shares (C$34.3 billion) on the TSX-V.

1.3   Issue activity
Total equity financing by listed issuers in 2010 was C$44.1 billion for TSX issuers and C$9.8 billion for TSX-V issuers.

1.4   Takeover activity
In 2009 and 2010, there were approximately 142 public takeover bids in Canada, with an aggregate value of approximately C$80 billion (Capital IQ).

1.5   Hostile takeover attempts
There were 17 attempted hostile takeover bids in the Canadian marketplace in 2009 and 2010 (Capital IQ).

2.   REGULATORY STRUCTURE
2.1   General
Securities regulation in Canada is a provincial responsibility. Each of Canada's 10 provinces and three territories has its own securities legislation and regulator. For example, the securities regulator in Ontario is the Ontario Securities Commission (OSC).

2.2   Regulation of the offering of new securities
The offering of new securities by an issuer will fall within the definition of a distribution under Canadian securities legislation and will be subject to the prospectus requirement. An issuer must either file and clear a prospectus with the appropriate regulators or rely on a prospectus exemption.

2.2.1 Public offering

In a typical public offering, an issuer will file a preliminary prospectus, which is reviewed by the securities regulators. Any resulting changes will be reflected in an amended preliminary prospectus or the final prospectus. Certain information, such as the price and size of the offering may be omitted at the preliminary prospectus stage. The issuer and the underwriters are prohibited from marketing the offering until a receipt for the preliminary prospectus has been obtained from the securities regulators. Issuance of this receipt is routine following only a pro forma review.

The preliminary prospectus is made public on the System for Electronic Document Analysis and Retrieval (SEDAR), which is the public repository of filed documents at *www.sedar.com*. The issuer and underwriters are then permitted to solicit expressions of interest and are required to deliver a copy of the preliminary prospectus to potential investors.

No sales may be made until the regulators' comments have been addressed and a receipt for the final prospectus is obtained. The final prospectus is required to contain full, true, and plain disclosure of all material facts related to the securities distributed. The final prospectus must be delivered to each purchaser and person who received the preliminary prospectus.

Purchasers have the right to withdraw from their agreement to purchase securities within two days of receipt of the final prospectus. If the final prospectus contains a misrepresentation, a purchaser will have rights of action for damages or rescission against the issuer, every director of the issuer, the underwriters, and any expert who consented to disclosure regarding a report, opinion or statement provided by them in the prospectus to the extent that the misrepresentation relates to that report, opinion or statement and any other person who signed the prospectus.

2.2.2 Private offering

Several prospectus exemptions permit securities to be distributed in a private placement. The majority of these exemptions apply in all Canadian jurisdictions; however, there are variations.

If an issuer is not a reporting issuer, any securities that it distributes under a prospectus exemption may generally only be resold pursuant to a further exemption. Securities of a reporting issuer distributed under a prospectus exemption may be subject to a four-month hold period. These securities may be resold on an exempt basis prior to the expiry of the hold period, and freely thereafter.

Examples of commonly used prospectus exemptions include:
- sales to accredited investors who are defined in terms of their assets or income;
- sales of securities of a private issuer to certain investors based on their relationship to the issuer; and
- sales of securities where the acquisition cost paid by the purchaser at the time of the distribution exceeds C$150,000.

An issuer distributing securities under an exemption may be required to pay a fee and file a form providing the regulators with information concerning the distribution, any agent and the purchasers.

The requirements and potential liability regarding documentation and disclosure to purchasers under a prospectus exemption vary depending on the exemption relied on and the jurisdiction. For example, in Ontario there is no requirement to provide any particular form of disclosure. However, a misrepresentation in any disclosure that is provided may be actionable. If an issuer chooses to provide disclosure, it is required to include a description of statutory rights of the purchaser for misrepresentation in the disclosure and to deliver a copy of the disclosure to the OSC.

2.3 Differences between local and foreign companies

Foreign issuers may be required to appoint a local agent for service and to agree to submit to the jurisdiction of the Canadian courts and securities regulators and, if listing on an exchange, to meet higher listing standards and to adopt Canadian-equivalent corporate governance and investor protection regimes, if not otherwise applicable.

Issuers subject to disclosure requirements in Australia, France, Germany, Hong Kong, Italy, Japan, Mexico, The Netherlands, New Zealand, Singapore, South Africa, Spain, Sweden, Switzerland or the United Kingdom having less than 10 per cent of their securities, on a fully diluted basis, held by Canadian residents are exempt from many of the Canadian continuous disclosure requirements if they file in Canada the documents required in their home jurisdiction.

Issuers regulated by the United States Securities & Exchange Commission (the SEC) may satisfy their Canadian filing requirements with their US filings, regardless of the level of Canadian ownership. US issuers may also rely on the Multi-jurisdictional Disclosure System (MJDS), a bilateral arrangement between Canada and the United States. A US issuer relying on MJDS is required to file its US documents in Canada at the same time as it files them with the SEC, with additional disclosure. These documents are not subject to the normal review process and the Canadian regulators will rely on the SEC review.

2.4 Admission to trading on a regulated market

Each exchange establishes and administers its own standards for listed issuers. Completion of a public offering does not automatically result in listing on an exchange.

2.5 Financial promotion

Registration with a securities regulator may be required by persons engaged in the business of financial promotion. In addition, under Canadian securities law, a person who directly or indirectly takes the initiative in founding, organising, or substantially re-organising an issuer's business may be considered to be a promoter. Disclosure regarding a promoter is required in a prospectus and the promoter may be required to accept liability in a public offering by signing a prospectus certificate.

2.6 Rule books

Each jurisdiction in Canada has its own securities legislation and regulations. National and multi-lateral instruments and policies are adopted by all or a subset of the Canadian jurisdictions, resulting in similar rules for key areas of securities regulation, such as prospectus offerings and continuous disclosure.

Stock exchanges have rules that apply to its listed issuers. Market participants may be subject to the rules of the Investment Industry Regulatory Organisation of Canada (IIROC) and the Mutual Fund Dealers Association (MFDA).

3. REGISTRATION OF THE ISSUER AND SECURITIES
3.1 Registration requirements

Issuers that distribute securities to the public will become reporting issuers under the securities legislation of one or more jurisdictions. Most commonly, an issuer will become a reporting issuer by obtaining a receipt for a prospectus or by listing on an exchange. The regulators may also designate that an issuer is a reporting issuer.

Persons who engage in the business of trading in securities, providing advice regarding securities or managing investment funds are required to register with the securities regulators.

3.2 Other requirements

A reporting issuer is subject to many requirements, such as the regular disclosure of financial information and other material information, and prompt disclosure of material changes to its business operations or capital. Holders of securities of a reporting issuer may be subject to the insider reporting, early warning and takeover bid rules.

3.3 Nature of securities

There are no limitations regarding the types of securities that can be issued. Specific requirements for commonly issued types of securities have been incorporated in the prospectus and continuous disclosure forms. Securities regulators may impose requirements for novel types of securities or offering structures under their general public interest jurisdiction. Derivatives are covered by separate legislation or rules in some jurisdictions.

4. SUPERVISORY AUTHORITIES
4.1 Conduct: prudential, cooperation, self-regulation of stock exchange

Stock exchanges have the status of Self-Regulatory Organisations (SROs), which operate under the supervision of one of more of the securities regulators. IIROC is an SRO that regulates the activities and prudential requirements for investment dealers. The MFDA is an SRO that regulates mutual funds dealers.

4.2 New measures for listings in connection with credit crisis

Several new rules in response to the global financial crisis are under consideration; however, there have been no changes related to listings or going public in Canada. Dealers in the exempt market have greater suitability and know your product obligations. Prospectus exemptions may be tightened.

5. OFFERING DOCUMENTATION OR PROSPECTUS REQUIREMENTS

5.1 Nature and statutory requirements of the offering document or disclosure document

See the discussion of a public offering in section 2.2.1

5.2 Exemptions

Securities regulators have discretion to grant exemptions from requirements of the prospectus forms. The issuance of a receipt for the final prospectus may serve as evidence that an exemption has been granted.

See section 2.2.2 for a discussion of prospectus exemptions.

5.3 Preparation of the offering document, general contents

A prospectus is prepared by the issuer in consultation with the lead underwriter for an offering and their respective advisers. The goal is to provide full, true and plain disclosure of all material facts related to the securities offered, as well as complying with the specific form requirements, and to avoid misrepresentations. A misrepresentation is an untrue statement of a material fact or an omission to state a material fact that is required to be stated or that is necessary to make a statement not misleading in the light of the circumstances in which it was made.

Reporting issuers may, subject to certain qualifications, use a short form prospectus or shelf prospectus, which allows them to satisfy prospectus disclosure requirements though incorporation by reference of their previously filed continuous disclosure documents.

5.4 Due diligence

Due diligence provides the basis for one of the key defences to statutory liability for a misrepresentation in a prospectus, and is a key activity of the underwriters and their advisers in the process of prospectus preparation. A defendant is not liable with respect to any part of the prospectus unless it failed to conduct investigations to provide reasonable grounds for a belief that there was no misrepresentation or unless it believed that there was a misrepresentation. The due diligence defence is not available to the issuer or any selling security holder.

5.5 Responsibility

Prospectus liability applies to the issuer, any selling security holders, the signing officers, the directors, the underwriters, any promoters that sign the prospectus, and experts who consent to disclosure regarding their report, opinion or statement in the prospectus.

5.6 Disclaimer/selling restrictions

A preliminary prospectus contains red herring language indicating that it is subject to change. During the waiting period, between the issuance of a receipt for the preliminary prospectus and the issuance of a receipt for the final prospectus, the underwriters may solicit expressions of interest from potential investors. The underwriters cannot accept binding subscriptions before a receipt for the final prospectus is issued. A final prospectus contains a disclaimer that no securities regulator has approved its contents.

5.7 Recognition of prospectuses by other exchanges

Stock exchanges are not the lead regulators for the public offering process. Prospectuses are reviewed primarily by the securities regulators, although issuers are also required to deliver copies of the prospectus to the exchange in connection with the listing of new securities.

Canadian securities regulators cooperate to a degree on prospectus review. An issuer distributing securities in several Canadian jurisdictions must pay fees and comply with certain obligations in each jurisdiction. If the issuer is based in Ontario and distributing in several jurisdictions, only the OSC is required to review the prospectus. However, if the issuer is based in another Canadian jurisdiction but is also offering in Ontario, the regulator in the home jurisdiction and the OSC are required to review the prospectus. Foreign issuers select their principal regulator based on connecting factors to a Canadian jurisdiction.

5.8 Supplementary prospectuses

A preliminary prospectus must be amended if a material adverse change occurs before a receipt for the final prospectus is obtained. A final prospectus must be amended if any material change occurs before the distribution is completed.

Alternative forms of prospectuses, such as a shelf prospectus or a prospectus using the post-receipt pricing system, allow information to be omitted from a final prospectus, provided that a supplement containing the omitted information is filed.

5.9 Issuing of bonds

Bonds fall within the definition of a security and are subject to the same requirements as equity securities. There are specific prospectus exemptions and eligibility criteria for use of the short form prospectus system for certain debt securities. Many large bond offerings are completed using prospectus exemptions.

6. DISTRIBUTION SYSTEMS
6.1 Normal structure of a distribution group

Since any person in the business of trading in securities must be registered, issuers generally distribute securities through a registered dealer.

6.2 Methods of distribution
Dealers may act as an agent for the issuer and arrange for investors to purchase securities, or purchase the securities as principal and resell them to the ultimate purchaser.

6.3 Underwriting
Regardless of whether a dealer is acting as an agent or principal, it is considered to be an underwriter. Underwriting arrangements involve the underwriter agreeing to use best efforts to sell the securities or making a firm commitment to sell a certain number of securities. The underwriters may agree to a bought deal where they agree to purchase the full offering at a fixed price and bear the risk of finding substitute purchasers. Underwriters are permitted to make limited market inquiries prior to a bought deal.

6.4 Fees and commission
Underwriters' fees, commissions and expenses can range up to 7 per cent (or more) of the gross proceeds of an offering. Underwriters may receive compensation options of up to 10 per cent of the deal size.

6.5 Stabilisation
Market stabilisation is permitted in connection with public offerings. An underwriter may receive an over-allotment option to facilitate stabilisation. The option is exercisable for no more than 60 days and only to the lesser of the amount that the offering was oversold as of closing and 15 per cent of the total securities distributed.

6.6 Involvement of a distributor in the preparation of the offering document
Underwriters are typically involved in all stages of the offering document preparation.

6.7 Timing of distribution process
Key determinants for the timing of a distribution include the review period for the prospectus and the expiry of the purchasers' two-day right of withdrawal. For a long-form prospectus, initial comments are issued within 10 days and the review typically ranges from two to four weeks. For a short-form prospectus, comments are issued within three days and the review may take less than a week.

6.8 Rules on distribution to the public
See section 2.2.1.

7. PUBLICITY
No publicity regarding a public offering is permitted before a preliminary prospectus is filed. Limited advertising is permitted after a preliminary prospectus receipt has been obtained.

8. LISTING

8.1 Special listing requirements, admission criteria

An issuer must meet the minimum listing requirements of an exchange to list its securities. For the TSX, an issuer must have at least 1 million freely tradeable shares, having an aggregate market value of at least C$4 million. The securities must be held by at least 300 public holders, each holding at least one board lot. The TSX also has minimum criteria based on the financial resources and management of an issuer. The TSX will expect companies to show evidence of successful operation or, for new companies, management experience and expertise.

There are different listing criteria for profitable companies, companies forecasting profitability, technology companies, research and development companies and mining companies. For example, a mining company that will not require sponsorship, must have three years of proven and probable reserves as estimated by an independent qualified person, adequate working captital to carry on the business, C$7.5 million in net tangible assets, pre-tax profitability in the last fiscal year, and pre-tax cash flow in the last fiscal year of C$700,000, and an average of C$500,000 for the past two fiscal years as well as an upto date comprehensive technical report.

Also, a technology company must have a minimum of C$10 million in aggregate market value of freely tradeable shares, C$10 million of treasury resources, adequate funds for at least one year of planned expenses and satisfactory evidence that its products and services are at an advanced stage of development.

Junior exchanges have more relaxed listing criteria.

8.2 Mechanics of the review process

An issuer must submit an application for listing. The application will be reviewed for eligibility under the minimum listing conditions and may be approved conditionally pending obtaining a receipt for the issuer's final prospectus from the securities regulators. As part of the review, directors, officers and significant shareholders must submit personal information forms and the exchange will conduct background checks. For the TSX and TSX-V listing decisions are made by a committee composed of senior management of the exchange.

8.3 Prospectus obligation, due diligence, exemption

The regulators review prospectuses to determine whether it would be in the public interest to issue a receipt for the final prospectus. The regulators are required to refuse to issue a receipt if any of a number of specific grounds are present, such as: the prospectus fails to comply with securities law; the issuer's resources are not sufficient to meet its stated aims; the issuer cannot be expected to be financially responsible in the conduct of its business; or the business may not be conducted with integrity in the best interests of the security holders.

8.4 Appeal procedure in the event of a prospectus refusal

If the regulator refuses to issue a receipt for a prospectus, the issuer has rights to challenge this decision under the relevant securities legislation. For example, in Ontario, the regulator may not refuse to issue a receipt without giving the filer an opportunity to be heard and the decision may be reviewed before a panel of the OSC within 30 days. Any decision of the OSC may be appealed to the Divisional Court of Ontario and the higher courts.

8.5 Authority of the exchange

The exchanges obtain their authority over listed issuers through agreements entered into in connection with the initial listing and may suspend or terminate an issuer's listing.

8.6 Sponsor

Sponsorship is not a significant requirement for listing in Canada, except for junior issuers on the TSX-V.

8.7 Special arrangements for smaller companies such as ALTERNEXT, AIM or SPACs

A company that is not listed on the TSX or a market outside of Canada (other than AIM or the PLUS markets) is a venture issuer and has lower standards for certain reporting requirements.

The TSX-V permits the listing of capital pool companies, which are similar to SPACs but are limited to raising between C$200,000 and C$4,750,000. The TSX adopted a listing standard for SPACs; however, none have yet been listed.

8.8 Costs of various types

There are various listing and listing maintenance fees that issuers must pay to the exchange and regulators.

9. SANCTIONS AND DISPUTES
9.1 Disciplinary and administrative sanctions

The securities regulators have powers to investigate and enforce securities law requirements and to issue orders and sanctions in the public interest. SROs oversee regulated conduct of their members. For example, IIROC may impose monetary penalties and suspend or revoke IIROC membership and registration for a contravention of the Universal Market Integrity Rules (UMIR).

Disciplinary and administrative law issues may be escalated to the court level and a breach of securities law may pursued as a criminal offence.

9.2 Civil actions

Purchasers under a prospectus have civil rights of action if the prospectus contains a misrepresentation. Participants in the secondary market may have rights of action for a misrepresentation in a document filed or statement made by, or on behalf of, a reporting issuer. Purchasers of securities distributed pursuant to a prospectus exemption may have rights of action for misrepresentations contained in documents provided to them, depending on the jurisdiction and the exemption relied on.

9.3 Criminal penalties
It is a criminal offence to make misleading or untrue statements in connection with an investigation by, or in a document filed with, a Canadian securities regulator. Breaches of securities law, such as fraud and insider trading, may be criminal offences.

10. CONTINUING OBLIGATIONS
10.1 Disclosure and transparency rule
The primary continuous disclosure rules are National Instrument 51-102 – *Continuous Disclosure Obligations* (NI 51-102) and National Instrument 81-106 – *Investment Fund Continuous Disclosure* (NI 81-106). Disclosure obligations are contained in many of the securities rules.

10.2 Information
Reporting issuers must file annual audited and quarterly unaudited financial statements, together with management discussion and analysis, as well as their information circulars. Reporting issuers that are not venture issuers are also required to file an annual information form, with a detailed description of the issuer's business. Annual and interim filings, together with internal controls and disclosure controls, must be certified by the chief executive officer and chief financial officer.

Prompt disclosure of material changes in the business, operations or capital of a reporting issuer are also required. (See section 2.3 for foreign issuers.)

10.3 Listing rules
The exchanges also require timely disclosure of all material facts regarding the affairs of a listed issuer, which can be more extensive than the disclosure requirements under securities law.

10.4 Obligations regarding proxy solicitation
Where the management of a reporting issuer gives or intends to give to holders of its voting securities notice of a meeting, management is required to send to all security holders who are entitled to notice of a meeting, a form of proxy for use at the meeting, in compliance with corporate and securities law. A reporting issuer is not permitted to solicit proxies unless it sends an information circular with prescribed disclosure.

10.5 Continuing requirements of reporting and notification of substantial shareholdings or a substantial transaction
Certain reporting insiders of a reporting issuer are required to disclose any direct or indirect beneficial ownership of, or control or direction over, securities of the reporting issuer. Any holdings of related financial

instruments involving a security of the reporting issuer, such as derivatives, that affect their economic interest in, or economic exposure to, the reporting issuer must also be disclosed. Examples of reporting insiders include directors and certain senior executive officers of the issuer and shareholders who hold more than 10 per cent of the voting rights associated with the securities of the issuer. An initial report is required within 10 calendar days of becoming a reporting insider. Subsequent reports are required to be filed within five calendar days of any change in ownership or control.

Under the early warning system, any person who acquires more than 10 per cent of any class of voting or equity securities of a reporting issuer is required to promptly issue a press release and file a report on SEDAR within two days with prescribed disclosure. Subsequent reports are required on the acquisition of an additional two per cent of the class of securities or if there is a material change to the information disclosed in a prior report. Where a takeover bid for securities of the issuer is outstanding, the threshold for initial early warning reporting is five per cent.

Eligible institutional investors, such as pension funds and investment fund managers, can use an alternative reporting system that permits disclosure on a monthly basis in lieu of early warning reports. Eligible institutional investors may also be exempt from insider reporting.

Under both the insider reporting and early warning requirements, securities that may be acquired within 60 days, regardless of the conditions, are considered to be held and to be outstanding for the purpose of the reporting thresholds and required disclosure.

A reporting issuer must file a business acquisition report within 75 days of an acquisition that is considered to be a significant acquisition, determined by prescribed tests based on assets, income or purchase price. The business acquisition report is required to contain audited financial statements of the acquired business.

10.6 Clearing
CDS Clearing and Depository Services Inc (CDS) is Canada's national securities depository, clearing and settlement hub. CDS is regulated primarily by the Ontario and Quebec securities regulators and the Bank of Canada.

10.7 Requirements for unlisted issuers
Unlisted reporting issuers are fully subject to securities law requirements, except where relaxed rules apply to venture issuers. An issuer that is not a reporting issuer will generally only be subject to the conditions of applicable prospectus exemptions.

11. CORPORATE GOVERNANCE
11.1 Law and/or code
The statute under which an issuer is incorporated is the primary source of corporate law regarding its organisation, management and shareholder rights. Companies may incorporate under the Canada Business Corporations Act or one of the provincial and territorial corporate statutes, and foreign

incorporated companies may register as extra-provincial corporations. Non-corporate issuers are subject to the requirements of their organising statute or constating documents.

Securities regulators have adopted rules that apply to corporate governance, such as: National Instrument 52-110 *Audit Committees* (NI 52-110), National Instrument 58-101 *Disclosure of Corporate Governance Practices* and National Policy 58-201 *Corporate Governance Guidelines* (NP 58-201).

11.2 Management structure
Management structure is determined by the issuer's organising statute and/or constating documents; however, it may be influenced by securities requirements. For example, NI 52-110 requires that a reporting issuer (other than a venture issuer) have an audit committee composed of at least three directors, all of whom are independent. The certification requirement under National Instrument 52-109 *Certification of Disclosure in Issuers' Annual and Interim Filings* requires that a reporting issuer have people in the role of chief executive officer and chief financial officer to provide the required certificates.

The securities law definitions of officers and directors apply to any person performing a similar function or occupying a similar function as a particular officer or a director of a corporation, regardless of their actual title or the organisation of the issuer.

11.3 Obligations to publish information on the Internet
Most documents filed by a reporting issuer will be made available on the Internet through SEDAR.

11.4 Responsibility of inside/outside directors
Inside directors will not be considered to be independent directors for the purpose of NI 52-110 and may not be members of the audit committee of a reporting issuer (other than a venture issuer).

11.5 Committees
Reporting issuers are required to have an audit committee. NP 58-201 recommends nominating and compensation committees.

11.6 Obligation to ask for consent of a shareholders' meeting
Multilateral Instrument 61-101 *Protection of Minority Securityholders in Special Transactions* (MI 61-101) imposes the requirement to obtain disinterested shareholder approval for certain related party transactions and business combinations. MI 61-101 also prescribes disclosure and may require an independent valuation of the subject matter of the proposed transaction. MI 61-101 has been adopted only in Ontario and Quebec; however, since all TSX listed issuers are reporting issuers in Ontario and the TSX-V has adopted a policy requiring compliance with MI 61-101, it applies to all listed issuers.

Exchange rules also include specific requirements to obtain shareholder approval for private placements of more than 25 per cent of issued shares, other significant transactions and transactions with related parties.

11.7 Depth of information – proxy solicitation

A management information circular for a meeting to elect directors is required to contain substantial detail, particularly with respect to executive compensation and corporate governance. A circular for a special meeting to approve a transaction is required to provide full details of the transaction and, in some cases, must provide prospectus-level disclosure of the parties to, or resulting from, the transaction.

11.8 Appointment/dismissal of directors

The election and dismissal of directors is not governed by securities law; however, National Instrument 54-101 *Communication with Beneficial Owners of a Reporting Issuer* impacts on the timing and process for shareholder meetings.

11.9 Income and options for directors

There are no specific limitations on the compensation of directors; however, all compensation must be disclosed. There is a prospectus exemption for the issuance of options to directors, employees and consultants of an issuer. Listed issuers are subject to exchange rules on the volume of options permitted and related shareholder approval requirements.

11.10   Earnings guidance

Reporting issuers are required to identify forward-looking financial information and financial outlooks (such as earnings guidance), disclose the material factors and assumptions used, describe the issuer's policy for updating such information and include cautionary language. The issuer is only permitted to disclose such information if it is based on assumptions that are reasonable in the circumstances and must disclose the date that management approved the information (if the document is undated) and describe its purpose.

11.11   Management discussion and analysis (MD&A)

Issuers must prepare and file annual and interim MD&A in the prescribed form. MD&A is intended to provide a narrative explanation, through the eyes of management, of how the issuer performed during the period covered by the accompanying financial statements and of the issuer's financial condition, future prospects and material risks.

11.12   Directors' liability

Directors have statutory liability under corporate law and may be liable for a misrepresentation contained in the public disclosure of a reporting issuer.

12. MARKET ABUSE

12.1 Insider trading

No person in a special relationship with a reporting issuer may:

*   purchase or sell securities of the reporting issuer with the knowledge of a material fact or material change with respect to the reporting issuer that

has not been generally disclosed; or
- inform, other than in the necessary course of business, another person of a material fact or a material change before the material fact or material change has been generally disclosed.

A person in a special relationship with a reporting issuer includes any insider, affiliate, associate, officer or employee of the issuer or an insider, any person that has engaged, is engaging in or proposes to engage in any business or professional activities with or on behalf of the reporting issuer, or any director, officer or employee of any other person in a special relationship with the reporting issuer.

Trading on undisclosed material information and tipping of undisclosed material or information are offences, and also give rise to statutory civil liability in favour of persons adversely affected by such actions.

12.2 Market manipulation

Market manipulation is contrary to securities legislation and could give rise to criminal offences. Potentially manipulative actions are also prohibited under rules such as UMIR.

12.3 Miscellaneous

Securities regulators have a broad jurisdiction to make orders that are in the public interest. Actions that would tend to undermine confidence in the public markets may be prohibited by a regulator regardless of whether there is a specific breach of securities law.

13. MUTUAL OR INVESTMENT FUNDS

13.1 Introduction to these two categories

An investment fund can mean a mutual fund or a non-redeemable investment fund. A mutual fund is an issuer whose primary purpose is to invest money provided by its security holders and whose securities entitle the holder to receive an amount computed by reference to the value of a proportionate interest in the whole or in part of the net assets of the issuer on demand (or within a specified period after demand). A non-redeemable investment fund is an issuer whose primary purpose is to invest money provided by its security holders and does not seek control of the entities it invests in and that is not a mutual fund.

13.2 Investment companies, open-ended, close-ended

Investment funds can be distributed pursuant to a prospectus. A mutual fund is typically in continuous distribution and open for redemptions daily or weekly; a non-redeemable investment fund is typically only distributed periodically and may be open for redemptions infrequently, if at all, so liquidity comes from listing on an exchange.

13.3 Licence requirements

A dealer registered as a mutual fund dealer may act as a dealer in respect of any security of a mutual fund. Except in Quebec, mutual fund dealers are required to be members of the MFDA. Portfolio managers of investment funds must generally be registered as advisers, and fund managers must generally be registered as investment fund managers.

13.4 Continuing requirements
Mutual funds and non-redeemable investment funds that are reporting issuers have continuous disclosure obligations pursuant to NI 81-106. These continuous disclosure obligations can include the filing of annual information forms, annual financial statements, management reports of fund performance, quarterly portfolio disclosure, proxy voting records, material change reports and information circulars.

13.5 Custodians
Unless there is an exemption, all portfolio assets of a mutual fund must be held under the custodianship of a custodian who satisfies certain requirements.

13.6 Undertakings for Collective Investments in Transferable Securities (UCITS)
Not applicable.

13.7 Non-UCITS funds
Not applicable.

13.8 Hedge funds
Alternative investment funds such as hedge funds are principally distributed under prospectus exemptions, although a few are reporting issuers who sell under a prospectus. The distributor must in most cases be registered as a dealer, the portfolio manager as an adviser and the fund manager as an investment fund manager.

13.9 Marketing and distribution requirements
Public distribution of investment fund securities is subject to the prospectus regime, but there are different prospectus forms than ordinary issuers. Marketing and distribution to the public is conducted through registered dealers.

13.10　Manager
Investment fund managers are regulated as registrants and have capital and proficiency requirements.

14.　SECURITIES INSTITUTIONS
14.1 Market executive undertaking
Not applicable.

14.2 Securities clearing house
CDS is the primary clearing agency in Canada.

14.3 Central securities depository
CDS is the primary depository in Canada.

14.4 Investment services providers (ISP)
Investment services are delivered to the public principally by registered dealers.

15. NOTIFICATION OBLIGATIONS
15.1 Notification of major shareholding
See section 10.5.

16. PUBLIC TAKEOVERS
16.1 Applicable laws and regulations or regulatory framework
In Ontario, public takeovers are governed by Part XX of the Ontario *Securities Act*, as supplemented by the rules adopted by the OSC. Equivalent rules have been adopted in other jurisdictions in Multilateral Instrument 62-104 *Takeover Bids and Issuer Bids* (MI 62-104).

16.2 Competent authorities
There are several competent authorities in Canada that regulate public takeovers. These authorities include securities regulators, stock exchanges, and the federal and provincial governments.

16.3 Dealing with disclosures and stake building
See the discussion of the early warning system in section 10.5.

16.4 Types of takeover bids
A takeover bid is defined as an offer to acquire voting or equity securities of any class of securities of an offeree issuer (target company) that, together with the securities already held by the offeror and any joint actors, would result in the offeror holding 20 per cent or more of the class of securities. In determining whether the takeover bid threshold has been crossed, any securities that the offeror, or joint actor of the offeror, has the right to acquire within 60 days, regardless of conditions, are considered to be held and to be outstanding.

Anyone who makes a takeover bid is required to comply with the formal takeover bid requirements.

Exemptions to the formal takeover bid requirements are available for normal course market purchases of up to 5 per cent of the class of securities in a 12 month period, private agreements with up to five sellers at a premium of no more than 15 per cent, purchases of securities of non-reporting issuers, purchases of securities of foreign issuers that have limited Canadian shareholders.

An offer by an issuer to acquire its own securities is an issuer bid and must comply with the formal issuer bid requirements and be made to all holders on the same terms. Purchases made pursuant to corporate law or the issuer's constating documents are exempt from these requirements, as are normal course issuer bids made on an exchange, subject to certain conditions.

16.5 Procedural aspects

An offeror may commence a bid by either delivering a takeover bid circular or by advertisement.

A formal takeover bid must be made to all holders of the class of securities. A takeover bid must be open for at least 35 days and the bidder is not allowed to take up any securities deposited under the bid until after 35 days. A press release must be issued upon expiration of the bid. Bids are typically extended for longer than the minimum period.

The target issuer must respond to a bid with a directors' circular.

Securities deposited under a bid must be taken up, if all terms and conditions of the bid have been complied with or waived, within 10 days. Any securities taken up under the bid must be paid for within three business days after take up. Where the bid is for less than all of the class of the targeted securities and the bid is over-subscribed, the securities must be taken up on a pro rata basis.

There are pre- and post- bid integration rules that prevent an offeror from acquiring securities of the class at a different price within 90 days before or 20 business days after the takeover bid.

16.6 Nature and value of consideration offered

Identical consideration must be offered to all holders of the class of securities subject to a bid. If a bid is varied to increase the value of the consideration offered, the offeror must pay the increased consideration to all sellers.

Collateral agreements that result in any security holder receiving greater value than the other holders of the same class are prohibited. There are exemptions for certain common employment arrangements.

16.7 Timetable and variations

Takeover bids must be open for at least 35 days. If a variation is made, a takeover bid must be extended for at least 10 days.

16.8 Strategy

An offeror launching a takeover bid is subject to considerable expense and risk. Typically, a bidder will seek prior approval of the issuer and negotiate for a break fee in the event the issuer's approval is withdrawn in the face of a higher bid. It is also common for a bidder to negotiate an agreement with holders of a significant number of shares to tender to the bid prior to making the offer. These agreements are permitted; however, no additional consideration can be offered.

16.9 Irrevocable

There is no specific prohibition on a bidder deciding not to proceed with a takeover bid. However, announcing an intention to make a takeover bid could be considered to be market manipulation if the intention is not genuine. Negative variations to a takeover bid that make it less favourable to target security holders may be considered to be contrary to the public interest and attract intervention from securities regulators if sufficient time is not provided for target security holders to react to the variation.

16.10 Share dealings, buying shares

A bidder cannot acquire shares other than pursuant to its bid. However, limited normal course purchases of up to 5 per cent of the class of securities subject to the bid on a published market may be made, provided that required disclosure is made.

16.11 First announcement

See section16.5.

16.12 Drafting of offer documents

The primary offering document in a bid is the takeover bid circular, which is drafted by the offeror in consultation with its legal and financial advisers.

16.13 Further announcements

Announcements are required from both the bidder and target throughout the process. There is an obligation to update required documents for material changes.

16.14 Responsibility

Takeover bid circulars and directors' circulars must be certified. The bidder and target, and their respective officers and directors, may be subject to statutory liability if these documents contain a misrepresentation.

16.15 Despatch

A depository is appointed for the purpose of collecting securities tendered to the bid and releasing the consideration for the securities taken up. Deposited securities may be withdrawn:

- any time prior to take up;
- within 10 days of a change to the bid; or
- if not paid for within three business days of take up.

16.16 Due diligence in advance of a takeover bid

Due diligence must be negotiated with management of the target. If the target is not willing to provide access, a bidder may be forced to proceed based on publicly available information.

16.17 Conditions to the offer

Conditions to a takeover bid are not expressly regulated. However, if unreasonable conditions are included or if the bidder is effectively retaining discretion regarding proceeding with a bid, the regulators may intervene under their public interest jurisdiction.

16.18 Financing

Where the consideration offered under the bid includes cash, the offeror must make adequate arrangements prior to making the bid to ensure that the required funds will be available to pay for all securities the offeror has offered to acquire.

16.19 For cash/for shares/mixed
Consideration in a takeover bid can be cash, shares or a combination thereof. If a choice of consideration is offered, the same choice must be offered to all holders of the class of securities. If the consideration is in the form of shares, then prospectus level disclosure must be made in respect of the entity that is issuing the shares. Issuing shares as consideration may result in the issuing entity becoming a reporting issuer in certain Canadian jurisdictions.

16.20 Inducement
See section 16.6.

16.21 Defence mechanisms
Responses by the board of directors and management to an unsolicited takeover bid, such as shareholder rights plans, are dealt with under the securities regulators' public interest jurisdiction. National Policy 62-202 *Takeover Bids – Defensive Tactics,* provides that the primary objective of the Canadian takeover bid regime is to protect the interests of target security holders. The regulators consider that unrestricted auctions produce the most desirable results in takeover bids. However, they will intervene if target security holders are being deprived of the ability to respond to a bid.

16.22 Nature of listed securities
The bid must be made to all holders of the targeted class of securities who are in the local jurisdiction and delivered to all security holders and holders of securities convertible into the targeted class of securities.

16.23 Squeeze-out
The squeeze-out of remaining target security holders following a takeover bid may trigger the business combination provisions under MI 61-101. However, the votes attached to securities tendered in a takeover bid may be counted in favour of a second step acquisition and there is an exemption available to these requirements if the bidder obtains 90 per cent of the outstanding securities.

16.24 Schemes of arrangement
Statutory arrangements are frequently used in lieu of formal bids, with the cooperation of the target. Among other benefits, they avoid second step acquisitions and, since they include court fairness hearings, can be useful where targets have US investors. A statutory arrangement may trigger the minority approval and valuation requirements under MI 61-101 if related parties are involved in the transaction.

17. FOREIGN INVESTMENT CONTROLS
17.1 Foreign investments
Foreign investment in Canada is regulated primarily under the Investment Canada Act. However, there are a number of regulated industries that have Canadian control requirements, such as financial institutions, telecommunications, and air transportation.

17.2 Exemptions
The Investment Canada Act applies to an acquisition of control of a Canadian business by a non-Canadian, which includes any person that is not a Canadian citizen or permanent resident of Canada and any entity that is not controlled or beneficially owned by Canadians.

17.3 Exemptions of notification or prior authorisation
If a non-Canadian acquires control of a Canadian business, the non-Canadian must either file: (i) a straight-forward notification of the investment; or (ii) a much more in-depth application for review. A notification must be filed within 30 days after a non-Canadian acquires control of an existing Canadian business, unless an application for review is required.

The acquisition of control of an existing Canadian business by a non-Canadian will require an application for review and will be subject to a net benefit review to be completed prior to implementation of the acquisition, if the book value of the assets being acquired exceeds one of the applicable thresholds. The basic threshold in 2011 for an acquisition by an investor from a WTO member country is C$312 million, but this is reduced to C$5 million for industries of particular interest such as uranium production, the provision of financial or transportation services or the conduct of a cultural business.

17.4 Notification in order to establish a balance of payments
Canada does not have foreign exchange controls.

England & Wales

Macfarlanes LLP Robert Boyle & Mark Slade

1. GENERAL DESCRIPTION OF THE CAPITAL MARKETS
1.1 Number of companies listed; division in markets
Some 1,420 companies were admitted to trading on the Main Market (the 'Main Market') of London Stock Exchange plc (LSE) as of 28 February 2011, and 1,178 on the AIM (smaller market) of the LSE.

Of the 1,420 companies admitted to trading on the Main Market, 371 were incorporated outside of the UK.

1.2 Total volume and market value; percentage of gross national product
(2009 figures in brackets throughout this section) In 2010, the equity market value of the Main Market was approximately £4,065 billion (£3,600 billion), representing approximately 280 per cent of UK gross domestic product in 2010 (approximately 260 per cent).

In 2010, the volume of shares traded on the Main Market was 380.3 billion (534.4 billion).

1.3 Issue activity
In 2010, there were 72 (36) initial public offers on the Main Market, raising £8,775.31 million (£1,059.35 million) and 232 (418) secondary issues, raising £15,139.61 million (£75,987.57 million).

1.4 Takeover activity (data available as of publication date)
In the year to 31 March 2010 (year to 31 March 2009 in brackets) there were 90 (104) resolved takeover proposals (where an announcement of a firm intention to make an offer was made and the offer period has ended). Of these, 88 (101) resulted in a takeover and the remainder were withdrawn before the issue of documents or were otherwise unsuccessful.

1.5 Hostile takeover attempts (data available as of publication date)
In the year to 31 March 2010, 25 offers (out of the 90 resolved takeover proposals) (21/104) were not recommended at the time that the announcement of a firm intention to make an offer was made. Twenty-one (13) remained so at the time the offer document was posted.

2. REGULATORY STRUCTURE
2.1 Laws/regulatory framework for offering of securities and the sale of and subscription for securities
The principal governing piece of securities law in the UK is the Financial

Services and Markets Act 2000 (FSMA). There are a myriad of rules and regulations made under FSMA. Some of the key rules and regulations which affect the offering of securities and the sale of and subscription for securities include the Prospectus Rules, the Disclosure Rules and Transparency Rules (the DTRs) and the Financial Services and Markets Act 2000 (Financial Promotion) Order 2005 (SI 2005/1529) (the FPO).

2.2 Regulation of the offering of new securities

Public offerings of securities are governed by the Prospectus Rules which implement the EU Prospectus Directive. There are two 'triggers' requiring a prospectus to be published in the UK, namely where:

- transferrable securities are offered to the public in the UK (the 'Public Offer Limb') (section 85(1) FSMA); or
- admission of transferrable securities to trading on a regulated market situated or operating in the UK is requested (the 'Regulated Market Limb') (section 85(2) FSMA), in which case an approved prospectus must be made available to the public before the offer/request (as applicable) is made.

Non-compliance is a criminal offence.

Commonly used exemptions for the (i) Public Offer Limb include offers made to or directed at qualifying investors only and where the offer is made to or directed at fewer than 100 persons, other than qualified investors, per EEA state; and (ii) Regulated Market Limb include shares representing, over a period of 12 months, less than 10 per cent of the number of shares of the same class already admitted to trading on the same regulated market and under employee/board incentive schemes.

It is also a criminal offence for a person ('A') in the course of business to communicate an invitation or inducement to engage in investment activity (the 'Financial Promotion Prohibition') (section 21, FSMA) unless:

- A is an authorised person (ie, authorised by the Financial Services Authority (FSA) under FSMA); or
- the content of the communication is approved for the purposes of section 21 FSMA by an authorised person.

The FPO sets out certain exemptions, including promotions made to investment professionals, high net worth individuals and companies and sophisticated investors, together with certain types of investment activity such as the sale of a body corporate or 'one-off non-real-time communications' or when a prospectus is required to be published.

2.3 Differences between local and foreign companies

Foreign companies are generally subject to the same obligations as local companies, except when certain corresponding rules apply in their home member state.

The Prospectus Rules provide for mutual recognition of prospectuses within the EEA. They also allow the FSA to approve a prospectus relating to an issuer that has its registered office outside the EEA which is drawn up in accordance with the legislation of that country if:

- the prospectus has been drawn up in accordance with international standards set by international securities commission organisations, including the International Organisation of Securities Commission (IOSCO) disclosure standards; and
- the information requirements, including information of a financial nature, are equivalent to the requirements under Part VI of FSMA, Regulation (EC) No. 8009/2004 (the 'Prospectus Directive (PD) Regulation') and the Prospectus Rules.

3. REGISTRATION OF THE ISSUER AND SECURITIES

3.1 Registration requirements
It is not necessary for a (foreign) company to be locally registered or licensed; or to have a local formal presence in the UK but such companies often appoint local agents to accept legal process on their behalf.

3.2 Other requirements
Securities do not need to be registered with any securities regulator in the UK.

3.3 Nature of securities
Securities admitted to trading on UK markets are generally in registered form.

3.4 Clearing institutions
A body recognised as a clearing house under Part XVIII of FSMA is exempt from the general prohibition in FSMA on carrying on any regulated activity that is carried on for the purposes of, or in connection with, the provision of clearing services. The Recognised Investment Exchanges and Recognised Clearing Sourcebook sets out recognition requirements and notification requirements for clearing institutions.

4. SUPERVISORY AUTHORITIES

4.1 Laws that create competency/authority for supervisory authorities (exchange and others)
The FSA is designated as the competent authority under Part VI of FSMA (official listing) and is delegated a broad range of other authorities under FSMA. The UK has an atypical listing regime in that it has a split structure. A listing comprises two parts: (i) admission to the official list (the 'Official List') (which is maintained by the UK Listing Authority (part of the FSA) and is governed by the listing rules made by the FSA pursuant to FSMA (the 'Listing Rules')); and (ii) admission to trading on a regulated market (which is governed by the rules of the relevant market). In the case of the Main Market, the relevant rules are the Admission and Disclosure Standards of the LSE (enforced by the LSE). The LSE is itself listed on the Official List and has its shares admitted to trading on the Main Market.

4.2 Responsibility supervisory authorities
The FSA has responsibility for a very broad range of securities law matters,

including maintaining and enforcing the Listing Rules, the DTRs and the Prospectus Rules, as well as maintaining a supervisory role in relation to regulated activities.

5. OFFERING DOCUMENTATION OR PROSPECTUS REQUIREMENTS

5.1 Nature and statutory requirements of the offering document or disclosure document for each type of security

The overriding contents requirements for a prospectus are contained in section 87A FSMA and support the general duty of disclosure set out in section 80 FSMA, namely the information necessary to enable investors to make an informed assessment of:

- the assets and liabilities, financial position, profits and losses, and prospects of the issuer of the transferrable securities and of any guarantor; and
- the rights attaching to the transferrable securities.

A prospectus must also be drawn up using one or a combination (depending on the type of security that is the subject of the prospectus) of schedules and building blocks set out in the PD Regulation, which set out detailed contents requirements, and in accordance with the recommendations of the European Securities and Markets Authority. Generally, key information in a prospectus includes: audited historical financial information for the latest three financial years; a detailed overview of the business; a description of the business' organisational structure; an operating and financial review; and miscellaneous information concerning matters such as share capital and constitutional documents.

If, at any time after its submission for approval and before the commencement of dealings in the securities concerned, there is a significant change in any matter contained in the prospectus the inclusion of which was required by section 80, FSMA, the Listing Rules or the FSA (as the competent authority) or a significant new matter arises the inclusion of which would have been required if it had arisen at the time the prospectus was prepared, the issuer must submit a supplementary prospectus of the change or new matter to the FSA for its approval and, if they are so approved, publish them (section 81, FSMA).

5.2 Preparation of the offering document

A prospectus is usually prepared by the issuer's legal counsel or its financial adviser, with input from reporting accountants and the issuer's sponsor.

5.3 Due diligence

A full due diligence exercise is generally undertaken by the issuer's legal counsel (shadowed by underwriters' counsel) (in relation to legal matters) and by the reporting accountants (in relation to financial matters) in connection with an offering. Whether a formal due diligence report (addressed to the issuer, the sponsor and the underwriters) is issued depends on the nature of the underwriting syndicate. Generally, US houses prefer not to have such a report produced. In addition, the issuer (in connection with its legal counsel) will carry out a verification exercise on the offering documents. On transactions with a US element, the underwriting syndicate will almost inevitably request Rule 10b-5 and no registration opinions from both the issuer's counsel and underwriters' counsel.

The underwriting syndicate will also undertake management due diligence through a management questionnaire and detailed question and answer sessions.

5.4 Responsibility for statements and liability for misstatements
Under the Prospectus Rules, the following people have statutory liability for a prospectus relating to equity shares:
- the issuer;
- if the issuer is a body corporate, its directors (and anyone who has agreed to become a director or is named as a director in the prospectus);
- the offeror and any director of the offeror (if a body corporate) if the prospectus is in relation to an offer;
- anyone who accepts and is stated in the prospectus as accepting responsibility for the prospectus; and
- anyone else who authorises the contents of the prospectus.

Under section 90 FSMA (subject to certain statutory defences), any person responsible for a prospectus is required to pay compensation to any person who has acquired securities to which the prospectus applies if they suffer loss as a result of:
- any untrue or misleading statement in the prospectus; or
- the omission from the prospectus of any matter required to be included by section 80 (general duty of disclosure) or section 81 (supplementary prospectus), FSMA (see 5.1 above).

Outside of the statutory liability regime, there may be liabilities for breach of contract and in tort for misstatement/misrepresentation.

Criminal liability under section 397 FSMA attaches to a person who deliberately or recklessly makes a misleading statement or dishonestly conceals material facts in connection with a statement for the purpose of inducing another to acquire or dispose of securities.

5.5 Type of current and historical financial information
Issuers have to provide audited historical financial information covering the latest three financial years (or such shorter period that the issuer has been in operation) and the audit report in respect of each year. The financial information must be prepared according to Regulation (EC) No 1606/2002, or if not applicable, to a member state's national accounting standards for issuers from the European Community. For third country issuers, the financial information must be prepared in accordance with (or restated using) international accounting standards recognised under Regulation (EC) No 1606/2002.

The prospectus must include an operating and financial review, which explains in detailed narrative form the issuer's financial condition and operating results.

The issuer is also obliged to describe any significant change in the financial or trading position which has occurred since the end of the last financial period for which either audited financial information or interim financial information has been published or to provide a negative statement. A working capital statement and a capitalisation and indebtedness statement must also be provided.

5.6 Future projects required or permitted

Whilst there is no requirement per se for issuers to disclose future projects in the prospectus, issuers must be mindful of their obligations under section 80 FSMA (see 5.1 above).

5.7 Disclosure of policy on dividends

The prospectus must contain a description of the issuer's policy on dividend distributions and any restrictions thereon, along with the amount of the dividend per share for the period covered by the historical financial information adjusted, where the number of shares in the issuer has changed, to make it comparable.

5.8 Disclaimer/selling restrictions

Prospectuses published in the UK generally contain extensive disclaimers and selling restrictions. Typical examples include, *inter alia*:

- a disclaimer of responsibility for the prospectus by the underwriting syndicate;
- a statement of the principal jurisdictions in which the securities have not been registered (eg, the US);
- a statement excluding the distribution of the prospectus from all jurisdictions where it would be unlawful to distribute it or to make any offer contained therein and, in addition (subject to certain exceptions), specifically excluding its distribution and the general making of any such offer from certain problematic jurisdictions such as the US, Canada, Australia, South Africa and Japan; and
- a statement limiting any reliance in relation to the accuracy of forward-looking statements and the obligation to update such statements.

5.9 Recognition of prospectuses by other exchanges

If an issuer wishes to 'passport' a prospectus which has been approved by the FSA into another member state, the issuer must apply to the FSA who will send a certificate of approval to the host member state. The host member state does not undertake any approval process.

6. DISTRIBUTION SYSTEMS
6.1 Practice of distribution

Distributors are normally investment banks or other financial institutions. The main method of distribution in the UK is through an institutional bookbuild (either traditional or accelerated) which involves the circulation of placing documentation (either a prospectus or an announcement if no prospectus is required) which does not contain a price or the size of the offering (a 'Pathfinder Prospectus'). The size and price of the offering are fixed at the end of the bookbuild once demand for the shares from potential investors has been ascertained.

On a primary issue, securities are frequently over-allocated by the underwriting syndicate at the time of allocation (creating a short position). The stabilising manager is usually protected from the consequences of that short position by the operation of the 'Greenshoe', which is a call option allowing the stabilising manager to acquire up to a certain number (usually 15 per cent of the offering) of additional shares. The stabilising manager will generally utilise a stock loan at admission to satisfy over-allocations and then repay that stock loan either by exercising the Greenshoe (if the price has remained above the offer price) or by acquiring shares in the market (if the price is below the offer price).

6.2 Dealers in another role
See 6.3 below.

6.3 Normal structure of distribution group
On larger underwritten securities offerings in the UK, the distributing group is generally known as the 'underwriting syndicate'. Typically, an underwriting syndicate might comprise:
- listing sponsor (see 8.8 below): liaises with, and has statutory duties to, the FSA in relation to a premium listing;
- global co-ordinator: manages the underwriting syndicate and brings together the global offer;
- financial adviser: provides strategic advice to the issuer on issues such as timing, price and size of the offering, corporate governance and employee incentivisation (often the same as the listing sponsor);
- bookrunner: maintains the book of demand for shares and determines allocations therein;
- underwriter: subscribes for or purchases (as the case may be) securities to the extent that there is insufficient demand in the market;
- stabilising manager: takes action in the market in the 30-day period after the offering has closed to support the share price of the issuer; and
- research analyst: provides an independent report on the issuer.

6.4 Range of fees or commissions on different types of securities
Fees and commissions on securities offerings vary considerably depending on the type of offering and the nature of the securities. On an initial public offering (IPO), aggregate commissions are typically between two and five per cent, often with an additional discretionary element.

6.5 Requirement of registration of distributor
Distributors are almost invariably required to be authorised by the FSA because the activities which they undertake, including underwriting, are

regulated activities for the purposes of FSMA. Application for authorisation can be made directly to the FSA.

6.6 Distributor active in preparation offering document and/or settlement of it with regulatory agency

The listing sponsor will be heavily involved with the preparation of the offering document as, even though it will make every effort not to be a 'person responsible' for the offering documents, the sponsor will want to avoid the reputational embarrassment of being involved with an offering in which false or misleading information is disseminated. The listing sponsor will also want to have significant input into the equity story set out in the offering document. Distributors will also want to ensure the accuracy of the offering documents, although they will not often be involved directly in its preparation. They will, however, seek the benefit of a diligence comfort package (both legal and financial).

6.7 Timing of distribution process

On a bookbuild, a pathfinder (or sometimes price-range) prospectus is published, typically two weeks before the pricing of the offering (unless the bookbuild is an accelerated bookbuild, where it would be usual for a book to be built overnight or over a few days). Any retail element of an offering will generally close a day or so before the institutional offering due to the larger volume of applications to be processed.

6.8 Distribution normally made to the public or to financial intermediaries

Most IPOs are only made to institutional investors, although retail offers are not unknown.

7. DEBENTURES, SPECIFIC ASSETS
7.1 Requirement to register

Fiscal agents and trustees are required to be authorised by the FSA as the activity they undertake is a regulated activity for the purposes of FSMA.

7.2 Paying agent

The paying agent in the UK will generally be a fiscal agent who is responsible for paying principal and interest to debenture holders under the terms of a fiscal agency agreement. This agreement sits alongside a deed of covenant which grants debenture holders direct rights of enforcement against the issuer in certain circumstances.

7.3 System for a representative for debenture holders

Common law trust deeds are recognised in the UK.

8. LISTING
8.1 Special listing requirements; capital, track-record, profit, lock-up

The listing requirements applicable to an issuer proposing to list its shares on the Official List depend on the proposed nature of that issuer's listing. The Official List comprises two segments, namely a standard listing (under which the minimum EU standards apply) and a premium listing (under which UK super-equivalent standards apply). Only voting equity shares may be listed on the premium segment. The standard segment is further divided into five sub-categories (shares, debt and debt-like securities, certificates representing certain securities, securitised derivatives and miscellaneous securities). Open-ended investment companies and closed-ended investment funds can only list their equity securities on the premium segment.

There are some listing requirements which are applicable to all securities, including that the securities:

- conform with the laws of the issuer's place of incorporation, are duly authorised under the issuer's constitution and have the necessary statutory or other consents;
- (subject to limited exceptions) are admitted to trading on a regulated market for listed securities operated by a recognised investment exchange;
- are freely transferrable and fully paid; and
- that (subject to certain exceptions) the aggregate market capitalisation of the securities to be listed is £700,000 in respect of shares and £200,000 for debt securities.

Additional requirements are applicable to issuers applying for the admission of equity shares to a premium listing (being commercial entities, ie, not investment companies or funds). Some of the key requirements include:

- a three-year track record of audited accounts;
- 75 per cent of the issuer's business being supported by a historic revenue earning record covering the period;
- working capital requirements; and
- that at least 25 per cent of the shares to be admitted are in public hands.

There are specific listing requirements for mineral companies and scientific research based companies.

8.2 Mechanics of the review process

A prospectus must be submitted to, and be approved by, the FSA prior to its publication. On a primary listing, the FSA aims to provide comments on the initial proof of a prospectus within 10 working days and to provide comments on subsequent proofs within five working days. Typically, a prospectus is approved between six and eight weeks after submission of the first proof.

8.3 Prospectus obligation, due diligence, exemptions

See 5 above.

8.4 Appeal procedure in the event of a prospectus refusal

Decisions of the FSA in relation to prospectus approval and FSA authorisations and permissions can be appealed to the Tax and Chancery Chamber of the Upper Tribunal.

8.5 Requirements and availability for listing
See 8.1 above.

8.6 Authority of the Exchange
See 4.1 above.

8.7 General nature of listing agreement
The listing agreement, normally referred to as the underwriting agreement, generally contains an obligation on the underwriting syndicate to procure subscribers/purchasers under the offering (usually using reasonable endeavours) and (if underwritten) containing an underwriting obligation. In return, the issuer agrees to pay the fees and commissions of the underwriting syndicate and give a broad general indemnity, together with certain warranties and undertakings. The underwriting syndicate is typically afforded very broad termination rights. The agreement also typically contains contractual obligations in respect of the mechanics for obtaining the listing.

8.8 Obligations for a sponsor
There is no ongoing requirement for an issuer to have a sponsor. The Listing Rules require an issuer with, or applying for, a premium listing of its equity shares to appoint a sponsor on each occasion that it:
- makes an application for admission of equity securities; or
- is required to produce a class 1 circular; or
- is producing a circular that proposes a reconstruction or a refinancing which does not constitute a class 1 transaction; or
- is producing a circular for the proposed purchase of its own shares which does not constitute a class 1 circular and which is required to include a working capital statement; or
- is required to do so by the FSA because it appears to the FSA that there is, or there may be, a breach of the Listing Rules or the DTRs by the issuer.

An issuer is also required to appoint a sponsor where it applies to transfer the category of listing of its equity shares to and from certain listing categories.

8.9 Appeal to regulator or court
See 9.4 below.

8.10 Costs of various types
The cost of obtaining a listing is £225 plus £100 for each additional issue of securities with its own International Securities Identification Number. In addition, document vetting fees apply. The fees for a prospectus are currently £6,270 (in respect of equity) and £2,750 (in respect of non-equity).

The ongoing listing fees (for all issuers other than issuers of securitised derivatives, depository receipts and global depository receipts) comprise a minimum fee of £3,700 plus an additional fee worked out on a sliding scale by reference to market capitalisation.

9. SANCTIONS AND DISPUTES
9.1 Rights of purchasers of securities

To rescind for no reason
The purchase contract usually excludes the potential right at law for purchasers of securities to rescind the purchase contract.

To rescind based on misrepresentation by the issuer or distributor
A contract to acquire shares is potentially voidable (ie, capable of rescission) if induced by a material misrepresentation, provided that the person acquiring the shares acts within a reasonable amount of time of becoming aware of the misrepresentation. The contract will remain valid until rescission but, when rescinded, becomes void so that it is deemed never to have had effect.

To sue the issuer, its directors, distributor or others (lawyers, auditors) for misstatements
Where a prospectus forms part of a contract between an issuer and those acquiring shares, those investors may have a claim for damages against the issuer/vendors of shares for breach of contract if any statement in the prospectus is untrue or misleading.

If a person is negligent in making any statement in a prospectus or any other marketing documentation or presentation they may be liable in an action for damages brought by a person who has suffered loss as a result of acting on that statement (notwithstanding the fact that the person making that statement is not party to a contract with the person who has suffered loss). In addition, damages may be recovered under the Misrepresentation Act 1967.

Other cure sanctions
Under section 90A, FMSA, statutory liability potentially applies in relation to specified information (which is broadly information published via a regulatory information service or by other recognised means). The regime provides for the payment of compensation to investors suffering loss (where they acquire, continue to hold or dispose of securities) where that loss is caused by: (i) untrue or misleading statements or omissions in published information; or (ii) a dishonest delay in publishing information.

Compensation may also be available under section 90 FSMA (see 5.4 above).

Under section 87Q FMSA, if a supplementary prospectus is published and a person has agreed to purchase or subscribe for transferrable securities to which the supplementary prospectus relates prior to its publication, that person may withdraw its acceptance before the end of the period of two working days beginning with the first working day after the date on which the supplementary prospectus was published.

9.2   Time limits for legal actions

The principal statutory source of temporal limitations for legal actions in the UK is the Limitations Act 1980. For both contractual and tortious claims, the limitation period is (subject to certain exceptions) six years. In the case of breach of contract, the limitation period runs from the act giving rise to the breach of contract. In tortious claims, it runs from the date that the damage is sustained by the claimant. Parties may (subject to certain exceptions) contract out of statutory limitation periods.

9.3   Dispute settlement and court procedure

Disputes are normally litigated in the High Court and are instigated by the issue and service of a claim form. Disputes are frequently resolved using alternative dispute resolution processes such as arbitrations (which are usually legally binding) and mediations.

9.4   Possible criminal penalties

Potential criminal sanctions include, amongst other things, offences under the Fraud Act 2006, the Theft Act 1968 (eg, the offence of obtaining a pecuniary advantage by deception) and under section 397 FSMA (see 5.4 above).

10.   CONTINUING OBLIGATIONS

10.1 Nature of current requirements

The continuing obligations of issuers whose shares are admitted to the Official List and to trading on the Main Market are found in a number of different sources. Chapters 7 to 13 (inclusive) of the Listing Rules set out continuing obligations for companies with a premium listing (see 10.8 below) and Chapter 14 of the Listing Rules sets out continuing listing obligations for companies with a standard listing. Continuing obligations with respect to certain specialist types of issuer (eg, Chapter 15 in relation to closed-ended investment funds) or securities (eg, Chapter 17 in relation to debt and debt-like securities) are set out in other chapters of the Listing Rules. The DTRs provide rules on, inter alia, when and what information issuers should disclose to the market. Issuers with securities admitted to trading on the Main Market must also comply with the Admission and Disclosure Standards of the LSE. Finally, issuers must have regard to the corporate governance matters set out in 11 below.

10.2 Quarterly, half-yearly and yearly financial statements

The DTRs require issuers to make public an annual financial report at the latest four months after the end of each financial year, which includes:
* audited financial statements;
* a management report containing a fair review of the issuer's business and the principal risk and uncertainties facing the issuer; and
* responsibility statements from persons responsible within the issuer.

   Detailed contents requirements for issuers' annual report and accounts are also set out in the Companies Act 2006, the Listing Rules and institutional codes and guidance.

Issuers must also make public a half-yearly report covering the first six months of the financial year not later than two months after the end of the period to which it relates. The report must include:

- condensed financial statements;
- an interim management report giving an indication of important events that have occurred during the first six months of the financial year, and their impact on the condensed set of financial statements and a description of the principal risks and uncertainties for the remaining six months of the financial year; and
- responsibility statements from persons responsible within the issuer.

Whilst quarterly reporting does not formally exist in the UK market, the requirement to produce interim management statements (see 10.3 below) means that financial reports are produced by issuers four times per annum.

10.3 Required interim disclosure
An issuer is required to make public a statement by its management during the first six-month period of the financial year and another statement by its management during the second six-month period. The relevant statement must be made in a period between 10 weeks after the beginning, and six weeks before the end of the relevant six-month period.

The interim management statement must provide:
- an explanation of material events and transactions that have taken place during the relevant period and their impact on the financial position of the issuer and its controlled undertakings; and
- a general description of the financial position and performance of the issuer and its controlled undertakings during the relevant period.

Issuers may also be required to make a disclosure under DTR 2, DTR 3 and DTR 5, as explained at 10.5 and 15 below.

10.4 Obligations regarding proxy solicitation
Proxy solicitation rules do not apply in the UK, although some issuers use proxy solicitation agents.

10.5 Disclosure
Under DTR 2, information must be immediately announced to the market broadly if it is precise, it affects the issuer and/or its securities and its announcement would be likely to have a significant effect on the price of the issuer's shares (including that it is information of that kind which a reasonable investor would be likely to use as part of the basis of its investment decisions) ('Inside Information').

The announcement of Inside Information may be delayed by an issuer so as not to prejudice its legitimate interest (eg, when it is negotiating a contract) provided that:
- such an omission would not be likely to mislead the public;
- any person receiving the information owes the issuer a duty of confidentiality; and
- the issuer is able to ensure the confidentiality of that information.

10.6 Continuing requirements of reporting and notification of substantial shareholdings
See 15 below.

10.7 Requirements of transfer agent, clearing, paying agent
The Listing Rules require that all listed shares be eligible for electronic settlement. See 3.4 above for details on clearing institutions.

The DTRs require issuers to appoint, as their agent, a financial institution through which members may exercise their financial rights. This is widely understood to mean that issuers need to appoint a registrar. A registrar will usually fulfil the role of transfer agent and paying agent. Transfer agents maintain issuers' records of members and transfers and administer share certificates. Paying agents accept payments from issuers (eg, dividends, coupons and principal payments) and distribute the proceeds to the issuer's members.

10.8 Other continuing obligations
The principal continuing obligations under Chapters 7 to 13 of the Listing Rules are as follows:
- Chapter 7 sets out generic overarching principles which issuers must follow;
- Chapter 8 relates to the appointment of a sponsor (see 8.8 above);
- Chapter 9 prescribes a number of continuing obligations, including compliance with the Model Code (see 12.7 below), pre-emption rights for existing shareholders, provisions as to how certain transactions should be carried out, various notification provisions and provisions relating to information to be included in accounts;
- Chapter 10 sets out various restrictions in relation to significant transactions. Entering into transactions which are of a significant size (which is measured by reference to percentage ratios known as 'class tests') require various levels of consents and formalities, ranging from a Class 1 transaction which requires prior shareholder approval, notifications and an explanatory circular (which entails significant cost) to a Class 3 transaction, which may only require notification of limited prescribed information to a regulatory information service;
- Chapter 11 sets out restrictions in relation to transactions with related parties which, dependent on the value of the transaction (judged by reference to the class tests), may require notifications to be made and obtaining the prior approval of shareholders to the proposed transaction;
- Chapter 12 contains rules applicable to an issuer that purchases its own securities, sells or transfers treasury shares, purchases or redeems its own securities during a prohibited period or purchases its own securities from a related party; and
- Chapter 13 sets out the contents requirements for circulars to shareholders.

11. CORPORATE GOVERNANCE

11.1 Law and/or code

Corporate governance in the UK operates on a 'comply or explain' basis. A listed company incorporated in the UK must explain in its annual report to shareholders whether it has complied with the Combined Code on Corporate Governance published by the Financial Reporting Council (the 'Combined Code') and, to the extent it has not, it must explain the reasons for non-compliance. For financial years beginning on or after 29 June 2010, a new code, the UK Corporate Governance Code will apply to all companies with a premium listing of equity securities regardless of whether they are incorporated in the UK or elsewhere.

Whilst the Combined Code is the main corporate governance investment source for UK listed companies, various shareholder bodies and institutional representative groups have issued extensive guidance, to which (whilst not legally binding) UK listed companies also need to pay careful attention.

11.2 One-two tier; CEO-Chairman separate

Boards in the UK have a single structure. There is no equivalent of a management board and a supervisory board, although many companies have an operating board below the main board of the issuer. The Combined Code provides that the roles of chairman and chief executive should not be exercised by the same individuals.

11.3 Obligations to publish information on the Internet

The Combined Code provides that the terms of reference of an issuer's audit committee, remuneration committee and nomination committee should be made available and that this requirement would be met by including the information on a Web site that is maintained by or on behalf of the issuer.

11.4 Responsibility of inside/outside directors

The Combined Code provides that the board should include a balance of executive and non-executive directors (and in particular independent non-executive directors) such that no individual or small group of individuals can dominate the board's decision taking. It further provides that non-executive directors should, *inter alia*, scrutinise the performance of management and satisfy themselves on the integrity of financial information and that financial controls and systems of risk management are robust and defensible.

All directors are collectively responsible for the success of the issuer. The Combined Code further recognises that, whilst non-executive directors have the same legal duties and responsibilities as executive directors, they are likely to have less detailed knowledge about the business than the executive directors and that this may be relevant in assessing the knowledge, skill and experience expected of them.

11.5 Committees

The Combined Code recommends the appointment of:

- a nomination committee which should lead the process for board appointments and make recommendations to the board;
- a remuneration committee which should have responsibility for setting remuneration for all executive directors and the chairman as well as recommending and monitoring the level and structure of remuneration for senior management; and
- an audit committee which should consider how to apply financial reporting and internal control procedures and establish arrangements for maintaining an appropriate relationship with the issuer's auditors.

11.6 Obligation to ask for consent of a shareholders' meeting

The Listing Rules set out certain circumstances where shareholder approval is required (in addition to any approval required by company law). Key areas in which shareholder approval is required include:

- significant transactions (Chapter 10, Listing Rules) and Related Party Transactions (Chapter 11, Listing Rules) see 10.8 above;
- employees' share schemes and long term incentive schemes must (subject to certain exceptions) be approved by shareholders; and
- directors' remuneration report, which must be laid before shareholders at the issuer's annual general meeting.

11.7 Appointment/dismissal of directors

Although directors are generally initially appointed by the board, the Combined Code provides that all directors should be subject to election by shareholders at the first annual general meeting after their appointment and thereafter at intervals of no more than three years. This obligation is typically enshrined in the issuer's constitutional documents. The UK Corporate Governance Code further provides that all directors of FTSE 350 companies should be subject to annual election by shareholders.

Directors may be appointed by shareholders (by ordinary resolution) but an issuer's constitutional documents usually allow the board to fill casual vacancies.

Under the Companies Act 2006, shareholders may by ordinary resolution remove a director before the expiration of the period of office, notwithstanding anything in any agreement between the issuer and the director. The resolution requires special notice (28 days) and the director is afforded the opportunity to be heard on the resolution at the meeting and to make representations in writing, which must be sent to every member of the issuer to whom notice of the meeting is sent.

11.8 Income and options for directors

The Combined Code recognises that levels of remuneration should be sufficient to attract, retain and motivate directors of the quality required to run the issuer successfully, but issuers should avoid paying more than is necessary for this purpose. Executive share options should not be issued at a discount (save to the extent permitted by the Listing Rules). The Combined Code further provides that the performance elements of remuneration should form a significant proportion of the total remuneration package of executive directors and sets out provisions on the design of performance related remuneration.

Non-executive director's remuneration should reflect the time commitment and responsibilities of the role and should not include share options as this goes to their independence.

11.9 Earnings guidance

Whilst there is no rule preventing an issuer from giving earnings guidance, issuers in the UK market generally seek to avoid doing so. This is because the Listing Rules provide that where an issuer publishes any unaudited financial information in a class 1 circular or a prospectus or any profit forecast or profit estimate, it must, in its next annual report, reproduce the same, produce and disclose the actual figures for the same period and provide an explanation of the difference if there is a difference of 10 per cent or more between the two sets of figures. The Prospectus Rules further provide that, *inter alia*, an independent accountant or auditor must report on any profit forecast given. Reports on profit forecasts must also be made under the Takeover Code. Giving earnings guidance clearly heightens the risk of the issuer disseminating false or misleading information and therefore potential liability for the issuer and its directors.

If earnings guidance is given, issuers should take utmost care in preparing the figures and make clear to the market that forward-looking figures are inherently uncertain and that the issuer is under no obligation to update those figures.

11.10   Management discussion and analysis (MD&A)

An MD&A is not produced in the UK market.

11.11   Directors' liability

Set out below is a non-exhaustive list of civil and criminal liability directors can face:

Directors' duties: under the Companies Act 2006, any director may be liable for a breach of statutory duties, which are:

- to act in accordance with the company's constitution and only exercise powers for the purpose for which they are conferred;
- to act in the way the director considers, in good faith, would be most likely to promote the success of the company for the benefit of its members as a whole;
- to exercise independent judgment;
- to exercise reasonable care, skill and diligence;
- to avoid conflicts of interest;
- not to accept benefits from third parties; and
- to declare interests.

Fraud Act 2006: introduces three basic fraud offences:

- fraud by false representation;
- fraud by failure to disclose information (which there is a legal duty to

disclose); and
- fraud by abuse of position.

A director can be liable under the Fraud Act if the offence is committed with the director's consent or connivance. The offences require dishonesty on the part of the perpetrator and an intention to cause gain or loss;

Assumption of personal liability: a director may be personally liable to either the company or to third parties in the following circumstances:
- where the director fails to disclose the company's interest or involvement in a contract;
- where the director fails to disclose the full name of the company when issuing certain documents (such as cheques and orders for goods) and the company defaults; and
- where a director exceeds the powers granted.

Insolvency-related liabilities: directors risk incurring personal liability to contribute to the assets of the company available to creditors where it is found in the course of winding up the company that the directors have been guilty of wrongful or fraudulent trading;

Sections 90, 90A and 397, FSMA: see 5.4 and 9.1 above;

Market abuse/insider dealing: see 12 below;

Section 21, FSMA, see 2.2 above; and

Failure to publish a prospectus: see 2.2 above.

12. MARKET ABUSE

12.1 Laws and regulations
The two principal pieces of legislation governing insider trading (known as insider dealing in the UK) are Part V of the Criminal Justice Act 1993 (CJA) and Part XIII of FSMA (the 'Market Abuse Regime'). In addition to insider dealing, the Market Abuse Regime also covers other abusive conduct in relation to prescribed markets.

12.2 Codes of conduct
The FSA has (using its powers under FSMA) issued the Code of Market Conduct which gives guidance to those determining whether or not behaviour amounts to market abuse in respect of the Market Abuse Regime.

12.3 Definitions and description
Outline of the CJA offence
Under Part V of the CJA, an individual (the offence only applies to individuals) commits the primary insider dealing offence if the person:
- has information as an insider;
- deals in securities (which are widely defined) that are price-affected securities in relation to the information; and
- the dealing takes place on a regulated market (as prescribed by the Treasury) or the person dealing relies on a professional intermediary or acts as a professional intermediary.

There are also two secondary insider dealing offences being 'encouraging' and 'disclosing'.

The 'encouraging' offence is committed if an individual has information as an insider and encourages another person to deal in securities that are (whether or not that other knows it) price-affected securities in relation to the information, knowing or having reasonable cause to believe that the dealing would take place on a regulated market or the person dealing would rely on a professional intermediary or act as a professional intermediary.

The 'disclosing' offence is committed if an individual has information as an insider and discloses the information, otherwise than in the proper performance of the function of employment, office or profession, to another person.

Key definitions
An insider is an individual who has information as an insider if and only if:
- it is, and the individual knows that it is, inside information; and
- the person has it and knows the information is from an inside source.

An individual has information from an inside source if and only if:
- the individual has it through: (i) a director, employee or shareholder of an issuer of securities; or (ii) having access to the information by virtue of the individual's employment, office or profession; or
- the direct or indirect source of the information is such a person.

Inside information means information which:
- relates to particular securities or to particular issuers of securities and not to securities generally or to issuers of securities generally;
- is specific and precise;
- has not been made public; and
- if it were made public would be likely to have a significant effect on the price of any securities.

Securities are price-affected securities in relation to inside information if and only if the information would, if made public, be likely to have a significant effect on the price of the securities.

Territorial scope
The insider dealing offence is only committed if the relevant behaviour took place in the UK.

The Market Abuse Regime
Insider dealing under the Market Abuse Regime is similar to the CJA offence, although slightly more widely drawn. A breach of the Market Abuse Regime is a civil offence (as opposed to the CJA, which is a criminal offence). Under the Market Abuse Regime, insider dealing can be committed anywhere in the world as long as it relates to qualifying investments admitted to trading on a prescribed market and further it can be committed by corporations as well as individuals. Insider dealing under the market abuse regime has a civil law burden of proof (ie, the balance of probabilities) whereas the CJA offence has a criminal burden of proof (the case against the defendant must be proved beyond reasonable doubt).

12.4 Sanctions

The CJA offence of insider dealing is punishable by a fine not exceeding the statutory maximum (currently £5,000) and/or imprisonment for a term not exceeding seven years.

Under the Market Abuse Regime the FSA may impose on the person committing market abuse a penalty of such amount as it considers appropriate or publish a statement to the effect that the person has engaged in market abuse.

12.5 Are there defences?

The CJA provides for three general defences in relation to the primary offences of insider dealing (the burden of proof for each defence falls on the defendant on the balance of probabilities):

- no profit expected, ie, the individual did not at the time expect the dealing to result in a profit attributable to the fact that the information in question was price-sensitive information in relation to securities; or
- sufficiently wide disclosure, ie, at the time, the individual believed on reasonable grounds that the information had been disclosed widely enough to ensure that none of those taking part in the dealing would be prejudiced by not having the information; or
- the individual would have traded anyway, ie, that the individual would have acted the same way even if the individual had not had the information.

Similar defences are available for the secondary offences of 'encouraging' and 'disclosing'.

There are also special defences covering market makers, market information and price stabilisation.

Whilst there are no defences to market abuse, the FSA may not impose a penalty on a person if, having considered any representations made to it in response to a warning notice, there are reasonable grounds for the FSA to be satisfied that the person: (i) believed on reasonable grounds that the behaviour did not amount to market abuse; or (ii) took all reasonable precautions and exercised all due diligence to avoid behaving in a manner which constitutes market abuse.

12.6 Consulting major shareholders in light of major transaction; irrevocables

Issuers will often consult major shareholders before engaging in significant corporate actions. In doing so, an issuer may be passing price-sensitive information to those shareholders and will therefore have to rely on the limited disclosure provisions contained in DTR 2, as described in 10.5 above.

Similarly, bidders will be passing price-sensitive information to shareholders when seeking irrevocable undertakings (see 16.7 below for further details). Accordingly, they will have to make those shareholders insiders.

In each case, the issuer and the bidder will respectively need to be sensitive to shareholders not wanting to be restricted from dealing for any significant amount of time (as they will not be able to deal in the shares of the target until that information ceases to be price sensitive) and they should therefore consider not approaching shareholders until late in the process.

12.7 Trading in certain periods

The Listing Rules provide that issuers must adopt a share dealing code no less exacting than that set out in the Model Code, which is annexed to Chapter 9 of the Listing Rules. The Model Code applies to persons discharging managerial responsibilities (PDMRs) (being: (i) directors; and (ii) senior executives of the issuer who (a) have regular access to inside information relating, directly or indirectly, to the issuer and (b) have the power to make managerial decisions affecting the future development and business prospects of the issuer).

As well as providing that PDMRs cannot deal without obtaining clearance to do so in advance, the Model Code also provides (with limited exceptions in extremis) periods in which PDMRs cannot deal in the securities of the issuer (a 'Prohibited Period'). A Prohibited Period means: (i) any close period; or (ii) any period in when there exists any matter which constitutes inside information in relation to the issuer.

Close period means:

- the period of 60 days immediately preceding a preliminary announcement of the issuer's annual results or, if shorter, the period from the end of the relevant financial year up to and including the time of announcement; or
- the period of 60 days immediately preceding the publication of its annual financial report or, if shorter, the period from the end of the relevant financial year up to and including the time of such publication; and
- if the issuer reports on a half-yearly basis the period from the end of the relevant financial period up to and including the time of such publication; and
- if the issuer reports on a quarterly basis the period of 30 days immediately preceding the announcement of the quarterly results or, if shorter, the period from the end of the relevant financial period up to and including the time of the announcement.

A PDMR must also seek to prohibit any dealings in the securities of the issuer during a close period by or on behalf of any connected person of the issuer or by an investment manager on the issuer's behalf or on behalf of any person connected with the issuer.

These restrictions are in addition to any prohibition on dealings that may apply under the CJA or Market Abuse Regime.

12.8 Buying before launch takeover bid

In respect of the CJA, a special bid defence to insider dealing is available to those stakebuilding. An individual is not guilty if it is shown that:

- the individual acted in connection with a bid which was under

consideration or the subject of negotiation with a view to facilitating the accomplishment of the bid; and
• the information the individual had as an insider was market information.

The 'market information test' is generally satisfied by an individual demonstrating that the individual had, at the time of dealing, knowledge that the bidder was going to make or was considering making a bid.

If the bidder has information which is not market information (for example, through the bidder's due diligence) the special bid defence does not apply and the insider dealing issue becomes more acute as the share price will not be supported by the bid price at this time and, accordingly, the information is more likely to affect the price of the securities in question.

Whilst there are no defences to market abuse, the FSA's Code of Market Conduct creates 'safe harbours' in relation to market abuse. In the context of a bid, behaviour based on inside information does not itself amount to market abuse so long as: (i) the information is relevant information viz, either information that the bidder is going to make or is considering making a bid for the target or information the bidder may obtain through due diligence; and (ii) the stakebuilding is for the purpose of the bidder gaining control of the target.

The special bid defence and the market abuse safe harbours do not apply to stakebuilding using derivative products such as contracts for difference.

12.9 Buying after close of takeover bid
Similar issues apply to those outlined in 12.8 above once the bid has been made, although the share price of the target is likely to be supported by the bid price and the other information in relation to the transaction by then made available to the market, making it less likely that other information will affect the price of the securities in question.

12.10 Analysts
Analysts' reports on issuers provide a useful source of information for the market as they look in detail at an issuer and benchmark the issuer against its peer group. Accordingly, issuers frequently arrange briefings for analysts that follow them. Whilst some of the information given to analysts will not be price-sensitive, there is an obvious concern that analysts will be primarily interested in receiving price-sensitive information.

Arguably, once the analyst's report is published, the information has been made public and therefore is no longer price-sensitive. Practically, issuers and their analysts should adopt procedures for checking the factual basis of information and determining whether or not it is price-sensitive information.

13. MUTUAL FUNDS
13.1 Special regulation for mutual fund
Mutual funds established in the UK must be authorised to be marketed to the public in the UK. Such funds may be established as authorised unit trusts (AUTs) or open-ended investment companies (OEICs).

13.2 Controlling power of competent authority/exchange
The FSA is responsible for authorising and regulating AUTs and OEICs and their functionaries.

13.3 Regulated functions
In respect of an AUT, the fund has a manager, and in the case of an OEIC, an authorised corporate director (ACD). In respect of an AUT, the fund has a trustee, and in respect of an OEIC, a depositary. The manager/ACD may appoint a separate investment manager/adviser. All of the functionaries must have the appropriate permissions from the FSA to act in the relevant capacities.

13.4 Exemptions
There are no exemptions from the requirement for a UK established AUT or OEIC to be authorised in order to be marketed to the public in the UK.

13.5 Requirements
For an AUT or OEIC to become authorised by the FSA, the manager/ACD must demonstrate, and the FSA must be satisfied, that the proposed fund complies with the relevant rules in the UK. The rules are very prescriptive and include: independence and competence of functionaries; having appropriate constitutional documents in place and having appropriate investment and borrowing powers and appropriate procedures for valuation, pricing and dealing of units/shares. Information regarding the fund will also need to be filed with the FSA in certain circumstances throughout the life of the fund eg, if changes are to be made to the fund or the fund is to be wound up.

13.6 Special requirements for foreign entities
A mutual fund which has been established in another EEA state as an Undertaking for Collective Investment in Transferable Securities (UCITS) may be marketed to the public in the UK provided the FSA has first 'recognised' the scheme in the UK. The FSA will also recognise certain classes of mutual funds established in certain designated territories (the Channel Islands, the Isle of Man and Bermuda).

Mutual funds established outside of these jurisdictions may apply to the FSA for individual recognition, but this is rare in practice. Subject to that, non-UK mutual funds may only be marketed in the UK in accordance with UK legislation regarding the promotion of unregulated collective investment schemes (broadly, to more experienced/wealthy/institutional investors).

13.7 Relation with clients
The instrument of incorporation of an OEIC and the trust deed of an AUT are the documents which constitute those respective types of fund and by which investors are bound. Those documents set out the technical details of how the fund is to operate. The prospectus is the more relevant document for the benefit of the investors and sets out full information about the fund. An abbreviated version, known as the 'Simplified Prospectus', is normally also produced.

13.8 Reporting/guarantee systems
A short report (sent to investors) and a long report (available on request) must be prepared by the manager/ACD both half-yearly and annually.

13.9 Extra disclosure requirements
Changes to the fund may be made by the manager/ACD. The nature and significance of a proposed change will dictate whether FSA approval is needed to implement the change and also whether prior investor approval is required, or advance notice to investors, or merely notification to investors after the change has taken effect (in the case of minor changes).

13.10 Typical mutual fund
Mutual funds in the UK are most commonly structured as OEICs, however AUTs are also used.

13.11 Registration and requirements for manager
The manager/ACD is responsible for operating the fund and must be authorised by the FSA to do so. The manager/ACD must be independent from the trustee/depositary, be incorporated in the UK or another EEA state and have a place of business in the UK.

13.12 Registration and requirements for custodian
The trustee/depositary is responsible for safe custody of the fund's assets and overseeing certain functions of the manager/ACD and must be authorised by the FSA in order to do so. The trustee/depositary must be independent from the manager/ACD, incorporated in the UK or another EEA state and have a place of business in the UK. The trustee/depositary is at liberty to delegate the custody function to a third party.

13.13 Registration and requirements of redemption agent
Applications for redemption are made to the manager/ACD.

13.14 Regulation on investment powers
There are three types of funds with different investment and borrowing powers in the UK (UCITS schemes, non-UCITS retail schemes and Qualified Investor Schemes (QIS)). UCITS schemes have the tightest investment and borrowing powers, non-UCITS retail schemes have slightly wider powers and QISs have the widest powers as they are only available to investors who are prepared to accept a higher degree of risk or have a higher degree of experience and expertise.

13.15 Any other specific features
None.

14. SECURITIES INSTITUTIONS
14.1 Separate regulation for securities institutions
A person may not undertake a 'regulated activity' in the UK unless the

individual is authorised by the FSA or the activity is exempt. Securities institutions undertake regulated activities and are therefore caught by this requirement.

14.2 Controlling power of competent authority/exchange
The FSA is the regulator of securities institutions as 'authorised persons' under the UK regulatory regime.

14.3 Regulated functions
The obligation to obtain FSA authorisation is triggered when a person undertakes an activity of a specified kind in respect of a 'specified investment' (together constituting a regulated activity). The list of specified investments includes securities and other financial instruments. Specified activities cover a broad range of financial activities relating to investments.

14.4 Exemptions
A number of exemptions from the requirement to obtain FSA authorisation exist, some of which apply to a number of regulated activities and others of which are specific to just one activity. Certain of the exemptions are subject to override by European legislation in respect of firms that are covered by the scope of the relevant EU legislation. Some key exemptions include:
- an exemption in the context of activities undertaken within a corporate group;
- the 'appointed representative' and 'tied agent' exemptions – these enable an entity that has been appointed as an appointed representative (for purely domestic firms) or tied agent (for firms subject to relevant European legislation) by another entity (its principal) to undertake certain regulated activities under the regulatory umbrella of the principal without the need for direct authorisation; and
- an exemption for activities undertaken in the context of the sale of a body corporate.

14.5 Requirements
A number of ongoing compliance requirements apply to a securities institution that is regulated by the FSA. Amongst the most important of these is that the FSA's consent is required prior to any change in control over an FSA authorised firm. This can have timing implications for a transaction in respect of a securities institution. In addition, FSA authorised firms are required to maintain regulatory capital calculated in accordance with a detailed framework of rules, based in part upon the international Basel II standards in addition to applicable European legislation. FSA authorised firms must also comply with detailed conduct of business rules; restrictions on outsourcing 'critical or important' operational functions; rules relating to senior management arrangements, systems and controls (including the composition of senior management); and a regime designed to ensure that only 'fit and proper persons' perform certain 'controlled functions' on behalf of an authorised firm.

14.6 Special requirements for foreign entities

A European 'passporting' regime applies to enable certain European regulated firms to provide services in the UK either on a cross-border basis or by establishing a UK branch. Such entities are treated as authorised in the UK for the purposes of the general prohibition on undertaking a regulated activity, but are subject only to limited supervision by the FSA.

Third-country securities institutions may apply to authorise a branch with the FSA, although as a matter of market practice most such institutions wishing to undertake regulated business in the UK tend to establish a regulated UK subsidiary instead.

14.7 Relation with clients

FSA authorised firms are required to enter into a 'client agreement' before providing regulated services to a client which must contain certain prescribed regulatory disclosures and must categorise the client as either 'retail', 'professional' or an 'eligible counterparty' for regulatory purposes. This affects the type of business that a firm may undertake with that client and the level of regulatory protection afforded to the client.

14.8 Reporting/guarantee systems

An FSA authorised securities institution is subject to detailed ongoing reporting and notification requirements. These cover both conduct of business and prudential matters. Certain reports must be filed on a periodic basis, whilst other notification obligations are event-triggered.

15. NOTIFICATION OBLIGATIONS
15.1 Notification of substantial shareholdings

Under DTR 5, a person must notify the issuer and the FSA (using the prescribed form TR-1) of the percentage of voting rights that person holds as a shareholder or is deemed to hold through direct or indirect holding of certain financial instruments if the percentage of those voting rights reaches, exceeds or falls below certain thresholds. The notification must be made as soon as possible but broadly within four trading days in the case of a non-UK issuer and two trading days in the case of a UK issuer of the event which changed that person's voting rights. The issuer is then obliged to make public all of the information contained in the notification by the end of the trading day following receipt of the notification if it is a UK issuer and not later than the end of the third trading day following receipt of the notification if it is a non-UK issuer.

Under DTR 3, all PDMRs and their connected persons must notify all transactions conducted on their own account in the shares of the issuer or derivatives or any other financial instruments relating to those shares within four business days of the day on which the transaction occurred. The issuer must then release the information via a regulatory information service by no later than the end of the business day following the receipt of the information by the issuer.

15.2 Which thresholds?

Under DTR 5, for UK issuers, the relevant thresholds are three per cent and each 1 per cent threshold thereafter up to 100 per cent. For non-UK issuers, the relevant thresholds are 5 per cent, 10 per cent, 15 per cent, 20 per cent, 25 per cent, 30 per cent, 50 per cent and 75 per cent.

15.3 Are notifications public?

See 15.1 above.

15.4 Notification of substantial holdings in a credit institution

Entities authorised by the FSA are subject to the change of control notification procedures set out in FSMA and in the FSA Handbook. Those rules distinguish between two types of firm: (i) firms that are subject to the European Markets in Financial Instruments Directive (2004/39/EC), credit institutions subject to the European Banking Consolidation Directive (2006/48/EC) or certain other European legislation relating to the regulation of the financial services sector (such firms being 'directive firms'); and (ii) 'non-directive firms' that are not subject to such European legislation. A directive firm that is authorised by the FSA must notify the FSA of any of the following events concerning the firm:

- a person acquiring control;
- an existing controller increasing control;
- an existing controller reducing control; and
- an existing controller ceasing to have control.

Non-directive firms must notify the FSA of a person becoming a controller of the firm or an existing controller ceasing to be controller of the firm.

An overseas firm must notify the FSA if a person becomes a controller of the firm, increases or reduces control over the firm or ceases to have control over the firm.

Notification must also, in all cases, be made by the person acquiring, increasing or reducing control or ceasing to have control. For this reason, notifications are often jointly made.

For UK domestic firms (other than non-directive firms), control starts at 10 per cent (broadly by reference to shareholding or voting control, including through chains of ownership). For non-directive firms, control starts at 20 per cent.

In broad summary, control is then increased through a series of bands (the legislation provides a number of additional tests):

- from less than 20 per cent to 20 per cent or more;
- from less than 30 per cent to 30 per cent or more; or
- from less than 50 per cent to 50 per cent or more.

Control is decreased in a similar manner:

- from 50 per cent or more to 50 per cent or less;
- from 30 per cent or more to 30 per cent or less; or
- from 20 per cent or more to less than 20 per cent.

Notification must be made in writing and contain the prescribed information set out in the FSA Handbook and must be made as soon as the party with the notification obligation has become aware that a person, whether alone or acting in concert, has decided to acquire control or to increase or reduce control. If the change of control takes place without the knowledge of the firm, the notification must be made within 14 days of the firm becoming aware of the change of control concerned.

16. PUBLIC TAKEOVERS
16.1 Applicable laws and regulations
Regulation of takeovers in the UK has a statutory footing in Part 28 of the Companies Act 2006. The Companies Act 2006 requires the Panel on Takeovers and Mergers (the Panel) to make rules giving effect to certain provisions of the Takeover Directive as well as affording it general powers to regulate takeover bids, merger transactions and transactions which have or may have, directly or indirectly, an effect on the ownership or control of companies and certain matters relating to each transaction. The rules made by the Panel are set out in the City Code on Takeovers and Mergers (the Code).

The Code applies to companies which have their registered offices in the UK, the Channel Islands or the Isle of Man if their securities are admitted to trading on a regulated market in the UK or on any stock exchange in the Channel Islands or the Isle of Man. It also applies to certain other companies (both public and private) who meet tests in relation to central management and control and certain other tests in relation to private companies.

16.2 Competent authorities
The UK has designated the Panel as its competent authority to supervise bids for the purposes of the Takeover Directive.

16.3 Corp NV or Country Co buying up to 25 per cent in target or 30 per cent or 50 per cent
The Code contains a general prohibition on a bidder and its concert parties from acquiring more than 30 per cent of the voting rights in a target (Code, Rule 5). There are, however, certain exemptions available, which have conditions attached to them. If a bidder relies on those exemptions and acquires more than 30 per cent of such voting rights, the bidder will be obliged to make a mandatory offer for the entire equity share capital of the target in cash (or with a full cash alternative) at a price which is not less than the highest price paid by the bidder for shares of the same class during the 12 months prior to the announcement of that bid (Code, Rule 9). The only condition allowed to the mandatory offer (unless the Panel consents) is the acceptance of sufficient shareholders of the offer for the bidder to hold 50 per cent of the voting rights in the target.

16.4 Obligation of same price for offer
If a bidder or its concert parties have acquired interests in shares in the period commencing three months before the offer period commences and the date on which the bid closes for acceptances, Rule 6 of the Code sets a floor for the consideration of a bid at the highest price paid for such interests during that period.

16.5 Timing

The table below sets out a typical bid timetable. 'D' represents the day on which the offer document is posted.

Date	Milestone
D - 28	Transaction announced.
D	Offer document posted.
D + 21	First closing date of the bid (ie, the earliest date on which the offer could become wholly unconditional).
D + 24	Earliest date on which compulsory acquisition notices could practically be posted (if the bid has become wholly unconditional and the 90 per cent threshold is reached by D + 21).
D + 35	Earliest day on which the bid may close (assuming the offer becomes or is declared wholly unconditional on D + 21).
D + 39	Latest date on which the target can publish new information.
D + 42	Shareholders may withdraw acceptances of the offer if the offer is not unconditional as to acceptances.
D + 46	Latest date on which any revised offer document may be posted.
D + 60	Latest possible date for the bid becoming or being declared unconditional as to acceptances.
D + 65	Earliest date on which the compulsory acquisition of non-accepting shares could be completed (if the bid has become unconditional and the 90 per cent threshold is reached by D + 21).
D + 74	Earliest day on which the bid may close (assuming the offer becomes or is declared unconditional as to acceptances on D + 60).
D + 81	Latest possible date on which the bid can become or be declared unconditional in all respects.
D + 95	Latest date on which target shareholders can be paid if the offer is declared unconditional on D + 81.
D + 125	Earliest practical date for the compulsory acquisition procedure to be completed if the bid is declared wholly unconditional on D + 81. 16.10

Strategy

It is critical that a bidder's strategy is thought through at the outset of a bid, as the likely success or failure of the bid will depend, to a large measure, on the bidder's tactics. Key strategic decisions for a bidder to take include:

* Will the bid be hostile or will the bidder seek a recommendation from the target board?
* Will the bid be by way of contractual offer or by scheme of arrangement (a court sanction scheme, voted upon by shareholders, which is binding on all shareholders)?
* What commercial protections will the bidder seek from the target (eg, a break-up fee – see paragraph 16.18)?
* Should the bidder stakebuild in the target?
* How will the bidder finance the bid?
* What price will the bidder offer and what form will the consideration take?

The defensive strategy of a target board is considered in detail at 16.20 below. In addition, issuers will usually have a defence manual (known as a 'black book') prepared by a combination of its lawyers and financial advisers which sets out at a high level the action required and the issues which need to be addressed by the board of the issuer and its advisers prior to or in the event of an announcement of a bid for that company.

16.6 Irrevocables
A bidder will usually seek irrevocable undertakings from shareholders in the target to send a positive message to the market, other shareholders and potential competitors with a view to increasing the bidder's chances of meeting the acceptance condition.

Irrevocable undertakings generally take one of three forms:
* a hard irrevocable is an undertaking to accept the offer with no provision for release, which binds the shareholder until the offer lapses;
* a soft irrevocable is an undertaking to accept the offer with a provision for release if there is a higher offer; and
* semi-soft irrevocable is an undertaking to accept the offer with a provision for release if there is a higher offer which exceeds the offer by a certain magnitude eg, if the higher offer is at least five pence higher than the original offer.

Bidders usually seek irrevocable undertakings in the 24-hour (or 48-hour) period prior to the bidder's announcement of a firm intention to make a bid. This is because, by virtue of the approach to it, a shareholder will be made an insider (and will therefore be restricted from dealing); consequently the time between the approach and announcement of the bid should be kept to a minimum. In addition, the bidder must disclose any irrevocable undertakings gathered by midday on the business day after they are gathered. They must also be disclosed in the bidder's announcement of an intention to make a firm bid. Before seeking the irrevocable undertakings, the bidder will need to consult the Panel.

16.7 Buying on exchange prohibited
Other than the restriction under Rule 5 (as explained in 16.3 above) and pursuant to the insider dealing and market abuse regimes (see 12 above), there are no legal restrictions on a bidder buying shares in a target in the market (although there may be tactical reasons for, or for not, doing so). Purchasing shares in the market may (depending on the time of purchase) give rise to difficulties in meeting the threshold for the compulsory acquisition of shares or the threshold for shareholder approval in a scheme of arrangement.

16.8 First announcement
The first announcement made on a takeover is generally either the announcement of a possible offer (Code, Rule 2.4) or the announcement of a firm intention to make an offer (Code, Rule 2.5).

A bidder should announce a firm intention to make an offer only when the bidder has every reason to believe that it can and will be able to implement the offer. That announcement has detailed contents requirements.

The announcement of a possible offer is generally much shorter and can be limited to announcing that talks are taking place (there is no requirement to name the offeror).

16.9 Period between first announcement and offer document
The offer document should normally be distributed within 28 days of announcement of a firm intention to make an offer.

16.10   Offer document content
Whilst the detailed contents of the offer document will vary from transaction to transaction, each offer document will always include (in general terms), without limitation:
*   the general terms of and conditions to the offer;
*   details of the bidder's intention as regards target;
*   financial information relating to the bidder (and, if recommended, the target;
*   disclosure of interests and dealings; and
*   responsibility statements.

The Code sets out in detail contents requirements in relation to each of these headings (as well as some more technical contents requirements).

16.11   Drafting of offer document
The offer document is generally drafted by the bidder's legal counsel and its financial adviser. If the offer proceeds as a scheme of arrangement, then the target's legal counsel and financial adviser will draft the scheme documents. Notwithstanding the identity of the draftsman of the offer documents, responsibility must be accepted by the directors of the bidder and, where appropriate, the directors of the target in respect of the information contained in each document issued to shareholders or each advertisement published in connection with a bid.

16.12 Addressees of offer document
The offer document should normally be sent to shareholders of the target and persons with information rights and, for information, holders of options/awards under the target's employee incentive schemes. At the same time, both bidder and target must make the offer document readily available to their employee representatives or, where there are no such representatives, to the employees themselves.

16.13 Due diligence
A bidder often wishes to conduct due diligence prior to making a firm announcement of a takeover bid because once that announcement has been made, the Panel will insist that the bid be made. It is not possible for due diligence to be a condition or a pre-condition to a bid.

The purpose of bidder due diligence is three-fold (with the ultimate aim in each case of allowing the bidder to assess whether or not it should make a bid for the target and, if so, on what terms), being to allow the bidder to assess:

- whether the target holds the assets which the bidder thought it held;
- whether the target has any hidden liabilities; and
- whether the target is performing in line with the bidder's expectations.

The approach to diligence depends on whether the bid is hostile or not. If it is not hostile, the scope of diligence will be a matter of negotiation between the bidder and the target. If it is hostile, then the bidder will have to rely on publicly available information on the target, subject to the caveat that the Code requires that any information given to one bidder must, on request, be given equally and promptly to another bona fide potential offeror, no matter how unwelcome the bid may be. Accordingly, target companies frequently adopt a position of minimum disclosure.

16.14 Conditions

The Code draws a distinction between pre-conditions and conditions. A pre-condition is an event or circumstance to which the posting of the offer document is made subject. A condition is set out in the offer document and is a consent, approval or other event or circumstance to which the bid itself is subject.

Pre-conditions

The Panel must be consulted whenever a bidder proposes to include in its announcement a pre-condition to the posting of the offer document. The Panel only allows very limited pre-conditions concerning references made to the Competition Commission or the European Commission or the need to obtain other material official authorisation or regulatory clearance in relation to the bid.

Conditions

A bid must not be made subject to conditions which depend solely on subjective judgements by the directors of the bidder or the target, nor should the fulfilment of the conditions be in the hands of the bidder or the target. Typical categories of conditions in UK takeovers include:

- the acceptance condition (the percentage of shareholders who must accept the offer, which must be at least 50 per cent);
- UK or EC competition clearance;
- other legal or regulatory conditions (such as shareholder consent under the Listing Rules); and
- other conditions designed to benefit the offeror, such as conditions relating to the status or performance of the target's business.

The bidder is obliged to use all reasonable endeavours to ensure the satisfaction of any conditions or pre-conditions to which the bid is subject. Other than the acceptance condition and any UK or EC competition condition, the bidder may not invoke a condition unless the circumstances which give rise to the condition or pre-condition are of material significance to the bidder in the context of the bid, material for these purposes being of such significance as, broadly, amounting to the frustration of a contract.

16.15 Obligations of financing
The Code does not generally allow bids to be subject to a financing condition. It requires that a bidder must only announce a bid after ensuring that they can fulfil any cash consideration, if such is offered, and after taking all reasonable measures to secure the implementation of any other type of consideration.

If the bid is for cash or includes an element of cash, both the announcement of the firm intention to make an offer and any subsequent offer document must include confirmation by the financial adviser or another appropriate third party that resources are available to the bidder sufficient to satisfy full acceptance of the bid.

The offer document must contain a description of how the bid will be financed and the sources of that finance. It must also name the principal lenders or arrangers of that finance.

16.16 For cash/for shares/mixed
Generally (subject to certain exceptions) the consideration for an offer can be in cash or shares or a mixture of both, although stakebuilding in a target can in certain circumstances require either a cash offer or a securities offer to be made.

16.17 Break-up fees
Bidders often seek break fees on bids which are not hostile. Reasons for obtaining a break fee include:
* to recover costs if the bid does not proceed through no fault of its own (albeit that the break fee cannot be structured as an indemnity for costs, as this would constitute unlawful financial assistance);
* to persuade the target to continue to negotiate with the bidder;
* to make the target think carefully before entertaining bids from other bidders;
* to dissuade other bidders from making a bid (as, if they are successful, their subsidiary will have to pay the break fee).

If a break fee is proposed, the Panel must be consulted at the earliest possible opportunity and the target board and its financial adviser must confirm to the Panel that they believe the fee to be in the best interests of shareholders.

Principally for the reason set out on the fourth bullet point above, the Code provides that break fees must be de minimis (normally no more than 1 per cent of the value of the target, calculated by reference to the offer price).

16.18 Introduction 13th Directive
The 13th Company Law Directive was introduced into UK law in 2007. Only limited changes were made as a result, as the Directive was largely modelled on the UK takeover regime.

16.19 Traditional and current legal and practical defence mechanisms
In defending a bid, directors must have regard to their statutory duties under

the Companies Act 2006, most relevantly the duty to act within their powers and to promote the success of the company. The Code also provides that the target may not take certain action which may result in the frustration of the bid unless it obtains shareholder approval (Rule 21).

Within this framework, directors might commonly consider the following grounds of defence and adduce evidence to support them:

- the bid undervalues the target;
- the bid offers insufficient premium for control;
- there is insufficient rationale for the merger;
- the target board might introduce a new business strategy or model for growth;
- showing evidence of having returned value to shareholders; and
- attacking the bidder.

The target's directors may also wish to take certain steps to strengthen the target's position, such as:

- making a major acquisition or disposal;
- ensuring that there are change of control provisions in the target's key contracts;
- using the regulatory authorities to the target's advantage eg, the antitrust authorities;
- soliciting a rival bid from a more acceptable bidder (known as a white knight);
- arranging for a friendly shareholder to acquire a blocking stake;
- although rare in the UK, making a bid for the bidder (known as the Pac-Man defence);
- inserting a 'poison pill' mechanism into the target's articles (this is also rare in the UK); and
- lobby support eg, from the media, political groups and analysts, in defence of the bid.

16.20 Nature of listed securities
Securities of UK listed companies in registered form.

17. FOREIGN INVESTMENT CONTROLS
17.1 Any restrictions in foreign control
Foreign investment controls in the UK are significantly less onerous than in comparable jurisdictions, such as mainland Europe, the US and Canada. Foreign ownership is occasionally restricted in specific companies where the government considers that foreign ownership of such a company would constitute a risk to national security. For example, no single foreign individual or company may own more than 15 per cent of the shares in either BAE Systems or Rolls-Royce.

All air operators based in the UK are required to be majority owned and effectively controlled by EEA states or nationals of EEA states. Companies with a controlling shareholding in a company that holds an operating licence granted by the Civil Aviation Authority must also be owned and effectively controlled by EEA states or nationals of EEA states.

17.2 Any foreign exchange control or filing
The UK has no foreign exchange control or foreign investor filing regime.

Finland

Roschier Paula Linna, Elisa Heinonen & Essi Rimali

1. GENERAL DESCRIPTION OF THE CAPITAL MARKETS

The official name of the Helsinki Stock Exchange is NASDAQ OMX Helsinki Ltd., following the acquisition of OMX by NASDAQ in February 2008. NASDAQ OMX Helsinki is part of NASDAQ OMX Nordic, which includes stock exchanges in Stockholm (Sweden), Copenhagen (Denmark) and Rekjavik (Iceland). These stock exchanges share the same trading system, provide common listing and index structures, enable cross-border trading and settlement and provide one market source of information. Further, NASDAQ OMX Nordic is a part of the global NASDAQ OMX Group. The level of foreign ownership is very high in Finland. In recent years, typically 50 to 60 per cent of the market value of NASDAQ OMX Helsinki has been in foreign hands.

1.1 Numbers of companies listed

NASDAQ OMX Helsinki has some 130 listed companies.

1.2 Total volume and market value

According to the latest statistics, the value of the aggregate annual share trading on NASDAQ OMX Helsinki amounted to approximately EUR 133.7 billion in 2010.

1.3 Issue activity

During 2008, the initial public offering (IPO) markets plummeted worldwide, due to the severe economic downturn, and similarly during 2009 there were only a few IPOs worldwide. The Nordic countries were not an exception to this market trend. However, the development of the stock markets during 2010 indicates that investors are restoring confidence in the valuation of the markets. As a consequence, there are signs of a gradual reawakening of the IPO markets.

1.4 Takeover activity

During the economic downturn, the number of takeovers has been modest with only a few takeovers per year, but there have been signs of increasing activity also in the mergers and acquisitions (M&A) market.

1.5 Hostile takeover attempts

The continuing uncertainty in the market may also result in a rising number of hostile takeover attempts due to a certain level of discrepancy in the valuation of target companies by the major shareholders and boards of directors of the target and, on the other side, potential offerors.

2. REGULATORY STRUCTURE

2.1 General

The main law regulating the capital markets is the Securities Market Act (495/1989, as amended, the SMA). The SMA contains provisions, amongst other things, on the issuance of securities to the public, public tender offers, public trading in securities and the clearing and settlement of trades. More specific rules and recommendations can mainly be found in decrees issued by the Ministry of Finance and in the standards issued by the Finnish Financial Supervisory Authority (the FSA).

In addition, listed companies must comply with the rules and regulations of NASDAQ OMX Helsinki, which include, *inter alia*, Harmonised Disclosure Rules, Guidelines for Insiders and the Finnish Corporate Governance Code. Further, in the context of takeovers of public companies, the Helsinki Takeover Code is applicable. The Helsinki Takeover Code is a non-binding, self-regulatory recommendation issued by the Finnish Takeover Panel and drafted in co-operation with issuers, leading law firms, investment bankers and other market players.

The SMA implements, *inter alia*, the EU directive on Markets in Financial Instruments (2004/39/EC) (the MiFID), the EU Transparency Directive (2004/109/EC), the EU Prospectus Directive (2003/71/EC) and the EU Takeover Directive (2004/25/EC).

Currently the SMA is in the process of being revised and a working group established in February 2009 published its report on the proposed amendments in February 2011. The proposed revision of the current SMA is part of a broader reform of Finnish securities markets regulations which aims, *inter alia*, to improve the clarity, comprehensibility and competitiveness of the securities market legislation, to increase the effectiveness of the custody and settlement operations and to ease the administrative burden of listed companies.

The reform also aims to enhance investor protection eg through the introduction of clearly stricter administrative sanctions to be imposed by the FSA. As part of the revision, the current SMA is proposed to be split into several acts, namely the new, amended SMA, the Act on Trading in Financial Instruments, the Investment Services Act and the Act on the Book-entry System and Clearing Operations. Among many other substantive amendments being proposed, the new SMA will also introduce wider exemptions to the obligation to publish a prospectus in accordance with the Prospectus Directive as amended by the Directive 2010/73/EU.

2.2 Regulation of the offering of new securities

2.2.1 Public offering

The concepts of 'public offering' and 'private offering' are not defined under Finnish law. However, according to the guidelines issued by the FSA, the concept of public offering depends on the target group of the offering.

Anyone who offers securities to the public shall be under an obligation to publish a prospectus approved by the FSA before the launch of the offering, unless the offering of the securities falls within an exemption from the prospectus requirement under the SMA and the supplementing Government Decrees on Prospectuses (Decrees 818/2007 and 452/2005). As a main rule, offerings targeted at more than 99 investors are considered public offerings. (See also section 5).

2.2.2 Private offering
According to the FSA, an offering qualifies as a private offering, if the addressees of the offering consist of a group of pre-selected potential investors whose number does not exceed 99 and if the issuer ensures that no other investors than the named, pre-selected potential investors can participate in the offering. Such an offering falls under the exemption of the Decree 452/2005 on Prospectuses and does not trigger the prospectus requirement.

There are generally no Finnish filing or authorisation requirements with respect to an offer qualifying as a private offering. However, the general marketing and duty of disclosure provisions of the SMA apply and the issuer must provide the FSA upon request with a list of the potential investors that are to be approached in Finland.

2.3 Differences between local and foreign companies
The same regulatory framework governing offering of new securities applies to both local and foreign companies.

2.4 Admission to trading on a regulated market
See section 8 (in particular section 8.1).

2.5 Financial promotion
See section 7.

2.6 Rule books
In addition to the Helsinki Takeover Code and the rules and guidelines issued by NASDAQ OMX Helsinki, Euroclear Finland Ltd (Euroclear), the Federation of Finnish Financial Services, the Finnish Financial Ombudsman Bureau and the Securities Market Association have, *inter alia*, issued self-regulation to be observed by publicly listed companies. See also sections 2.1, 3.1 and 4.1.

3. REGISTRATION OF THE ISSUER AND SECURITIES
3.1 Registration requirements
In order for the securities of Finnish companies to be admitted to public trading, they must be issued by a public limited liability company and be registered in the Finnish book-entry securities system. In addition to the registration requirements applicable to Finnish issuers, there is no specific local registration or licensing requirement for the offering of securities to the

public by foreign issuers or the admission of securities issued by such issuers to regulated markets in Finland, nor are there requirements of a formal presence or a local agent.

3.1.1 Finnish book-entry securities system

The book-entry securities system is centralised at the Central Securities Depository, in Euroclear, which is part of the international Euroclear Group. Euroclear provides national clearing and registration services for issuers of securities. Such services include the technical maintaining of shareholder lists and insider registers, general meeting services, assistance with corporate actions and yield payments. Euroclear has securities links to the central securities depositories in Sweden, Germany, France and Estonia. The book-entry system is also linked to Switzerland via the German central securities depository. The links enable the transfer and handling of both Finnish and foreign equities and debt instruments.

Registration with the Finnish book-entry securities system is mandatory for shares listed on NASDAQ OMX Helsinki. However, foreign issuers that intend to list securities on NASDAQ OMX Helsinki may use Finnish depositary receipts or direct links from securities depositories outside Finland. In practice listed debt securities are also registered with the book-entry securities system.

3.1.2 Clearing and trading systems

The Act on Book-Entry Accounts (827/1991) and the Act on the Book-Entry System (826/1991) together with the rules of Euroclear govern the settlement of securities in the book-entry system. Euroclear's clearing and settlement system is a real-time settlement system that enables the settlement of trades on the trading date (T+0). The standard clearing time of exchange trades is three days (T+3). The common trading platform for NASDAQ OMX Nordic, called INET Nordic, is used for share trading on NASDAQ OMX Helsinki.

3.2 Nature of securities

The SMA applies to all types of securities, which are transferable and issued (or intended to be issued) to the public, together with several other securities with similar rights. See section 13 regarding mutual funds.

4. SUPERVISORY AUTHORITIES

4.1 Conduct: cooperation, self-regulation of stock exchange

Generally, the Ministry of Finance (the Ministry) is responsible for ensuring that the legislative framework for financial markets is stable and efficient. The SMA authorises the Ministry to issue supporting regulations. For example, the contents of prospectuses are regulated by Ministry Decrees. The Ministry must also approve stock exchange rules and amendments after having requested a statement from the FSA.

Supervision of the securities markets and the entities operating in such markets is solely within the authority of the FSA, while supplementary regulation is divided between the Ministry and the FSA. Unlike the Ministry, which is only authorised to issue supporting regulations, the FSA has a general authority to issue regulations. The regulations and guidelines issued by the FSA are not subject to the approval of other governmental authorities, even though the FSA operates in connection with the Bank of Finland. The main tasks of the FSA are to oversee financial market operations, to supervise and guide market participants and to maintain trust in the market.

In addition to the FSA, the disciplinary committee of NASDAQ OMX Helsinki supervises compliance with securities market regulation, primarily with the rules of NASDAQ OMX Helsinki, and may impose disciplinary sanctions in the case of non-compliance. See also section 8.5.

The Takeover Panel is an independent self-regulatory body operating at the Central Chamber of Commerce of Finland, which has statutory footing in the SMA. The Takeover Panel promotes compliance with good securities market practice and ensures fair and equal treatment for all shareholders by issuing recommendations and statements regarding listed and private companies. Accordingly, in December 2006 the Takeover Panel issued the Helsinki Takeover Code containing recommendations on the procedures to be complied with in public tender offers. The prerequisites for the Takeover Panel to continue its operations in their current form have been under scrutiny in connection with the pending reform of the Finnish securities markets regulations and it is possible that the Panel will be abolished and potentially replaced by another self-regulating body in the future

5. OFFERING DOCUMENTATION OR PROSPECTUS REQUIREMENTS

5.1 Nature and statutory requirements of the offering document or disclosure document

The SMA, supplemented by Ministry Decrees, contains provisions on the obligation to publish a prospectus and the approval of the prospectus. A prospectus shall be prepared and published when securities are offered to the public or when an application is made to admit securities to public trading. The prospectus shall be approved by the FSA before its publication.

The Ministry Decree on EU prospectuses (452/2005), applies when the offering of securities amounts to at least EUR 2.5 million (calculated for a preceding 12-month period) and always when admission to public trading is sought. Where the total amount of the offer is less than EUR 2.5 million and the offer therefore falls outside the scope of the Prospectus Directive, the Ministry Decree on national prospectuses (818/2007) will apply.

5.2 Exemptions

When the securities offering does not involve the admission of securities to public trading, by operation of law the prospectus requirement does not apply, *inter alia*, in the following situations:

- the securities are offered to qualified investors only (as defined in the Prospectus Directive);
- the total subscription price of the securities offered during 12 months does not exceed EUR 100,000;
- the securities are offered to fewer than 100 investors in Finland;

- the securities offered can be acquired only for consideration of not less than EUR 50,000 per investor or in denominations of not less than EUR 50,000.

Upon application, the FSA may also grant a partial or complete exemption from the obligation to publish a prospectus in certain situations. For a particular reason, eg, if the information is considered of minor importance, the FSA may agree to the omission of information generally required in a prospectus.

5.3 Preparation of the offering document, general contents

According to the SMA, a prospectus can be drawn up either as a single document or as separate documents consisting of a registration document, a securities note and a summary note. Information may be incorporated in the prospectus by reference to previously or simultaneously published documents approved by or filed with the competent authority of the home member state. An approved prospectus is valid for 12 months.

The issuer or offeror and the manager of the issue or the offering are responsible for the preparation and content of the prospectus. As a rule, a prospectus is prepared to comply with the minimum content requirements in the European Commission's Regulation on Prospectuses no 809/2004. Domestic regulations may be applied with respect to offerings limited in size. Further, in accordance with the Prospectus Directive, Finnish law recognises the concept of prospectus passporting.

5.4   Due diligence

As required under the guidelines of NASDAQ OMX Helsinki and the FSA, it is customary to conduct a business, financial and legal due diligence review of the issuer in connection with an IPO. A due diligence is customarily also conducted prior to a public offering, a merger, an acquisition or a public takeover. See also section 8.3.

5.5   Responsibility

According to the SMA and the guidelines issued by the FSA, the underwriter, the distributer of the securities as well as the issuer itself are liable for the accuracy of the information presented in the prospectus, which shall be published prior to the public offering. See also section 9.2.

5.6   Disclaimer/selling restrictions

There are no explicit Finnish law requirements as to country-specific selling restrictions or other disclaimers to be inserted into the marketing materials or other securities offer documentation. In general, a company cannot restrict its liability through disclaimers in Finland. However, especially foreign issuers nevertheless tend to use short disclaimers when offering securities to Finnish investors.

5.7   Issuing of bonds

As a general rule, the offering documentation and prospectus requirements are relatively similar for equity and debt securities.

6. DISTRIBUTION SYSTEMS
6.1 Normal structure of a distribution group
The manager or arranger of a capital markets transaction or an international cross-border transaction with a Finnish dimension is typically a well-recognised investment bank. Depending on the size and nature of a contemplated transaction, the bank chosen will usually be: (i) a local investment bank; (ii) a Nordic investment bank with a presence in the Finnish market; or (iii) an international investment bank.

Larger transactions usually involve more than one manager. A typical syndicate could include an internationally recognised investment bank together with a local bank that will be in charge of the retail tranche.

Equity offerings executed in the past few years have included both large rights offerings and offerings directed at selected domestic and international institutional investors.

6.2 Underwriting
Rights offerings are often fully underwritten and may involve fairly complex underwriting structures. Offerings directed at institutional investors are typically conducted on the basis of exemptions from the prospectus requirements in different jurisdictions. In offerings targeted at US investors, the Rule 144A exemption is mostly used. However, certain offerings have also been registered with the US Securities and Exchange Commission (the SEC).

6.3 Stabilisation
Stabilisation is possible in Finland. According to the SMA, the provisions on the use of insider information or market manipulation shall not apply to trading in securities where an investment firm or a credit institution stabilizes the price of securities in accordance with Article 8 of the Market Abuse Directive.

6.4 Rules on distribution to the public
See section 2.2.

7. PUBLICITY
A marketing brochure or other marketing materials can be published in connection with the publication of a prospectus. The marketing materials must always include a reference to the prospectus and should also indicate where and when the prospectus is available. The marketing materials must be prepared so that their contents or form of presentation cannot be confused with the actual prospectus, nor are they allowed to contain information that is inconsistent with the contents of the prospectus. Such marketing materials shall be submitted to the FSA.

All actions intended to promote the sale of securities, including, for example, equity offerings or tender offers for securities, are considered marketing of securities under the SMA. According to the general provision of the SMA, securities shall not be marketed or acquired in business by giving false or misleading information or by using a procedure that is contrary to good practice or otherwise unfair. Furthermore, the Consumer Protection Act (38/1978, as amended) and Unfair Business Practices Act (1061/1978, as amended), may become applicable in the context of marketing of securities.

8. LISTING
8.1 Special listing requirements, admission criteria
The listing requirements on NASDAQ OMX Nordic, including NASDAQ OMX Helsinki, are in all material respects the same for the Nordic countries Finland, Sweden, Denmark and Iceland.

On NASDAQ OMX Nordic, listed companies are first presented by market capitalisation and then by industry sector following the international Global Industry Classification Standard. Listed companies are divided into three segments: Large Cap for companies with a market capitalisation of at least EUR 1 billion; Mid Cap for companies with a market capitalisation of between EUR 150 million and EUR 1 billion; and Small Cap for companies with a market capitalisation of less than EUR 150 million.

NASDAQ OMX Helsinki may admit to public trading a security that is likely to be subject to sufficient demand and supply and the price formation of which can thus be expected to be reliable.

In brief, the main listing criteria include the following:
- a history of three years;
- documented earnings capacity or sufficient working capital for at least 12 months ahead;
- 25 per cent of the share capital held by the public (free float); and
- the required adequacy with respect to the company's organisation, management and board of directors.

Debt instruments may be admitted to public trading provided that:
- the face value of a debt issue is at least EUR 200,000;
- they are freely transferable;
- their issuer is sufficiently financially sound; and
- the issuer's reporting and supervision processes are arranged in an appropriate manner.

8.2 Mechanics of the review process
The issuer will need to publish a prospectus prior to listing. The legal advisers for the offering typically arrange for the filing of the prospectus with the FSA and are involved in related communication with the FSA during the review process. The fees payable to the FSA for approval of the prospectus depend on the type of securities in question.

Further, a listing application will need to be filed with NASDAQ OMX Helsinki. The application shall contain a description of the issuer's corporate activities and financial position, and include, for example, the following:
- a statement of the issuer's board of directors on the outlook for the current and following financial period;
- confirmation by the board of directors that the issuer is able to comply with the requirements for listed companies; and

- an opinion by the lead manager on the preconditions for the listing of issuer and its ability to operate as a listed company.

Before filing the listing application, a company presentation will be given issuer and its ability to operate as a listed companyby the issuer (assisted by their advisers) to the listing committee. An issuer must promptly disclose both their intent to apply for listing and the filing of the listing application. They will then be considered an applicant for listing and be under an obligation to adhere to the same disclosure requirements as listed companies. The issuer must also pay a registration fee prior to submitting the application and, in addition, an annual fee to NASDAQ OMX Helsinki.

Further, the issuer must conclude a listing agreement with NASDAQ OMX Helsinki and undertake to comply with the rules and guidelines of NASDAQ OMX Helsinki.

8.3 Prospectus obligation, due diligence, exemption

In general, anyone applying for the admission to public trading of a security must publish a prospectus before the securities can be admitted to public trading. However, according to the Ministry Decree on EU prospectuses (452/2005) there are certain exemptions from this obligation. An exemption is, for example, available where the shares that are sought to be admitted to public trading represent, together with shares of the same class admitted to trading during the last 12 months, less than 10 per cent of the total number of shares of the same class admitted to trading on the same stock exchange. An exemption is likewise available where the securities have been admitted to trading maintained by another stock exchange – provided that the issuer fulfils certain conditions (eg, securities of the same class have been subject to this trading for more than 18 months).

As required under the guidelines of NASDAQ OMX Helsinki and the FSA, it is customary to conduct a business, financial and legal due diligence review of the issuer in connection with an IPO. See also section 5.

8.4 Appeal procedure in the event of a prospectus refusal

In the event of a prospectus refusal by the FSA, the issuer may appeal to the Market Court within 30 days of the receipt of the FSA decision.

8.5 Authority of the Exchange

Decisions regarding the admission to listing and de-listing of securities are made by the listing committee of NASDAQ OMX Helsinki. Supervision of compliance with the rules of NASDAQ OMX Helsinki is exercised by NASDAQ OMX Helsinki, which has certain disciplinary powers that are enforced by the disciplinary committee. NASDAQ OMX Helsinki is supervised by the FSA.

8.6 Special arrangements for smaller companies

NASDAQ OMX First North is an alternative marketplace for small and medium-sized growth companies with fewer disclosure and other obligations and lighter listing requirements compared to the main market discussed above.

8.7 Costs of various types

Companies are required to pay a registration fee to NASDAQ OMX Helsinki prior to submitting their application for listing. Furthermore, all companies whose shares are listed on NASDAQ OMX Helsinki are required to pay an annual fee to the stock exchange. The applicant company may also incur various types of advisor fees in connection with the listing.

9.   SANCTIONS AND DISPUTES
9.1   Disciplinary and administrative sanctions

There are two types of disciplinary and administrative sanctions that may be imposed by the respective authorities on the Finnish market. The FSA has the right to impose administrative sanctions for breach of the provisions relating, for example, to market abuse and disclosure requirements. The FSA may, *inter alia*, issue a public notice or warning or impose monetary penalties. In addition, the disciplinary committee of NASDAQ OMX Helsinki may impose certain sanctions, such as a warning, monetary penalty or, ultimately, de-listing of the company, mainly for the breach of its own rules. See also section 8.5.

9.2   Civil actions

The provisions of the SMA set forth the basis for civil liability for non-compliance with rules governing, *inter alia*, disclosure requirements in connection with securities offerings and listings of securities. Accordingly, any person who causes damage through actions violating the SMA or regulations issued pursuant to the SMA shall be liable for the damage.

In principle, a subscription for or purchase of securities is irrevocable. However, Finnish courts are empowered to mitigate or nullify unreasonable contract terms, particularly in cases of stringent and/or unusual terms and conditions of standard contracts.

9.3   Criminal penalties

Both the issuer of securities and the manager may be fined for failure to comply with the SMA's general disclosure requirement to make available sufficient information on factors that may have a material effect on the value of the securities or for using false or misleading information in the marketing of securities. Non-compliance with certain provisions of the Act on Investment Funds (48/1999, the 'AIF') may also result in criminal liability and a fine or imprisonment.

9.4   Additional protection

The Finnish Securities Complaint Board offers advice regarding securities market regulations, the application of contractual terms, good commercial practices in securities trading and other issues related to securities practices. This service is free of charge and available to all non-professional investors who are customers of banks, investment firms or mutual fund companies. The Securities Complaint Board also issues recommendations in disputes relating to investment services and investment funds that involve providers of such services and non-professional investors.

Further, the Consumer Ombudsman has the authority to supervise the marketing of securities to consumers. Finally, the Market Court may order a person marketing, acquiring or trading in securities in breach of the SMA to cease or correct such operations.

10. CONTINUING OBLIGATION
10.1 Disclosure and transparency rule
The regular and continuing disclosure requirements for publicly listed companies are set forth in the SMA, complemented by Ministry Decrees, the FSA guidelines and the NASDAQ OMX Helsinki rules and recommendations. This regulation is largely based on EU directives, most importantly the EU Market Abuse Directive (2003/6/EC) (the MAD) (implemented as of 1 July 2005 by amendments to the SMA and the Act on the FSA) and the EU directive on the Admission of Securities to Official Stock Exchange Listing and on Information to be Published on those Securities (2001/34/EC).

10.2 Information
The SMA sets forth requirements for publicly listed companies to disclose to the market significant matters relating to their operations in an orderly and open manner. Under the SMA, information to be disclosed on a regular basis consists of interim reports, annual accounts and account statements. Further, all decisions and other information on the issuer and their operations that are likely to have a material effect on the value of the securities issued must be disclosed without undue delay. This disclosure obligation also applies to issuers whose securities are subject to a pending application for admission to public trading. The FSA guidelines give certain examples of decisions and information to be disclosed. The NASDAQ OMX Helsinki rules also specify certain matters that need to be disclosed. According to the SMA, an issuer may, with acceptable grounds, postpone the disclosure of information if doing so does not endanger the investor's position and the issuer is able to ensure the confidentiality of the information.

10.3 Listing rules
See sections 10.1 and 10.2.

10.4 Obligations regarding proxy solicitation
There are no proxy solicitation provisions in Finland that would directly correspond to the rules issued by the SEC. Dissemination of information to shareholders is regulated in the Finnish Companies Act (624/2006, as amended, the FCA), securities markets legislation and in the Finnish Corporate Governance Code of 2010 (the CG Code). It is generally held that the board of directors should not engage in soliciting proxies using the company's funds if the proxy would be the board itself or a party related to the board.

10.5 Continuing requirements of reporting and notification of substantial shareholdings or a substantial transaction

Shareholders are obligated to disclose their holdings in Finnish limited companies, the shares of which are publicly traded on the market either in Finland or in the European Economic Area (the EEA), when such holding reaches, exceeds or falls below 5, 10, 15, 20, 25, 30, 50 or 66.7 per cent of the voting rights or of the share capital in the company. Such changes in ownership must be disclosed to the FSA and to the target company, which must publish the change by way of a stock exchange release.

See also section 15.

10.6 Requirements for unlisted issuers

Similarly to a listed issuer, an unlisted issuer is required to publish a prospectus and to comply with the general marketing provisions of the SMA if it offers securities to the public (see section 7). However, there are no similar continuing disclosure obligations applicable to unlisted issuers as there are for listed issuers.

11. CORPORATE GOVERNANCE
11.1 Law and/or code

Corporate governance in listed companies is mainly regulated by the FCA, which includes provisions on the relationship between the board of directors (the board), the managing director and the shareholders, and sets forth their respective rights and obligations. The duties of the company and the board towards the market are regulated by the SMA and other securities market legislation, such as the guidelines and regulations issued by the FSA and the rules of NASDAQ OMX Helsinki. A company whose shares are listed on NASDAQ OMX Helsinki shall comply with the CG Code on a comply-or-explain basis, ie, listed companies must either adhere to the rules of the CG Code or explain publicly the reasons for any possible deviations.

11.2 Management structure

Companies can have either a one-tier or a two-tier board structure. The board is the mandatory corporate body elected by the shareholders' meeting (or by the supervisory board if so designated in the articles of association), whereas the supervisory board is a special corporate body that may be elected if so determined in the articles of association. In practice, the use and the significance of supervisory boards have been limited and have declined even further in recent years.

The board is responsible for the management and proper organisation of the operations of the company. The board appoints the managing director, is responsible for the supervision of the bookkeeping and is in control of the company's financial matters. The Code recommends the board adopt a written charter for its work and to describe the main contents of the charter to the market.

11.3 Obligations to publish information on the Internet
The FCA and the SMA require that relevant documentation relating to the annual general meeting and the annual and interim reports of the company are kept available on the company's Web site. In addition, a variety of investor information must be published on the company's Web site, such as the statutory corporate governance statement and the stock exchange releases published by the company.

11.4 Responsibility of inside/outside directors
There are no differences in the responsibilities or liability of inside and outside directors of a company. However, the Code refers in several recommendations to outside directors, for instance by stating that the boards of listed companies and the board committees should mainly consist of non-executive directors (ie, directors who have no employment relationship or service contract with the company). See also section 11.8.

11.5 Committees
According to the Code, the board should consider establishing committees in order to enhance the effectiveness of its work. The Code addresses the roles of the audit, nomination and remuneration committees. The committees are considered merely preparatory bodies of the board with no independent decision-making power.

11.6 Obligation to ask for consent of a shareholders' meeting
Under the FCA, certain decisions must be made by the shareholders. The annual general meeting of shareholders decides, among other things, upon the adoption of the financial statements and the use of the profit shown on the balance sheet. In addition, the shareholders decide amendments to the articles of association, any share issue, a decrease of share capital, a merger, de-merger or liquidation.

11.7 Depth of information – proxy solicitation
Although there are no specific provisions in Finland regarding proxy solicitation, there are substantial disclosure requirements in the FCA, securities markets legislation and the Code.

11.8 Appointment/dismissal of directors
The members of the board are elected by the shareholders' meeting (unless stipulated otherwise in the articles of association). The Code recommends that a majority of the members of the board shall be independent of the company, and at least two of such members shall, in addition, be independent of significant shareholders (ie, shareholders holding at least 10 per cent of all shares or votes in the company). The shareholders' meeting can, at any time, remove from office an elected board member with an unlimited right. See also section 11.4.

11.9 Income and options for directors

The shareholders' meeting also determines the board members' remuneration. The Code recommends that non-executive directors do not participate in share-related compensation systems.

11.10 Earnings guidance

There are no obligations for listed companies to disclose earnings guidance and profit forecasts. However, the directors' report and the explanatory statement to interim reports and annual accounts shall contain an assessment of the likely future development of the issuer. Actual profit forecasts (numerical or verbal) are always voluntary and at the sole discretion of the company. However, the FSA recommends the publication of profit forecasts.

In December 2010 the FSA issued guidance on the manner in which companies should publish their earnings guidance and how the companies should present the assessments of expected future development. The FSA recommends that earnings guidance would be given for the entire financial period and emphasises that any guidance given should be as unambiguous as possible. The underlying assumptions, as well as the risks and uncertainties relating to the reaching of the forecasted targets, must also be disclosed as do any reasonably expected material deviations from them. (See sections 10.1, 10.2 and 10.6).

11.11 Management discussion and analysis (MD&A)

A management discussion and analysis – commenting on the changes in financial key ratios between financial periods – is only required in relation to financial information in prospectuses, not in relation to other financial information disclosed by a listed company, such as interim reports. However, the directors' report must contain an account of material events that have occurred during (and to some extent after) the reported financial period. The Finnish Accounting Board (*Kirjanpitolautakunta*) operates under the auspices of the Ministry of Employment and the Economy, and gives instruments and opinions on the application of the Accounting Act (1336/1997). The Accounting Board has issued guidelines for the preparation of a directors' report. These comprehensive guidelines include instructions on how to report the material events that have occurred during and after the financial period; estimates of expected future developments; estimates of the most significant underlying risks; uncertainties from the company's perspective; estimates of the company's upcoming business activity; and its financial result. Publicly listed companies tend to comply diligently with these guidelines.

11.12 Directors' liability

A member of the board (or managing director) who wilfully or negligently breach their duties may be held liable for compensation for any damage caused to the company. A member of the board (and the managing director) may also be held directly liable toward a shareholder or another third party if that party has suffered damage through the member's breach of the FCA or the articles of association. Breach of the SMA and the directors' duties towards the market (eg, in fulfilling the company's disclosure obligation) may also result in liability. (See also section 9.3).

12. MARKET ABUSE

12.1 Insider trading

The prohibitions relating to insider information and market manipulation under the MAD have been implemented in the SMA. Misuse of insider information and market manipulation are criminalised under the Penal Code (39/1889) and, furthermore, the Act on the FSA (878/2008) contains certain administrative sanctions relating to market abuse. The SMA regulates on a general level the use of insider information, disclosure of holdings and insider registers. These provisions are supplemented by the FSA guidelines on insider information and insider registers, by the insider guidelines issued by NASDAQ OMX Helsinki and by various self-regulatory guidelines regarding insiders, including securities dealers.

The definition of insider information in the SMA corresponds to the definition under the MAD. The basic principle concerning the use of insider information is that insider information may not be used in any manner, directly or indirectly, in the purchasing or selling of securities or by advising somebody else in securities trading. Insider information cannot be disclosed to anyone unless the disclosure is part of the customary performance of the work, profession or assignment of the person disclosing the information. Under certain circumstances, the disclosure of insider information to the major shareholders of the company may be allowed (eg, when company management is contemplating a measure or transaction which later would require the shareholders' approval).

12.2 Market manipulation

The definition of market manipulation in the SMA corresponds substantially to the definition under the MAD. The prohibition of undue market manipulation covers all actions directly or indirectly affecting the price of a security in an artificial manner and deviating from the normal course of trading or disclosure on the securities market.

12.3 Miscellaneous

12.3.1 Disclosure obligations

The ownership of shares and securities entitling the holder to shares of publicly listed companies shall be made public if the shareholder is, *inter alia,* a member of the company's board of directors or upper management. Also, information on share ownership of certain persons related to the company management must be included in the public insider register. The company has an obligation to maintain a public register of such ownership information. In addition to this register, companies are obliged to maintain a non-public, company-specific insider register of persons who regularly receive insider information because of their positions or duties.

12.3.2 Sanctions

The Penal Code imposes sanctions for the misuse of insider information, market manipulation and breach of disclosure duty. A person who wilfully or through gross negligence breaches the prohibition to misuse insider information, may be ordered to pay a fine or given a prison sentence. These sanctions may also be imposed on a person breaching the prohibition of market manipulation or failing to comply with the disclosure duty. For minor breaches, certain administrative sanctions, such as an admonition, a warning or a monetary penalty, may be imposed under the Act on the FSA. (See also section 9).

13. MUTUAL OR INVESTMENT FUNDS

13.1 Introduction to these two categories

Mutual funds are governed by the AIF (the Act on Investment Funds (48/1999) referred to earlier, in section 9.3). The AIF implements the undertakings for collective investments in transferable securities directives I-III (1985/611/EC, 2001/107/EC and 2001/108/EC). Finnish mutual funds can either be UCITS funds or so-called special mutual funds (typically hedge funds). A special mutual fund differs from a UCITS fund in that a special mutual fund is not subject to the investment restrictions set forth for a UCITS fund under the AIF.

13.2 Licence requirements

The entity marketing and offering investment funds in Finland may be required to be licensed by the FSA where the marketing of the fund constitutes provision of investment services. However, there is an exemption from this licence obligation with regard to fund managers.

13.3 Custodians

Custodians are responsible for safeguarding the assets of the mutual/investment funds. The name of the custodian must be explicitly stated in the rules of the fund as well as in its prospectus(es). The fund itself cannot act as its own custodian but it is nevertheless possible that both the fund and the custodian are members of the same group of companies. The FSA grants authorisations to custodians. Furthermore, custodians holding securities in the Finnish book-entry system must have an account operator license granted by Euroclear. The account operator license entitles the custodian to operate in the Finnish book-entry system.

13.4 Undertakings for collective investments in transferable securities (UCITS)

The marketing and selling of units in non-Finnish mutual funds that qualify as AIF funds will, as a rule, be governed by and subject to AIF filing requirements. EEA funds authorised in accordance with the UCITS directives are always governed by the AIF. A non-Finnish UCITS fund may be marketed to the public two months after filing the notification with the FSA, unless the FSA forbids marketing within that period. The Finnish or Swedish language must be used in the marketing of units in a mutual fund to non-professional investors. If a UCITS fund publishes a simplified prospectus in connection with the marketing of the fund to investors in Finland, only the simplified prospectus will need to be translated into Finnish or Swedish. Further, non-Finnish UCITS funds are required to prepare a so-called Finland-specific marketing document. Reporting requirements under the AIF correspond to those set forth in the UCITS directives.

13.5 Non-UCITS funds

Should such foreign mutual funds not qualify as funds under the AIF (eg, where the funds are close-ended), they will only be subject to the general provisions governing securities contained in the SMA. If units in a non-UCITS fund are marketed solely to professional investors in Finland, the AIF does not apply. However, if a non-UCITS fund is marketed (even partly) to non-professional investors, it may not be marketed in Finland without the authorisation of the FSA. The authorisation can only be granted if the foreign legislation provides unit holders protection that is sufficiently comparable with that of the AIF. Furthermore, the fund shall, according to its home state regulations, be subject to supervision comparable to that set forth in the EU regulations, and sufficient co-operation between the supervising authority and the FSA must be ascertained.

13.6 Hedge funds

There are no specific regulations in Finland governing hedge funds, in particular.

14. SECURITIES INSTITUTIONS

14.1 Stock Exchanges

NASDAQ OMX Helsinki is the only stock exchange (regulated market) in Finland. NASDAQ OMX Helsinki has issued rules that, in addition to statutory rules and regulations, govern securities exchange and other activities conducted on NASDAQ OMX Helsinki.

14.2 Securities clearing house

The securities clearing house in Finland is Euroclear Finland Ltd. For more details on Euroclear as well as the provisions covering the settlement of securities in the book-entry system, see sections 3.1 and 14.3.

14.3 Central securities depository

The central securities depository in Finland is Euroclear Finland Ltd. (See sections 3.1 and 14.2.)

14.4 Investment service providers (ISP)

The offering and marketing of investment services to the public in Finland is subject to the Act on Investment Firms (922/2007, IFA) and the Act on

Foreign Investment Firms (580/1996, FIFA).

Further, investment services can be offered by banks and credit institutions pursuant to the Credit Institutions Act (121/2007 as amended) which applies to the conduct of banking business on a professional basis.

The SMA includes code of conduct rules to be observed in the provision of investment services. The FSA has also issued guidelines for the marketing of financial instruments to Finnish investors. Further, the IFA contains code of conduct rules concerning eg, the separation of assets, prevention of money laundering and confidentiality.

Under the FIFA, an EEA investment firm that intends to provide investment services in Finland, on a cross-border basis or by establishing a branch office, shall notify the competent home state regulator of this intention. The home state regulator shall then notify the FSA thereof under the MiFID. The investment firm may commence the operations of a branch office in Finland in reliance on the passport within two months from the receipt of the home state regulator's notification by the FSA. The FSA shall within that time period issue any provisions it deems necessary regarding the duty to disclose information relating to the supervision of the activities of the investment firm and regarding specific operational conditions necessary for the general good. Further, once the FSA has received the respective notification, cross-border operations conducted without establishing a branch office may be commenced immediately.

According to the FIFA, a foreign investment firm authorised in a state outside the EEA may be granted an authorisation by the FSA to establish a branch office in Finland if the firm: (i) is subject to sufficient supervision in its home state; and (ii) has sufficient operating conditions and a management that fulfils the requirements for the reliable provision of investment services. In order to offer cross-border investment services without establishing a branch office or subsidiary, a foreign non-EEA investment firm must apply to the FSA for authorisation.

15. NOTIFICATION OBLIGATIONS
15.1 Notification of major shareholding
Notification obligations are set forth in the SMA and complemented by a related Ministry Decree and by FSA regulations.

Under the SMA, a shareholder whose holding reaches, exceeds or falls below the thresholds of 5, 10, 15, 20, 25, 30, 50 or 66.7 per cent of the voting rights or share capital in a Finnish company, and whose shares are subject to public trading within the EEA, is obliged to disclose the holding to the target company and the FSA.

To determine the proportion of voting rights and share capital referred to above, the following are also to be regarded as shares held by a shareholder:
- shares held by a controlled undertaking;
- shares held by a pension fund or foundation of the shareholder or of a controlled undertaking; and
- shares carrying voting rights, the exercise of which, on the basis of an agreement or otherwise, is dependent on a decision by the shareholder

alone or together with a third party.

Disclosure is also required where a shareholder is a party to an agreement or other arrangement that, if enforced, will cause their holding to reach, exceed or fall below one of the above thresholds.

The target company and the FSA must be notified without delay once the shareholder has or should have become aware of the change in their holding or on the day the agreement concerning such holding is entered into. The target company is obliged to publish the information without delay.

Additional disclosure requirements apply to holdings in Finnish credit institutions, investment firms and insurance companies as well as in companies within the defence industry. The relevant thresholds for credit institutions, investment firms and insurance companies are 10, 20, 30 or 50 per cent and the intended change in holdings must be filed with the FSA prior to effecting the change. The FSA may prohibit the acquisition should it be likely to jeopardise the careful and sound management of the target institution's business.

16. PUBLIC TAKEOVERS

16.1 Applicable laws and regulations and Competent Authorities

The acquisition of publicly traded shares (or other securities) through a public tender offer is largely governed by the SMA. The provisions of the SMA set forth, *inter alia*, requirements on the information to be published in connection with a public tender offer and the main principles relating to the offer. The FCA regulates the redemption of minority shareholdings (squeeze-out) and sets forth the rights and duties of the target board.

Public tender offers are also governed by the Helsinki Takeover Code (the Takeover Code) and the FSA's standards (partly binding and partly recommendatory procedural and application guidelines on the provisions of the SMA). The Takeover Code is not legally binding, but rather a recommendation recording best practices and good conduct on the securities market in connection with public tender offers. The Takeover Code has been issued by the Takeover Panel, a self-regulatory body that has statutory footing in the SMA and operates in connection with the Finnish Central Chamber of Commerce.

Further, the rules and regulations of NASDAQ OMX Helsinki govern, in addition to disclosure matters and trading, other issues such as, for example, the de-listing of securities.

See also sections 2.1 and 4.1.

16.2 Dealing with disclosures and stake building

If an offeror builds a stake in the target company before launching an offer, they must comply with the regulations on disclosure of holdings and insider regulations.

16.3 Types of takeover bids

The SMA contains provisions regarding both voluntary and mandatory offers. The threshold triggering a mandatory offer is reached when a shareholder's holding in a Finnish listed company exceeds 30 or 50 per cent of the total voting rights in the target company. A shareholder's holding includes the voting rights held by any undertakings controlled by the shareholder and the voting rights held by the shareholder together with a third party, as well as the voting rights held by parties acting in concert with the shareholder to exercise control over the target company.

Finnish law does not draw a distinction between friendly and hostile public tender offers.

16.4 Procedural aspects

In a friendly transaction it is customary for the offeror to enter into a so-called combination agreement with the target board. The combination agreement governs the transaction process and includes the main terms and conditions of the offer as well as the conditions and prerequisites under which the target board will recommend the offer to the shareholders. The offeror may quite freely decide on the terms and conditions of the offer, with the exception of the mandatory provisions mainly relating to the offer price, the duration of the offer period and the equal treatment of all holders of shares and/or other securities that are tendered for.

16.5 Nature and value of a consideration offered

The offer consideration shall, as a general rule, be the market price of the shares in question. In mandatory offers, the market price is defined as the highest price paid by the offeror during the six months preceding the date when the obligation to make a mandatory offer was triggered, or, in the absence of such purchases, at least the volume-weighted average price paid for the securities in question in public trading during the three months preceding said date. In a voluntary offer made for all the securities in the target company, the offer consideration must be at least equivalent to the highest price paid by the offeror during the six months preceding the announcement of the offer. In the absence of such purchases, the offeror is free to determine the offer consideration.

The offer consideration can be cash, securities or a combination. However, in mandatory offers cash must always be offered at least as an alternative, whereas in voluntary offers the offeror may decide upon the form of consideration to be offered (except for certain situations in which the offeror is required to offer a cash consideration at least as an alternative).

According to the SMA, all shareholders must be treated equally in a tender offer, ie, shareholders must be offered equal consideration on equal terms. In particular, the SMA imposes a statutory top-up obligation, requiring the offeror to adjust the offer terms if target securities are acquired by the offeror for a higher price than the initial offer price after the announcement of the offer and prior to the expiry of the offer period. The adjustment will need to reflect the higher price paid. A similar top-up obligation will apply if target securities are acquired by the offeror for a higher price than the initial offer price during a period of nine months from the end of the offer period.

16.6 Timetable and variations

The statutory minimum offer period is three weeks and maximum is 10 weeks. The offer period may, on special grounds, exceed the 10-week maximum, provided that this does not impede the operations of the target company for an unreasonably long period. The FSA may order an extension of the offer period in order for the target company to convene a general meeting of shareholders to consider the offer.

16.7 Irrevocable

In practice, it is fairly common for the offeror to approach major shareholders prior to the announcement of a tender offer to solicit irrevocable undertakings to accept the contemplated offer. Such undertakings have to be disclosed in the tender offer announcement and in the offer document but do not have to be disclosed prior to the announcement of the offer. Any contact with shareholders should be taken with due care, taking into consideration confidentiality and insider issues. The terms of any irrevocables may not be more favourable than the terms of the offer to the rest of the shareholders.

16.8 Share dealings, buying shares

The offeror may during or after the offer period, at times determined by the offeror, acquire the securities subject to the offer also outside of the tender offer. However, when acquiring such securities, the offeror must ensure that all shareholders are treated equally and that all actions comply with applicable insider regulations. The offeror must also acknowledge that the price paid for any such shares outside the tender offer must not be higher than the consideration offered in the tender offer in order not to trigger the top-up obligation described in section 16.5.

16.9 Announcements

The offeror must disclose their decision to launch a tender offer immediately after such a decision has been made. The decision to launch the offer must also be communicated to the target company and the FSA. The disclosure shall include the main terms of the forthcoming offer.

After the decision has been disclosed, it must, without delay, be communicated also to the representatives of the employees or to the employees in the target company and the offeror.

Similarly after the expiration of the offer period, the offeror shall, without delay, make the result of the offer public.

16.10   Drafting of offer documents

In connection with the tender offer, the offeror must also publish a tender offer document, which discloses the terms and conditions of the offer as well as all other relevant information. The offeror shall, in the offer document, present its strategic plans regarding the target company and an assessment on the likely affect on the operations and employment of the target company. Additional information about the target is also required.

16.11 Responsibility

The offeror must in the tender offer document also make a specific statement to the effect that to the best of its knowledge, all the information provided in the offer document is correct and that nothing has been left out of the document that may have an impact when evaluating the merits of the tender offer. The offeror is liable for the contents of the offer document. However, to the extent information presented on the target company is based on public information, the offeror is only liable for the correct restatement thereof.

16.12 Due diligence in advance of a takeover bid

In friendly transactions, it is common to conduct a due diligence review of the target company prior to making a decision to make an offer. There are no explicit rules of law on whether due diligence should be allowed by the target board and to what extent, but the Takeover Code provides some guidance. If conducting a due diligence review is a precondition imposed by the offeror for launching an offer, and the target board considers the contemplated offer to be in the shareholders' best interest, allowing the review would generallly be considered to be in the interest of the shareholders. If the board does not consider a proposal for a contemplated offer to be of a serious nature nor in the best interests of the shareholders, due diligence should generally not be allowed.

When due diligence is permitted, special attention must always be paid to confidentiality and insider issues in relation to disclosure of information, taking into account the possibility that the offer will never be completed.

16.13 Conditions to the offer

The completion of a voluntary offer can be made conditional upon the fulfilment of certain conditions, eg, reaching a certain acceptance level. Legislation does not regulate the kinds of conditions that are permitted in a tender offer, but the Takeover Code and the FSA's guidelines on takeover bids and mandatory bids provide further guidance in this respect. The conditions should be unambiguous, so that their satisfaction may, when necessary, be clearly determined, thus ensuring that the completion of the offer does not effectively occur at the offeror's discretion. Further, in order to invoke a condition to completion, the non-fulfilment of the condition must be of material relevance to the offeror in relation to the contemplated transaction.

16.14 Financing

The offeror is obligated to secure financing for the tender offer before announcing its decision to make the offer.

16.15 Inducement

According to the Takeover Code the board of directors of the target company should be careful in agreeing to so-called 'break-up fees', which refer in general to an arrangement where the target company agrees to pay the offeror a pre-agreed compensation in case the offer is not completed because of certain pre-defined reasons.

However, in some situations a break-up fee may be justifiable. For example, if the offeror sets the break-up fee as a pre-condition for launching the offer and, in the opinion of the target's board of directors, receiving the offer is in the best interests of the shareholders, the break-up fee may be acceptable provided *inter alia* that the amount of the break-up fee is reasonable (merely a cost compensation). However, the target company may not agree to a break-up fee in a situation where the offer will not be completed due to a reason arising from the offeror. A break-up fee is usually agreed upon in the combination agreement between the parties or otherwise.

16.16   Defence mechanisms
In a takeover context the target board is generally prevented from making decisions that could endanger the completion of any tender offer that is likely to be in the interests of the target shareholders. In the case of an unwanted takeover attempt, the most common and acceptable forms of defence are either to seek a 'white knight' (ie, a more favourable competing offer) or for the board to recommend declining the offer. Generally speaking, the board should be careful in taking any other concrete measures that could endanger the completion of an attractive tender offer without submitting such meansures to the general meeting. However, the FCA permits many kinds of pre-arrangements that could in practice complicate the successful completion of a tender offer, such as the use of multiple voting shares or voting caps.

16.17   Squeeze-out
An offeror who has acquired more than 90 per cent of the shares and votes in the target company has the right to redeem the remaining minority shareholdings under squeeze-out proceedings governed by the FCA.

16.18   Schemes of arrangement
Finnish law does not recognise the concept of a scheme of arrangement. An alternative transaction structure for a public tender offer in Finland would be a statutory merger, which requires the decision to be made in a general meeting of shareholders of the target company by a qualified majority (ie, the proposal must be supported by at least two-thirds of the votes cast and the shares represented at the meeting). In practice, a statutory merger is, however, not a commonly used alternative for a public tender offer in Finland.

17.   FOREIGN INVESTMENT CONTROLS
The Act on the Monitoring of Foreigners' Corporate Acquisitions in Finland (1612/1992, as amended) imposes certain restrictions on foreign investments in Finnish companies of significant size where important national interests, such as securing national defence, preventing significant economic, social or environmental difficulties or safeguarding public order, might be at

risk. However, a proposal on a new Act on the Monitoring of Foreigners' Acquisitions in Finland (272/2010) that would repeal the Act of 1992 was issued in late 2010. The proposal would extend the authority of the Ministry of Employment and the Economy to monitor that no 'essential national interests' are jeopardised where a foreign company intends to acquire a stake in a Finnish company. A foreign company would comprise all companies with registered offices in non-EU/non-EEA countries. Acquisitions representing at least 10 per cent of the voting power carried by all the shares of the company or a 'corresponding actual influence in the monitored entity' would have to be notified to the Ministry beforehand.

France

De Pardieu Brocas Maffei
Antoine Maffei & Guillaume Touttée

1. GENERAL DESCRIPTION OF THE CAPITAL MARKETS
France's stock exchanges are operated by Euronext Paris, the NYSE
Euronext's French subsidiary.

1.1 Number of companies listed
At the end of November 2010, a total number of 695 companies were listed
on Euronext Paris (compared to 654 in 2009, ie +6.3 per cent, and to 792 in
2008, ie -12.3 per cent).

1.2 Total volume and market value
At the end of November 2009, the market capitalisation of the companies
listed on Euronext Paris amounted to approximately EUR 1,275 billion.
The average daily market capitalisation for the year 2009 amounted to
approximately EUR 3.6 billion.

1.3 Issue activity
In 2008, the issue activity on Euronext Paris resulted in a global amount of
approximately EUR 136 billion (ie, +16 per cent compared to 2007, and -16
per cent compared to 2005).

1.4 Takeover activity
A total number of 29 public takeovers were completed in France in 2009,
versus 41 in 2008 and 67 in 2007.

1.5 Hostile takeover attempts
Three hostile takeovers were launched in 2008 and two in 2009 (including a
successful one and an unsuccessful one).

2. REGULATORY STRUCTURE
2.1 General
In France, the trading of securities on a stock market is governed by the
French Monetary and Financial Code (MFC) and the *Autorité des Marchés
Financiers* (AMF) General Regulation and its implementing instructions.
   More recent laws and regulations are the consequence of the incorporation
of EU directives. Within the last five years, four main EU directives were
implemented under French law, in addition to the Markets in Financial
Instruments Directive (MiFID), which came into effect on 1 November 2007.

Takeover Directive

The Takeover Directive of 21 April 2004 (Directive 2004/25/EC) was incorporated into French law by the Public Takeover Act of 31 March 2006. The purpose of this directive is to facilitate takeover activity in the member states.

Prospectus Directive

The Prospectus Directive of 4 November 2003 (Directive 2003/71/EC) harmonised requirements for the drafting, approval and distribution of the prospectus to be published when securities are offered to the public and/ or admitted to trade on a regulated market situated or operating within a member state.

Market Abuse Directive

The Market Abuse Directive of 28 January 2003 (Directive 2003/6/EC) provides for harmonised definitions of inside information and market manipulation in EU member states. Three other EU market abuse directives were enacted on 22 December 2003 and 29 April 2004. The implementation of the market abuse directives into French law started as early as 1 August 2003 with the adoption of the Financial Security Act.

Transparency Directive

The Transparency Directive of 15 December 2004 (Directive 2004/109/EC) was incorporated into French law by the 'Breton Act' of 26 July 2005 and the amendments to the AMF General Regulation approved by the decree of 4 January 2007. This directive supplements the rules set out in the Market Abuse Directive and the Prospectus Directive by harmonising the periodic and ongoing reporting obligations for issuers whose securities are admitted to trade on a regulated market and the notification obligations for major shareholdings.

2.2   Regulation of the offering of new securities

Public offering

Under French law, a public offering (*offre au public*) is defined as:
- any communication of any form brought to the attention of any person or legal entity by any means, which contains sufficient information about the conditions of the offer so as to allow an investor to decide to purchase or subscribe for the offered securities;
- the offer of securities through financial intermediaries.

Pursuant to French rules, every issuer making a public offering of securities (as defined above) or applying for the listing of securities on a regulated market must file a prospectus with the AMF.

Private offering

A private offering consists of the offer of securities to 'qualified investors' (ie, individuals and legal entities that possess the necessary competence and means to appreciate the risks of securities transactions) or among a 'restricted group of investors' (ie, group composed of less than 100 natural or legal persons).

2.3 Differences between local and foreign companies

The private placement of foreign shares and bonds in France requires no prior authorisation of the French authorities. The MFC prohibits the solicitation of investors in France for the purchase of securities that are not admitted to trade on a French regulated market or on a recognised foreign market (ie, a market deemed to have sufficient levels of regulatory oversight and investor protection).

2.4 Admission to trade on a regulated market

Pursuant to the EU Prospectus Directive, a prospectus is required for admission to trade on regulated markets of the EU member states.

2.5 Financial promotion

Démarchage is defined in the French regulations as: (i) any unrequested solicitation of a person, by any means, for the purpose of recommending or encouraging the subscription, purchase, exchange or sale of, or the participation in, transactions involving securities or providing such recommendations or encouragement to the general public; or (ii) visiting persons at their homes or places of work for the same purpose.

Under the MFC, *démarchage* may be carried out by: (i) French credit institutions; (ii) registered French investment service providers (ISPs); (iii) French insurance companies; or (iv) equivalent entities in EU member states authorised to conduct *démarchage* activities in their home states.

2.6 Rule books

The trade of securities on French stock markets is ruled by three main rulebooks: the Euronext Rule Books, the Alternext Rule Book and the AMF General Regulation.

3. REGISTRATION OF THE ISSUER AND SECURITIES
3.1 Registration requirements

Companies do not have to be locally incorporated in order to offer securities on a French financial market. No local formal presence on French territory is even required. However, in addition to being subject to European passport rules, foreign issuers have to comply with local regulations relating to securities and offerings.

3.2 Other requirements

Requirements that have to be met by issuers who apply to have their securities admitted to be listed on Euronext Paris are detailed below in section 8.

3.3 Nature of securities

Following the Executive Order of 8 January 2009, a new classification of financial instruments was adopted by dividing them into two sub-categories: 'financial securities' *(titres financiers)* and 'financial contracts' *(contrats financiers)*. Financial securities include equity and debt securities, as well as shares and units in collective investment schemes. Financial contracts are forward financial instruments.

Financial securities issued in France are 'dematerialised', ie, registered with the issuer or recorded with a financial intermediary in book entry form.

4. SUPERVISORY AUTHORITIES

4.1 Conduct: prudential, cooperation, self-regulation of stock exchange

The French supervisory authorities are the *Autorité des Marchés Financiers* (AMF) and the *Autorité de Contrôle Prudentiel* (ACP).

The AMF is an independent public agency, which is responsible for ensuring the protection of investments and the proper functioning of France's financial markets.

The AMF oversees and regulates transactions involving the securities of listed companies.

The ACP is an independent public agency, created in 2010 as a result of the merger of the *Commission Bancaire*, the *Autorité de Contrôle des Assurances et des Mutuelles* and the *Comité des Etablissements de Crédits et des Entreprises d'Investissement*. It may grant and withdraw approval of credit institutions, investment companies and custodians authorised to operate in France.

The ACP supervises credit institutions and investment and insurance firms. It operates with the support of the Bank of France *(Banque de France)*.

4.2 New listing measures in connection with the credit crisis

As a result of the credit crisis, the AMF decided to introduce exceptional provisions on short-selling. These measures, which apply to equity securities issued by credit institutions and insurance companies traded on the French regulated market, prohibit naked short-selling transactions and provide for transparency of short positions. Initially implemented for a three-month period, the AMF decided to extend the application of these provisions for an undefined period.

5. OFFERING DOCUMENTATION OR PROSPECTUS REQUIREMENTS

5.1 Nature and statutory requirements of the offering document or disclosure document

Every issuer that makes a public offering of securities or applies for the admission to trade securities on a regulated market must file a prospectus with the AMF in order to obtain its approval *(visa)*.

5.2 Exemptions

French law provides two types of exemptions:
- the first exemption is for private placements; and
- the second concerns offerings to ISPs performing asset management services for third parties.

5.3   Preparation of the offering document, general contents
The prospectus may be drawn up as a single document or as separate documents, ie:
- a registration document (*document de référence*) containing general information about the issuer;
- an information memorandum regarding the financial instruments being offered to the public (*note d'opération*); and
- a summary note (summary of the prospectus).

The prospectus must contain all information necessary for an investor to make an informed decision. The prospectus must be made generally available to the public and transmitted to any person solicited in connection with the offering.

5.4   Due diligence
Where a prospectus has to be filed with the AMF, a due diligence investigation must be undertaken by ISPs and statutory auditors of the issuer who shall communicate a completion letter to the AMF in order to confirm that their review did not reveal any mistake or omission in the prospectus that may be misleading to investors.

5.5   Responsibility
The legal representative of the issuer takes responsibility for the information contained in the prospectus. He is required to certify in a statement that, to the best of his knowledge, the information contained in the prospectus is true and reflects the true situation of the issuer, and contains no fact or omission which may be misleading. Auditors also take responsibility for the information they have produced in the prospectus.

5.6   Disclaimer/selling restrictions
It is customary to include disclaimers and specific selling restrictions in relation to the marketing of the securities where the offer of securities is limited to France.

5.7   Recognition of prospectuses by other exchanges
Issuers having their headquarters in an EU member state and intending to offer their products to investors in France may benefit from the European single passport system. As a result, no prospectus will be required from such issuers provided that the AMF receives proper notification by the competent supervisory authority of the prospectus drafted by the issuer in its own member state.

5.8   Supplementary prospectuses
Every significant new factor that is capable of affecting the assessment of the securities and that arises between the time when the prospectus is approved and the time when trading on a regulated market begins shall be disclosed by the issuer in a supplement to the prospectus.

5.9 Issuing of bonds
In order to issue bonds or to have such bonds listed, issuers must prepare a prospectus. Issuers may prepare either:
- a standalone prospectus, to be prepared for each listing application; or
- a base prospectus, to be prepared annually and supplemented with a document setting out the financial terms of the issuance.

6. DISTRIBUTION SYSTEMS
6.1 Normal structure of a distribution group
A distribution group usually involves between one and four financial institutions. These financial institutions must be licensed as ISPs.

6.2 Methods of distribution
The distribution depends on the structure of the transaction. The distribution may consist of a placement with selected persons, an offer to intermediaries, or a retail offer. The distribution is usually performed through the book-building method.

6.3 Underwriting
If the issue consists of a public offer, it will be guaranteed by an ISP (usually also licensed as a bank) through an underwriting agreement. Such an agreement usually contains, among other specific provisions, representations and warranties of the issuer, lock-up of the shareholders and the fees and commissions of the ISP.

6.4 Fees and commission
Fees and commissions depend on the structure and the size of the issuance. Such fees are in line with market practices and vary regarding the commitments of the ISP (underwriting or guarantee agreement).

6.5 Stabilisation
The underwriting agreement may contain a stabilisation provision according to which the ISP will stabilise the price of the shares on the market during a defined period following the issuance of the securities.

6.6 Involvement of a distributor in the preparation of the offering document
The lead underwriter coordinates the preparation of the offering document, but the issuer is legally responsible for its drafting and filing with the AMF.

6.7 Timing of distribution process
The distribution process may usually vary between a few hours (accelerated book-building) and 15 days.

6.8 Rules on distribution to the public
Listed financial instruments may only be distributed to the public by an ISP, either registered in France or in another member state of the EU and duly 'passported' in France.

7. PUBLICITY

It is common practice that legal counsel of the issuer draft publicity guidelines providing for limitations and procedures for issuing any communication and marketing materials. Usually, such counsel also prepares research guidelines, which set out the procedures relating to the preparation of research reports by the analysts and the distribution of said research reports prior to and following the initial public offering (IPO).

Any form of publicity is prohibited before the approval of the prospectus by the AMF.

All information relating to the issuance shall be available on the Web site of the company.

After the approval of the prospectus, any press release, marketing material or publicity has to be first communicated to the AMF.

8. LISTING

8.1 Special listing requirements, admission criteria

	Euronext	Alternext
Minimum public offering	25 per cent shares distributed to the public or 5 per cent representing a value of at least EUR 5 million.	EUR 2.5 million
Accounting track record	Issuer must have published or filed audited annual financial statements for the preceding three financial years. If the fiscal year ended more than nine months before the date of the admission to listing, the issuer must have published or filed audited semi-annual accounts.	Audited annual financial statements for the preceding two financial years plus semi-annual accounts for the fiscal year ended more than nine months before the date of the admission to listing.
Accounting standards	Compulsory International Financial Reporting Standards (IFRS).	French (IFRS not compulsory)

8.2 Mechanics of the review process

The board of Euronext reviews applications and decides whether the financial instruments should be admitted or not. The admission committee processes the applications and advises the Euronext's board.

8.3 Prospectus obligation, due diligence, exemption

Please refer to sections 5.2, 5.3 and 5.4.

8.4 Appeal procedure in the event of a prospectus refusal

In the event of a refusal by the AMF to grant its visa to a prospectus, the issuer may appeal that decision before the Paris Court of Appeal, which has exclusive jurisdiction in such matters.

8.5 Authority of the exchange

The entity running the French stock exchange is Euronext Paris by NYSE Euronext, which is licensed as a market operator *(entreprise de marché)*.

8.6 Sponsor

Every issuer applying for a listing on a regulated market or offering securities on a regulated market has to be assisted by an ISP. For more details on ISPs, please refer to section 14.4.

An original feature of Alternext is that listed companies must have a 'listing sponsor'. The listing sponsor provides advisory services to the company throughout its life and assists it in meeting its legal and regulatory requirements.

8.7 Special arrangements for smaller companies such as Alternext, AIM or SPACs

NYSE Alternext was created by NYSE Euronext to meet the needs of small and medium-sized companies seeking simplified access to the stock market. NYSE Alternext is not a regulated market as defined by the MiFID. It is a multilateral trading facility, offering a lighter regulatory regime than Euronext Paris.

Mandatory bid procedures *(offres publiques d'achat)* do not apply on Alternext.

8.8 Costs of various types

The listing of financial instruments on Euronext Paris and Alternext implies the payment of two categories of fees:
- fees and costs relating to the IPO process; and
- admission fees paid to Euronext.

The admission fee calculation is based on the market capitalisation at the offering price and an annual fee.

9. SANCTIONS AND DISPUTES

9.1 Disciplinary and administrative sanctions

The power to impose disciplinary and administrative sanctions is distributed among the ACP and the AMF.

The ACP

The ACP is allowed to impose on credit institutions and investment firms one of the following disciplinary sanctions: a warning, blame, a temporary or definitive ban from exercising in whole or in part its activities, a compulsory resignation, the withdrawal of the licence of a credit institution or investment firm authorised to operate in France and monetary penalties.

The AMF

The AMF has the power to sanction any legal entity or natural person for the infringement of market rules or market intermediaries' professional duties by using the following sanctions: a warning, blame, a temporary suspension or withdrawal of a professional licence, a temporary or permanent ban on conducting some or all business activities and/or a fine.

In February 2011, the upper limit on AMF fines was raised from EUR 10 million to EUR 100 million, or 10 times the amount of any profits generated.

The respondents have two months to appeal the AMF's ruling.

9.2 Civil actions

Violations of the special prohibitions contained in the MFC and in the French Commercial Code (CC) relating to the issue of securities and the ability of a company to make a public offering may be sanctioned by the commercial courts through the award of damages to the plaintiff.

9.3 Criminal penalties

In addition to administrative sanctions, French courts may inflict criminal penalties to legal entities or individuals who violate specific French securities rules.

Those criminal penalties may consist of, *inter alia*, a fine and/or a jail sentence, a temporary or permanent ban on conducting some business activities, or a temporary or permanent ban on making a public offering of securities or applying for the listing of securities on a regulated market.

10. CONTINUING OBLIGATION
10.1 Disclosure and transparency rule

The main rules relating to disclosure and transparency obligations result from the transposition of the EU Transparency Directive into French law and are laid down in the AMF General Regulation.

10.2 Information

Listed companies must comply with two categories of disclosure obligations: continuous disclosure obligations and periodic disclosure obligations.

Continuous disclosure obligations

The duty of continuous disclosure applies to any financial transactions, as well as to any other company's significant facts, which are likely, if known, to have a material effect on the price of the securities of the issuer. Such information must automatically be brought to the attention of the public 'as soon as possible'.

Nevertheless, to protect business secrets and preserve the confidentiality required in structuring certain transactions, the AMF authorises the issuer to 'postpone the publication of insider information in order not to harm its legitimate interests, provided that such omission does not risk misleading the public and that the issuer is able to ensure that the information is kept confidential'.

In the event of any leak or rumour, a press release has to be published.

Periodic disclosure obligations

The periodic disclosure obligations imposed on issuers consist of the following:
- within four months following the end of the financial year and at least two weeks before the annual shareholders' meeting convened to approve the annual accounts, the publication of an annual financial report containing, among others, the annual and consolidated accounts for the past financial year;

- within 45 days following the approval of the accounts by the annual shareholders' meeting, the publication in the *Bulletin des Annonces Légales Obligatoires* (BALO) of a notice mentioning that the company's accounts were approved by the shareholders as stated in the annual financial report;
- within two months following the end of the first semester, the publication of a semi-annual financial report;
- within 45 days following the end of the first and third quarters, the publication of a quarterly report presenting their net quarterly turnover.

10.3 Listing rules
Please refer to question 8.

10.4 Obligations regarding proxy solicitation
The EU Shareholder Directive was implemented under French law in December 2010. Before its implementation, proxies could only be given to other shareholders of the company or to the shareholder's spouse. French listed companies' shareholders are now also entitled to give proxies to any individual or legal person, at their sole discretion, provided they are entitled to do so under the by-laws of the company. Blank proxies may also be sent by the shareholders to the company. In such cases, they are granted by law to the chairman of the board.

10.5 Continuing requirements of reporting and notification of substantial shareholdings or a substantial transaction
Any person who increases their shareholding in a French listed company to the point where they cross certain thresholds must notify both the issuer and the AMF. For more details, please refer to question 15 below.

10.6 Clearing
Clearing activities are regulated by the MFC. Clearing agents must be licensed as a credit institution. The rules of operation of clearing houses must be approved by the AMF.

10.7 Requirements for unlisted issuers
Not applicable.

11. CORPORATE GOVERNANCE
11.1 Law and/or code
French corporate governance is mostly governed by the French Commercial Code. The AMF also made several recommendations for listed companies. In addition, professional associations establish non-binding corporate governance codes for listed companies, such as the AFEP-MEDEF Code. Companies may choose not to apply these codes. Nevertheless, companies shall provide an explanation for any provisions they have chosen not to apply (the 'comply or explain' rule).

11.2 Management structure

For all French public limited companies (*sociétés anonymes*), including listed companies, French law offers an option between two different forms of organisation of management and supervisory powers:

- a management board *(directoire)* controlled by a supervisory board; or
- a board of directors *(conseil d'administration)*, chaired by a chairman of the board of directors *(Président du conseil d'administration)*. In such a structure, the roles of the chairman of the board and CEO can be separated (dual structure) or held by the same person (unitary structure).

11.3 Obligations to publish information on the Internet

Companies listed on Euronext Paris are required to publish specific financial information on their Web site (eg, annual financial reports, which contain information relating to corporate governance, must be posted on the company's Web site for a five-year period).

Listed companies must keep a record on their Web site of all of the regulated information that they disseminate.

11.4 Responsibility of inside/outside directors

In unitary structures, the board members are all executive directors. The chairman of the board is also the legal representative of the company.

In dual structures, only the members of the management board are executive directors, the members of the supervisory board being all non-executive directors.

There is no legal distinction between executive and non-executive in terms of liabilities.

11.5 Committees

The only specific requirement regarding committees of the board of directors consists in the obligation of French listed companies to have an audit committee, which is responsible for assisting the board in their financial and accounting obligations.

11.6 Obligation to ask for consent of a shareholders' meeting

The shareholders have exclusive authority to enact some specific decisions, in particular to modify the by-laws of the company, issue shares or other equity securities or approve the annual accounts of the company.

11.7 Depth of information – proxy solicitation

The conditions under which the meetings and the activities of the board are prepared and organised, as well as the internal control procedures set up within the company, must be specified in the annual report.

11.8 Appointment/dismissal of directors

Directors and members of the supervisory board are appointed and dismissed by the shareholders at the general meeting. The members of the management board are appointed and dismissed by the supervisory board.

11.9 Income and options for directors

A lump-sum amount of fees *(jetons de présence)* for the entire board
is approved each year by the shareholders' meeting. The board may
also allocate exceptional compensation to certain directors for special
assignments.

The compensation of the chairman of the board is set by the board of
directors. The chairman may be granted options, subject to the achievement
of performance targets.

11.10   Earnings guidance

In listed companies, the AFEP-MEDEF Code states that income and benefits
of any kind (including golden parachutes) granted to executive directors
must be disclosed to the shareholders and linked to the beneficiary's
performance.

11.11   Management discussion and analysis (MD&A)

Before each annual general meeting of shareholders, the board of directors
(or the management board) must establish a report containing specific
information about the company.

11.12   Directors' liability

Directors or members of the management board can be held liable to the
company and/or the shareholders for any breaches of applicable laws,
regulations or of the by-laws, and for mismanagement. In particular, they
may incur civil and criminal liability for breaches of securities law, whether
intentional or resulting from their negligence.

Directors only have individual liability towards third-parties if they have
personally committed a fault separate from their corporate duties.

12. MARKET ABUSE
12.1 Insider trading

Transactions carried out by persons having access to inside information are
regulated by the MFC and the AMF General Regulation.

Inside information

Inside information is defined as any information of a precise nature that has
not been made public, relating directly or indirectly to one or more issuers
or to one or more securities and which, if made public, would likely have a
material effect on the listing prices of the relevant securities.

Concerned persons

The laws and regulations relating to insider trading apply to any person
holding inside information and who knows, or should know, that it is inside
information.

Prohibited behaviours

French law prohibits any person benefiting from inside information to trade or allow someone to trade, either directly or indirectly, securities related to the inside information as long as such information has not been made public. The corresponding legal breach is known as 'insider trading' (*délit d'initié*).

'Insider breach' (*manquement d'initié*) is another prohibited behaviour, which has to be distinguished from insider trading. Indeed, an insider breach is determined objectively and can entail penalties even in the absence of a link between the insider information and the market transaction, and therefore does not require that the insider had an 'intention to use' the information.

Sanctions
Insider trading is punished by an administrative fine of up to EUR 100 million or the repayment of 10 times the profit made. In addition, a criminal fine of up to EUR 1.5 million or the repayment of 10 times the profit made may also be incurred, as well as a jail sentence of up to two years.

List of insiders
Issuers are under an obligation to draw up and regularly update a list of all persons working for the company, whether on a regular or occasional basis, or any other persons who have access, directly or indirectly, to inside information as a result of their professional relations with said company.

The list must be submitted to the AMF upon request.

12.2 Market manipulation
The French legislative and regulatory framework also prohibits anyone from disseminating false or misleading information or from manipulating prices.

Market manipulation encompasses, *inter alia*, transactions or orders to trade which:
• give, or are likely to give, false or misleading signals as to the supply of, demand for or price of financial instruments; or
• secure, by a person, or persons acting in concert, the price of one or several financial instruments at an abnormal or artificial level; or
• employ fictitious devices or any other form of deception or contrivance.

12.3 Miscellaneous
Specific disclosure requirements are imposed on corporate insiders within an issuer concerning all transactions conducted for their own account involving securities of the issuer.

Any trading professional who suspects that a transaction on a regulated market might involve insider trading or market manipulation must file a report with the AMF without delay.

13. MUTUAL OR INVESTMENT FUNDS
13.1 Introduction to these two categories
Undertakings for collective investment in transferable securities (UCITS) (Organismes de placement collectif en valeurs mobilières or OPCVM) are

primarily regulated by the provisions contained in the MFC, the AMF General Regulation and its implementing instructions.

UCITS encompass the two following categories:

- *sociétés d'investissement à capital variable* (SICAV); and
- *fonds communs de placement* (FCP).

The following rules are common to both categories.

Their constitution, just like their transformation, merger, spin-off or winding-up, requires the approval of the AMF. Approval is delivered by the AMF within one month from the filing of an application.

A UCITS must provide subscribers with an information document (prospectus) before any subscription to its shares/units. It is duty-bound to: (i) publish or make available annual or semi-annual reports; and (ii) inform the shareholders of any change in the units.

The assets of an FCP must be held by a custodian *(dépositaire)*. An FCP custodian is selected by the manager of the fund from a list established by the Minister of Economy.

13.2 Investment companies, open-ended, close-ended

Open-ended investment vehicles: SICAV
SICAVs are limited companies whose purpose is the holding and management of securities portfolios. The SICAV may manage itself and does not need a management company. However, for practical reasons, most SICAVs are managed by a management company.

Close-ended Investment: SICAF
New rules recently amended the rules for French *sociétés d'investissement à capital fixe* (SICAFs or 'closed-ended funds') and listing of French and foreign closed-ended funds. Final implementing measures are expected shortly.

A SICAF must be incorporated as a *société anonyme*.

A SICAF is now required to have a management company and a depositary. As it is closed-ended, shareholders cannot redeem their shares at any time.

Special rules for mutual funds: FCP
An FCP is defined under law as a co-ownership of securities with no legal personality. It is created under the common initiative of a management company and a depositary. The management company manages the assets of the FCP and represents the fund *vis-à-vis* third parties.

13.3 Licence requirements
Please refer to section 13.1.

13.4 Continuing requirements
UCITS must *inter alia* annually publish specific documents such as their asset structure, profit and loss account and balance sheet.

13.5 Custodians

The custodian shall have custody of the assets of the collective investments scheme and ensure that the regularity of the decisions of the FCP's manager complies with applicable laws and regulations.

The safeguarding duties of the custodian with regard to the assets of a collective investment scheme shall include:

- keeping the custody account for the financial securities; and
- recording in a position-keeping book the positions regarding assets of the collective investment scheme (other than in respect of financial securities).

Custodians are duty-bound to return to unit holders financial securities under custody. Subject to certain limitations, this is an obligation of result even where assets are held with a sub-custodian.

13.6 Undertakings for collective investments in transferable securities (UCITS)

To implement the 2009/65 CE European directive (UCITS IV), the AMF sets up an approach based on three steps:

- from June to October 2009: consultation of UCITS actors;
- from November 2009: constitution of working groups about regulation and marketing of financial securities; and
- from July 2010 to July 2011: implementation of the directive.

13.7 Non-UCITS funds

Under French law, non-co-ordinated funds must be authorised by the AMF except as regards certain vehicles that are generally open to qualified investors only, which are subject to a single declaration to the AMF.

13.8 Hedge funds

Different types of hedge funds are available under French law:

- *Fonds communs d'intervention sur les marchés à terme* (FCIMT);
- *OPCVM à règles d'investissement allégées* (ARIA): ARIA funds are mainly of three types, ie, non-leveraged ARIA funds, leveraged ARIA funds and ARIA funds of funds; and
- contractual funds.

13.9 Marketing and distribution requirements

The marketing of foreign UCITS in France requires prior approval of the AMF. Foreign UCITS in France must appoint one or more financial correspondents whose duties are *inter alia* the treatment of subscriptions, redemptions, payment of dividends, being the AMF correspondent, the information of shareholders and the payment of the AMF annual royalty.

13.10   Manager

A fund can be managed by one person, by two people as co-managers and by a team of three or more people. Fund managers are paid a fee for their work, which is a percentage of the fund's average assets under management.

14. SECURITIES INSTITUTIONS

The securities institutions in France are market executive undertakings, securities clearing houses, central securities depositories and investment firms.

14.1 Market executive undertaking

Euronext Paris SA is the only market executive undertaking in France. It provides price quotation and trading services. In addition to its duties as a market executive undertaking, Euronext has developed its own share indexes.

14.2 Securities clearing house

The purpose of a securities clearing house is to supervise positions, margin calls and, as the case may be, the liquidation of positions.

LCH.Clearnet is the leading independent financial clearing house in Europe, serving major international exchanges and platforms, as well as a range of over-the-counter (OTC) markets. It clears a broad range of asset classes and works closely with market participants and exchanges to identify and develop clearing services for new asset classes.

14.3 Central securities depository

Euroclear France is the French central securities depository (CSD). Its purpose is to act as a CSD and manage securities settlement and the ESES delivery versus payment system. Euroclear France, in its capacity as CSD, transfers securities by debit and credit of participant accounts opened in its books.

14.4 Investment services providers (ISP)

In order to conduct a placement of securities in France, a financial intermediary must be an authorised French ISP, or an equivalent entity in an EU member state that benefits from the EU single passport system. French ISPs must be approved by the ACP, which is in charge of granting appropriate licences (refer to section 4.1).

ISPs are investment firms and credit institutions authorised to carry out investment services.

15. NOTIFICATION OBLIGATIONS

Under French law, shareholders may be required to notify the AMF and/or the issuer the total number of shares and proportion of voting rights they hold in the share capital of the issuer, upon crossing certain thresholds set out in the law or in the company's by-laws.

15.1 Notification of major shareholding

Legal thresholds

Any individual or legal entity, acting alone or together with another person, who crosses the thresholds of 5, 10, 15, 20, 25, 30, 33.3, 50, 66.6, 90, or 95 per cent of the share capital or the voting rights of the company (by acquiring or selling shares in a company whose registered office is in France and admitted for trading on a regulated market), must notify the company and the AMF within four trading days from the date the shareholding threshold was reached.

Thresholds set out in by-laws
The same information must be provided to the company, within the same time constraints, upon crossing thresholds set out in the company's by-laws.

Sanction
If the crossing of a legal threshold is not declared, all shares in excess of the fraction that should have been declared are deprived of their voting rights at any shareholders' meeting that takes place within two years of the rectification of the notification.

Declaration of intention
Furthermore, any investor whose ownership interest exceeds thresholds of 10 per cent or 20 per cent of the shares or voting rights of a company also has to submit a statement of intent to the AMF and the issuer, within five trading days, describing the objectives it intends to pursue with respect to the company in the 12-month period following notification.

16. PUBLIC TAKEOVERS
16.1 Applicable laws and regulations or regulatory framework
Public takeovers are regulated by the MFC, the AMF General Regulation and its implementing instructions. The EU Takeover Directive, incorporated into French law by the Public Takeover Act of 31 March 2006, modified a number of significant aspects of French securities law.

16.2 Competent authorities
The entity which is empowered to regulate public takeovers is the AMF.

16.3 Dealing with disclosures and stake building
Before the offer: please refer to section 15.
    During the offer: any natural person or legal entity who acquires more than 1 per cent of the share capital of the target company shall notify the AMF.

16.4 Types of takeover bids
Takeovers of listed companies can be divided into two categories: voluntary takeover bids and mandatory takeover bids

Voluntary takeover bids
Such voluntary offers can be friendly or hostile.

Mandatory takeovers
The launch of a takeover addressed to all of the shareholders of the target

company is mandatory where a person, acting alone or in concert:

- acquires more than 30 per cent of the share capital or voting rights of a company (or an essential part of a company's assets); or
- increases their shareholding by more than 2 per cent within a rolling 12-month period if this person already holds between 30 per cent and 50 per cent of the company's share capital or voting rights.

This threshold of 30 per cent has been provided under French Banking and Financial Law 22 October 2010, entered into force 1 February 2011. The former threshold was 33.3 per cent. The Banking and Financial Law provides for a transitional period for shareholders holding more than 30 per cent and less than 33.3 per cent as of 1 January 2010.

16.5 Procedural aspects
The offeror must file a draft offer with the AMF.

The AMF General Regulation provides a simplified procedure for takeovers in particular circumstances, such as an offer by a person already owning a majority of the target's shares, an offer for no more than 10 per cent of the target's shares, or for self-takeovers.

16.6 Nature and value of consideration offered
The offer may be settled entirely in cash. Settlement of the offer may also consist of an exchange of shares (or any other type of securities) or in a mix of cash and shares (mix and match).

16.7 Timetable and variations
The length of an offer is usually between 10 and 35 trading days, depending on the specific terms and conditions of the offer.

16.8 Strategy
The strategy will depend on the nature of the takeover (friendly or contested).

16.9 Irrevocable
Once the offer has been filed by the bidder, commitment to acquiring the tendered securities is irrevocable.

Shareholders may commit to tendering their shares to the offeror; however, this commitment will be automatically void if a competing offer is filed with the AMF.

16.10 Share dealings, buying shares
Before the announcement of a takeover, there is no particular restriction on the offeror's ability to buy and sell the target company's shares (with the exception that it may not acquire securities on the market with a view to reducing its average share price if it has already decided to launch an offer).

During the pre-offer period (ie, after the announcement but before the filing of the offer), the offeror (and persons acting in concert with it) shall not acquire any of the securities of the target company, unless such acquisitions result from an agreement entered into before the beginning of the pre-offer period.

After the filing of the offer and until the opening of the offer, the offeror may acquire the securities of the target company, but these acquisitions are limited to 30 per cent of the securities targeted by the offer.

During the offer, the offeror may acquire the securities of the target company provided it consists of a cash offer. If the offeror purchases securities of the target company at a higher price than the price of the offer, then the price of the offer will be automatically increased to the amount paid for the corresponding securities.

After the closing of the offer and before the publication of the results, the offeror may purchase securities of the target company at the offer price.

16.11 First announcement
The AMF is empowered to require any person believed to be preparing a takeover to declare their intentions. The information supplied to the AMF in response to its request must be made public by means of a press release, which is controlled by the AMF prior to its publication.

If the potential bidder states that they do not intend to make an offer, or do not meet the deadline, either for the publication of a press release detailing its offer, or for the filing of their offer, they will be barred from doing so for a period of six months, unless they can justify the change in their decision by important developments in the market environment, the situation or the shareholding of one of the parties concerned.

16.12 Drafting of offer documents
The draft offer is prepared by the ISP together with the bidder and their legal counsel.

16.13 Further announcements
Any modification of the takeover conditions shall be subject to a further announcement.

16.14 Responsibility
The bidder and the presenting bank are responsible for the proper completion of the offer.

16.15 Despatch
The offer documents are filed with the AMF and made available on the Web sites of both the AMF and the issuer.

16.16 Due diligence in advance of a takeover bid
If the takeover is friendly the offeror may be allowed to carry out a due diligence review prior to the launch of the takeover. Any material information provided during the review will have to be disclosed in the prospectus filed by the target company.

16.17   Conditions to the offer
The offer may be subject to certain limited conditions, such as the acquisition of a defined level of the share capital of voting rights of the target company or the clearance of the anti-trust authorities.

16.18   Financing
The bidder may use financing provided, however, the offer is always guaranteed by the bank designated by the offeror.

16.19   For cash/for shares/mixed
Please refer to section 16.6.

16.20   Inducement
Inducement provisions, when applied in the context of a public takeover bid, may be characterised either as liquidated damages provisions or as a termination amount depending on the fact pattern under consideration. Those arrangements are within the scope of party autonomy. Case law has supported the validity of such arrangements and has characterised the same as a termination amount *(clause de dédit)*. If characterised as a liquidated damages clause, the level of inducements remains subject to judicial review where such inducements are deemed to be manifestly excessive or insufficient in light of the situation of the parties. Typically, inducement provisions may contemplate amounts payable in the order of magnitude of about 1 per cent to 2 per cent.

16.21   Defence mechanisms
Except in the case of a search for a white knight or the issuance of warrants through the use of a delegation of authority granted no later than 18 months before the bid and previously approved by the shareholders, any implementation by the target company of mechanisms of defence must be first approved by an extraordinary general meeting of shareholders.

16.22   Nature of listed securities
A takeover bid for a French target must be for the acquisition of 100 per cent of the share capital of the target company.

All of the securities issued by the target company shall be included in the scope of the takeover (ie, equity securities as well as any securities giving access to the capital and voting rights of the target company).

16.23   Squeeze-out
The bidder may implement a squeeze-out if, following the takeover, they hold at least 95 per cent of the share capital and the voting rights of the target company.

16.24   Schemes of arrangement
Not applicable.

17. FOREIGN INVESTMENT CONTROLS

Financial relationships between France and foreign countries are unrestricted. Nevertheless, the French government is allowed to submit specific operations to prior authorisation, notification, or review procedures.

17.1 Foreign investments

Foreign investments subject to prior authorisation

In France, a prior authorisation is required for investments in companies engaged in the following sectors and activities:
- companies participating in the exercise of public authority;
- companies engaging in activities that might endanger public order, public safety, or the interests of natural defence; and
- companies engaging in research, production or sales of arms, munitions or explosive powder and substances.

An authorisation must be sought by:
- individuals from the EU member states, from the European Economic Area or from third countries, but also by French citizens who are not located in France; and
- companies that have their registered offices outside of France.

Foreign investments subject to administrative notification

Moreover, foreign investors are required to notify the French Ministry of the Economy upon the occurrence of specific investments in France, including among others:
- the establishment in France of a company by a foreign company or individual;
- the acquisition, in whole or in part, of a French business by a foreign company or individual; and
- the acquisition of any capital in a French registered company that results in a foreign company or individual holding more than 33.3 per cent of its share capital or voting rights.

17.2 Exemptions

A notification exemption shall not be interpreted as an exemption to obtain any required prior authorisation or satisfy any requested conditions to exercise a regulated activity in France.

17.3 Exemptions of notification or prior authorisation

Some specific transactions (ie, extensions of an existing activity by a French company, purchase of additional capital or voting rights) may be exempted from notification.

17.4 Notification in order to establish a balance of payments

Foreign investors may also have to make declarations for statistical purposes to the Bank of France concerning their investments.

Germany

Hengeler Mueller Dr Wolfgang Groß & Dr Thomas Paul

1. GENERAL DESCRIPTION OF THE CAPITAL MARKETS

The capital markets in Germany, one of the biggest economies in the world, provide liquidity for domestic and foreign capital in a wide range of products such as equity securities, equity-linked securities (eg, convertibles and exchangeables), debt securities, hybrid securities, interests in trusts, funds and other recognised management investment schemes. There are six stock exchanges, of which Frankfurt is the largest. Since the Directive 2004/39/EC on markets in financial instruments has been implemented in 2007 the stock exchanges have two markets: the Regulated Market (*regulierter Markt*), governed by public law, and the Not Regulated Market (*Freiverkehr*), which is governed by civil law only.

The shares of more than 16,000 domestic and foreign companies were trading on the two different markets as of August 2009. For example, on the Frankfurt Stock Exchange 620 German and 73 foreign companies were on the Regulated Market, and 406 German and 9,048 foreign were on the Not Regulated Market (see DAI-Factbook).

There were about 21 takeover offers for listed German companies in 2010.

2. REGULATORY STRUCTURE

2.1 General

Since 1 July 2005 and the implementation of EU Directive 2003/71/EC (Prospectus Directive), the regulatory framework for the offering and sales of securities in Germany is set by the German Securities Prospectus Act (SPA) (*Wertpapierprospektgesetz*) and the European Commission Regulation No. 809/2004 (EC Prospectus Regulation), which govern the public offering of securities in Germany and the contents, format and publication of prospectuses. Apart from the prospectus requirement, governed by the rules mentioned above, the admission to trading and the admission to a quotation on any of the German stock exchanges is governed by the German Stock Exchange Act (SEA) (*Börsengesetz*) and the Stock Exchange Admission Ordinance (SEAO) (*Börsenzulassungsverordnung*) for the Regulated Market with some additional regulations contained in the Stock Exchange Rules (*Börsenordnung*) of the respective stock exchange. For the offering and sale of investments not represented in securities the German Sales Prospectus Act (*Wertpapier-Verkaufsprospektgesetz*) and the Investment Sales Prospectus Ordinance (*Vermögensanlagen-Verkaufsprospektverordnung*) apply. The offering and sale of interests in trusts, funds and other recognised management investment schemes is governed by the Law on Investments (*Invest-*

mentgesetz). The following description focuses on securities other than those governed by the Law on Investments.

2.2 Regulation of offerings

The SPA applies to any public offering of securities. In principal, every public offering of securities in Germany is required to be based on a prospectus. Although the SPA in line with the Prospectus Directive contains several exceptions where a prospectus does not need to be published, those exceptions are both fewer and more limited in scope compared to the situation before 1 July 2005. Under the current German regime, it is irrelevant to consider the distinctions between prospectuses prepared for a securities offering with/without a simultaneous admission to trading and between prospectuses for the admission to trading on the official and the regulated market.

3. REGISTRATION OF THE ISSUER AND SECURITIES

An offering of securities in Germany does not require that the issuer is locally registered or licensed, nor does the issuer have to have a formal legal presence or a local agent to accept legal process. A registration of the securities themselves is not required.

4. SUPERVISORY AUTHORITIES

The governmental authority responsible for the supervision of the German financial system is the Federal Financial Supervisory Authority (*Bundesanstalt für Finanzdienstleistungsaufsicht* or BaFin), which was created in 2002 by a merger of the former Federal Supervisory Authority for Financial Institutions (*Bundesaufsichtsamt für das Kreditwesen*), the Federal Supervisory Authority for Securities Trading (*Bundesaufsichtsamt für den Wertpapierhandel*) and the Federal Supervisory Authority on Insurances (*Bundesaufsichtsamt für das Versicherungswesen*) by the law on the Federal Financial Supervisory Authority (*Gesetz über die Bundesanstalt für Finanzdienstleistungsaufsicht*) (22 April 2002, as amended).

In securities offerings, the BaFin is competent for the approval of the prospectus, whether the prospectus is to be used for offerings or for admission to trading, while the management board (*Geschäftsführung*) of the relevant stock exchange remains the competent authority for the admission to trading of the securities and, in addition, for the start of the quotation which are two separate decisions, both governed by public law.

5. OFFERING DOCUMENTATION
5.1 Disclosure document

In principle, any public offering of securities in Germany needs a disclosure document. Contents, format and publication of the prospectus for investments represented in securities is governed by the EC Prospectus Regulation. No prospectus may be published prior to BaFin approval. The BaFin must decide on the approval within 10 working days (or 20 working days if the issuer's securities were not yet admitted to a regulated EU market and there had been no public offering of securities). It should be noted that, should the BaFin regard the document to be incomplete or that supplementary information is needed, the BaFin should notify the issuer accordingly within 10 working days. In this case, the time limit for approval will be counted as from the date such information is provided to the BaFin. As yet, no prospectus has been approved by the BaFin without a request by the BaFin for amendments or additional information so the 10/20 working-day time limit is theoretical.

5.2 General contents of the disclosure document

The main purpose of the disclosure document is to give potential investors a complete and accurate view of: the issuer; its business; its state of affairs and financial standing; a special description of the securities offered including the risks or liabilities attaching to the securities; and, the terms and conditions of the offer. According to the EC Prospectus Regulation (and based on the Prospectus Directive and the SPA) the prospectus may consist either of one single document or three separate documents: a summary, a securities note and a registration document. The EC Prospectus Regulation contains 17 annexes with schedules listing what particular information must be included for different types of securities such as shares, equity linked securities, debt etc.

5.3 Responsibility for the disclosure document

According to the specific prospectus liability provisions included in the SEA, and for securities offered but not to be listed the Sales Prospectus Act which refers to the provisions included in the SEA ('Statutory Prospectus Liability'), the issuer, any person assuming liability for the disclosure document, and any person who has commissioned the prospectus (in particular where there is a special economic interest such as a major shareholder) are responsible for the disclosure document *vis-à-vis* investors purchasing the securities within six months after the first quotation of the securities on the Regulated Market or up to six months after the publication of the disclosure document. This means, Statutory Prospectus Liability: (i) is not limited to the initial purchasers but protects any investor buying the securities over the counter or on the stock exchange within the period mentioned, even if such an investor has not even looked at the disclosure document; and (ii) covers when new shares are issued all shares outstanding of the same class including shares issued before the issue of the new shares.

In general, Statutory Prospectus Liability lies with the issuer and the banks signing the prospectus. Currently, no Statutory Prospectus Liability *vis-à-vis* investors lies with members of the management or supervisory board as such; board members are, however, liable under the Stock Corporation Act (SCA) *vis-à-vis* the issuer for any damage – including Statutory Prospectus Liability – the issuer incurs. Under German law there is no Statutory Prospectus Liability for auditors or advisers.

Prospectus liability attaches when material information contained in the disclosure document is incorrect or incomplete, provided that the responsible person acted with knowledge or gross negligence. Whether a disclosure document is incorrect or incomplete is measured by: (i) compliance with the rules on the contents of the disclosure document, eg, the EC Prospectus Regulation; and (ii) reference to the 'average investor'. Except in cases of gross negligence, persons will not be liable under Statutory Prospectus Liability who did not know of the incorrectness or incompleteness of the disclosure document. With these provisions in mind, it is usual in order to enable a 'due diligence defence' to carry out some sort of due diligence and ask for a comfort letter from the auditors, and legal and disclosure opinions from the legal advisers. There is, however, no general rule that these are always needed.

6. DISTRIBUTION SYSTEM

According to the German Banking Act, only banks or financial services providers are allowed to be underwriters or distributors of securities. In addition, the application for trading on the Regulated Market of a German stock exchange must be filed by the issuer and a bank or financial services provider.

7. PUBLICITY

With the implementation of the Prospectus Directive the restrictions on publicity contained in it were introduced. Due to liability concerns relating to publicity and due to the obligation contained in section 15 of the SPA that information contained in advertisements and other publications be consistent with the prospectus, usually the issuer's counsel drafts publicity guidelines detailing the limitations and setting up a clearance procedure for approving any corporate communications and marketing material to be released before an offering. In addition, the underwriters' counsel typically prepares research guidelines specifying the restrictions applicable to the syndicate banks' research reports.

When distribution focused on retail investors it was common practice in Germany to advertise share offerings and especially initial public offerings (IPOs) in the media (newspaper, magazines, radio and TV), which, as long as this advertisement does not constitute an offer or, if it does, as long as it refers to an approved prospectus, is legally not prohibited. With the shift of the focus from retail to institutional investors, advertising share offerings declined.

8. LISTING

The SEA and SEAO and, to a certain extent, the Stock Exchange Rules of the respective stock exchange regulate the filing process if admission to trading on the Regulated Market is sought.

The admission requires that an application be filed with the management board of the relevant stock exchange; such application to be sponsored by a bank or by a financial services provider.

Admission requirements (eg, free-float and minimum anticipated market value of security) are contained in the SEAO.

If there is no exception from the prospectus requirement under the SPA any application for admission to trading on the Official or Regulated Market must be accompanied with a prospectus already approved by the BaFin or to be approved before granting the admission.

Because the admission to trading on the Regulated Market is an administrative act, any appeal first has to go to the management board of the respective stock exchange and to the administrative court thereafter if the admission board does not redress the appeal.

The costs for the admission to trading and the additional costs for the quotation are regulated by the fee regulations of the prospective stock exchange. They are minimal, for instance, on the Frankfurt Stock Exchange the maximum fee for the admission to trading is EUR 3,000 and for the quotation is EUR 2,500.

9.   ONGOING COMPLIANCE REQUIREMENTS
9.1   Ongoing requirements for listed issuers

9.1.1 Obligations under the German Securities Trading Act

With the implementation of the European Directive 2004/109/EC on the harmonisation of transparency requirements (Transparency Directive) as of January 2007 the basic rules for the obligations arising from admission to the Regulated Market of a German stock exchange are contained in the German Securities Trading Act (STA).

The STA requires that an issuer whose shares are admitted to the Regulated Market publishes at least three interim reports per financial year containing information on the financial condition and the general business operation of the issuer during the reporting period. In addition it requires, among other obligations, that the issuer: (i) under similar circumstances treats equally holders of admitted securities; (ii) has at least one paying agent and depositary; (iii) informs the public and the management board of the respective stock exchange about new developments on the issuer and the admitted securities; and (iv) as required by the SEAO applies for admission of new shares of the same class as the admitted shares if those shares are publicly issued.

In addition, under the STA, the issuer of admitted shares must, *inter alia*, publish notices on certain corporate events, such as the convening of a shareholders' meeting, declaration and payment of dividends, issuance of new shares and changes in the rights arising from the securities; notify the management board of the respective stock exchange of any proposed amendments to its articles of association; as a rule, make its annual financial statements available to the public and the annual report to shareholders immediately upon approval; and, in general, publish in Germany at least the equivalent information relevant for the assessment of the securities as the issuer publishes in another country where the securities are also admitted to trading on an official market.

A breach of any of these obligations may trigger administrative fines and, if the violation continues after an appropriate cure period, the revocation of the admission.

9.1.2 Additional reporting obligations under the Frankfurt Stock Exchange rules for the 'Prime Standard'

In 2003, the Frankfurt Stock Exchange introduced two sub-sectors within the statutory Regulated Market segments: a General Standard, reflecting the respective minimum statutory requirements, and a Prime Standard, imposing further ongoing obligations in addition to the statutory requirements. Application to have securities listed on the Prime Standard is voluntary. Admission to the Prime Standard, however, is a precondition to be included in share indices such as the German Stock Exchange Index (DAX). The additional requirements are laid out in the Stock Exchange Rules issued by the Frankfurt Stock Exchange and are designed to enhance transparency in accordance with international standards.

9.1.3 Additional obligations and regulations under the Federal Securities Trading Act (FSTA) (*Wertpapierhandelsgesetz*)

In addition to the SEA and the SEAO, the FSTA contains further obligations and regulations for issuers, shareholders and investors of shares admitted to (or in the process of being admitted to) the Regulated Market of any German stock exchange.

Insider regulations

The FSTA contains a statutory prohibition of insider transactions, which implemented the EC Insider Trading Directive and which was amended several times thereafter mainly to implement EU legislation such as Directive 2003/06/EC on Insider Dealing and Market Manipulation (Insider Dealing and Market Manipulation Directive) and the Transparency Directive.

Ad hoc disclosure requirements

In addition, the FSTA obliges the issuer of securities which are admitted to trading on a domestic exchange to publish any inside information which directly concerns the issuer without undue delay, unless the issuer decides to delay the public disclosure so as not to prejudice his legitimate interests, provided that such an omission would not be likely to mislead the public and provided that the issuer is able to ensure the confidentiality of that information.

Reporting obligations of major shareholdings

The issuer must publish notice when a third party notifies a German issuer, whose securities are listed on an organised market in Germany, that it has acquired, or that its shareholding has exceeded or fallen below certain thresholds (3, 5, 10, 15, 20, 25, 30, 50 and 75 per cent of the company's voting rights). Notification must be made in writing to the issuer and the BaFin without undue delay, and within four stock exchange trading days from the increase or decrease. The target company is then itself obliged to publish the notification without delay and in any event within three stock exchange trading days from receipt of the notification. The BaFin keeps a publicly accessible database containing such information.

If, and for as long as, these notification requirements are not complied with, the voting rights attached to the respective shareholdings are suspended: ie, votes cast are null and void.

Directors' dealings

According to the FSTA, persons discharging managerial responsibilities within an issuer of shares admitted to trading on a domestic exchange or within a German issuer of shares admitted to an organised market of the EU and persons closely associated with them shall notify the issuer and the BaFin within five working days of any transaction conducted on their own account relating to shares of the issuer, or to derivatives or other financial instruments linked to them unless such transactions are below EUR 5,000 within the same calendar year.

9.1.4 Securities Prospectus Act

In line with the Prospectus Directive, the SPA currently requires (this was to change once the Prospectus Directive was changed), the issuer of listed securities to publish an annual document including or referring to information published by the issuer during the preceding fiscal year in connection with certain securities regulations such as directors' dealings, ad hoc publications, and publications required under the German stock exchange laws, etc.

9.2 Ongoing requirements for unlisted issuers

None of the requirements just mentioned applies to unlisted issuers. There is, however, an obligation contained in the SCA that shareholders of a stock corporation must notify it if their shareholding exceeds 25 per cent or 50 per cent of the shares in a German stock corporation. If, and for as long as, these notification requirements are not complied with, the voting rights attached to the respective shareholdings are suspended. The stock corporation itself has to publish the information received by its shareholder.

10. INSIDER TRADING

10.1 Regulatory regime

The FSTA of 1995, amended several times thereafter mainly to implement EU legislation such as the Insider Dealing and Market Manipulation Directive and the Transparency Directive, contains in sections 12 to 14 the regulatory regime on insider trading.

10.2 Insider trading prohibition

Section 14 of the FSTA contains the prohibition on insider trading. It prohibits: (i) using inside information by acquiring or disposing of insider securities for the insider's own account or for the account of a third party; (ii) disclosing inside information to any other person or granting access to inside information without authorisation; and (iii) recommending or inducing another person on the basis of inside information to acquire or dispose of financial instruments to which the information relates.

Exemption exists for repurchase of own shares and stabilisation methods organised and executed in accordance with EC Regulation 2273/2003.

Insider trading is a criminal offence that may be sanctioned with a fine or imprisonment of up to five years.

11. INVESTMENT FUNDS
11.1 Introduction
After almost continuous growth in sales since the early 1990s, the German investment fund industry managed assets with an aggregate value of EUR 1,375.7 billion at the end of 2009 (in 2007: EUR 1,422.6 billion and in 2008: EUR 1,217.4 billion). Of this amount, EUR 650.2 billion was managed as public (mutual) funds and EUR 725.6 billion as special funds (source: BVI). Special funds are investment funds exclusively for institutional investors and are subject to fewer investment restrictions than public mutual funds.

The regulation of investment funds in Germany had undergone an almost complete revision with the new Investment Act (IA) (*Investmentgesetz*), which came into force in Germany on 1 January 2004 implementing EU Directives 2001/107/EC and 2001/108/EC which amended EU Directive 85/611/EEC on Undertakings For Collective Investment in Transferable Securities (UCITS Directive). Subsequently, the IA was again substantially revised by the amendment act to the IA, which entered into force on 28 December 2007. This initiative was not primarily triggered by the need to implement any EU Directive but primarily serves the purpose of improving the competitive advantage of the German fund industry and to prevent further emigration to offshore locations, in particular to Luxembourg, while at the same time improving investor protection. The four key objectives of the amended IA are: (i) deregulation (in particular, the establishment of more flexible investment possibilities for German special funds, reduction of the regulatory burden on investment companies by no longer qualifying them as credit institutions and increased flexibility for the custody of German assets); (ii) the modernisation of open-ended real estate funds (eg, more flexibility for investments in real estate companies and real estate investment trusts (REITs)); (iii) the promotion of product innovations (introduction of infrastructure funds and 'Other Funds', establishing investment stock corporations as UCITS and introducing guarantee funds); and (iv) improvement of corporate governance and investor protection (introducing independent supervisory board members, enhanced organisational requirements for the avoidance of conflicts of interest between the investment companies (*Kapitalanlagegesellschaften*, KAG) and the depositary bank, limitation of sales charges in the case of savings plans and disclosure of transaction costs).

11.2 Investment companies
Investment companies are the only institutions which may launch and manage investment funds in contractual form (as opposed to investment stock corporations, section 11.7). Apart from this principal activity, investment companies may only engage in certain ancillary activities as

defined in the IA.

When managing the investment fund, the investment company must act in its own name but for the joint account of all unitholders within the scope of the management agreement (the so-called fund rules). The investment company cannot legally bind the investment fund or its unitholders. Thus, the investment company opens with the depositary bank different cash and securities accounts in its own name as blocked accounts on behalf of each investment fund. When the investment company enters into transactions on behalf of the investment fund, the investment company is entitled, in accordance with the terms of the fund rules, to reimbursement of its expenses by the depositary bank out of the assets of the investment fund.

11.2.1 Regulatory framework
Although German investment companies are no longer qualified as special credit institutions, numerous provisions of the German Banking Act (*Kreditwesengesetz*) apply to them by reference. Investment companies are supervised by the BaFin with a dual seat in Bonn and Frankfurt am Main.

11.2.2 Organisational requirements

Capital requirements
Investment companies must be established as either limited liability companies (GmbH) or stock corporations (AG). The statutory minimum paid in share capital is EUR 300,000 plus an additional capital of 0.02 per cent for the amount by which the assets under management exceed EUR 1,125 billion (with a maximum of EUR 10 million), but in no case less than 25 per cent of annual expenses. Fifty per cent of the additional capital can be substituted by a guarantee of a suitable credit institution or insurance company.

Board structure
The investment company must have at least two managing directors who are qualified for investment business as well as sufficient personnel to conduct and control its business. Mere letterbox companies are not permitted. In addition, a supervisory board of at least three members must be established, even in the case of an investment company in the legal form of a limited liability company, for which generally a supervisory board is otherwise not required. If the investment company manages one or more public mutual funds, at least one member of the supervisory board must be independent from the investment company's shareholders, their affiliates and the investment company's business partners.

Outsourcing
The outsourcing of functions by an investment company is permissible if the requirements of the IA, which are identical to the rules of delegation set out in the UCITS Directive, are met. In particular, the outsourcing of portfolio management,ie, the delegation of discretionary management to a third

party manager, requires that the asset manager is licensed to perform asset management services and that the asset manager is subject to effective public supervision. It can generally be assumed that such effective public supervision exists in all member states of the Convention on the European Economic Area (EEA member states) as well as in those jurisdictions where the competent regulatory authorities have entered into a memorandum of understanding with BaFin (which are listed in the BaFin Circular 18/2009 (WA)).

Outsourcing of portfolio management to the depositary bank or to other parties whose interests may conflict with those of the unitholders is prohibited. The investment company does not require prior approval for outsourcing from BaFin but must notify BaFin annually which functions were outsourced and must list in the prospectus (and simplified prospectus, if applicable) all functions which it has outsourced.

11.2.3 Branch offices and cross-border services

An investment company which manages at least one UCITS may use an EU passport to establish a branch office in, or to provide cross-border services into, another EEA member state after completion of a notification procedure. In the notification, the investment company must submit the name of the host member state, a programme of operations identifying the activities and services to be conducted in the host member state and, in the case of a branch office, some further information about the infrastructure of the branch, the head of the branch and an address in the host member state where documents may be obtained. In the case of the opening of a branch office, the home state regulator must transfer the notification to the host member state regulator within two months; the host state regulator must then notify the branch office within two months whether it may begin activities. When an investment company notifies BaFin of its intention to make use of the cross-border passport, BaFin must inform the host member state regulator within one month unless it has concerns regarding the appropriateness of the investment company's organisational structure or its financial situation; the investment company must await the notification within this one-month period.

Similarly, investment companies from other EEA member states may establish a branch office in, or provide cross-border services into, Germany. Although in principle these activities are subject to home state supervision, Germany reserves the right to impose certain regulatory requirements on the branch office or the provider of cross-border services. In the case of a branch office, these rules include certain reporting requirements pursuant to the Banking Act as well as compliance with the rules of conduct under the STA (*Wertpapierhandelsgesetz*). In the case of the provision of cross-border services, essentially the same requirements apply, with the exception of the reporting requirements.

The investment company (branch or cross-border) passport does not obviate the need for a product passport, ie, a UCITS passport for each individual investment fund. Consequently, if a German investment company wishes to distribute in another EEA member state a UCITS launched by it, it must also complete the notification procedure for the investment fund in that EEA member state.

11.3 Custodians
It is mandatory that the assets of investment funds are held in safekeeping by another credit institution, the depositary bank, which must be authorised to conduct deposit taking and custody business. In addition to the safekeeping of the assets belonging to the investment funds, the depositary bank's main function is the control of the investment company.

11.4 Investment funds
The IA distinguishes between UCITS and the various categories of non-UCITS.

11.5 UCITS
The rules in the IA with regard to the content of the UCITS mirror the rules set out in the UCITS Directive.

In line with the UCITS Directive, derivatives may be employed not only for the purpose of hedging but also for investment purposes. Unlike in most other EEA member states, there is a specific ordinance on the employment of derivatives for UCITS, which was issued by BaFin and became effective on 13 February 2004. This ordinance gives the investment company a choice between two approaches for the measurement of market risk. Under the 'qualified approach' the investment company must use a specific risk measurement model (value at risk) to measure its market risk. Under the 'simplified approach' the market risk must be measured on the basis of a quantitative analysis. Whichever approach is chosen, the investment company must conduct stress tests on at least a monthly basis.

The IA transposed into German law Directive 2007/16/EC implementing Directive 85/611/EEC on the coordination of laws, regulations and administrative provisions relating to UCITS as regards the clarification of certain definitions, OJ L 79/11 (Implementation Directive) as well as Article 10 paragraph 2 sentence 1 lit. a and b of Directive 2007/14/EC, laying down detailed rules for the implementation of certain provisions of the Transparency Directive in relation to information about issuers whose securities are admitted to trading on a regulated market.

11.6 Non-UCITS funds
Non-UCITS funds may be organised as special funds or as public (mutual) funds.

11.6.1 Real estate investment funds
Real estate investment funds may invest not only in developed and undeveloped real estate, hereditary building rights and different forms of part ownership rights, but also in participations in real estate companies and usufructs (*Nießbrauchrechte*) in real estate which serves the purpose of performing public services. Investment by real estate investment funds in real property situated outside the EEA is permitted without limitation. The

exposure to currencies other than the euro, however, is limited to 30 per cent of the value of the investment fund.

The investment in real estate companies as defined in the IA is geared to allow the use of the specific market expertise of local companies with respect to the acquisition and management of foreign real estate and to permit the use of potential tax advantages of direct investments (eg, property acquisition tax). The holding of participations in real estate companies is limited to 49 per cent of the value of the investment fund unless the real estate investment fund holds all of the holdings in the real estate company in which case the investment will be treated as a direct investment in the properties held by the real estate company. Minority holdings in real estate companies are permitted but limited to 30 per cent of the value of the investment fund. Multi-layered investments in real estate companies are also permitted and follow the aforementioned rules.

Although the property investments are generally not very liquid, investors have the right to redeem their units on a daily basis. As a consequence of the financial crisis and caused by massive redemption requests, several real estate investment companies had to suspend redemptions because of insufficient liquidity. The legislator is expected to introduce new rules for notice periods and for the liquidation of real estate investment funds which may have to be liquidated because they cannot redeem units on a sustainable basis.

11.6.2 Balanced funds
Balanced funds are investment funds which may invest not only in all the assets in which a UCITS may invest but also up to 100 per cent of their net asset value into German real estate investment funds and up to 10 per cent of their net asset value in German or foreign (single) hedge funds or so-called 'other funds'.

Balanced funds can also be established as index funds which do not have to comply with the concentration rules applicable to UCITS.

11.6.3 Old age provision investment funds
Old age provision investment funds also qualify as balanced funds. As they can invest up to 30 per cent of their net asset value in real estate investments funds, they do not qualify for a UCITS passport.

Unlike all other types of investment funds, old age provision investment funds are not characterised by the eligible investments but by their investment objective (ie, the provision of retirement savings). Old age provision investment funds therefore contain further special features, such as a prohibition against dividend distributions to unitholders.

The assets of an old age provision investment fund may only consist of securities, note loans, units in German real estate investment funds, real estate and participations in real estate companies.

11.6.4 Infrastructure investment funds
The IA introduced infrastructure investment funds as a new fund type. The legislative intention was the promotion of investments in public private

partnerships. These investment funds may invest in participations in private public partnerships, real estate, securities, money market instruments, cash deposits and investment fund units. Derivatives may only be employed for hedging purposes.

11.6.5 Other funds
The IA also introduced 'other funds' as a new fund type. 'Other funds' are intended to provide a non-harmonised investment vehicle particularly for investments in innovative financial products. As a consequence, these funds may acquire the same assets as UCITS, as well as units in UCITS, real estate investment funds, balanced funds, 'other funds' and hedge funds. In addition, the investment in participations in unlisted companies, precious metals and unsecuritised loan receivables (including those micro-finance institutions) are permissible. Derivatives not permitted for UCITS precious metals, and unsecuritised loans may constitute up to 30 per cent of the fund's value. Investments in units of hedge funds and 'other funds' are permissible also up to 30 per cent of the fund's value. Investments in unlisted securities and participations of unlisted companies are limited to 20 per cent of the fund's value. Borrowing is permitted up to 20 per cent of the fund's value.

11.6.6 Special funds
Special funds are available only to institutional investors. They customarily only have one investor or a small group of investors which are usually group companies. The investor determines the investment guidelines under which the special fund is managed. Special funds are traditionally established on the basis of a framework (or three-party) agreement between: the investor(s); the investment company; and the depositary bank. This framework agreement not only contains the investor's obligation to transfer units in the special fund only with the investment company's prior consent, but primarily establishes certain rights for the investor(s) such as the right to request an exchange of the investment company without the liquidation of the special fund, the right to determine whether profits should be distributed or retained and the right for representation in the investment committee. The investment committee is a body in which the investor and sometimes also the depositary bank are represented. The purpose of the investment committee is to review the past investment performance and the possible adjustment of the investment guidelines for the future. However, the investor cannot limit the investment company's discretion to manage the special fund within the investment guidelines by giving specific instructions, eg, to acquire or to sell certain assets or to employ certain derivative techniques, even if there is only one investor in a special fund.

The fundamental change introduced by the IA is the recognition that special fund investors do not require the same level of protection as investors in public mutual funds. While public mutual funds can always only be established as investment funds of a certain type which, by definition, limits their investment possibilities, special funds are no longer bound by such fund types. In other words, a special fund can invest in any of the assets available for the various fund types of the IA. As a consequence, a special fund can combine investments in securities, money market instruments, derivatives, cash deposits, real estate and real estate companies, participations in unlisted companies, precious metals, unsecuritised loan receivables and investments in 'other funds'.

Special funds may employ derivatives without having to comply with the UCITS limitations, except that they must not enter into short sales and they must not use leverage beyond the UCITS limitations unless they are set up as hedge funds. The risk diversification requirements applicable to UCITS, eg, the 5 per cent- and the 10 per cent-issuer limitations, the 5 per cent/10 per cent/40 per cent-rule, the 35 per cent-limit for certain public issuers, the 20 per cent-limit for cash deposits with one bank and investments in another investment fund do not apply to special funds. The only specific concentration limit is the 20 per cent-limit for investments in unlisted securities and participations in unlisted companies; consequently, a special fund constituted as a Master Fund may have a segment not exceeding 20 per cent of the Master Fund's aggregate net asset value acting as a private equity fund.

11.7 Investment stock corporations

Overview
The IA permits the establishment of open-ended investment stock corporation with variable capital, a vehicle hitherto unknown in German corporate law and similar to the Luxembourg *Société d'Investissement à Capital Variable* (SICAV) and the UK or Irish open-ended investment company (OEIC). The investment stock corporation can be established as a single fund or an umbrella fund. It can be self-managed or appoint a German investment company as a designated management company.

Organisational requirements and investment restrictions
The investment stock corporation must obtain a licence from BaFin and meet substantially the same requirements as an investment company, although the minimum initial capital is only EUR 300,000. The registered seat and head office must be in Germany. The directors (no less than two) must pass the same 'fit and proper' test as the managing directors of the investment companies.

Investment stock corporations may be established as public mutual funds, including UCITS, and can also be organised as special funds. The investment in real estate, however, is prohibited.

11.8 Hedge funds and funds of hedge funds

Hedge funds
Hedge funds are characterised by the leverage they get from the use of generally unlimited borrowing powers and the employment of derivatives and short selling. They must not invest in real estate or real

estate companies. Eligible investments include securities, money market instruments, cash at bank, investments in 'other funds' and derivatives (including commodity futures) but not direct investments in commodities other than precious metals. Investments in participations of unlisted companies are limited to 30 per cent of assets to avoid the creation of hedge funds which are substantially private equity funds. Investments in other hedge funds are limited to 50 per cent of assets to distinguish hedge funds from funds of hedge funds. German hedge funds are not subject to any other investment restrictions except for compliance with the principle of risk diversification, which is not specified any further in the IA but implies the general prohibition of master-feeder fund structures.

Hedge funds can be established as investment funds in contractual form (in which case they must be managed by an investment company) or as investment stock corporations. In either case a custodian and/or a prime broker must be appointed with much the same responsibilities as the custodian of a UCITS. The prime broker must have its seat in a member state of the EU, the EEA or a state which is a full member of the Organisation for Economic Cooperation and Development (OECD). Furthermore, it must be subject to an efficient public supervision and must have an appropriate credit rating.

Hedge funds can be established as special funds or public mutual funds. In neither case, however, can they be publicly distributed and the distributors must always be either credit institutions or financial services institutions. There are no minimum investment criteria or other requirements for private investors in hedge funds.

Funds of hedge funds
Funds of hedge funds may only invest in German and foreign single hedge funds and may hold only up to 49 per cent of their net asset value in cash, money market funds and money market instruments. The portfolio managers of a fund of hedge funds must, in addition to fitness for portfolio management in general, have sufficient experience in and practical knowledge of hedge fund investments. The fund of hedge funds must not use leverage (except for short term borrowings of up to 10 per cent of the net asset value) or short sales and may employ derivatives only for the purpose of currency hedging. Investment in any single hedge fund is limited to 20 per cent of net asset value; however, a fund may acquire all the units of a target fund. No more than two funds held by a fund of hedge funds may be managed by the same fund manager or issued by the same issuer. The funds may thus all have the same issuer as long as no more than two of them have the same individual as a fund manager.

Funds of hedge funds may be established as special funds or as public mutual funds. In the latter case they may be publicly distributed.

11.9 Marketing and distribution requirements
11.9.1 Distributors
While up to the mid-nineties the distribution of (German and foreign)

investment funds was effected predominantly through the branch networks of German banks, investment funds are increasingly marketed through other channels, such as fund supermarkets, fund shops and the Internet, as well as independent and tied agents who usually also distribute unit-linked life insurance policies and other financial products.

Investment companies may, if their articles of association so provide, also distribute investment units.

Since 1 January 1998, independent intermediaries and structured distribution networks require a special licence under the Banking Act if they qualify as financial services institutions. In this case, the rules of conduct set out in Directive 2004/39/EC on markets in financial instruments (MIFID), as implemented in the STA, apply to the distribution activities.

An exemption from the application of these rules applies, however, in accordance with MIFID, if the distributor: (a) only markets unit certificates of German investment funds (except single hedge funds) or foreign investment funds which are admitted for public distribution; (b) only acts as an intermediary between the investor and a credit institution supervised in Germany, a foreign investment company or a German branch of a foreign credit institution; and (c) is not authorised to obtain title to or possession of investors' money, unit certificates or units.

11.9.2 Required sales documentation

When distributing unit certificates of German investment funds, the distributor has to proactively offer the simplified prospectus to the interested investor before the conclusion of the subscription and free of charge. Upon request, the full prospectus together with the latest published yearly report, and, if already published, the subsequent half-yearly report must be made available free of charge to the unitholders and to interested investors. Making available means the unsolicited offer to provide these documents, not their automatic handing over, which is only required in the case of the sale of hedge funds and funds of hedge funds, where subscriptions must also always be made in writing. A copy of the subscription form must be handed over or a contract note must be sent to the investor.

11.9.3 Public distribution of foreign investment funds (notification procedure)

Foreign investment units are only eligible for public distribution after a notification procedure has been completed without BaFin having prohibited public distribution during a waiting period of two months (for UCITS) or three months (for non-UCITS) respectively following the filing of a complete notification. BaFin does not grant express approval for public distribution in order to avoid giving the impression of supervision, or even a guarantee of the good standing, of the foreign investment company by BaFin. Furthermore, the competent supervisory authority of the foreign state must be willing to cooperate with BaFin in a satisfactory manner.

No notification procedure is required for private placements, eg, the distribution of investment units to certain types of regulated institutional investors. Furthermore, no notification procedure is required where investment units are sold upon the (unsolicited) request of the investor.

Public distribution of foreign non-UCITS
Non-UCITS are all foreign investment companies and investment funds not structured pursuant to the UCITS Directive which have not received a UCITS certificate from asupervisory authority in an EEA member state. This includes foreign investment funds established in, for instance, Luxembourg or Ireland, but which due to their investment policy cannot qualify as UCITS, such as funds of hedge funds.

For non-UCITS, the IA contains minimum requirements as to the contents of both the fund rules/articles of association/trust deed and the sales prospectus. Foreign funds of hedge funds must be structured in a manner comparable to their German counterparts. This means, for example, that foreign funds of hedge funds may not invest in target funds which themselves invest in other hedge funds.

In addition, non-UCITS must provide documents to BaFin showing the company is subject to effective public supervision in its home state. Furthermore, the competent supervisory authority of the foreign state must be willing to cooperate with BaFin in a satisfactory manner.

Public distribution of foreign UCITS
UCITS are only subject to the supervision of their home state authorities. BaFin's supervision is limited to the manner of public distribution in Germany. For this purpose, the current versions of the (simplified and full) sales prospectus, the fund rules (or the articles of association or trust deed, as the case may be) and the financial reports must be submitted to BaFin in the original; documents in foreign languages must be submitted together with a German translation. The IA does not contain any specific requirements as to the contents of the fund rules (or the articles of association or trust deed); however, the sales prospectus must contain some specific Germany-related language. Furthermore, a guideline for the notification of foreign funds in Germany established by BaFin includes specific language for the declarations of the paying and information agent and for the explanation of the right of revocation which must be printed on the application form. The application form, however, does not have to be submitted to BaFin for review.

12. PUBLIC TAKEOVERS
12.1 Regulatory framework
The regulatory framework for takeovers is mainly set by the Act on Acquisition of Securities and Takeovers (*Wertpapiererwerbs- und Übernahmegesetz*, the Takeover Act of 2001, as amended) and regulations issued under the Takeover Act by the Federal Ministry of Finance, the SCA, the STA, the Law against Restraints of Competition (*Gesetz gegen Wettbewerbsbeschränkungen*), the Restructuring Act (*Umwandlungsgesetz*), with respect to investments of non-German investors by the German Foreign Trade and Payments Act and the German Foreign Trade and Payments

Regulation and the SPA and the SEA.

The main source of regulation is the Takeover Act (TA). When determining whether or not the TA applies, it is the nature of the offeree or potential offeree company which is relevant, not the nature of the offeror. In principle, the TA applies to all offers for shares or other convertible securities that have been issued by a German stock corporation (AG) or a partnership limited by shares (KGaA) or a European Company (SE), in each case having its registered office in Germany, provided that the securities for which the offer is made are listed on the Regulated Market of any of the German stock exchanges. Only certain provisions of the TA apply for German companies who only have securities listed on another regulated market in the EEA (currently EU member states plus Iceland, Liechtenstein and Norway), or for companies having their registered office in another EEA member state and securities listed either on a German Regulated Market only or on a German Regulated Market or on another regulated market in the EEA.

Pursuant to the TA, the Federal Ministry of Finance has adopted regulations, one of which contains important provisions governing the contents of an offer document, the consideration payable in a takeover bid and exemptions from the obligation to make a compulsory offer.

The TA itself and the SCA include provisions relating to defences against hostile takeovers.

Among other things, the German Act Against Restraints of Competition deals with the German antitrust regime, while the Restructuring Act contains the mechanics for a statutory merger between two German companies, which can be an alternative to a takeover offer. The SPA and the SEA set out prospectus requirements when issuing new shares as consideration in a takeover. The German Foreign Trade and Payments Act and the German Foreign Trade and Payments Regulation enables the German Federal Ministry of Economics and Technology to review the acquisition of 25 per cent or more of the voting rights in the field of military technology and in any other sector, if such an acquisition would endanger the 'public order or security' of Germany. While the regime for companies active in the field of military technology has a long history, the new provisions on other companies were enacted in 2009 and the application of these provisions was very low-key.

12.2 Competent authorities
The BaFin is the authority responsible for supervising compliance with the TA. It has powers to investigate suspected breaches of the TA and impose fines.

12.3 Takeover bids
12.3.1 Types of takeover bid

Voluntary bids
A bid may be either voluntary or compulsory. A voluntary bid may be 'simple' or a 'takeover' bid. It is simple if the acquisition of control is neither

the consequence of nor the reason for the offer; that is, the person acquiring the shares merely intends to acquire a shareholding of less than 30 per cent or to consolidate an existing controlling shareholding (over 30 per cent). A voluntary bid is a takeover bid if the acquisition of control (over 30 per cent) is intended.

Compulsory bids

A compulsory bid is required when a person acquires control of the target, that is, acquires, directly or indirectly, alone or in concert, shares carrying 30 per cent or more of the voting rights of the target company.

The BaFin may, on application, consider a waiver of the requirement to make a compulsory takeover offer, if: (i) the shares are held in the trading portfolio of a financial institution; (ii) the shares are acquired due to family succession or changes of corporate form/restructuring measures within a corporate group; (iii) the presumption that a 30 per cent shareholding confers controlling power does not hold true, either because another person holds a larger stake in the target, or because high turnouts at the last three general meetings mean that the offeror's shareholding cannot be expected to represent a simple majority at future votes; (iv) the controlling shareholding is a result of a cancellation of voting rights; (v) the transfer takes place only to secure a claim against the transferor (eg, under a share pledge); or (vi) the acquisition was part of a rescue restructuring of the target and the obligation to bid would be detrimental to the target and ultimately the outside shareholders as it would discourage or deter the rescuer.

Where exemptions from the obligation to make a compulsory bid are granted, they may be made subject to certain conditions. According to court decisions and the prevailing German legal literature any waiver granted by the BaFin may not be the subject of an appeal or subsequently challenged in court by outside shareholders.

The Act does not provide for any specific rules on takeovers after the acquisition of control by a concert party. Therefore, in theory, every concert party may be under a separate obligation to make a bid. However, since this would be confusing for shareholders, a single offer should be agreed between the concert parties and an exemption for the remaining parties should be sought.

Similarly, if the party acquiring the 30 per cent shareholding is a subsidiary of a parent company, the parent and the subsidiary and even any other subsidiary of the parent will technically be under an obligation to make the compulsory offer. It is unclear, in practice, which company will be required to make this bid and which will be exempted, which can pose difficult questions for acquisition vehicle structures.

Regulation of voluntary and compulsory bids

Voluntary takeover bids and compulsory bids are effectively governed by the same procedural rules. However, voluntary takeover bids can be made subject to any number of objective conditions, whereas compulsory takeover bids cannot be made subject to conditions, other than a condition relating to necessary regulatory clearances.

12.4 Procedural questions
12.4.1 Purchases of shares of the target in advance of a bid
Building a stake before making an offer is not forbidden in principle but subject to restrictions. Such purchases may also have an impact on the structure and pricing of the eventual offer.

The STA
There is no statutory defence which relates to the possession of information about the offeror's own intention to make a bid. However, in the context of stakebuilding, the general view of the authorities and legal commentators is that purchases made by the offeror to facilitate a contemplated bid would not violate the provisions of the STA.

If the offeror gains further information during the takeover process (for example, through due diligence), it is uncertain whether it may continue to acquire shares on the basis of that information without violating the provisions of the STA. It may be able to do so only if it can be demonstrated that it is following a pre-existing intention to buy/make the offer. Neither the number of shares bought nor the price paid for them may be increased as a result of the due diligence findings.

In addition, the STA prohibits any person, other than the offeror itself, who knows that an offer is being contemplated from dealing in target company shares prior to the announcement of the offer. This means that a director, adviser or employee of an offeror who is aware of the imminent offer would not be allowed to deal in target shares.

The TA
Pursuant to the TA, purchases of shares in a target before making a bid may have an impact not only on the pricing of the eventual offer but also on the ability to make a 'paper-only' offer. The offeror will also have to be aware of the provisions relating to compulsory offers.

12.4.2 Purchases of shares of the target during a bid

Offeror
An offeror may also purchase shares in the target once it has announced an offer, although it will obviously need to consider similar issues to those set out above. In addition, the effect of buying shares after the announcement of a bid on the consideration in the offer will be different.

There are no restrictions on sales of target shares by an offeror during an offer, except for insider dealing/market manipulation regulations.

Target
Acquisitions/sales of its own shares by the target during an offer may be restricted.

12.4.3 Disclosure obligations on purchases of shares in target

The STA
The STA provides that any increase or decrease in the percentage of a
person's direct or indirect shareholding in a German company either to,
above or below thresholds of 3, 5, 10, 15, 20, 25, 30, 50 and 75 per cent
of the company's total voting rights must be notified to the BaFin and the
target company, regardless of whether a takeover offer is contemplated.

The TA
Under the TA, notification of the acquisition of 'control' must be published
as soon as a person reaches the threshold of 30 per cent of voting rights.
This provision does not apply, however, where the threshold is reached in
consequence of a public takeover bid.

In addition, during the offer period, the offeror must publish its direct
or imputed interests (for instance, of any subsidiaries or any persons acting
in concert with it) on a weekly basis and, during the last week of the offer
period, on a daily basis. Immediately after the end of the offer period, an
additional disclosure of the final outcome of the offer must be made. The
information must be published in at least one supra-regional official stock
exchange gazette and on the Internet. The information (together with proof
of publication) must also be communicated to the BaFin.

12.5 Due diligence in advance of a takeover bid
Pre-takeover due diligence in Germany is usually limited in scope – more
limited than due diligence on a private acquisition.

In the case of a hostile offer, the due diligence exercise will normally be
limited to a review of publicly available information.

In the case of a recommended bid, the due diligence may be more
extensive, although the target board will have to decide carefully how much
information it is appropriate to disclose, taking into account its fiduciary
duties. More sensitive information may be withheld until the offeror has
proved its interest in the target.

German law is silent as to whether information given to one offeror
in a due diligence exercise must also be passed on to another offeror.
Previously the consensus was that no such obligation existed, but the issue
is now debated. Consequently, the target should be prepared to disclose
information revealed to one party to other potential offerors.

Where the offeror is offering its own shares as consideration, the target
may well also insist in carrying out due diligence on the offeror itself.

12.6 Price and consideration offered
12.6.1 Price
In general, an offeror making a voluntary takeover bid, or a compulsory bid,
must always offer a minimum price, which needs to be 'adequate'. However,
if the offeror is making a voluntary 'simple' bid (ie, one not intended to

acquire control), it is free to offer whatever price it wishes.

The offer price for a voluntary takeover or compulsory bid is generally 'adequate' if it is not less than the higher of: (i) the highest price paid by the offeror for shares in the target during the six months before the publication of the offer document; and (ii) the average market price (weighted in relation to turnover) of the target shares during the three months before publication of the decision to make an offer.

If the shares are not traded on a German market, but on a market in another EEA state, the offer price must also not be less than the unweighted average stock exchange price at the stock exchange with the highest turnover during the three-month period.

Where a company has more than one class of share capital, the consideration must be determined individually on the above basis for each class. Consequently, the price offered for each class is likely to be different.

If the offeror chooses to extend the offer to securities other than shares (for example, convertible bonds in the target) and if those securities are listed securities, the same rules also apply to the price offered for such securities.

In addition to the offer consideration, an obligation to make subsequent payments to shareholders who accept the offer will arise if the offeror pays a higher price than the offer price in buying outstanding minority shares within a year of completion of the bid.

12.6.2 Consideration
The types of consideration that may generally be offered comprise cash (in euros only) or shares (either ordinary or preference shares) or a combination of cash and shares. If shares are offered, and there is no cash alternative available, they must be traded on a liquid market within the EEA. If the offeror provides a cash alternative, it is also free to offer shares which are listed outside the EEA, so long as they are liquid. (These restrictions do not apply to simple offers, including partial offers).

The offeror must, in any event, also provide a cash offer (or alternative) if the offeror has acquired for cash during the six months before publication of the decision to make an offer and prior to the expiration of the acceptance period, shares which represent 5 per cent or more of the target company's voting rights.

12.7 Conditions of an offer
12.7.1 Level of acceptance
A voluntary offer may be made subject to a condition that it will lapse unless the offeror receives a certain level of acceptances. Acceptance level conditions are normally set at 50 per cent or 75 per cent of the voting rights of the target. An unusually high acceptance level condition might, depending on the circumstances (in particular, the initial holding of the offeror), be considered inappropriate. This is because, in effect, it could give the offeror a free option to withdraw the bid. The BaFin may, therefore,

prohibit an offer containing such a condition.

In practice, the offeror may decide to waive the acceptance condition, or lower the specified threshold once it has reached a sufficient percentage to give it control, since most shareholders will not continue to resist an offer once it becomes obvious that it will complete. There is no minimum acceptance level that must be achieved by the offeror.

However, if the offeror waives or lowers the acceptance threshold during the last two weeks of the offer, it must keep the offer open for a further two weeks, and it cannot lower the threshold again during that extended period.

12.7.2 Other conditions
The Act does not make provision for pre-conditions to an offer (ie, conditions which, once satisfied, will cause an offer to be made). The Act instead provides that, once a decision to make an offer has been reached, the offer must be submitted within a defined period of time.

The completion of the offer may, however, be subject to certain conditions, provided that they are not 'subjective'. Subjective conditions are those which can be fulfilled exclusively by the offeror, its concert parties, their subsidiary undertakings or their advisers.

Compulsory offers may not be conditional on shareholder resolutions or acceptance levels. However, it is generally accepted that they can be conditional on obtaining merger clearance.

12.7.3 Most common types of pre-conditions and conditions
As noted above, the concept of pre-conditions is not really provided for under German law. Common conditions attached to a voluntary bid include: (i) any resolutions necessary to implement the offer being passed by the shareholders of the offeror (and registered in the commercial register); (ii) where the consideration involves the issue of new listed securities in the offeror, the admission of those shares to listing on a regulated market; (iii) all necessary competition or antitrust approvals or clearances having been obtained; and (iv) the absence of specified defensive measures being implemented by the target (for instance, the sale of its most valuable assets).

Offerors may also seek to include some kind of objective *force majeure* or 'material adverse change' condition. However, such a condition may, depending on the drafting, be viewed as subjective by the BaFin.

If any 'unusual' conditions are being considered, it is advisable to consult the BaFin in advance.

12.8 Timetable
See Timetable and Variations of the Timetable at 12.8.1 and 12.8.2 below.

12.8.1 General

Publication day (no later than submission day + 10 working days)	Offer document must be published on the Internet and by announcement in the electronic Federal Gazette or by making it available for distribution free of charge at a suitable agency in Germany. Offer document may be approved earlier by the BaFin but is deemed approved if the BaFin does not comment within 10 working days.
	Transmission of proof of publication of offer document to the BaFin. Transmission of offer document to target management board.
Promptly following publication day	Management board notification to works council.
Promptly following publication day (normally within two weeks)	Publication of target management/supervisory boards' opinions on the offer and opinion of works council. (The opinions must also be reissued after any amendment to the offer document.)
Weekly intervals after publication day	Announcement of level of acceptances (minus, if applicable, any withdrawals).
Publication day + four weeks	First possible closing date for acceptance period.
Last week of acceptance period	Daily announcement of level of acceptances (minus, if applicable, any withdrawals).
Publication day + 10 weeks	Last possible closing date for acceptance period (unless offer increased in last two weeks). Last possible date for increase of the offer.
Publication day + 12 weeks	Last possible date for acceptance period (if offer increased in last two weeks of original acceptance period).
Offer wholly unconditional + two weeks	Acceptance period automatically extended for extra two weeks if the offer is unconditional by the end of the original acceptance period.

12.8.2 Variations of the timetable

Where a competing offer has been announced, both offers will normally be bound by the timetable established by the publication of the competing offer document, and the acceptance period for the first offeror will be extended accordingly.

Where it is not possible for an offeror to act within the timetable due to requirements relating to cross-border offers or the need to hold an offeror shareholder meeting (for instance, to increase share capital), the BaFin may extend the four-week period for submission of the offer document, up to a maximum of a further four weeks.

Where a shareholders' meeting of the target is called in connection with the offer, the acceptance period is automatically extended to 10 weeks from the publication of the offer document, provided that the notice of meeting is issued after the publication of the offer document and before the end of the original acceptance period.

Where an increase in the offer is published within the last two weeks of the acceptance period, the acceptance period is automatically extended by a further two weeks. However, no further increases in the offer are allowed during the extended acceptance period.

12.9 Main documents and offer documents

12.9.1 General overview

There are a number of key documents involved in a public takeover bid. Although in practice, depending on whether the bid is hostile or recommended, these can vary significantly in number, style and content, the main documentation for recommended and hostile offers does not differ.

Set out below is a *pro forma* illustrating the main relevant public documents:
- notification to BaFin and stock exchanges (offeror);
- announcement of offer (offeror);
- notification to target's management board in writing (offeror);
- notification to target's work council/employees (target);
- offer document (offeror);
- acceptance form (offeror);
- opinion of target board(s) (target);
- notification to offeror's works council/employees (offeror);
- invitation for a target shareholder meeting (if applicable) (target); and
- listing particulars for offeror shares where required (offeror).

In addition, there will be a number of press announcements; for example, weekly/daily announcements of acceptance levels. In a hostile bid, there are also likely to be further documents sent to target shareholders by both the offeror and target at regular intervals over the offer period, setting out their arguments.

12.9.2 Review of the documents by regulators

The offer document must be approved by the BaFin before publication to ensure that it complies with the requirements; however, if the BaFin does not disallow the bid within 10 working days after it has received the offer document it may be published. If the BaFin decides that the offer document does not comply, the offeror must amend the draft submitted.

If the offer document is not approved, the BaFin disallows the bid, in which case the offeror is barred from relaunching an offer for the same target for 12 months. Any share acquisitions and transfers effected as part of a disallowed bid are void.

12.10 Contents of the documents

Offer document
The offer document must be complete and correct. It must also contain all information necessary to allow a reasonably informed decision to be made about the offer, and be written in German in a style that is easy to read. There are many specific content requirements, including details of the offer, conditions of the offer and the offeror's plans for the target company. In the case of a recommended offer, the offer document may refer to the fact that the target management board has agreed to support the offer. If the consideration for the shares to be acquired consists of securities the information required with respect to these securities has to be the same as for public offerings of these securities, eg, the EC Prospectus Regulation has to be complied with.

Other
There are no specific content requirements for any other document to be published during an offer (including the opinion of the target board(s)), except for the listing prospectus which must comply with the relevant rules if no exception applies.

Ireland

Arthur Cox Stephen Hegarty

1. GENERAL DESCRIPTION OF THE CAPITAL MARKETS

1.1 Number of companies listed

At the end of December 2010, there were 36 companies traded on the main market for listed securities (the Main Market) of the Irish Stock Exchange (the ISE) and a further 23 companies traded on the Enterprise Security Market (the ESM). The ESM is a secondary market designed for smaller or newer companies that may not satisfy all the requirements for admission to the Main Market.

1.2 Total volume and market value

The market capitalisation of companies on the ISE grew to EUR 48 billion in 2010, an increase of 7 per cent on the prior year total of EUR 44.8 billion The ISE saw equity turnover fall to EUR 45.6 billion in 2010, a 14.6 per cent decrease on the 2009 total of EUR 53.4 billion. The fourth quarter saw a 21 per cent decrease in average daily turnover to EUR 157 million when compared to the 2009 daily average of EUR 198 million. The number of equity transactions being undertaken on the ISE also fell. 2,116,816 trades were done in 2010 representing a fall of 8 per cent compared to 2,289,956 in 2009. Quarter four saw a decrease of 1.3 per cent in the daily average number of trades to 8,176 from 8,288 in 2009.

1.3 Issue activity

There were no new companies listed in the 12 month period to 31 December 2010.

1.4 Takeover activity of listed companies

In the 12 month period to 31 December 2010, there were five takeover offers for listed companies. Four of the offers were recommended.

2. REGULATORY STRUCTURE

2.1 Regulatory framework

The EU Prospectus Directive, the Market Abuse Directive, the Transparency Directive, and the Markets in Financial Instruments Directive have all been implemented into Irish law.

The regulatory framework for the offering of securities, by sale or subscription, is contained in the Investment Funds, Companies and Miscellaneous Provisions Act, 2005, the Prospectus (Directive 2003/71/EC) Regulations 2005 and the Prospectus Rules (together the Irish Prospectus

Regulations). These provisions implement the EU Prospectus Directive 2003/71/EC. The provisions also include the provisions dealing with the issue of a prospectus for the purpose of an application for listing.

2.2 Regulation of the offering of new securities

2.2.1 Public offering

Any offer of securities to 100 natural or legal persons, not counting qualified investors, will constitute a public offering unless:

- the aggregate price of the securities being offered, together with the price of any other shares offered in the preceding 12 month period, is less than EUR 100,000; or
- the aggregate price of the securities being offered, together with the price of any other shares offered in the preceding 12 month period, is equal to at least EUR 100,000 but is less than EUR 2,500,000, and the offer is accompanied by a 'local offer document'; or
- the minimum consideration payable is at least EUR 50,000 per investor.

Where a company intends to make a public offering, it must prepare a prospectus and have it approved in accordance with the Irish Prospectus Regulations.

Brokers and other financial intermediaries must take care when placing shares with their customers as this can be regarded as a separate offer for the purposes of determining whether it is an offer of securities to the public within the meaning of the Irish Prospectus Regulations.

Irish law makes a distinction between private and public limited liability companies. Private companies are prohibited from making an offer of securities to the public. Private companies are not however prohibited from seeking to have their debentures listed on a stock exchange.

2.3 Differences between Irish and foreign companies

When offering securities to the public on the basis of a prospectus which has already been approved by a competent authority in another member state of the EU, companies incorporated outside of Ireland may avail of the mutual recognition regime provided for in the Irish Prospectus Regulations. This also applies to any company incorporated outside of the EU which has its prospectus approved by a competent authority in another EU member state.

2.4 Admission to trading on a regulated market

The Main Market of the ISE is the only regulated market in Ireland for the purpose of the EU Prospectus Directive, the Market Abuse Directive and the Transparency Directive.

Companies can elect either to have a primary listing or a secondary listing on the Main Market of the ISE. Chapter 11 of the Listing Rules of the ISE sets out provisions for overseas companies seeking a secondary listing. In Chapter 11 of the Listing Rules the requirements of the Listing Rules are substantially modified, both for the purpose of the admission to listing and the continuing obligations of the company applying for the secondary listing.

3. REGISTRATION OF THE ISSUER AND SECURITIES
3.1 Registration requirement
An overseas company is required to register as a branch in Ireland and deliver certain documents (including specifying an address for service of documents) to the Registrar of Companies if it establishes a place of business in Ireland. There is no legal requirement to register a place of business if the overseas company is merely seeking a listing or admission to trading on the Main Market or ESM.

When an Irish company has had a prospectus approved by the Central Bank for the purpose of offering shares to the public or obtaining a listing on the Main Market of the ISE, the prospectus must be registered with the Central Bank and the Registrar of Companies.

3.2 Nature of securities
Securities are widely defined in the Irish Prospectus Regulations to include shares, debt securities, warrants, certificates, options, exchange traded funds (ETFs) and other securities of any description. It is possible to list shares in registered or bearer form or in the form of depository receipts. Derivative securities can also be listed. Special rules are set out in Chapters 12 and 13, respectively, of the Listing Rules for the listing of depository receipts and derivative securities.

4. SUPERVISORY AUTHORITIES
4.1 The supervisory authority
The Irish Financial Services Regulatory Authority (the Financial Regulator) is the single regulator for all authorised and approved persons, for investment exchanges, clearing houses and collective investment schemes. The Central Bank has delegated its responsibility as the competent authority for the approval of a prospectus under the Irish Prospectus Regulations to the ISE.

The ESM is regulated by the ISE. As such, the ESM does not constitute a regulated exchange for the purpose of the EU Prospectus Directive 2003/71/EC. This means that ESM admission documents will not require vetting by the Central Bank or any other body but if a company proposes to offer securities to the public generally and it cannot fit within the relevant exemption, the company will have to prepare a prospectus and have it approved by the ISE on behalf of the Central Bank.

While the Central Bank regulates the ISE, it does not have responsibility for the Listing Rules published by the ISE. Through its rules, the ISE can sanction stockbrokers for improper conduct in the secondary markets. For this reason, the ISE monitors these markets to identify unusual trading activity, price movements, potential breaches of the ISE's rules, insider dealing, market abuse and other forms of market manipulation.

4.2 Conduct: prudential, cooperation, self-regulation of stock exchange
The European Communities (Markets in Financial Instruments) Regulations 2007 (numbers 1 to 3) set out the legal requirements regarding the conduct

of business, capital adequacy, cooperation and self regulations which must be complied with by all authorised and approved investment intermediaries, investment exchanges and clearing houses.

5. OFFERING DOCUMENTATION

5.1 Nature and requirements of offer documents

Where a company wishes to have its shares admitted to the Main Market or to make an offer of its shares to the public, it must produce a prospectus, the contents of which must comply with the Irish Prospectus Regulations.

A prospectus must contain the minimum information required under the Commission Regulation (EC) 809/2004 as well as all information which, according to the particular nature of the issuer and of the securities offered to the public or admitted to trading, is necessary to enable investors to make an informed assessment of:

* the assets and liabilities, financial position, profit and losses, and prospects of the issuer and of any guarantor; and
* the rights attaching to such securities.

A prospectus must also include a summary which, in a brief manner and in non-technical language, conveys the essential characteristics and risks associated with the issuer, any guarantor and the securities. The summary is required to also contain a warning that it should be read as an introduction to the prospectus and any decision to invest in the securities should be based on consideration of the prospectus as a whole by the investor.

A prospectus may be drawn up as a single document or separate documents. A prospectus composed of separate documents shall divide the required information into a registration document containing the required information relating to the issuer and a securities note containing the required information concerning the securities offered to the public or to be admitted to trading. A summary must also be produced.

The requirements for the issue of debt securities are substantially similar but less onerous. In addition to information about the issuer, details must be included of the debt securities for which application is being made as well as the tax treatment, withholding tax, the terms of the debt securities and details of the trustee or other security holders as well as the main provisions of the debt instrument including any conditions as to subordination, whether the debt securities are in registered or bearer forms, details of transfer and other information relating to payment, redemption and covenants.

5.2 Preparation of prospectus

The prospectus is prepared on the basis of information provided by the issuer. In the case of a new entrant without a primary listing elsewhere, an accountant's report will normally be prepared in respect of the company as this will provide most of the substantive information for the first draft of the prospectus. The drafting of the prospectus will commonly be delegated to the lawyers. After the preliminary drafts, the document will be developed through detailed discussions at drafting meetings.

5.3 Due diligence

Due diligence is integral to the preparation of a prospectus and there will be accountants, lawyers and other experts who will prepare due diligence reports in accordance with the terms of their engagement/instruction letters. Due diligence is also effected during the drafting meetings themselves. When the prospectus is nearing finalisation, it is subjected to a process of verification. This is done by the preparation of a detailed set of verification questions, designed to test statements of fact, expectation or belief contained in the draft prospectus.

5.4 Responsibility

Each prospectus must include a statement from the responsible persons that, to the best of their knowledge, the information contained in the prospectus is truthful and contains no omission likely to affect its import.

The responsible persons for prospectuses relating to equity securities are:

- the issuer;
- all persons that are directors of the issuer when the prospectus is published and those that have authorised themselves to be named as directors or having agreed to become directors of the issuer;
- each person that accepts, and is stated in the prospectus as accepting, responsibility for the prospectus;
- the offeror of the securities (if there is an offer to the public and the offeror is not the issuer);
- the person seeking admission of the securities (if not the issuer);
- every other person that has authorised the contents of the prospectus (other than the competent authority in Ireland).

However, the issuer is not responsible if it does not authorise the application for admission or the offer to the public. In addition, directors are not responsible when a prospectus is published without their consent and they have given reasonable public notice that it has been issued without their knowledge or consent.

Certain persons (for example, experts) can state in the prospectus that they accept responsibility for specific parts of the prospectus or only in specific respects, and such persons must give written confirmation regarding statements made by them in the prospectus. In these written confirmations such persons will state that they are only responsible to the extent specified and only if the material is included in (or substantially in) the form and context to which they had agreed.

In addition to the persons listed above, any guarantor and promoter of the issue is liable to pay compensation to all persons that acquire securities on the basis of a prospectus for any loss or damage sustained due to any untrue statements or omitted information. However, such persons are not liable if they do not consent to the issue of the prospectus (or withdrew their consent before publication or acquisition of any securities by an investor) or if they have reasonable grounds to believe that the information in the prospectus was true or that the omission causing loss was rightly omitted.

The punishment for an offence in relation to the publication of a
prospectus is a fine of up to EUR1 million or up to five years' imprisonment.

5.5 Disclaimer/selling restrictions
It is the custom to include disclaimers in relation to the marketing of the
securities in jurisdictions outside Ireland and in particular and specifically
in the USA, Japan, Canada and Australia. Appropriate disclaimers must be
included where the securities are not to be offered to retail investors.

5.6 Recognition of prospectuses by other exchanges
In circumstances where Ireland is the home member state and the Central
Bank has approved a prospectus, the Central Bank can be required by the
person responsible for drawing up the prospectus to provide the competent
authority of each host member state specified in the request with a copy
of the prospectus and a certificate confirming its approval. The certificate
must be issued within three working days of the approval and will confirm
that the prospectus has been drawn up in accordance with the Prospectus
Directive and recording whether any information has been omitted from the
prospectus in accordance with Article 8(2) and (3) of the Prospectus Directive
or the relevant provision of EU prospectus law implementing the said Article
and, if so, the justification for such omission.

5.7 Supplementary prospectuses
Where a prospectus has been issued and the offer is still open for acceptance
or trading on a regulated market has yet to commence, a supplementary
prospectus will have to be issued in the event of the person responsible for
drawing up the prospectus becoming aware of any significant new factor,
material mistake or inaccuracy relating to the information included in
the original prospectus which is capable of affecting the assessment of the
securities. If the person responsible for drawing up the prospectus does not
proceed to prepare the supplementary prospectus, the Central Bank can
require it to do so. The supplementary prospectus must disclose the new
information so that it is in accordance with the facts and does not omit
anything likely to affect the import of such information. The approval
procedure for the supplementary prospectus is the same as a prospectus but
those procedures shall, in general, be completed in a maximum of seven
working days. The supplementary prospectus must be published in the
manner in which the original prospectus was published.

When a supplementary prospectus is published everyone who has already
agreed to purchase or subscribe for the securities has the right, exercisable
within two working days after the publication of the supplement, to
withdraw their applications or acceptances by notice in writing to the issuer
or offeror.

5.8 Issuing of bonds
The issuer of bonds will normally not have to prepare a prospectus to
accompany the issue as the bonds will normally be sold to institutional

investors or for a minimum purchase price of EUR 50,000 per investor.
An application to list bonds on the Global Exchange Market (GEM) of
the ISE can be made by preparing listing particulars approved by the ISE.
A prospectus can also be used but this is not obligatory as the GEM is an
exchange regulated market.

6.   DISTRIBUTION SYSTEMS

6.1   Methods of distribution

Whether securities are offered to the public or placed with institutions, the
issuer will usually appoint an underwriter or small group of underwriters
who will agree to underwrite the offer or, more usually, undertake a book
building exercise whereby each underwriter builds a book of potential
purchasers and establishes the issue price by matching supply and demand.

6.2   Underwriting

The agreement which governs the book building process will be signed
before the underwriters contact potential placees, this agreement
may contain an underwriting commitment by the relevant bank or a
commitment that the securities will be placed on a 'reasonable endeavours'
basis only. If the deal is underwritten, the agreement will state a back stop
price and the company can therefore be certain of raising a minimum level
of proceeds. If the deal is done on a 'reasonable endeavours' basis there
will be no minimum price and therefore no guarantee of proceeds to the
company. Once the offering has been announced the 'book' is built up.
When the 'book' is closed, the underwriters will sign a placing or purchase
memorandum which will commit them to placing or purchasing a fixed
number of securities at the offer price.

6.3   Fees and commission

The bookbuilding or underwriting agreement will specify the commissions
which the underwriter will receive as well as the commission which will
be paid to the brokers and sub-underwriters. Typically placers of equity
securities earn commission of 2 to 3 per cent. The amounts vary depending
on the strength of the issuer and the volatility in the market.

6.4   Stabilisation

In Ireland, Regulation 9 of the Market Abuse (Directive 2003/6/EC)
Regulations 2005 recognises the safe harbours for stabilisation and
ancillary stabilisation activities carried out in accordance with Commission
Regulation (EC) No. 2273/2003.

6.5   Involvement of distributor in the preparation of the offering document

Where the securities are to be listed on the Main Market of the ISE, a sponsor
will have to be appointed by the company. The sponsor may often be one of
the underwriters to the offer. While the sponsor will not take responsibility
for the contents of the prospectus, the sponsor will supervise the drafting

of the prospectus and will usually do so by delegating the drafting to the lawyers. The sponsor will then be responsible for liaising with the ISE in respect of any comments the ISE may have on the draft prospectus.

6.6 Timing of distribution process and rules on distribution to the public

The timing of the distribution process and the rules governing the distribution to the public will depend on the way the offer is made. The principal ways of offering securities, to raise new capital or to widen the shareholding base are as follows.

Rights issue

A rights issue is an offer of new shares made to existing shareholders on a pre-emptive basis, pro rata to their existing holding.

The rights issue offer is required by the Companies Acts to be kept open for at least 21 days. However, Irish public companies annually seek an authority from shareholders which disapplies the statutory pre-emption rights including in respect of 'rights issues' so that the statutory 21 day period would not apply.

The listed company will be required to issue a prospectus where it is proposing to increase its share capital by more than 10 per cent. Regardless of the size of the issue, a rights issue by a company with more than 99 retail shareholders will also require the issue of a prospectus.

The right to subscribe for the new shares has a value itself and can be sold in the market. This is called a sale of 'nil paid rights'. Institutional investors expect companies to arrange their rights issues so that these nil paid rights can be traded during a period which is required by the Listing Rules to be kept open for 14 days (this period was reduced from 21 days in February 2009).

If a shareholder does not take up its 'rights', arrangements will be made to sell the shares that would have been allotted to it and it will receive any premium of the sale price over the subscription price net of expenses.

Open offer

An open offer is also an offer of new shares made to existing shareholders on a pre-emptive basis, pro rata to their existing holding except that shareholders do not have the ability to sell their pre-emption right. The fact that it is not necessary to offer rights on a nil paid basis means that an open offer can be concluded under a slightly quicker timetable than a rights issue.

Placing

A placing involves an issue of shares for cash on a non pre-emptive basis. Most Irish companies obtain a disapplication of the statutory pre-emption rights at their annual general meetings allowing for non pre-emptive issues up to 5 per cent of their issued ordinary share capital. This allows small placings of this size to be done very quickly and will usually be announced at the same time that the placees give their commitment to take up shares in the company.

Under the current institutional investor guidelines in Ireland, institutional investors are advised not to object to non pre-emptive issues which add no more than 5 per cent to historic non-diluted balance sheet equity in the period from annual general meeting to annual general meeting, and no more than 7.5 per cent in total over a period of three financial years. Notwithstanding this, some companies (particularly those trading on the ESM) have been given an authority by the shareholders to issue new shares for cash equivalent to 10 per cent of the company's issued share capital.

A prospectus will not be required for a placing as it is possible to exclude retail investors in any small placing. However, a prospectus will be required to be issued by the company where it is proposing to increase its share capital by 10 per cent or more in any 12 month period as this is a requirement for listing an issue of shares of this size.

The Listing Rules provide that any discount on a placing may be up to 10 per cent (without shareholder approval) or more than 10 per cent (if approved by the shareholders).

A placing could also be made on the basis that it is subject to a clawback. This refers to an arrangement whereby the new shares are 'placed' with institutional investors (who effectively underwrite the issue and ensure that it will be taken up), subject to an open offer being made to existing shareholders to take up their pro rata entitlements.

Convertible bond
The conversion right in a convertible bond is subject to all the pre-emption restrictions which are referred to above in the context of rights issues, open offers and placings. The pre-emption limits are calculated on the assumption of 100 per cent probability of conversion, using the figure of undiluted historic balance sheet share capital

Convertible bonds are normally issued to professional investors with the consequence that it will not be necessary for the company to issue a prospectus. Also, even if the exercise of the conversion right could result in an increase in the company share capital by more than 10 per cent, it will not be necessary to issue a prospectus on account of the exemption in the Irish Prospectus Regulation.

6.7   Companies law restrictions on the issue of new shares for cash
Before issuing any new shares, the company may need to increase its authorised share capital and if so, shareholder approval by ordinary resolution will be required under the Companies Acts. In assessing whether an increase is required or not, account should be taken of any existing obligations to issue shares out of the current authorised share capital, for example, share option schemes, convertible securities or deferred considerations.

In addition, the directors must have the requisite authority to allot the shares or securities. The authority to allot can be contained in a company's articles of association, although in practice most listed companies have a standing authority to allot shares. An ordinary resolution is required to provide the requisite authority. The authority must expire within five years (even if it is contained in the articles of association) and must be limited to a fixed number of shares. The authority can be given for a specific exercise of the power or generally. The practice of many Irish public companies is to renew this authority annually.

Unless pre-emption rights are specifically disapplied, issues of shares for cash must be done on a pre-emptive basis, with the shares being offered to holders of relevant shares in proportion to their existing holdings. The Companies Acts sets out detailed procedures with which the offer has to comply, including the form the offer should take and the length of time during which it may be accepted.

7. PUBLICITY

Once a prospectus has been approved and filed with the Central Bank and the Registrar of Companies, it must be available to the public as soon as practicable and in any case, at a reasonable time in advance of, and at the latest at the beginning of, the offer to the public or the admission to trading of the securities. Where the securities are being offered as part of an initial public offer of a class of shares not already admitted to trading, the prospectus must be made available to the public no later than six working days before the end of the offer.

Where a person has issued a prospectus relating to equity securities, the relevant person must publish a notice stating how the prospectus has been made available and where it can be obtained by the public.

8. LISTING
8.1 Listing requirements, admission criteria

It is possible to list shares, debt securities, warrants, and exchange traded funds. Shares can be listed in registered or bearer form or in the form of depository receipts. Derivative securities can also be listed.

The ISE operates three markets for the listing of securities:

* The Main Securities Market (the Main Market), the principal market for Irish and overseas companies, which admits a wide range of security types such as shares, bonds and funds to listing and trading. The Main Securities Market is a regulated market as defined by Markets in Financial Instruments Directive (MiFID);
* the Enterprise Securities Market (ESM), an equity market designed for growth companies. The ESM is an exchange regulated market and multi-lateral trading facility (MTF) as defined by MiFID; and
* the Global Exchange Market (GEM), a specialist debt market for professional investors. GEM is an Exchange regulated market and MTF as defined by MiFID.

In addition to having to publish a prospectus, the principal requirement when seeking a listing on the Main Market for an issuer's securities is to ensure that the issuer meets the conditions out in Chapters 3 and 4 of the Listing Rules (in the case of a primary listing) or Chapter 11 of the Listing

Rules (in the case of a secondary listing).

Subject to very limited exceptions, at least 25 per cent of any class of the issuer's listed securities must be in the hands of the public. In calculating this percentage all securities held by the directors or persons connected with them, by group pension schemes or by people interested in 5 per cent or more are to be disregarded.

The ESM has less onerous requirements. There is no equivalent of having to have a minimum amount of the share capital in public hands and there is no requirement for a trading record as for a full listing. Finally, there is no need to have the ESM admission document approved by any regulatory authority. Instead there must be a nominated adviser (the ESM Adviser) who is required to take responsibility for ensuring the company's compliance with ESM rules.

The Listing Rules set out application procedures and require certain documents to be lodged 48 hours before the final document is issued and other documents to be lodged on the day of issue. However, for the application for trading on ESM the only requirement is for the ESM Adviser to approve the ESM admission document. The ESM document would normally follow and contain much of the same material as contained in a prospectus but there is more flexibility in agreeing changes with the ESM Adviser.

A company applying for admission to the Main Market must have been independently carrying on its main revenue earning activity for at least three years. The ISE can accept a shorter trading period (for example, where a new holding company is set up for the purpose of floating a company that meets the minimum trading record). A company applying for admission to the ESM is not required to have a minimum trading record.

When the formal application for listing on the Main Market is submitted the company and its sponsor must confirm to the ISE that it has sufficient working capital for at least 12 months from the date the prospectus is approved.

The total market value of all securities (excluding treasury shares) to be listed must be at least EUR 1 million, except where securities of the same class are already listed. The ISE can admit securities of a lower value if satisfied that there will be an adequate market.

8.2 Mechanics of the review process

The prospectus must be submitted to the ISE (as delegate of the Central Bank) for approval where the securities are to be offered to the public or listed on the Main Market. A company can expect to have to submit at least several drafts of the prospectus to the ISE before it will be in a form capable of approval. The ISE will approve the prospectus where it is satisfied that it contains the information and disclosures specified in the Irish Prospectus Regulations. The contents of the prospectus will also have to comply with the requirements of the Listing Rules where the securities are to be listed on the ISE. To assist the ISE review, the draft prospectus must be annotated to show where the prospectus complies with each of the information and disclosure requirements specified in the Irish Prospectus Regulations and the Listing Rules.

In the case of an application for listing on the ESM, the ESM admission document has to be agreed with the ESM Adviser.

8.3 Appeal procedure in the event of a prospectus refusal

If the Central Bank refuses to approve a prospectus, an application may be made to the court within 28 days of the refusal to have the refusal reviewed.

8.4 Appointment of sponsor/ESM Adviser

In order to obtain a listing on the Main Market, an issuer is required to appoint a sponsor ie, an authorised person registered with the ISE, who has the necessary experience in market practice to advise the company of its responsibilities under the Listing Rules. The sponsor, as well as being responsible for assisting the issuer in complying with the Listing Rules, is required to confirm to the ISE at the time the application for listing is made that the Listing Rules have been complied with and that there are no matters known to the sponsor which should be taken into account by the ISE which are not disclosed in the prospectus.

Similarly companies seeking to have shares traded on the ESM are required to appoint a nominated adviser and broker to oversee the admission process and be available thereafter to offer advice to the company and to liaise with the ISE. When the application for admission is made, the role of the ESM Adviser is similar to that of the sponsor, but the ESM Adviser is required to continue its advisory role following admission to trading on the ESM. The ESM Adviser is appointed by the company but has a duty to the ISE to ensure compliance with the ESM rules. If the ESM Adviser resigns and is not replaced, trading will be suspended and, after a month, admission will be cancelled.

8.5 Costs of listing

The initial fee for listing a company on the Main Market depends on the market capitalisation of the company's securities. The fees are published on the Web site of the Irish Stock Exchange.

The annual listing fees payable depend on the market capitalisation of the company's securities, subject to a minimum of EUR 6,350. For example, a company with a market capitalisation of between EUR 12.7 million and EUR 31.7 million pays EUR 8,330, and a company with a market capitalisation over EUR 2.5 billion pays EUR 30,000.

9. SANCTIONS AND DISPUTES

9.1 Disciplinary and administrative sanctions

If any person fails to comply with the Irish Prospectus Regulations, the Central Bank may impose any of the following sanctions:
- a private caution or reprimand;
- a public caution or reprimand;
- a monetary penalty (not exceeding EUR 2,500,000);

- a direction disqualifying the person from being concerned in the management of, or having a qualifying holding in, any regulated financial service provider for such time as is specified in the order;
- a direction ordering the person to cease committing the prescribed contravention;
- a direction requiring the person to pay to the Central Bank all or a specified part of the costs incurred by the Central Bank in investigating the matter to which the assessment relates and in holding the assessment.

9.2 Civil actions

Purchasers of securities are protected by a number of statutory and common law rights. Under the Irish Prospectus Regulations, a prospectus is required to comply with the contents prescribed by the Irish Prospectus Regulations or alternatively in the case of ESM admission, by the ESM rules. More specifically, the Irish Prospectus Regulations provide that the person responsible for the prospectus can be liable to pay compensation to any person who acquires any securities concerned and who suffers loss in respect of them as a result of any untrue or misleading statements or omissions from the prospectus.

In addition, at common law, a purchaser can bring an action for negligent misstatement if it has suffered a loss as a result of acting on that statement, where the loss was a reasonably foreseeable consequence of a negligent statement and that person owed it a duty of care.

Liability can also arise under the common law of fraudulent misrepresentation.

In the case of companies on the Main Market or a listing on another regulated market in the EU, false or misleading statements made in the context of an offer of securities and/or an application for listing can constitute the offence of market abuse under the Investment Funds, Companies and Miscellaneous Provisions Act, 2005 and the Market Abuse (Directive 2003/6/EC) Regulations 2005. In the case of companies on the ESM a similar offence can be committed under Part V of the Companies Act 1990. The Central Bank has the power to investigate and to apply to the court for penalties to be imposed in the case of market abuse. Market abuse is, in essence, market manipulation or information abuse.

9.3 Criminal liability

It is a criminal offence under the Irish Prospectus Regulations to make a statement, promise or forecast which a person knows to be misleading, false or deceptive in a material particular, or to dishonestly conceal any material facts or recklessly make (dishonestly or otherwise) a statement, promise or forecast which is misleading, false or deceptive in a material particular, where this is done for the purpose of inducing, or the person is reckless as to whether it may induce, another person to buy shares.

It is an offence under the Market Abuse (Directive 2003/6/EC) Regulations 2005 to engage in a course of conduct which gives a false or misleading impression as to the market in or the price or value of any relevant investments.

10. CONTINUING OBLIGATIONS

10.1 Disclosure and transparency rules

The disclosure obligations (the Disclosure Rules) of Irish public companies listed on the Main Market of the ISE are primarily contained in the Market Abuse (Directive 2003/6/EC) Regulations, 2005 (the Irish MAD Regulations), Chapter 6 of the Irish Listing Rules, Part 4 of the Investment Funds, Companies and Miscellaneous Provisions Act, 2005, the Transparency (Directive 2004/109/EC) Regulations 2007 and the Central Bank's Market Abuse Rules and Transparency Rules (the Central Bank Rules). In interpreting the Central Bank Rules regard must also be made to Commission Regulation (EC) 2273/2003 of 22 December 2003 (the Market Abuse Regulation) and CESR Guidance and Information on the Common Operation of the Market Abuse Directive (CESR/04-505b).

10.2 Directors' details

A company listed on the ISE must notify a Regulatory Information Service (RIS) of certain information about directors including all directorships held in a publicly quoted company in the previous five years, any unspent convictions, any bankruptcies, voluntary arrangements and any public criticism by a statutory or regulatory authority.

10.3 Lock-up arrangements

The Listing Rules include rules requiring a listed company to announce details of any lock-up arrangements that have not already been disclosed and changes to any lock-up arrangements previously disclosed.

10.4 Change of date of financial year end

Listed companies must notify a RIS as soon as possible of any change in their financial year end. If the change in the company's financial year end leads to an extension of the accounting period to more than 14 months, the company must produce a second interim report.

10.5 Proxy forms

Together with the notice of meetings, listed companies must send a proxy form containing prescribed information to each person entitled to vote at the meeting and ensure that the proxy form provides for at least three-way voting on all resolutions intended to be proposed with the exception of procedural resolutions. This requirement for at least three-way proxy voting was introduced as a consequence of the implementation of the Shareholders' Rights Directive 2007/36/EC.

10.6 Use of the Internet to send documents

The Electronic Commerce Act 2000 and Transparency (Directive 2004/109/ EC) Regulations 2007 allows companies to send documents, such as annual reports and accounts, to a shareholder in electronic format or by making them available on the company's Web site.

10.7 Significant transactions

In the event of transactions, the Listing Rules will require the company to issue either an announcement or a circular to shareholders and in the case of a substantial acquisition or disposal or a transaction with a related party, obtain prior shareholder approval. A substantial acquisition or disposal is calculated by a comparison of assets to assets, profits to profits, turnover to turnover, consideration to market capitalisation or gross capital to gross capital where the assets or business to be acquired or to be disposed of would exceed 25 per cent on various tests. There are further requirements on reverse takeovers or transactions with related parties. Related parties include directors and significant shareholders. Any circular to shareholders will normally have to be approved by the ISE before being sent to shareholders.

The ESM regime for continuing obligations is considerably lighter, approval of shareholders is required only in the event of a reverse takeover ie, where the target company is larger than the offeror.

10.8 Financial information

A listed company is required to issue an annual report and accounts within four months of the end of the financial period to which it relates. The accounts must be audited by an independent accountant whose report should confirm that the accounts give a true and fair view of the state of affairs, profit and loss and changes in the financial position of the company and its subsidiaries or the equivalent in the relevant jurisdiction. Listed companies must also produce half yearly reports which must be published within 90 days of the end of the period to which they relate, together with a comparison for the same period for the previous year.

10.9 Interim disclosure

Under the Market Abuse Regulations, listed companies must publicly disclose without delay inside information:
* which directly concerns the issuer; and
* in a manner that enables fast access to and complete, correct and timely assessment of the information by the public.

The Transparency Regulations add to these requirements by placing an obligation on a listed company to ensure that information is disseminated in a manner which ensures it is capable of reaching as wide a part of the public as possible and as close to simultaneously as possible in each relevant member state. Market practice in Ireland indicates that release of information without delay via a RIS is considered sufficient to meet this obligation.

Under the Disclosure Rules, companies on the Main Market, persons discharging managerial responsibilities (PDMRs) and their connected persons are also under an obligation to provide to the ISE as soon as possible following a request for:

- any information that the ISE considers appropriate to protect investors or ensure the smooth operation of the market;
- any other information or explanation that the ISE may reasonably require to verify whether the Disclosure Rules are being or have been complied with.

At any time, the ISE may require a listed company to publish such information in such form and time limits as it considers appropriate to ensure the smooth operation of the market.

The Disclosure Rules provide that a listed company must announce any significant changes concerning already publicly disclosed inside information without delay after these changes occur.

10.10   Other continuing requirements

The other continuing requirements are set out in Chapter 6 and also Chapter 8 (Related Party Transactions), Chapter 9 (Dealing in own Securities and Treasury Shares), and Chapter 10 (Content of Circulars). There are similar, but much less onerous, requirements under the ESM rules.

11.   CORPORATE GOVERNANCE
11.1 The Combined Code

Companies listed on the Main Market are expected to comply with the principles of good governance set out in the Combined Code published by the UK Financial Reporting Council. It is attached to, but does not form part of, the Listing Rules and sets out how companies should conduct themselves in order to comply with the principles of good governance. The Combined Code does not have the force of law. Companies are expected to comply with the Combined Code or explain the areas where they do not comply and the reasons therefore.

In addition, all companies are required to adopt the Model Code for Dealings in Securities by directors and PDMRs.

As well as the Combined Code, there are other corporate governance guidance notes which listed companies seek to apply, the main ones being the Turnbull Guidance on Internal Control, the Smith Guidance on Audit Committees, the Higgs Suggestions for Good Practice and the Walker Review of Corporate Governance in Banks and other financial industry entities.

For financial years commencing after November 2010, companies listed on the Main Market are expected to comply with the principles of good governance set out in the UK Corporate Governance Code and the Irish Corporate Governance Annex in the ISE Listing Rules.

11.2 Directive 2006/46/EC

Directive 2006/46/EC on corporate reporting has been implemented into Irish law. This requires companies listed on the Main Market to produce an annual corporate governance statement.

11.3 One or two-tier board

Whilst it is possible to adopt a structure similar to a two-tier board, most

Irish companies have a unitary board; all directors therefore having equal fiduciary duties. Executive directors in addition will have their areas of executive responsibility and the chairman of the board has a particular role as head of the company.

11.4 Publication of internal regulations
The memorandum of association (which sets out the name and objects of the company) and the articles of association (which sets out the regulations for directors and shareholders) of an Irish company are available for inspection at the Companies Registration Office.

11.5 Responsibility of directors
An Irish company has a board of directors, the members of which have similar fiduciary duties, primarily to act at all times in the best interests of the company. Some will be executives, employed in the business of the company and others will be non-executive directors and, if an issue arises, it is expected that the executive directors would have the primary responsibility to resolve the problem because of their closer knowledge of the business.

The internal regulations of the company (not the articles of association but the resolutions of the board and terms of reference of committees) are usually structured such that certain matters are dealt with by non-executive directors and they will, for example, comprise the membership of the audit committee, the remuneration committee and the nomination committee. However, both executives and non-executives can sign the accounts.

11.6 Consent of shareholders' meeting
There is a requirement to have an annual general meeting (AGM) and to put the accounts, the dividend and the re-appointment of the auditors up for approval by the meeting.

In addition, under the Combined Code, directors are expected to put themselves up for re-election every three years (soon to be every year for accounting periods commencing on or after 18 December 2010) and any director appointed by resolution of the board since the date of the last AGM is also required to be put up for election at that AGM. Each of those matters requires an ordinary resolution, namely a vote in favour by 50 per cent plus of those attending (in person or by proxy) and voting at the meeting.

Certain resolutions require a special resolution and some require extraordinary notice. Special resolutions require a 75 per cent vote of those attending (in person or by proxy) and voting at the meeting.

The Listing Rules require shareholder approval to be sought for certain transactions whilst ESM rules require shareholder approval only on a reverse takeover.

11.7 Appointment/dismissal of directors
In practice all appointments, and for the most part dismissals, of directors are dealt with by resolution of the board of directors. There is no different

treatment for executive directors from non-executives.

If executive directors are dismissed from their executive position, the provisions of their service agreement usually state that they also cease to be a director. However, any such resolution will not prejudice a claim by the individual director for breach of contract.

The articles of association contain provisions for circumstances where directors lose office, usually relating to misconduct or breach of duty, bankruptcy or other offence. Many articles of association provide that a resolution calling upon a director to resign and signed by all other directors will force that director to resign.

11.8 Directors' remuneration and share options
The Combined Code provides, as a general principle, that the levels of directors' remuneration should be sufficient to attract, retain and motivate directors of the quality required to run the company successfully but the company should avoid paying more than is necessary for this purpose. A proportion of the executive directors' remuneration should be structured so as to link rewards to corporate and individual performance.

The Listing Rules require companies on the Main Market to include with their annual report a report to the shareholders by the board which sets out the information in regard to the remuneration and other benefits afforded to directors. Under the Listing Rules for the Main Market, prior shareholder approval is required for the grant of any new shares, share options or long term incentive awards to directors.

11.9 Directors' liability
All directors, executive and non-executive, owe duties of care to the company and have fiduciary duties relating to that duty of care. There is no particular distinction drawn between executive and non-executive directors.

11.10 Depth of information – proxy solicitation
When a company convenes a shareholders meeting, it must send the same information to all shareholders and remind them of their right to appoint a proxy. An Irish company may not canvass the return of proxy appointments on a selective basis.

11.11 Earnings guidance
As companies must now comment on their prospects in their annual report and interim management statements, they will also go further and give some guidance in regard to their expected earnings in the current year.

11.12 Management discussion and analysis
The directors' report in the annual report of an Irish company listed on the Main Market must contain the following information:
* a fair review of the development and performance of the group's business and of its position during the financial year together with a description of the principal risks and uncertainties that the group faces;

- references to, and additional explanations of, amounts included in the company's annual financial statements, where appropriate;
- particulars of any important events affecting the company or any of its subsidiaries, if any, which have occurred since the financial year end;
- an indication of likely future developments in the business of the group;
- an indication of the activities, if any, of the group, in the field of research and development; and
- an indication of the existence of branches of the company outside the state and the country in which each such branch is located.

12. MARKET ABUSE, INSIDER TRADING AND OTHER SHARE DEALING RESTRICTIONS

12.1 Overview

For companies with securities listed on a regulated market in the EU, the Market Abuse Directive 2003/6/EC has been implemented by the Market Abuse (Directive 2003/6/EC) Regulations 2005, the IFSRA Market Abuse Rules and the Investment Funds, Companies and Miscellaneous Provisions Act 2005. These regulations impose significant criminal and civil penalties in the event of any breach. In addition, significant powers have been conferred on the Central Bank for the purpose of preventing, investigating and remedying the breaches. The insider dealing prohibitions in the Companies Act 1990 continue to apply to companies listed on the ESM.

The key aspects of these regulations are as follows:
- A person who possesses inside information shall not use that information by acquiring or disposing of, or by trying to acquire or dispose of for the person's own account or for the account of a third party, directly or indirectly, financial instruments to which that information relates.
- A person shall not disclose inside information to any other person unless such disclosure is made in the normal course of the exercise of the first-mentioned person's employment, profession or duties or recommend or induce another person, on the basis of inside information, to acquire or dispose of financial instruments to which that information relates.

12.2 Insider dealing offences

Insider dealing offences include the following:
- dealing, or attempting to deal, (whether on a person's own account, or for the account of a third party) on the basis of inside information;
- disclosing inside information to any person unless such disclosure is made in the normal course of the exercise of the disclosing person's employment, profession or duties; and
- recommending or inducing another person, on the basis of inside information, to acquire or dispose of financial instruments to which that information relates.

12.3 What is 'inside information'?

Inside information is information:

- of a precise nature;
- relating directly or indirectly to one or more issuers of financial instruments or to one or more financial instruments;
- which has not been made public; and
- which, if it were made public, would be likely to have a significant effect on the price of those financial instruments or on the price of related derivative financial instruments.

12.4 Exempted transactions
The following transactions are exempted from some of the market abuse prohibitions:
- exemption for actions taken in conformity with takeover rules (Regulation 8 of the Market Abuse (Directive 2003/6/EC) Regulations 2005);
- implementation of a decision to deal where the decision is the only inside information;
- implementation of a pre-existing obligation; and
- certain buy back or stabilisation measures.

12.5 Market manipulation offences
The following transactions are specifically identified as constituting Market Manipulation offences:
- transactions or orders to trade which give, or are likely to give, false or misleading signals as to the supply of, demand for or price of financial instruments;
- transactions or orders to trade which secure, by a person, or persons acting in collaboration, the price of one or several financial instruments. The 'accepted market practices' defence is available to this offence;
- transactions or orders to trade which employ fictitious devices or any other form of deception or contrivance;
- dissemination of information through the media, including the Internet, or by any other means, which gives, or is likely to give, false or misleading signals as to financial instruments, including the dissemination of rumours and false or misleading news, where the person who made the dissemination knew, or ought to have known, that the information was false or misleading.

12.6 Trading in certain periods
The Model Code set out in the Listing Rules provides that a director should not deal in securities of a listed company during the close periods for the company. These comprise the period of 60 days immediately preceding the preliminary announcement of the full year results, the period of 60 days preceding the publication of the half yearly results and, if the company issues results on a quarterly basis, the period of 30 days immediately preceding that announcement. In addition, the Model Code provides that a director should not deal in securities when it is in possession of unpublished price sensitive information.

12.7 Takeovers

The Irish Takeover Panel Act, 1997 (as amended) and the rules made thereunder (the Irish Takeover Panel Rules) deal with acquisitions of shares in the context of takeovers. The Irish Takeover Rules contain various prohibitions on dealings in certain circumstances.

If an offer has closed and has been unsuccessful, the Irish Takeover Rules prohibit the acquisition of shares for 12 months, if such acquisition would result in a holding of 30 per cent or more and would therefore require a Rule 9 mandatory offer. The Irish Takeover Rules also prohibits the offeror if the offer has been unsuccessful, from subsequently within a 12 month period, making a second offer to acquire shares on better terms than those made available under the original offer.

12.8 Analysts

There is no specific exemption for analysts in terms of committing offences under the Market Abuse Rules.

13. MUTUAL FUNDS

13.1 Fund structure

A fund may be established as a single fund or as an umbrella fund comprising one or more sub-funds, each with a different investment objective and policy. A sub-fund may comprise different classes of shares which share in the same pool of assets of the sub-fund. Typically classes of shares are distinguished by matters such as the minimum initial and subsequent subscription, differing management charges and differing entry and exit fees, differing currencies of denomination or differing policies on distributions.

13.2 Authorisation of Irish funds

Irish funds are authorised by the Central Bank. Certain parties involved with the fund and all the material documents of the fund must be approved in advance by the Central Bank in order for an Irish fund to be established.

13.3 Parties to a fund structure

The promoter of an investment fund must be approved by the Central Bank to act as such. Although there is no definition of a promoter it is the entity responsible for the establishment of the fund, the selection of the service providers and the production of the prospectus. In considering such an application the Central Bank will consider the financial status of the proposed promoter, its regulatory status, ownership, management structure and experience in managing collective investment schemes or assets generally.

Similarly, the investment manager of a fund must also be approved to act as such by the Central Bank. Only promoters or investment managers established in a regulated jurisdiction are acceptable to the Central Bank

Investment decisions are taken by the investment manager who is appointed by the investment company or, in the case of the unit trust, the management company. The calculation and determination of the net asset value per share and the registrar and transfer agency functions are carried out by an administrator. The fund's assets are held by the custodian (and its sub-custodians appointed by it pursuant to its global custodial arrangements). An Irish fund must have an Irish administrator and an Irish custodian.

13.4 Types of funds

Irish funds can take one of four forms; an investment company, a unit trust, an investment limited partnership and, more recently, a common contractual fund (CCF). Investment limited partnerships and CCFs are less common than investment companies and unit trusts.

The non-UCITS category of fund (ie, funds which are established pursuant to Irish law and are not therefore undertakings for collective investment in transferable securities as recognised by EU law) comprises retail, professional and qualifying investor funds. The investment restrictions and borrowing requirements for professional funds are more relaxed than those that apply to UCITS and non-UCITS retail funds, with typically a doubling of the restrictions imposed on UCITS funds (ie 20 per cent of the fund's net asset value may be invested in the securities of any one issuer and the fund may borrow up to 25 per cent of its net asset value for any purpose). There is a minimum subscription requirement for these types of funds of EUR 125,000.

A qualifying investor fund is the least restrictive of all the funds in that the investment objectives and policies are framed by the promoter and not by the Central Bank and are agreed to on a case-by-case basis. This type of fund provides maximum flexibility for the promoter of the fund. It can be leveraged significantly and the concentration of investments in any one issuer can be considerable. However in the case of these funds each investor must make a certification about its net worth (in the case of individuals) or the level of assets under discretionary management or ownership and the minimum investment is EUR 250,000.

13.5 Listing

The ISE provides a technical listing for shares or units of Irish funds. The application process with the ISE would parallel the approval process with the Central Bank. There would be initial and ongoing fees payable to the ISE.

13.6 Tax status

An Irish authorised fund is not subject to income, corporate or capital gains taxes. However, certain Irish investors are chargeable to Irish tax on transfers or redemptions of shares or payments of dividends.

14. SECURITIES INSTITUTIONS
14.1 Market executive undertaking

The Central Bank has responsibility for the trading of Irish government bonds. The National Treasury Management Agency (NTMA) has responsibility for borrowing moneys for the Exchequer subject to the control and general superintendence of the Minister for Finance. In this role, the NTMA also has responsibility for the recognition of primary dealers in Irish government bonds.

The Central Bank has responsibility for the approval of stock exchanges in Ireland. The Irish Stock Exchange is the only stock exchange in Ireland. Anyone who has been authorised (or exempted from authorisation) to act as an investment firm can apply to become a member of the ISE. The ISE may at its sole discretion admit as a member firm a person who satisfies the ISE that it has appropriate capital and appropriate arrangements in place and sufficiently meets the suitability requirements in the membership rules of the ISE. Where the ISE exercises this discretion, the firm may be admitted as a Restricted Trading Member Firm.

14.2 Securities clearing house and central securities depository
There are no clearing houses or central securities depositories in Ireland for the clearing and holding of securities.

Irish bonds (including Irish government bonds) are deposited with and cleared through Euroclear.

Irish shares can be held and transferred in either certificated or uncertificated form. Euroclear UK & Ireland Limited (as the operator of the CREST system) have been approved in Ireland as an operator of a relevant system for the transfer of uncertificated securities. Certificated shares can be converted into uncertificated shares by depositing the underlying share certificates into the CREST system. Once shares have been deposited into the CREST system, they can be transferred by CREST members in accordance with the CREST rules and all such transfers are given the same legal recognition as conventional paper-based share transfers.

Derivatives over Irish shares are cleared through Eurex AG.

14.3 Investment services providers
The MiFID Directive as well as Directive 2006/73/EC on the organisational requirements and operating conditions for investment firms have been implemented by the European Communities (Markets in Financial Instruments) Regulations 2007 (numbers 1 to 3) (the MiFID Regulations).

It is an offence under the MiFID Regulations for any person operating in the state (see definition below), who is not authorised under regulation 11 of the MiFID Regulations or otherwise exempted under the MiFID Regulations, to act as an investment firm (see definition below). An offence under the MiFID Regulations is punishable by a term of imprisonment not exceeding 10 years and/or a fine not exceeding EUR 10,000,000. In addition, the guilty party may not be able to enforce any resulting investment agreement and may be required to repay or return any money or property transferred to it as a consequence of the investment agreement.

Regulation 8 of the MiFID Regulations provides that an investment firm will not be regarded as 'operating in the state' if the firm has no branch in the state and: (a) the firm's head or registered office is (i) in a state other than a member state, or (ii) in a member state outside the state and the firm does not provide any investment services in respect of which it is required to be authorised in its home member state for the purposes of the Directive; or (b) the firm is authorised in a member state outside the state, under the Directive, but provides only investment services of a kind for which authorisation under the Directive is not available during the provision of the investment services. However, if such a firm provides investment services to individuals in Ireland who do not themselves provide investment services on a professional basis, that firm will be regarded as 'operating in the state'.

14.4 Mergers and acquisitions
It is not necessary for a person to be authorised or exempted under the MiFID Regulations in regard to the giving of advice to an undertaking on structure, industrial strategy and related matters and advice relating to mergers and the purchase of an undertaking. This is so only when the advice is given to the undertaking involved in these matters.

14.5 Press releases
A press release should not fall within the definition of investment advice in the MiFID Regulations where the purpose of the press release taken as a whole is not to recommend to the persons to sell or invest in any particular investment, instrument or deposit or to recommend to any particular provider of investment business services.

15. NOTIFICATION OBLIGATIONS
15.1 Notification of substantial shareholdings
Under the Transparency (Directive 2004/109/EC) Regulations 2007 and the Transparency Rules of the Central Bank, a person is obliged to notify the company and the Central Bank when it acquires control over securities carrying 3 per cent or more of the voting rights attaching to shares in an Irish company listed on a regulated market in the EU.

Under Chapter 2 of Part IV of the Companies Act 1990 a person or other legal entity is obliged to notify the company when it becomes aware that it has acquired an interest in 5 per cent or more of the issued share capital of any Irish company. Interest is defined very widely and is not limited to the control of voting rights.

Subsequent transactions which change the percentage voting control or interest by a whole number (up or down) must also be notified. When such a person ceases to have a notifiable interest that cessation should also be notified. In the case of companies listed on a regulated market in the EU, the obligation to notify must be performed within the period of two trading days next following the day on which the transaction was concluded. In all other cases, the notification must be made within five business days of the interest being acquired. The notification must be made using Standard Form (TR-1) which is available in electronic form on the Web site of the Central Bank at www.financialregulator.ie

Under the articles of association of most public companies, the company may issue a person with a disclosure notice (requiring the disclosure of any interests in the company's share capital). Failure to comply with this notice can result in restrictions being placed on the rights attaching to the relevant shares.

Under the Listing Rules, the company is required to notify the ISE of the particulars of any legal entity who holds 3 per cent or more in the issued share capital of the company where it has been notified of it. The ISE must be notified as soon as possible and in any event by the end of the business day following receipt of the notification by the company. Where the company has issued a Section 81 Notice requesting disclosure of beneficial and other holdings in its shareholding it is required to notify the ISE as soon as possible and in any event by the end of the business day following receipt of the information where it is apparent that an interest exists or has been increased or reduced or ceased and should have been disclosed and which has not been previously been disclosed.

Under the Substantial Acquisition Rules of the Irish Takeover Panel, a person who holds 15 per cent or more but less than 30 per cent of the voting rights in a company and who acquires shares which increases its holding beyond a further 1 per cent is obliged to notify the company, the ISE and the Irish Takeover Panel not later than noon on the business day following the date of the acquisition. Failure to do so is a breach of the Takeover Rules and could lead to a censure or fine from the Irish Takeover Panel.

15.2 Register
There is an obligation on a company to keep a register of notifications and similarly in the event that the company sends a Section 81 Notice, the company is required to register any interests so disclosed. These registers are available for inspection without charge. A copy of the relevant register can be obtained on payment of a fee.

16. PUBLIC TAKEOVERS
16.1 Applicable laws and regulations
The European Communities (Takeover Bids (Directive 2004/25/EC)) Regulations 2006 (the 2006 Takeover Regulations), which transposed the EU Takeovers Directive into Irish Law, came into effect on 20 May 2006. Under the 2006 Takeover Regulations Ireland has made Article 9 (frustrating action) a mandatory provision. Ireland has exercised its right under the Directive not to make Article 11 (break-through right) a mandatory provision. Furthermore, the 2006 Takeover Regulations, do not allow companies to take advantage of the (so-called) reciprocity provisions in Article 12 (optional arrangements). The 2006 Takeover Regulations only apply to Irish companies listed on a regulated market within the EU. Except where the 2006 Takeover Regulations apply, all listed Irish companies are subject to the Irish Takeover Panel Act 1997 (the Irish Takeover Panel Act).

16.2 Competent authority
The Irish Takeover Panel is the statutory body responsible for monitoring

and supervising takeovers and other relevant transactions in Ireland.

The Irish Takeover Panel has extensive powers under the Irish Takeover Panel Act to make rulings and give directions, to hold hearings, to summon witnesses and to require production of documents and other information, where these are appropriate in the discharge of its statutory functions.

16.3 Announcements/secrecy/disclosure
The Irish Takeover Panel Rules are designed to ensure that an announcement of an offer or possible offer is made at the earliest moment if there is any risk of a leak (and hence of insider dealing). Prior to an approach to the board of the offeree, the responsibility for making an announcement of a possible bid lies with the offeror. Once the board of the offeree has received an approach that may or may not lead to an offer, the primary responsibility for making an announcement passes to the board of the offeree. It is essential that an announcement in relation to an offer or potential offer is accurate, unambiguous and not misleading in any way.

16.4 Shareholdings and dealings
The shareholdings and dealings of persons discharging managerial responsibilities, a category comprising directors and certain senior executives of the company, the offeree, and their connected persons (under the UK regime), and persons closely associated with them (under the Irish regime), in shares of the offeree and offeror immediately before and during an offer period are subject to various restrictions under the market abuse legislation, the Stock Exchange Model Code (the Model Code) and the Irish Takeover Panel Rules. In addition, all such dealings will have to be disclosed to the market and to shareholders.

16.5 Conflicts of interest
If a director has a potential conflict of interest that may prevent it from properly being involved in considering and advising shareholders about an offer, it should notify the board and its advisers at the earliest possible moment. In this case, an independent board committee consisting of all the directors except the director or directors with a conflict of interest should be constituted to consider the potential takeover offer and whether or not to recommend shareholders to accept the offer.

16.6 Frustrating action
The General Principles set out in the 2006 Takeover Regulations prohibit the board of a target company from doing anything which might deny the shareholders the opportunity to decide on the merits of a bid. Rule 21 of the Irish Takeover Panel Rules contains detailed provisions concerning actions which must not be taken by the board of a target company once the board has reason to believe that an offer may be imminent.

16.7 Supply of information and public statements during an offer period
Detailed rules are set out in the Irish Takeover Panel Rules in regard to the

provision of information. It is a fundamental principle of the Irish Takeover Panel Rules that information about companies involved in an offer must be made equally available to all shareholders as early as possible at the same time and in the same manner. Statements must not be issued which, while not factually inaccurate, may mislead shareholders and create uncertainty in the market.

16.8 Employees
The bidder is required to include in its offer document a statement of its intentions regarding the future business of the target and its subsidiaries, its strategic plans for the target and their likely repercussions on employment and on the locations of the target's place of business. The board of the offeree is then required to give its views on the implementation of these plans and the effect it will have on employment in the group.

The board of the offeree is also required to append to the response document a separate opinion from the representatives of its employees on the effects of the offer on employment, provided the opinion is received 'in good time' before the despatch of that document.

16.9 General principles in the Irish Takeover Panel Act
In addition to the fiduciary duties of directors referred to above, the target, its directors and all other parties to the takeover are required to observe the general principles. The 'general principles' derive from the EU Takeovers Directive. A key theme of the general principles is that shareholders in the target company should not be disadvantaged and should have access to all relevant information concerning that company so as to allow them to properly consider the merits of the offer. Under the Irish Takeover Panel Rules the directors of the target company are expected to advise the target shareholders on the merits and demerits of an offer or to state that they have not formed a view on the offer. If necessary, the Irish Takeover Panel can direct the directors of a target company to give such advice and such a direction is legally enforceable by the Irish Takeover Panel.

16.10   Profit forecasts
The Irish Takeover Panel Rules contain strict requirements in regard to statements that constitute profit forecasts, asset valuations or concern the financial benefits of a proposed offer. The company's financial advisers should be consulted in each case prior to any statement being made which could potentially be regarded as falling within such categories.

16.11   Inducement Fees
Except with the consent of the Irish Takeover Panel, an offeree may not enter into any contract or any arrangement to pay any compensation to the offeror where the obligation to pay is contingent in any respect on the relevant offer or proposed offer lapsing or not being made.

16.12 Stake building

If any company is buying shares in a potential target company, it first has to consider the Rules on Substantial Acquisition of Shares (the SARs) which effectively prohibit any person from acquiring shares carrying 10 per cent or more of the voting rights which, in aggregate with shares held, takes the person to over 15 per cent in any seven day period. There are exceptions, if the purchase is from a single shareholder or immediately prior to the announcement of a firm intention to make an offer.

An offer period for a company begins with an announcement of a possible offer and thereafter there is an obligation to disclose any dealings whatsoever by the offeror, and any person acquiring or selling more than 1 per cent of the shares (or class of shares) is also obliged to make a disclosure (Rule 8).

The principal provision is, however, Rule 9 of the Irish Takeover Panel Rules, which requires any person acquiring shares resulting in a holding of 30 per cent or more of the voting rights (or increasing his stake above 30 per cent) to make a mandatory cash offer conditional only on statutory merger approval and achieving a 50 per cent level in the target company, aggregating the shares held and accepted. All shareholders in the target therefore have the opportunity to sell.

The insider dealing law applies to purchases of shares in the course of an offer but an offeror may use the safe harbour of buying for the purpose of the offer in accordance with the Irish Takeover Panel Rules and the SARs. The offeror is prohibited by Rule 4 from selling securities in the target except with the prior consent of the Irish Takeover Panel and following 24 hours' public notice that sales may be made. Once any sales have been made, the offeror cannot then make purchases.

Otherwise the offeror can purchase shares in the market, although if it purchases shares at above the offer price, it is obliged to increase the consideration per share to the cash price paid in the market.

16.13 Obligation on price

The Irish Takeover Panel Rules require an offeror to make a cash offer, either if 10 per cent or more of the voting rights of the target shall have been acquired in the 12 months immediately preceding the relevant offer period, or if there is any purchase of shares for cash in the offer period itself. The cash consideration under the offer then must be at the highest price paid by the offeror or any concert party during the relevant period. If any shares have been acquired in the three months preceding, or during, the offer period for any consideration other than cash, then Rule 6 requires an offer to be made on no less favourable terms. Similarly, Rule 9 provides that the offeror must offer not less than the highest price paid for shares by the offeror or any concert party within the 12 months prior to the commencement of the Rule 9 obligation.

16.14 Timetable

The Irish Takeover Rules prescribe a clear timetable for an offer which begins with the making of the firm offer announcement (called a Rule 2.5 announcement) specifying the principal terms and all conditions; that imposes on the offeror a mandatory obligation to proceed with the offer. Once the Rule 2.5 announcement has been made, the offeror has up to 28 days to despatch the offer document.

Typically the offer document specifies a first closing date that cannot be less than 21 days after the date of posting and again, typically, the target would respond within 14 days. Other relevant dates include the right to withdraw which arises no earlier than 21 days after the first closing date; day 39 from the posting of the offer document which is the last date when the target company is allowed to provide new information; and day 46 which is the last date on which an offer can be increased. All offers must become unconditional as to acceptances by no later than the 60th day from the posting of the offer document and all conditions to the offer have to be satisfied by the 21st day following the later of the date that the offer has become unconditional as to acceptances or the first closing date. Finally the consideration must be posted within 14 days of the offer becoming unconditional or the date of receipt of the acceptance complete in all respects.

The timetable is complicated if there is a competing bidder when it is restarted on the basis of the date of the competing offer document, or if the competition clearance procedure is slower than expected, then the process can be frozen.

16.15 Irrevocables

A major shareholder has the alternative of seeking to sell its shares immediately prior to the offer (the acquisition of shares from a single vendor taking an offeror over 30 per cent is permitted by both the SARs and Rule 5).

More typically, the major shareholder would be asked to give an irrevocable undertaking agreeing to accept the offer, when made on agreed terms, and it may be prepared to sign this to ensure that an offer is made. Irrevocable undertakings vary between 'hard' undertakings, committed to accept the offer, and 'soft' undertakings, allowing the shareholder to escape from its commitment in the event of a higher offer.

16.16 First announcement

There are varying announcements prescribed for in the Irish Takeover Panel Rules, but the key announcement is what is called a Rule 2.5 announcement, which is the announcement of a firm intention to make an offer. That announcement must contain the terms of the offer, the identity of the offeror, details of any holding in the target or options, details of any derivatives relating to target shares, all conditions including normal conditions relating to acceptances, listing and increase of capital, details of any agreements or arrangements to which the offeror is party which may be relevant and details of any special indemnity arrangements.

If on the other hand an announcement is of a possible offer but there is no commitment, the target company may request the Irish Takeover Panel to require the offeror to make an offer or withdraw by a specified date.

Until the offeror has approached the target, it is under an obligation to make an announcement, in the event of a rumour of a bid or an untoward movement in the share price of the target. Once the approval has been made, the making of an announcement becomes the responsibility of the target.

16.17 Announcement to posting

There is a maximum 28 day period permitted between the date of the Rule 2.5 announcement and the posting of the offer document, although a much shorter period is usual. The offer document constitutes the making of the offer in law and starts the offer timetable.

16.18 Contents

The offer document will typically contain a letter from the chairman of the offeror and, if recommended, from the offeree. It will also contain a letter from the financial adviser setting out the terms of the offer in general, including price and reasons and other information. The offer document will contain appendixes with details which comply with the detailed requirements of the Irish Takeover Rules.

The offer document is required by Rule 24 to set out the offeror's intentions regarding the target and its employees, financial and other information on the offeror, the offeree company and the offer (although the degree of financial information on the offeror is dependent on whether it is an Irish company and whether the consideration for the offer is securities or cash). It is also required by Rule 24 to include details of the securities for which the offer is made, the consideration being offered, middle market quotations for the securities being offered, details of any special agreements or arrangements in relation to the conditions, a description as to how the offer was financed, and a recommendation from the target (if recommended). It will also include shareholders and dealings of the offeror and offeree, together with a statement as to directors' emoluments and special arrangements.

16.19 Responsibility

All documents or advertisements sent to shareholders are required by Rule 19.1 to satisfy the highest standard of accuracy and care as if they were prospectuses. The directors of the offeror and target are each required to accept responsibility for the contents of their documents and for there to be included a statement to the effect that they accept responsibility for the information contained therein and that, to the best of their knowledge and belief (having taken all reasonable care to ensure that such is the case) the information contained in the document is in accordance with the facts and that it does not omit anything likely to affect the import of such information.

16.20 Due diligence

Due diligence is a matter to be discussed between the offeror and the offeree.

The offeree sometimes takes the view that, since any material information is required to be put into the public domain by the offeree, under the Market Abuse Regulations, there is no material information that the offeree needs to make available. However this is a matter for discussion and frequently due diligence information is provided by the offeree to the offeror, subject to appropriate confidentiality undertakings.

Rule 20.2 requires a target to provide, if asked, the same information provided to any favoured offeror to a hostile offeror.

16.21 Conditions
Although there are a number of conditions set out in the Rule 2.5 Announcement and repeated in the offer document, the Irish Takeover Panel under Rule 13 will not allow an offeror any subjective conditions and, more importantly, will not let an offer lapse due to conditions unless the circumstances are of material significance to the offeror.

16.22 Financing
The offer document has to contain a cash confirmation statement from the financial advisers to the offeror to the effect that resources are available to the offeror sufficient to satisfy full acceptance of the offer.

16.23 Mixed consideration
It is possible to offer a variety of forms of consideration and typically consideration is either a cash consideration per share or a number of shares in the offeror, credited as fully paid.

17. FOREIGN INVESTMENT CONTROLS
There are no controls on foreign investment into Ireland.

Italy

Ughi e Nunziante Marcello Gioscia & Gianluigi Pugliese

1. GENERAL DESCRIPTION OF THE CAPITAL MARKETS

Under Italian law, a 'financial product' is an umbrella term including very different instruments, such as debentures, managed investment schemes or ordinary equities and certain derivatives.

Both the market and the financial products are basically regulated by Legislative Decree No 58 of 24 February 1998, ie, Consolidated Financial Act (the Consolidated Financial Act).

The *Commissione Nazionale per le Società e la Borsa* (Consob) is the public authority responsible for regulating the Italian securities market.

The Stock Exchange, the primary market, is managed by *Borsa Italiana* SpA (the Italian Stock Exchange Management Company, now part of the London Stock Exchange Group). There are 332 listed companies on the regulated equity markets, and between 2009 and the first quarter of 2010, seven companies had been listed on the recently launched stock regulated multilateral trading facility named AIM Italia. Domestic market capitalisation is approximately EUR 457 billion, equivalent to 30.3 per cent of the gross domestic product.

The main Italian markets are listed below.

i)   The Stock Exchange, which is divided into the following markets:
*   **Electronic Share Market** (MTA). The MTA is the regulated electronic market on which shares, convertible bonds, warrants and option rights are traded. It in turn has four segments:
    a)   Blue Chip (dedicated to companies with a capitalisation above EUR 1 billion);
    b)   STAR (dedicated to companies with a capitalisation between EUR 1 billion and EUR 40 million, operating in the traditional sectors of the economy which voluntarily comply with strict requirements on liquidity, transparency and corporate governance);
    c)   Standard, which groups all small and mid size companies with a capitalisation of between EUR 1 billion and EUR 40 million and not complying with the requirements to be listed on the STAR segment;
    d)   MTA International. In this segment, companies are eligible to admit – without the requirement to publish a prospectus – shares that have been listed on another European regulated market for at least 18 months upon the request by any of *Borsa Italiana*'s market intermediaries, by an issuer or by *Borsa Italiana* itself. Admission is announced in a notice which specifies the trading start date and other relevant details. Dedicated procedures and specific disclosure

obligations (both initial and ongoing, for the care of the applicant) apply.

- **Investment Vehicles Market** (MIV). The MIV is a regulated market on which securities issued by investment vehicles are traded. It is divided into three segments according to the types of financial instruments traded:
  a) Units of closed-end funds segment, where the units of closed-end securities and real estate funds are traded;
  b) Investment companies segment, where shares of investment companies are traded; and
  c) Real Estate Investment Companies (REIC) segment, where shares of the REICs are traded.

- **Electronic Securitised Derivatives Market** (SEDEX), where, through authorised intermediaries, both leverage and investment derivatives are traded. In order to assure investors of the transparency of negotiated products, SEDEX is divided into four segments: plain vanilla covered warrants; structured/exotic covered warrants; leverage certificates; and investment certificates.

- **After-Hours Market** (TAH), the market for trading listed shares that satisfy liquidity requirements established by the Italian Stock Exchange Management Company, covered warrants and certificates outside of MTA and SEDEX trading hours. Securities are traded at the request of the issuer. It is the first regulated European market for trading financial instruments after the closing of the daily market. It has two segments:
  a) Trading After Hours (TAH), for trading shares of the Mib30, S&P/MIB and Midex and covered warrants; and
  b) Trading After Hours *Nuovo Mercato* (TAHX), for trading shares mandatorily assisted, on a compulsory basis, by a liquidity specialist operator during evening hours.

Shares belonging to Blue Chip and Star segments of the MTA can be traded on this market, provided that a liquidity specialist operator is in charge.

ii) the electronic open-end funds and ETCs market (ETFplus) which is the *Borsa Italiana* electronic regulated market where, through authorised intermediaries, it is possible to trade the following financial instruments: ETFs (Exchange Traded Funds), ETCs (Exchange Traded Commodities) and Structured ETFs;

iii) the electronic bond and government securities market (MOT), which is divided into two segments:
  - Domestic MOT, within which financial instruments are divided into two classes according to their characteristics, trading procedures and hours: (i) BOT; BTP; BTPi; CCT; CTZ; and (ii) debt securities in euros or in a currency other than euros; and
  - EuroMOT, which provides for a single market class within which eurobonds, ABSs, foreign securities and other debt securities are traded.

iv) the Derivatives market (IDEM) for trading futures and options contracts whose underlying assets are financial instruments, interest rates, foreign currencies, goods or related indexes.

v) the Alternative Capital Market (MAC) which is a stock regulated multilateral trading facility dedicated to small enterprises. Trading is restricted among professional investors. Admission to the MAC market shall be restricted exclusively to ordinary shares that are not – and have not been in the past – subject to a public offering or traded on other alternative trading systems or on regulated markets. Trading began on 17 September 2007, but so far the number of companies listed has been very low.

vi) AIM Italia which is Borsa Italiana's market dedicated to small and medium-sized Italian enterprises with strong growth potential and is based on the successful model of the London Stock Exchange's AIM. This is a stock regulated multilateral trading facility launched on 1 December 2008. Trading is open to the public and this is one of the key differences from MAC. Following admission, the company's market operations are guided by a Nominated Adviser (Nomad), responsible both for assessing whether the company is appropriate for the market, and for supporting and advising it throughout its membership of the market. The Nomad is regulated by Borsa Italiana.

2. FINANCIAL SERVICES AND MARKETS
2.1 Italian financial services licence
The provision of investment services to the public is reserved to investment firms (SIM, EU investment firms and non-EU investment firms) and banks.

EU investment firms may provide services in Italy according to the principle of mutual recognition by acting cross-border without establishing branches in Italy, provided the Bank of Italy and Consob have been informed by the competent authority of the home country, or by setting up a branch in Italy. The establishment of the first branch by an EU investment firm shall be subject to prior notification to the Bank of Italy and Consob by the competent authority of the home country and the branch will be entitled to commence its business two months after the notification.

Similarly, non-EU investment firms may provide investment services and non-core services without establishing branches in Italy or by means of a branch, subject to the fulfilment of the requirements of the Consolidated Financial Act for Italian investment firms and Consob authorisation.

2.2 Supervisory authorities
In the Italian legal system and with regard to investment firms, Consob and Bank of Italy play a key role in ensuring the correct functioning of the market.

2.2.1 Consob
Consob is the supervisory authority over investment firms and listed companies. It is the public authority responsible for regulating the Italian securities market and for ensuring compliance with the rules for transparency and proper conduct to protect investors. Consob aims to

ensure:
* transparency and correct behaviour by securities market participants;
* disclosure of complete and accurate information to the investing public by listed companies;
* accuracy of prospectuses for offerings of transferable securities to the investing public; and
* compliance with regulations by auditors entered in the Special Register.

2.2.2   Bank of Italy (*Banca d'Italia*)
As the central bank, Bank of Italy has broad powers of supervision not only over banks but also, *inter alia*, over non-bank financial intermediaries, mainly investment firms and collective investment undertakings.
Its responsibilities include the supervision of the sound and prudent management of banking and financial institutions. The supervisory function is based on authorisation, regulation, analysis of companies' situations, inspections, on-site controls and crisis management. The Bank lays down prudential rules on capital adequacy, risk limitation, permissible holdings and company organisation, especially as regards internal controls.

Because properly functioning money and financial markets are needed to limit systemic instability and for an effective monetary policy, the Bank of Italy has been vested with important supervisory powers, particularly with regard to the wholesale markets in government securities, the inter-bank market and trading support services (clearing and final settlement of transactions, central securities depositories, and guarantee systems) and payment systems (the instruments, operators and rules of money transfer).

2.3   The Italian Stock Exchange Management Company
The Italian Stock Exchange Management Company is *Borsa Italiana* SpA, part of the London Stock Exchange Group and is responsible for the organisation and management of the Italian Stock Exchange. In particular, it is responsible for:
* defining and organising the functioning of the markets;
* defining the rules and procedures for admission to listing on the market for issuing companies and brokers;
* managing and overseeing the market; and
* management of listed companies' disclosure.

The Italian Stock Exchange Management Company aims to ensure the development of managed markets, maximising liquidity, transparency and competitiveness while achieving high levels of efficiency and profitability. A fundamental principle is the separation of responsibility for supervision (which rests with Consob and Bank of Italy) from that of market management (Italian Stock Exchange Management Company).

Further to the Italian Stock Exchange there are other regulated markets authorised in Italy which are managed by the company MTS SpA (controlled by *Borsa Italiana* SpA) and on which bonds and government bonds are traded.

2.4 Multilateral trading facilities
The Market in Financial Instruments Directive (MiFID) has extended the
trading venues and opened the way to multilateral trading facilities which
are not regulated markets, but are nevertheless subject to limited supervision
by Consob. *Borsa Italiana*, as well as other companies, has opened a number
of multilateral trading facilities, such as the MAC and AIM Italia (see above)
or EUROTLX (managed by EuroTLX SIM SpA), etc.

3. PUBLIC OFFERING
3.1 Definition and contents
Companies planning a public offering must give notice to Consob, attaching
a prospectus.

This prospectus should contain information necessary for investors to
make an informed assessment of the issuer's assets and liabilities, profits
and losses, financial position and prospects and of the financial products
and related rights and shall be compliant with the forms set out in the EU
Regulation 809/2004/CE.

With regard to non-equity securities issued by banks, the prospectus is
valid until the securities concerned are no longer issued in a continuous or
repeated manner. It is worth noting that Article 100 of the Consolidated
Financial Act states that financial instruments offered only to institutional
investors are exempted from the obligation to publish a prospectus.
However, in order to prevent some form of circumvention of the obligation
to publish a prospectus, Article 100-bis of the Consolidated Financial Act
states that should the institutional investors resell such securities to the
retail investors within one year from their issuance and without publishing a
prospectus, the retail investor may challenge the nullity of the purchase and
the institutional investors remain liable for damages *vis-à-vis* retail investors.

Under Article 98 of the Consolidated Financial Act, implementing in Italy
the Directive 2003/71/CE on the prospectus to be published when securities
are offered to the public or admitted to trading, the prospectus and any
supplements approved by Consob are valid for the purposes of offering EU
financial instruments in other EU member states ('passport'). To this end,
Consob shall issue notice in compliance with the procedure pursuant to EU
provisions. Where the offer of EU financial instruments is provided for in
Italy, the host member state, the prospectus and any supplements approved
by authority of the member state of origin may be published in Italy, as
long as they observe the notification procedures pursuant to European
provisions. Consob may inform the competent authority of the member
state of origin of the need to supply new information. On 11 April 2007
d'Amico International Shipping SA was the first company admitted to listing
only on the Italian market (MTA, Star segment) on the basis of a prospectus
passported in another EU country (Luxembourg).

3.2 Responsibility for defective documents
The persons who usually prepare the offering document are: the offeror;
the issuer; and the person entrusted with the placement (distributor). These

persons shall observe principles of proper conduct and transparency and equal treatment of the addressees of the offering and shall abstain from disseminating information conflicting with the prospectus or likely to influence acceptances.

Under Article 94 of the Consolidated Financial Act, the issuer, offeror and any guarantor, depending on the case, as well as the person responsible for the information contained in the prospectus answer, each in relation to the parts of pertinence, for damages endured by the investor who has reasonably relied on the truthful and complete nature of the information contained in the prospectus, unless they are able to present proof that they took every precaution to ensure that the information in question was conformant with the facts and there were no omissions such as to alter the meaning. The responsibility for false information or for omissions such as to influence the decisions of a reasonable investor, is held by the intermediary responsible for placement, unless they are able to present proof that they took every precaution, as indicated above. No one may be called upon to answer exclusively on the basis of the summary, including any translations, unless the summary is misleading, imprecise or inconsistent when read along with other parts of the prospectus. Claims for compensation must be made within five years of publication of the prospectus, unless the investor can prove the false nature of the information or omissions within the two years prior to the exercise of such claim.

With respect to the liability deriving from a false or incorrect prospectus, Article 173-bis of the Consolidated Financial Act establishes that whoever, with a view to obtaining an undue profit for themselves or for others, in prospectuses required for public offerings or for admission to trading on regulated markets, with the intention of deceiving the recipients of the prospectus, includes false information or conceals data or news in a way that is likely to mislead such recipients, shall be punished by imprisonment for between one and five years.

In addition, according to the general principles of Italian civil law, there are two other types of responsibilities for an incomplete, incorrect, false or misleading prospectus: (i) the civil liability of the person who prepared the prospectus; and (ii) the liability of Consob due to a lack of control.

Since the prospectus is signed by the issuer, the offeror and the placer, liability will fall on them according to their respective roles in providing defective information. The limited case law on this issue indicates that liability for a false prospectus shall be subject to general rules governing the violation of the duty to behave in good faith between the parties to a contract.

Damages may include lost profits.

In addition, case law establishes that Consob may be held liable if it does not accurately exercise its control over the prospectus and is negligent in verifying the completeness and correctness of the information provided.

4. LISTING

4.1 Requirements for stock exchange listing

In order to go public on the Stock Exchange, companies must fulfil both regulatory requirements set down by Consob and market requirements set forth by the Italian Stock Exchange Management Company. The market requirements relate both to the issuer and the shares.

The issuer must have:

- the ability, directly or through its subsidiaries, to generate revenues;
- published and filed consolidated annual accounts for the last three financial years – companies resulting from extraordinary corporate actions or whose assets and liabilities underwent material changes in the financial year preceding may provide pro forma data;
- its latest annual accounts (at least) audited;
- should assets or revenues of the issuer consist of an investment, the issuer must: (i) inform and update the public on its investment policy, specifying the criteria adopted in investment management and in diversification of risks; and (ii) invest and manage its own assets in compliance with the published investment policy;
- appoint an auditing firm to audit its annual accounts enrolled in a special register held by Consob or to a foreign auditing firm having equivalent requirements; and
- if it is controlled by another company, the issuer must have: (i) independent decision-making powers in dealings with customers and suppliers; (ii) a separate treasury or, should its treasury be centralised with that of the controlling company, such cash management must be in the interest of the issuer, pursuant to a justified statement of the board of directors verified by the board of statutory auditors; and (iii) an internal control committee composed of independent directors complying with the requirements laid down by Consob in its regulations.

In addition, there must be:

- free transferability of all shares;
- a free float of shares equal to at least 25 per cent of the company's share capital. *Borsa Italiana* may, however, deem this requirement to be satisfied where the market value of the shares held by the public suggests that the conditions for regular operation of the market can be met by a smaller percentage than that specified above; and
- a foreseeable market capitalisation of at least EUR 40 million. *Borsa Italiana* may admit shares with a smaller market capitalisation where it deems an adequate market for such shares will develop.

Companies must also fulfil disclosure and transparency obligations, such as periodic and price sensitive information, dividends calendar and information concerning extraordinary operations and corporate governance requirements, which basically entail acceptance of the Code of Conduct containing the Corporate Governance Rules of Listed Companies.

Further market requirements are based on real growth and business prospects and include:

- positive economic and financial track record;
- an ambitious but realistic business plan;
- quality and continuity of management;
- adoption of the Code of Conduct regulating internal transactions;
- transparency of ownership and accounting;
- appointment of an investor relations manager.

In order to obtain and maintain the Star status, additional requirements shall be fulfilled. Issuers, among others, must:

- make their quarterly reports available to the public within 45 days of the end of each quarter;
- have received a favourable auditor's report on their latest annual financial statements;
- have assets or revenues that do not preponderantly consist of an investment in, or the results of an investment in, a listed company;
- make available, in Italian as well as in English and on their Web site their financial documentation, price sensitive events and other documents established by the Stock Exchange;
- have identified within their organisation a person with appropriate qualifications specifically charged with investor relations (investor relator);
- have adopted the organisational, operational and control models provided for in Article 6 of legislative decree 231/2001;
- apply, in relation to the composition of the board of directors and the role and functions of non-executive and independent directors, the principles and criteria of the Corporate Governance Code;
- to implement a stock option plan for the remuneration of directors;
- have appointed an internal control committee; and
- have strictly forbidden the members of its management and supervisory bodies, persons performing functions of direction and managers from engaging – directly or by way of nominees – in so-called 'internal dealing'.

It is mandatory to appoint a sponsor to assist the company with the listing process. The sponsor shall also support the listing for at least one year producing research reports and organising meetings with investors.

4.2 Cost of listing

Admission and listing costs for a medium size company can be roughly estimated at between 4 and 5 per cent of the value of the global offer and include:

- fees to the Italian Stock Exchange Management Company: EUR 75 for every EUR 500,000 of market capitalisation, calculated on the basis of the offer price and the company's share capital after the offering, with a floor of EUR 20,000 (for the AIM Italia) and a cap of EUR 500,000 (for any of the MTA, MIV or AIM Italia);
- commissions to the global co-ordinator and other syndicate members;
- fees to legal advisers, public relations and auditors; marketing and roadshow costs, costs of publishing and distributing the prospectus and

Consob fees.

Annual fees to the Italian Stock Exchange Management Company include a fee between EUR 10.70 and 9.60 (depending of the market capitalisation) every six months for every EUR 500,000 of market capitalisation, calculated on the basis of the average for the six preceding months (with a floor of EUR 6,300 and a cap of EUR 215,000 per half-year). There are different fees for Italian and foreign companies already listed on other stock exchange markets.

5. CONTINUING COMPLIANCE REQUIREMENTS
5.1 Obligation to lodge financial documents (introduction)
Issuers of financial instruments and entities controlling them shall promptly inform the public and the market of certain facts. Moreover, they must prepare financial reports for each financial year. Communications with the market shall comply with criteria of correctness, clarity and equal access to information. Issuers of shares listed on regulated markets must prepare half-year and quarterly financial reports. They shall also make certain information regarding a merger or a division available to the public and to the market.

5.2 Continuous disclosure
Issuers of financial instruments, within one day of the approval of the company's annual accounts, shall make the following information available to the public at the authorised storage device (pursuant to the Transparency Directive 2004/109/EC) and on the issuer's Web site, among others:
- annual accounts, the report on operations, the report of the board of auditors, and the minutes of shareholders' and supervisory board meetings (where the minutes are not available within one day of the shareholders' or supervisory board meeting, they shall be made available to the public within seven days);
- the consolidated accounts, if any;
- the reports containing the opinion of independent auditors;
- an integral copy of the annual accounts of subsidiary companies; and
- the summary document showing the essential data of the latest annual accounts of associate companies.

In addition, within four months from the end of the first six months of the financial year, issuers of shares shall make their half-yearly report (with any observations of the internal control body and, if prepared, the report containing the opinion rendered by the independent auditors) available to the public at the authorised storage device (pursuant to the Transparency Directive 2004/109/ EC) and on the issuer's Web site. Half-yearly reports shall comprise:
- for issuers not required to prepare consolidated annual accounts: the financial statements and the notes thereto; or
- for issuers required to prepare consolidated annual accounts: the financial statements of the parent undertaking on a solo basis and the consolidated financial statements of the group and the notes thereto.

Where the notes to the financial statements of the parent undertaking are indispensable for the public to be correctly informed, these shall also be included.

Issuers of shares, within 45 days from the end of each quarter of the financial year, shall make a quarterly report prepared by the board of directors available to the public at the authorised storage device (pursuant to the Transparency Directive 2004/109/ EC) and on the issuer's Web site.

5.3 Disclosure of price sensitive information

Pursuant to Article 114 of the Consolidated Financial Act, listed issuers and the persons that control them shall make available to the public, without delay, inside information, that is 'information of a precise nature which has not been made public relating, directly or indirectly, to one or more issuers of financial instruments or one or more financial instruments and which, if it were made public would be likely to have a significant effect on the prices of those financial instruments'. In addition, persons performing administrative, supervisory and management functions in a listed issuer and managers who have regular access to inside information and the power to make managerial decisions affecting the future development and prospects of the issuer, persons who hold shares amounting to at least 10 per cent of the share capital, and any other persons who control the issuer must inform Consob and the public of transactions involving the issuer's shares or other financial instruments linked to them that they have carried out directly or through nominees. Such disclosures must also be made by the spouse, unless legally separated, dependent children, including those of the spouse, cohabitant parents and relatives by blood or affinity of the persons referred to above and in the other cases identified by Consob in a regulation implementing Directive 2004/72/EC on market abuse.

These disclosure requirements concern both the activities of such persons and the listed financial instruments.

Such inside information should be disclosed by issuing a press release to the Italian Stock Exchange Management Company by the dissemination of regulated disclosures system (SDIR) and also published on the issuer's Web site and in the authorised storage device, which shall immediately make it available to the public. Among other things, listed companies should disclose: (i) accounting data that will be reported in their company or consolidated annual accounts, half-yearly reports or quarterly reports when such data have been communicated to third parties and in any case as soon as the information is sufficiently certain; and (ii) resolutions whereby the competent body approves the draft company annual accounts, the proposed dividend, the consolidated accounts, the half-yearly report, and the quarterly reports.

Italian listed companies that are also listed on a foreign stock exchange should ensure that Italian investors have equal access to any information disclosed to the foreign exchange, even where it goes beyond Italian market requirements.

6. PROHIBITED CONDUCT
6.1 Insider trading
Insider trading can be defined as unauthorised use of inside information. This conduct is unlawful and mainly regulated by Articles 180-184, 186-187-*bis* and 187-*quater*-187-*septies* of the Consolidated Financial Act. Insiders, ie, those who possess inside information by virtue of holding an interest in a company's capital or exercising public or other duties, a profession or an office are prohibited from:

- carrying out transactions on listed instruments (trading);
- the communication of inside information to third parties (tipping); and
- the transmission of investment advice to third parties on the basis of the privileged information or pushing third parties to trade (*tuyautage*).

Law no 62 of 18 April 2004 (the 2004 Community Law) has depenalised any conduct of tippees. As a result, any tippee cannot be punished with imprisonment, even if they committed the offence prior to the depenalisation of the relevant rule (that is to say, 12 May 2005).

However, according to Article 187-bis, paragraph 4, of the Consolidated Financial Act, the conduct of tippees remains subject to pecuniary administrative sanctions of between EUR 100,000 and EUR 15 million.

As mentioned above, Article 181 of the Consolidated Financial Act defines inside information as 'any information having a precise content concerning financial instruments or issuers of financial instruments that has not been made public and that, if made public, would be likely to have a significant effect on the price of such instruments'. The offence is committed by virtue of the use of such particular information and through its simple possession. In particular, paragraph 3, of Article 181 of the Consolidated Financial Act specifies that information shall be deemed to be of a precise nature if:

- it refers to a set of circumstances which exists or may reasonably be expected to come into existence or an event which has occurred or may reasonably be expected to occur; and
- it is specific enough to enable a conclusion to be drawn as to the possible effect of the set of circumstances or events referred to above on the prices of financial instruments.

In addition, the following paragraph 4 clarifies that information which, if made public, would be likely to have a significant effect on the prices of financial instruments, shall mean information a reasonable investor would be likely to use as part of the basis of its investment decisions.

As to the scope of application of the provision, Article 182 of the Consolidated Financial Act establishes that the offence is committed where the trading is carried out: (i) in Italy, in respect of financial instruments admitted, or for which an application has been made for admission, to trading on an Italian regulated market; (ii) in Italy, in respect of financial instruments admitted to trading on an Italian regulated market, even if the instruments are traded in EU regulated markets; and (iii) abroad, provided that the instruments are traded in any Italian regulated market.

In addition, by virtue of paragraph 4 of Article 184 of the Consolidated Financial Act, which includes in the definition of financial instruments also non-listed financial instruments whose value depends on a listed financial instrument, it seems that the criminal offence of insider trading has been extended to this type of non-listed financial instruments.

Consob has the power to investigate insider trading. Article 187-octies of the Consolidated Financial Act establishes that Consob may require information, data or documents from and hear anyone who appears to be acquainted with the facts, and set time limits for the fulfilment of these requirements. Consob can avail itself of the cooperation of governmental bodies and have access to the information system of the taxpayer register.

Insider trading may result in both criminal and civil liability. It can be penalised by imprisonment for up to six years and a fine of between EUR 20,000 and EUR 3 million, which may be tripled depending on the seriousness of the offence. The means used to commit the offence and profits may be confiscated under Article 187 of the Consolidated Financial Act.

6.2 Market manipulation

Market manipulation is considered an offence under Italian law. The new Article 2637 of the Italian Civil Code provides that 'any person who disseminates false information, or sets up sham transactions or other devices concretely likely to produce a significant alteration in the price of financial instruments not admitted, or for which an application has not been made for admission, to trading or to significantly undermine the public's confidence in the soundness of banks or banking groups shall be punished by a term of imprisonment from one to five years.' The aim of the prohibition is to avoid artificial securities prices.

The same prohibition applies where listed securities are concerned; in which case the sanctions set forth under Article 185 of the Consolidated Financial Act are more severe (imprisonment from one to six years and fines from EUR 20,000 to EUR 5 million).

7. TAKEOVERS

7.1 Overview

Public takeovers in Italy are regulated by the Consolidated Financial Act. In addition, Law 287 of 10 October 1990 (the Antitrust law) regulates merger control in Italy in cases not governed by the EU Merger Regulation. The Italian Antitrust Authority examines the effects of takeovers and mergers on competition.

In 2007, Italy implemented Directive 2004/25/EC of the European Parliament and of the Council of 21 April 2004 on takeover bids.

7.2 Takeover process

In Italy, the decision or the arising of the obligation to launch a takeover bid shall be communicated to Consob without delay. In this respect, Consob has established that such communication must contain: (i) the draft offer document and the acceptance form; as well as (ii) the guarantee securing the payment of the consideration or, alternatively, the undertaking to obtain such guarantee prior to the start of the offering period. The communication must contain the essential elements of the offer, the purposes of the offer, details of how the offer will be financed, the guarantees, if any, the offer conditions, the shareholdings already held by the bidder or persons acting in concert with it, and the name of the advisors. The communication shall be released to the market and to the target company.

The offer document must include, *inter alia*:
- information on the bidder and the target (such as major shareholders, members of the board of directors and of board of statutory auditors, and description of the business carried out by the bidder);
- details of the shares being bid for, the consideration offered and the acceptance procedure;
- details of target's securities held by the bidder;
- dealings in the target's securities by the bidder in the last two years;
- consideration offered to the target shareholders and details of how it was calculated;
- bidder's reasons for the bid and its future intentions; and
- agreements, if any, between the bidder and the target or its shareholders or directors.

Consob has 15 days from the filing of the draft document to comment upon it and approve the offer document. Should the documents filed with Consob be incomplete, the bidder shall be informed by Consob and must complete the documentation within 15 days. Should the information be not completed within such term, the offer is stopped and the bidder cannot launch a new offer on the same financial products for the following 12 months. The acceptance period cannot start until the bidder has delivered to Consob the appropriate documentation confirming that the bid is fully guaranteed.

Following Consob's approval, the offer document is published by sending it to the target company and making it available to the market through publication in the press and by Consob. The bidder must agree with the stock exchange the start of the acceptance period and its duration. If the offer is voluntary and for 100 per cent of the target's shares, the period shall be between 25 and 40 market days. Otherwise, the period will range between 15 and 25 market days.

Once the offer plan is publicly announced, the target company becomes subject to the 'passivity rule'.

Until the enactment of Law 2 of 2009, the passivity rule provided for by Italian law required: (i) prior authorisation of the shareholders' meeting (resolving with a favourable vote of at least 30 per cent of the corporate capital) for any act or transaction, other than seeking alternative bids, which may result in the frustration of the public bid; and (ii) a breakthrough rule on lock-up and limitation on voting rights of shares in any shareholders' meeting called to resolve on defensive measures and on the first appointment of the board of directors when, after completion of the bid, the bidder succeeds in holding at least 75 per cent of the voting capital (both through implementation of Articles 9 and 11 of the EU Takeovers

Directive (2004/25/EC)). In addition, in the case of the issue of shares vested with a voting right conditional upon the launch of a public bid, the Italian passivity rule prescribed that such voting right was also conditional upon prior authorisation of the shareholders' meeting as mentioned above (for which shares with conditional voting rights cannot be voted on).

However, implementation of part of the European passivity rule provided by Articles 9 and 11 of the Directive 2004/25/EC was optional for EU member states, which are entitled not to adopt such restrictions and instead to allow local companies to decide whether to apply the passivity and breakthrough regime (Article 12). Even after the implementation of the Directive 2004/25/EC in Italy, Article 13 of Law 2 of 2009 replaced and amended the existing regime, providing that the corporate by-laws of Italian listed companies may provide for the abovementioned prior authorisation of the shareholders' meeting and breakthrough rule. In addition, the restriction on voting rights of shares issued with voting rights conditional to the launch of a public bid no longer applies, with the effect that shares which automatically become voting shares if a public bid is launched are allowed as a defensive measure. Law 2 of 2009 also provides that even if the corporate by-laws of an Italian listed company provide for prior authorisation of the shareholders' meeting and breakthrough rule, a reciprocity principle shall apply. As a result, in the event that an Italian listed company which has adopted such rules becomes the subject of an offer launched by a company which does not apply the passivity and breakthrough rules, or by a company controlled, directly or indirectly, by the latter, the relevant Italian company will automatically become exempt from the passivity and breakthrough rules, even though they are contained in its by-laws.

Finally, additional minor measures to increase the possibility for Italian listed companies to adopt defensive measures against takeover bids, were introduced by Article 7 of Law Decree no. 5 of 10 February 2009, converted into Law no. 33 of 9 April 2009: (i) shareholders vested with stakes higher than 30 per cent but lower than the majority of the voting shares, become subject to the obligation to launch a mandatory public bid, if they consolidate their participation by purchasing more than 5 per cent of the voting capital during a period of 12 months (while the previous threshold was of 3 per cent of the voting capital); and (ii) the maximum number of treasury shares (for both listed and non listed companies) was increased from 10 per cent to 20 per cent of the corporate capital.

The takeover bid transaction is essentially between a bidder and target shareholders. Negotiations with target shareholders are possible and may lead to the execution of an irrevocable undertaking to sell at a certain price. However, the Consolidated Financial Act makes clear that where a competing offer is launched, shareholders who have already accepted an offer may withdraw their acceptances and accept the competing bid instead. Therefore, if during the offer period (ie, from the filing of the draft offer document with Consob until the payment date) the bidder purchases target shares, or acquires the right to purchase them after the offer closes, at a higher price than the offer price, the offer price will have to be increased to this higher price (best price rule).

Shareholders accept the offer by signing an acceptance form made available at the bidder's offices. Such acceptance is irrevocable unless a competing bid is announced. From the bidder's side, Italian law provides that a takeover offer is irrevocable and any clause to the contrary is void.

Subjective conditions (ie, 'conditions which depend on the mere will of the offeror') are not permitted. Therefore, a bid cannot, for example, be conditional on financing, but can be conditional on the attaining of a certain threshold of acceptances (eg, 50 per cent plus one share of the voting capital).

Nevertheless, conditions could include antitrust clearances, regulatory authorisations, no material adverse change in the target and no frustrating action by the target.

Should a person or entity by one or more purchase transaction, acquire a stake made of shares having voting rights in a meeting called to appoint or revoke directors and which is higher than 30 per cent, such person or entity becomes subject to the obligation to launch a takeover bid for 100 per cent of all classes of shares of the same issuer which are listed on a regulated market. Such mandatory bid shall be for a price at least equal to the highest price paid by the bidder in the past 12 months. Mandatory bids cannot be subject to any kind of condition.

8. MANAGED INVESTMENTS SCHEMES (MUTUAL FUNDS)
8.1 Overview (data, evolution of the market and definition)
In Italy, mutual funds shall mean OICR (acronym for *'organismi di investimento collettivo del risparmio'*, ie, undertakings for collective investment in tradable securities – UCITS).

According to Consob, the most popular funds in Italy are open-ended. Harmonised funds (ie, EU investment funds falling within the scope of the directives on collective investment undertakings) that essentially invest in open-ended funds are by far the most common funds in the Italian market.

8.2 Regulation of Managed Investment Schemes (creation, registration, statutory duties, conditions of retiring)
The regulation of mutual funds is basically contained in Chapter II of Title II of the Consolidated Financial Act, ie, Articles 34 to 40.

A mutual investment fund is validly established when two basic conditions are met:

- the fund is promoted and managed by an asset management company duly authorised by the Bank of Italy to provide the service of collective portfolio management;
- the fund rules have been approved by the Bank of Italy, as prescribed by Article 39.

Pursuant to Article 34 of the Consolidated Financial Act, Italian management companies shall fulfil the following main conditions:

- the legal form adopted is that of a joint stock company (*società per azioni*);

- the registered office and the head office of the company are in Italy;
- the paid-up capital is not less than that established on a general basis by the Bank of Italy;
- the persons performing administrative, managerial or control functions fulfil certain experience, independence and integrity requirements;
- the owners of shareholdings fulfil certain integrity requirements;
- the structure of the group of which the company is part is not prejudicial to the effective supervision of the company;
- a programme of initial operations and a description of the organisational structure have been submitted together with the instrument of incorporation and the by-laws;
- the name of the company contains the words '*società di gestione del risparmio*'.

Italian management companies shall also be entered into a special register kept by the Bank of Italy.

Asset management companies are required to organise themselves in a way as to minimise the risk of conflict of interests, bearing in mind that conflict can also arise between portfolios under the same management.

In this respect Article 40 of the Consolidated Financial Act provides that Italian asset management companies must:

- operate diligently, correctly and transparently in the interests of the unit-holders and the integrity of the market;
- organise themselves in such a way as to minimise the risk of conflicts of interest, including conflicts between the pools of assets under management and, where a conflict of interest exists, act in such a way as to ensure the fair treatment of the collective investment undertakings; and
- adopt measures to protect the rights of the unit-holders and have sufficient resources and suitable procedures for the efficient provision of services.

In Italy the custodian must be a bank. In addition, the depository bank must fulfil two kinds of requirements:

- organisational requirements: the bank must be an Italian bank or an EU one with, at least, one branch in Italy; and
- independence requirements: in order to guarantee the independence of the Italian management companies (SGR) the managing director, the chief executive and the members of the management committee of the SGR are not able to assume similar roles within the custodian bank.

Consob regulation No 16190 of 29 October 2007 (Consob Regulation), implementing *inter alia* the provisions of Article 40, requires, *inter alia*, management companies to:

- operate with due diligence, accuracy and transparency in the interests of the investors and market integrity;
- ensure that management activities are performed independently, in compliance with the objectives, investment policy and specific risks of the fund, as indicated in the prospectus;
- acquire adequate knowledge of the financial instruments, assets

and other securities for investment of the managed assets and their liquidation conditions;

- refrain from conduct that could benefit managed assets to the detriment of a third party or customer; and
- operate with a view to limiting costs charged to the managed funds.

Public control of the funds is entrusted to Consob and the Bank of Italy. The Consob is responsible for ensuring compliance with conduct rules and transparency requirements.

Every manager wanting to offer a mutual fund shall draft a prospectus containing the most relevant information to the public, such as the issue, the benchmark or the risk. This prospectus must be approved by the Consob.

The Bank of Italy, after consulting Consob, authorises the management company. In addition, the Bank of Italy shall approve the fund rules containing the main characteristics of the fund (ie the name and duration of the fund; the manner of participating in the fund, the time limits and procedures for the issue and cancellation of certificates and for the subscription and redemption of units, as well as the procedures for winding up the fund; the bodies responsible for the selection of investments and the criteria for the apportionment of investments; the types of goods, financial instruments and other assets in which the fund's assets may be invested; the methods for determining the fund's operating income and profits and, where appropriate, the manner in which the latter are allocated and distributed; details of the expenses to be borne by the fund and those to be borne by the Italian management company; the amount of, or the methods for determining, the commission due to the Italian management company and the charges to be borne by unit-holders; and the manner of making public the value of units).

8.3 Foreign collective investment schemes

The rules for foreign collective investment schemes are different for EU and non-EU entities.

The marketing in Italy of the units of EU investment funds falling within the scope of the directives on collective investment undertakings must be notified in advance to the Bank of Italy and Consob. Marketing may begin following a two-month period running from the date of notification. Among the main requirements for such funds are that they cannot invest more than 5 per cent of their assets in securities offered by a single issuer.

The marketing in Italy of the units of investment funds not falling under the directives on collective investment undertakings shall be authorised by the Bank of Italy, after consulting Consob, provided the operating arrangements are compatible with those prescribed for Italian undertakings.

Japan

Anderson Mori & Tomotsune Kunihiko Morishita*

1. GENERAL DESCRIPTION OF THE CAPITAL MARKETS
1.1 Number of companies listed
Japan's capital markets have remained an important source of funding despite the recent downturn in market conditions. As of 1 December 2010, there were 1,675 companies listed on the First Section of the Tokyo Stock Exchange (TSE), 436 on the Second Section, and 181 companies listed on Mothers, the market for the high-growth and emerging stocks. With its current market capitalisation of about Yen 306 trillion and a daily trading value of around Yen 2.7 trillion (as of 10 December 2010), the TSE, founded in 1949, continues to drive Japan's capital markets. The country has five other stock exchanges, the Osaka Securities Exchange, the Nagoya Stock Exchange, the Sapporo Securities Exchange, the Fukuoka Stock Exchange and the Jasdaq Securities Exchange (integrated into the Osaka Securities Exchange in October 2010). Foreign companies are also eligible for listing on the TSE. According to the TSE's Web site, as of 1 December 2010, there were 12 foreign companies listed on the TSE (including the First Section and Mothers). Many Japanese companies have a global presence and several are listed on markets abroad.

In 2009, Tokyo AIM was established as an alternative investment market for professional investors, open also to foreign issuers. As of 1 December 2010, however, no issuer has been listed on Tokyo AIM.

1.2 Total volume and market value
See 1.1

1.3 Issue activity
See 1.1

1.4 Takeover activity
The number of takeover bids against Japanese companies has been generally increasing since late 1990s (information as of the writing of this book).

1.5 Hostile takeover attempts
See 1.4

2. REGULATORY STRUCTURE
2.1 General
Key statutes and regulations affecting the securities markets include:

- the Financial Instruments and Exchange Act (FIEA) (Law No. 25 of 1948, as amended) which regulates the issuance, placement and trading of category I securities, such as corporate shares, corporate bonds and interests or shares in investment trusts and investment corporations, and of category II securities, such as interests in collective investment schemes, as defined by the FIEA, (collectively, FIEA Securities) and regulates the primary and secondary markets of FIEA Securities in Japan; the FIEA regulates financial transactions in a cross-sectoral manner including various derivatives, commodity funds, partnerships, investment advisory/management services, investment trusts, etc.; the FIEA also regulates the dealing, brokering, underwriting and distribution (acting as a selling group member in a public offering), and arranging of private placement of FIEA securities by foreign securities firms;
- the Law Concerning Investment Trusts and Investment Corporations (ITICL) (Law No. 198 of 1951), which regulates investment trusts and investment corporations, both domestic and foreign, including the establishment and operation of investment corporations registered as such under the ITICL, while the operation of domestic investment trust management companies registered as such under the FIEA are primarily regulated by the FIEA;
- the Foreign Exchange and Foreign Trade Act (FEA) (Law No. 228 of 1949, as amended), which regulates, among others, the issuance and sale in Japan of securities denominated in foreign currencies by non-residents to residents; and
- the rules of the Japan Securities Dealers Association (JSDA Rules).

The Financial Instruments Business regulated under the FIEA is defined to collectively include engaging in derivative transactions, providing investment advisory/management services, as well as various securities-related businesses.

Those who are engaged in the Financial Instruments Business must be registered pursuant to the FIEA. The relevant key registration requirements are illustrated in the chart below.

Classification	Major requirements for registration
Financial Instruments Business (Type I)	Adequate staffing is required. Minimum capital requirement of Yen 50 million. Capital adequacy requirement is applicable. The scope of eligible business is restricted.
Financial Instruments Business (Type II)	Adequate staffing is required. Minimum capital requirement of Yen 10 million. Depositing requirement of Yen 10 million.
Investment Management Business	Adequate staffing is required. Minimum capital requirement of Yen 50 million. The scope of eligible business is restricted.
Investment Advisory Business	Depositing requirement of Yen 5 million.

Trading (dealing, brokering, distribution) of category I securities falls under the Financial Instruments Business (Type I), and trading of category II securities falls under the Financial Instruments Business (Type II). Also, public offering or private placement by the issuer ('self offering') of certain category II securities as well as that of certain category I securities such as interests in investment trusts (see 3.3 below) falls under Financial Instruments Business (Type II).

2.2 Regulation of the offering of new securities
See 3.1

2.3 Differences between local and foreign companies
See 3.1

2.4 Admission to trading on a regulated market
Each stock exchange in Japan has established its rules and standards for admitting securities for trading. The rules to be promulgated by stock exchanges (and any amendment thereto) are subject to the approval of the Financial Services Agency (FSA).

2.5 Financial promotion
Not relevant.

2.6 Rule books
Not relevant.

3. REGISTRATION OF THE ISSUER AND SECURITIES
3.1 Registration requirements
The following is a summary of the Japanese regulatory regime applicable to primary public offerings of category I securities. Similar regulations are applicable to secondary public offerings of category I securities.

Definition of public offerings
A 'primary public offering' is defined in the FIEA to mean any solicitation of offers to purchase newly issued FIEA Securities which is made: (i) to 50 or more persons (calculated by counting persons solicited (offerees), rather than actual subscribers, and excluding qualified institutional investors (as defined below) if such a placement satisfies certain requirements under the FIEA); or (ii) otherwise in a manner which does not qualify as a private placement.

If FIEA Securities are simultaneously offered in and outside Japan, only offerees in Japan are counted for the purpose of the above threshold. If any FIEA Securities of the same kind as are the subject of solicitation have been issued during the six-month period preceding the scheduled issue date, then offerees in Japan of the preceding issue will count towards the threshold.

Filing of a securities registration statement (SRS)
In addition to obtaining informal prior approval from the relevant Local

Finance Bureau (LFB) of the Ministry of Finance through prior discussions of the outline and structure of the public offering, a primary public offering of FIEA Securities requires the issuer, except in certain limited cases, to file with the relevant LFB (via an electronic filing system) an SRS. Non-compliance with the requirement or misrepresentation or omission of material facts in an SRS may open the issuer to liability for damages incurred by investors (see 9.2). If any such material misrepresentation is found in an SRS, or in certain other circumstances, the issuer will be required to file an amendment to the SRS. FIEA Securities offered in a public offering may be acquired or sold only after the registration has become effective, which in principle will occur 15 days after the filing of the relevant SRS.

Detailed information regarding the securities (including the terms and conditions of offering) and the issuer must be disclosed in the SRS. Generally speaking, the disclosure requirements for foreign issuers are similar to those for Japanese issuers, but certain additional information, including a brief summary of the legal system of the issuer's jurisdiction (ie, company law, foreign exchange and tax regulations), will also be required. In addition, the financial statements for the latest two fiscal years of the corporate issuers included in the SRS must be audited and certified by an independent certified public accountant or an audit corporation licensed to practice in Japan or registered in Japan as a foreign audit corporation.

3.2 Other requirements
See 3.1

3.3 Nature of securities
FIEA Securities are defined to include: (i) category I securities, such as shares of stock corporations, and debt securities, such as corporate bonds, as well as interests or shares in investment trusts or investment corporations which invest primarily in 'specified assets' (which are defined in the ITICL to be, among other things, FIEA Securities, derivatives (including securities derivatives, currency derivatives, commodity derivatives, etc), ownership or leasehold of real property, monetary claims, promissory notes, commodities); and (ii) category II securities, such as beneficial interests in trusts and interests in collective investment schemes (including a certain type of domestic and foreign partnership, etc), whereby participants contribute money or equivalent non-monetary assets to a certain project, the profit/loss of which are distributed among such participants.

Category II securities are, in principle, exempt from the public disclosure requirements. However, interests in collective investment schemes investing mainly in FIEA Securities are not exempt. The primary public offering of such non-exempt category II securities is defined in the FIEA to mean any solicitation of offers to purchase newly issued securities which causes such securities to be held by 500 or more persons who respond to the solicitation.

4. SUPERVISORY AUTHORITIES
As summarised by the chart below, powers rest primarily with the Prime

Minister (*naikaku souri daijin*), who heads the Cabinet Office (*naikaku fu*) in Japan. However, some powers are delegated to the Commissioner of the FSA, which is established as an external organ of the Cabinet Office. Other powers of the Prime Minister are delegated to the Securities and Exchange Surveillance Commission (*shoken torihiki tou kanshi iinnkai*) which is established as a lower commission of the FSA, and to the Director-General of the LFB.

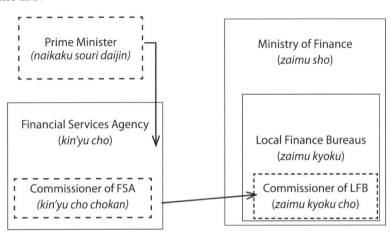

The Japan Securities Dealers Association has, as an authorised self-regulated organisation, certain supervisory powers over its member firms.

4.1 Conduct: prudential, cooperation, self-regulation stock exchange
See 1 and 4 above.

4.2 New listing measures in connection with the credit crisis
See question 8.

5. OFFERING DOCUMENTATION OR PROSPECTUS REQUIREMENTS
5.1 Nature and statutory requirements of the offering document or disclosure document
Under the FIEA, a prospectus complying with FIEA regulations must in principle be prepared and delivered to investors in connection with a public offering of FIEA Securities. The information to be contained in the prospectus (including amendments or supplements thereto) is virtually identical to that required in the main part of the relevant SRS (except in the case of a prospectus for domestic and foreign investment trusts, where a simplified 'summary' prospectus must be used). Any misrepresentation or omission of material facts in a prospectus may expose the issuer to liability for damages incurred by investors (see 9.2). If an amendment to the SRS is filed with the relevant LFB, the issuer will in practice be required to also prepare a supplementary prospectus and deliver it to investors in due course.

5.2 Exemptions
5.2.1 SRS exemption
Under the FIEA, an issuer of FIEA Securities with an aggregate issue or offer price of less than Yen 100 million, or to which certain circumstances apply, may be exempt from the SRS filing and prospectus delivery requirements applicable to primary public offerings. However, they will be required to file with the relevant LFB a securities notification (SN) outlining the issue in a prescribed form. The information to be included in an SN is much simpler than that required in an SRS. An SN is not available for public inspection, as opposed to an SRS. With regard to the voluntary use of an explanatory memorandum describing the offered securities, see (2)(b) below.

5.2.2 Private placement

Definition of private placement
The following is a summary of the Japanese regulatory regime applicable to the private placement in Japan of category I securities.

A 'private placement' is defined in the FIEA to mean, in essence, the solicitation of offers to purchase newly issued FIEA Securities which is made either: (i) to fewer than 50 offerees (a 'small number placement'); (ii) only to certain qualified institutional investors (a 'professional placement'); or (iii) subject to certain other circumstances as prescribed in the FIEA.

All of these instances are subject to conditions including restrictions on transferability, which vary depending on the type of FIEA Securities.

'Qualified institutional investors' (*tekikaku kikan toshika*) are defined under the FIEA and include: financial instrument firms, investment corporations, banks, insurance companies, certain other government-owned financial institutions and credit associations; and large corporations, foreign financial institutions and government agencies, etc that meet certain requirements prescribed under the FIEA.

As mentioned in 4.1 above, the number of qualified institutional investors will be excluded in calculating compliance with the 50-offeree threshold applicable to primary public offerings, if the relevant placement also satisfies certain other requirements under the FIEA. If any FIEA Securities of the same kind as the subject of the relevant placement have been issued during the six-month period preceding the scheduled issue date of such a placement, then offerees in Japan of the preceding issue will count towards the threshold.

Other requirements
There is no requirement to file an SRS or to deliver a prospectus in the case of a private placement of FIEA Securities.

Although a prospectus is not required, the issuer may choose to use an explanatory memorandum and other offering materials. If such documents are used, the issuer will be liable for damages incurred to investors due to a misstatement or omission of a material fact.

5.3 Preparation of the offering document, general contents
See question 5.1

5.4 Due diligence
Not relevant.

5.5 Responsibility
See question 9.

5.6 Disclaimer/selling restrictions
Not relevant.

5.7 Recognition of prospectuses by other exchanges
Not relevant.

5.8 Supplementary prospectuses
See question 5.1

5.9 Issuing of bonds
See question 3.1

6. DISTRIBUTION SYSTEMS
Not relevant in our material.

7. PUBLICITY
Not relevant in our material.

8. LISTING
8.1 Special listing requirements, admission criteria
A foreign entity seeking to list on the TSE must meet certain requirements including:

8.1.1 Numeral criteria

Shares
The TSE listing rules stipulate that at least 4,000 'trading units' must be listed. A trading unit is fixed according to the average closing price of shares on the entity's home stock exchange on a record date before the listing application.

Shareholders in Japan
At least 800 shareholders in Japan must be expected by the time of listing.

Market capitalisation
The market capitalisation must be expected to be Yen 2 billion or more at the time of listing.

Shareholders' equity
Net assets on a consolidated basis of Yen 1 billion or more as of the end of the latest business year is required.

Profit or total market capitalisation
The foreign entity must satisfy either the profitability or the market capitalisation criteria.

Amount of profit test
The foreign entity must satisfy either of the following:
- two-year standard
  - the first year: Yen 100 million or more
  - the most recent year: Yen 400 million or more
- three-year standard
  - the first year: Yen 100 million or more
  - the most recent year: Yen 400 million or more
  - total for three years: Yen 600 million or more

Profits (pre-tax profit on a consolidated basis) are calculated in accordance with the TSE listing rules.

Total market capitalisation
The total market capitalisation of such a foreign entity is expected to be Yen 100 billion or more at the time of listing, with revenues in the latest business year exceeding Yen 10 billion.

Audited financial statements
There shall be no misstatements contained in the latest two year financial statements. In principle, an 'unqualified' or 'qualified' opinion must be issued by an independent auditor for the latest two year financial statements. An 'unqualified opinion' must be issued by an accounting firm for the latest financial statement.

Corporate history
The entity should operate its business with a board of directors on a continuous basis for at least three years.

8.1.2 Other criteria
These include good corporate management, going concern and good business prospects and appropriate corporate disclosure in accordance with the TSE listing rules. The TSE will consider if an applicant meets the above-mentioned requirements. The applicant will normally have many discussions with the TSE officers in order to demonstrate its eligibility for listing.

8.2 Mechanics of the review process
Generally speaking, a foreign applicant should arrange for a preliminary examination of its application at least several months prior to the targeted

listing date. After the examination, the foreign entity should file its application for listing well before the targeted listing date, with sufficient time for the statutory timeline of a public offering as set out in section 3 above.

8.3 Prospectus obligation, due diligence, exemption
See question 5.1

8.4 Appeal procedure in the event of a prospectus refusal
Not relevant.

8.5 Authority of the Exchange
See question 8.1

8.6 Sponsor
Securities firms which have a Type I Financial Instruments Business registration normally act as a sponsor and provide necessary support to an issuer for listing.

8.7 Special arrangements for smaller companies such as Alternext, AIM or SPACS
See question 1.1.

8.8 Costs of various types
The TSE requires the following fees to be paid by the applicant: (i) listing examination fee; (ii) fee for initial public offering and listing; and (iii) annual listing fee and fee for issuance and listing of new shares.

9. SANCTIONS AND DISPUTES
9.1 Disciplinary and administrative sanctions

Rescission rights of purchasers and legal actions
The rescission of a purchase of securities is covered by the Civil Code (Law No. 89 of 1896, as amended) (Civil Code) and the Consumer Contracts Law (CCL) (Law No. 61 of 2000, as amended). The Civil Code applies when the rescission is between general purchasers and sellers; the CCL where the purchaser is a consumer. Under the Civil Code, rescission can be exercised in cases of fraud (which has a legal limitation of five years from the time the fraud became possible to detect, or 20 years from the time of the occurrence of fraud), or mistake (which has no written limitation).

Administrative sanctions
A surcharge (administrative penalty) system was introduced on 1 April 2005. The system of the surcharge was reviewed and amended in 2008, raising the amount of penalties imposed and expanding the coverage of violations. Those subject to the surcharge include:
- those who offered securities by disclosing documents containing

misstatements;
* those who failed to file ongoing disclosure documents;
* those who conducted a tender offer by disclosing documents containing misstatements;
* those who failed to make a public notice for commencing a tender offer, or to file a tender offer notification;
* those who sold or purchased the securities by spreading rumours or by fraud;
* those who sold or purchased securities for the purpose of manipulation (including illegal market stabilisation); and
* those who were involved in a company and sold or purchased securities with the knowledge of undisclosed material facts about the company (in short, those who committed insider trading).

The amount of surcharge is based on the economic benefit obtained.

There is a system for reduced surcharge (in the case of early reporting).

9.2 Civil actions

If an SRS contains a material misstatement or an omission of a material fact, the issuer of the FIEA securities will be liable, pursuant to the provisions of the FIEA, for damages sustained by a purchaser of such FIEA securities through the public offering, unless the purchaser was aware of the untruth or omission at the time of purchase. Strict liability applies; therefore there is no need to prove the issuer's negligence. Damages are calculated as being the difference between the purchase price of the securities and the current market price (or the estimated sales price if no market price is available). If the purchaser has already sold the securities, the price obtained will be used as the basis of the calculation. The issuer can reduce the damages by proving that there was some reason for the fall in the value of the securities other than the misstatement or omission. Liability may also attach directly to the responsible officers of the issuer, the vendor of shares in the secondary offerings, and independent auditors who certified false financial statements. In this context, 'officers' is defined in the FIEA to include directors, corporate auditors or any other officers of the issuer.

Unlike the issuer, officers, selling shareholders and independent auditors may only be liable if damage was actually caused by the material misstatement or omission. In their case, the measure of damages is not provided for in the statute. Also, officers and shareholders who are selling their shares have a defence if they did not know, and despite exercising reasonable care could not have known, of any material misstatement or omission. Independent auditors similarly have a defence if their certification of false financial statements was neither intentional nor negligent. It is possible that the liability of officers and independent auditors for misstatements or omissions in an SRS may extend to purchases not made in a public offering (such as purchases in the secondary market).

Although the FIEA is silent on this issue, and there is no judicial precedent on point, an argument for such liability could be made based on general tort principles. Statutory liability under the FIEA is also applicable to material misstatements or omissions in continuous disclosure documents incorporated by reference into an SRS of a seasoned issuer and certain documents for a 'shelf' registration and the reports for continuous disclosure referred to in such documents. The FIEA provides for similar liability with respect to a 'securities report' and other documents which are prepared as part of the ongoing disclosure requirements (see 9.1).

There are no special court procedures for liability under the FIEA or for the criminal penalties described below. Regular Japanese civil or criminal procedures are applicable.

9.3 Criminal penalties
Issuers and officers of issuers knowingly responsible for material misstatements in an SRS filed for a public offering of securities in a foreign corporation may be punished by penal servitude of up to 10 years and/or a fine of up to Yen 10 million, under the FIEA. Failure to file an SRS is punishable by penal servitude of up to five years and/or a fine up to Yen 5 million. Failure to file an amendment to an SRS is punishable by penal servitude of up to one year and/or a fine of up to Yen 1 million. Violations of the 'shelf' registration system attract similar penalties. When a representative, agent or other employee of a juridical person is guilty of any such offences on behalf of that person, the juridical person may be fined as well. For example, if a representative, officer or employee of the issuer knowingly prepared and filed with the LFB an SRS containing a material misstatement, they would be subject to penal servitude and/or a fine, and the issuer would be subject to a fine of up to Yen 700 million.

Issuers and officers of issuers knowingly responsible for material misstatements in a tender offer notification filed for a tender offer may be punished by penal servitude of up to 10 years and/or a fine of up to Yen 10 million, under the FIEA. Failure to file a tender offer notification is punishable by penal servitude of up to five years and/or a fine up to Yen 5 million.

Penalties for insider trading include penal servitude for up to five years and/or a fine of up to Yen 5 million. Confiscation of property acquired through insider trading, or an amount equivalent to the value of such property, is another possible penalty.

10. CONTINUING OBLIGATIONS
10.1 Disclosure and transparency rule
The foreign issuer of FIEA Securities is required to make continuous disclosure by filing a securities report for every annual fiscal period and a semi-annual report for the first six months, within six months and three months respectively from the end of the period (in addition, a quarterly report and internal control report (on an annual basis) is required under the FIEA for companies whose shares are listed in a stock exchange in Japan). Filing may only be discontinued if the number of holders of the FIEA Securities in Japan falls to 25 or fewer and with approval from the authority. Like the SRS, the securities report must contain audited financial statements certified by an independent certified public accountant or an auditing corporation licensed in

Japan or a foreign audit firm etc registered with the FSA. In addition, audited reports on internal control procedures are required under the FIEA for listed companies. Interim financial statements of a foreign filer as a component of the semi-annual report (or, as the case may be, a quarterly report) need not be audited or reviewed, although a domestic issuer must file audited or reviewed interim financial statements. The accountant's report does not need to be attached to a semi-annual report or a quarterly report, regardless of the rules in the foreign filer's jurisdiction. Upon the occurrence of certain material events, the foreign filer should file an extraordinary report.

10.2 Information
Japanese versions of the SRS, securities reports, semi-annual reports, quarterly reports, internal control reports and extraordinary reports are made generally available for inspection on the FSA's Web site. SNs, however, are not open for public review, as mentioned above.

10.3 Listing rules
Listing rules require a listed issuer to make timely disclosure, in which an issuer is required to make announcements of certain material events as soon as such an event is decided or occurs.

10.4 Obligations regarding proxy solicitation
Not relevant.

10.5 Continuing requirements of reporting and notification of substantial shareholdings or a substantial transaction
See questions 10.1 and 10.3

10.6 Clearing
Not relevant.

10.7 Requirements for unlisted issuers
See question 10.1.

11. CORPORATE GOVERNANCE
11.1 Law and/or code
The Companies Act (CA) (Law No. 86 of 2005, as amended) which came into effect as of 1 May 2006, modified a number of corporate systems previously existing under the former Commercial Code.

Flexibility in internal governance system
The CA allows for a wide variety of selection and combination of internal governance systems for a Japanese stock corporation (*kabushiki kaisha*), particularly in the case of small and medium sized companies, however the choice of the internal governance scheme for large sized companies and public companies (see definition in 11.2) remains substantially the same as those permitted under the former Commercial Code.

Establishment of internal control system

The CA requires large size companies without committees, as well as those with committees, to establish internal control systems with respect to particular matters as described in the ordinances. A 'large size' company is a company having either: (i) Yen 500 million or more paid-in capital; or (ii) Yen 20 billion or more debt on its balance sheet as of the end of the immediately preceding fiscal year. A company with committees must establish an audit committee, a nominating committee and a compensation committee. More than half of the members of each committee must be outside directors. A large size company with committees must have one or more executive officers (*shikkoyaku*) and one or more representative executive officers who represent the company. A large size company without committees must have one or more representative directors from the board of directors who represent the company. The board of directors appoints one or more representative directors from among its directors. In addition, a large size company without committees must have a board of corporate auditors that consists of one or more corporate auditors that supervise the directors' performance of their duties. Half or more of the members of the board of corporate auditors must be outside corporate auditors.

Under the CA, an 'outside director' is a director of any stock corporation who is neither an executive director nor an executive officer, nor an employee of the company or its subsidiaries, nor who has ever been an executive officer, or an employee of the company or any of its subsidiaries.

11.2 Management structure

Public companies (any company that issues at least one class of shares without restrictions on transfers) need to establish a board of directors. The board of directors, which consists of individuals appointed at the shareholders' meeting, determines the company's business and supervises the actual business operations. The relationship between the company and its directors is governed by the law relating to fiduciary relationships, and directors have a duty to conduct the business of the company 'faithfully' with the standard of care of a good manager. The standard of care is higher than that expected in one's own business. Directors also have a duty to abide by the law, the articles of incorporation of the company and the resolutions of the general meetings of the shareholders.

11.3 Obligations to publish information on the Internet

Not relevant.

11.4 Responsibility of inside/outside directors

See question 11.1.

11.5 Committees

See question 11.1.

11.6 Obligation to ask for consent of a shareholders' meeting
Certain material events (such as amendments to a company's articles of incorporation and most corporate reorganisation transactions) are subject to shareholders' approval in accordance with the CA.

11.7 Depth of information - proxy solicitation
The CA requires a stock corporation to provide in its convocation notice for a shareholders' meeting certain information that is important for the voting of shareholders.

11.8 Appointment/dismissal of directors
See question 11.2.

11.9 Income and options for directors
Directors' and other officers' compensation can be paid either in cash or options but are subject to shareholders' approval and detailed disclosure requirements under the laws and regulations.

11.10   Earnings guidance
Earnings are calculated in accordance with generally accepted accounting standards of Japan and dividends are subject to limitation based on a complicated calculation of adjusted retained earnings under the CA.

11.11   Management discussion and analysis (MD&A)
A detailed description of MD&A is required in a securities report. See question 10.1.

11.12   Directors' liability
Directors, corporate auditors and executive officers who violate the CA may face severe penalties such as criminal fines of up to Yen 10 million and/or penal servitude for up to 10 years in cases of serious and deliberate breaches of trust against the company and causing damage to the company. Several less serious offences attract lighter penalties. Third parties dealing in good faith with a company in transactions in the ordinary course of business will be protected even when such transactions were not duly authorised by the board of directors and, in principle, the company will be bound by actions taken on behalf of the company by a representative director.

12. MARKET ABUSE
12.1. Insider trading

Overview
The FIEA prohibits an affiliate of a listed company who obtains significant inside information as a result of the affiliate's relationship to the listed company from purchasing or selling any listed securities of the company until the information has been publicly disclosed. The FIEA also prohibits the purchase or sale of such listed securities by recipients of significant inside

information who have obtained such information from affiliates.
Affiliates include:

- directors, executive officers, corporate auditors, agents and employees of a listed company;
- shareholders or members of a listed company who hold 3 per cent or more of the company's shares and are entitled to inspect its financial records;
- persons entitled by law to obtain certain information concerning the company, including government officials in charge of licences and reports relevant to the listed company;
- persons who have entered into or are negotiating a contract with the company; and
- officers and employees of companies who meet the criteria in the second or fourth points above.

Recipients
A recipient is any person to whom an affiliate in possession of any significant inside information knowingly transmits such information. Where the recipient is an officer or employee of a company who has received the significant inside information in connection with their employment functions or duties, the insider trading rules will apply *mutatis mutandis* to any other officers and employees of the company who have received the significant inside information in connection with their employment functions or duties.

Listed securities
Listed securities include corporate bonds (including convertible bonds and bonds with warrants), warrants, shares (stock) or securities representing a subscription right to new shares that are listed on a securities exchange or are traded in an organised over-the-counter market in Japan. (As of writing this chapter, there was no eligible over-the-counter market in Japan).

Listed company
A listed company is a company that issues one or more types of listed securities. The definitions of 'affiliates' and 'significant inside information' of a listed company may include affiliates and significant inside information of the parent company or a subsidiary of the listed company.

Significant inside information
Significant inside information is any information that has not been publicly disclosed regarding the operations, business or assets of a listed company that would have a material influence on an investor's decision to buy or sell the company's securities. It includes: dividend changes; release of earnings estimates; changes in previously released earnings estimates; significant merger or acquisition proposals or agreements; significant new product developments; product recalls; major litigation; financial or liquidity problems and extraordinary management developments. Significant inside information with respect to straight bonds is limited to certain information regarding the issuer's

credit standing (such as the filing of a petition for insolvency procedures).

Disclosure

Significant inside information is disclosed to the public when it is included in certain disclosure documents filed pursuant to the FIEA or after 12 hours has passed since an announcement (eg, by a press release) made by the listed company to any two or more media outlets such as daily, general topic newspapers, news wire services, daily industrial or economic newspapers or radio and television service companies. If the press release is made through an electronic disclosure system operated by a stock exchange (such as the TDnet system operated by the TSE), the information is regarded to have been 'disclosed' immediately.

12.2 Market manipulation

Market manipulation (both informational and transactional) is strictly prohibited under FIEA.

12.3 Miscellaneous
Codes of conduct

Some companies bolster their insider dealing controls with internal codes of conduct. Generally, employees must keep the information confidential, and only disclose significant inside information to other employees who need to know it, and refrain from trading in the company's listed securities. Corporate compliance departments monitor the market for prohibited trades.

13. MUTUAL OR INVESTMENT FUNDS
13.1 Introduction to these two categories

There is no distinction between mutual funds and investment funds under the FIEA and the ITICL. Instead, the FIEA and the ITICL broadly classify these funds as contractual type funds (investment trusts) and corporate type funds (investment corporations). A foreign investment fund is usually categorised as either one of these two types according to its structure and nature. A domestic contractual type fund is further sub-classified into investment trusts managed: (i) by investment trust management companies; and (ii) by trustees in Japan. An investment fund which takes the form of a limited partnership is categorised as a collective investment scheme and will be subject to significantly different requirements. See questions 2.1 and 3.3.

13.2 Investment companies, open-ended, close-ended

Although both open-ended and closed-ended types of investment funds are accepted in Japan, open-ended type funds are more commonly seen than closed-ended type funds, whereas corporate type funds (such as real estate investment trust (REIT) funds) are mostly closed-ended type funds.

13.3 Licence requirements

An issuer of interests or shares in a foreign investment trust or an investment corporation must file a notification with the FSA pursuant to the ITICL prior to the marketing of such interests or shares (regardless of whether it is a primary public offering or a private placement), in addition to the filing of an SRS or an SN, where applicable.

The establishment and management of a foreign investment trust or investment corporation outside Japan itself does not require a licence or registration in Japan. There is no notable difference between undertakings for collective investments in transferable securities (UCITS) funds and non-UCITS funds in regard to the licence requirements as well other requirements. See questions 2.1 and 3.3 for other requirements.

13.4 Continuing requirements
Publicly offered investment funds are subject to ongoing disclosure requirements that are similar to those of corporations. See section 10.

In addition to the above, in accordance with the ITICL, certain modifications to the terms and conditions of investment funds are subject to procedural requirements, including prior notification to the FSA and prior notice to the investors in Japan.

13.5 Custodians
Not relevant.

13.6 Undertakings for collective investments in transferable securities (UCITS)
See question 13.3.

13.7 Non-UCITS funds
See question 13.3.

13.8 Hedge funds
Currently there are no regulations which are specifically applicable to hedge funds.

13.9 Marketing and distribution requirements
See question 2.1 for the licence (registration) requirements in respect of the marketing and distribution of fund interests in Japan. See question 13.3 concerning the prior notification requirement under the ITICL.

13.10   Manager
See question 13.3.

14. SECURITIES INSTITUTIONS
Not relevant.

15. NOTIFICATION OBLIGATIONS
15.1 Notification of major shareholding

Large holding report
In the case where an investor acquiring voting shares of a listed company (the 'issuer') has become, either solely or jointly with certain 'joint holders' (as defined below), a holder of more than 5 per cent of the total outstanding shares of the issuer, the investor must file a large holding report with the competent LFB within five business days from the date when the aggregate holding ratio of the investor and its joint holders crosses the 5 per cent threshold holding.

A 'holder' for this purpose includes not only a party who beneficially holds the shares, whether in its own name or in the name of others, but also the following:
- a party who is empowered by contract (eg, trust agreement) or law to exercise, or otherwise instruct others to exercise, voting rights of the shares and has the intention of controlling the business operations of the issuer; and
- a party who has discretionary authority to invest in the shares pursuant to a contract (eg, a discretionary investment management contract) or law.

A holder further includes a person who (i) has the right to demand delivery of the shares under a purchase agreement or other contract; (ii) has made an advance engagement for the purchase of shares; or (iii) has acquired a call option for the purchase of shares.

The large holding report requirement also applies to an acquisition of voting shares of a foreign company, as long as the relevant shares are listed on a stock exchange in Japan and the acquisition of the relevant shares is effected in Japan.

'Joint holder' means a holder of voting shares of the issuer:
- with whom a holder has agreed to jointly acquire, transfer or exercise the voting shares; or
- who is directly or indirectly controlling, controlled by or under common control with the holder.

Report on change
A holder who is required to file a large holding report must file a report ('report on change') within five business days when the aggregate holding ratio of the holder and its joint holders increases or decreases by 1 per cent or more of the total outstanding shares of the issuer as compared with the percentage at the time of the previously filed large holding report or report on change. A report on change also needs to be filed within five business days upon the occurrence of any change to certain matters, including the following:
- the trade name or address of the reporting company;
- a material arrangement/agreement concerning the shares of the issuer held by the holder (eg, provision of the shares as collateral); or
- a decrease or increase in the number of joint holders.

Special report

In lieu of the large holding reports and the reports on change, a holder who meets certain requirements: (i) as an institutional investor (including one that has Type I Financial Instruments Business registration, investment management company, bank, insurance company, or foreign equivalents of the foregoing); or (ii) as a non-institutional joint holder of an institutional investor and who has no intention of controlling or making certain material proposals on the business activities of the issuer, may elect to file a much simplified 'special report' on a bi-weekly basis, with regard to a holding over 5 per cent or an increase or decrease of a holding by 1 per cent or more. In order to be eligible to file a 'special report', the aggregate holding ratio of the holder and its non-institutional joint holders must not exceed 10 per cent, and the holding ratio of the non-institutional joint holders must not exceed 1 per cent of the total number of outstanding shares of the issuer.

16. PUBLIC TAKEOVERS

16.1 Applicable laws and regulations or regulatory framework

When an investor wishes to acquire: (i) shares of a listed company or other companies subject to continuous disclosure obligations (see 10.1); or (ii) bonds convertible into, warrants exercisable over, options for purchase of or depository receipts for such shares (otherwise than through trading on a stock exchange or an organised over-the-counter market, which does not currently exist), the acquisition must be made by means of a tender offer bid and the procedures stipulated in 16.5 below must be followed. In this context, 'investor' includes not only a party who beneficially acquires securities, whether in its own name or in the name of others, but also:

- a party who is empowered by contract or by law to exercise voting rights of shares (regardless of whether it has the intention of controlling the business operations of the issuer);
- a party who has discretionary authority to invest in securities pursuant to a contract or by law;
- a party who has the option right to conclude a share purchase agreement regarding the shares;
- a party who has the option to purchase the shares pursuant to a call option agreement;
- a party who has the option to acquire the right of the purchaser under a sale and purchase agreement pursuant to a call option agreement; or
- a party who acquires a bond exchangeable to shares.

(Note: certain acquisitions that involve both: (i) trading on the stock exchange or the organised over-the-counter market; and (ii) out-of-market transactions, must also be made by means of a tender offer bid if the combined transactions take place within three months, and the resulting holding of the investor and its special affiliated parties exceeds one-third of the outstanding shares of the issuer and certain other tests are met.)

16.2 Competent authorities

See question 16.5 below.

16.3 Dealing with disclosures and stake building
See question 16.5 below.

16.4 Types of takeover bids
See question 16.5 below.

16.5 Procedural aspects
A foreign investor must appoint an agent in Japan, customarily a Japanese law firm, who shall be responsible for filing the tender offer registration statement. An investor must also appoint a tender offer agent who handles custody of the shares tendered and payment of the purchase price. When an investor commences a tender offer bid, the investor must publish a public notice regarding the tender offer in a newspaper in Japan. Following the publication of the public notice (usually on the same date), the investor must file with the relevant LFB (via an electronic filing system) a tender offer registration statement for public inspection. The investor must also deliver a prospectus for the tender offer to offerees. The tender offer period starts on the date of the public notice and lasts for a period between 20 and 60 business days.

The target company is required to express an opinion about the tender offers. They must file an opinion statement with the relevant LFB for public inspection within 10 business days from the date of the public notice regarding the tender offer. Along with its opinion, the target company may file a written inquiry for the investor and a request to extend the tender offer period up to 30 business days if the original period is shorter, and such a request will be effective even against the investor's will. If formal inquiries are initiated by the target company, the investor must file a written response with the relevant LFB within five business days of the inquiry. At the end of the tender offer period, the investor must issue a public notice or press release disclosing the results of the tender offer, and submit the results to the relevant LFB. Some of the terms of tender offers may be amended by filing an amendment to the tender offer registration statement, resulting in a mandatory extension of the tender offer period. Changing terms to the disadvantage of offerees is prohibited.

Revocation or withdrawal of a tender offer is prohibited unless some exceptions are applicable.

The investor and its 'special affiliated parties' (as defined below) must not buy the shares of the target company during the tender offer period other than by way of the tender offer, subject to certain exceptions.

An exchange offer is permissible provided that a securities registration statement for securities as consideration is filed simultaneously. Cash and other assets, such as securities may be used as consideration for the acquisition of shares of the target company, but the type and nature of consideration must be disclosed.

The investor must demonstrate its source of funds by bank statement (in case of bank deposits) or other financing agreements.

Tender offer procedures are not required, however, in the following cases:
• where the number of securities to be beneficially held by the investor

and the 'special affiliated parties' as defined in the FIEA following the acquisition is not more than 5 per cent of the total number of outstanding shares of the issuer;
- where the investor acquires securities from not more than 10 persons (excluding those who have been special affiliated parties for at least one year since the date of acquisition of the shares), outside a stock exchange or an organised over-the-counter market during a period of not more than 60 days, and the number of securities to be beneficially held by the investor and special affiliated parties following the acquisition is more than 5 per cent but not more than one-third of the outstanding shares of the issuer;
- where an investor who already holds more than 50 per cent of the total outstanding shares of the issuer acquires securities from not more than 10 persons outside a stock exchange or an organised over-the-counter market during a period of not more than 60 days (provided that if the total holding would exceed two-thirds of the outstanding shares of the issuer, a tender offer is still required);
- where the investor acquires securities from its special affiliated parties, subject to certain exceptions; or
- in certain other exceptional cases.

Special affiliated parties of the investor include:
- family (a spouse or a relative within the first degree);
- an entity in which the investor (or the investor and its subsidiary jointly) owns 20 per cent or more of the voting shares, or an officer (director, corporate auditor, etc) of such an entity;
- an officer of the investor;
- an owner (alone or jointly with its subsidiary) who holds 20 per cent or more of the voting shares of the investor; or
- a party who has agreed to jointly acquire, transfer or exercise voting rights under such reportable securities.

16.6 Nature and value of consideration offered
See question 16.5.

16.7 Timetable and variations
See question 16.5.

16.8 Strategy
See question 16.5.

16.9 Irrevocable
See question 16.5.

16.10 Share dealings, buying shares
See question 16.5.

16.11 First announcement
See question 16.5.

16.12   Drafting of offer documents
See question 16.5.

16.13   Further announcements
See question 16.5.

16.14   Responsibility
See question 9.

16.15   Despatch
See question 16.5.

16.16   Due diligence in advance of a takeover bid
See question 16.5.

16.17   Conditions to the offer
See question 16.5.

16.18   Financing
See question 16.5

16.19   For cash/for shares/mixed
See 16.5.

16.20   Inducement
See question 16.5.

16.21   Defence mechanisms
As with other jurisdictions, a number of defence mechanisms have been proposed and introduced, especially pre-bid defences, however such mechanisms are often challenged by a hostile takeover bidder.

16.22   Nature of listed securities
Not relevant.

16.23   Squeeze-out
Squeeze-out schemes often take the form of a combination of the tender offer bid and the cash-out merger.

16.24   Schemes of arrangement
See question 16.5.

17. FOREIGN INVESTMENT CONTROLS
17.1 Foreign investments
Foreign issuers must file a *post facto* report regarding any offering of newly-issued FIEA Securities in Japan under the FEA with the Minister of Finance through the Bank of Japan, if the offering amount is equivalent to Yen

1 billion or more (regardless of whether it is a primary public offering or private placement).

A non-resident investor must file a *post facto* report under the FEA with respect to certain acquisitions of shares of Japanese companies (listed or unlisted). For some industries, a prior authorisation is required rather than a *post facto* report.

17.2 Exemptions
See question 17.1.

17.3 Exemptions of notification or prior authorisation
See question 17.1.

17.4 Notification in order to establish a balance of payments
See question 17.1.

* The author would like to acknowledge the assistance of Shinji Nakamura, Takehiro Shibuya, Hiroko Tsurumaru, Shinya Takizawa, Toshihiro Nakamura and Claudia Hoeben.

Luxembourg

Arendt & Medernach François Warken & Laurence van Zuylen*

1. GENERAL DESCRIPTION OF THE CAPITAL MARKETS

There are various ways to enter into the international capital markets. Each of them reflects a different strategy (eg, using a specific registered issuing entity, making a public offering, applying for a listing, etc) and is subject to different rules and regulations. Entering into the international capital markets is often about selecting the right location and the right structure. In this respect, there are various reasons for choosing Luxembourg.

Luxembourg is a leading financial and investment centre in Europe with an innovative and evolving legal and regulatory framework. Many of the most recent legal and regulatory changes were in response to an ever-growing interest in the Luxembourg securities market, while others were the result of the implementation of recent European securities law directives.

The Luxembourg markets have proven to be an attractive location for international and domestic issuers as their legal and organisational framework structure accommodate a range of specific legal entities, including the investment company in risk capital (the *société d'investissement en capital risque* (SICAR)), the specialised investment fund (SIF) and the undertaking for collective investment (UCI) that are able to meet the most diversified demands.

Issuers may also choose to apply for the listing and admission to trading of their securities on the Luxembourg Stock Exchange (LuxSE), as the latter which was founded in 1927, is a globally leading market for listing securities with over 3,500 issuers from more than 105 different jurisdictions and a trading volume of EUR 219.15 million (as of 31 December 2010). Since its establishment, the LuxSE has historically taken a liberal, innovative and flexible approach to the securities industry. In 1963, the LuxSE was the first stock exchange to list a Eurobond and, since 1969, it has listed and allowed the trading of bonds in their issuing currency.

As a result of its rich history, its dedication to changing with the evolution of the global securities marketplace and its accommodating approach to this industry, the LuxSE has become the foremost stock exchange for the listing of debt securities in Europe with 42 per cent of international bonds in Europe listed thereon. The LuxSE is also a global leader for the listing of sovereign debts of other countries. At least 60 countries have turned to the LuxSE for listed debt. Additionally, the LuxSE is a dominant market for both bonds and investment funds, with more than 20,000 debt securities listed on the market in 2010 and more than 480 issuers listing over 7,000 lines of UCIs in 2010. In addition to debt securities, the LuxSE lists the broadest ranges of securities in Europe: shares, units of investment funds, warrants, certificates and global depositary receipts (GDRs). The equity market capitalisation of the LuxSE totalled over EUR 300 billion by the close of the market at the end of 2010 with more than two-thirds of this equity market capitalisation originating in Asia.

The LuxSE is the only operator of a stock exchange in Luxembourg and operates two markets: a regulated market within the meaning of Directive 2004/39/EC (the Markets in Financial Instruments Directive, (MiFID)); and the EuroMTF, a multilateral trading facility within the meaning of the MiFID. Issuers whose securities are listed on the regulated market of the LuxSE are subject to the requirements set out in Directive 2003/71/EC (the Prospectus Directive) and in Directive 2004/109/EC (the Transparency Directive). They are also able to benefit from a European passport which, on the basis of an already approved Prospectus Directive-compliant prospectus, allows them to apply for the admission to listing and trading of their securities on the regulated market of another European member state or to conduct a public offer of their securities in any such other member state. The EuroMTF was launched in 2005 to enable issuers not interested in the European passport mentioned above not to be subject, in particular, to the requirements of the Prospectus and Transparency Directives and has proven to meet most notably the requirements of issuers being established outside the European Union.

2. REGULATORY STRUCTURE

2.1 Supervisory authorities

The *Commission de Surveillance du Secteur Financie*r (CSSF) is the competent supervisory authority for the supervision of the securities markets and their operators. The CSSF has delegated specific supervisory powers to the LuxSE, in particular regarding the applications for listing and trading on the LuxSE and compliance with disclosure and reporting obligations for issuers having securities listed on the EuroMTF.

2.2 Legal and regulatory framework

Most of the current rules and regulations in connection with the offering, sale and distribution of securities, their admission to trading and the related ongoing and periodic disclosure obligations for issuers of securities is derived from European securities law directives. The most relevant pieces of legislation are the law of 10 July 2005 on prospectuses for securities (the Prospectus Law, implementing the Prospectus Directive), the law of 11 January 2008 on transparency requirements in relation to information about issuers whose securities are admitted to trading on a regulated market (implementing the Transparency Directive) and the law of 5 April 1993, as amended, on the financial sector.

These laws have been completed by a number of circulars and other guidelines issued by the CSSF and containing in most cases practical implementation measures. When applying those laws, the CSSF generally tends to follow the guidelines issued by the Committee of European

Securities Regulators (CESR). Other laws may be relevant depending on the type of issuer or the type of product. Additionally, the Internal Rules and Regulations of the LuxSE (ROI) apply in particular as regards the application for admission to listing and trading on the LuxSE and as regards certain disclosure and reporting obligations for issuers of securities listed and admitted to trading on the market operated by the LuxSE.

3. REGISTRATION OF THE ISSUER AND THE SECURITIES
Without prejudice to a prospectus requirement which may apply in the case of a public offering of securities or an application for listing and trading on a market operated by the LuxSE, domestic and international issuers are generally not required to be licensed in view of offering their securities to the public or applying for the admission to listing and trading of their securities. However, specific registration requirements apply to certain types of specialised issuers such as investment funds, specialised investment funds, investment companies in risk capital and registered securitisation vehicles (Luxembourg law also offers the possibility to set up unregistered securitisation vehicles). In contrast, marketing activities performed by professional intermediaries cannot be carried out in Luxembourg without a licence (please refer to item 5 below).

4. OFFERING DOCUMENTATION OR PROSPECTUS REQUIREMENTS
An offer of securities to the public is defined by the Prospectus Law, as being a communication to persons in any form and by any means presenting sufficient information on the terms of the offer and the securities to be offered, so as to enable an investor to decide to purchase or subscribe to these securities. The definition of an offer to the public as set out under the Prospectus Law no longer allows a distinction between an 'offer to the public' and a 'private placement' according to the means of communication used or the persons concerned. For the distribution of units in investment funds, the concept of the private placement still exist. Offers which do not qualify as offers to the public because they do not, for example, offer sufficient information on the securities offered and therefore fall outside the scope of the Prospectus Law, can take place on the Luxembourg territory without the prior publication of a duly approved prospectus. However, specific rules apply to eg, offers of certain types of securities in investment funds, investment companies in risk capital and registered securitisation vehicles.

4.1 Prospectus regimes
Offers of securities to the public and admissions to trading are regulated by the Prospectus Law. The Prospectus Law sets forth three different prospectus regimes:
* A first regime (Part II of the Prospectus Law) with respect to prospectuses for offers of securities to the public and admissions of securities to trading on a regulated market, which are subject to Community

harmonisation, and transposing the rules of the Prospectus Directive including the possibility to apply for a so called passport of the prospectus;

• A second regime (Part III of the Prospectus Law) defining the rules that apply to prospectuses for offers to the public in Luxembourg and admissions to trading on the regulated market of securities and other comparable instruments, which are outside the scope of the Prospectus Directive, and providing for a simplified prospectus regime; and

• A third regime (Part IV of the Prospectus Law), setting up a Luxembourg specific regime applying to prospectuses for admissions of securities to listing and trading on a market which is not included in the list of regulated markets published by the European Commission. To date, the EuroMTF is the only such market operated in Luxembourg. The rules which apply to prospectuses for admissions of securities to listing and trading on the EuroMTF are set out in the ROI.

4.2 Content of the prospectus

The rules that are applicable to the content and approval of a prospectus will depend on the regime applying under the Prospectus Law as discussed above. The relevant rules can be summarised as follows:

• Prospectuses approved under the first regime have to be drawn up in accordance with and contain all information mentioned in the annexes of Commission Regulation (EC) No. 809/2004. The CSSF is the competent authority to approve these prospectuses;

• The content of prospectuses approved for the purposes of an offer to the public under the second regime is governed by the CSSF circular 05/210 which refers to the ROI. These prospectuses are called simplified prospectuses and are approved by the CSSF. The content of prospectuses approved for the purposes of an admission to trading on a regulated market only under the second regime is governed by the ROI and these prospectuses are approved by the LuxSE; and

• Prospectuses approved under the third regime in view of admission to trading on the EuroMTF must contain information set out in the annexes of the ROI. The disclosure requirements for prospectuses which are set out in the ROI are mainly derived from Directive 2001/34/EC (which has been repealed). For debt securities nearly all of which, because of their nature, are normally purchased and traded in by a limited number of investors who are particularly knowledgeable in investment matters, also commonly known as Eurobonds, issuers are only required to disclose limited financial information in their prospectus. The LuxSE is the competent authority to approve these prospectuses.

An admission to trading on the EuroMTF is furthermore always possible on the basis of a Prospectus Directive-compliant prospectus.

Finally, prospectuses drawn up for: (a) offers to the public of units issued by UCIs other than the closed-end type; and (b) for admissions to trading on a regulated market of units issued by UCIs other than the closed-end type governed by Luxembourg law, of units issued by UCIs governed by law other than Luxembourg law transposing harmonised Community law and commercialised in Luxembourg and of units issued by other foreign UCIs other than the closed-end type and offered to the public in Luxembourg, are subject to the sole provisions of the laws dated 30 March 1988 and 20 December 2002 relating to UCIs. The CSSF is the competent authority to approve these prospectuses.

4.3 Supplements to the prospectus
Every significant new factor, material mistake or inaccuracy relating to the information included in a prospectus which is capable of affecting the assessment of the securities and which arises or is noted between the time when the prospectus is approved and the final closing of the offer to the public or, as the case may be, the time when trading on a regulated market begins triggers the obligation to draw up a supplement to the prospectus. The content of a supplement is governed by the same rules that apply in respect of the content of the relevant prospectus. Also the approval process for a supplement is analogous to the approval process of a prospectus.

4.4 Exemptions from the obligation to draw up a prospectus
Without prejudice to the requirements resulting from other laws for certain types of securities issued by specialised issuers (see above), offers of securities which are subject to a prospectus requirement pursuant to the Prospectus Law are exempt from the obligation to publish a prospectus when the offer is made: (i) to qualified investors; (ii) to fewer than 100 investors (either natural or legal persons) per member state other than qualified investors; (iii) to investors acquiring securities of more than EUR 50,000 per investor, for each separate offer; (iv) for securities where the denomination per unit amounts to at least EUR 50,000; and (v) for a total consideration of less than EUR 100,000 calculated over a period of 12 months.

Similarly, applications for the admission to listing and trading of securities on the regulated market are exempt from the obligation to publish a prospectus if the securities are *inter alia* shares representing, over a period of 12 months, less than 10 per cent of the number of shares of the same class already admitted to trading on the same regulated market or shares issued in substitution for shares of the same class already admitted to trading on the same regulated market, if the issuance of such shares does not involve an increase in the issued capital.

The Prospectus Directive has been amended in December 2010 by Directive 2010/73/EC and the above mentioned exemptions will therefore be modified at least in part once this directive is implemented in Luxembourg.

4.5 Procedure for approval of prospectuses
The procedure for the approval of a prospectus varies depending on the authority which is competent for approving the prospectus. If the CSSF is competent, it must notify the person having filed the prospectus for approval of its decision regarding the approval of the prospectus or its

comments on the prospectus within 10 working days of the submission of the draft prospectus, if the file is complete. This time limit is extended to 20 working days if the public offer involves securities issued by an issuer which does not yet have any securities admitted to trading on a regulated market and which has not previously offered securities to the public.

If the LuxSE is the competent authority, the ROI does not provide for specific delays for the approval of the prospectus. However, the delays are *de facto* the same.

5. PUBLICITY

5.1 Marketing materials
Luxembourg law does not require the prior communication to or formal approval of marketing material by the CSSF. However, this does not exclude the possibility of submitting draft advertisements to the CSSF in order to obtain an opinion with regard to its compliance with the principles laid down in the Prospectus Law.

It should be noted that material information provided by an issuer and addressed to qualified investors or special categories of investors must be disclosed to all qualified investors or special categories of investors to whom the offer is exclusively addressed.

5.2 Licence requirements
Certain marketing activities (including brokerage, underwriting and placing) carried out in Luxembourg require prior authorisation from the Minister of Treasury and Budget and subject the entity engaged in such activities to the prudential supervision of the CSSF. In addition, the marketing must ordinarily be carried out in accordance with the Luxembourg financial sector conduct of business rules.

However, if a professional intermediary incorporated in a member state establishes a permanent presence in Luxembourg, it will be able to carry out certain marketing activities (under the regime of the MiFID as implemented in the jurisdiction of its member state of incorporation) in Luxembourg using its existing authorisation (in accordance with the EU passporting regime for the freedom of establishment by setting up a local branch – ie, without the need to obtain any further authorisation in Luxembourg). The marketing must be carried out in accordance with Luxembourg financial sector conduct of business rules.

If, on the other hand, a professional intermediary incorporated in a member state does not have a permanent presence in Luxembourg (a local office of a dealer is deemed a 'permanent presence' in this respect), it will be able to carry out certain marketing activities (under the regime of the MiFID as implemented in the jurisdiction of its member state of incorporation) in Luxembourg using its existing authorisation (in accordance with the EU 'passporting' regime – ie, without the need to obtain any further authorisation in Luxembourg). In such a case the professional intermediary would not need to be concerned by the Luxembourg conduct of business rules but would need to ensure that it complies with the equivalent requirements under the law of its member state of incorporation.

In principle, a professional intermediary incorporated in a country other than a member state may not carry out any marketing activities (including brokerage, underwriting and placing) in Luxembourg on a cross-border basis or by way of a local establishment without the prior authorisation from the Minister of Treasury and Budget and hence become subject to the prudential supervision of the CSSF. Moreover, the marketing must ordinarily be carried out in accordance with Luxembourg financial sector conduct of business rules.

These rules also apply to a roadshow if the roadshow is organised or conducted by a person other than the issuer.

5.3 Overallotment
An overallotment option (greenshoe) gives underwriters the right to sell additional shares at the offering price, if demand for the securities exceeds the original amount offered. The greenshoe can vary in size up to 15 per cent of the original number of shares offered. In some cases, an overallotment and stabilisation agent is designated.

6. LISTING
As discussed above, the LuxSE offers broad listing options via its two markets, the regulated market of the LuxSE and the EuroMTF.

Applications to listing and trading on the LuxSE (regulated market or EuroMTF) must be submitted to the admission committee of the LuxSE. An application for admission must be accompanied by a complete admission file and comply with the admission criteria set out in the ROI.

6.1 Admission documents
Any application for admission must be accompanied *inter alia* by a duly approved prospectus, the constitutional documents of the issuers, historical financial reports and the most relevant agreements relating to the issuance of the securities for which an application is being made. It is possible to make the application for admission on the basis of draft agreements if the agreements are not yet in final form by that time.

6.2 Admission criteria
There are two different types of admission criteria, criteria relating to the issuer and criteria relating to the securities. These criteria vary depending on the type of issuer and the type of securities. Some criteria are common to all applications for admission:
- criteria relating to the issuer, ie, the legal position of the issuer must always conform to the laws and regulations to which it is subject as regards both its incorporation and under its articles; and
- criteria relating to the securities, ie, (i) the legal position of the securities must always conform to the laws and regulations to which they are subject. (ii) the securities must be freely transferable, (iii) the physical form of the securities must offer sufficient safeguards for the investors' protection, (iv) the application for admission to the official list must

cover all securities of the same category already issued (v) and in the case of a public issue preceding admission to the official list the end of the period during which the subscription applications may be submitted must precede the first listing.

The following additional conditions apply to shares/units:
- the foreseeable stock market capitalisation of the shares/units, or if this cannot be assessed, the capital of the company, including the results from the last financial year, must amount to at least EUR 1,000,000 or the equivalent value in any other currency;
- the company must have published or filed, in accordance with national law, its annual accounts for the three financial years preceding the application for admission to the official list. However, the LuxSE may waive this condition; and
- a sufficient distribution of shares/units to the public of one or more member states must be achieved at the latest at the time of the admission to the official list (this condition does not apply to units issued by open-ended funds).

The following additional conditions apply to bonds:
- the minimum amount of the issue may not be less than EUR 200,000 or its equivalent value in any other currency; and
- convertible bonds, exchangeable bonds and bonds with warrants may only be admitted to the official list if the shares or units to which they relate have previously been admitted to this list or admitted to trading to another market that operates in a legitimate, recognised and open manner or are admitted at the same time.

6.3   Clearing and settlement
A pre-requirement for the listing and admission to trading on the LuxSE is that the securities to be listed and admitted to trading are accepted for clearing and settlement by a system recognised by the LuxSE, eg, Clearstream Banking S.A. (Clearstream) and Euroclear Bank S.A./N.V. (Euroclear). For securities which are not admissible for clearing and settlement through Clearstream and Euroclear (eg, due to specific selling restrictions), the LuxSE may by way of derogation authorise specific settlement procedures.

7.   CONTINUING OBLIGATIONS
Once securities are listed and admitted to trading on the LuxSE (regulated market or EuroMTF), the issuer must comply with ongoing and periodic disclosure and reporting obligations.

7.1   Regulated market
Disclosure and reporting obligations applying to issuers of securities listed on the regulated market of the LuxSE are set out in the Transparency Directive as implemented in their home member state for the purposes of this Directive to the extent applicable. The Transparency Directive does

not apply to units issued by collective investment undertakings other than the closed-ended type, the law of 9 May 2006 (the Market Abuse Law, implementing directive 2003/6/EC) and the ROI.

An issuer having securities listed and admitted to trading on the regulated market of the LuxSE has to comply with the disclosure and reporting obligations set out in the law implementing the Transparency Directive in its home member state for the purposes of that Directive.

According to the Transparency Directive, issuers are required to disclose annual and half-yearly financial reports. Financial information must be compliant with international financial reporting standards (IFRS) or equivalent reporting standards. Issuers are furthermore required to publish information on new loan issues which are admitted to trading on a regulated market and in particular information on any guarantee or security in respect thereof as well as information necessary for holders of securities to exercise their rights.

As far as issuers of equity securities are concerned, they are additionally required to publish: (i) interim financial statements; (ii) changes in the rights attaching to the various classes of shares; (iii) the proportion of their own shares they acquire or dispose of where that proportion reaches, exceeds or falls below the thresholds of 5 per cent or 10 per cent of the voting rights; and (iv) the total number of voting rights and capital at the end of each calendar month during which an increase or decrease of such total number has occurred. Issuers of debt securities are required to publish changes in the rights of holders.

Most information to be disclosed in accordance with the Transparency Directive qualifies as 'regulated information' and must be disclosed in three different ways: (i) it must be published in order to be disseminated in a fast and non-discriminatory manner on a pan-European basis; (ii) it must be stored with an officially appointed mechanism; and (iii) it must be sent to the competent financial authority in the home member state of the issuer for the purposes of the Transparency Directive.

Issuers having securities listed on the regulated market of the LuxSE must furthermore disclose as soon as possible inside information, ie, information of a precise nature, which has not been made public, relating, directly or indirectly, to one or more issuers of financial instruments or to one or more financial instruments, and which, if it were made public, would be likely to have a significant effect on the prices of those financial instruments or on the price of related derivative financial instruments. Inside information also qualifies as regulated information for the purposes of the Transparency Directive (see above).

The ROI contains certain residual reporting obligations for issuers having securities listed and admitted to trading on the regulated market of the LuxSE (among which the obligation to communicate to the LuxSE all regulated information for the purposes of the Transparency Directive).

7.2 EuroMTF
Disclosure and reporting obligations applying to issuers of securities listed on the EuroMTF are set out in the ROI. Except for financial information,

where the disclosure obligations on the EuroMTF are far less stringent, the disclosure and reporting obligations are similar to those applying to issuers of securities listed on the regulated market of the LuxSE. However, compared to the rules that apply when securities are admitted to listing and trading on the regulated market of the LuxSE, the rules regarding the dissemination of information the disclosure of which is required pursuant to the rules of the ROI are less onerous.

8. CORPORATE GOVERNANCE

The LuxSE has published 10 principles of corporate governance which are intended to apply to Luxembourg registered issuers having shares listed and admitted to trading on the regulated market of the LuxSE. However, they may also serve as a reference framework for all other issuers. These 10 principles are as follows:

- The company must adopt a clear and transparent corporate governance framework for which it will provide adequate disclosure;
- The board must be responsible for the management of the company. As a collective body, it must act in the corporate interest and serve the common interests of the shareholders ensuring the sustainable development of the company;
- The board must be composed of competent, honest and qualified persons. Their choice must take account of the specific features of the company. The board must establish the special committees necessary for the proper performance of its task;
- The company must establish a formal procedure for the appointment of directors and executive managers;
- The directors must take decisions in the best interest of the company. They must disclose to the board potential conflicts between their direct or indirect personal interests and those of the company or any subsidiary controlled by the company. They must refrain from participating in any deliberation or decision involving such a conflict, unless they relate to current operations, concluded under normal conditions;
- The board must regularly evaluate its performance and its relationship with the executive management;
- The board must set up an effective structure of executive management. It must clearly define the duties of executive management and delegate to it the necessary powers for the proper discharge of these duties;
- The company must secure the services of qualified directors and executive managers by means of a suitable remuneration policy that is compatible with the long-term interests of the company;
- The board must establish strict rules, designed to protect the company's interests, in the areas of financial reporting, internal control and risk management; and
- The company must respect the rights of its shareholders and ensure they receive equitable treatment. The company must establish a policy of active communication with the shareholders.

Luxembourg companies whose securities are listed and admitted to trading on a regulated market in a member state must include in their management report a declaration on their corporate governance, ie, *inter alia* the corporate governance code they apply.

9. MARKET ABUSE

The provisions of the Market Abuse Law apply to securities which are listed and traded on the regulated market of the LuxSE and on the EuroMTF or to securities for which a request for an admission on such a market has been made. The prohibitions set out under the Market Abuse Law are those which are derived from Directive 2003/6/EC (the Market Abuse Directive), ie, insider dealing and market manipulation. The definition of insider dealing and market manipulation as a matter of Luxembourg law is very similar to the definition provided by EU legislation and relevant CESR guidance.

Issuers of securities being admitted to listing and trading on the regulated market of the LuxSE or for which an application for such an admission has been made are required to disclose inside information as soon as possible. By way of derogation, an issuer may, under his own responsibility, delay the public disclosure of inside information so as not to prejudice the issuer's legitimate interests, provided that such an omission is not likely to mislead the public and that the issuer has put the necessary measures in place to ensure the confidentiality of that information. No prior authorisation from the CSSF is required for a delayed disclosure of inside information.

9.1 Insider lists

Issuers of securities being admitted to listing and trading on the regulated market of the LuxSE or for which an application for such an admission has been made are required to draw up insider lists. The list of insiders must include in particular the persons who, due to their involvement at management decision level, have regular access to inside information and the power to make managerial decisions affecting the future developments and business prospects of the issuer. Moreover, this list must include those persons working regularly on sensitive issues and, where applicable, those persons working on an occasional basis on files containing inside information. The list of insiders should not include persons that might have access to inside information by accident. However, where it has been confirmed that those persons indeed had access to such information, those persons shall of course be included on the list.

9.2 Management transactions

Persons discharging managerial responsibilities within an issuer having its registered office in Luxembourg and, where applicable, persons closely associated with them, must declare, within five working days of each transaction's execution date, to the CSSF and to the issuer the existence of transactions conducted on their own account relating to shares of the issuer having its registered office in Luxembourg and which are admitted to trading on a regulated market, or to derivatives or other financial instruments linked to them.

9.3 Recent amendments of the Market Abuse Law

The Market Abuse Law has been modified by the law of 26 July 2010 on market abuse, completing the implementation of the Market Abuse Directive. The scope of the powers and authority of the CSSF has been extended and the catalogue of administrative sanctions has been strengthened.

10. MUTUAL OR INVESTMENT FUNDS

With approximately EUR 2,199 billion assets under management, Luxembourg's market share of the overall European investment fund industry represented 27.4 per cent at the end of 2010, which made Luxembourg the largest investment fund domicile in Europe.

Luxembourg investment funds may be created as: (i) UCIs subject to the provisions of Part I of the law of 20 December 2002 on UCIs (the 2002 Law) implementing Directive 85/611/EC, as amended (the Undertakings for Collective Investment in Transferable Securities (UCITS) Directive); (ii) UCIs subject to the provisions of Part II of the 2002 Law; or (iii) SIFs subject to the provisions of the law of 13 February 2007 on specialised investment funds (the '2007 Law').

10.1 UCITS

UCITS are open-ended funds that are required to directly or indirectly repurchase their units or shares at the request of the investors. UCITS benefit from the right to be freely marketed in other member states on the basis of the European passport. The exclusive object of UCITS is the investment in transferable securities and/or in other eligible liquid financial assets as set out in the 2002 Law. Investments have to be made in accordance with the restrictions mentioned in the 2002 Law.

UCITS are subject to specific substance requirements and requirements regarding the qualification of managers as well as restrictions on delegation of duties.

10.2 UCIs

UCIs are investment funds: (i) that are closed-ended (to redemptions); or (ii) that raise capital without promoting the sale of their units or shares to the public within the EU or any part thereof; or (iii) that sell their units only to the public in countries which are not members of the EU; or (iv) that fall under one of the categories of UCIs for which the investment rules of Part I of the 2002 Law are inappropriate (typically real estate funds, venture capital funds or hedge funds).

UCIs do not benefit from the European passport, meaning that the sale of the units or shares of such vehicles should only be made on the basis of the rules applicable in each country where they are sold on a public or on a private placement basis.

As a general rule, the 2002 Law does not restrict the types of investment strategies which can be used by UCIs.

10.3 SIFs

SIFs are subject to the 2007 Law. SIFs are exclusively dedicated to sophisticated investors, ie, institutional investors, professional investors or well-informed investors. In contrast with UCIs governed by the 2002 Law, a SIF is not required to have a promoter with significant financial means. SIFs are characterised by a more flexible framework than funds subject to the 2002 Law and may invest in a very broad range of eligible assets with a lower risk diversification principle, which accommodates to various types of funds, in particular hedge funds, real estate funds and private equity funds.

10.4 Legal forms of UCITS and UCIs

The 2002 Law and the 2007 Law permit the creation of UCITS and UCIs in contractual form (*fonds communs de placement* (FCP)), which is in certain aspects similar to the unit trust in the United Kingdom and the mutual fund in the United States.

Investors subscribing for units of an FCP do not, in principle, have voting rights and are only entitled to a proportional share of the net assets of the relevant FCP. FCPs are managed by a management company domiciled in Luxembourg, which decides on the investment policies and strategies and generally manages the FCP on behalf of its joint owners.

UCITS and UCIs may also be created under the corporate form either as: (i) a *société d'investissement à capital variable* (SICAV) (the capital of which is always equal to its net assets) or (ii) a *société d'investissement à capital fixe* (SICAF).

10.5 Umbrella structures

UCITS and UCIs may be created as umbrella funds with several compartments which may have different investment policies and be denominated in different currencies as well with different classes of units or shares.

10.6 Prudential supervision

The CSSF is entrusted with the supervision of UCIs and UCITS. No Luxembourg UCI or UCITS may be registered without the approval of the CSSF. In order to set up a Luxembourg UCI or UCITS, a written application must be filed with the CSSF, containing drafts of the constitutional, sales and ancillary documents.

The approval of a UCI or UCITS is effected by its inscription on the official list of Luxembourg UCIs or UCITS. This list is published in the Official Gazette. The CSSF supervises UCIs or UCITS on a continuous basis.

10.7 Service providers

The management of an FCP is carried out by a management company established under Luxembourg law. The board of directors/board of managers of a corporate-type UCI or UCITS carries out the management functions of such an entity. The day-to-day management of any UCI or UCITS may be carried out from outside Luxembourg, either through individuals (general managers) or through legal entities (investment managers and advisers).

The CSSF will, however, review the reputation and professional expertise of all persons involved in the management of a Luxembourg UCI or UCITS (except for a SIF where only the board members are subject to CSSF approval).

Furthermore, the central administration of a UCITS or UCI must be carried out in Luxembourg. This means that accounts are kept and made available in Luxembourg, issues and redemptions are processed in Luxembourg, the register of units or shares is kept in Luxembourg, the prospectus and financial reports are established in co-operation with the central administration in Luxembourg, the dispatch of notices and reports is made from Luxembourg and the calculation of the net asset value is made in Luxembourg.

All Luxembourg UCIs or UCITS must appoint a custodian bank, which must be a bank established either as a Luxembourg corporation or as a Luxembourg branch of a foreign bank. In compliance with the UCITS Directive, Luxembourg branches of foreign banks, the registered offices of which are not located in another member state, may not act as custodian banks for UCITS.

The custodian bank must be entrusted with the physical custody of the assets of the UCI or UCITS.

Any Luxembourg UCI or UCITS is obliged to have its books audited at least once a year by a *réviseur d'entreprises agréé* (authorised independent auditor) designated by the UCI or UCITS with the approval of the CSSF.

11. NOTIFICATION OBLIGATIONS

Shareholders who acquire or dispose of shares of an issuer whose shares are admitted to trading on a regulated market and for which Luxembourg is the issuer's home member state for the purposes of the Transparency Directive and to which voting rights are attached must notify the issuer and the CSSF if the proportion of voting rights of the issuer held by this shareholder as a result of this acquisition or disposal reaches, exceeds or falls below the thresholds of 5, 10, 15, 20, 25, 33 1/3, 50 and 66 2/3 per cent. The issuer must in turn publish the notification received. It is possible for issuers to foresee additional thresholds in their constitutional documents.

The Transparency Law foresees (under certain conditions) exemptions for shares acquired for the sole purpose of clearing and settlement within the usual short settlement cycle, to acquisitions and disposals by a market maker, to acquisitions and disposals of voting rights held in the trading book and if the notification has already been made by a parent undertaking. Further exemptions (under certain conditions) are available in respect of the aggregation of voting rights by the parent undertaking of a management company or the parent undertaking of an investment firm.

12. PUBLIC TAKEOVERS

The Luxembourg law of 19 May 2006 on public takeovers (the Takeover

Law implementing Directive 2004/25/EC) applies to the securities of a Luxembourg company, where all or some of those securities are admitted to trading on a regulated market in one or more EU member states or EEA member states. The term 'securities' as referred to in this section applies to shares, units and other transferable securities carrying voting rights and the term 'member state' refers to an EU or European Economic Area (EEA) member state. The Takeover Law does not apply to takeover bids for open-ended funds, issuers being established in a jurisdiction other than a member state or issuers not having their securities admitted to trading on a regulated market, eg, the EuroMTF.

If the target company's securities are admitted to trading on a regulated market in a member state other than the member state in which the company has its registered office, the competent authority to supervise the bid shall be the authority of the member state on the regulated market of which the company's securities are admitted to trading.

Matters relating to the consideration offered in the case of a bid, in particular the price, and matters relating to the bid procedure, in particular the information on the bidder's decision to make a bid, the content of the offer document and the disclosure of the bid shall be governed by the law of the EU member state on the regulated market of which the company's securities are admitted to trading.

In matters relating to the information to be provided to the employees of the target company and in matters relating to company law, in particular the percentage of voting rights which confers control (in Luxembourg the threshold is fixed at 33 1/3 per cent of the voting rights) and any derogation from the obligation to launch a bid, as well as the conditions under which the board of the target company may undertake any action which might result in the frustration of the bid, the applicable rules and the competent authority shall be those of the member state in which the target company has its registered office.

12.1 Squeeze-out

No general principle of squeeze-out is provided for by Luxembourg law. However, under the Takeover Law, if any natural or legal person holds a total of at least 95 per cent of a company's share capital carrying voting rights and 95 per cent of such a company's voting rights as a result of a public bid regarding the securities of a target company (in the course of which the bidder acquires control of the company), such a person may acquire the remaining securities in the target company by exercising a squeeze-out against the holders of the remaining securities. The price shall take the same form as the consideration offered in the bid or shall be in cash. Cash shall be offered at least as an alternative. Following a voluntary bid, the consideration offered in the bid shall be presumed to be fair where, through acceptance of the bid, the bidder has acquired securities representing not less than 90 per cent of the capital carrying voting rights comprised in the bid. Following a mandatory bid, the consideration offered in the bid is presumed to be fair. The CSSF ensures that a fair price is guaranteed. The squeeze-out must be exercised by the bidder no later than three months after the end of the period of acceptance of the bid.

12.2 Sell-out

According to the Takeover Law, if any natural or legal person, alone or together with persons acting in concert with it, hold(s) a total of at least 90 per cent of a company's share capital carrying voting rights and 90 per cent of such company's voting rights as a result of a public bid regarding the securities of a target company, any shareholder may exercise a sell-out with respect to his securities. Such a right must be exercised no later than three months after the end of the period of acceptance of the bid. The price shall be determined in the same manner as the one described above in respect of squeeze-out procedure.

13. FOREIGN INVESTMENT CONTROLS

There are currently no limitations under the laws of Luxembourg on the rights of non-residents to hold or vote securities issued by a Luxembourg issuer. Cash distributions, if any, payable in euro or US dollars may, in principle, be transferred from Luxembourg and converted into any other currency without Luxembourg legal restrictions. However, no payments, including dividend payments, may be made to jurisdictions subject to certain sanctions, adopted by the government of Luxembourg, implementing resolutions of the Security Council of the United Nations or regulations of the European Union.

*The authors would like to thank Anne-Marie Reuter, avocat à la Cour, for her support in drafting this chapter.

The Netherlands

NautaDutilh NV Arjan J J Pors, Fleur S M van Tilburg, Lotte van de Loo & Pim Heemskerk

1. GENERAL DESCRIPTION OF THE CAPITAL MARKETS
1.1 General description of the capital markets
The Dutch capital market provides for domestic and foreign capital in the form of ordinary equity, debt securities and other securities. The only recognised stock exchange in the Netherlands is Euronext Amsterdam NV, whose indirect parent company is NYSE Euronext, Inc., formed pursuant to a 2007 merger between the operator of the New York Stock Exchange and Euronext NV. Together with the NYSE Euronext group companies, NYSE Euronext (International) BV, NYSE Euronext (Holding) BV and Euronext NV, Euronext Amsterdam received a joint licence to operate the stock exchange in the Netherlands. Together with these NYSE Euronext group companies, Euronext Amsterdam is also licensed to operate the Amsterdam derivatives market LIFFE and the multilateral trading facilities NYSE Alternext and NYSE Arca Europe.

1.2 Regulatory structure
On 1 January 2007, the Financial Supervision Act (FSA) entered into effect. The FSA provides for a general framework of combined legislation for prudential supervision and conduct supervision. The FSA and further regulations pursuant to the FSA govern the offering of securities, the supervision of financial institutions that exist in the Netherlands (supervision of banks, insurers, collective investment schemes etc), the providing of services by financial institutions (eg, securities brokers or portfolio managers) and public takeover bids.

If offered securities are admitted or are likely to be admitted in the near future to the stock exchange of Euronext Amsterdam, the rules established by Euronext are also applicable.

2. SUPERVISORY AUTHORITIES
2.1 AFM – conduct supervision
The Netherlands Authority for the Financial Markets (the AFM) is the conduct supervisor. Licences for institutions that are largely subject to conduct supervision (ie, investment firms and investment institutions) are granted by the AFM.

2.2 DNB – prudential supervision
The Dutch Central Bank (*De Nederlandsche Bank* or DNB) is the prudential

supervisor. Licences for institutions that are largely subject to prudential supervision, such as banking institutions and insurance companies, are exclusively granted by DNB.

2.3 Cooperation

The FSA lays down rules for cooperation between the AFM and DNB. The AFM and DNB will cooperate with a view to drawing up joint rules and policy in respect of matters that are relevant in terms of both conduct supervision and prudential supervision. The AFM and DNB will furthermore have to involve each other in certain decisions by asking the point of view of the other party or advice. The FSA also provides for the exchange of information between the supervisory authorities and for the right of the supervisory authorities to ask the other supervisory authority for certain information. The AFM and DNB have a contract specifying their cooperation in more detail.

2.4 Controlled self-regulation stock exchange – Euronext

The FSA provides a legal framework for the self-regulation of recognised stock exchanges. The recognised stock exchange is responsible for establishing adequate rules and ensuring compliance with them. In turn the AFM supervises, among others, recognised stock exchange and market personnel, such as clearing members, market makers, liquidity providers and traders.

3. OFFERING DOCUMENTS OR PROSPECTUS REQUIREMENTS

3.1 Prohibition on the offering of securities

The EU Prospectus Directive (2003/71/EC) (the Directive) was implemented in the Netherlands in July 2005. The rules implementing the Directive are contained in the FSA and further regulations pursuant to the FSA. The most important change brought by the implementation of the Directive was the introduction of a European passport for prospectuses.

The FSA prohibits the offering of securities to the public, or to have securities admitted to trading on a regulated market, unless a prospectus approved by the AFM (or supervisory authority in another member state as defined in the FSA) is generally available with regard to such offering or admission.

The definition of securities includes negotiable shares or other negotiable documents of value or rights considered equivalent to negotiable shares, negotiable bonds or other negotiable debt instruments and any other negotiable document of value issued by a legal entity, company or institution with which a security as referred to above can be acquired by exercising the rights attached thereto or through conversion, or which can be settled in cash.

3.2 Non-applicability of prohibition – exceptions

The prohibition on the offering of securities without a prospectus does not apply to (i) money market instruments having a maturity of less than 12 months and (ii) negotiable participations in an open-end investment institution. Furthermore, the prohibition on the offering of securities without a prospectus does not apply to the offers of securities to the public, in respect of an offer of securities:

- addressed solely to qualified investors;
- addressed to less than 100 individuals or legal entities, other than qualified investors;
- addressed to investors who acquire securities for a total consideration of at least EUR 50,000 per investor;
- whose denomination per unit amounts to at least EUR 50,000; and/or
- with a total consideration of less than EUR 100,000, which limit shall be calculated over a period of 12 months.

In 2008, the AFM issued an interpretative statement regarding the '50,000 exceptions'. Pursuant to this statement: (i) each investment (the initial investment and each subsequent investment) must have a consideration of at least EUR 50,000; and (ii) if securities are not offered in accordance with the aim and purpose of the Directive, the investor must pay the amount of EUR 50,000 in a lump sum.

The FSA provides for further exceptions to the prohibition on the offering of securities upon issue or having securities admitted to trading on a regulated market without a prospectus in respect of certain types of securities, including but not limited to exceptions in respect of:

- shares or certificates of shares issued in substitution for shares or certificates of shares of the same category or class already issued, if the issuing of such new shares or certificates of shares does not involve any increase in the issued capital;
- securities offered in connection with a takeover by means of an exchange offer, provided that a document is available containing information being equivalent to that of the prospectus; and
- securities offered, allotted or to be allotted in connection with a merger, provided that a document is available containing information being equivalent to that of the prospectus.

3.3 Non-applicability of prohibition – exemptions

The Exemption Regulation pursuant to the FSA provides for certain exemptions from the prohibition on the offering of securities or having securities admitted to trading on a regulated market without a prospectus, including but not limited to exemptions in respect of:

- non-equity securities issued by an EEA state or by one of an EEA's regional or local authorities, by public international bodies of which one or more EEA states are members, by the European Central Bank or by a central bank of an EEA state;
- shares in the capital of a central bank of an EEA state;
- securities unconditionally and irrevocably guaranteed by an EEA state or by one of an EEA state's regional or local authorities;
- securities issued by associations or non-profit-making bodies with a

view to their obtaining the means necessary to achieve their non-profit-making objectives;

- non-equity securities issued by banks, provided that these securities: are offered or form part of an offer to the public or admissions to trading on a regulated market in a continuous manner where over a period of 12 months at least two separate offerings or admissions to trading of securities of a similar category and/or class are made; are not subordinated, convertible or exchangeable; do not give a right to subscribe to or acquire other types of securities and that they are not linked to a derivative instrument; materialise reception of repayable deposits; and are covered by a deposit guarantee scheme under the EU Directive on deposit-guarantee schemes (94/19/EC);
- non-equity securities issued by banks where the total consideration of the offer is less than EUR 50,000,000, which limit shall be calculated over a period of 12 months, provided that these securities: are offered or form part of an offer to the public or admissions to trading on a regulated market in a continuous manner where over a period of 12 months at least two separate offerings or admissions to trading of securities of a similar category and/or class are made; are not subordinated, convertible or exchangeable; do not give a right to subscribe to or acquire other types of securities and that they are not linked to a derivative instrument; and
- securities included in an offer where the total consideration of the offer is less than EUR 2,500,000, which limit shall be calculated over a period of 12 months.

In line with the Directive, the Exemption Regulation FSA provides for certain exemptions in respect of offerings to the public of securities in the secondary market and for an exemption in respect of offerings to persons other than qualified investors who entered into a discretionary portfolio management agreement with a regulated portfolio manager. Furthermore, an exemption is available under certain conditions in respect of offerings to the public if such offering is solely in connection with trading on a multilateral trading facility and such securities have already been admitted to trading on a trading venue.

3.4 Issuing of bonds – prohibition to act as a bank without a licence and prohibition on receiving repayable funds from the public

As mentioned above, the issuing of securities falls within the scope of the regulatory framework for the offering of securities described above. However, if the issuer of securities receives repayable funds, eg, in case of issuing bonds, and the funds are used by the issuer to on-lend, the issuer may qualify as a bank within the meaning of the FSA.

The FSA prohibits acting as a bank without a licence. Those who make their business from receiving repayable funds outside a restricted circle from persons who do not qualify as professional market parties on the one hand, and on-lending such funds on the other hand, qualify as a bank.

As appears from the definition of bank, those who make their business from receiving repayable funds solely from professional market parties and/ or within a restricted circle, do not qualify as bank and, therefore, do not fall within the scope of the prohibition referred to above. The definition of professional market parties includes qualified investors and certain natural or legal persons appointed as such by governmental decree. In this connection it should be noted that persons or legal entities who or which provide repayable funds qualify as professional markets parties in their legal relationship with the person or legal entity that receives the repayable funds from them if the nominal value of the first receivable or the first jointly acquired receivables together, is at least EUR 50,000 (or its equivalent in a foreign currency) and this amount is provided at once or the first receivable or the first jointly acquired receivables together can only be acquired or are acquired for an amount of at least EUR 50,000 (or its equivalent in a foreign currency) at once.

The FSA furthermore provides that the prohibition to receive repayable funds outside a restricted circle from persons who do not qualify as professional market parties without a licence is not applicable if:

- the repayable funds are received as a consequence of the issuing of securities in accordance with the applicable laws and regulations;
- the issuer on-lends at least 95 per cent of its balance sheet total within the group of companies to which it belongs; and
- a guarantee by or other arrangement with a parent company having a positive net worth during the term of such guarantee or other arrangement or a bank guarantee is in place.

In addition, subject to certain exceptions and possible exemptions by ministerial regulation, any person is prohibited from inviting, receiving or having, in the course of its business, repayable funds from outside a restricted circle from persons who do not qualify as professional market parties. The FSA provides, among other things, for an exception for the situation that repayable funds are received as a consequence of the issuing of securities in accordance with the applicable laws and regulations.

4. LISTING REQUIREMENTS EURONEXT AMSTERDAM
4.1 General
In order for securities to be admitted to the official listing on the stock exchange of Euronext Amsterdam a request to admission has to be filed with Euronext Amsterdam by the issuer and:
- the admission criteria must be met;
- a listing agreement must be entered into; and
- the issuer must appoint a listing agent.

4.2 Admission criteria

General listing requirements for securities
In order for securities to be admitted to listing, among other things, the following general criteria need to be met:
- the legal form and structure of the issuing company need to be in accordance with applicable laws and regulations both as regards its

formation and its operation under its articles of association;
- the issuer must comply with the requirements of the relevant competent authority (ie the governmental or self-regulating authority in the specific case); and
- adequate procedures must be available for the clearing and settlement of transactions in respect of such securities.

The issuer shall ensure that securities of the same class have identical rights and are validly issued in a form in accordance with applicable laws and regulations. The issuer shall ensure that securities are freely transferable and negotiable.

An application for admission to listing must cover all issuer's securities of the same class issued at the time of the application or proposed to be issued.

Addditional listing requirements for shares
In order for shares, depository receipts for shares and equity securities to be admitted to listing, the following criteria need to be met:
- a sufficient number of shares must be distributed to the public. This means that 25 per cent of the subscribed capital must be in the hands of the public. This percentage may be lower (but not less than 5 per cent), provided that the market will function with the lower percentage and provided that the lower percentage represents a value of at least EUR 5,000,000 calculated on the basis of the offering price;
- the issuer must have published or filed audited annual financial statements for the preceding three financial years. Euronext Amsterdam may grant dispensation from this requirement. In that case Euronext Amsterdam may subject the admission to listing to additional requirements in respect of market capitalisation, shareholders' equity and/or lock-up requirements.

Additional listing requirements for securities other than shares
In order for corporate bonds to be admitted to listing, the nominal value must be at least EUR 200,000, except in the case of tap issues where the amount of the issue is not fixed. Euronext Amsterdam may as a condition to admission to listing require that the relevant corporate bonds be rated by a rating agency or require that a guarantee for the principal amount and interest be issued by a parent company or by a third party.

In order for participations in an investment institution or other securities to be admitted to listing, a number of additional listing requirements relating to market capitalisation and adequate public distribution need to be met. Additional listing requirements are also applicable with respect to trackers, warrants and other transferable securities.

4.3 Listing agreement – listing rules
If a company wishes to obtain a listing for securities on Euronext Amsterdam, it must enter into a listing agreement. By entering into the listing agreement the company agrees to be bound by and to comply with the rules in the Euronext Rule Book (as amended from time to time).

4.4 Listing agent

In order to obtain a listing for securities on Euronext Amsterdam, a listing agent is required to be involved. The listing agent needs to make a written statement to Euronext Amsterdam declaring that it shall guide and council the issuer throughout a period of no less than six months following the listing. In principle, the listing agent needs to be a member of Euronext. In exceptional cases where securities have already been listed on the NYSE market, Euronext Amsterdam may decide that the listing agent does not need to be a Euronext member. The listing agent needs to be authorised by Euronext to perform the following tasks:

- to take part in the admission of securities to listing;
- to assist the issuer with preparing the information documents and with the application procedure as set out in the Euronext Rule Book;
- if need be, carry out the placement of the securities.

The listing agent needs to have at its disposal sufficient and experienced human resources to ensure the proper fulfilment of the abovementioned obligations. The obligations of the listing agent are laid down in an agreement signed by the issuer. A copy of this agreement must be provided to Euronext Amsterdam at its request.

5. PROSPECTUS REQUIREMENTS

5.1 Prospectus requirements

The prohibition under the FSA to offer securities to the public or to have securities admitted to trading on a regulated market is not applicable if a prospectus that has been approved by the AFM or by a supervisory authority in another member state is generally available with regard to such offering or admission.

The prospectus must comply with the rules of the Directive (as implemented in the Netherlands in the FSA and further regulations pursuant to the FSA).

The prospectus shall contain all information which, according to the particular nature of the issuer and of the securities offered to the public or admitted to trading on a regulated market, is necessary for the purposes of making an informed assessment of the assets and liabilities, financial position, profit and losses, prospects of the issuer and of any guarantor and of the rights attaching to such securities, including the information referred to in Articles 3 up to and including 23 of the Commission Regulation (809/2004/EC) of 29 April 2004 implementing the Directive (the Prospectus Regulation).

In relation to securities of a specific category, the Prospectus Regulation provides for schedules and building blocks listing the information which must be included in the prospectus. Article 21 and Annex XVIII of the Prospectus Regulation provide for mandatory combinations of schedules and building blocks for specific types of securities. The AFM may require, in a specific case, the inclusion of additional information if necessary for the purposes referred to above.

Information contained in the prospectus shall not conflict with any other information contained in it or other information available to the AFM and shall be presented in an easily analysable and comprehensible form.

If information to be included in a prospectus is inappropriate to the issuer's sphere of activity or to the legal form of the issuer or to the securities to which the prospectus relates, the prospectus shall contain information, if available, equivalent to the required information.

5.2 Summary

The prospectus should contain a summary. The summary shall in a brief manner convey the essential characteristics and risks associated with the issuer, any guarantor and the securities, in the language in which the prospectus was originally prepared. The summary will contain a warning that:

- it should be read as an introduction to the prospectus;
- any decision to invest in the securities should be based on the prospectus as a whole;
- if a claim with respect to the information contained in the prospectus is brought before the courts, the investor may, under applicable national law, have to bear the cost of translating the prospectus before the commencement of legal proceedings; and
- those persons who have tabled the summary, including any translation of it, and requested a confirmation by the AFM that the prospectus complies with the requirements of the Directive, can be held liable only if the summary is misleading, inaccurate or inconsistent when read together with the rest of the prospectus.

5.3 Prospectus consisting of separate documents

The prospectus may consist of either one document or three separate documents. If the prospectus consists of three separate documents, these will include:

- a registration document containing information about the issuer;
- a securities note with information on the securities offered or issued in a specific transaction; and
- a summary.

Once approved, a registration document may be used for new transactions without re-approval. The issuer only needs to submit the securities note and a summary for each new offering of securities to the public or admission to trading on a regulated market. If a material change or a recent development has occurred which could affect the assessment of investors, the securities note shall contain the information to be included in the registration document and update the registration document.

5.4 Offer price or exchange ratio and volume of securities

If the final offer price or exchange ratio and the volume of securities to be offered to the public are not included in the prospectus, the prospectus must indicate the criteria and/or conditions in accordance with which the offer price or exchange ratio and volume of securities to be offered will be determined or, in the case there is no final offer price, the maximum price. If the prospectus does not include the above information on the price and volume of the offered securities, this information must be filed with the AFM and made generally available to the public.

5.5 Language
As a general rule, the prospectus must be drafted either in Dutch or in a language deemed customary in international financial circles if the prospectus is to be approved by the AFM. If the prospectus is approved by a supervisory authority in another member state, the AFM may require that the summary is translated into Dutch.

5.6 Omission of information
The AFM may authorise the omission from the prospectus of certain information, if:
- disclosure of such information would be contrary to the public interest; or
- disclosure of such information would be seriously detrimental to the issuer, provided that the omission would not be likely to mislead the public with regard to facts and circumstances essential for an informed assessment of the issuer, the person requesting admission to trading on a regulated market or guarantor, if any, and of the rights attached to the securities to which the prospectus relates; or
- such information is of minor importance, only relates to a specific offer or admission to trading on a regulated market and will not as such influence the assessment of the financial position and prospects of the issuer, the person requesting admission to trading on a regulated market or guarantor, if any.

5.7 Supplements to the prospectus
If following the approval of a prospectus and prior to the offering of securities to the public or admission to trading on a regulated market a significant new development relating to the information contained in the prospectus occurs or a material error or inaccuracy in the prospectus which could affect the assessment of the securities is identified, a document supplemental to the prospectus will be required. This document supplemental to the prospectus must be approved by the AFM and made generally available to the public. Investors who have already agreed to purchase or subscribe to the securities (prior to publication of the supplement) shall be entitled to withdraw their acceptance within a given period of time.

5.8 Prospectus requirements for open-end investment institutions
As explained in 3.2 above, the prohibition on the offering of securities without a prospectus does not apply to participations in an open-end investment institution. Consequently, managers of open-end investment institutions or open-end investment companies which do not have a

manager, need not publish a prospectus as described above. However, licensed managers of investment institutions or investment companies which do not have a manager must, *inter alia*, satisfy the rules laid down by further regulations pursuant to the FSA in respect of information to be supplied to the public. This means that each manager must have available a prospectus within the meaning of the FSA about any investment institution, which it manages and investment companies which do not have a separate manager must have a prospectus available within the meaning of the FSA about the investment company.

Such prospectus must contain the information which is necessary for the investors to come to an informed judgement about the investment institutions or investment companies and the costs and risks in connection with it. Apart from this general rule, the rules set by or pursuant to the FSA provide in detail (among other things, in a Schedule) the issues which need to be included in the prospectus.

6. ONGOING COMPLIANCE REQUIREMENTS – DUTY TO DISCLOSE INFORMATION

Pursuant to the Euronext rules and the FSA, as amended following the implementation of directive 2004/109/EC (the Transparency Directive) as per 1 January 2009, following the admission to listing and trading on Euronext Amsterdam, an issuer of securities which issued securities that have been admitted to trading on a regulated market has to comply with ongoing obligations, subject to certain exceptions and exemptions.

These ongoing obligations include, but are not limited to, the following:
- publication of annual financial reports within four months after the end of the financial year;
- publication of the half-yearly financial reports within two months from the end of the first half of each financial year;
- publication of an interim management statement during the first and second half of each financial year within 10 weeks after the beginning and six weeks before the end of the relevant period, containing an explanation of important events and transactions that have taken place during the relevant period and the impact on the financial position of the issuer and its controlled undertakings and a general description of the financial position and performances of the issuer and its controlled undertakings during the relevant period;
- publication of a document annually including or referring to the information disclosed in the 12 months preceding the publication of the annual report pursuant to: (a) the relevant European directives as implemented in Dutch securities and company law; and (b) applicable securities laws of other countries;
- immediately publishing any changes in the rights attached to the various classes of securities of the issuer;
- immediate publication of price sensitive information about the issuer and its securities or other financial instruments by means of an official press release in the Netherlands and in any other state where that

company's securities or financial instruments are admitted to trading on a regulated market or where such admission has been requested;

- ensuring equal treatment of all holders of securities in the same position and provide all necessary information and facilities to enable holders of securities to exercise their rights; and
- communicating any proposed amendment of it articles of association to both the AFM and Euronext.

The FSA furthermore provides for certain rules on information to be made available periodically for financial institutions, eg, investment institutions or investment firms.

An exception to the above obligations is available for, among others, issuers offering non-equity securities with a nominal value per unit of at least EUR 50,000.

7. MARKET ABUSE
7.1 Insider trading
The rules on insider trading are incorporated in the FSA. Persons with inside information are prohibited from carrying out transactions or causing transactions to be carried out:

- in or from the Netherlands or a non-EEA state, in financial instruments (including securities) that are admitted or are likely to be admitted in the near future to a regulated market or multilateral trading facility in the Netherlands;
- in or from the Netherlands in financial instruments that are admitted or are likely to be admitted in the near future to a regulated market or a multilateral trading facility in another EEA state or a system comparable to a regulated market or a multilateral trading facility in a non-EEA state; and
- in or from the Netherlands or a non-EEA state in financial instruments which value is at least in part determined by the financial instruments mentioned above in or from another EEA state in financial instruments that are admitted to a multilateral trading facility in the Netherlands.

Inside information is an awareness of information that is concrete and that directly or indirectly concerns the legal entity, company or institution to which the financial instruments pertain or to the trade in those financial instruments, which information has not been publicly disclosed and which public disclosure might have a significant influence on the price of the financial instruments or on the price of financial instruments derived from those financial instruments (and as regards financial instruments whose value partly depends on the value of commodities, information investors in those securities or other financial instruments may expect to be disclosed based on market practices that are customary on the regulated market or the multilateral trading facility where those financial instruments are traded).

The FSA makes a distinction between 'primary insiders' (for example directors and members of the supervisory board and persons with a qualifying shareholding) and 'secondary insiders'. For primary insiders it is irrelevant whether they should reasonably suspect that they possess

inside information. For secondary insiders it has to be proven that they
know or should reasonably suspect that their knowledge qualifies as inside
information within the meaning of the FSA.

The FSA provides for certain exceptions and exemptions to the
prohibition on insider trading, including exceptions in respect of
repurchases of own shares under a repurchase programme and price
stabilisation immediately following an initial public offering.

The FSA furthermore provides for a prohibition on passing on inside
information or recommending transactions to third parties by primary or
secondary insiders.

7.2 Market manipulation

The FSA contains a prohibition on market manipulation. It is prohibited to:

- carry out a transaction or cause a transaction to be carried out,
  in financial instruments, which gives or is likely to give a false or
  misleading signal as to the supply of, demand for or price of such
  financial instruments;
- carry out a transaction or cause a transaction to be carried out, in
  financial instruments, which secures the price of one or several of such
  financial instruments at an artificial level;
- carry out a transaction or cause a transaction to be carried out, in
  financial instruments, which employs deception or contrivance;
- disseminate information which gives or is likely to give a false or
  misleading signal as to as to the supply of, demand for or price of
  financial instruments while the person disseminating the information
  knows or should reasonably know that the information is incorrect or
  misleading.

The FSA provides for certain exceptions and exemptions to the
prohibition on market manipulation, including exceptions in respect
of repurchases of own shares under a repurchase programme and price
stabilisation immediately following an initial public offering.

The Dutch Criminal Code also contains a more general provision that
prohibits any person from (and penalises) unlawfully forcing the price of
merchandise, securities or valuable paper to rise or fall by disseminating
untruthful information.

7.3 Miscellaneous

The FSA furthermore provides for notification obligations or reporting
duties for certain insiders, an obligation to draw up rules governing the
holding of and transactions in its own securities by its directors, members
of its supervisory board and its employees, an obligation to keep a list of
insiders, and an obligation for investment firms and others responsible for
carrying out transactions to report transactions where there is a suspicion
that the client is acting with inside information or that the client is acting in
violation of the rules on market manipulation.

8.   INVESTMENT INSTITUTIONS

8.1 Prohibition

The FSA prohibits the offering of a participation in an investment institution in the Netherlands if that investment institution's manager or in case of an investment company without a separate manager, the investment company itself, has not obtained a licence from the AFM.

8.2 Non-applicability of the prohibition – exceptions

The prohibition does not apply in respect of:

- offers to less than 100 individuals or legal entities other than qualified investors;
- offers to qualified investors only;
- offers concerning investment institutions which are established in a state which has been designated for that purpose by the Minister of Finance (ie France, Guernsey, Ireland, Jersey, Luxembourg, Malta, the United Kingdom and the United States of America to the extent the investment institution is registered with the SEC, provided that a notification procedure is followed and unless in the relevant state the investment institution is subject to restrictions concerning the parties to whom its participations may be offered); or
- offers concerning investment institutions which are 'registered' as undertakings for collective investments in transferable securities (UCITS) in another EEA state and have followed a notification procedure.

Reliance on the first two exceptions requires that the offer and each advertisement and document announcing the offer contain a selling restriction stating that:

- the investment institution does not require a licence pursuant to the FSA and is not supervised pursuant to Part 3 (Prudential Supervision of Financial Undertakings) and Part 4 (Conduct of Business Supervision of Financial Undertakings) of the FSA (for the first exception); and
- the offer is or shall be solely addressed to qualified investors (for the second exception).

8.3 Non-applicability of the prohibition – exemptions

The Exemption Regulation FSA provides for certain exemptions to the prohibition, including an exemption for offers of participations for a total consideration of or at a denomination of at least EUR 50,000 per investor.

If a party wants to rely on one of these exemptions, that party's advertisements and the documents in which the participations are offered must contain a selling restriction stating that it is not required to obtain a licence under the FSA and that it is not subject to supervision by the AFM.

8.4 Licence requirements

If no exemption or exception applies, the manager of the investment institution or the investment company itself (if it does not have a manager) will have to apply for a licence. A licence will be granted by the AFM if the manager or the investment company meets certain criteria, for instance in

respect of:
- expertise;
- trustworthiness;
- administrative organisation;
- minimum own funds; and
- a registration document (containing information about the investment institutions which such manager manages or about the investment company).

Dispensation from certain licence requirements may be granted if the manager or investment company shows that it is not reasonably possible to meet such requirements, and that the aims which the FSA seeks to accomplish have been adequately achieved in other ways.

A licence may be made subject to certain restrictions and stipulations.

8.5 Continuing requirements
A licensed manager or a licensed investment company must on a continuing basis comply with certain rules, including the rules described in 9.4 above. Persons who are excluded from the prohibition still may have to comply with the conduct rules or part of them, such as rules intended to ensure that the manager or investment company acts in the interests of its clients and the proper operation of the securities markets.

9. INVESTMENT FIRMS
9.1 Prohibition
The FSA prohibits the provision of investment services or the performance of investment activities in the Netherlands without having obtained a licence from the AFM. This includes, among other things, securities brokerage (including intermediation and market making), the provision of investment advice, individual portfolio management (collective portfolio management is covered by the prohibition referred to in 9.1 above) and the exploitation of a multilateral trading facility.

9.2 Non-applicability of the prohibition – exceptions
The FSA provides for certain exceptions to the prohibition, for instance in respect of investment institutions, credit institutions, financial institutions and investment firms established in another EEA state (if a notification procedure is followed). Most of these exceptions are subject to certain conditions.

9.3 Non-applicability of the prohibition – exemptions
The Exemption Regulation FSA provides for certain exemptions to the prohibition, for instance in respect of investment firms from certain non-EEA states which are subject to supervision in their home country, private venture capital companies (regarding shares in their own subscribed capital) and family companies and foundations. Most of these exemptions are subject to certain conditions.

9.4 Licence requirements

A licence will be granted by the AFM if the applicant meets certain criteria, for instance in respect of:

* expertise;
* trustworthiness;
* administrative organisation;
* minimum own funds;
* adequate measures to protect investors rights; and
* adequate policy to prevent conflicts of interest.

Dispensation from certain licence requirements may be granted if the investment firm shows that it is not reasonably possible to meet such requirements and that the aims which the FSA seeks to accomplish have been adequately achieved in other ways.

A licence may be made subject to certain restrictions and stipulations.

9.5 Continuing requirements

A licensed investment firm must on a continuing basis comply with certain rules, including the rules described in 10.4 above. Investment firms which are excluded from the prohibition still may have to comply with the conduct rules or part of them, such as rules intended to ensure that the investment firm acts in the interests of its clients and the proper operation of the securities markets.

10. NOTIFICATION OBLIGATIONS/DECLARATIONS OF NO OBJECTION FOR QUALIFYING SHAREHOLDINGS

10.1 The Act on the Prevention of Money Laundering and the Financing of Terrorism

Pursuant to the Act on the Prevention of Money Laundering and the Financing of Terrorism, financial institutions and other institutions which offer financial and other services listed in this act as part of their profession or business are required to report any unusual transactions to the disclosure office.

10.2 The External Financial Relations Act 1994

A company can be appointed by DNB as a reporter under the External Financial Relations Act 1994 and the further regulation Reporting Requirements Balance of Payments Reports 2003 pursuant thereto. If appointed it will be obliged to comply with certain notification and registration requirements in connection with any possible payments to or from non-residents. Certain financial institutions are required to notify DNB in order for DNB to assess whether the financial institution should be appointed as a reporter.

10.3 The disclosure of voting rights and capital interest in issuers of shares which have been admitted to trading on a regulated market

The FSA provides for certain disclosure duties, *inter alia*, for issuers of shares or certificates of shares which have been admitted to trading on a regulated market and for holders of shares or voting rights, including:

- a disclosure duty for issuers of shares or certificates of shares which have been admitted to trading on a regulated market in respect of changes in the issued capital or in the number or nature of voting rights on the shares in its capital;
- a disclosure duty for a legal or natural person holding shares or voting rights in respect of achieving, exceeding or falling below certain levels of capital interest and/or voting rights in a listed company;
- a disclosure duty for a legal or natural person that acquires or disposes of shares with special voting rights; and
- a disclosure duty for a legal or natural person that has a substantial interest (5 per cent or more in shares or voting rights).

For managing directors and members of the supervisory board of listed companies there are additional disclosure requirements.

10.4 Insider trading
The FSA provides for rules relating to insider trading and market manipulation (see above), including notification obligations or reporting duties for certain insiders.

10.5 Declaration of no objection for qualifying shareholdings
Unless a declaration of no objection has been obtained from DNB, the following are prohibited: the holding or acquisition of, or increase in a 'qualifying shareholding' (10 per cent capital interest or voting rights) in a Netherlands-established bank; a manager of a Netherlands-established investment institution; a Netherlands-established investment firm; a Netherlands-established entity for risk acceptance; a Netherlands-established insurance company; and the exercise of any control connected with a qualifying shareholding in such entities. The holding or acquisition of, or increase in a qualifying shareholding in an operator of a regulated market licensed in the Netherlands and the exercise of any control connected with a qualifying shareholding in such entities requires a declaration of no objection from the Minister of Finance.

Pursuant to the FSA it is furthermore prohibited for a bank established in the Netherlands to:

- acquire or increase a qualifying shareholding in a bank, an investment firm, a financial institution or an insurance company, if at the time of such acquisition or increase in the balance sheet total of that bank, investment firm, financial institution or insurance company represents more than 1 per cent of the consolidated balance sheet total of the bank; or
- to acquire or increase a qualifying shareholding in an undertaking other than referred to above, if the amount paid for such acquisition or increase together with the amounts of previous acquisitions and increases of that qualifying shareholding amount to more than 1 per cent of the consolidated own funds of the bank, unless a declaration of no objection has been obtained from DNB.

11. PUBLIC TAKEOVER BIDS
11.1 Prohibition
The FSA prohibits making a public offer for securities admitted to trading on a regulated market in the Netherlands, unless an offering document which has been approved by the AFM or the supervisory authority of another EEA state is made generally available. All announcements concerning the public offer should refer to this offering document. An invitation to make an offer by means of which the bidder has the intention of acquiring securities qualifies as a public offer within the meaning of the FSA as well.

Public offers are also subject to workers' participation rules, such as the rules laid down in the Works Council Act. These workers' participation rules will not be discussed further.

11.2 Mandatory offer
The FSA obliges parties (acting alone or in concert) that acquire 'dominant control' in a Dutch company (basically 30 per cent or more of voting rights), of which the shares or depositary receipts for shares are issued with the company's cooperation and trading on a regulated market, to make an offer at a fair price for the remaining shares and depositary receipts for shares issued with the company's cooperation. The offer must in principle be made within 30 days after the dominant control is acquired. However, this period may be prolonged by the Enterprise Chamber of the Amsterdam Court of Appeal at the request of the bidder, the target company or the target's investors.

11.3   Non-applicability – exemptions/dispensations
Certain exemptions to the above prohibition and obligation exist. Furthermore, the AFM may grant, upon request, a dispensation from the prohibition on making a public offer.

11.4 Requirements offering document
The FSA and further regulations pursuant to the FSA set out in detail the ssues or information which need to be included in the offering document in case of a firm offer, a partial offer or tender offer, for example, information in respect of the bidder, the offer, the target and reasons for and intentions of the bidder.

The offer can be made subject to certain conditions, provided that the fulfilment of such conditions does not depend on the will of the bidder.

11.5 Rules of conduct
The FSA and further regulations pursuant to the FSA provide for rules of conduct which, subject to possible dispensations, have to be complied with by the bidder, the target company and their executive directors, supervisory directors and other officers. This includes rules on how and when to make public announcements, to give notices to the AFM and/or the target company (of transactions by the bidder or insiders or other information), to make the offering document, other documents and information available

and on the tender period and on how and when to declare the offer unconditional. Specific rules of conduct apply to mandatory offers (eg, the fulfilment of a mandatory offer may not be made conditional).

12. SANCTIONS

12.1 Criminal sanctions

Violation of the rules set by or pursuant to the FSA is – in most cases – an economic offence. Violation of the rules, if committed intentionally, is a serious offence or, if committed unintentionally, a minor offence. Violation of insider trading rules and market manipulation rules is – in all cases – a serious offence. Offenders can face monetary penalties and/or imprisonment if convicted of an economic offence. In case of a legal person, persons giving instructions and *de facto* directors can be prosecuted as offenders. In addition, the court may order an offender to pay to the state an amount equal to the benefit which the offender obtained as a result of its offence.

12.2 Administrative sanctions

In case of a violation of the rules set by or pursuant to the FSA, the AFM or DNB can – in most cases – impose an administrative fine or an order for periodic penalty payments. All violations have been classified in one of the three fine categories, which provide for a principal amount of the fine. For the two highest categories the fine may be increased or decreased based on the severity and duration of the violation and degree of blame. In all cases, the amount of the fine may be doubled for a repeated violation within five years after a fine was imposed for the same violation. The maximum amount of a fine is either EUR 4,000,000 or EUR 8,000,000 for a repeated violation within five years after a fine was imposed for the same violation, or (if it is higher) twice the amount of the benefit which the violator obtained as a result of the violation.

The right to impose an administrative fine lapses if the public prosecutor has commenced criminal proceedings against the offender for the same offence. The opposite also applies; the right to prosecute lapses if the AFM or DNB has already imposed an administrative fine for an offence.

Depending on the circumstances, the AFM or DNB can also take the following measures:

- give instructions;
- revoke dispensations, licences and/or declarations of no objection granted by it;
- appoint an administrator;
- give public warnings (eg, it can disclose directions given by it or it can disclose its refusal to grant a licence etc); and
- in the case of a public takeover bid, the AFM can instruct institutions not to co-operate with the implementation and settlement of a public offer.

Furthermore, under the FSA, all decisions will be disclosed whereby the AFM or DNB impose a fine or an order for periodic penalty payments (unless disclosure of the decision is contrary to the purpose of the AFM or DNB supervision); and the periodic penalty payment will be forfeited.

12.3 Civil law consequences

The FSA provides that legal acts performed in violation of the rules set by or pursuant to the FSA are not void or voidable for that reason, unless otherwise provided for in the FSA. However, transactions (eg, agreements on brokerage or portfolio management or the issuing of securities) in violation of the rules set by or pursuant to the FSA may be void or voidable on the basis of deceit or error. Furthermore, issuers of securities or investment firms or any other person could be held liable on the basis of tort.

12.4 Consequences of breaches of Euronext rules

In the case of non-compliance with the listing rules, Euronext Amsterdam can take measures with regard to the listing. The measures include suspension and cancellation of the listing.

13. PENDING LEGISLATION
13.1 General

Securities laws and regulations are continuously subject to change, particularly since the European Commission, against the backdrop of financial crisis, adopted important draft legislation to strengthen supervision of the EU financial sector in late 2009.

In this section, some of the legislation pending in the Netherlands is described in broad outline.

13.2 Bill on the supervision of clearing and settlement services

A bill on the supervision of clearing and settlement services was submitted in 2009. The aim of this bill was to introduce a system of direct supervision over institutions providing clearing and/or settlement services in the Netherlands and to set out rules on the provision of such services.

Under the bill, a provider of clearing and/or settlement services must, in principle, obtain a licence from DNB. In order to do so, the provider must meet certain requirements relating to, for example, the integrity and expertise of its policymakers, the transparency of its control structure, risk control and conflicts of interest.

13.3 Bill on the corporate governance of listed companies

In July 2009, a bill providing for a number of changes in the corporate governance of listed companies was submitted to the Dutch Parliament. Relevant elements of the bill – which consists of amendments to the FSA, the Dutch Securities Book-Entry Administration and Transfers Act, the Dutch Civil Code and the Dutch Economic Offences Act – are:
*   the introduction of a mechanism to identify the 'ultimate investors' (ie, shareholders or holders of depositary receipts for shares) of a company (Dutch or non-Dutch) whose securities are admitted to trading on a regulated market or multilateral trading facility in the Netherlands and to enable direct communications to and among the identified shareholders;
*   the introduction of a new minimum threshold for the disclosure of

substantial interests in Dutch companies whose shares are admitted to trading on a regulated market in the Netherlands;

- the imposition of a requirement on companies whose securities are admitted to trading on a regulated market and whose jurisdiction of origin is the Netherlands to disclose their strategy on their Web site;
- the imposition of a requirement on holders of a substantial interest in a Dutch company whose shares are admitted to trading on a regulated market in the Netherlands to publicly disclose whether or not they agree with the company's overall strategy; and
- the raising of the threshold for the right of shareholders of Dutch public limited liability companies to place items on the agenda for a shareholders' meeting.

13.4 Bill introducing standardised notice requirements for exempt offers of securities

As discussed under 3.2, offers of securities to the public are in certain cases exempted from the prospectus requirements contained in the FSA. Under a bill to amend the FSA, offers under some of those exemptions require a notice to potential investors stating that the offer is exempt. The notice must be given in the offer itself, in all advertisements and announcements relating to the offer and in all documents indicating that such an offer will be made. The exempt offers covered by the bill are:

- offers to less than 100 individuals or legal entities other than 'qualified investors';
- offers under which the securities can only be acquired for a total consideration of at least EUR 50,000 per investor;
- offers of securities with a denomination per unit of at least EUR 50,000; and
- offers the total consideration for which is less than EUR 100,000, calculated over a period of 12 months.

The FSA already contains a similar requirement in respect of offers of participations in investment institutions (see 8.3 above).

Portugal

Morais Leitão, Galvão Teles, Soares da Silva & Associados, Sociedade de Advogados
Ricardo Andrade Amaro & Diana Ribeiro Duarte

1. GENERAL DESCRIPTION OF THE CAPITAL MARKETS
1.1 Number of companies listed
There are 52 listed companies currently on the Lisbon stock exchange, named (although not officially) Eurolist by New York Stock Exchange (NYSE) Euronext Lisbon (hereafter Eurolist), the official quotation market managed by Euronext Lisbon (Sociedade Gestora de Mercados Regulamentados, S.A.). Additionally, there are 17 listed companies on the Portuguese multilateral trading facility (MTF) EasyNext Lisbon.

1.2 Total volume and market value
In 2010, 15.608.620.049 shares were traded in the Euronext Lisbon regulated markets and in the EasyNext Lisbon MTF, corresponding to a market value of 40.7 billion EUR, and, additionally, an amount of EUR 591,065,019.00 concerning to public debt.

1.3 Issue activity
According to the Fact Book Euronext 2010, one company was admitted to trading on Eurolist, whilst in 2009 no company was admitted and in 2008 three companies were admitted to trading.

1.4 Takeover activity
According to the Portuguese Securities Market Commission (CMVM) annual report for 2008, only one mandatory takeover was launched in 2008. In reference to 2009, the CMVM annual report lists four mandatory takeovers launched during that year.
There was no official information available for 2010 at the time of writing.

1.5 Hostile takeover attempts
Recently, significant hostile takeovers have been attempted, mostly concerning companies related to relevant sectors of the Portuguese economy, notably telecommunications banking in 2006, and cement in 2009.

2. REGULATORY STRUCTURE
2.1 General
The Portuguese securities market is mainly governed by the Portuguese Securities Code (CVM), by orders issued by the Ministry of Finance,

regulations issued by the CMVM and technical regulations issued by Euronext Lisbon. EU law, including regulations in respect of offerings, prospectuses and, more generally, securities markets also applies.

2.2 Regulation of the offering of new securities

The offer of new securities in Portugal is made either through public offers or private placements.

2.2.1 Public offering

An offer of securities shall be deemed to be a public offer in Portugal whenever any of the following events occurs:

- the offer is, totally or partially, addressed to undetermined Portuguese residents;
- the offer is addressed to all the shareholders of a Portuguese listed company, even if the share capital is represented by nominative shares;
- the offer is, partially or totally, preceded or executed with prospecting or marketing activities in Portugal; or
- the offer is addressed to more than 99 non-qualified investors located and/or resident in Portugal.

An offer falling under the category of a public offer can only be validly and legally addressed to investors resident and/or located in Portugal when: (i) an offer prospectus is approved by (in the case of a distribution offer) or the offer is registered with (in the case of a tender offer) the CMVM; or (ii) an offer prospectus (in the case of both a distribution offer and a tender offer for securities admitted to trading in a regulated market in Portugal) has been approved by another EU member state regulatory authority, a recognition procedure is commenced with the CMVM and the offer prospectus is passported into Portugal.

In the case of a tender offer, the offeror has to register the tender offer with the CMVM. Following the registration of the offer, the offeror has to disclose: (i) an announcement launching the offer; and (ii) the offer prospectus duly approved by the CMVM.

A mutual fund is deemed to be incorporated through the public subscription of participation units if such subscription is: (i) addressed to undetermined addressees; (ii) preceded or disclosed simultaneously with marketing activities or a collection of investment intentions addressed to undetermined addressees; or (iii) addressed to at least 100 addressees.

2.2.2 Private offering

Where there is no advertisement, prospecting or marketing activities in Portugal in relation to an offer and the offer is exclusively addressed to qualified investors and/or 99 or less non-qualified investors resident and/or located in Portugal, the offer should qualify as a private placement.

The following entities are considered as qualified investors: (i) credit institutions; (ii) investment companies; (iii) insurance companies; (iv) collective investment institutions and their respective managing companies; (v) pension funds and their respective managing companies; (vi) other authorised or regulated financial institutions, such as securitisation companies or funds; (vii) financial institutions of states outside the European Union performing activities similar to those indicated in (i) to (vi) above; (viii) entities negotiating financial instruments on commodities; and (ix) national and regional governments, central banks and public agencies managing state debt, such as the European Central Bank, European Investment Bank, International Monetary Fund and World Bank.

Other entities may also be deemed as a qualified investor for the purpose of determining an offer as a private placement, notably: (i) entities whose main activity is to invest in securities; (ii) companies that, in accordance with their annual accounts, fulfil at least two of the following criteria: (a) an average of 250 or more workers during the relevant year, (b) assets in an amount above EUR 43 million, and/or (c) a turnover of more than EUR 50 million; (iii) small and medium sized companies, if registered with the CMVM, having their registered offices in Portugal and that, in accordance with their annual accounts, fulfil one of the criteria mentioned in (a), (b) and (c) above; and (iv) individuals resident and/or located in Portugal, if registered with the CMVM, that fulfil at least two of the following criteria: (a) have, in the past, made significant market transactions over securities with a frequency of at least 10 operations per quarter in the past year, (b) have a portfolio of securities in an amount of more than EUR 500,000, and/or (c) have performed any activity, at least during one year, in the financial sector, in a position that demands knowledge of investment in securities.

An offer qualifying as a private placement would not be subject to: (i) registration with; or (ii) prospectus approval by the CMVM.

2.3 Differences between local and foreign companies
There is no need for a foreign company offering securities to be locally registered or licensed, or to have local presence in Portugal.

A prospectus specifically prepared for an offer in Portugal or prepared for a pan-European offer and passported into Portugal should be disclosed, if a public offer is envisaged to be launched in Portugal.

2.4 Admission to trading on a regulated market
An issuer seeking the listing of its securities in Eurolist must comply with the prerequisites set out in section 8.1.

A prospectus is required for admission to trading on Eurolist.

2.5 Financial promotion
Advertising and prospecting with the purpose of entering into financial intermediation agreements or gathering information on current or potential clients may only be carried out by:
- an authorised financial intermediary; or
- a tied agent representing the financial intermediary.

2.6 Rule books
The rules regarding prospectuses and listing are set out in the CVM,

Directive 2003/71/EC and EC Regulation 809/2004, which implements the former Directive.

3. REGISTRATION OF THE ISSUER AND SECURITIES

3.1 Registration requirements

There are no specific requirements in respect of the registration of the issuer, either local or foreign, other than the commercial registration applicable to all Portuguese companies.

The registration of a branch in Portugal requires the delivery of certain documents to the commercial registry authorities if a place of business is established in Portugal.

The issuance of a book entry form and titled securities is mandatorily registered with the issuer.

Titled securities may be deposited with a financial intermediary in, or out, of the centralised system. Alternatively, titled securities may be kept by their respective holders. In any case, titled securities of listed companies must be deposited with a financial intermediary within the centralised system.

Book-entry form securities may be registered under: (i) an account with the financial intermediary, in the centralised system; (ii) an account with a single financial intermediary appointed by the issuer; or (iii) an account with the issuer or with a financial intermediary representing the issuer.

3.2 Other requirements

Not applicable.

3.3 Nature of securities

Pursuant to the CVM, the capacity to issue securities and the representation form of the securities are governed by the issuer's personal law and types of securities are extensively (although not exhaustively) listed in the CVM and include:

(a) shares;
(b) bonds;
(c) equity instruments;
(d) units in undertakings for collective investments;
(e) warrants;
(f) rights detached from the securities described in a) to d); and
(g) other documents representing fungible legal positions provided they may be traded on the market.

Securities may be titled or in book-entry form if they are, respectively, registered in an account or represented by certificates. Furthermore, securities are nominative or in bearer form, respectively, if the issuer has the ability to know its holders or not.

4. SUPERVISORY AUTHORITIES

4.1 Conduct: prudential, cooperation, self-regulation of stock exchange

The CMVM has the power to supervise the Portuguese securities market.

The regulatory duties of the CMVM relate mainly to the development of the broad principles set out in the CVM by means of issuing: (i) regulations; (ii) instructions, which aim to regulate proceedings of an internal nature; (iii) general recommendations; and (iv) official legal opinions.

The CMVM also has powers to investigate infractions to the securities market's rules and apply sanctions.

The CMVM's supervisory duties also include prudential supervision aiming, in general, to: (i) preserve the solvency and liquidity of the institution, as well as to prevent risks; (ii) to prevent systemic risk; and (iii) to oversee the ethical standards of the members of the management bodies and holders of qualifying shareholdings.

Banking and insurance sectors are additionally supervised and regulated by, respectively:
- the Bank of Portugal (BP); and
- the Portuguese Insurance Institute (ISP).

In the context of its attributions, Euronext Lisbon also has supervisory powers, being responsible for defining the operating rules of its markets and adopting any action deemed necessary to defend the integrity, proper functioning, safety and market transparency.

4.2 New listing measures in connection with the credit crisis

The CMVM has issued Regulation no. 1/2009 establishing a particular information regime for complex financial products in order to allow the public to acknowledge the real features of such products; and Regulation no. 1/2010 setting out new recommendations on corporate governance, aiming to improve the levels of transparency of the securities market.

5. OFFERING DOCUMENTATION OR PROSPECTUS REQUIREMENTS

5.1 Nature and statutory requirements of the offering document or disclosure document

As a general rule, public offers must be preceded by the disclosure of a prospectus.

Any prospectus must contain complete, true, up-to-date, clear, objective and lawful information, allowing the addressees to make an informed assessment about the offer, and must comply with information requirements contained in Directive 2003/71/EC and EC Regulation 809/2004.

Any prospectus must include, among others, the following information:
- persons who are responsible for its contents;
- the purpose of the offer;
- about the issuer and its business;
- about the offeror and its business;
- corporate governance structure of the issuer;
- about the members of the corporate bodies of the issuer and the offeror; and
- about the financial intermediary.

5.2 Exemptions

Certain types of public offers do not require a prospectus, notably:

- offers of securities, as a result of a merger, to at least 100 shareholders who are not qualified investors;
- payment of dividends in the form of shares of the same class as those that granted the right to dividend; and
- offers of securities to members of the management bodies or employees, to the extent that the offeror has securities listed in a regulated market and that there is a document containing information on the securities being offered.

5.3 Preparation of the offering document, general contents

The prospectus of a public distribution offer must include a summary describing the essential features of the offer and the risk factors associated with the issuer, the guarantor (if applicable) and the securities that are the object of the offer. Such a prospectus may be a single document or composed of separate documents (ie, register document, information on the securities and summary).

In limited circumstances, the issuer may alternatively prepare a base prospectus, which will be subject to an addendum whenever updated information is available, and which must also include statements of responsibility issued by the persons who are responsible for its contents.

5.4 Due diligence

Although Portuguese law does not expressly govern the exercise of due diligence, it is common that the financial intermediary, assisted by its legal advisors, exercises due diligence and issues a report, which is usually made available to the issuer and its advisors in the offer.

5.5 Responsibility

The following persons or entities may be held responsible for the contents of the prospectus:

- the offeror;
- the members of the management board of the offeror;
- the issuer;
- the members of the management board of the issuer;
- the promoters, in the case of a subscription offer for the incorporation of a company;
- the members of the auditing corporate body, accounting firms, chartered accountants and any other individuals that have certified or, in any other way, verified the accounting documents on which the prospectus is based;
- the financial intermediaries of the offer; and
- any other entities appointed in the prospectus as responsible for any information, forecast or study included in the prospectus.

5.6 Disclaimer/selling restrictions

In the case of private offers, disclaimers in respect of selling restrictions are

commonly used in respect of:
- restrictions on the distribution of the offer prospectus and other offer materials;
- the addressees; and
- the absence of registration and approval of the prospectus by the CMVM.

5.7 Recognition of prospectuses by other exchanges

A prospectus approved by the competent authority of an EU member state for a public distribution offer can be validly used in Portugal, so long as a passport procedure of such a prospectus is complied with. To that purpose, the CMVM must receive a prospectus approval certificate from the competent authority and a copy of the aforementioned approved prospectus and, in some circumstances, a translation into Portuguese of the summary.

A prospectus approved in another member state for a takeover offer to be made in relation to securities listed in a regulated market in Portugal can be recognised by the CMVM and used in Portugal if the prospectus is translated into Portuguese and the CMVM receives the relevant certificate from the authority of the other member state.

5.8 Supplementary prospectuses

If, between the moment of the approval of the prospectus and the term of the offer, any inaccuracy in the prospectus is noticed, or any new fact occurs, or any fact not previously considered is acknowledged and is relevant to the assessment to be made by the addressees, an addendum or rectification to the prospectus must be filed with the CMVM for approval.

5.9 Issuing of bonds

Issuance of bonds is subject to the rules mentioned in sections 5.1, 5.2 and 5.3 in respect of public and private offers, in particular in relation to prospectus obligation, although the level of required disclosure may vary in accordance with EC Regulation 809/2004.

6. DISTRIBUTION SYSTEMS
6.1 Normal structure of a distribution group

Securities offerings are traditionally distributed by banks. Such entities must be authorised to perform financial intermediation activities by the BP and be registered with the CMVM and fall under the joint supervision of both these entities.

6.2 Methods of distribution

The distribution of the securities may be made through the entering into of a placement agreement with a financial intermediary or through the entering into of an underwriting agreement.

6.3 Underwriting

By entering into an underwriting agreement, the financial intermediary is obliged to acquire the securities that are the object of the public offer and, subsequently, place them, on its own account and risk.

The financial intermediary must transfer to the final acquirers all the patrimonial rights inherent to the securities issued after the date of the underwriting.

Pre-emption rights in the subscription or acquisition of the securities are not affected.

6.4   Fees and commission

The direct consideration for the rendering of financial intermediation services is not subject to particular restrictions, except those in connection with loyalty duties towards the client. Commissions and fees vary on the type of agreement and commitment taken by the financial intermediary.

Proper fees necessary to the rendering of the financial intermediation services are allowed if they do not damage the client's interests.

Inducement fees granted to third parties may only be charged if the client is informed and the quality of the service is improved.

6.5   Stabilisation

In general, transactions likely to produce stabilisation effects on the prices of a certain type of securities are prohibited, as per Regulation 2273/2003/EC. However, buy-back programmes and the stabilisation of financial instruments may be exempted, notably in the context of an initial public offer.

As an additional means of facilitating a public offer, a stabilisation agent, acting on behalf of the managers, may engage in transactions that stabilise, support, maintain or otherwise affect the price of the shares for a maximum period of 30 calendar days from the date the shares are admitted to listing on a regulated market. The stabilisation agent may over-allot the total number of shares comprised in a certain public offer or effect transactions with a view to supporting the market price of the shares at a level higher than that which might otherwise prevail in the open market.

6.6   Involvement of a distributor in the preparation of the offering document

The distributor may be a different entity from the financial intermediary who rendered the assistance services during the offer.

6.7   Timing of distribution process

The distribution of securities in the context of an offering generally occurs in the term defined by the financial intermediary but always in compliance with the nature of the offer (ie, public offer or private placement, see sections 2.2.1 and 2.2.2).

6.8   Rules on distribution to the public

The prospectus shall not be disclosed to the public until its approval by the CMVM.

The prospectus shall be disclosed:

- in the event of a distribution public offer preceded by a negotiation of rights, no later than the working day before the day on which the rights are detached; or
- in all other distribution public offers, no later than the commencement of the relevant public offer.

In the event of a public offer of a class of shares not yet admitted to trading on a regulated market and which is intended to be admitted to trading on a regulated market for the first time, the prospectus must be available at least six working days before the expiry of the offer period.

If the prospectus is made available in electronic form, a paper copy must be delivered to the investor, upon his request and free of charge, by the issuer, the offeror or the financial intermediaries placing the securities.

Again, distribution of securities must conform to the applicable rules depending on the type of the offer (ie, public offer or private placement, see sections 2.2.1 and 2.2.2).

7. PUBLICITY

All advertising materials related to public offers are subject to prior approval by the CMVM.

All marketing materials shall: (i) be comprehensive, true, current, clear, objective and lawful, even if the information is inserted in an advice, a recommendation, an advertisement or a rating notice; (ii) mention the existence or future availability of a prospectus and indicate the means to obtain it; and (iii) be consistent with the contents of the prospectus.

8. LISTING

8.1 Special listing requirements, admission criteria

The issuer seeking listing of its securities must:

- be incorporated and functioning in accordance with the law under which it is governed;
- have been conducting business for at least three years;
- have published its annual financial statements for the prior three years; and
- prove that its financial and economic condition is compatible with the nature of the securities to be admitted and with the market to which listing is requested.

Only those shares in relation to which an adequate level of dispersion among the public can be verified and a minimum amount of EUR 1 million of market capitalisation is forecast (or, if such forecast is not possible, when the own funds of the company are at least equal to such an amount) shall be admitted to trading.

8.2 Mechanics of the review process

The application for the admission to trading on a regulated market is served to the regulated market operator of the market on which the securities will be traded and must include evidence that the prerequisites referred to in section 8.1 are met (or how and when they will be met) and may be

requested by:
- the issuer;
- the holders of at least 10 per cent of the issued securities of the same category, if the issuer is already a listed company; and
- the Public Credit Management Institute, if it relates to bonds issued by the Portuguese state.

The regulated market operator shall decide on the admission to trading of the securities or its refusal up to 90 days after the submission of the application.

In any case, admission to trading shall be deemed refused if the approval decision is not notified within 90 days following the admission application.

8.3 Prospectus obligation, due diligence, exemption
In general, a prospectus is mandatory for the admission to trading of securities, in line with the general prospectus exemptions we have stated above, and is subject to the CMVM's approval.

Due diligence, although not legally regulated, is a common proceeding.

8.4 Appeal procedure in the event of a prospectus refusal
In the event that the CMVM refuses to approve the prospectus or register an offer, the issuer may bring the case before the Portuguese administrative courts, although there is no precedent of such an appeal procedure.

8.5 Authority of the Exchange
Eurolist is managed by Euronext Lisbon, which supervises and provides rules for the market agents of the Exchange. Euronext Lisbon holds an exchange licence granted by the CMVM and operates under its supervision.

8.6 Sponsor
Not applicable.

8.7 Special arrangements for smaller companies such as Alternext, AIM or SPACs
Euronext Lisbon operates Eurolist, the official quotation market, and the Euronext Lisbon Futures and Options Market, ie the Lisbon market of the New York Stock Exchange (NYSE) Liffe.

Euronext Lisbon also operates a multilateral trading facility (MTF) – EasyNext Lisbon – that does not fall within the EU definition of 'regulated markets'.

NYSE Alternext is a pan-European market designed specifically for small and medium-sized companies which may benefit from a market with less stringent listing requirements and innovative operating rules which Portuguese companies may access. In any case, a local platform in Portugal is to be created briefly.

8.8 Costs of various types
The costs of listing may vary considerably and, in general, include adviser

fees (lawyers, accountants and financial intermediary), marketing and distribution costs and fees related to the application with the CMVM and Euronext Lisbon.

9. SANCTIONS AND DISPUTES
9.1 Disciplinary and administrative sanctions
The most relevant infractions are:
* the breach of information duties by entities subject to the CMVM's supervision;
* the breach of the obligation to constitute the required sinking funds and the failure to make the adequate contributions to them;
* the breach of rules concerning the disposal, listing, negotiation, trading and registration of securities;
* the breach of rules concerning public offers' proceedings;
* the usurpation of powers of authorised clearing houses and the breach of rules regarding the intermediation activity; and
* the breach of the professional secrecy duty, the asset segregation obligation, the rules concerning the use of securities and the duty to defend the market and the failure to comply with lawful orders issued by the CMVM.

There is a distinction between: (i) very serious infractions, punishable with administrative fines between EUR 25,000 and EUR 5,000,000; (ii) serious infractions, punishable with administrative fines between EUR 12,500 and EUR 2,500,000; and (iii) less serious infractions, punishable with administrative fines between EUR 2,500 and EUR 500,000. In the event of negligence, the minimum and maximum amounts of the administrative fines are halved.

In addition to the administrative fines, the CMVM may also apply accessory penalties.

9.2 Civil actions
Any person who suffers damage by reason of a conduct undertaken in breach of the obligations provided in the CVM may file a legal suit in order to obtain damage compensation.

However, there are specific provisions in relation to civil liability actions in the CVM, such as those concerning: (i) the civil liability for the content of the prospectus; and (ii) the civil liability of the financial intermediaries.

9.3 Criminal penalties
Insider trading, market manipulation and disobedience to legitimate orders issued by the CMVM are deemed as crimes.

Such crimes are only punishable when wilfully committed.

10. CONTINUING OBLIGATIONS
10.1 Disclosure and transparency rule
Information relating to financial instruments, organised forms of trading, financial intermediation activities, clearing and settling of transactions,

public offers of securities and issuers must be comprehensive, true, up-to-date, clear, objective and lawful.

For each regulated market or multilateral trading system, the managing entity must disclose:

*   information on the financial instruments admitted to trading or selected for trading, the transactions carried out and respective price;
*   price, quantity, time and other details concerning each share transaction; and
*   total amount of shares traded.

10.2 Information

Issuers must disclose: (i) annual (consolidated and individual, when required) management reports and accounting documents and accounts, including a report from an authorised auditor; (ii) annual report on corporate governance; (iii) each semester, management and financial information; (iv) in certain circumstances, quarterly management and financial information; and (v) any privileged information of a price sensitive nature.

10.3 Listing rules

Listing rules comprise, amongst others, the obligation to serve to the CMVM information on several company elements; such as the share capital composition, certain shareholders' agreements, acquisition of qualifying shareholding, the dividends paid to the shareholders and the composition of the corporate bodies.

In addition, listing rules also compel the issuer to publicly disclose its financial standards and information on the corporate governance practices adopted.

Finally, and in accordance with the Rule Book I issued by Euronext, when trading on the market, listed companies shall always: observe high standards of integrity, market conduct and fair dealing; act with due skill, care, and diligence; and refrain from any act or course of conduct which is likely to harm the market's reputation.

10.4 Obligations regarding proxy solicitation

Proxy solicitation is subject to the following rules:

*   the proxy shall be granted only for a specified meeting, either on first or on second call;
*   the proxy may be revoked, being automatically revoked with the presence of the represented person in the shareholders' meeting; and
*   the request for representation must contain all the necessary elements for the exercise of the voting rights.

In the case of listed companies, the proxy letter shall also mention the voting rights attributable to the requestor, as well as the justification for the voting position.

The notice convening the shareholders' meeting shall mention the availability of a proxy form, indicating the means to request it, or include said form, which shall be submitted to the CMVM two days before being sent to the shareholders.

10.5 Continuing requirements of reporting and notification of substantial shareholdings or a substantial transaction

Any entity reaching or exceeding a holding of 10 per cent, 20 per cent, one-third, half, two-thirds and 90 per cent of the voting rights in the share capital of a listed company subject to Portuguese law or reducing its holding to a value lower than any of the above limits, should, within four trading days of the occurrence of said fact or the knowledge thereof, inform the CMVM and the relevant company.

Also, any entity reaching or exceeding a holding of: (i) 5 per cent, 15 per cent and 25 per cent of the voting rights in the share capital or reducing its holding to a value lower than any of the above limits with regard to a listed company, subject to Portuguese law, a company with its head offices in an EU member state with securities exclusively admitted to trading in Portugal and a company with its head offices outside the EU with securities admitted to trading in Portugal and subject to the supervision of the CMVM; or (ii) 2 per cent and reducing its holding to a value lower than said percentage of the voting rights in the capital of a listed company subject to Portuguese law must inform the CMVM and the relevant company.

Issuers with securities admitted to trading on a regulated market must disclose information directly concerning them or their securities, which is of a precise nature and has not been made public and, if it were made public, would be likely to have a significant effect on the prices of such securities, their underlying instruments or related derivatives (including substantial transactions).

Shareholders' agreements that have as their purpose the acquisition, maintenance or reinforcement of a qualified holding in a listed company or securing or frustrating the success of a takeover must be disclosed to the CMVM.

10.6 Clearing

The organisation, functioning and operational proceedings relating to each settlement system are included in the incorporation agreement of the system and the rules approved by the managing entity, the latter being subject to registration with the CMVM.

10.7 Requirements for unlisted issuers

Unlisted issuers are subject to less stringent rules than listed companies, being, in any case, obliged to disclose certain financial and corporate information and to comply with certain proceedings in respect of incorporation, amendments to bylaws, mergers, demergers and winding-up.

11. CORPORATE GOVERNANCE

11.1 Law and/or code

The relevant provisions in relation to corporate governance are set forth in the Portuguese Companies Code, the CVM and, in particular, in the CMVM's Regulation no. 1/2010 and in the CMVM Corporate Governance Code (2010).

11.2 Management structure
A Portuguese company (*sociedade anónima*) can adopt one of the following corporate governance models:
- board of directors and audit board;
- board of directors (including an audit committee) and chartered accountant; or
- executive board of directors, supervisory board and chartered accountant.

11.3 Obligations to publish information on the Internet
Issuers must disclose on their Internet page information in respect of: (i) shareholders' meetings; (ii) bylaws and regulations of corporate bodies; (iii) accounting documents and reports of activities; and (iv) members of corporate bodies.

11.4 Responsibility of inside/outside directors
Pursuant to the Corporate Governance Code of the CMVM, the board of directors of a listed company shall include a number of non-executive members that ensure the efficient supervision, auditing and assessment of the executive members' activity.

The CMVM also recommends that non-executive members include an adequate number of independent members and that non-executive members are not less than one-quarter of the total number of directors.

Directors, regardless of their nature (executive or non-executive), are jointly and severally liable, there being no differences between the liability regimes of executive and non-executive directors, although in the first case, due to the nature of their duties and their responsibilities concerning the day-to-day company's business, there is a higher risk of exposure.

11.5 Committees
The board of directors or the general and supervisory board, depending on the corporate governance model adopted, shall create committees to: (i) ensure a competent and independent assessment of the performance of the management bodies; (ii) evaluate the effectiveness of the corporate model adopted and propose measures aiming for its improvement; and (iii) identify potential candidates with the adequate profile for the performance of the directors' duties.

11.6 Obligation to ask for consent of a shareholders' meeting
The following matters, among others, are subject to approval by the shareholders' meeting:
- annual accounts;
- distribution of annual earnings;

- amendments to the bylaws;
- mergers and demergers; and
- appointment of corporate bodies.

11.7 Depth of information – proxy solicitation
Please see section 10.4.

11.8 Appointment/dismissal of directors
Directors may be appointed in the company's incorporation deed, through shareholders' resolution or, in particular circumstances, by the court.

In general terms, directors may be dismissed by the shareholders with or without legitimate cause. In this context, shareholders, the corporate body with legal competence for the appointment and dismissal of the members of the board of directors, may resolve on the election of a substitute director. However, in the case of inertia of the shareholders, when a director waives, is dismissed or for any other reason must be replaced before the end of the term for which he was appointed, such a director shall be replaced, if applicable and subsidiary: (i) if there is a list of directors to serve as substitutes, by the substitute director previously appointed for such a purpose; (ii) if there is no list of directors to serve as substitutes, by cooptation of the remaining directors, subject to the shareholders' ratification; (iii) by appointment of the supervisory board or of the audit committee, also subject to the shareholders' ratification; or (iv) by an *ad hoc* appointment of a new director to be resolved by the shareholders.

In the case of inadequate performance, director's dismissal shall not entitle the relevant director to receive compensation.

11.9 Income and options for directors
The CMVM recommends that the executive directors must maintain the holding of the shares that were allotted to them by virtue of variable remuneration schemes, up to an amount corresponding to the double of the respective annual global remuneration, with the exception of those shares that are required to be sold for the payment of taxes on the gains of said shares.

11.10 Earnings guidance
The directors' remuneration shall be structured to avoid extreme risk taking and so that the current interests may be aligned with the long-term interests of the company.

Therefore, it is recommended by the CMVM that the directors' remuneration includes a variable part (such as, for instance, stock options) which shall be determined by a performance assessment, carried out by the company's competent bodies, according to pre-established quantifiable criteria and maximum limits, and taking into consideration the company's growth and the increase of value for the shareholders. The CMVM also recommends that a significant part of such variable component of the remuneration shall be deferred for three years and its payment shall depend on the company's steady and positive performance.

On the contrary, the CMVM recommends that the remuneration of non-executive board members must not include a variable component indexed to the assessment on the company's performance.

The Corporate Governance Code recommends that agreements for purposes of mitigating the variability of the remuneration shall not be entered into.

11.11 Management discussion and analysis

The directors must prepare an annual management report and accounts containing a true and fair exposure of the evolution of the business, the performance and the position of the company, as well as a description of the risks and uncertainties which the company is facing, the shareholders' meeting being responsible for its approval.

11.12 Directors' liability

The directors, being bound by duties of care and loyalty, shall consider, in addition to the company's best interest, the interests of employees and other entities with significant interests in the company.

Therefore, in the case of a breach of such duties, directors may be held liable before the company and, in certain circumstances, before the shareholders, the company's creditors and third parties for any damage caused in the course of their activity. The shareholders and the company's creditors may also exercise certain rights the company may have against its directors which have not been exercised by the company, by means of subrogation.

12. MARKET ABUSE

12.1 Insider trading

Whoever holds privileged information (non-public information that, being accurate and with respect to any issuer, securities or other financial instruments, would be capable, if disclosed, of influencing in a sensitive manner their price in the market) as a result of: (i) its position as a member of a corporate or supervisory body of an issuer or as a shareholder; (ii) any work or services provided to an issuer or to another entity; (iii) its profession or public function; or (iv) having otherwise obtained the information illicitly; and discloses such information to someone outside the regular scope of their functions or, based on this information, trades or advises someone to trade in these securities or other financial instruments, or, directly or indirectly, orders their subscription, purchase, sale or exchange for their own account or for the account of another person, shall be punished by imprisonment for a maximum of five years or by a fine.

Any other person having become aware of inside information, and who discloses it, shall be punished by imprisonment for a maximum of four years or by a fine.

12.2 Market manipulation

Whoever discloses false, incomplete, exaggerated or biased information, carries out operations of a fictitious nature or executes other fraudulent practices capable of altering artificially the regular functioning of the securities market or of other financial instruments (ie, acts that may change the conditions of price development, the regular conditions of offer or demand of securities or other financial instruments or the normal conditions of issue and acceptance of a public offering), shall be punished by imprisonment for a maximum of five years or by a fine.

12.3 Miscellaneous
Both crimes of inside information and market manipulation may be subject to supplementary penalties such as disqualification, for a maximum period of five years, from the practice as agent of the profession or activity connected with the crime.

13. MUTUAL OR INVESTMENT FUNDS
13.1 Introduction to these two categories
Funds are generally divided into two main categories: mutual funds (FIM) and real estate funds (FII).

Certain types of mutual funds are governed by special law: private equity funds, re-structuring and company internationalisation funds, securitisation funds and pension funds.

Special funds combining several investment structures and objects may also be created, pursuant to the CMVM's authorisation.

Only funds defined in the law or in special regulations may be incorporated through the subscription by the public of participation units.

13.2 Investment companies, open-ended, close-ended
The concept of collective investment institutions includes investment funds and investment companies.

Except for securitisation companies and private equity investment companies which were already governed by the respective legal framework, the general rules for mutual and real estate investment companies have only been approved on June 2010.

In fact, securitisation operations may be performed either through a fund managed by a managing entity or by a securitisation company, which, after acquiring the assets, manages them and issues debt securities that are acquired by the investors. Also, in accordance with the regime applicable to private equity, investments may be structured through a private equity company or by a private equity fund or by a business angel.

FIMs and FIIs may be open-ended, close-ended or of a mixed nature.

Mutual funds companies (SIM) and real estate funds companies (SIIMO) may be incorporated with a fixed or variable share capital, the minimum incorporation share capital being of EUR 300,000 for SIM and EUR 375,000 for SIIMO, represented by shares without nominal value.

These companies may be self managed or may designate a third entity to perform the management. The relationship between the managing entity and the investment company must be regulated by an agreement. Self managed companies are subject to the rules applicable to FIIs and FIMs.

Certain information and disclosure obligations are still subject to further regulation by the CMVM.

13.3 Licence requirements

The CMVM must grant prior simplified authorisation for the incorporation of FIIs and FIMs, as for the SIMs and SIIMOs.

The application for the authorisation must be presented, amongst others, with the drafts of the management regulation, the simplified and complete prospectus and the agreements to be signed with the proposed custodian credit institution and marketing agents.

The incorporation of private equity funds and the commencement of activity of private equity investments and private equity companies whose capital is not subject to a public offer and whose capital holders are exclusively qualified investors or, irrespectively of its nature, when the minimum amount of the capital to be subscribed is equal or above EUR 500,000 by each investor, is subject to prior communication to the CMVM.

13.4 Continuing requirements

Amendments to the simplified prospectus, to the complete prospectus and to the management regulation are subject to prior notification to the CMVM.

Managing entities of mutual funds must prepare, disclose and send to the CMVM the annual and biannual accounting documents.

Information in respect of transactions involving the fund's assets must also be notified to the CMVM.

13.5 Custodians

Custodians are notably subject to the following duties: (i) hold the assets in escrow; (ii) custody or registration of the assets, as applicable; (iii) perform the operations related to the assets upon request by the managing entity; and (iv) supervise the participants and the managing entity.

13.6 Undertakings for collective investments in transferable securities (UCITS)

EU harmonised funds may be directly offered in the EU market and their assets may include securities, instruments of the currency market or financial derivatives. Such funds are mandatorily open-ended and are subject to particular ratios applicable to the relative percentage of certain types of assets included in the funds' assets.

13.7 Non-UCITS funds

Non-UCITS funds are of several different natures and are subject to less strict requisites as to their underlying assets.

13.8 Hedge funds

Hedge funds are a special type of fund which have not yet been fully recognised and regulated by Portuguese law.

The incorporation of special funds – like hedge funds – is subject to the CMVM's approval and is regulated by Regulation no. 15/2003 of the CMVM, as amended.

13.9 Marketing and distribution requirements
Managing entities, custodians and authorised financial intermediaries are allowed to place participation units in investment funds.

13.10 Manager
Domestic funds may only be managed by companies limited by shares with their registered offices in Portugal.

In addition, open-ended FIMs and FIIs must be managed by companies specifically incorporated for such a purpose, while close-ended FIMs and FIIs may also be managed by certain credit institutions.

Management fees due by the fund may be fixed or variable (based on the fund's performance).

14. SECURITIES INSTITUTIONS
14.1 Market executive undertaking
The regulated markets are: (i) the official quotation market, Eurolist, on which most significant Portuguese equity securities are listed; (ii) the derivatives market (*Mercado de Futuros e Opções*), which is the market for equities futures and options (both of these markets are managed by Euronext Lisbon); and (iii) the special market for public debt (*Mercado Especial de Dívida Pública*), managed by MTS Portugal – *Sociedade Gestora do Mercado Especial de Dívida Pública, SGMR, S.A.*

The multilateral trading systems are: (i) the non-quotation market for shares and the structured securities (warrants and bonds) market (jointly named as EasyNext Lisbon) managed by Euronext Lisbon; and (ii) the PEX market managed by OPEX – *Sociedade Gestora de Mercado de Valores Mobiliários Não Regulamentado, S.A.*

14.2 Securities clearing house
Transactions in securities traded on Eurolist are cleared by LCH Clearnet and settled by Interbolsa's Settlement System. LCH Clearnet interposes itself between the buyer and seller in a covered transaction and becomes a transaction counterparty in order to eliminate counterparty risk.

14.3 Central securities depository
The Portuguese Settlement System is managed by Interbolsa (*Sociedade Gestora de Sistemas de Liquidação e de Sistemas Centralizados de Valores Mobiliários, S.A.*), a company that is wholly owned by Euronext Lisbon and which also manages *Central de Valores Mobiliários* (Central VM). The Central VM is the centralised system for the registration and control of securities, including custody of certificated securities and registration of book-entry securities, in which all securities admitted to trading on a Portuguese regulated market, either in certificates or in book-entry form, must be deposited or registered. Any trading of securities listed on a Portuguese

regulated market that takes place over the counter must be cleared through financial institutions and physically settled through the Central VM, where such securities are registered or deposited.

Under the procedures of the Portuguese Settlement System, physical settlement takes place at 11:00 a.m. (CET) on the third business day after the trade date and is provisional until financial settlement, which takes place at the BP at 12:30 p.m. (CET) on the same day.

14.4 Investment services providers (ISP)
The professional exercise of any financial intermediation activity depends on: (i) authorisation to be granted by the competent authority (eg, the BP for credit institutions); and (ii) pre-registration with the CMVM.

15. NOTIFICATION OBLIGATIONS
15.1 Notification of major shareholding
Please see section 10.5.

16. PUBLIC TAKEOVERS
16.1 Applicable laws and regulations or regulatory framework
Public takeovers are governed by the CVM.

16.2 Competent authorities
A takeover must be authorised and previously registered with the CMVM.

16.3 Dealing with disclosures and stake building
Anyone whose holding in a listed company exceeds, directly or indirectly, one-third (unless evidence is given that such a percentage does not give them control over the company, or that such an entity is involved with it in a group relationship) or half of the voting rights attributable to the share capital, has the obligation of launching a takeover for the totality of shares (and other securities issued by the company granting the right to their subscription or acquisition). The limit of one-third may be eliminated by the by-laws of listed companies that do not have shares or securities granting the right to their subscription or acquisition listed on a regulated market (see section 10.5).

The duty to launch a takeover shall be suspended if the person under such a duty undertakes in writing before the CMVM to cause such events to cease within the following 120 days.

16.4 Types of takeover bids
Takeovers may be voluntary or mandatory. Voluntary takeovers must be addressed to all the holders of securities that are the object of the offer.

Mandatory takeovers must occur in accordance with the circumstances described in section 16.3.

16.5 Procedural aspects
In voluntary takeovers, as soon as the decision to launch a takeover

is made, the offeror must send the preliminary announcement to the CMVM, to the targeted company and to the operators of the regulated markets, immediately proceeding with the publication of the preliminary announcement. The publication obliges the offeror to: (i) launch the offer in terms no less favourable to the addressees than those contained in the preliminary announcement; (ii) apply for registration of the offer with the CMVM within the term of 20 days (extendable up to 60 days in takeover offers for exchange of securities); and (iii) inform the employees of the contents of the offer documents, as soon as these are made public.

In mandatory takeovers, the publication of the preliminary announcement of the offer must take place immediately after the fact that gives rise to such an obligation, and the registration must be applied for within 20 days.

Simultaneously with the launching of the takeover, the offeror must deposit the consideration in cash, or have a bank guarantee securing the amount of the consideration, or order the blockage of the securities that are the object of the consideration, as applicable.

The announcement of the launching of the offer shall be published simultaneously with the disclosure of the prospectus. The offer period may vary between two and 10 weeks and during this period the acceptance statement of the offer by the addressees is made through an order addressed to a financial intermediary. At the end of the offer period, the offer's results are immediately assessed and published by a financial intermediary that collects all the acceptance declarations, or in a special regulated market session.

16.6 Nature and value of consideration offered

The consideration in voluntary takeovers may consist of:

* cash;
* securities already issued or to be issued; or
* a mixed nature.

If the consideration consists of cash, the offeror should deposit the total amount with a financial institution or present an appropriate bank guarantee, before the registration of the offer. If the consideration consists of securities, these should have appropriate liquidity and must be easy to evaluate.

The consideration for a mandatory takeover must be the higher of the following two prices:

* the highest price paid by the offeror or companies connected to the offeror for the acquisition of securities of the same class, in the six months immediately prior to the date of publication of the preliminary announcement of the offer; or
* the average price of these securities in a regulated market during the same period.

The offeror may review the consideration as to its nature and amount up to five days before expiry of the takeover period but such a reviewed offer cannot contain conditions making it less favourable than the original offer and its consideration must be at least 2 per cent higher than the preceding offer as to its amount.

16.7 Timetable and variations
The period between the preliminary announcement and the acceptance of the offer by the addressees can vary between six to 22 weeks, including: (i) the application for registration of the offer; (ii) the approval of the prospectus, registration or its refusal; and (iii) the offer period (also including a possible offer suspension, each for a period of 10 days).

16.8 Strategy
The strategy will mostly depend on whether the takeover is 'hostile' or 'friendly'.

16.9 Irrevocable
A takeover may only be revoked in the case of an increase in the risks of an offer due to an unforeseen and substantial change of circumstances, which is known by the addressees and upon which the decision to launch the offer is based. In this case, the offeror may, within a reasonable period and subject to the CMVM's authorisation, modify or revoke the offer.

16.10 Share dealings, buying shares
From the publication of the preliminary announcement until the assessment of the offer's result, the offeror and related entities cannot trade outside regulated markets any securities of the class of those which are the object of the offer or those which comprise the consideration, except if authorised by the CMVM with a previous opinion from the target company, and shall inform the CMVM daily of the transactions relating to the securities issued by the target company or the class of those which comprise the consideration.

16.11 First announcement
Please see section 16.3.

16.12 Drafting of offer documents
The prospectus of a takeover shall, *inter alia*, contain information on:
- the consideration offered, its justification and method of payment;
- the minimum and maximum amounts of securities that the offeror intends to acquire;
- the percentage of voting rights that may be exercised by the offeror in the target company;
- the percentage of voting rights that may be exercised by the target company in the offeror company;
- related parties to the offeror or the offeree;
- the securities of the same class as those that are the object of the offer, which have been acquired in the previous six months by the issuer or by a related entity;

- the offeror's intentions with regard to the business of the offeree;
- implications for the financial condition of the offeror;
- the shareholders' agreements entered into by the offeror or by a related entity, with significant influence on the offeree;
- the agreements entered into between the offeror or a related entity and the members of the corporate bodies of the offeree;
- the compensation proposed in the event of a removal of rights;
- the domestic legislation that shall apply to agreements entered into by the offeror and holders of securities in the offeree company; and
- any charges to be borne by the addressees of the takeover.

16.13 Further announcements
The CMVM's decisions on approval of prospectuses and registration of takeovers shall be disclosed through its information disclosure system. Moreover, the modification and the review of the consideration shall be disclosed immediately by the same means used to disclose the prospectus.

16.14 Responsibility
Please see section 5.5.

16.15 Despatch
Please see section 16.5 on procedural aspects.

16.16 Due diligence in advance of a takeover bid
Portuguese law does not govern the exercise of due diligence, therefore it is a matter subject to discussion between the offeree and the offeror.

16.17 Conditions to the offer
The offer may only be subject to conditions that correspond to a legitimate interest of the offeror and do not affect the market's normal course; never to conditions whose verification depends only on the offeror (*potestativas*).

16.18 Financing
The offeror has to provide evidence that it has sufficient financing guarantees for the payment of the consideration under the offer (see section 16.6).

16.19 For cash/for shares/mixed
An offer may consist of a takeover proposing the purchase of the target company's securities, their exchange for existing or new securities, or a payment in securities and cash.

16.20 Inducement
Please see section 6.4.

16.21 Defence mechanisms
From the moment the target company has knowledge of the launch of the

offer until the completion of the process, the management body of the target company may not perform acts that materially affect the net equity of the target company and which may significantly affect the purposes disclosed by the offeror.

The defence mechanisms are generally limited to the issue by the target company of a reasoned opinion on: (i) the type and amount of the consideration offered; (ii) the offeror's strategic plans for the offeree; and (iii) the effects of the takeover on the interests of the offeree.

16.22 Nature of listed securities
Securities which may be the object of a takeover are composed by shares and by all other securities which may grant the right to subscribe or purchase shares of the offeree.

16.23 Squeeze-out
The offeror who acquires 90 per cent of the voting rights of a company subject to a takeover offer may acquire the remaining shares within three months after the assessment of the offer's result.

If the squeeze-out procedure is not timely initiated, the holders of the remaining shares can give rise to a compulsory sale.

16.24 Schemes of arrangement
Not applicable.

17. FOREIGN INVESTMENT CONTROLS
17.1 Foreign investments
Foreign investment operations do not need to be registered with, or authorised by, the Portuguese central or local authorities.

Banks must report to the BP any transactions with foreign entities made on their own account or on behalf of their clients. However, when providing information on behalf of their clients, banks may benefit from an exemption threshold up to the amount of EUR 50,000, in relation to payments made within the European Union, if they previously inform the Bank of Portugal of their intention to benefit from the exemption. In these cases, banks must provide the Bank of Portugal with a list of all the clients who performed transactions with foreign entities, during the relevant year (irrespective of the amounts involved), as well as the global amount of payments and receipts in relation to each client.

In addition, direct declarants (all economic agents) performing transactions with foreign entities without involving a resident bank, must inform the Bank of Portugal of the following: (i) opening and termination of foreign bank accounts or settlement of current account with non-resident entities; and (ii) transactions with foreign entities without involving a resident bank.

General direct declarants (economic agents), as designated by the Bank of Portugal, must inform this entity of all operations performed with non-resident entities, including those intermediated by resident banks.

However, persons travelling into, or from Portugal, coming from, or into, a non-EU country carrying net moneys in an amount equal to or in excess of EUR 10,000, must report that fact to the Portuguese custom authorities. For these purposes the following assets are, amongst others, deemed as net moneys: (i) payment means in bearer form, including monetary instruments, traveller's cheque and negotiable securities, such as cheques, promissory notes and other payment orders; (ii) cash; (iii) banknotes or hard money with legal tender in the respective issuing states; and (iv) banknotes or hard money without legal tender (although still in the period of time in which such banknotes or hard money are accepted for exchange).

17.2 Exemptions
Please see section 17.1.

17.3 Exemptions of notification or prior authorisation
Please see section 17.1.

17.4 Notification in order to establish a balance of payments
Please see section 17.1.

Russia

Egorov Puginsky Afanasiev & Partners
Alexey Andrusenko, Tatyana Boyko, Nikita Gurin,
Daria Izotova, Julia Kulyamina, Elena Kuznetsova,
Valentin Osipov, Alexander Rudyakov, Nadezhda
Rybinskaya, Irina Skidan, Alexey Vasilyev & Uliana Volina

1. GENERAL DESCRIPTION OF THE CAPITAL MARKETS
There are a number of registered stock exchanges in the Russian Federation.
The principal stock exchanges are the Moscow Interbank Currency Exchange
(MICEX) and the Russian Trading System (RTS).

Established in 1992, MICEX is the largest stock exchange with a total
value of approximately 64 trillion roubles (approximately EUR 1.5 trillion)
representing almost 700 issuers as of January 2011. Established in 1995, the
RTS is the second largest exchange with a total value of approximately 46
trillion roubles (approximately EUR 1.1 trillion) as of January 2011. Russian
issuers generally rely on MICEX for stock trading and on the RTS for its futures
and options market and derivatives trading. Foreign issuers are allowed to list
their securities on Russian stock exchanges under certain conditions.

The MICEX and the RTS are in the process of merging, with the merger
expected to be completed by mid-2011.

Public offerings of securities in the Russian securities markets in 2010
increased significantly compared to 2009. There were three offerings in 2009
with an aggregate value of approximately EUR 195 million and 13 offerings
in 2010 with an aggregate value of approximately EUR 1.4 billion. The
largest issuers on MICEX and the RTS in 2010 were OJSC 'Transcontainer'
(transport industry) with an offering value of approximately EUR 276
million, OJSC 'Protek' (pharmaceutical industry) with offering value of
approximately EUR 275 million and OJSC LSR (construction) with an
offering value of approximately EUR 274.5 million.

In addition, in 2010 a number of Russian companies placed securities
in the international securities markets through their offshore holding
structures, including UC RUSAL with a EUR 1.5 billion offering on the Hong
Kong Stock Exchange, Mail.ru Group with a EUR 630 million offering on the
London Stock Exchange and Mechel with a EUR 158 million offering on the
New York Stock Exchange.

2. REGULATORY STRUCTURE
2.1 General
Securities offerings are regulated by the Federal Financial Markets Service
of the Russian Federation (the FFMS) and also by the Central Bank of the

Russian Federation in cases involving the issuance of securities by financial institutions and the Ministry of Finance of the Russian Federation in cases involving the issuance of governmental securities.

The FFMS licenses and supervises professional participants in the securities market, regulates the registration of securities issuances and related prospectuses and issues rulings regulating the conduct of market activities. It also approves securities of Russian issuers for issuance outside of the Russian Federation and the classification of different securities by type.

Securities issued in the Russian Federation and subject to Russian law may be issued in dematerialised form. Their ownership is generally recorded in book-entry form in the register of shareholders maintained by a professional share registrar.

2.2 Regulation of the offering of new securities

Russian law recognises two different types of securities: bonds and equity securities *(emissionnye tsennye bumagi)* and other non-equity securities. Bonds and equity securities include shares, debt obligations, state obligations, issuer's options, mortgage-backed securities and Russian depositary receipts, while other non-equity securities include consignment notes, cheques, certificates of deposit, savings certificates and mortgage certificates, among others. Issuers are required to publicly register the issuance of bonds and equity securities with the FFMS whether or not they are intended to be publicly offered. The issuance of other non-equity securities does not require their placement with investors and, consequently, their issuance is not specifically regulated by Russian securities laws.

2.2.1 Public offering

In order to issue bonds and equity securities, after completing corporate formalities, the issuer must apply to the FFMS and submit the documents specified in the FFMS regulations for the issuance and distribution of securities in order to publicly register the issuance. A securities prospectus is required to be registered if:
* the securities are intended to be distributed by means of an offering to the public; or
* the securities are intended to be distributed by means of a private offering among existing security holders, whose number exceeds 500.

Once the issuance of securities has been registered with the FFMS, the issuer has one year during which it may offer and sell them to existing shareholders or new investors.

An issuer must publicly register the results of the placement of its securities by filing a report with the FFMS within 30 days after the placement is completed.

Issuers that are required to register a securities prospectus with the FFMS must disclose certain financial and other relevant information in the prospectus. Documents confirming the information disclosed in the prospectus must be submitted by the issuer to the FFMS at the time the securities issuance is registered. This information includes the issuer's quarterly reports, which must be prepared in compliance with FFMS requirements, and any material facts that may affect the finances or the business activities of the issuer.

The FFMS adopted disclosure requirements in 2006. Generally, information regarding the issuance of the securities must be disclosed through an authorised news agency, on the issuer's Web site and, in certain cases, relevant disclosure must also be published in a printed publication that complies with FFMS requirements.

2.2.2 Private offering

Registration of a prospectus in connection with a securities issuance is not required if the total number of potential investors does not exceed 500. In accordance with Russian law, it is illegal to advertise the issuance of securities that are not intended to be publicly offered.

2.3 Differences between local and foreign companies

In 2009, the Federal Law on the Securities Market was amended in order to allow foreign issuers to distribute securities in the Russian Federation.

In order for securities of a foreign issuer to be publicly traded in the Russian Federation, they must be admitted to trading by decision of a Russian stock exchange or of the FFMS. The FFMS grants admission to trading upon application from a Russian stock exchange if the foreign securities are not listed on a foreign stock exchange. A Russian stock exchange can admit foreign securities to trading if they meet the listing requirements of a recognised foreign stock exchange and they may be publicly offered and traded in accordance with foreign law.

The FFMS must qualify the foreign securities as being of a type recognised by Russian law. The FFMS must also assign an international identification code for securities and an international classification code for financial instruments to the foreign security.

Securities of foreign issuers are eligible to be publicly offered and traded in Russia if they are issued by any one of the following:
- legal entities incorporated in a member state of either the Organisation for Economic Cooperation and Development (OECD), the Financial Action Task Force (FATF) and/or the Council of Europe Committee of Experts on the Evaluation of Anti-Money Laundering Measures and the Financing of Terrorism; or
- OECD, FATF and/or Council of Europe Committee of Experts on the Evaluation of Anti-Money Laundering Measures and the Financing of Terrorism member states or their central banks; or
- legal entities incorporated in a jurisdiction whose securities market regulator has entered into a cooperation agreement with the FFMS; or
- international financial organisations included in the list approved by the Russian government.

The foreign issuer must register a securities prospectus with the FFMS. The foreign issuer must also notify the FFMS of the results of the placement and comply with applicable information disclosure requirements.

2.4   Placement of securities by Russian issuers in foreign markets

In accordance with the Federal Law on the Securities Market, Russian companies may distribute their shares outside of the Russian Federation after obtaining approval from the FFMS. In order to obtain approval, Russian companies must submit the documents specified in the applicable regulation to the FFMS.

The maximum number of shares of Russian issuers that may be offered outside of the Russian Federation (including by way of depositary receipts) must fall within the quotas established by the FFMS, which vary from 5 per cent to 50 per cent of the total amount of the issuer's outstanding shares, depending on the issuer's category as established by the FFMS.

The issuer (or selling shareholder) must notify the FFMS about the results of the securities placement in Russia and outside of Russia within 30 days after the end of the distribution period.

2.5   Admission to trading on a regulated market

Securities that go through the listing process of a specific Russian stock exchange may be included in its quotation lists. The rule books of the various exchanges set out the specific listing criteria for securities. Please refer to the discussion about listing in section 8 below.

2.6   Financial promotion

Advertising a public offering of securities before the prospectus has been registered by the FFMS is prohibited. In addition, Russian laws prohibit the advertisement of public offerings of securities by issuers who do not comply with information disclosure requirements.

2.7   Rule books

The Federal Law on the Securities Market requires stock exchanges to disclose information on the rules for trading securities, entering into and registering transactions with securities and other related information. Each Russian stock exchange has its own rule book containing the requirements and other criteria for listing and trading securities on the exchange. Companies whose securities are admitted to trading on a stock exchange must comply with the regulations of the FFMS and that exchange.

3.   REGISTRATION OF THE ISSUER AND SECURITIES
3.1   Registration requirements

Securities may be issued by a legal entity, a state executive body or a local government body (issuers). Russian law does not contain any specific registration requirements relating to issuers, except for the requirements relating to the issuers of bonds discussed in section 5.7 below.

3.2   Other requirements

Specific listing requirements are detailed in section 8 below.

3.3 Nature of securities

The two different types of securities recognised by Russian law are described in section 2.2 above. Public registration is required only for the issuance of bonds and equity securities. Such securities may be issued in certificated or uncertificated form.

4. SUPERVISORY AUTHORITIES

4.1 Conduct: prudential, cooperation, self-regulation of stock exchange

The FFMS is the federal executive body that is primarily responsible for securities market regulation and the enforcement of securities laws.

The FFMS licenses professional securities market participants (including brokers, dealers, depositories, registrars, clearing houses and stock exchanges) and certifies the qualified experts they must employ as part of their licensing requirements. Self-regulatory organisations consisting of market participants are granted this status by permission of the FFMS, which keeps a registry of these organisations and supervises them.

The FFMS also regulates professional activity on the securities market by establishing rules of professional conduct and the rights and obligations of companies involved in certain types of market activities.

In accordance with Russian securities laws and related government decrees, the FFMS establishes standards for issuing securities, the procedures for registering prospectuses in connection with the issuance of securities and conducts their registration. It also establishes the terms that qualify securities to be legally offered to the public, traded, listed and cleared by clearing houses.

The FFMS regulates and supervises the procedure for initial public offerings of securities of Russian issuers abroad. Before such an offering can take place, a Russian issuer must apply for and receive the permission of the FFMS, which is usually granted if all preliminary conditions for the offering were met in Russia (initial national listing, volume of securities traded in Russia, etc).

The FFMS may issue formal prescriptions to issuers in connection with the exercise of its enforcement authority. If there is a significant violation of the securities laws by security market participants, the FFMS has the right to bring a civil enforcement action that may result in suspension/revocation of their licence issued by the FFMS that enables them to conduct professional securities market operations (eg, a broker's or dealer's licence). If a violation occurs in the course of the securities issuance process, the FFMS has the right to suspend the securities issuance or to cancel it. In some cases where the securities trading does not comply with the law, the FFMS has the right to bring an action to declare those transactions void.

4.2 New listings measures in connection with the credit crisis

The Russian Duma did not adopt any laws that were aimed at addressing specific aspects of the 2008 global financial and credit crisis but did take certain measures to enhance the stability of the Russian markets and economy generally.

5. OFFERING DOCUMENTATION OR PROSPECTUS REQUIREMENTS

5.1 Nature and statutory requirements of the offering document or disclosure document

All issuers offering securities to the public must submit a resolution of the issuer authorising the issuance of the securities and a prospectus to the FFMS. The prospectus must be registered by the FFMS. Russian securities laws specify requirements for the resolution and the prospectus and establish rules for making disclosures.

Issuers must make disclosure at each stage of the securities issuance process. Disclosure must be published in two media sources – a news wire and on the issuer's Web site. In certain cases an issuer may also be required to publish disclosure in an official periodical.

Specific disclosure requirements depend on the form of the document, as different forms of disclosure documents must be used at various stages of the securities issuance process.

5.2 Exemptions

The Federal Law on the Securities Market contains a number of exemptions from the requirements to prepare a prospectus and to make disclosures. Neither requirement applies in the case of a private placement of securities where an offer is made to fewer than 500 persons. The FFMS can also exempt an issuer from disclosure obligations if all necessary requirements set out by the Federal Law on the Securities Market are met. These requirements include, among other things, the issuer's shares not being included in a quotation list of securities being traded on an exchange or by any other securities market operator.

5.3 Preparation of the offering document, general contents

The resolution of the issuer must be signed by the CEO and approved by the Board of Directors.

The resolution must include, among other things: (i) information on the issuer and its place of business; (ii) the date on which the decision to issue the securities was taken; (iii) the type of securities to be issued; (iv) a description of the rights of the security holders; and (v) the amount and face value of the securities to be issued.

The prospectus must contain information on: (i) the members of the management bodies of the issuer, the issuer's bank accounts, its auditor and financial consultant and those persons who sign the prospectus; (ii) the amount of securities being offered and the terms and conditions of the offer; (iii) the issuer's financial standing; (iv) its employees; and (v) its accounts and other financial information, and meet the other requirements set forth in the Federal Law on the Securities Market.

5.4 Due diligence

The issuer's CEO and chief accountant must sign the prospectus in order to confirm the completeness and truthfulness of the information included in it.

The prospectus must also be signed by the issuer's auditor and independent appraiser (if there is one) and may additionally be signed by its financial consultant for the purposes of confirming the completeness and truthfulness of the information included in the parts of the prospectus that relate to them.

Furthermore, the issuer's Board of Directors must approve the prospectus.

5.5 Responsibility

The issuer may be held liable for damages caused to investors by untruthful, incomplete or misleading information included in the prospectus. In addition, the issuer's CEO and any persons who signed the prospectus have joint secondary liability for such damages.

Furthermore, if the issuer violates the Federal Law on the Securities Market in the course of issuing and placing the securities, it will also be subject to penalties and other sanctions under the Administrative Offences Code of the Russian Federation.

Individuals who signed a prospectus containing misleading information may also face criminal sanctions.

5.6 Supplementary prospectuses

The resolution on issuing securities and/or the prospectus may be amended or supplemented at any time prior to the end of the placement period. The placement period is determined in accordance with the resolution of the issuer referred to in section 5.3 above, but may not exceed one year from the date of registration of the securities issuance.

If the issuer experiences a change in circumstances prior to the date on which the securities issuance is registered which could significantly impact on an investor's investment decision, the issuer must submit a revised issuance resolution and/or prospectus to the FFMS.

Amendments to the issuance resolution and/or the prospectus are permitted after the date of the state registration of the securities issuance if they extend the placement period or they are necessary to protect the interests of investors and do not violate their rights. Amendments which reduce the placement period or the scope of investors' rights are not permitted.

The issuer must suspend the placement of the securities from the time it decides to amend or supplement the resolution on their issuance or the prospectus. The placement resumes either after the amendments have been registered by the FFMS or the FFMS has refused to register them.

5.7 Issuing of bonds

The procedure for issuing bonds is almost identical to the procedure for issuing equity securities. Equity securities and bonds issued by the Russian Central Bank are not required to be registered by the FFMS.

If the bonds are secured by collateral or guaranteed, the person providing the security or guarantee must sign the prospectus to confirm the accuracy and truthfulness of the information it contains on the security or guarantee.

Currently, the requirements for issuing shares are not as strict as the requirements for issuing bonds. As a general rule, the face value of the bonds may not exceed the amount of the issuer's charter capital. In order to issue bonds, the issuer must be in existence for more than three years and have duly approved annual accounting reports, unless the bonds are secured by a third party. These requirements do not apply to: (i) bonds secured by a mortgage; (ii) issuers whose securities were listed on a stock exchange; (iii) issuers and bonds that have a credit rating issued by an accredited rating agency; and (iv) bonds intended for qualified investors, such as brokers, dealers, banks and insurance companies.

The Federal Law on the Securities Market contains specific requirements applicable to guarantors. Only the following persons may act as guarantors: profit-making organisations, as long as the value of their net assets is equal to or exceeds the amount of the guarantee; state corporations or a state company; and the international financial organisations included in the list approved by the Russian government.

Bonds may not be publicly offered earlier than six months after the formation of the company, unless one of the following requirements is met: the bonds are guaranteed by the state or the Bank for Development and Foreign Economic Affairs (*Vnesheconombank*); the bonds are issued by a mortgage agent; or the bonds are issued by a Russian legal entity that has entered into a concession agreement with the Russian Federation or one of its regions.

6. DISTRIBUTION SYSTEMS
6.1 Normal structure of a distribution group
Under Russian law, only financial institutions licensed as brokers may act as underwriters of an initial offering of securities. As a general matter, a reputable investment bank will coordinate the distribution process. Depending on the offering volume, additional banks may participate in the distribution and form part of a distribution syndicate, with one bank acting as coordinator.

6.2 Methods of distribution
A Russian joint stock company may place its shares by means of a private placement among a limited number of investors or a public offer.

6.3 Underwriting
Underwriters are licensed financial organisations, usually investment banks, that provide services aimed at organising and guaranteeing the successful issue and placement of securities for a fee that is usually based on a percentage of the total value of the offering. Typical services include:
• acting as the issuer's agent and selling the issued securities in the process of their initial offering in the interests of the issuer;
• undertaking to purchase shares that have not been placed; and
• acting as a market maker.
In addition, an underwriter will guide the issuer through the entire

offering process, assist in the preparation of the prospectus and act as the financial and marketing adviser to the issuer.

6.4 Fees and commission

The underwriting agreement usually determines the fees and commission for the performed services depending on their scope and type of issue. In addition, the underwriting agreement provides for specific warranties from the company in order to provide comfort to the distributor, who acts as the issuer's agent in the market.

6.5 Stabilisation

A distributor may be appointed to act as stabilising manager (market maker) in order to ensure that the price for the issued shares stays at a certain level immediately after the offering commences. To keep the price of the offered securities at the desired level, the stabilisation manager enters into a series of transactions to purchase the offered securities on the open market for a certain limited period of time.

Measures to counter market abuse have been enacted in Russia recently. Consequently, currently there is no court or other practice addressing whether the 'market-making' activities of a distributor constitutes market abuse.

6.6 Timing of the distribution process

The distribution process usually takes from two to three weeks, depending on discussions with potential investors prior to the actual distribution taking place.

7. PUBLICITY

It is unlawful to advertise an issuance of securities prior to its state registration. Accordingly, it is illegal to distribute information regarding the securities using any means or forms of communication for the purpose of attracting investors, directing their attention to the securities, creating or maintaining an interest in the securities, or promoting the securities in the market.

The securities can be freely advertised after the FFMS registers their issuance. In addition to general principles that require advertisements to be correct and made in good faith, advertisements relating to securities cannot contain: (i) promises of dividends or other profit payments (except for minor exceptions); and (ii) predictions on their increase in market value.

From the date on which the prospectus is registered, the issuer must provide all interested persons with access to the information contained in the prospectus, regardless of their reason for requesting this information.

8. LISTING
8.1 Special listing requirements, admission criteria

The admission of securities to trading on the RTS or MICEX is carried out by including them in the 'List of securities admitted for trading'. In order to have its securities admitted, the issuer must file an application, complete a questionnaire and provide numerous other documents (such as securities registration documents, cooperation agreement, listing services agreement, market-maker cooperation undertaking, the issuer's corporate documents, by-laws, balance sheets, etc) to the Department of Listing and Non-Listed Securities Market of the RTS or the Listing Committee of MICEX. After the documents are reviewed, the Department or Listing Committee will issue a decision on admission or deny admission of the securities to trading.

The general criteria for admission of securities to trading are as follows. For the RTS: (i) registration of the prospectus or privatisation plan as a substitute for the prospectus; (ii) registration of the report on the results of the issuance or notification to the FFMS regarding the issuance; and (iii) compliance by the issuer with Russian securities laws and disclosure requirements. For MICEX: in addition to the foregoing, (iv) the securities must be transferred to a depositary; and (v) a clearing house must be engaged.

The specific listing for each security varies depending on the stock exchange quotation list category (A1, A2, B, V, I) and relates to the terms of the quotation, capitalisation of the issuer, monthly trading volume, whether the issuer prepares US Generally Accepted Accounting Principles/ International Accounting Standards (IAS) financial statements, etc.

Securities are included in the trading list by decision of the general director of the stock exchange, which is notified to the FFMS.

Over-the-counter (non-listed) securities are traded upon their admission to trading and are not placed in a quotation list.

8.2 Mechanics of the review process

The RTS must review the issuer's application and accompanying documents within 10 days of filing and prepare a formal decision on their admission or denial of admission. MICEX follows a similar process, but also requires a separate expertise agreement to be entered into between MICEX and the issuer. The MICEX expertise process takes 20 days for initially placed securities and 45 days for securities that have been trading previously in the over-the-counter market.

8.3 Prospectus obligation, due diligence, exemption

Registration of the securities prospectus with the FFMS is a prerequisite for having securities admitted to trading on the RTS or MICEX. MICEX must approve the draft prospectus before it is submitted to the FFMS if the securities are planned to be traded on that exchange.

8.4 Appeal procedure in the event of a prospectus refusal

If the issuer disagrees with a decision by MICEX not to admit its securities to trading, it can file an action with the Arbitration Commission of MICEX.

The rules of the RTS also provide for a special appeal procedure. The issuer is given one month from the date of receipt of the denial to send a complaint to the board of directors of the RTS. After due consideration, the board of directors may exercise its authority to admit the securities to trading.

8.5 Authority of the Exchange

Both MICEX and the RTS have the authority to: (i) admit securities to trading on their exchange; (ii) delist the securities; (iii) regulate trading in the securities; and (iv) adopt measures against the illegal use of insider information and market manipulation, monitor suspected trades and request relevant documents from market participants.

The stock exchange also determines the amount of fees, dues and other payments for its services, as well as the size of any fines imposed in the event of a violation of its rules.

8.6 Sponsor

Issuers frequently employ the services of a securities market professional in order to conduct the securities placement more efficiently. The underwriting agreement generally provides for either a 'best efforts' or a 'firm commitment' undertaking on the part of the underwriter. In contrast to best efforts, a firm commitment guarantees the issuer that all of the securities will be purchased by the underwriter even if no other purchaser appears. In this situation the underwriter acts as the sponsor of the issue.

There are no detailed regulations governing an underwriter's status as sponsor. The Federal Law on Joint Stock Companies exempts stock market professionals acquiring securities as part of their services to issuers in connection with securities placements from having to conduct a mandatory offer (see section 16 below) for the remaining securities as long as the stock market professional does not hold the securities being placed for longer than six months. Standards for underwriting activity and other services related to securities placement have been widely discussed, but not yet adopted by the FFMS.

8.7 Special arrangements for smaller companies such as Alternext, AIM or SPACs

In 2007 the RTS established its START platform for small and medium-sized companies targeted at admitting for trading shares of issuers with capitalisations of up to 5 billion roubles (EUR 123 million) and accepting corporate bond issues not exceeding 500 million roubles (EUR 12 million). MICEX has similar platforms, such as SECTOR IRK and SECTOR MICEX Discovery, which is more focused on technological and innovative start-up companies.

8.8 Costs of various types

The inclusion of securities in quotation lists A1, A2, B, V, I (with listing) on MICEX costs approximately 105,000 – 265,000 roubles (EUR 2,500 – 6,500) as of March 2011, depending on the type of security and issuer. The admission of non-listed securities to trading on MICEX is free of charge. Listing securities on the RTS is less expensive, although the RTS does charge a small fee for admitting non-listed securities to trading and small annual payments to maintain securities listings.

9. SANCTIONS AND DISPUTES

Persons violating the securities laws of the Russian Federation may be subject to civil, administrative or criminal penalties. Losses resulting from securities law violations are compensated in the manner established by Russian civil law.

9.1 Disciplinary and administrative sanctions

The FFMS is empowered to impose disciplinary and administrative sanctions in respect of securities law violations.

With respect to issuances of securities that fail to satisfy legal requirements, the FFMS is entitled to:

- suspend further placement of the securities;
- publish information in the mass media regarding the fact that the issuance failed to satisfy legal requirements and the grounds for its suspension;
- notify the issuer in writing of the need to cure the securities law violations and establish the cure period;
- deliver materials to the prosecutor's office if there are grounds for criminal sanctions; and
- file a claim with an arbitration court for the purpose of declaring an issuance of securities void.

Participation in the securities markets by unlicensed securities professionals is illegal. With respect to such persons, the FFMS is entitled to:

- adopt measures to terminate unlicensed activities;
- publish information in the mass media regarding the fact that a stock market participant is engaged in unlicensed activities;
- inform the market participant in writing of the need to obtain a licence and establish the cure period;
- deliver materials to a court of law for the purpose of enforcing administrative sanctions against the unlicensed professional's officials in accordance with law;
- file a claim with an arbitration court to recover income received from the unlicensed market activity for the benefit of the state; and
- file a claim with an arbitration court on the forcible liquidation of the professional market participant if it fails to obtain the requisite licence within the established cure period.

9.2 Civil actions

In accordance with Russian civil law, the person found to have committed securities law violations must compensate the resulting losses. Losses include the expenses incurred by the person whose rights have been violated to restore those rights, the loss or damage to its property (compensatory damages) and the ordinary profits that would have been earned by such person had the securities law violations not occurred (lost profits).

9.3 Criminal penalties

Securities law violators may also be subject to criminal sanctions under the

Criminal Code of the Russian Federation. Insider trading, communication of privileged information, market manipulation, market abuse in the issuance of securities and persistent refusal to disclose or provide information required by the Russian securities laws are included among the offences that can result in criminal penalties. Criminal penalties are imposed only on individuals (management and employees).

10. CONTINUING OBLIGATIONS
10.1 Disclosure and transparency rule
Rules for making requisite disclosure are set forth in the Federal Law on the Securities Market and the FFMS Regulation on Information Disclosure.

For this purpose disclosure means making information available to all persons concerned, regardless of their purpose for receiving it, in a manner that guarantees its delivery and receipt.

In cases where a securities prospectus must be registered, each stage of the issuance process must be accompanied by disclosure of particular information by the issuer. The relevant information must be disclosed:
- within one day of the occurrence of the relevant event – through the news wire of at least one of the FFMS authorised information agencies, and
- within two days – on the issuer's Web site.

In addition, notice of the registration of an issuance of securities must be published in a periodical with a circulation of not less than 10,000 copies (in case of a public placement) or 1,000 copies (in case of a private placement) within 10 days from the date on which the issuer was notified of the registration of the issuance or this information was published on the FFMS Web site.

After a prospectus is registered, issuers are required to report significant facts (as defined below) and facts that may influence the price of the securities ('price sensitive facts') and prepare quarterly reports.

10.2 Information
The types of information subject to disclosure are described below.

10.3 Obligations regarding proxy solicitation
Russian law does not currently regulate the procedure for soliciting proxies.

10.4 Continuing requirements of reporting and notification of substantial shareholdings or a substantial transaction

Reports on Significant Facts
Issuers must disclose certain information in the form of Reports on Significant Facts. This duty arises on the date following the prospectus registration date and terminates on the date following the date on which any of the following information is published by news wire (the 'termination date'):
- the securities issuance is declared to be invalid;

- a securities prospectus registered after the date of the state registration of the report on securities issuance is declared to be invalid;
- the securities with respect to which the prospectus was registered are cancelled; and
- certain other information specified in the Regulation on Information Disclosure.

The following significant information must be disclosed in the Report on Significant Facts:

- the corporate reorganisation of the issuer or its subsidiaries or dependent companies;
- circumstances that lead to: (i) a one-time increase or decrease of the issuer's assets by more than 10 per cent; or (ii) a one-time increase of net profits or net losses of the issuer by more than 10 per cent;
- one-off transactions the value of which is equal to 10 per cent or more of the assets of the issuer as of the date of the transaction;
- information on the stages of the securities issuance process, suspension or recommencement of an issuance and declaration of the invalidity of the issuance; and
- certain other facts specified in the Regulation on Information Disclosure.

Reports on Price Sensitive Facts
Issuers are required to report price sensitive facts from the date of any of the following events:

- certain decisions made by the issuer's board of directors;
- the expiration of the term of office of the CEO or directors of the issuer;
- changes in the shareholdings of the CEO (general director), directors or members of the issuer's management board in the issuer or its subsidiaries;
- an interested party transaction where the price of the transaction is equal to 5 per cent or more of the issuer's asset book value; or
- the initiation of bankruptcy proceedings by a Russian court against the issuer or its subsidiaries.

The obligation to report price sensitive facts expires on the termination date (see Reports on Significant Facts above).

Quarterly Reports
The duty to file quarterly reports arises in the quarter in which the securities prospectus was registered. A quarterly report must contain extensive information on the issuer, including its management, auditors, bank accounts, economic situation, business, material transactions, major shareholders and related party transactions.

Quarterly reports must be provided to the FFMS within 45 days following the end of the relevant quarter and published on the Internet.

Quarterly reports must be available on the Internet for three years from the date of their publication. A quarterly report must be signed by the CEO (general director) and the chief accountant of the issuer. Quarterly reports (as well as any other reports that are required to be produced by an issuer) must be generally available to any security holder and must be provided within seven days of the date on which a request is received.

10.5 Clearing

Currently, clearing operations are mainly regulated by the Federal Law on the Securities Market and the FFMS Regulation on Clearing. However, in February 2011, the Federal Law on Clearing was adopted. This law introduces changes into the legal framework for the regulation and supervision of clearing activities by the state. The Federal Law on Clearing will not become effective until January 2012.

Clearing activity is subject to licensing and may be conducted only by clearing organisations. In accordance with the new Federal Law on Clearing, these organisations may not engage in certain specified activities, including trading, insurance, or the maintenance of securities registers. If a clearing organisation combines clearing activity with other permitted services it must conduct a review of conflicts of interests to avoid potential violations of the rights of clearing participants.

Once the Federal Law on Clearing becomes effective, clearing organisations will be required to maintain minimum capital of 100 million roubles (EUR 2.5 million). They will also be required to establish a risk management system that must be stress-tested on a regular basis. The information on the results of these stress-tests will be required to be submitted to the Central Bank of Russia and to the FFMS.

11. CORPORATE GOVERNANCE

11.1 Law and/or Code

The general rules of corporate governance in the Russian Federation are set out in the Federal Law on Joint Stock Companies and certain orders of the FFMS. Additional guidance is provided in the FFMS's Corporate Governance Code (CGC). The provisions of the CGC are not mandatory, but they are recommended. Certain corporate governance provisions may also be contained in a company's charter.

11.2 Management structure

The management structure of a company typically consists of three governing bodies – the general meeting of shareholders (GM), which is the supreme management body of the company, the Board of Directors (BoD) and the executive bodies of the company (very often the company's general director, but companies are also entitled to adopt a collegial executive body in the form of a management board).

In a company with less than 50 shareholders, the charter of the company may provide that the functions of the BoD be carried out by the GM. If this is the case, the charter must also contain provisions specifying who has authority to convene a GM and approve its agenda.

11.3 Obligations to publish information on the Internet

Generally, companies required to disclose information must disclose it on

their Web sites. An open joint stock company is obliged to disclose:
- its annual report and annual financial statements;
- the prospectus for the company's shares in certain cases;
- announcements of forthcoming general meetings of shareholders; and
- other information required by the FFMS.

11.4 Responsibility of inside/outside directors
There are no differences between the responsibilities of inside and outside directors. The CGC recommends that independent directors be included in the BoD and their presence be disclosed.

The RTS and MICEX listing rules contain requirements for the number of independent directors that a listed company must have, depending on the applicable quotation list and the type of security. That number is generally either one or three independent directors.

11.5 Committees
The types of committees and their membership composition should be specified in the company's charter and other internal documents. The CGC also contains recommendations regarding establishing committees, including those for strategic planning, nomination and remuneration, audit, corporate conflicts settlement, risk management and ethics.

The existence of an audit committee and a nomination and remuneration committee are required by the RTS and MICEX listing rules, depending on the applicable quotation list and the type of security.

The CGC recommends that BoD members play an active role in the meetings of the BoD and its committees, but recommends that the participation of directors in multiple committees be limited.

11.6 Obligation to ask for consent of a shareholders' meeting
A number of matters are relegated to the exclusive competence of the GM, unless otherwise specified in the Federal Law on Joint Stock Companies, including, but not limited to,
- adopting or amending the charter of the company;
- reorganising the company;
- liquidating the company;
- determining the number of directors, electing them to the BoD and terminating their powers prior to the expiration of their term;
- determining the number, face value and type of shares and the rights attributed to them;
- increasing or decreasing the authorised capital of the company in certain cases;
- approving the company's auditor;
- paying annual, first quarter, semi-annual and third quarter dividends;
- approving annual reports; and
- establishing procedures for holding a GM.

11.7 Depth of information – proxy solicitation
Shareholder representatives participating in a GM must act in accordance with

their powers of attorney and other legal acts. A power of attorney entitling the holder to vote at a GM must contain certain information on the holder and the shareholder being represented. This power of attorney must be in the form prescribed by the Russian Civil Code or certified by a notary.

If shares are transferred after the cut-off date for the GM attendance list and prior to the date of the GM, the person included in the list, but who no longer owns shares, must issue a power of attorney to the purchaser to permit the purchaser (or its representative) to vote at the GM.

11.8 Appointment/dismissal of directors

The members of the BoD must be elected by the GM for a term ending on the date of the next annual GM. If the next annual GM is not convened as scheduled, the powers of the BoD terminate, except for the power to convene and hold the annual GM.

Shareholders owning in the aggregate at least 2 per cent of the voting shares are entitled to nominate candidates to the BoD, the number of whom cannot exceed the number of BoD members.

Persons elected to the BoD may be re-elected an unlimited number of times.

The members of the management board may not comprise more than one-quarter of the members of the BoD. A person exercising the functions of a general director may not be the same person as the chairman of the BoD.

The GM may terminate the powers of all of the directors, but not those of a particular director or directors, earlier than the end of the BoD's term.

The number of directors is determined by the charter or by decision of the GM, but must be at least five. For a company with more than 1,000 shareholders, the number of directors may not be less than seven, and for a company with more than 10,000 shareholders, the number of directors may not be less than nine.

Directors are elected by cumulative voting. The number of votes belonging to each shareholder is multiplied by the number of candidates to be elected and the shareholder is entitled to cast all of the votes for one candidate or to distribute them among two or more candidates. The candidates who receive the largest number of votes are elected to the BoD.

11.9 Income and options for directors

Directors may be compensated for their services as directors and have their BoD-related expenses reimbursed. The amount of compensation is established by the GM. The CGC contains recommendations on the compensation of directors.

Directors are allowed to receive options to acquire the company's shares.

11.10   Earnings guidance

Open joint stock companies must publish their annual reports on a regular basis. Listed companies, credit organisations and insurance companies must also publish their consolidated financial statements prepared in accordance with IAS.

11.11 Management discussion and analysis (MD&A)
The content of the MD&A section of the prospectus is not prescribed by law or regulation.

11.12 Directors' liability
Members of the BoD, general directors and members of the management board must exercise their rights and perform their duties in the interests of the company, reasonably and in good faith.

Otherwise, they are generally liable to the company for losses caused on account of their faulty actions or omissions. Directors and members of the management board who voted against or did not participate in the voting on the decision that entailed losses to the company are not liable to the company.

Actions taken or omissions made in the ordinary course of business and other circumstances bearing on the matter must be taken into account when determining the grounds and the extent of a director's, general director's or management board member's liability to the company for the losses resulting from such actions or omissions.

If several directors are liable, their liability is joint and several.

The company or shareholder(s) possessing in the aggregate not less than 1 per cent of the issued ordinary shares have the right to file a derivative action against the BoD, general director or management board members to obtain compensation for the company's losses.

12. MARKET ABUSE
12.1 Insider trading

Law and regulations
The legal framework for combating unlawful use of insider information and market manipulation is contained in the recently enacted Federal Law on Insider Trading.

Code of conduct
The Federal Law on Insider Trading prohibits any person from entering into, or recommending or inducing a third party to enter into, a transaction involving financial instruments, foreign currencies and/or commodities if this person received insider information prior to entering into, or recommending or inducing a third party to enter into, the transaction.

Notification of transactions
Insiders included in the list of insiders of an issuer, a management company, a legal entity holding a dominant position in a particular market, certain securities market participants or any of their contractors that may have access to inside information must notify such entities and the FFMS of any insider trading.

Inside information
Inside information includes any precise and specific non-public information,

the disclosure of which may significantly affect the price of a particular financial instrument, foreign currency and/or commodity. Insider information also includes any information that is included in the list of insider information to be formulated by the FFMS.

Sanctions

Criminal liability for unlawful use of insider information will only commence in 2013. A fine in the amount of 300,000-1,000,000 roubles (approximately EUR 7,000-25,000) or three to four years' worth of salary or other income of the convicted person may be imposed for the illegal use of insider information. A person found guilty may also face imprisonment for up to four (maximum of six) years together with the imposition of a fine.

Administrative fines can be imposed for the unlawful use of insider information and market manipulation in the absence of criminal intent. An administrative fine for an individual amounts to 3,000-5,000 roubles (approximately EUR 74-123), for an officer – 30,000-50,000 roubles (approximately EUR 738-1,300) or a prohibition against holding certain offices for a period of one to two years, and for a legal entity – a fine in the amount of the extra gain earned as a result of the illegitimate use of inside information, but not less than 700,000 roubles (approximately EUR 18,000).

The Federal Law on Insider Trading contains certain exemptions from liability for the inadvertent use of inside information and/or market manipulation, including, but not limited, to cases involving the media publishing false data, if this data were accurately reproduced from announcements, interviews and press-releases of individuals or legal entities or from data published elsewhere in the media, provided that the source of the data is referred to, or by a person using inside information if this person was unaware of its nature.

12.2 Market manipulation

Market manipulation primarily refers to:

- the intentional dissemination of false information through the media, including the Internet;
- transactions or bids; and
- sham transactions or bids made or issued without any intention to execute them,

that create or secure the price, demand, offer or trading volume of a financial instrument, foreign currency and/or commodity at a level significantly different from that created in usual market conditions. Some market activities, such as market maker services, are specifically excluded from the list of manipulative practices.

13. MUTUAL OR INVESTMENT FUNDS

13.1 Introduction to these two categories

Under the Federal Law on Investment Funds, an investment fund is a property portfolio owned by a joint stock company or that is owned by means of participatory share ownership interests by persons and/or entities (jointly referred to as the 'grantors'), and which is administered by a management company solely in the interests of the joint stock company's shareholders or the grantors. Investment funds in Russia are classified into joint stock investment funds (JSIFs) and unit investment funds (UIFs).

A JSIF is an open joint stock company that is only entitled to invest assets in securities and other facilities listed in the Federal Law on Investment Funds and may not pursue any other types of entrepreneurial activities.

A UIF is a property portfolio that does not have the status of a legal entity. A UIF is composed of property transferred by a grantor (or grantors) to a management company to be held in trust. Accordingly, a UIF is a form of collective investment which involves pooling together the assets (monetary funds and other assets) of natural persons and legal entities and transferring them to a management company for the purpose of deriving a profit from the management of those assets. The property is managed in accordance with the management rules adopted by the management company with respect to the UIF.

By investing funds in a UIF, an investor acquires investment shares issued by the management company, which are registered securities giving their holder the right to own the assets constituting the UIF, as well as the right to demand proper fund management of the UIF and the right to claim monetary compensation upon the redemption of the investment shares. An investment share may be sold, donated, pledged or bequeathed by will.

The assets of a UIF are the common property of the grantors. Division of the UIF property and the apportionment of participatory shares in kind is not permitted.

13.2 Investment companies, open-ended, close-ended

The Federal Law on Investment Funds establishes three types of UIFs: open-end funds, interval funds and closed-end funds. The principal difference between these types is the procedure by which a grantor exercises its right to terminate the management contract entered into between the grantor, the UIF and the management company.

In the case of an open-end mutual fund, the grantor is entitled to redeem the investment shares it owns in whole or in part on any business day and receive *pro rata* compensation for them from the management company. Accordingly, investment shares are exchanged and redeemed on a daily basis and their value is also calculated on a daily basis.

In the case of an interval fund, the grantor is entitled to redeem investment shares only during a specified period.

In the case of a closed-end fund, the grantor may either redeem investment shares or, in certain cases, attend the general meeting of the UIF grantors, and may have the right to receive income from the management of the property portfolio, if this right is contained in the management rules of the UIF.

13.3 Licence requirements
A JSIF requires a licence to engage in its activities issued by the FFMS. Because UIFs are not legal entities, it is the management company that must obtain the licence.

A JSIF and a UIF management company must meet certain requirements before they can receive a licence from the FFMS. By way of example, the JSIF and the UIF management company must own assets equal to or exceeding 35 million (EUR 860,000) and 60 million (EUR 1.5 million) roubles, respectively, on the day they apply for the licence.

The licence is issued without any limitations as to its term.

13.4 Continuing requirements
Russian legislation establishes continuing requirements applicable to JSIFs and UIF management companies. In general these continuing requirements include (but are not limited to): periodic reporting; annual audits; and requirements relating to the composition and structure of the portfolio assets.

Depending on the composition and structure of its assets, a JSIF/UIF may be any one of a long list of sub-types of funds, such as a money market fund, bond fund, stock fund, fund of funds, etc. Separate requirements for the composition and structure of assets are established for each type of investment fund.

13.5 Custodians
Under the Federal Law on Investment Funds, the property owned by a JSIF or the property constituting a UIF (the 'fund property') must be recorded and retained by a specialised custodian (a professional securities market-maker engaged in custody activities). Only a legal entity created in the form of a joint stock company or a limited liability company and which holds a specialised custodian licence may act as the custodian for a JSIF or a UIF.

The custodian performs its functions on the basis of a custody agreement entered into between the custodian and the JSIF or the UIF management company.

The custodian must act only in the interests of the JSIF shareholders or the UIF grantors.

The custodian is not entitled to use or dispose of the fund property. It is also prohibited from owning shares in an investment fund of which it is a custodian.

13.6 Undertakings for Collective Investment in Transferable Securities (UCITS)
UCITS refers to a set of European Union directives that aim to establish a single regulatory regime across the European Union for open-ended funds investing in transferable securities, such as shares and bonds, with a view to establishing high levels of investor protection.

Because the UCITS directives are addressed only to the member states of the European Union, and the directives not applicable in Russia, there are no UCITS funds in Russia. However, since the UCITS concept is globally recognised as providing a stable, high quality and well-regulated investment product with significant levels of investor protection, certain major Russian investors have established UCITS funds outside of Russia.

13.7 Hedge funds
Only in 2008 did it become legally possible to create a hedge fund in Russia when the FFMS enacted its Regulation on the Composition and Structure of Assets of Joint Stock Investment Funds and Assets of Shared Investment Funds.

Under the Regulation, a hedge fund may only be a JSIF, or a closed or interval share investment fund. Its assets may only be comprised of the property that is specified in the Regulation.

Only qualified investors may invest in hedge funds. In accordance with the Federal Law on the Securities Market, the category of 'qualified investor' includes brokers, dealers, managers, credit institutions, JSIFs and UIFs, non-governmental pension funds and other persons specified in the Law.

As of March 2011, only six hedge funds have been established in Russia.

13.8 Dissemination of information on investment funds
The Federal Law on Investment Funds contains rules on the dissemination, delivery and disclosure of information about a JSIF's, UIF's, its management company's or custodian's activity. Among the information required to be disseminated is the name of the JSIF/UIF and its management company, the number and date of registration of the share prospectus of the JSIF, the licence number of the JSIF, as well as the number and date of registration of the UIF management rules and the licence number of the UIF management company.

The information subject to dissemination must comply with the JSIF charter, its investment declaration, the share prospectus, or with the UIF management rules (as appropriate), and must not contain any:
- unfair, unethical or misleading information;
- any guarantees or promises of would-be effectiveness and yield level of the investment activity of the JSIF or the UIF management company; in particular, those based on their actual past performance;
- information not supported by documents; or
- reference to approval or endorsement of any information on the activities of the JSIF or the UIF management company by the state authorities.

In certain cases, the information must be filed with the FFMS prior to its dissemination.

14. SECURITIES INSTITUTIONS
Professional market participants must be licensed in accordance with the Federal Law on the Securities Market. Licensing requirements and applicants' qualifications are set forth in FFMS regulations.

14.1 Market executive undertaking

Obligations are undertaken and performed on the organised securities markets in accordance with a system operated by professional market participants with the support of a stock exchange (market executive undertaking). A market executive undertaking in Russia is generally organised as a non-commercial partnership or a joint stock company. The RTC and MICEX are among the most significant market executive undertakings.

14.2 Securities clearing house

Under the Federal Law on the Securities Market, clearing houses are professional securities market participants that supervise positions and clear settlements in connection with securities transactions. Clearing houses in Russia must be licensed. They typically work in close tandem with stock exchanges (eg, the MICEX National Settlement Depositary and the RTS Clearing Centre).

14.3 Central securities depository

Depositories in Russia are professional securities market participants that hold securities in certificated form and/or record the transfer of rights to securities. The same entity can act as both a clearing house and a depositary for securities. Securities depositories in Russia must be licensed.

The process of establishing a central securities depository in Russia has begun. This institution is proposed to be one of the core organisations necessary to transform Moscow into an international financial centre under a programme currently being implemented by the Russian government.

14.4 Investment services providers (ISP)

Russia has not adopted specific ISP legislation. However, there is special regulation of the activities of professional securities market participants that encompasses the provision of investment services.

Under the Federal Law on the Securities Market, brokers are professional securities market participants who engage in market operations with securities on behalf of and at the expense of their clients (investors or issuers) or in proprietary trading.

Dealers are professional securities market participants who engage in transactions with securities for their own account by publicly declaring the bid and ask prices for securities with the obligation to buy and/or sell securities at the appropriate price.

Trust managers are professional securities market participants who manage the securities of their clients under a trust management agreement. Trust management may be exercised over securities, money for investment in securities and also assets and securities derived from such management activities.

15. NOTIFICATION OBLIGATION
15.1 Notification on major shareholding
A number of Russian securities laws and regulations require that significant shareholders and their percentage shareholdings be publicly identified.

Issuer obligation
The issuer must disclose information regarding a shareholder holding at least 5 per cent of its outstanding ordinary shares and regarding any event that causes an increase in such shareholding above 5, 10, 15, 20, 25, 30, 50 or 75 per cent or a commensurate decrease.

This information must be disclosed in the form of notification of significant facts referred to in section 10.4 above.

The information must be disclosed in the news wire not later than one day after any such threshold is crossed and on the issuer's Web site not later than two days after such event. The information must be available for six months after its publication date.

Shareholder obligation
The shareholder must disclose information regarding its acquisition of 5 per cent of an issuer's outstanding ordinary shares and regarding any event that causes an increase in such shareholding above 5, 10, 15, 20, 25, 30, 50 or 75 per cent or a commensurate decrease.

The shareholder must notify the issuer and the FFMS of these facts.

16. PUBLIC TAKEOVERS
16.1 Applicable laws
Public takeovers are regulated by the Federal Law on Joint Stock Companies.

16.2 Competent authorities
The FFMS exercises control over voluntary and mandatory offer documents, buyout notifications and squeeze-outs, as well as any amendments made to such documents.

16.3 Types of takeovers
In accordance with the Federal Law on Joint Stock Companies:
*   a person who intends to acquire over 30 per cent of the shares of a company may make a voluntary offer to purchase the shares from their owners (a 'voluntary offer'); and
*   a person who, together with its affiliated persons, has already acquired more than 30 per cent (or more than 50 or 75 per cent, as the case may be) of a company's shares must offer to purchase the remaining shares from their owners (a 'mandatory offer').

16.4 Procedural aspects
Both a voluntary offer and a mandatory offer must be sent to the remaining shareholders by the company. Offers are considered to be duly made by the prospective purchaser upon receipt of the relevant offer by the company.

A mandatory offer must be made within 35 days of: (i) more than 30 per cent of the shares being recorded in the name of the prospective purchaser; or (ii) the day on which the prospective purchaser learned, or should have learned, that it alone or together with its affiliates owned the relevant number of shares.

The same provisions apply in the case of acquisitions of more than 50 per cent and more than 75 per cent of the shares.

The prospective purchaser may amend the terms of a voluntary offer or a mandatory offer to increase the purchase price or to shorten the payment period.

The deadline for accepting a voluntary offer is not less than 70 and not more than 90 days from the time the offer is received by the company. Similarly, the deadline for accepting a mandatory offer is not less than 70 and not more than 80 days. The prospective purchaser may not acquire the shares prior to the expiration of the acceptance period on terms different from those contained in the offer.

The obligation of the prospective purchaser to pay the purchase price for the shares must be secured by an irrevocable bank guarantee, which must remain in force for at least six months after the end of the period fixed for payment. The bank guarantee must be attached to the voluntary offer and mandatory offer documents.

The Federal Law on Joint Stock Companies contains certain restrictions on the application of, as well as certain exemptions from the requirement to make, a mandatory offer.

16.5 Nature and value of consideration offered

Determination of purchase price for a voluntary offer
The purchase price for the shares or the procedure for determining it is proposed by the prospective purchaser. If a procedure is indicated, it must ensure that the same per share purchase price is established for all owners of this class and type of shares.

Determination of purchase price for a mandatory offer
The price specified in the mandatory offer may not be less than:
- the weighted average price of the shares as quoted on a stock exchange for a period of six months prior to the delivery of the mandatory offer to the company; or
- if the shares have not been traded on a stock exchange for at least six months, or are not traded on a stock exchange, the price determined by an independent professional appraiser; and
- the maximum price for the relevant shares paid (or undertaken to be paid) by the prospective purchaser or its affiliates within the six months prior to the delivery of the mandatory offer to the company.

16.6 Financing/payment method
Both a voluntary offer and a mandatory offer must stipulate cash payment

for the shares, but may also provide the remaining shareholders with the opportunity to elect to receive the payment in cash or other securities.

16.7 Title transfer

Title to the shares passes to the prospective purchaser at the time the newly acquired shares are recorded in its account by the share registrar in accordance with the transfer deed provided by the selling shareholder.

16.8 Drafting of offer documents

Voluntary offer

A voluntary offer must include the following information:
- the number of shares in the company already owned by the prospective purchaser and its affiliates, and the affiliates must be identified;
- the type, category and number of shares the prospective purchaser intends to acquire;
- the purchase price or its calculation method;
- the payment period and the form of consideration for the shares;
- the time period for accepting the offer (70 to 90 days from receipt of the voluntary offer by the company); and
- information on the terms of the bank guarantee securing the prospective purchaser's payment obligations, as well as the name of the bank providing the guarantee.

A voluntary offer may include other terms and conditions as well.

Mandatory offer

Among other things, the following additional or substitute information must be included in the mandatory offer document:
- period of time for accepting the offer (70 to 80 days from the receipt of the mandatory offer by the company);
- the payment period (which cannot exceed 15 days from the date on which the acquired shares are recorded in the prospective purchaser's account); and
- the purchase price or its calculation method, as well as the justification for the purchase price, including data on the price's compliance with the requirements of the Federal Law on Joint Stock Companies.

Unlike a voluntary offer, a mandatory offer cannot contain any conditions other than those clearly set out in the Federal Law On Joint Stock Companies.

16.9 Defence mechanism

The minority shareholders are protected by the following means:
- the prospective purchaser must notify the other shareholders of its mandatory offer; and
- a special regulation defines the price to be paid for the shares subject to the mandatory offer.

16.10   Buyout

A person who has acquired more than 95 per cent of the shares in a company as a result of a voluntary offer for the purchase of all of the remaining shares or a mandatory offer (the 'controlling shareholder') must buy out all of the remaining shares of the company at the demand of the minority shareholders. A person who has acquired more than 95 per cent of the shares as a result of a voluntary offer for the purchase of some of the company's shares is not required to buy out the remaining minority shareholders.

16.11   Squeeze-out

The controlling shareholder has the right to squeeze-out the remaining shareholders by filing a demand to purchase all of the remaining shares with the company (the 'squeeze-out demand'). However, prior to being allowed to submit a squeeze-out demand, the controlling shareholder must buy out the shares proffered in the buyout.

The squeeze-out demand can only be filed by a shareholder who, as a result of a voluntary offer or mandatory offer, acquired more than 95 per cent of the voting shares of a company; provided that the shares acquired during the voluntary offer or mandatory offer represented at least 10 per cent of the total number of issued shares.

As in the case of a mandatory offer, the principal means of protecting the remaining minority shareholders during a squeeze-out is a special regulation on determining the price to be paid for the shares subject to the forced squeeze-out.

The purchase price must not be less than the market value of the shares, as determined by an independent professional appraiser. In addition, the price may not be less than:

- the price paid for the shares acquired in a voluntary offer or mandatory offer; or
- the maximum price that the prospective purchaser paid or undertook to pay for the shares subsequent to the expiration of the acceptance period for the voluntary offer or mandatory offer.

The shares may only be paid for in cash. A minority shareholder who disagrees with the purchase price may submit a claim for damages within six months from the date on which it became aware of the transfer of its shares from its account to the account of the prospective purchaser maintained by the share registrar.

17.   FOREIGN INVESTMENT CONTROLS
17.1 Foreign investments
Russian regulations governing foreign investments in Russian companies were substantially amended in 2008 with the adoption of the Federal Law on Foreign Investments in Strategic Enterprises.

The Federal Law on Foreign Investments in Strategic Enterprises applies to investments in strategic companies (which are Russian companies conducting at least one of the 42 strategic activities specified in the Law) by foreign investors. A foreign investor includes a legal entity established in any jurisdiction or territory outside of Russia, a legal entity established in Russia but controlled by a foreign investor (or a group of persons which includes a foreign investor), as well as foreign governments, international organisations and organisations directly or indirectly controlled by them.

Under the Federal Law on Foreign Investments in Strategic Enterprises, acquisition of strategic control over a strategic company by a foreign investor requires the prior approval of the Governmental Commission for Control over Foreign Investments in the Russian Federation (the Governmental Commission). Acquisition of strategic control includes:

• acquisition of more than 50 per cent of the votes or the right to appoint more than 50 per cent of the BoD or management board in a strategic company;

• acquisition of at least 10 per cent of the votes or the right to appoint at least 10 per cent of the BoD or management board in a strategic company engaged in geological survey or exploration and development of subsoil areas of federal significance (a 'Strategic Subsoil Company');

• acquisition of any additional votes in a Strategic Subsoil Company by a foreign investor already controlling at least 10 per cent of it;

• assumption of managing company functions or entering into any other transactions leading to the establishment of control over a strategic company; and

• acquisition by a foreign state, international organisation or organisation under its control of more than 25 per cent or other blocking rights in a strategic company or more than 5 per cent in a Strategic Subsoil Company (in either case, the law prohibits a foreign state, international organisation or organisation under its control from acquiring control over a strategic company).

17.2 Exemptions

Under the Federal Law on Foreign Investments in Strategic Enterprises, the following transactions may be entered into without the prior approval of the Governmental Commission:

• transactions completed before the enactment of the law; and

• acquisition of control over companies in which a foreign investor or a group of persons which includes a foreign investor already directly or indirectly controls more than 50 per cent of the votes. (This exception does not apply to Strategic Subsoil Companies).

17.3 Notification

The Federal Law on Foreign Investments in Strategic Enterprises requires foreign investors acquiring at least 5 per cent of the shares in a strategic company to notify the Russian Federal Antimonopoly Service of this fact within 180 days of the acquisition.

South Korea

Lee & Ko Je Won Lee & Mark B Rolfson

1. GENERAL DESCRIPTION OF THE CAPITAL MARKETS

1.1 Number of companies listed
As of December 2010, 1,807 corporations were listed on the Korea Exchange (KRX), 779 with the Stock Market Division and 1,028 with the Korea Securities Dealers Automated Quotations system (KOSDAQ) Market Division.

1.2 Total volume and market value
The various securities issued by KRX-listed corporations reached a total of 1,998 separate securities listings (953 securities listings with the Stock Market Division and 1,045 securities listings with the KOSDAQ Market Division) at the end of 2010. At the end of 2009, the aggregate market value of securities listed on the KRX was KRW 974 trillion, while the aggregate trading value came to KRW 1,232 trillion.

In the Derivatives Market Division, the trading volume consisted of 3.617 billion contracts (including a total of 3 billion equity-index products, 20 million interest-rate products and 41.7 million currency and other products). The Derivatives Market Division trading value totalled approximately KRW 10,813 trillion (including an aggregate of KRW 7,907 trillion for equity-index products, KRW 2,210 trillion for interest-rate products and KRW 696 trillion for currency and other products). Open interests consisted of a total of 60.1 million contracts (including a total of 50 million equity-index products, 1.9 million interest-rate products and 8.22 million currency and other products).

With respect to bonds, as of the end of 2009, the number of listed issues was 9,527, and the aggregate par value of listed bonds that remained outstanding was KRW 1,014 trillion. The aggregate trading volume for the year 2009 was KRW 504 trillion.

1.3 Issue activity
See 1.2

1.4 Takeover activity
No well-defined/standardised public data sets are available.

1.5 Hostile takeover attempts
No well-defined/standardised public data sets are available.

2. REGULATORY STRUCTURE

2.1 General

Regulated markets

In 2005, a new market structure was instituted in Korea, pursuant to which the Korea Stock Exchange, KOSDAQ and the Korea Futures Exchange (each of which had previously operated as independent markets) became divisions of a single exchange system formally designated as the Korea Exchange (KRX). These market divisions are currently referred to, respectively, as the Stock Market Division, the KOSDAQ Market Division and the Derivatives Market Division (formerly known as the Futures Market Division) of the KRX. While this consolidation did not result in any major changes in the basic operations and functions of the respective market divisions, it has led to significant gains in efficiency and convenience, including, for example, the ability of customers to use a single trading account for transactions in all KRX market divisions, rather than requiring separate accounts for trading in each market category.

The Financial Investment Services and Capital Markets Act

The Financial Investment Services and Capital Markets Act (FSCMA) and regulations promulgated thereunder govern such matters as public offerings and tender offers of securities, restrictions against insider trading (see section 12) and market price manipulation, as well as requirements for the filing of reports on substantial shareholdings (see section 10.5).

Regulatory agencies for FSCMA-related matters

At the ministerial level, the Financial Services Commission (FSC) is responsible for the implementation of the provisions of the FSCMA and related regulatory matters. At the administrative level, the FSC and its administrative arm, the Financial Supervisory Service (FSS), are the principal governmental agencies responsible for enforcement and supervision of matters governed by the FSCMA and related regulations. Each of these organisations is also responsible for formulating related guidelines and rules within the scope of discretion granted to them under the FSCMA.

Within this overall regulatory scheme, the KRX has the authority to establish listing requirements, public disclosure requirements and various detailed rules applicable to KRX listings and trading activities.

Other relevant laws

In addition to the FSCMA, other laws that are particularly relevant to the capital market include the Monopoly Regulation and Fair Trade Act (MRFTA), the Foreign Exchange Transaction Act (FETA) and the Foreign Investment Promotion Act (FIPA).

The MRFTA governs anti-trust/fair-trade issues and the Korean Fair Trade Commission is the governmental body principally responsible for overseeing compliance with MRFTA provisions and related regulations.

The FETA and related regulations govern transactions involving foreign parties, foreign currencies and/or foreign-currency denominated securities.

The Ministry of Strategy and Finance (MOSF) and the Bank of Korea (BOK) are responsible for overseeing compliance with the various requirements imposed under the FETA and related regulations, which are of particular relevance to foreign investment in Korean securities. It should be noted that the FETA regulations pertaining to foreign exchange transactions have become increasingly lenient in recent years, generally shifting away from a system requiring MOSF or BOK approvals toward a more simplified reporting system, including simplified reporting requirements that can be satisfied by filing with the filer's designated foreign exchange bank in Korea.

FIPA (which is further discussed in section 17 below) governs various categories of investment by foreigners deemed to be particularly beneficial to the Korean economy. The Ministry of Knowledge Economy (MKE) oversees compliance and implementation matters relating to FIPA.

2.2   Regulation of the offering of new securities
2.2.1 Public offering

Definition of public offering
In Korea, a public offering is defined as occurring, and related public offering regulations become applicable, when, within any six-month period: (i) with regard to newly issued securities, 50 or more persons have received solicitations for bids to buy the relevant securities; or (ii) with regard to outstanding securities, 50 or more persons have received solicitations for bids to buy or offers to sell the relevant securities outside the KRX system. Financial institutions and specially related parties of the issuer of the securities are excluded when calculating whether the 50-person threshold has been reached in any particular case.

However, in the case of newly issued securities, even if the solicitations for bids to buy the securities in question are made to fewer than 50 persons, an issuance may still be legally 'deemed' as constituting a public offering if there is any possibility that the securities can be transferred to 50 or more persons within one year from the date of issuance. The determination of whether there is a deemed public offering is made by reference to such factors as the type of security involved, the minimum denomination and applicable restrictions set forth in the terms and conditions of the security.

Public disclosure obligations (filing of material change reports, etc)
Under the Securities Exchange Act (which has been replaced by FSCMA), any domestic or foreign corporation intending to issue securities (except for certain securities such as beneficiary certificates or bonds issued by securities companies) in a public offering for the first time in Korea was required to register with the FSC. This requirement has been abolished under the FSCMA.

Under the current system, a corporation is required to make public disclosures whenever any of the following events occurs: (i) when any bank drafts or promissory notes issued by the corporation are dishonoured; (ii) when the corporation's banking transactions/privileges are suspended or prohibited; (iii) when all or materially all of the substantial business activities of the corporation are discontinued; or (iv) the occurrence of any other event having a material effect on the corporation, such as a resolution by the board of directors of the corporation for an increase or reduction of capital. Additionally, (i) issuers who have certain types of securities (such as convertible bonds, bonds with warrants and exchangeable bonds) listed on the KRX, (ii) issuers who, in connection with a public offering, provide shares or the types of securities referred to in (i), and (iii) all corporations that have 500 or more shareholders and are subject to external audit requirements are required to submit to the FSC and KRX standard corporate documents, such as the corporation's balance sheet, profit-and-loss statement, and surplus appropriation statement within 90 days following the end of each fiscal year.

Filing of registration statement and offering documents for publicly offered securities

Corporations that intend to sell securities in a public offering (or in circumstances that would constitute a deemed public offering) in which the total trade value is to be KRW 1 billion or more are required to file a securities registration statement (SRS) with the FSC. The SRS will then become effective only at the end of a prescribed waiting period following the date of the FSC's formal acceptance of the SRS. The applicable prescribed waiting period is determined as follows: (i) a period of 15 days in the case of an offering or sale of unlisted stock, a period of 10 days with respect to an offering or sale of the stock of a corporation whose stock is listed with the KRX (Stock-Listed Corporation) or a period of seven days with respect to a Stock-Listed Corporation's allocation of shares for distribution to shareholders for consideration or subscription by a third-party investor; (ii) a period of seven days with respect to an offering or sale of debt securities; (iii) a period of 10 days with respect to an offering or sale of a closed-end collective investment scheme's collective investment securities (ie, investment interests issued by a fund of limited duration) or a period of seven days with respect to a closed-end collective investment scheme's allocation of collective investment securities for distribution to investors (eg, shareholders in the case of a fund organised with corporate form) for consideration or subscription by a beneficiary; and (iv) 15 days with respect to the offering or sale of all other types of securities. Accordingly, the issuer must wait until the end of the applicable waiting period, at which time the SRS becomes effective, before proceeding with the offering or issuance of the relevant securities.

The above-mentioned SRS must be submitted in the Korean language using the standard form prescribed by the FSC, and attaching any required supporting documentation. Electronic filings are permitted.

The issuer of securities must also prepare a prospectus and related offering documents that are consistent with the information provided in the SRS filing. On or after the date on which the SRS becomes effective, the formal prospectus may be used in connection with the offering and sale of the securities. Between the date on which the FSC accepts the SRS filing and the effective date of the SRS, however, a preliminary prospectus should be used in lieu of the formal prospectus.

In the event that a corporation makes an offering for which the aggregate offering price is less than KRW 1 billion (a 'low-amount offering'), the corporation is not required to file an SRS with the FSC. In such cases, however, the corporation is still required to submit to the FSC documentation describing the corporation's financial and business status, as well as the offering method and offering documents to be used in connection with the planned offering. (The aforementioned requirement for submission of documentation concerning the corporation's financial and business status applies generally to unlisted corporations and must be submitted prior to proceeding with the relevant low-amount offering. The requirement for submission of information concerning the documents and offering method to be used in the relevant low-amount offering applies to both listed and unlisted corporations and must be submitted promptly after the offering is made.)

Brokerage/intermediary system
In Korea, only dealers or brokers (ie, entities that have been duly licensed to engage in securities dealing or brokerage business activities) are permitted to act as brokers/intermediaries in handling securities subscriptions, transfers, marketing and other related activities with respect to offerings of securities to Korean investors.

If an issuer desires to place securities in a public offering, a dealer or broker must be involved in the role of underwriter. If the securities issuance is relatively small, a single dealer or broker would be sufficient to handle the transaction; in the event that the issuance is relatively large, however, multiple dealers or brokers may form a consortium of underwriters, with one of the companies taking on the role of lead manager for the issuance.

In a typical public offering procedure for shares of stock, investors are required to submit, to the subscription handling department of the designated dealer or broker, on the date of subscription, two copies of the subscription agreement for the relevant stock, together with the deposit of an amount equal to the subscription price stated for such stock (which is required to be held in escrow as evidence of the ready availability of funds for the payment of the subscription price). The fees payable to any dealer or broker in respect of a particular offering and issuance of new shares can be deducted and paid from the subscription price paid for the shares only after the full amount of the subscription price (as stated in the board resolutions authorising the stock issuance) has been paid into the relevant bank account of the issuer and the related capital increase of the issuer has been formally registered.

2.2.2 Private offering
The above-discussed SRS filing requirement does not apply to privately offered securities (ie, private placements of newly issued securities made *vis-*

à-vis limited numbers of investors and otherwise conducted so as to avoid constituting a public offering (see 2.2.1 above)). On the other hand, privately offered securities are subject to the general requirement that only (Korea-licensed) dealers or brokers are permitted to act as brokers/intermediaries in handling securities subscriptions, transfers, marketing, and other related activities with respect to offerings of securities to Korean investors.

2.3 Differences between local and foreign companies

Pursuant to the KRX's adoption in 2005 of a policy of actively encouraging new listings on the KRX by eligible foreign corporations, the KRX has developed related rules and guidelines aimed at promoting reliability and transparency for the benefit of investors with respect to such foreign corporation listings. In this regard, the KRX has instituted a system to promote accounting reliability and transparency by, among other things: (i) requiring that auditors responsible for audited accounts of foreign companies that are listed (or to be listed) on the KRX must be incorporated accounting firms that meet or exceed specified threshold qualifications; and (ii) imposing restrictions on changes to the generally accepted accounting principles (GAAP) standards used by a listed foreign company and its auditor subsequent to the company's listing on the KRX. Additionally, with regard to cases where a foreign corporation is applying to be listed on the KRX and the nominally largest shareholder of the foreign corporation is a special purpose company or paper company, the KRX has instituted systems that take into account special issues and concerns related to multi-level and nominal ownership structures of listed companies. For example, the standard requirement for the largest shareholder of a company seeking to be listed on the KRX to deposit its shares with a custodian at the time of the company's initial public offering (IPO) (for a period of six months in the case of the Korea Composite Stock Price Index (KOSPI) and one year in the case of the KOSDAQ) is extended to apply also to the largest shareholder of the special purpose company/paper company. These requirements apply to both domestic and foreign corporations where such multi-level ownership structures exist.

2.4 Admission to trading on a regulated market

See relevant discussion in section 8 (Listing).

2.5 Financial promotion

Not applicable.

2.6 Rule books

Not applicable.

3. REGISTRATION OF THE ISSUER AND SECURITIES

3.1 Registration requirements

See relevant information in section 2.

South Korea

3.2 Other requirements
See relevant information in section 2

3.3 Nature of securities
Under the FSCMA, securities are broadly and conceptually defined to include any financial investment instrument issued by a citizen of Korea or a foreigner, for which investors do not owe any obligations of payment on any grounds beyond the acquisition price paid at the time of acquiring the instrument (excluding any obligations to pay when the investor assumes such an obligation as a result of exercising an option or right to purchase an underlying asset). Securities may be generally divided into the following categories: debt securities; equity securities; beneficiary certificates; investment contract securities; derivatives-combined securities; securities depositary receipts.

4. SUPERVISORY AUTHORITIES
4.1 Conduct: prudential, cooperation, self-regulation of stock exchange
Please see relevant information in section 2.1 above.

4.2 New listing measures in connection with the credit crisis
Not applicable.

5. OFFERING DOCUMENTATION OR PROSPECTUS REQUIREMENTS
5.1 Nature and statutory requirements of the offering document or disclosure document
Please see relevant information in section 2.2.1.

5.2 Exemptions
Please see relevant information in section 2.2.1.

5.3 Preparation of the offering document, general contents
Please see relevant information in section 2.2.1.

5.4 Due diligence
Please see relevant information in section 8.3.

5.5 Responsibility
Offering documentation is primarily the responsibility of the issuer and, if applicable, the underwriter or lead manager who participates in the preparation of the offering documentation.

5.6 Disclaimer/selling restrictions
A disclaimer is not required by law and provides no intrinsic legal protection (other than limited evidentiary value) with respect to any transaction(s) that violate applicable regulations, but is often included in private placement documentation to expressly state that no public offering is intended.

EUROPEAN LAWYER REFERENCE SERIES 389

5.7 Recognition of prospectuses by other exchanges
Not applicable.

5.8 Supplementary prospectuses
Changes to any material information set out in a filed registration statement are required to be disclosed through supplementary report filings.

5.9 Issuing of bonds
See relevant information in section 2.2.1.

6. DISTRIBUTION SYSTEMS
See Brokerage/Intermediary System content in section 2. Otherwise, not applicable.

7. PUBLICITY
Not applicable.

8. LISTING
8.1 Special listing requirements, admission criteria

Stock market division
The listing requirements of the Stock Market Division of the KRX that are applicable to domestic and foreign corporations can be divided into two broad categories, namely: (i) quantitative requirements based upon objectively applied standards; and (ii) qualitative requirements, which rely on the judgement and analysis of the KRX with regard to a corporation's general suitability for listing, as determined from the perspective of policies intended to serve general public interests and the protection of investors.

There are a total of 16 quantitative requirements, including, for example, requirements in relation to the following: (i) the corporation's operating history (three years or more must have passed since incorporation); (ii) the corporation's equity capital and minimum share listing (the corporation must have at least KRW 10 billion (apx $10 million) in equity capital and one million or more shares to be listed); (iii) the sales requirement (the total sales/business volume of the corporation's most recently concluded fiscal year must be at least KRW 30 billion (apx $30 million) and the average annual sales/business volume for the past three fiscal years should be KRW 20 billion (apx $20 million); and (iv) various matters relating to share distribution.

KOSDAQ market division
The listing requirements of the KOSDAQ Market Division of the KRX tend to be less demanding, with consideration being given to the technology and growth potential of venture companies, since the purpose of the KOSDAQ is to facilitate the listing of venture-type companies and small and medium sized companies.

Special lock-up requirement for the largest shareholder of the corporation to be listed
In cases where a corporation intends to make an initial listing with the KRX, such a corporation's largest shareholder (and specially related persons to it) must deposit their voting shares (including certificates representing any securities convertible into new voting shares, such as convertible bonds, bonds with warrants, warrants and exchangeable bonds; hereinafter, together with voting shares and ordinary voting shares, collectively referred to as Equity Securities) with the Korea Securities Depository: (i) for a period of six months following the date of listing, in the case of a listing with the Stock Market Division of the KRX; and (ii) for a period of one year in the case of a listing with the KOSDAQ Market Division of the KRX.

8.2 Mechanics of the review process
The listing process essentially consists of three major phases: (i) the preparation phase; (ii) the preliminary listing application phase; and (iii) the IPO and listing phase.

During the preparation phase: (i) auditors approved by the Securities and Futures Commission carry out an audit with respect to the corporation's most recently concluded fiscal year; and (ii) the corporation appoints a lead manager/arranger for the listing and IPO, and amends the company's articles of incorporation to reflect and accommodate provisions of the FSCMA and other relevant laws and regulations applicable to listed corporations.

In principle, a contract with the lead manager must be executed three months before the request for the preliminary regulatory review of the listing is made. Subsequent to their appointment as lead manager, the lead manager, together with a law firm retained by the lead manager, performs financial, business and legal due diligence on the listing corporation, and, depending on the outcome, the company makes appropriate amendments to its articles of incorporation in anticipation of the IPO and listing. Although the request for the preliminary regulatory review is submitted at the end of the preliminary listing application phase, the corporation must keep in close contact and communication with the related regulatory authorities such as the KRX, the FSC and the FSS, and make appropriate changes if requested by the regulatory authorities to the preliminary application documentation, the corporation's articles of incorporation or the corporation's SRS, as the case may be.

During the preliminary listing application period: (i) the corporation's board of directors or shareholders' meeting passes relevant resolutions to authorise the listing; (ii) a commitment letter for the required deposit of the Equity Securities of the largest shareholder (and specially related persons to it) is obtained from the shareholder; and (iii) a preliminary regulatory review of the proposed listing is requested. The preliminary regulatory review usually takes one to one and a half months to complete. Following receipt of the results of the KRX's preliminary regulatory review, the process moves into the IPO and listing phase.

During the IPO/listing period, the corporation files the SRS, makes the IPO and then submits the application for listing.

8.3 Prospectus obligation, due diligence, exemption
See relevant information in 8.2 above.

8.4 Appeal procedure in the event of a prospectus refusal
See relevant information in 8.2 above.

8.5 Authority of the Exchange
See relevant information in 8.2 above.

8.6 Sponsor
See comments in 8.2 regarding the appointment of a lead manager.
Otherwise not applicable.

8.7 Special arrangements for smaller companies such as Alternext, AIM or SPACs
See relevant information in 2.3 above regarding additional requirements that
apply to the largest shareholders of special purpose companies (such as SPACs).

8.8 Costs of various types
Costs associated with a listing include fees payable to the KRX for: (i)
preliminary review of the proposed listing; and (ii) for the listing itself. The
preliminary review fee is KRW 5 million and applies only with respect to the
listing of shares of stock. The listing fees are assessed based on the type and
the price of the listed securities (eg, Korea Depositary Receipts, foreign stock,
bonds, beneficiary securities and equity-linked warrants). The listing fee rates
applicable to the listing of shares of domestic corporations fall in the range
of 0.03 per cent to 0.001 per cent (depending on the aggregate price of the
stock to be listed). In the event that the total amount of listing fees exceeds
the amount of preliminary review fees paid to the KRX, the preliminary
review fee amount is applied towards the listing fees by deducting such an
amount from the total amount of listing fees to be paid.

For the listing of stock of foreign companies and depository certificates
based on underlying share certificates of foreign companies, the listing fees
are determined by reference to the number of shares and depository receipts
to be listed.

Additionally, where a corporation is offering securities in a public offering
and has filed the required SRS with the FSC, it must pay a fee in the amount
of: (i) 1.8/10,000 (ie 0.018 per cent) of the total issue price, in the case of
an offering of stock; and (ii) 4/10,000 – 9/10,000 (ie 0.04 per cent – 0.09 per
cent) of the total issue price depending on the length of the maturity, in the
case of an offering of debt securities.

9. SANCTIONS AND DISPUTES
9.1 Disciplinary and administrative sanctions
Regulatory authorities may impose a fairly broad range of disciplinary and
administrative sanctions, including, without limitation, warnings, advisory
notices, licence suspensions, penalties, fines etc, depending on the various

factors that the regulatory authorities may take into account in determining the appropriate response to any particular violation and related set of circumstances.

9.2 Civil actions
Various civil actions are possible, depending on the circumstances, relationships and arrangements between the relevant parties. Although a full discussion of such matters is beyond the scope of this material, some examples of potential civil action causes may include negligence, fraud, breach of fiduciary duty, etc.

9.3 Criminal penalties
Various criminal actions are possible, depending on the circumstances, culpability of the party to be charged, nature of harm/violation, etc.

10. CONTINUING OBLIGATIONS
10.1 Disclosure and transparency rule

Relevant statutory/regulatory requirements
Pursuant to the FSCMA and related disclosure regulations, as well as the KRX's disclosure regulations, corporations that have listed securities with the KRX (Listed Corporations) are required to satisfy certain public disclosure obligations. Such disclosures are usually done by way of electronic filings. A dual filing system is currently in place with respect to public disclosures of significant business or managerial matters ('material change report'). Under this system a separate disclosure report is submitted to the FSC and the KRX.

Additionally, pursuant to fair disclosure regulations, whenever a Stock-Listed Corporation intends to provide material information, such as future business plans, management plans and operational results (which has not been disclosed or made available to the public) to any select investor or group of investors, such information must also be disclosed immediately to the public.

10.2 Information
Quarterly, semi-annual and annual financial statements
Listed Corporations are required to: (i) prepare and file, within 90 days from the end of each fiscal year, an annual report; (ii) prepare and file, within 45 days following the end of each of the first, second and third quarters of each fiscal year, a quarterly report or a semi-annual report, as the case may be; and (iii) corporations that are classified as belonging to a large enterprise group (conglomerate) are required to file consolidated annual financial statements to the FSC and KRX within six months following the end of each fiscal year.

Disclosures of material facts
A Stock-Listed Corporation must publicly disclose all material facts and developments related to the Listed Corporation that may affect the investment decisions of a reasonable investor, such as significant matters

proposed to be resolved at the corporation's shareholders' meetings or the nature of any significant resolutions adopted by any meeting of the board of directors or shareholders. Although the regulatory provisions governing disclosure provide an illustrative list of relevant types of events that should be disclosed, the list is by no means exhaustive. With regard to the material change report to be submitted to the FSC, the submission of the report is a statutory requirement and the report submission must generally be completed no later than the end of the day following the date on which the relevant change or matter occurred. Certain types of extraordinary events, however, must be reported on the day of occurrence. Failure to comply may lead to the imposition of certain penalties under the relevant statute. (By contrast, the filing of disclosure reports to the KRX exists as a voluntary disclosure system rather than as a statutorily required reporting system.)

A Stock-Listed Corporation making a public offering of new securities, or a public offering of existing securities, in connection with corporate restructuring events such as mergers, business transfers, comprehensive transfers of stock, exchanges of stock or corporate spin-offs, must include the essential details of the relevant restructuring in the SRS filed in respect of the offering, along with the standard disclosures regarding the securities transaction and parties involved, etc.

10.3 Listing rules
See relevant information in 10.2 above.

10.4 Obligations regarding proxy solicitation
Not applicable.

10.5 Continuing requirements of reporting and notification of substantial shareholdings or a substantial transaction
See relevant information in section 15.1.

10.6 Clearing
Not applicable.

10.7 Requirements for unlisted issuers
Not applicable.

11. CORPORATE GOVERNANCE
11.1 Law and/or code
The Korean Commercial Code provides the general statutory and regulatory framework for corporate organisation and governance.

11.2 Management structure

Directors, representative director and the board of directors
In Korea, commercial enterprises are predominantly organised in the form of stock corporations. In principle, a corporation must have three or more

directors on its board, with each serving a three-year term. Those corporations with less than KRW 1 billion aggregate par value of issued stock, however, may have only one or two directors. Stock-listed corporations must also appoint a number of outside directors in order to ensure greater transparency in corporate management and a healthy system of checks and balances in corporate governance. If the total asset value of a stock-listed corporation exceeds KRW 2 trillion, then its board must have no fewer than three outside directors and such outside directors must constitute a majority of the board. If the total asset value of a stock-listed corporation does not exceed KRW 2 trillion, then outside directors must comprise more than a quarter of the board's directors. To qualify as an outside director, a person must meet certain minimum standards of professional expertise and experience deemed essential to the performance of their duties as directors and must not have any special interests or conflicts of interests with respect to the corporation on whose board they serve.

For a corporation with two or more directors, the corporation must have at least one representative director with the authority to conduct the business of the corporation. The representative director or their designee (by way of an appropriate power of attorney) has the power to represent and act for the corporation in accordance with decisions and policies adopted by the board of directors or as generally delegated to the representative director by the board. The representative director's name, resident registration number and address must be registered with the corporate registry in Korea, in order to ensure that the public can independently confirm who has been appointed to serve as representative director of the corporation and who is authorised to act on behalf of the corporation.

Corporations having two or more directors are generally required to place ultimate decision-making authority in the hands of the board of directors for all matters related to the day-to-day and general operations of the company. However, a corporation's board of directors may also delegate some areas of decision-making authority to the representative director.

Auditors and audit committees
Corporations whose total capital equals KRW 1 billion or more must have full- or part-time auditors or establish an audit committee responsible for auditing the corporation's operations. Stock-Listed Corporations must have at least one or more full-time auditors or an audit committee, if the corporation's total asset value is KRW 100 billion or more. (If the corporation's total asset value is KRW 2 trillion or more, an audit committee is required.) When voting on the appointment of an auditor or member of an audit committee, shareholders who hold more than 3 per cent of the outstanding voting stock of the corporation cannot exercise their voting rights in respect of any more than 3 per cent of the voting shares of the corporation.

12. MARKET ABUSE
12.1 Insider trading
The FSCMA contains several provisions against the use of inside information by insiders (such as management and major shareholders) to gain an unfair

advantage or profits in securities transactions.

More specifically, the FSCMA prohibits any person who acquires inside information (ie, information of the corporation that has not been publicly disclosed) in connection with their duties or position within a corporation, as well as any persons who have received such information from an insider, from using such information in connection with specified securities transactions or allowing a third party to use such information in a specified securities transaction. Specified securities means: (i) securities issued by the corporation; (ii) depositary receipts related to the securities referred to in (i); (iii) securities issued by another entity, which may be converted into the securities referred to in (i) or (ii); or (iv) financial investment products using only the securities referred to in (i) through (iii) as underlying assets.

The specific categories of persons who are subject to such insider-trading prohibitions are listed in the FSCMA, and include the corporation and the corporation's officers, employees and major shareholders. Insiders continue to be subject to insider-trading restrictions for up to a year after the termination of the employment or insider status of the relevant insider. With respect to the foregoing, the following is not classified as insider information: (i) information that has been disclosed pursuant to relevant disclosure regulations and thereby has been publicly available for a period of 24 hours or more; (ii) information made public through electronically transmitted media (eg, Internet Web sites) established and operated by the FSC or KRX that has been publicly accessible through such media for at least three hours; (iii) information published through not less than two nationwide newspapers among general daily newspapers or daily newspapers specialising in economics/business coverage (provided that such information is not deemed to have been publicly disclosed until 6am of the day immediately following the date of the relevant newspapers in which the disclosure was published); (iv) information that has been broadcast by broadcast media having a national audience and six hours or more have passed since the time of the relevant broadcast; or (v) information that has been made available through the Yonhap News Agency and six hours or more have passed since the time that it became available.

12.2 Market manipulation

Deceptive or otherwise intentionally misleading acts or practices engaged in for the purpose of manipulating market prices are prohibited.

12.3 Miscellaneous

Officers, employees or major shareholders of a stock-listed corporation are prohibited from engaging in short-swing trading with respect to the specified securities of the stock-listed corporation. In cases where such short-swing trading occurs, the corporation may demand that the relevant persons disgorge to the corporation any profits gained from such trading within the six-month period immediately following the relevant transaction. In this context 'major shareholder' refers to any person who: (i) holds, or for whose account are held, 10 per cent or more of the outstanding voting shares (whether such shares are formally held in the name of the shareholder or in some other name); and/or (ii) has substantial actual influence with respect to material managerial decisions affecting the corporation, such as influence over the appointment/termination of directors.

13. MUTUAL OR INVESTMENT FUNDS
13.1 Introduction to these two categories
Korean laws do not make any specific distinction between mutual funds and investment funds *per se*. Instead the focus of the FSCMA statutory and regulatory framework is on 'collective investment schemes' and all of the various arrangements that fall within that broadly defined term.

More specifically, the FSCMA governs various forms of indirect collective investment activities, such as the management of funds collected from various investors for investment in securities, derivatives and/or other assets (including real estate) and distribution of profits derived therefrom back to the investors. Presently, there is some overlapping of laws and regulations that are applicable to indirect investment activities and relevant indirect investment vehicles, which may be established and operated under applicable provisions of the Real Estate Investment Company Act, the Support for Small and Medium Enterprise Establishment Act, the Industrial Development Act, the Act on Private Participation in Infrastructure, the Overseas Resources Development Business Act and the Act on Special Measures for the Promotion of Venture Businesses. The various statutory and regulatory provisions that govern indirect investment matters, such as types of investment vehicles allowed, management methods and supervising regulatory authority, are to some extent inconsistent.

Establishment of collective investment schemes
The forms of legal entities prescribed under the FSCMA for use as collective investment schemes are *chusik hoesa* (standard stock corporations), *yuhan hoesa* (limited liability companies), *johap* (partnership), *ik-myung johap* (dormant/undisclosed association), *hapja hoesa* (similar to limited partnerships) and investment trusts.

13.2 Investment companies, open-ended, close-ended
Not applicable.

13.3 Licence requirements
All collective investment schemes must file a report with the FSC after establishment of the collective investment scheme entity/organisation.

Foreign collective investment schemes that desire to sell interests to Korean investors must register with the FSC.

13.4 Continuing requirements
Reports must be filed regarding any material changes that occur with regard to matters initially disclosed to the FSC at the time of the establishment or registration of a collective investment scheme.

13.5 Custodians
Licensed trustee companies may act as custodians.

13.6 Undertakings for collective investments in transferable securities (UCITS)
Not relevant – no particular legal distinction is made between UCITS and Non-UCITS funds.

13.7 Non-UCITS funds
Not relevant – no particular legal distinction is made between UCITS and Non-UCITS funds.

13.8 Hedge funds
Hedge funds are not generally allowed in Korea. However, hedge funds may be set up for the purpose of investing in financially distressed companies.

13.9 Marketing and distribution requirements
When any collective investment scheme's securities are publicly offered, it must file a registration statement with respect to the securities issued by it (eg, shares, beneficiary certificates or investment units). Furthermore, any prospectus to be used in the marketing of such securities must be prepared and filed with the FSC or Korea Financial Investment Association (KoFIA) (in applicable cases) before it can be distributed to potential investors. Licensed dealers and brokers (which may be securities companies, banks, insurance companies, futures brokerage firms, merchant banks, securities finance companies etc) are permitted to market the securities issued by collective investment vehicles (Collective Investment Securities).

Private placements of Collective Investment Securities issued by private funds are subject to significantly fewer regulatory restrictions than publicly offered funds. Such private placements can be divided into two categories: (i) placement with 49 or fewer investors other than professional investors (as defined in the FSCMA); and (ii) placement with 49 or fewer 'qualified professional investors' (ie, a more limited class of investors within the professional investors grouping).

The latter category (private placement limited to qualified professional investors) is subject to fewer regulatory requirements than the former (private placement not limited to non-professional investors). For example, in the case of a private placement that is not limited to professional investors only, registration of the collective investment scheme with the FSC is required. In the case of a private placement that is limited to qualified professional investors only, registration of the collective investment scheme is not required, except in the case of foreign collective investment schemes, which must be registered with the FSC before any kind of public offering or private placement of fund interests is made vis-à-vis Korean investors.

Furthermore, private placements that are limited to only qualified professional investors are subject to fewer restrictions with regard to the investment of fund assets. For example, leveraged investments and related borrowing are permitted for funds limited to qualified professional investors, but are not permitted for funds that include non-professional investors.

Sales of foreign collective investment securities

In the event that a foreign collective investment scheme intends to market Collective Investment Securities to Korean investors, the relevant collective investment scheme must first be registered with the FSC and must appoint a domestic contact person whom the regulatory authorities can contact for inquiries, communications etc, related to investor protection concerns. Additionally, the investment interests issued by a foreign collective investment scheme can only be marketed in Korea through a 'local sales agent' (ie, a dealer or broker licensed in Korea). The investment interests of a foreign collective investment scheme (Foreign Collective Investment Securities) can be sold in Korea through either a public offering or in a private placement. In the case of a public offering, a registration statement must be filed in Korea and the relevant Foreign Collective Investment Securities must also be publicly offered outside of Korea. If the placement of the relevant Foreign Collective Investment Securities in Korea will be limited to only certain specified professional investors (as defined in the FSCMA), the above-mentioned registration of the foreign collective investment scheme with the FSC can be carried out under a simplified registration process.

13.10   Manager

The FSCMA regulates the activities of Collective Investment Business Entities (ie fund asset managers).

In principle, only companies that are licensed by the FSC are permitted to manage the assets of collective investment schemes. The law does not, however, require the licensing of managers of private equity funds. Under the FSCMA, a private equity fund is a collective investment scheme that issues equity securities only through private placement as an investment limited partnership or limited liability company established for the purpose of investing in and managing equity holdings etc, in order to participate in the management and improvement of the business structure or corporate governance of the company or companies whose Equity Securities are acquired by it.

Because Collective Investment Business Entities play such a central role in the collective investment market, they are required to meet certain minimum standards designed to protect investors. For instance, a Collective Investment Business Entity must have a minimum paid-in capital of KRW 1-8 billion (depending on the scope of financial investment products and form of investments involved) and must have at least one compliance auditor responsible for monitoring the company's compliance with applicable regulatory requirements. Strict statutory and regulatory standards apply with respect to the liabilities of Collective Investment Business Entities in cases where they have breached their obligations under relevant laws and regulations, a relevant trust agreement or the articles of incorporation of the investment vehicles they manage, or where they have otherwise been negligent. Collective Investment Business Entities are also liable if they are materially in breach of representations made in an applicable investment prospectus.

14. SECURITIES INSTITUTIONS
14.1 Market executive undertaking
Not applicable.

14.2 Securities clearing house
Not applicable.

14.3 Central securities depository
The Korea Securities Depository performs the role of central securities depository for the Korean securities market.

14.4 Investment services providers (ISP)

Investment advisors/discretionary investment managers
Under the FSCMA, any person engaged in the business of evaluating investment assets and providing advice on investment decisions is classified as an investment advisor, and a person entrusted with making all or some discretionary investment decisions on behalf of a client/investor is classified as a discretionary investment manager. Under the FSCMA, investment advisors and discretionary investment managers must be registered as such with the FSC and must meet related standards established by the FSC.

Foreign persons who intend to provide investment advisory or discretionary investment management services to Korean residents must also be registered with the FSC and meet the applicable standards. Discretionary investment managers who do not maintain business offices in Korea are allowed to provide services only to professional investors (as defined in FSCMA).

15. NOTIFICATION OBLIGATIONS
15.1 Notification of major shareholding

Substantial shareholdings in stock-listed corporations
Upon reaching a shareholding ratio of 5 per cent or more of the issued and outstanding equity securities of a stock-listed corporation, a shareholder is required to file a report to the authorities within five days following the date on which the shareholding threshold was reached. Thereafter, any change, whether by reduction or increase, in the shareholding ratio of the shareholder, where the net reduction or increase accounts for 1 per cent or more of the issued and outstanding equity securities of the relevant corporation, must also be reported within five days following the date on which the 1 per cent change threshold was reached. The scope of such substantial shareholding reporting requirements includes any particular holder of equity securities together with specially related persons thereof who also hold equity securities of the relevant stock-listed corporation.

Accordingly, by way of example, if a parent corporation and its wholly owned subsidiary each own equity securities of a stock-listed corporation, the shareholding ratios (including in such a calculation all equity securities held) of both the parent corporation and the subsidiary will be counted together for the purposes of calculating whether the 5 per cent or 1 per cent thresholds have been reached. Similarly, if two members of the same family own equity securities in a particular stock-listed corporation, their combined shareholding ratios will be counted for the purpose of determining whether the relevant shareholding ratio threshold has been reached.

Specially related persons

In this context, the term 'specially related person' refers to: (i) with respect to natural persons, persons related by blood; (ii) with respect to corporate entities, corporate affiliates, shareholders or persons in positions of managerial influence; and (iii) other parties to any agreement regarding the purchase and disposal of equity securities and/or the exercise of voting rights with respect to the target corporation. Additionally, for the purposes of determining whether any special relationship exists based on shareholding relationships, the concept of shareholding is interpreted broadly to include not only shareholders of record, but also beneficial owners of equity securities and various types of arrangements where stock may be held by one person for the account of another.

Required content of substantial shareholding reports

The required content of the substantial shareholding reports differs according to the purpose behind the acquisition of the relevant equity securities (ie, whether the equity securities are obtained for purely investment purposes or to acquire managerial control with respect to the relevant stock-listed corporation).

In cases where the reporting shareholder has acquired the equity securities for investment purposes only, the substantial shareholding report must include: (i) basic information on the reporting party; (ii) a description of the issuer of the equity securities; (iii) information on the reporting party's shareholding status; and (iv) a detailed description of the circumstances of any change of shareholding status (in respect of any change relating to 1 per cent or more of the issued and outstanding equity securities of the relevant stock-listed corporation).

In cases where the reporting shareholder has acquired the equity securities in order to gain influence over the management of the stock-listed corporation, in addition to the content described above for the investment-purpose substantial shareholding report, various other matters must be included, such as a more detailed description of the purpose of shareholding, a description of agreements entered into in connection with the relevant equity securities acquisition and shareholding, and a description of the source of funding for the relevant equity securities acquisition. Shareholders who have filed a substantial shareholding report relating to the acquisition of managerial influence are not allowed to exercise voting rights pertaining to the acquired equity securities or to acquire any additional equity securities for a period of five days following the date of the filing of the report.

Report on officer and major shareholder status

In addition to the above-described reporting requirements: (i) any person who becomes a director, auditor or officer of similar status in a stock-listed corporation must file a report to the Securities and Futures Commission and the KRX, regarding the person's shareholding status (including all shares held for the account of the person, regardless of the name under which such shares are held) within five days from the date of their appointment to such a position; and (ii) any person who becomes a major shareholder (as defined in 12.3 above) must report such major shareholder status to the Securities and Futures Commission and the KRX within five days from the date that the major shareholder status was attained.

Substantial shareholding in financial institutions

A person cannot acquire and hold 10 per cent or more of the voting shares of a bank unless otherwise expressly permitted by the FSC. A holder of shares issued by a bank must file a report to the FSC in each of the following cases: (i) where the shareholder comes to hold 4 per cent or more of the voting shares of the bank; (ii) pursuant to the filing of the report described in (i), where there is a change of the shareholder's shareholding ratio relating to 1 per cent or more of the issued and outstanding shares of the bank; or (iii) where the shareholder becomes the largest shareholder of the bank.

Any person who desires to be the controlling shareholder of a securities company, Collective Investment Business Entity (eg, an asset management company) or insurance company must obtain prior approval from the FSC. The precise definition of controlling shareholders may vary somewhat in each context. Generally the persons who may constitute the controlling shareholders will include the largest shareholder, major shareholders and any shareholders who have special relationships to the largest shareholder.

16. PUBLIC TAKEOVERS

16.1 Applicable laws and regulations or regulatory framework

Tender offer

If any person intends to acquire, participate in bidding for or otherwise obtain or purchase the equity securities of a stock-listed corporation from 10 or more persons outside the KRX market mechanisms, pursuant to which such a person will come to own 5 per cent or more of the issued and outstanding equity securities of such a corporation, the acquisition(s) must be made through a tender-offer process. No tender-offer process is required in the following cases: (i) acquisition through the KRX of equity securities in a stock-listed corporation; (ii) acquisition of equity securities in a corporation other than a stock-listed corporation; or (iii) acquisitions involving the sale and purchase of equity securities among affiliates within a large enterprise group or between members of the same family by an insider of a corporation.

Any person who plans to proceed with a tender offer is required to publish the relevant tender-offer plan in a public newspaper and submit a tender-offer statement to the FSC and the KRX on the same day. A copy of the tender-offer statement should subsequently be sent to the issuer of the stock to be acquired. In principle, any person who makes a tender offer should acquire the relevant stock only during the relevant tender-offer period (ie, the period starting on the filing date of the tender-offer statement and ending on the tender-offer termination date stated in the tender-offer statement).

In the event that a hostile merger and acquisition is contemplated to be made through the tender-offer process, the existing controlling shareholder of the target company can make a counter tender offer. Furthermore, the issuer of the target securities may undertake to issue additional voting shares to counter such a tender offer; provided, however, that the directors who approve the issuance of new shares may be liable for a breach of fiduciary duties to other shareholders if the purpose of the new issuance is solely to protect the controlling interest of the existing controlling shareholder.

Business combination report/approval
Under the MRFTA, an acquisition of a company or a substantial portion of a company's business by another company requires the filing in certain circumstances of a business combination report to the Fair Trade Commission in accordance with the relevant provisions of the Monopoly Regulation and Fair Trade Act.

16.2 Competent authorities
See 16.1 above.

16.3 Dealing with disclosures and stake building
See 16.1 above.

16.4 Types of takeover bids
See 16.1 above.

16.5 Procedural aspects
See 16.1 above.

16.6 Nature and value of consideration offered
See 16.1 above.

16.7 Timetable and variations
See 16.1 above.

16.8 Strategy
See 16.1 above.

16.9 Irrevocable
See 16.1 above.

16.10   Share dealings, buying shares
See 16.1 above.

16.11   First announcement
See 16.1 above.

16.12   Drafting of offer documents
See 16.1 above.

16.13   Further announcements
See 16.1 above.

16.14   Responsibility
See 16.1 above.

16.15   Despatch
See 16.1 above.

16.16   Due diligence in advance of a takeover bid
See 16.1 above.

16.17   Conditions to the offer
See 16.1 above.

16.18   Financing
See 16.1 above.

16.19   For cash/for shares/mixed
See 16.1 above.

16.20   Inducement
See 16.1 above.

16.21   Defence mechanisms
See 16.1 above.

16.22   Nature of listed securities
See 16.1 above.

16.23   Squeeze-out
See 16.1 above.

16.24   Schemes of arrangement
See 16.1 above.

17. FOREIGN INVESTMENT CONTROLS
17.1 Foreign investments
Under the FIPA, investment by a foreigner (individual or company) of KRW 50 million or more into a Korean company will qualify as a FIPA foreign investment (foreign investment) if it falls into any one of the following circumstances: (i) acquisition by the foreign investor of 10 per cent or more of the voting shares of a Korean company; (ii) acquisition of a managerial role in a Korean company (eg, acquiring the right to appoint directors or key managers of the company in cases where less than 10 per cent of the company's voting shares are acquired); (iii) entering into an agreement with a Korean company to provide qualifying raw materials and products or to purchase the same over a period of one year or more; and (iv) entering into an agreement with a Korean company regarding technology transfers or joint research and development projects. In order to obtain formal classification as a Foreign Investment, a related report should be filed to a designated foreign exchange bank or the Korea Trade Investment-Promotion Agency. Direct investment made pursuant to such a report and classification as a Foreign Investment is entitled to certain FIPA tax benefits and enhanced investor protection and support that are not available in the context of ordinary investments in securities.

In the event that an investment by a foreign investor does not qualify as a Foreign Investment, the foreign investor is required to open a dedicated securities investment account in Korea for use in connection with the purchase or sale of certain types of Korean securities. In other cases, the foreign investor may be required to file a prior report to a designated foreign exchange bank in Korea, or to the Bank of Korea, depending on the nature of the particular purchase or sale of Korean securities.

Additionally, in order for a foreign entity to acquire listed securities, such an entity must first register as a foreign investor with the FSS and obtain an investor registration number. Unless a limited range of compelling reasons can be proven, the Korean securities acquired by a foreign investor are required to be deposited with a domestic custodian. In connection with the above, it should be noted that, except for the acquisition of listed securities pursuant to the filing of a FIPA report for a qualifying Foreign Investment and except for a very limited range of other circumstances, it is nearly impossible for a foreign investor to acquire the securities of a listed corporation outside of the KRX market system.

17.2 Exemptions
See 17.1.

17.3 Exemptions of notification or prior authorisation
See 17.1.

17.4 Notification in order to establish a balance of payments
See 17.1.

Spain

J&A Garrigues Javier Ybáñez & José Luis Palao

1. GENERAL DESCRIPTION OF THE CAPITAL MARKETS
1.1 Number of companies listed
There were 170 companies listed on the Spanish stock markets, according to the 2009 Spanish Securities Market Commission (or CNMV) annual report.

The Spanish Stock Exchange Interconnection System (*Mercado Continuo*), which is an interstate stock exchange linking system that integrates the four existing securities exchanges of Barcelona, Bilbao, Madrid and Valencia, for the trading of securities approved by the CNMV, had 133 companies.

The figures above do not include companies included in the Madrid alternative market called *Mercado Alternativo Bursátil* (MAB).

1.2 Total volume and market value

Total volume
Trading (in cash) amounted to EUR 897 billion, and the number of securities traded in 2009 amounted to EUR 114 billion, according to the 2009 annual report prepared by Stock Exchange Company (*Sociedad de Bolsas*).

Market value
According to the 2009 CNMV annual report, the market value of companies listed on Spanish stock markets stood at EUR 549.8 billion at the end of 2009.

1.3 Issue activity
The total amount of capital increases (issuances) was EUR 11.4 billion, down 30.3 per cent compared with the previous year, according to the 2009 CNMV annual report. Share issues for cash stood at EUR 7.8 billion – 68.6 per cent of the total. As of 15 September 2010 the total amount of capital increases (issuances) was EUR 7.1 billion, according to the CNMV Bulletin for 3Q 2010.

From January 2010 to September 2010 there were only two Initial Public Offerings (IPOs).

1.4 Takeover activity Takeover bids

(EUR million)	2009
Authorised	
Number	5
Potential amount	9,952
Potential amount plus agreements prior to acquisition	18,516
Carried out	
Number	5
Amount	7,201
Amount plus agreements prior to acquisition	17,605

Source: CNMV's annual report 2009.

The five takeover bids involved cash consideration, and all met the fair price rules defined in regulations. None of the takeover bids met the squeeze-out and sell-out conditions.

1.5 Hostile takeover attempts
No information was made public on hostile takeover attempts.

2. REGULATORY STRUCTURE
2.1 General
The main regulation of the Spanish capital market is Law 24/1988, 28 July 1988 (as amended), the Securities Market Act (or LMV).

2.2 Regulation of the offering of new securities
The main regulations for offering (both public and private) of securities are the following:
- LMV;
- Royal Decree 1310/2005, dated 4 November; and
- Ministerial Order EHA/3537/2005, 10 November 2005.

2.3 Differences between local and foreign companies
Except for corporate requirements, there are no differences in legal requirements for offerings of Spanish and non-Spanish EU companies.

Where there is an offer of shares in Spain from an issuer that is not resident in an EU member state, or a listing on a Spanish secondary market of shares in a company which is not resident in an EU member state, the following rules apply to the prospectus that should be registered with the CNMV:
- the prospectus must be drawn up in accordance with international standards set by the International Organisation of Securities Commissions (IOSCO), including the IOSCO disclosure standards; and
- information requirements, including financial information, must be at

least equivalent to the requirements under Spanish regulations.

Specific rules are applicable within the EU on the competent authority to approve a prospectus among the different EU authorities.

2.4 Admission to trading on a regulated market

The main regulations on admission to trading on regulated markets are those listed in section 2.2 above.

2.5 Financial promotion

Advertising regarding public offers and/or admission to trading may be distributed by any interested party. Advertisements can be published in any media and at any time, including before approval of the prospectus by the CNMV. However, advertisement is subject to the following conditions:

- it must be clearly recognisable as such;
- the information contained therein must not be inaccurate or misleading; and
- if a prospectus is required, the advertising should mention that a prospectus has been or will be published and where it can be obtained; and the information in the advertisement must be consistent with the information in the prospectus.

When a prospectus is not required by Spanish regulations, material information provided by the issuer or an offeror and addressed to qualified investors or special categories of investors must be disclosed to all investors to whom the offer is addressed.

For private placements which do not require a prospectus, addressed to the public in general, using any form of publicity, Spanish law requires the participation of an entity authorised to render investment services, in order to market the securities.

2.6 Rule books

There are no rule books officially published in Spain on securities regulation.

3. REGISTRATION OF THE ISSUER AND SECURITIES

3.1 Registration requirements

The public offer of negotiable securities in Spain is subject to the following requirements:

- registration of the issuer's corporate resolutions approving the issuance of the securities;
- registration of the financial statements and audit reports of the issuer, for the last three years for equity securities and two years for debt securities. The CNMV may accept exceptions to the above, when it considers that the investors do have the required information to decide on the investment; and
- registration of a prospectus.

3.2 Other requirements

There are no other additional significant requirements.

3.3   Nature of securities

Spanish offerings regulations are applicable to negotiable securities to be issued or sold by Spanish issuers or to be sold within the Spanish territory including, among others: shares; bonds; notes; commercial papers; warrants; participations in collective investment institutions; and, in general, any economic right that may be able to be traded or negotiated on a secondary market.

4.   SUPERVISORY AUTHORITIES

4.1   Conduct: prudential, cooperation, self-regulation of stock exchange

The main regulatory body is the CNMV, which is entrusted with the supervision and surveillance of the securities markets and of the trading activities of all individuals and legal persons in those markets, and the exercise of the power to sanction them, among others. The CNMV shall seek to ensure the transparency of the securities markets, the correct formation of the prices on these markets and the protection of investors.

4.2   New listings measures in connection with the credit crisis

No new measures regarding listings in connection with the credit crisis have been implemented in Spain so far.

5.   OFFERING DOCUMENTATION OR PROSPECTUS REQUIREMENTS

5.1   Nature and statutory requirements of the offering document or disclosure document

The following documents must be filed and registered for a public offering or admission to trading:
*   a statement of the legal status of the issuer and the securities to be admitted to trading or offered;
*   financial statements of the issuer prepared and audited in accordance with the applicable law; and
*   the prospectus, which must also be published.

5.2   Exemptions

The following offers are not considered public offers and therefore no documentation will be required to be registered:
*   offers of securities addressed solely to qualified investors;
*   offers of securities addressed to fewer than 100 natural or legal persons per EU member state, other than qualified investors;
*   offers of securities addressed to investors who acquire securities for a total consideration of at least EUR 50,000 per investor, for each separate offer;
*   offers of securities whose denomination per unit amount to at least EUR 50,000; and
*   offers of securities with a total consideration of less than EUR 2,500,000, which limit shall be calculated over a period of 12 months.

In addition, the following public offers of securities do not require a prospectus:

- shares issued in substitution for shares of the same class already issued, provided the issue of the new shares does not involve any increase in the issued capital;
- securities offered in connection with a takeover by means of an exchange offer, provided that a document is available containing information which is regarded as being equivalent to that of the prospectus;
- securities offered, allotted or to be allotted in connection with a merger; provided that a document is available containing information which is regarded as being equivalent to that of the prospectus;
- shares offered, allotted or to be allotted free of charge to existing shareholders, and dividends paid out in the form of shares of the same class as the shares in respect of which the dividends are paid, provided that a document is made available containing information on the number and nature of the shares and the reasons for and details of the offer; and
- securities offered, allotted or to be allotted to existing or former directors or employees by their employer which has securities already admitted to trading on a regulated market or by an affiliated undertaking provided that a document is made available containing information on the number and nature of the securities.

Anyhow, if the securities were to be listed on Spanish Stock Exchanges then there might be a requirement for a listing prospectus.

5.3 Preparation of the offering document, general contents
The content of a prospectus should be drafted following the formats in Commission Regulation (EC) NO 809/2004 of 29 April 2004 implementing the EU Prospectus Directive.

Among others, the prospectus should include details on:
- the persons responsible for providing the information contained in it;
- the company's auditors;
- selected financial information;
- risk factors;
- general information about the issuer;
- business overview;
- organisational structure;
- property, plant and equipment;
- operating and financial review;
- trend information;
- board practices; and
- major shareholders.

Legal advisers, auditors, global coordinator and other advisers normally intervene in the prospectus preparation, based on the information provided by the issuer.

5.4 Due diligence

There is no legal requirement or obligation for the issuer or placement entities to conduct due diligence of the issuer. However, regarding public offers conducting due diligence of the issuer and its group is market practice in Spain for placement entities.

5.5 Responsibility

Responsibility for the information contained in a prospectus shall attach, at least, to:
- the issuer or offeror or person that requests the listing of the securities;
- the directors of the issuer or offeror;
- those that agree to assume responsibility for the prospectus, and are named as such in the prospectus;
- persons that gave their authorisation for the content of the prospectus, and are named as such in the prospectus;
- the guarantor, for the information that it must provide.

In case there is a global coordinator of the offer (*entidad directora*), it will be responsible for the information contained in the securities note (a part of the prospectus, which contains the information concerning the securities offered to the public or to be admitted to trading).

5.6 Disclaimer/selling restrictions

In addition to rules described in section 2.5, according to Spanish law, where it is not mandatory to register a prospectus, it is convenient to include in any offering materials a legend stating that the offer will not be registered in Spain. Likewise, if the offer does not require the prior registration of a prospectus, all the advertising materials provided by the issuer or offeror shall be disclosed to all prospective investors to whom the offer is addressed.

5.7 Recognition of prospectuses by other exchanges

A prospectus approved by the CNMV, and its supplements, shall be valid for admission to trading in any other EU country, provided that the CNMV notifies the competent authority of each EU country in accordance with regulations.

A prospectus approved by the competent authority of another EU country, and its supplements, shall be valid for admission to trading in Spain, provided that said competent authority notifies the CNMV accordingly.

5.8 Supplementary prospectuses

Every significant new factor, material mistake or inaccuracy relating to the information included in the prospectus which is capable of affecting the assessment of the securities and which arises or is noted between the time when the prospectus is approved and the time when trading begins, shall be mentioned in a prospectus supplement.

5.9 Issuing of bonds

Public offer regulations apply both to equity and to bonds. Any public offering of negotiable securities in Spain is subject to the same statutory requirements, regardless of the type of securities to be offered.

It should be noted that documentation that must be filed with, and registered by, the CNMV for a public offering or admission to trading of bonds includes financial statements of the issuer for the last two years. However, the accounts must usually cover a three-year period for the listing of equity securities.

6. DISTRIBUTION SYSTEMS

6.1 Normal structure of a distribution group

The normal structure of securities distribution for large IPOs is divided into: (i) a local investor's tranche; and (ii) an international tranche.

Local investor's tranche is normally divided into two sub-tranches: a qualified investors' tranche (or 'institutional tranche'); and retail investors' tranche (which sometimes includes a sub-tranche addressed to the issuer's employees). Sometimes the retail tranche is also registered in other EU countries.

The international tranche is normally only addressed to qualified investors.

For mid- and small-sized IPOs, it is also becoming a practice to have a unique qualified investors' tranche, including both the Spanish and the international investors.

6.2 Methods of distribution

An indicative price range is usually published in the prospectus and the final price is agreed between the offeror and global coordinator after the book building period. As for the retail investors' tranche, usually after a week-long offer period, a maximum price is fixed and the retail investors that do not revoke their orders agree to acquire the securities at such maximum price.

Securities are allocated to retail investors using systems which allow a proportionate distribution, mixed with minimum allocations. Sometimes chronological preferences are granted.

On the institutional tranche investors are allowed to confirm their purchase order once the final price is fixed. Allocations are at the discretion of the issuer and global coordinator.

6.3 Underwriting

Public offers of equity securities to be listed in Spain are usually underwritten by a syndicate of financial institutions, although this is not a legal requirement.

6.4 Fees and commission

Distribution and placement of securities normally entails different fees, such as management, underwriting, placement, agency and success fees.

6.5 Stabilisation

Stabilisation activities are governed by the EU market abuse directive and regulations.

Public offer prospectuses in Spain normally include a reference to the potential stabilisation activities of the global coordinator. Green shoe over-allotment options are usually granted on qualified investor tranches.

6.6 Involvement of a distributor in the preparation of the offering document
There is no statutory provision on the involvement that a distributor may have in the preparation of the offering document, however, in practice global coordinators actively participate in the preparation of prospectuses.

6.7 Timing of distribution process
In the institutional tranche, the distribution process starts with the opening of the book-building period, after the prospectus is registered, and finishes on the date of termination of such book-building which lasts between one and two weeks. Once the book building period has ended, the price is determined by the issuer and global coordinator, and orders are allocated to investors who then are required to confirm them.

Retail tranche distribution in Spain starts after the registration of the prospectus, with the opening of the period for submitting revocable orders, before the maximum price is fixed (which usually lasts seven to 10 days). Then another period for submitting binding orders is opened for a period of three or four days.

6.8 Rules on distribution to the public
No offer or distribution of securities to the public will be allowed without prior approval and publication of a prospectus.

The Markets in Financial Instruments Directive (MiFID) and regulations should be complied with by the placement entities.

7. PUBLICITY
It should be noted that once approved, the prospectus must be made available to the general public by the issuer, offeror or person asking for admission to trade. Prospectuses are usually published using CNMV and issuer Web sites, and delivered on paper, if required by the investors.

Advertising public offers is in practice limited to retail tranches, and should mention that a prospectus has been or will be published and where it can be obtained. The information in the advertisement must be consistent with the information contained in the prospectus.

8. LISTING
8.1 Special listing requirements, admission criteria
The admission of securities to trading on a Spanish stock exchange requires prior verification by the CNMV. Listing on each stock exchange also requires a resolution from the stock exchange in question.

In addition to offering requirements (prospectus, financial statements, and issuer resolutions), the following requirements are also applicable:

- the issuer must be duly incorporated;
- each class of securities issued by the issuer must afford identical rights to all shareholders in that class;
- the securities must have been issued in accordance with the legal regime to which they are subject;
- the securities must be represented by book entries;
- the securities must be freely negotiable and transferable; and
- the total amount of the securities which admission to trading is requested shall be, at least: (i) for shares: EUR6,000,000; (ii) for debt securities: EUR200,000; and no minimum amount is required for the remaining securities;
- as for shares, a sufficient distribution of them must be made prior to the listing date in one or more EU countries, or in non-EU countries. Spanish regulations require a minimum free float of 25 per cent, although the CNMV may accept a reduced percentage in some cases.

Foreign companies must meet the same eligibility requirements as Spanish companies. However, in the case of companies already listed on an EU exchange, the CNMV does not review compliance with requirements that have already been reviewed by the supervisory authority of the home country.

8.2 Mechanics of the review process

The issuer, its legal advisers, accountants, placement entities, if any, and their legal advisers normally intervene in the prospectus preparation process.

After submitting the first draft to the CNMV, the CNMV review process normally consists of comments received verbally by the CNMV analyst in charge of the review. Such process may last between four and eight weeks.

8.3 Prospectus obligation, due diligence, exemption

As mentioned, the registration of a prospectus is required for the listing of securities in a Spanish Stock Exchange.

The following exceptions apply to the prospectus registration:

- shares representing, over a period of 12 months, less than 10 per cent of the number of shares of the same class already admitted to trading on the same regulated market;
- shares issued in substitution for shares of the same class already admitted to trading on the same regulated market, if the issuing of such shares does not involve any increase in the issued capital;
- securities offered in connection with a takeover by means of an exchange offer, provided that a document is available containing information which is regarded as being equivalent to that of the prospectus;
- securities offered, allotted or to be allotted in connection with a merger, provided that a document is available containing information which is regarded as being equivalent to that of the prospectus;
- shares offered, allotted or to be allotted free of charge to existing shareholders, and dividends paid out in the form of shares of the same

class as the shares in respect of which such dividends are paid, provided that the said shares are of the same class as the shares already admitted to trading on the same regulated market and that a document is made available containing information on the number and nature of the shares and the reasons for and details of the offer;

- securities offered, allotted or to be allotted to existing or former directors or employees by their employer or an affiliated undertaking, provided that the said securities are of the same class as the securities already admitted to trading on the same regulated market and that a document is made available containing information on the number and nature of the securities and the reasons for and details of the offer;
- shares resulting from the conversion or exchange of other securities or from the exercise of the rights conferred by other securities; provided that the said shares are of the same class as the shares already admitted to trading on the same regulated market; and
- securities already admitted to trading on another regulated market, provided that certain conditions are met (18 months trade, compliance with reporting obligations, etc).

8.4 Appeal procedure in the event of a prospectus refusal
In case the CNMV refuses to register a prospectus, its decision may be appealed before the contentious-administrative courts.

8.5 Authority of the exchange
Each stock exchange is a private company governed by a limited liability management company which carries out the management activities prescribed by law for each stock exchange (*Sociedades Rectoras de las Bolsas*).

8.6 Sponsor
There is no legal obligation to use sponsors for a listing in Spain.

8.7 Special arrangements for smaller companies such as Alternext, AIM or SPACs
The MAB for companies undergoing expansion is a market created to facilitate the access by small and medium sized companies to the stock markets, and began to operate in 2009.

No special purpose acquisition companies have been listed in Spain.

8.8 Costs of various types
- Stock exchange fee – fixed fee of EUR 1,160 plus a variable amount calculated on the nominal value of the shares: up to EUR 230 million – 0.1 per cent; and over EUR 230 million – 0.01 per cent.
- CNMV fee – for admission to listing, 0.003 per cent of the price of the shares; if the listing is executed together with an IPO, 0.014 per cent of the price of the shares, with a floor of EUR 1,742.78 and a cap of EUR 69,727.25.
- Iberclear fee – 0.003 per cent of the price of the shares, with a floor of

EUR 500 fixed fee and a cap of EUR 30,000.

Once listed, the stock exchange charges an annual fee of 0.045 per cent of the capitalisation of the company to the last trading day of each year, with a floor of EUR 100 and a cap of EUR 325,000.

The costs of sponsors, brokers, lawyers, accountants and other advisers, advertising, mercantile registry and public notaries should also be taken into account.

9.   SANCTIONS AND DISPUTES
9.1   Disciplinary and administrative sanctions
A person or legal entity subject to the LMV, as well as those directors or managers of such entities that breach any of the obligations under the LMV, will be subject to sanctions and fines.

Infringements vary from very serious, serious to minor.

Examples of very serious infringements are the offering of securities without registering a prospectus, misleading information or lack of relevant information in the prospectus, market abuse and insider trading, among others.

Examples of fines that may entail very serious infringements are:
*   a fine in the amount highest of the following: (i) five times the gross profit obtained as a result of the acts or omissions of which the infringement consists; (ii) 5 per cent of the offender equity ; (iii) 5 per cent of the offender equity used in the acts or omissions of which the infringement consists; or (iv) EUR 600,000;
*   suspension or restriction of the type or volume of transactions which the offender may carry out in the securities markets for a period not longer than five years;
*   exclusion of a financial instrument from trading on the stock exchange;
*   suspension of the offender from directorships or executive posts in a financial institution for a period not longer than five years; and
*   removal of the offender from directorships or executive posts in a financial institution and disqualification from holding directorships or executive posts at the same institution for a period not longer than five years.

9.2   Civil actions
Civil liability attaches to those persons listed in section 5.5 above when the information contained in the prospectus is false, misleading, inaccurate or inconsistent. Legal actions to claim liability based on those grounds will be heard by the ordinary courts following the declaration procedure.

9.3   Criminal penalties
The following conducts may be considered as criminal offences under the Spanish Criminal Code:
*   to disseminate false information, using violence, threat or deception, to try to distort the free formation of prices of tradable products, goods, securities, services or any other movable or fixed assets; and

- to misuse negotiable instruments or price sensitive information that has been known in the normal course of the exercise of their employment, profession or duties (inside information), or to disclose that information to obtain any economic benefit exceeding the amount of EUR 600,000 or causing an equivalent damage.

10. CONTINUING OBLIGATIONS
10.1 Disclosure and transparency rule
Listed companies are required to disclose:
- periodic financial information;
- price sensitive information;
- major shareholdings, including directors' shareholdings and dealing by the issuer of treasury stock;
- total existing number of shares and voting rights; and
- annual report on corporate governance.

10.2 Information
Periodic financial information
Listed companies are required to disclose the following financial information:
- yearly-annual accounts, management report and auditors' report for each financial year within four months from year closing;
- half-yearly-complete financial statements within two months from the end of the corresponding period; and
- quarterly-preview of results and other relevant information (only equity issuers) within 45 days of the end of the first and second quarter.

Price sensitive information
Issuers of securities must also disclose all price-sensitive information to the market immediately, by means of a communication to the CNMV which is also required to be published on the issuer's Web site.

There are cases when issuers may be allowed to delay the public disclosure of price sensitive information, mainly because publication could affect its legitimate interests (for instance during negotiation of a relevant transaction), provided that such omission would not be likely to mislead the public and provided that the issuer is able to ensure the confidentiality of that information.

10.3 Listing rules
There are no listing rules in Spain which require the publication of further information by the issuers than the one contained in the regulations, as described above.

10.4 Obligations regarding proxy solicitation
There are no specific proxy solicitation obligations in Spain except for the following:
- corporate requirements which require that the agenda of the meeting,

the request of voting instructions and the indication of the way in which the proxy will vote in the event of precise instructions are not granted, are included in the proxy request; and
- corporate governance legal requirements which establish that directors, who make proxy solicitation, could not exercise such proxies when conflicts of interest arise.

10.5 Continuing requirements of reporting and notification of substantial shareholdings or a substantial transaction
Major shareholdings
Any shareholder who, directly or indirectly, acquires or disposes of shares with voting rights in a listed Spanish company, with the result that the voting rights of the shareholder exceed or fall below some percentage thresholds (3, 5, 10, 15, 20, 25, 30, 35, 40, 45, 50, 60, 70, 75, 80 and 90 per cent) must notify the issuer and the CNMV of the resulting proportion of voting rights held.

The entry into certain voting, deposit, temporary transfer or usufruct agreements regarding the relevant shares or the existence of custodians or proxy-holders having the ability to exercise discretion over the voting of the relevant shares are considered equivalent to the acquisition of shares.

Holders have similar disclosure obligations in connection with the acquisition or disposition of financial instruments entitling the holder to acquire shares of the issuer, such as options, futures, and swaps.

Special thresholds apply when the person that is obligated to give the notification is a resident of a tax haven (as specified in Spanish law) or of a country or territory where there is no taxation or where the authorities decline to exchange information for tax purposes.

Director's shareholdings
Members of the board of directors of a listed company must inform the CNMV of their voting interest in an issuer's securities upon joining the board and, thereafter, must notify the CNMV of any transaction by them involving the shares or other securities of the issuer. Senior executives of a listed company must report any such transactions as well.

Treasury stock
In addition, a Spanish issuer listed on a Spanish Stock Exchange must report any acquisition of the issuer's own shares if the acquisition, together with any other acquisitions since the date of the issuer's last report (without deducting sales), results in the issuer holding its own shares in excess of 1 per cent of the total voting power.

10.6 Clearing
Transactions carried out on the Spanish Stock Exchanges are cleared and settled through Iberclear and its participating entities.

10.7 Requirements for unlisted issuers
Unlisted issuers are not legally subject to the above mentioned requirements.

11. CORPORATE GOVERNANCE

11.1 Law and/or code

The Spanish system on corporate governance includes both legal requirements and code requirements.

Legal requirements include, among others:
- comply or explain principle;
- audit committee;
- general shareholders' meeting regulations;
- board regulations;
- annual corporate governance report;
- issuers Web site;
- shareholders' rights;
- directors' duties and conflicts of interest; and
- information on related-party transactions.

The Corporate Governance Code which follows the 'comply or explain' principle was published on 19 May, 2006 by the CNMV setting out recommendations in the following areas, among others:
- by-laws and powers of the general shareholders' meeting;
- board of directors (competences, size, structure, number of independent directors, functions of the chairman and secretary, frequency of board meetings, evaluation of the board, information to directors, dedication, selection, appointment and renewal of directors, remuneration); and
- committees of the board (executive committee, audit committee, nomination and remuneration committees): functions and composition.

11.2 Management structure

The Corporate Governance Code recommends that in the interest of maximum effectiveness and participation, the board of directors should ideally comprise no fewer than five and no more than 15 members.

It also recommends, among others, that: external directors, proprietary and independent, should occupy an ample majority of board places; and the number of independent directors should represent at least one-third of all board members.

11.3 Obligations to publish information on the Internet

Listed companies must have a Web site for shareholders to exercise the right to information, and to disseminate the significant or price-sensitive information.

Such Web sites must contain, among others:
- corporate by-laws;
- shareholders' meeting and board regulations;
- board of directors composition;
- annual corporate governance reports;
- financial information required to be published;
- price sensitive information; and
- information on shareholders' meetings.

11.4 Responsibility of inside/outside directors

There is no specific legal regime for responsibility of inside directors as opposed to the one of outside directors.

For general directors' liability, please refer to section 11.12.

11.5 Committees

Issuing companies whose shares or bonds are listed on official secondary securities markets must have an audit committee, which must consist of a majority of non-executive directors appointed by the board of directors.

The Corporate Governance Code recommends that in addition to the audit committee, the board of directors should form a committee, or two separate committees, of nomination and remuneration.

11.6 Obligation to ask for consent of a shareholders' meeting

The Corporate Governance Code recommends that even when not expressly required under corporate law, any decisions involving a fundamental corporate change should be submitted to the general shareholders' meeting for approval or ratification. Besides, the Corporate Governance Code recommends that the board should submit a report on the directors' remuneration policy to the advisory vote of the general shareholders' meeting, as a separate point on the agenda.

Corporate law generally requires a shareholders' resolution for, among others, any amendment of the by-laws (including increase or reduction of capital and change of corporate purpose), appointment and remuneration of directors, annual accounts, dividends, issue of bonds, or mergers.

11.7 Depth of information – proxy solicitation

Please refer to section 10.4.

The Corporate Governance Code recommends that detailed proposals of the resolutions to be adopted at the general shareholders' meeting should be made available at the same time as the publication of the meeting notice.

11.8 Appointment/dismissal of directors

Directors do not need to be shareholders of the company, unless the by-laws provide to the contrary.

Appointment of directors corresponds to the general shareholders meeting, for a maximum term of six years, or as provided in the by-laws. Shares which are voluntarily pooled so that they constitute an amount of share capital greater than or equal to that which results from dividing total share capital by the number of board members shall have the right to appoint those which result from the corresponding proportion.

Where during the term for which the directors have been appointed, vacant positions arise, the board may appoint from among the shareholders the persons to occupy them until the next following general meeting is held.

A resolution to remove directors may be passed at any time by the company in a general meeting.

Corporate Governance Code recommendations as described in section 11.2 should also be taken into account.

11.9 Income and options for directors

The remuneration (if any) of directors shall be established in the by-laws. Where it consists of a share in profits, it may only be paid out of profits after tax, after setting aside the required amounts for compulsory reserves and after declaring a dividend to the shareholders of 4 per cent or of such higher rate as is established in the by-laws.

Remuneration consisting of shares or options over shares, or referenced to the value of the shares, must be expressly provided for in the articles of association, and its application will require a resolution by the shareholders in a general meeting.

11.10   Earnings guidance

The Corporate Governance Code recommends that: (i) remuneration comprising the delivery of share-based instruments, payments linked to the company's performance or membership of pension schemes should be confined to executive directors, adding that the delivery of shares should be excluded from this limitation when directors are obliged to retain them until the end of their tenure; (ii) external directors' remuneration should sufficiently compensate them for the dedication, abilities and responsibilities that the post entails, but should not be so high as to compromise independence; (iii) in the case of remuneration linked to the company earnings, deductions should be computed for any qualifications stated in the auditor's report; and (iv) in the case of variable awards, remuneration policies should include technical safeguards to ensure they reflect the professional performance of the beneficiaries and not simply the general progress of the markets or the company's sector, atypical or exceptional transactions or circumstances of this kind.

11.11   Management discussion and analysis (MD&A)

MD&A sections of prospectuses approved by the CNMV are not as detailed as others published in the US or UK.

11.12   Directors' liability

Directors shall be liable to the company, the shareholders and the creditors of the company for any damage they cause through acts or omissions contrary to the law or the by-laws or carried out in violation of the duties inherent in their office. All the members of the board shall be jointly and severally liable, except those who prove that, since they did not take part in its passing and implementation, they were unaware of its existence or, if they were aware of it, did everything appropriate to avoid the damage or at least expressly opposed it.

12. MARKET ABUSE

Spanish regulations on market abuse are in line with EU regulations (Directive 2003/6/EC of the European Parliament and of the Council of 28 January 2003 on insider dealing and market manipulation (market abuse), and further implementing directives and regulations).

12.1 Insider trading

Inside information is defined as information of a precise nature which has not been made public, relating, directly or indirectly, to one or more issuers of negotiable securities or financial instruments or to one or more negotiable securities or financial instruments and which, if it were made public, would be likely to have a significant effect on the prices of those negotiable securities or financial instrument.

All those who possess inside information must refrain from performing any of the following activities, directly or indirectly, on their own account or for third parties:

* preparing or carrying out any type of transaction on the negotiable securities or financial instruments to which the information refers;
* disclosing inside information to any other person unless such disclosure is made in the normal course of the exercise of its employment, profession or duties; and
* recommending or inducing another person, on the basis of inside information, to acquire or dispose of instruments to which that information relates.

It should be noted that misuse of inside information may constitute a criminal offence.

12.2 Market manipulation

All persons or entities that act in, or are connected to, the securities market must refrain from preparing or engaging in practices that distort market prices. Such practices shall be understood to include:

* transactions or orders to trade which give, or are likely to give, false or misleading signals as to the supply of, demand for or price of financial instruments, or which secure, by means of a person or persons acting in collaboration, the price of one or several financial instruments at an abnormal or artificial level; unless the person who entered into the transactions or issued the orders to trade establishes that its reasons for so doing are legitimate and that these transactions or orders to trade conform to accepted market practices on the regulated market concerned;
* transactions or orders to trade which employ fictitious devices or any other form of deception or contrivance; and
* dissemination of information through the media, including the Internet, or by any other means, which gives, or is likely to give, false or misleading signals as to financial instruments, including the dissemination of rumours and false or misleading news, where the person who made the dissemination knew, or ought to have known, that the information was false or misleading.

In particular, the following practices should be understood to be market manipulation:

* conduct by a person, or persons acting in collaboration, to secure a dominant position over the supply of or demand for a financial instrument which has the effect of fixing, directly or indirectly, purchase

or sale prices or creating other unfair trading conditions;
- the buying or selling of financial instruments at the close of the market with the effect of misleading investors acting on the basis of closing prices; and
- taking advantage of occasional or regular access to the traditional or electronic media by voicing an opinion about a financial instrument (or indirectly about its issuer) while having previously taken positions on that financial instrument and profiting subsequently from the impact of the opinions voiced on the price of that instrument, without having simultaneously disclosed that conflict of interest to the public in a proper and effective way.

12.3 Miscellaneous
Market manipulation and insider trading could constitute a criminal offence and are subject to administrative fines.

13.   MUTUAL OR INVESTMENT FUNDS
13.1 Introduction to these two categories
Financial investment funds are collective investment schemes (IIC) without legal personality, the object of which is the collective investment in transferable securities of capital raised from the public.

Any other types of investment funds are deemed to be non-financial. The most important type of non-financial investment funds are those mainly devoted to investing in real estate assets for sub-leasing.

13.2 Investment companies, open-ended, close-ended
Investment companies are legal entities in the form of a corporation having equivalent purposes to the investment funds described in section 13.1.

Financial investment companies may be open-ended (*Sociedad de Inversión de Capital Variable* or SICAV), structured as a company with variable capital. SICAVs continually issue new shares to investors and must stand ready to buy back shares from them redeeming their shares at the then current net asset value per share.

On the other hand, close-ended investment companies are those having a fixed capital, devoted to investing in real estate assets (*Sociedad de Inversión Inmobiliaria* or SII).

13.3 Licence requirements
Formation/incorporation of investment funds and investment companies is subject to prior authorisation by the CNMV. Services rendered by their managers and custodians are reserved activities as well.

13.4 Continuing requirements
Detailed continuing obligations apply to IICs so as to ensure the timely disclosure of all relevant information. IICs shall also have to meet requirements to maintain their authorisation as set forth under relevant regulations.

13.5 Custodians

IICs (except for SIIs) must have a depositary to which its assets and cash must be entrusted, which is in charge of the surveillance of the manager and, where applicable, the IIC's directors.

The depositary shall be liable to the IIC and the investors for any loss suffered by them as a result of its unjustifiable failure to perform its obligations, or its improper performance of them.

13.6 Undertakings for Collective Investment in Transferable Securities (UCITS)

Please refer to section 13.1 above as a very general basis and bearing in mind certain exceptions stated below.

13.7 Non-UCITS funds

Non-UCITS funds are those undertakings without legal personality for collective investment in transferable securities which do not comply with the requirements of the UCITS Directive as amended.

Another category of IIC is the so called free-investment IIC or Spanish hedge funds (*Instituciones de Inversión Colectiva de Libre Inversión*), which have more flexible requirements than ordinary IICs and are not considered to be UCITS compliant. In addition, non-financial IICs (real estate) are also not considered to be UCITS.

13.8 Hedge funds

Please refer to section 13.7 above.

13.9 Marketing and distribution requirements

All kinds of marketing or distribution of IICs are regulated activities under Spanish regulations. The concept of marketing is broad and includes telephone or other telematic contacts. Marketing and distribution of IICs is therefore reserved to authorised entities such as banks, management companies or investment firms.

13.10   Manager

Managers of IICs are legal entities in the form of a corporation in charge of administrating, representing and managing the investments and reimbursement of funds and redeeming of investment companies shares.

14. SECURITIES INSTITUTIONS

14.1 Market executive undertaking

The LMV establishes a general prohibition on performing, on a professional basis, investment services and ancillary services by non-authorised entities. In addition, the marketing of investment services and attraction of clients can only be carried out on a professional basis by institutions authorised to provide such services acting in their own name or through agents.

14.2 Securities clearing house

Iberclear is in charge of the clearing and settlement of all trades from the Spanish Stock Exchanges.

14.3 Central securities depository

Iberclear is the Spanish Central Securities Depository which is in charge of the register of securities, held in book-entry form.

While Iberclear maintains the Securities Registry by means of book-entry form, its participants are in charge of the custody of the securities belonging to clients.

14.4 Investment services providers (ISP)

Investment firms are companies whose principal activity consists of providing investment services and ancillary services, on a professional basis, to third parties with respect to financial instruments.

The following are considered to be investment services, among others:
- placing financial instruments, with or without a firm commitment basis;
- underwriting the issuance or placement of financial instruments;
- operation of multilateral trading facilities;
- reception and transmission of orders;
- discretionary portfolio management; and
- financial investment advice.

The following are considered to be ancillary services, among others:
- the custody and administration of financial instruments for the account of clients; and
- services related to underwriting issues or placements of financial instruments.

15. NOTIFICATION OBLIGATIONS
15.1 Notification of major shareholding

Please refer to section 10.1 above.

16. PUBLIC TAKEOVERS
16.1 Applicable laws and regulations or regulatory framework

The main regulations for public takeovers are the following:
- LMV; and
- Royal Decree 1066/2007, of 28 July.

The Spanish system on takeovers follows EU Directive 2004/25/EC of the European Parliament and of the Council of 21 April 2004 on takeover bids.

16.2 Competent authorities

The CNMV is the competent authority on takeover bids for Spanish companies listed on Spanish stock exchanges.

16.3 Dealing with disclosures and stake building

Apart from the requirements on disclosing major shareholdings as described in section 10.1 above, there are no further requirements to disclose any stake building previously to a takeover.

16.4 Types of takeover bids

The Spanish regime distinguishes between mandatory takeover bids, when control of the target company has already been acquired, and voluntary takeover bids, when the control has not been acquired. The voluntary takeover bid may fulfil the role of the mandatory takeover bid and, therefore, the person who acquires control of a company after a voluntary takeover bid shall not be under the obligation to launch a mandatory takeover bid if the voluntary takeover bid was made for all of the securities, and either an equitable price was offered or it was accepted by at least 50 per cent of the voting rights to which it was addressed.

The takeover bid is mandatory when control of a listed company is acquired. Such control may be acquired either: (i) by acquiring shares or other securities, which directly or indirectly confer voting rights in the company; or (ii) under shareholders agreements; or (iii) as a result of the cases in which control is acquired indirectly or unexpectedly.

Control is deemed to be acquired by a natural or legal person, individually or jointly with persons acting in concert, when:
- a percentage of voting rights equal to or in excess of 30 per cent is directly or indirectly acquired; or
- a lower percentage of voting rights is directly or indirectly acquired and a number of directors who, jointly, if appropriate, with those already designated, representing more than half the members of the company's board, is designated within 24 months subsequent to the date of acquisition of the lower percentage.

Regulations contain: (i) specific rules on how to calculate the stake in a listed company, in order to determine whether the obligation to make a takeover bid exists or not; and (ii) express rules on the designation of directors.

The percentage of voting rights is calculated on the basis of all the shares carrying voting rights, excluding treasury stock of the target company.

Specific rules apply for mergers or taking indirect control of another company that holds a direct or indirect stake in the share capital of a listed company and other cases referred to as unexpected acquisition of control, which are characterised because the percentage of control is acquired, not as a result of the acquisition of shares or voting rights, but for other reasons.

Some exceptions apply under certain conditions to the mandatory takeover bid such as the mere redistribution of voting rights when the shares are still allocated to one single person, the existence of another shareholder with a higher stake, or a merger in which the listed company participates.

The takeover bid be should be addressed to all of the holders of voting shares in the listed company, all holders of pre-emptive rights if any, and all the holders of convertible bonds.

Mandatory takeover bids should be made at an equitable price. The equitable price is generally the highest that the offeror or persons acting in concert with it have paid or agreed for the same securities during the 12 months prior to the announcement of the takeover bid. In case that neither the offeror nor persons acting in concert with it have acquired shares in the target company during the 12 months prior to the announcement of the takeover bid, the price shall be determined in accordance with the rules established for the price of delisting bids.

16.5 Procedural aspects

Announcement of the takeover bid
In the case of mandatory takeover bids, the event that renders it obligatory to make the takeover bid should be made public as soon as it occurs, by means of a communication to the CNMV and through the issuer's Web site. In the case of voluntary takeover bids, as soon as the decision has been adopted to make a takeover bid and provided that it has been guaranteed that any cash consideration can be paid in full or after adopting all reasonable measures to secure any type of consideration, the offeror should make public and publish that decision.

Filing of the takeover bid
The application for authorisation of the takeover bid is submitted in writing by the offeror, attaching the relevant documentation (including the offer document).

Admission to procedure
CNMV should admit it to procedure within a period of seven working days from the date on which the documentation on the takeover bid is completed.

Authorisation of the takeover bid
CNMV should authorise or reject the takeover bid within a period of 20 working days as of the date on which the application for authorisation is filed.

Publication of the takeover bid
After the offeror has been notified that the takeover bid is authorised, it should, within a maximum period of five working days, make public the takeover bid by way of placing the appropriate announcements.

The offer document should be made available to interested parties, from the working day after the first announcement is published.

Acceptance period
The acceptance period may not be less than 15 calendar days nor exceed 70 days.

Publication of the report to be issued by the board of the target
The board of the target company is required to draft a detailed and well-

founded report on the takeover bid, which needs to be published within a maximum of 10 calendar days from the date on which the acceptance period commences.

Publication of the results
Once the acceptance period has lapsed, the CNMV shall publish the offer result.

Settlement
For cash takeover bids, the settlement shall be made through the procedure established to that end by the Spanish settlement system (Iberclear), and the trade date shall be the date of the session to which the Stock Exchange Bulletin in which the result of the takeover bid is published refers.

When the consideration consists of an exchange, the takeover bid shall be settled in the form provided for in the offer document.

16.6 Nature and value of consideration offered
The takeover bid may be made as a sale and purchase, as an exchange or transfer of securities or as both simultaneously, provided that the equal treatment of the security holders who are operating under equal circumstances is guaranteed.

Notwithstanding, mandatory takeover bids require (as in other cases) that the takeover bid includes at least, as an alternative, consideration in cash financially equivalent to the exchange offered.

16.7 Timetable and variations
Please refer to section 16.5 above.

16.8 Strategy
Normal practice shows that hostile takeover bids are scarcely used in Spain, as they have not usually been successful. Hostile takeover bids have usually been converted into friendly takeover bids reaching agreements with the board of the target company.

It has sometimes proved useful to hold a significant stake of the target before the takeover bid, or to reach agreements with significant shareholders.

16.9 Irrevocable
The takeover bid shall be irrevocable as from the public announcement and may not be modified, withdrawn of the effects therefore cease, except in the cases and manner stipulated by the regulations.

16.10   Share dealings, buying shares
The offeror is entitled to acquire securities of the target company at any time, outside the takeover bid, but such acquisitions shall have the following consequences:
- if the takeover bid is subject to obtaining a minimum percentage, the elimination of said condition and any other condition that might have

been established;

- when the consideration of the takeover bid consists of securities in the offeror or of a combination of cash and securities in the offeror, the obligation to offer cash to all the addressees of the takeover bid, as alternative consideration; and
- when the consideration of the takeover bid exclusively consists of cash, the automatic rise in price offered up to the highest price paid for the securities.

The offeror or the persons acting in concert with it may not transfer shares in the target company until the takeover bid has been liquidated.

In the case of a takeover bid, reporting requirements on major shareholdings are reduced to 1 per cent of voting rights, and those shareholders owning more than 3 per cent of the voting rights should report any transaction which modifies their shareholding.

16.11 First announcement

The intention to make a takeover bid should be published:

- in the case of mandatory takeover bids as soon as the obligation is triggered; and
- in the case of voluntary takeover bids, as soon as the decision has been adopted to make a takeover bid and provided that it has been guaranteed that any cash consideration can be paid in full or after adopting all reasonable measures to secure any type of consideration, the offeror should make public and publish that decision.

16.12 Drafting of offer documents

The prospectus has to be drafted in accordance with the content requirements set forth under annexes to the Royal Decree 1066/2007.

The offeror and the offeror's legal advisers normally intervene in the prospectus preparation process.

16.13 Further announcements

Further announcements refer basically to:

- any amendment to the terms and conditions of the bid, if legally possible;
- the results of the offer; and
- any other information relevant to the offer.

16.14 Responsibility

The offer document should indicate the name and position of the persons responsible for the offer document and, as the case may be, the specific portions of the offer document for which they assume responsibility.

16.15 Despatch

Please refer to section 16.5 above on the publication of the takeover's announcements, the takeover's authorisation and the offer document.

16.16   Due diligence in advance of a takeover bid

There is no requirement or legal obligation to conduct due diligence of the target company. However, a prior due diligence is market practice in Spain for friendly takeover bids. A non-disclosure agreement is normally executed between the offeror and the target company before the due diligence period starts.

Spanish regulations provide for equal information amongst competing offerors, so that, when specifically required by an offeror or bona fide potential offeror, the target company should make the information requested available to it, provided that such information has already been provided to other offerors or potential offerors.

In any case, the delivery of information should be subject to the recipient guaranteeing its confidentiality, that the information will exclusively be used to make a takeover bid and that the information is necessary to make the bid.

16.17   Conditions to the offer

Mandatory takeover bids may not be subject to any condition, other than those which require authorisations form other supervisory bodies and by antitrust authorities. Voluntary takeover bids, on the other hand, may be subject to the following conditions: (i) authorisations form other supervisory bodies and by antitrust authorities; (ii) approval of modifications of articles of association or structural modifications or the adoption of other resolutions by the general shareholders' meeting of the target company; (iii) acceptance of the takeover bid by a certain minimum number of securities of the target company; (iv) approval of the takeover bid by the general shareholders' meeting of the offeror company; and (v) any other which may be considered to conform to law by the CNMV.

16.18   Financing

There are no restrictions on obtaining financing from credit institutions so as to pay the purchase price of the shares or to comply with the relevant consideration.

The bidder should file a guarantee (usually a bank guarantee, in the event of a cash consideration) which secures the fulfilment of its obligations under the takeover bid.

16.19   For cash/for shares/mixed

Please refer to section 16.6

16.20   Inducement

Any inducement by the target company is subject to the requirements established in section 16.21 below. The offeror should respect the equal treatment principle of all shareholders to which the offer is addressed.

16.21   Defence mechanisms

From the date on which the public announcement of the decision to make the takeover bid is made, up to the date on which the result of it is published, the board and management of the target company shall refrain from engaging in any activity that might result in the frustration of the takeover bid, with the exception of: (i) the search for competing takeover bids; and (ii) any activity or transaction which is expressly authorised by its general shareholders' meeting.

16.22   Nature of listed securities
All listed securities must be book entry securities.

16.23   Squeeze-out
Squeeze-out and sell-out (for the benefit of the minority shareholders of the target company) procedures are applicable, after a takeover bid, provided that: (i) the offeror becomes the owner of securities representing at least 90 per cent of the voting share capital of the target company; and (ii) the takeover bid has been accepted by securities representing, at least, 90 per cent of the voting rights to which it was addressed. Said procedures shall be executed at an equitable price, construed as the price corresponding to the consideration of the takeover bid.

16.24   Schemes of arrangement
Schemes of arrangement are not regulated under Spanish law.

17. FOREIGN INVESTMENT CONTROLS
17.1 Foreign investments
Foreign investments in Spanish listed companies are not subject to any prior control (with some exceptions such as companies devoted to national defence or weapon manufacture activities), but must be declared after the investment is made and after it has been settled. Foreign investment declarations are submitted solely for administrative and census purposes. The general rule for investment in Spanish listed companies is that the declaration is made by the entity where the securities account is opened, or where the securities are deposited is located in Spain.

17.2 Exemptions
Not applicable.

17.3 Exemptions of notification or prior authorisation
There are no exemptions under Spanish law to the obligation to declare foreign investments.

17.4 Notification in order to establish a balance of payments
Please see section 17.1.

Sweden

Roschier Ola Åhman, Mattias Friberg & Malin Karvonen

1. GENERAL DESCRIPTION OF THE CAPITAL MARKETS
The official name of the Stockholm Stock Exchange is NASDAQ OMX
Stockholm AB (NASDAQ OMX Stockholm), following the acquisition of
OMX by NASDAQ in February 2008. NASDAQ OMX Stockholm, with some
260 listed companies, is part of NASDAQ OMX Nordic, which includes stock
exchanges in Helsinki (Finland), Copenhagen (Denmark) and Reykjavik
(Iceland). These stock exchanges share the same trading system, provide
common listing and index structures, enable cross-border trading and
settlement and provide one market source of information. Further, NASDAQ
OMX Nordic is a part of the global NASDAQ OMX Group.

In addition to NASDAQ OMX Stockholm there are a number of
alternative exchanges and other markets in Sweden:
- NASDAQ OMX First North (First North), a multilateral trading facility
  (MTF) with some 125 listed companies;
- Nordic Growth Market (NGM), a stock exchange with some 20 listed
  companies;
- Aktietorget, an MTF with some 130 listed companies; and
- Nordic MTF, an MTF with some 20 listed companies.

1.1 Numbers of companies listed
There are some 550 listed companies in Sweden.

1.2 Total volume and market value
According to the latest statistics the value of the aggregate annual share
trading on NASDAQ OMX Stockholm amounted to approximately EUR 415
billion in 2010.

1.3 Issue activity
In 2008 the initial public offering (IPO) markets plummeted worldwide, due
to the severe economic downturn, and similarly during 2009 there were few
IPOs worldwide. The Nordic countries were not an exception to this market
trend. However, the recent relative stability of the stock markets during 2010
indicates that confidence in the valuation of the markets is in the process of
being restored. As a consequence there are signs of a reawakening of the IPO
markets.

1.4 Takeover activity
During the economic downturn the number of takeovers has been modest

with only a few takeovers per year, but during 2010 the activity increased in the mergers and acquisitions (M&A) market.

1.5 Hostile takeover attempts

The uncertainty in the market may also result in a rising number of hostile takeover attempts, eg, due to a certain level of discrepancy in the valuation of target companies by, on one side, the major shareholders and board of directors of target companies and, on the other, potential offerors.

2. REGULATORY STRUCTURE

2.1 General

The Swedish legislation regulating the capital markets is to a great extent based on European Union (EU) directives.

The main act regulating the capital markets is the Securities Market Act (SFS 2007:528, SMA). The SMA contains provisions on, *inter alia*, the operation of a stock exchange or an MTF and regulates what requirements a stock exchange or an MTF shall pose on its members and listed companies. New provisions have been introduced in order to implement the EU directive on Markets in Financial Instruments (2004/39/EC) (MiFID). Furthermore, certain amendments have been introduced for purpose of implementing the EU Transparency Directive (2004/109/EC), in particular with respect to the information to be regularly disclosed by listed companies.

The Financial Instruments Trading Act (SFS 1991:980, FTA) contains statutory provisions regulating the duty to publish prospectuses and offer documents as well as the duty to disclose ownership of shares.

The Takeover Act (SFS 2006:451, Takeover Act) was introduced through the implementation of the EU Takeover Directive (2004/25/EC) and imposes an obligation on the offeror to enter into an agreement with the stock exchange operating the market where the target company is listed before a takeover bid is launched. The Takeover Act also contains rules on the obligation to publish an offer document, mandatory bids, information to employees, defence measures and breakthrough provisions.

Another relevant piece of legislation regulating the capital markets is the Financial Instruments Accounts Act (SFS 1998:1479) containing provisions relating to the authorisation requirements for central securities depositories. Furthermore, the Swedish Companies Act (SFS 2005:551, Companies Act) provides rules on, *inter alia*, the issue of shares and certain other financial instruments.

The legislation forms the basis of the regulatory structure, being supplemented with an extensive structure of self-regulation. For example, the FTA and the SMA are supplemented by the Swedish Financial Supervisory Authority's (SFSA) statutory regulations with regard to, *inter alia*, clearing and the disclosure of information by listed companies, as well as disclosing obligations for holders of shares and other financial instruments issued by a listed company.

2.2 Regulation of the offering of new securities
2.2.1 Public offering
The concepts of 'public offering' and 'private offering' are not as such
defined under Swedish law. However, the FTA contains provisions according
to which anyone who offers securities to the public shall be under an
obligation to publish a prospectus describing the issuer and the securities
and obtain the SFSA's approval of that prospectus before the launch of
offering unless the offering of the securities falls within an exemption from
the prospectus requirement under the FTA. As a general rule, offerings
targeted at more than 99 non-qualified investors are considered public
offerings. The active marketing of securities such as the marketing of
securities in the public media is likewise always considered to constitute a
public offering.

See also section 5.

2.2.2 Private offering
If certain requirements are met, the offering will not be considered to
constitute a public offering in Sweden and will not trigger the prospectus
requirement imposed by the FTA but will be viewed as a private offering.
According to the FTA, an offering qualifies as a private offering eg, if the
addressees of the offering consist of qualified investors and/or not more than
99 potential non-qualified investors.

There are generally no Swedish filing or authorisation requirements
with respect to an offer qualifying as a private offering. However, general
marketing and duty of disclosure provisions apply (section 7).

2.3 Differences between local and foreign companies
In Sweden, there are no differences in the regulatory structure that applies to
local and foreign companies.

2.4 Admission to trading on a regulated market
See section 8 and in particular section 8.1.

2.5 Financial promotion
See section 7.

2.6 Rule books
The Takeover Act is supplemented by the takeover rules issued by eg,
NASDAQ OMX Stockholm (referred to hereafter as the 'takeover rules'), see
also section 16. Furthermore, NASDAQ OMX Stockholm has adopted a set of
rules and regulations concerning the different participants on the exchange
(such as the NASDAQ OMX's rulebook for issuers). The rules and regulations
include, *inter alia*, listing requirements for all instruments and disclosure
rules for issuers and members. Furthermore, as part of the self-regulatory
framework, a Swedish code of corporate governance (referred to hereafter as
'the code') has been published, following co-operation among regulators and
several private organisations.

3. REGISTRATION OF THE ISSUER AND SECURITIES

3.1 Registration requirements

In order for the securities of a Swedish company to be admitted to public trading, they must be issued by a public limited liability company and be defined as a so-called Euroclear company (*avstämningsbolag*), ie, the company being obliged to have a record day provision in its articles of association as well as being required to admit its securities for trading and be affiliated to a central securities depository. In Sweden, the only central securities depository is Euroclear Sweden AB (Euroclear), the trade name of which was changed from VPC AB in February 2009.

It is possible to affiliate both public and private limited liability companies to Euroclear even though companies affiliated to Euroclear are primarily public limited liability companies. There are no special requirements for a foreign company to be affiliated to Euroclear. In addition to those applicable to Swedish issuers, there are in principle no special registration or licensing requirements for the offering of securities to the public by foreign issuers or the admission to trading of securities issued by such issuers on markets in Sweden, nor are there requirements of a formal presence or a local agent.

3.1.1 Swedish book-entry securities system

The Swedish book-entry securities system is centralised at Sweden's central securities depository, Euroclear, part of the international Euroclear Group. Euroclear provides national clearing and registration services for issuers of securities. Such services include the technical maintaining of shareholder lists, general meeting services, assistance with corporate actions and yield payments.

Registration with the Swedish book-entry securities system is mandatory for shares listed on NASDAQ OMX Stockholm. However, foreign issuers that intend to list securities on NASDAQ OMX Stockholm may use Swedish depositary receipts or direct links from securities depositories outside Sweden. In practice, listed debt securities are also registered with the book-entry securities system.

3.1.2 Clearing and trading systems

The Financial Instruments Accounts Act (SFS 1998:1479) together with the rules of Euroclear govern the settlement of securities in the book-entry system. Euroclear's clearing and settlement system is a real-time settlement system that enables the settlement of trades on the trading date (T+0). The standard clearing time of exchange trades is three days (T+3). The common trading platform for NASDAQ OMX Nordic, called INET Nordic, is used for share trading on NASDAQ OMX Stockholm.

3.2 Nature of securities

The SMA applies to securities, which are transferable and may be subject to trade on the capital markets. It may also be noted with respects to units of non-UCITS funds that in case these non-UCITS funds are not viewed to resemble Swedish investment funds to a sufficient extent, they may be classified as financial instruments as defined in the SMA instead. This means that they would need to comply with eg, the FTA's prospectus requirements. See also sections 5 and 13.

4.   SUPERVISORY AUTHORITIES
4.1   Conduct: prudential, cooperation, self-regulation of stock exchange

The supervisory authority in relation to the Swedish capital market is the SFSA. The legislative framework regulating the capital markets is provided by the Swedish parliament and is thereafter supplemented and regulated in more detail by the SFSA via statutory regulations as well as general guidelines and recommendations. Throughout this process the SFSA, following recent EU legislation such as the EC Prospectus Directive (2003/71/EC), works closely together with other competent authorities in the EU, by adopting guidelines in the European Securities and Markets Authority (ESMA), previously the Committee of European Securities Regulators (CESR). The main tasks of the SFSA are to oversee financial market operations, to supervise and guide market participants and to maintain trust in the market. The SFSA is furthermore the authority authorising the operation of regulated markets (stock exchanges) or MTFs and the competent authority approving, inter alia, prospectuses.

The Swedish Securities Council (*Aktiemarknadsnämnden*) has an important role in contributing to the development of good stock market practice, by issuing statements in individual cases. In addition, both the SFSA and NASDAQ OMX Stockholm have delegated certain decision-making powers to the Swedish Securities Council, such as the granting of exemptions from the provisions on mandatory bids, exemptions from the provisions on defensive measures and the interpretation of the takeover rules.

See section 2.6 regarding the self-regulation of NASDAQ OMX Stockholm.

5.   OFFERING DOCUMENTATION OR PROSPECTUS REQUIREMENTS
5.1   Nature and statutory requirements of the offering document or disclosure document

Pursuant to the statutory provisions of the FTA, a prospectus shall be prepared and published when securities are offered to the public or when an application is made to admit securities to trading. The prospectus shall be approved by the SFSA before publication.

5.2   Exemptions

Exemptions from the obligation to prepare a prospectus apply in, *inter alia*, the following situations:
*   the securities are offered to qualified investors only;
*   the total subscription price of the securities offered during 12 months does not exceed EUR 1,000,000;
*   the securities are offered to fewer than 100 investors; and

- the securities offered can be acquired only for a consideration of not less than EUR 50,000 per investor or in denominations of not less than EUR 50,000.

Upon application, the SFSA may also grant a partial or complete exemption from the obligation to publish a prospectus in certain situations. For a particular reason, eg, if the information is considered of minor importance, the SFSA may also agree to the omission of information generally required in prospectuses.

5.3 Preparation of the offering document, general contents

According to the FTA, a prospectus can be prepared either as a single document or as separate documents consisting of a registration document, a securities note and a summary note. Information may be incorporated into the prospectus by reference to previously or simultaneously published documents approved by or filed with the competent authority of the home member state. An approved prospectus is valid for 12 months.

The issuer or offeror are responsible for the preparation and content of the prospectus. As a general rule, a prospectus is prepared to comply with the minimum content requirements in the European Commission's Regulation on Prospectuses no 809/2004 (Prospectus Regulation). Further, in accordance with the Prospectus Directive, Swedish law recognises the concept of prospectus passporting. The fees payable to the SFSA for approval of the prospectus depend on the type of securities in question.

5.4 Due diligence

It is customary to conduct a business, financial and legal due diligence review in connection with a public offering. In connection with an IPO, it is required under the NASDAQ OMX's rulebook for issuers to conduct a legal due diligence review. It is customary to conduct a due diligence also prior to a merger, an acquisition or a public takeover. Section 16.13.

5.5 Responsibility

The board of directors of the issuer is normally liable for the accuracy of the information presented in the prospectus, which shall be published prior to the public offering. Section 9.2.

5.6 Disclaimer/selling restrictions

There are no explicit Swedish law requirements as to country-specific or other disclaimers to be inserted into the marketing materials or other securities offer documentation (section 7). Generally, a company cannot restrict its liability through disclaimers in Sweden. However, especially foreign issuers nevertheless tend to use short disclaimers when offering securities to Swedish investors.

5.7 Issuing of bonds

As a general rule, the offering documentation and prospectus requirements are relatively similar for equity and debt securities.

6. DISTRIBUTION SYSTEMS

6.1 Normal structure of a distribution group

The manager or arranger of a capital market transaction or an international cross-border transaction with a Swedish dimension is typically a well-recognised investment bank. Depending on the size and nature of a contemplated transaction, the bank chosen will usually be either: (i) a local investment bank; (ii) a Nordic investment bank with a presence on the Swedish market; or (iii) an international investment bank. Larger transactions usually involve more than one manager.

Equity offerings executed in the past few years have included both large rights offerings and offerings directed at selected domestic and international institutional investors.

6.2 Underwriting

Rights offerings are often fully underwritten, and may involve fairly complex underwriting structures. Offerings directed at institutional investors are typically conducted on the basis of exemptions from the prospectus requirements in different jurisdictions. In offerings targeted at US investors, the Rule 144A exemption is mostly used.

6.3 Stabilisation

Stabilisation is possible in Sweden: according to the Market Abuse Act (SFS 2005:377, MAA), the provisions of the use of inside information or market price distortion shall not apply to stabilisation of financial instruments provided that the trading is carried out in accordance with the European Commission's Regulation on Stabilisation no 2279/2003.

6.4 Rules on distribution to the public

See section 2.2.

7. PUBLICITY

Pursuant to the FTA, an advertisement regarding an offer of securities to the public or regarding an application to admit securities to trading shall contain information that a prospectus has been or will be published and where it is or will be available. Furthermore, the advertisement shall be formatted and presented so that it is clear that it is an advertisement. The information in the advertisement shall not be erroneous or misleading and shall conform to the information in the prospectus.

The provisions of the Swedish Marketing Act (SFS 1995:450) as well as general marketing principles shall be observed when publishing a prospectus or an offer document. Accordingly, the marketing of the instrument must be compatible with good marketing practice. Further, all marketing of financial instruments must be designed and presented so that their marketing nature is evident and they must not be misleading.

8. LISTING

8.1 Special listing requirements, admission criteria

The listing requirements on NASDAQ OMX Nordic, including NASDAQ OMX Stockholm, are in all material respects the same for the Nordic countries Sweden, Finland, Denmark and Iceland. On NASDAQ OMX Nordic, listed companies are first presented by market capitalisation, then by industry sector following the international Global Industry Classification Standard. Listed companies are divided into segments: Large Cap for companies with a market capitalisation of at least EUR 1 billion; Mid Cap for companies with a market capitalisation of EUR 150 million to EUR 1 billion; and Small Cap for companies with a market capitalisation of less than EUR 150 million.

In brief, the main listing criteria for the NASDAQ OMX Nordic include the following:

• a financial and operating history of three years;
• documented earnings capacity or sufficient working capital for at least 12 months;
• 25 per cent of the share capital held by the public (free float); and
• the required adequacy and suitability with respect to the company's organisation, management and board of directors.

Debt instruments may be admitted to trading provided that:

• the face value of a debt issue is at least SEK 2,000,000;
• they are freely transferable;
• their issuer is sufficiently financially sound; and
• the issuer's reporting and supervision processes are arranged in an appropriate manner.

8.2 Mechanics of the review process

In accordance with the FTA, the issuer will need to publish a prospectus prior to listing, unless any exemption to this requirement is applicable. A listing application will need to be submitted to NASDAQ OMX Stockholm.

The issuer must also conclude a listing agreement with NASDAQ OMX Stockholm and undertake to comply with the NASDAQ OMX's rulebook for issuers. The issuer must pay an application fee prior to the submission of the application and an annual fee to NASDAQ OMX Stockholm.

8.3 Prospectus obligation, due diligence, exemption

In general, anyone applying for the admission to public trading of a security must publish a prospectus before the securities can be admitted to public trading. However, according to the FTA, there are certain exemptions from this obligation. Among the most commonly utilised exemptions is the case where the shares that are sought to be admitted to public trading, together with shares of the same class admitted to trading during the last 12 months, represent less than 10 per cent of the number of shares of the same class admitted to trading in the same stock exchange at the beginning of the 12 month period. An exemption is likewise available where the securities have been admitted to trading maintained by another stock exchange – provided that the issuer fulfils certain conditions (eg, securities of the same class have been subject to this trading for more than 18 months).

See also section 5.

8.4   Appeal procedure in the event of a prospectus refusal

In the event of a prospectus refusal by the SFSA, the issuer may appeal the decision to the Administrative Court.

8.5   Authority of the Exchange

Decisions regarding the admission to listing and the de-listing of securities are made by the listing committee of NASDAQ OMX Stockholm. Supervision of compliance with the rules of NASDAQ OMX Stockholm is exercised by the bodies of the exchange itself, which has certain disciplinary powers that are enforced by its disciplinary committee. NASDAQ OMX Stockholm is supervised by the SFSA.

8.6   Special arrangements for smaller companies

NASDAQ OMX First North, *Aktietorget* and Nordic MTF are alternative marketplaces for small and medium-sized growth companies and have fewer disclosure and other obligations and lighter listing requirements compared to the main market discussed above.

8.7   Costs of various types

Companies are required to pay a listing application fee to NASDAQ OMX Stockholm prior to submitting their application for listing. This application fee is non-refundable. Furthermore, listed companies are required to pay a follow-up fee approximately one year following the first day of listing as well as quarterly fees to the stock exchange. The applicant company may also incur various types of advisor fees in connection with the listing.

9.   SANCTIONS AND DISPUTES

9.1   Disciplinary and administrative sanctions

Certain disciplinary and administrative sanctions may be imposed on the board of directors of the issuer following a public offering. In accordance with the FTA, the SFSA may impose fines following violations of the FTA with regard to, *inter alia,* the non-fulfilment of the prospectus requirements or the disclosure requirements. A listed company may be issued a warning, be imposed monetary penalties or, ultimately, be de-listed in the event of the company not complying with the rules of NASDAQ OMX Stockholm.

9.2   Civil actions

A shareholder who has suffered damage has primarily to base a claim on the Companies Act. Under the Companies Act an incorporator, a board director or a managing director who, in the performance of their duties, intentionally or negligently causes damage to the company shall be liable for such damage. The same liability applies where damage is caused to a shareholder or other person as a consequence of a violation of the

Companies Act, the applicable annual reports legislation or the articles of association of the company.

Furthermore, a director is responsible for observing the duty to publish a prospectus or an offer document as well as the minimum content requirements in such documents set out in the Prospectus Regulation. Pursuant to the Companies Act, liability applies where damage is caused to a shareholder or other person through violation of these obligations.

In principle, a subscription for or a purchase of a security is irrevocable. However, Swedish courts are empowered to mitigate or nullify unreasonable contract terms, particularly in cases of stringent and/or unusual terms and conditions of standard contracts.

9.3 Criminal penalties

Most of the Swedish provisions that regulate the Swedish capital markets and that can inflict criminal penalties have reference to market abuse. Pursuant to the MAA, a person is prohibited from trade, or from inducing others to trade, in the event that the person has insider information, ie, information that is materially price sensitive. Furthermore, the person is prohibited from disclosing such insider information. Failure to obey these rules may result in a criminal penalty. The MAA also contains provisions against measures designed to manipulate market prices. The prohibition covers all actions made to influence such prices improperly.

See also section 12.

10. CONTINUING OBLIGATIONS
10.1 Disclosure and transparency rule

A company listed on an exchange shall enter into an agreement with the exchange. The agreement with NASDAQ OMX Stockholm requires the company to observe the NASDAQ OMX's rulebook for issuers, which sets out the continuing disclosure requirements for publicly listed companies. These requirements are to a large extent based on EU directives, most importantly the EU directive on the Admission of Securities to Official Stock Exchange Listing and on Information to be Published on those Securities (2001/34/EC), as well as MiFID.

10.2 Information

The NASDAQ OMX's rulebook for issuers sets forth requirements for publicly traded companies to disclose to the market significant matters relating to their operations in an orderly and open manner. Under the SMA, information to be disclosed on a regular basis consists of interim reports, annual accounts and account statements. Further, all decisions and other information on the issuer and its operations that are likely to have a material effect on the value of the securities issued must be disclosed without undue delay. The SFSA regulations and guidelines as well as the NASDAQ OMX's rulebook for issuers give certain examples of decisions and information to be disclosed. According to the SMA, an issuer may, exceptionally and with acceptable grounds, postpone the disclosure of information if this does not endanger the investors' positions and the issuer is able to ensure the confidentiality of the information.

10.3 Listing rules
See sections 10.1 and 10.2 above.

10.4 Obligations regarding proxy solicitation
There are in principle no proxy solicitation provisions in Sweden. The main rule in the Companies Act is that the company may not bear the expense of collecting proxies, unless a specific provision has been made in the company's articles of association in this regard. If that is the case, proxies may be collected on the company's expense, following a specific form and procedure.

10.5 Continuing requirements of reporting and notification of substantial shareholding or a substantial transaction
Shareholders are obligated to disclose their holdings in Swedish companies whose shares are publicly traded on the market either in Sweden or in the European Economic Area (EEA), when such holding reaches, exceeds or falls below 5, 10, 15, 20, 25, 30, 50, 66.7 and 90 per cent of the voting rights or of the share capital in the company. Such changes in ownership must be reported to the SFSA, which will publish the change, and to the company.
    See also section 15.

10.6 Requirements for unlisted issuers
Similarly to a listed issuer, an unlisted issuer is required to publish a prospectus if it offers securities to the public. However, there are no similar continuing disclosure obligations for unlisted issuers as there are for listed issuers. An unlisted issuer must comply with general marketing provisions (see section 7) and refrain from marketing the securities by giving false or misleading information or by using procedures that are contrary to good practice or otherwise unfair. There are no requirements to report substantial shareholdings in unlisted issuers.

11. CORPORATE GOVERNANCE
11.1 Law and/or code
Corporate governance in listed companies is mainly regulated by the Companies Act, which includes provisions on the relationship between the shareholders, board of directors and the managing director, and sets forth their respective rights and obligations. The duties of the company and the board of directors towards the market are regulated by the SMA and other securities market legislation, such as the SFSA's regulations and guidelines and the NASDAQ OMX's rulebook for issuers. A company whose shares are listed on a regulated market (NASDAQ OMX Stockholm and NGM) shall comply with the code, on a comply-or-explain basis, ie, listed companies must either adhere to the rules of the code or explain publicly the alternative solutions and the reasons for any deviations.

11.2 Management structure

From a structural point of view, the Swedish corporate governance model is neither one-tier nor two-tier. The division of powers and responsibilities is hierarchic and strict between the bodies of a Swedish limited liability company, ie, the shareholders' meeting, the board of directors, the executive management and the auditors. The shareholders' meeting is the superior body followed by the board of directors. A superior body may instruct subordinated bodies but cannot, however, give instructions to an extent that deprives the subordinated bodies of the actual responsibility and control in the field of competence assigned to those bodies by law.

The shareholders' meeting appoints the board of directors. However, in contrast to the predominant situation in the Anglo-Saxon jurisdictions, Swedish boards of directors are entirely or predominantly non-executive. The board of directors, which has ultimate responsibility for the management of the company, appoints the managing director (such an appointment is mandatory in public companies) and is responsible for the supervision of the book-keeping and in control of the company's financial matters. The Companies Act requires the board of directors to adopt a written charter for its work. The managing director is responsible for the day-to-day management of the company and its business.

11.3 Obligations to publish information on the Internet

The NASDAQ OMX's rulebook for issuers requires a listed company to have its own Web site on which all disclosed information shall be published. The information shall be made available on the Web site as soon as possible following the public disclosure. In addition, the code requires that a listed company publishes on this Web site a yearly report on, *inter alia*, the corporate governance of the company, in which it describes its compliance with the code or the reasons for any deviation.

11.4 Responsibility of inside/outside directors

There are no differences in the responsibilities or liability of inside and outside directors of a company. However, the code recommends that a majority of the board directors shall be independent of the company and its management, and that at least two of such directors shall be independent of significant shareholders (ie, shareholders holding at least 10 per cent of all shares or votes in the company).

11.5 Committees

The Companies Act contains a statutory provision for the board of directors of a listed company to have an auditing committee, which shall, *inter alia*, supervise the financial reporting of the company and follow up on the accounting of the company as well as the work carried out by the company's auditor. Furthermore, the code recommends that a listed company has a nomination committee appointed by the shareholders' meeting, which proposes the election of new board directors and auditors, as well as a remuneration committee established by the board of directors, which prepares matters related to salary and other forms of remuneration for the company management. A limited liability company may also, as a general rule, appoint other committees within the board of directors, since the board of directors can organise its work as it deems appropriate.

11.6 Obligation to ask for the consent of a shareholders' meeting
Under the Companies Act, certain decisions shall be made by the shareholders' meeting. The annual general meeting of shareholders decides, *inter alia*, upon the adoption of the annual profit and loss statement, the balance sheet and the appropriation of the company's results. In addition, certain other decisions relating to a range of issues, from share- and share-price-related incentive programmes to the executive management, amendment of the articles of association, the increase or decrease of share capital, a merger, a de-merger or the entering into liquidation, shall be taken by the shareholders' meeting.

11.7 Depth of information – proxy solicitation
There are substantial disclosure requirements in the Companies Act, securities markets legislation and the code.
    See section 10 above.

11.8 Appointment/dismissal of directors
The board's directors are elected by the shareholders' meeting (unless stipulated otherwise in the company's articles of association). The shareholders' meeting can at any time remove from office a director it has elected.

11.9 Income and options for directors
The shareholders' meeting also determines the board of directors' remuneration. The code stipulates that non-executive directors should not participate in share-related compensation schemes.

11.10   Earnings guidance
There are no obligations for listed companies to disclose forward-looking information such as earnings guidance and projections. However, NASDAQ OMX's rule book for issuers requires listed companies that make such disclosures to disclose also the underlying assumptions and to immediately disclose as soon as there is reason to expect any material deviation from the projection. Sections 10.1, 10.2 and 10.6.

11.11   Management discussion and analysis (MD&A)
A management discussion and analysis – commenting the changes in financial key ratios between financial periods – is only required in relation to financial information in prospectuses, not in relation to other financial information disclosed by a listed company, such as annual reports and interim reports. However, as a general rule, listed companies are required to disclose material events that have occurred during (and to some extent

after) the reported financial period as well as to disclose detailed notes to the financial statements for the reported period.

11.12   Directors' liability

A board director or managing director who wilfully or negligently breaches their duties may be held liable for compensation for any damage caused to the company. A director may also be held directly liable towards a shareholder or another third party if that party has suffered damage through the director's breach of the Companies Act, the applicable annual accounts legislation or the articles of association. See also section 9.

12. MARKET ABUSE

12.1 Insider trading

The MAA contains, *inter alia*, criminal law provisions on insider trading and market manipulation. Furthermore, the FTA contains provisions regarding the obligation of shareholders in listed companies to, under certain circumstances, disclose their shareholding in such companies. These provisions are supplemented by regulations on insider registers, as well as by the NASDAQ OMX Stockholm guidelines and by various self-regulation guidelines.

The basic principle concerning the use of insider information is that it may not be used, directly or indirectly, in the purchasing or selling of securities. Insider information is defined in the MAA as 'information regarding a circumstance that has not been made public or that is not generally known and is likely to affect materially the price of financial instruments'. Insider information cannot be disclosed to anyone other than a person who receives such insider information as part of the customary performance of their work, profession or assignment. In addition, under certain circumstances, the disclosure of insider information to major shareholders of the company may be allowed (eg, when a company's management is contemplating a specific measure or transaction which later would require the approval of the shareholders' meeting).

12.2 Market manipulation

Undue market manipulation is basically defined as actions that directly or indirectly affect the price of a security in an artificial manner and that deviate from the normal course of trading on the securities market. The prohibition on undue market manipulation covers all actions made to influence improperly the price of a security. As the mere action is prohibited, the action that is intended to influence the share price is not required to have actually influenced the share price.

12.3 Miscellaneous

12.3.1   Disclosure obligations

The ownership of shares and securities in publicly traded companies shall be reported to a public insider register maintained by the SFSA if the shareholder is a member of the company's executive, administrative or supervisory body. Also, information on shareholdings of certain persons related to the company's management must be reported to the public insider register. In addition to this register, listed companies are obliged to maintain a non-public, company-specific insider register of persons who from time to time possess insider information due to their positions or duties.

12.3.2 Sanctions

The MAA imposes sanctions for the misuse of insider information and other breaches of the provisions concerning insiders. A person who wilfully or through gross negligence breaches the prohibitions may be ordered to pay a fine or face imprisonment. Moreover, with regard to the disclosure obligations, certain administrative sanctions, such as an administrative fine or a sanction fee, may be imposed by the SFSA.

13. MUTUAL OR INVESTMENT FUNDS

13.1 Introduction to the two categories

Investment funds are governed by the Act on Investment Funds (SFS 2004:46, AIF). The AIF implements the undertakings for collective investments in transferable securities (UCITS) directives I-III (1985/611/EC, 2001/107/EC and 2001/108/EC). Swedish mutual funds can either be UCITS funds or so-called special funds (typically hedge funds). A special fund differs from a UCITS fund, for example, in that a special fund is not subject to the investment restrictions set forth for a UCITS fund under the AIF.

13.2 Licence requirements

The entity marketing and offering investment funds in Sweden may be required to be licensed by the SFSA (see section 14) where the marketing of the fund constitutes provision of investment services. However, there is an exemption from this licence obligation with regard to fund managers.

13.3 Custodians

Custodians are responsible for safeguarding the assets of the funds. SFSA grants authorisations to custodians. The name of the custodian must be explicitly stated in the rules of the fund as well as in its prospectus(es). The fund itself cannot act as its own custodian but it is nevertheless possible that both the fund and the custodian are members of the same groups of companies. Furthermore, custodians holding securities in the Swedish book-entry system must have an account operator licence. The account operator licence gives the custodian the right to operate in the Swedish book-entry system.

13.4 Undertakings for collective investments in transferable securities (UCITS)

The Swedish regulations that apply to the marketing and selling of funds in Sweden depend primarily on: (i) whether the fund would qualify as an investment fund under the Investment Funds Act (SFS 2004:46, AIF); (ii) whether they would qualify as financial instruments under the FTA; or (iii)

whether the fund would qualify as neither an investment fund under the
AIF nor a financial instrument under the FTA. The AIF is generally applicable
to Swedish and foreign investment funds operating in Sweden. It always
applies to undertakings for collective investments in transferable securities
(UCITS) funds, whether Swedish or foreign.

13.5 Non-UCITS funds
The applicability of the AIF to non-UCITS investment funds is usually
subject to at least some uncertainty as there is no clearly established practice
as to what kind of foreign investment vehicles qualify as foreign non-UCITS
investment funds for the purposes of the AIF.

If foreign funds that do not qualify as funds under the AIF are sold in
Sweden, the FTA, including certain prospectus, filing and notification
requirements, will, as a general rule, become applicable. However, if such
funds were not sold but only marketed in Sweden, such requirements would
again not be applicable. Furthermore, the marketing in Sweden of a fund
that falls under neither the AIF nor the FTA, is regulated merely by general
marketing regulations and principles.

13.6 Hedge funds
There are no specific regulations in Sweden governing hedge funds.

14. SECURITIES INSTITUTIONS
14.1 Stock Exchanges
NASDAQ OMX Stockholm and NGM are the only stock exchanges (regulated
markets) in Sweden. They issue rules that, in addition to statutory rules and
regulations, govern activities conducted on NASDAQ OMX Stockholm and
NGM, respectively.

14.2 Securities clearing
The securities clearing house in Sweden is Euroclear Sweden AB. The SMA
and the Financial Instruments Accounts Act, together with the SFSA's
general guidelines as well as the rules of Euroclear, govern the settlement of
securities in the electronic book-entry system. For more details on Euroclear
(sections 3.1 and 14.3).

14.3 Central securities depository
The central securities depository in Sweden is Euroclear Sweden AB. For
more details on the organisation (sections 3.1 and 14.2.

14.4 Investment service providers (ISP)
The offering and marketing of financial investment services to the public
in Sweden is regulated by the Act on Financial Advice to Consumers
(SFS 2003:862) and, to a limited extent, the SMA and the FTA, which are
supplemented by the SFSA's guidelines on financial advice to consumers.

The SMA includes code of conduct rules to be observed in relation to
investment services and the SFSA has issued guidelines for the marketing

of financial instruments to Swedish investors. Under the SMA, an EEA investment firm may, after observing certain procedures and obtaining approval from the relevant financial supervisory authority, provide investment services in Sweden, on a cross-border basis or by establishing a branch office. Furthermore, a foreign investment firm authorised to conduct investment services in a state outside the EEA may be granted an authorisation by the SFSA to establish a branch office in Sweden on condition that the firm: (i) is subject to sufficient supervision in its home state; and (ii) has sufficient operating conditions and a management fulfilling the requirements for the reliable provision of investment services. In order to offer cross-border investment services without establishing a branch office or a subsidiary, a foreign non-EEA investment firm must apply to the SFSA for authorisation.

15. NOTIFICATION OBLIGATIONS
15.1 Notification of major shareholding
Under the FTA, a shareholder, or any of their related parties, whose holding reaches, exceeds or falls below the thresholds of 5, 10, 15, 20, 25, 30, 50, 66.7 and 90 per cent of the voting rights or the share capital in a Swedish company whose shares are subject to trading on a regulated market, is obliged to disclose their shareholding to the company and the SFSA. Disclosure is also required where a shareholder is a party to an agreement or other arrangement that, if enforced, will cause their holding to reach, exceed or fall below one of the above thresholds. The disclosure shall be made, at the latest, the trading day after the trade has been effected or the agreement has been entered into.

16. PUBLIC TAKEOVERS
16.1 Applicable laws and regulations
The acquisition of publicly traded shares and other securities is regulated by a combination of legislation and self-regulation. The statutory framework consists mainly of the Takeover Act, which states that a takeover bid for a company listed in Sweden may only be launched if the offeror has entered into an agreement with the stock exchange operating the regulated market where the company is listed. In addition, the Companies Act regulates, *inter alia*, redemption of minority shareholdings ('squeeze-out').

The self-regulation supplementing the legislation consists of the takeover rules, which apply to bids for shares and other financial instruments issued by companies listed on the regulated markets operated by NASDAQ OMX Stockholm or NGM. By signing the agreement with the stock exchange the offeror is obliged to adhere to the takeover rules, including good stock market practice as interpreted by the Swedish Securities Council. If the target company is a foreign company that has a majority of its shares listed outside Sweden, the offeror may in certain situations obtain an exemption from complying with the takeover rules, since it could be burdensome to comply with the regulations of more than one jurisdiction. The takeover rules apply accordingly, as a matter of good stock market practice, to takeover offers concerning companies listed on NASDAQ OMX First North, Aktietorget and Nordic MTF.

16.2 Competent authorities
See section 4.

16.3 Dealing with disclosures and stake building
If an offeror builds a stake in the target company before launching a bid, they must comply with the regulations on the disclosure of shareholdings and insider regulations in accordance with the FTA and the MAA as well as good stock market practice.

16.4 Types of takeover bids
Swedish law does not distinguish between friendly and hostile takeover bids. Furthermore, the legal framework contains provisions for both voluntary and mandatory takeover bids.

The threshold triggering a mandatory bid is reached when a shareholder's holding exceeds 30 per cent of the total voting rights in the listed target company. A shareholder's holding includes the voting rights held by a company within the same group, a party with whom an agreement has been reached to take a long-term common position for the purpose of achieving a controlling influence over the management of the company through a coordinated exercise of voting rights and a party who co-operates with the offeror for the purpose of achieving control over the company.

16.5 Procedural aspects
The offeror must disclose their decision to launch a takeover bid immediately after such a decision has been made. The disclosure shall include the main terms of the takeover bid. Further, pursuant to the Takeover Act, the offeror must publish an offer document in connection with the bid.

In the Swedish market it is generally considered an unfriendly action not to contact the board of directors of the target company in advance of the launch of a takeover bid, in order to seek a recommendation of the takeover bid and sometimes to enter into agreements with the target board of directors relating to the takeover bid. In addition, it is customary, in advance of the launch of a takeover bid, to contact major shareholders in order to secure acceptances and obtain support for the bid.

16.6 Nature and value of a consideration offered
As a general rule, the value of the consideration offered in a takeover bid shall be determined on the basis of the market value of the shares. However, in the event that the offeror and/or their related parties have acquired target company shares in the periods: (i) six months prior to the offer announcement; (ii) after the offer announcement, but outside the takeover bid and prior to the commencement of settlement of the takeover bid; or (iii) six months after the commencement of settlement, the offer price in

the takeover bid must normally not be lower than the highest price paid for such shares. This means that acquisitions prior to the takeover offer announcement set a 'floor price' for the takeover bid and that the offer price in the takeover bid may have to be increased subsequent to the offer announcement.

The consideration offered in a takeover bid can consist of cash, equity or debt securities or a combination of these. Regarding mandatory bids, there is a requirement for the offeror to provide the target company shareholders with an all-cash alternative.

Shareholders within the same class of shares shall be offered the same consideration, whereas shareholders with different classes of shares shall be offered the same form of consideration. If the bid includes the acquisition of shares of different classes and the classes are different from each other with respect to economic rights, the difference in value of the consideration offered for the different classes of shares must not be unreasonable. In cases where shareholders have shares of different classes that only differ regarding voting rights and where not all classes of shares are subject to trading on the exchange, the shareholders shall be offered a consideration of the same value.

If the bid includes the acquisition of different classes of shares and the classes differ only as regards voting rights and all classes of shares are subject to trading on the exchange, the principal rule is that the value of the consideration shall be the same for all shares.

16.7 Timetable and variations
The statutory offer (acceptance) period is a minimum of three weeks and maximum of 10 weeks. The offer period may, on special grounds, exceed the 10-week maximum in the event that the offeror has reserved a right to extend it.

16.8 Irrevocable undertakings
The commonly used contractual arrangement for enhancing the chances of a successful takeover bid is to receive irrevocable undertakings from major shareholders of the target company to accept the bid. Such an irrevocable undertaking has to be disclosed in the takeover offer announcement and in the offer document but does not have to be disclosed ahead of time as it is typically not considered a financial instrument. Soft irrevocable undertakings that allow shareholders to accept a higher competing takeover bid are typically the norm in Sweden. Any contact with shareholders should be taken with due care, taking into consideration confidentiality and insider issues.

16.9 Share dealings, buying shares
The offeror may during or after the offer period, at times determined by the offeror, acquire the securities subject to the bid also outside of the takeover bid. However, when acquiring such securities, the offeror must ensure that all shareholders are treated equally and that all actions comply with the insider regulations. The offeror must also acknowledge that the price offered for these shares outside the bid cannot be higher than the consideration

offered outside of the bid during the offer period or during a period of six months after the completion of the bid. If the price offered is higher, the top-up obligation will apply (see section 16.6).

16.10   Announcements
The offeror must disclose their decision to launch a takeover bid immediately after such a decision has been made. The decision to launch a takeover bid shall also be communicated to the target company, the relevant stock exchange (eg, NASDAQ OMX Stockholm), the Swedish Securities Council and the SFSA. After the decision is disclosed, it shall, without delay, be communicated to the representatives of the employees or to the employees in the target company and the offeror. The disclosure shall include the main terms of the forthcoming bid. The bidder may quite freely decide on the terms and conditions of the bid, with the exception of the mandatory provisions mainly relating to the offer price, the duration of the offer period and the equal treatment of all holders of shares or securities subject to the bid. Similarly, after the expiration of the offer period, the offeror shall, without delay, make the result of the bid public.

16.11   Drafting of offer documents
The offeror must also publish an offer document in connection with the bid, which discloses the terms and conditions of the bid as well as all other relevant information regarding the bid. The offeror shall in the offer document present eg, its strategic plans regarding the target company and its assessment on their likely effects on the operations and employment of the target company. Certain additional information regarding the target company is also required to be provided in the offer document.

16.12   Responsibility
The offeror shall make an affirmation in the offer document stating that for example, to the best of its knowledge, the information provided in the offer document is correct. In friendly bids, the target company's board of directors normally assumes responsibility and provides a similar affirmation in respect of the description of the target company.

16.13   Due diligence in advance of a takeover bid
The takeover rules permit the target company's board of directors to invite the offerors to, prior to the announcement of a takeover bid, conduct a due diligence review on the target company. In the event of competing takeover bids, all offerors must, as far as possible, be given access to the same information during the due diligence review.

16.14   Conditions to the offer
A takeover bid may be subject to conditions regarding completion. Such conditions may, however, not be designed arbitrarily. It must be possible to determine objectively whether or not they have been fulfilled. Further, a condition must not be dependent on the offeror's subjective judgment or on

any actions that are within the discretion of the offeror. The takeover rules state that a condition may not be invoked unless the non-fulfilment thereof is of material importance to the offeror's acquisition of the target company.

16.15   Financing
The offeror is obliged to have secured sufficient financial resources to be able to implement the takeover bid. A takeover bid may be financed with debt, in which case the takeover bid may, to a limited extent, be made conditional on the disbursement of the funds.

16.16   Inducement
The takeover rules state that target company's board of directors should, when evaluating an offeror's request to enter into agreements with the target company, for instance regarding arrangements where the target company or the offeror promises to pay the other party a certain pre-agreed compensation in case the bid is not completed because of certain pre-defined reasons (a so-called 'break-up fee'), see to it that the conditions of such agreements not only conform to the legal requirements but are also formulated taking into account the interests of all the shareholders to whom the bid is directed.

16.17   Defence mechanisms
The Takeover Act prohibits the management and board of directors of the target company from taking defence measures without the prior approval from the shareholders' meeting when a takeover bid has been launched or the target company's board of directors having good reason to assume that a serious takeover bid is imminent. Defence measures are defined as any action involving the company which is designed to frustrate the launch or implementation of a takeover bid. It should be noted that the prohibition does not affect the right of the board of directors to seek alternative offerors.

16.18   Squeeze-out
An offeror who has acquired more than 90 per cent of the shares in the target company has, in accordance with the Companies Act, the right to acquire compulsorily the remaining minority shares through squeeze-out proceedings. The minority shareholders have a corresponding right to request a squeeze-out.

16.19   Schemes of arrangement
Swedish law does not recognise the concept of scheme of arrangement.

17.   FOREIGN INVESTMENT CONTROLS
17.1 Foreign investments
Practically all restrictions on foreign investments in Sweden have been abolished. There is no maximum transferable amount either to or from Sweden, although there are certain reporting requirements relating to cross-border payments.

Switzerland

Schellenberg Wittmer
Martin Lanz, Lorenzo Olgiati & Philippe Borens

1. GENERAL DESCRIPTION OF THE CAPITAL MARKETS

Switzerland is a major centre not only for investment but also for private banking, in particular wealth management. Asset management and investment advice are important businesses for Swiss banks. Swiss banks are estimated to have a 27 per cent share of the world market for cross-border wealth management business. As of 31 December 2009, the assets managed by Swiss banks amounted to an aggregate of CHF 5.6 trillion. Switzerland's low nominal interest rates, comparatively low transaction costs and large base of private and institutional investors attract, despite the financial crisis and the banking secrecy discussions, many high-quality foreign issuers of equity and debt securities and derivative instruments.

As Switzerland is not a member state of the European Union or the European Economic Area, it is not bound by EU capital markets legislation. This leaves Switzerland with a certain autonomy to regulate its capital market as it sees fit.

The Financial Market Supervisory Authority (FINMA), which is, *inter alia*, the supervisory authority for banks, stock exchanges, securities dealers and collective investment schemes, has a broad remit and the power to issue rules and regulations to flesh out legislation. There is, however, no regulatory authority for public offerings of securities (other than collective investment schemes) in Switzerland (see section 2.1).

Currently, there is no comprehensive federal act that would regulate the Swiss capital market in its entirety. The most important pieces of legislation are: the Federal Stock Exchange Act (SESTA), which applies to Swiss exchanges, securities dealers, stock exchange trading and takeover offers; the Federal Banking Act (the Banking Act); and the Federal Act on Collective Investment Schemes (CISA) (see section 6). The issuing of equity and debt securities is subject to the Federal Code of Obligations (the CO), while the listing of securities at the main Swiss exchange, the SIX Swiss Exchange (the SIX), is governed by the SIX listing rules (the SIX LR).

In Switzerland, there are three major regulated exchanges: the SIX (the principal trading platform in Switzerland for equity and debt securities), EUREX (the automated trading platform for standardised derivative instruments) and Scoach (the trading platform for structured products). In 2009, the turnover of the SIX and of Scoach amounted to CHF 1.131 trillion (as at the end of November 2010 CHF 1.104 trillion); approximately 36,905 securities were listed at the SIX and Scoach as at the end of November 2010 (split up into approximately 329 equity securities, 2,045 debt securities (including funds) and 34,531 derivatives). Out of the 276 listed companies, approximately two-thirds are Swiss. EUREX is the world's leading derivatives exchange with 1.68 billion contract trades in 2009 (as at the end of November 2010: 1.77 billion).

Financial instruments specifically tailored to the requirements of an individual counterparty are not considered securities under the SESTA. Since Switzerland has no compulsory exchange trading rule (*Börsenzwang*), securities may also be traded off-exchange. In addition, derivatives, which are not standardised for mass trading but tailor-made, are traded over the counter (OTC). The OTC markets are not subject to any specific supervision or regulation. In these markets, the rights and duties of the market participants are subject to the general rules of contract law and obligations based on the participant's special status (eg securities dealer in the meaning of the SESTA).

2.   FUNDRAISING
2.1 General
Compared with other jurisdictions, the process of offering equity or debt securities in Switzerland is fairly informal, due to a lenient regulatory framework. A more comprehensive regime applies if such securities are listed at the SIX (see section 3), or if units of collective investment schemes are offered or distributed (see section 6). In particular, as long as equity and debt securities are not listed at the SIX, their public offering is not subject to authorisation by, or registration with, any governmental or self-regulatory body (except that newly issued shares of Swiss companies need to be registered with the competent commercial register, which is no more than a formality).

Debt securities are normally issued in bearer form; equity securities are in either bearer or registered form. The issuance of physical certificates is still customary for debt securities (typically as global certificates) but as for equity securities, uncertificated securities (*Wertrechte*) have become the market standard. Listed securities typically qualify as book-entry securities (*Bucheffekten*) under the Federal Act on Book-Entry Securities (BESA). There are no foreign exchange restrictions or controls applying to the offering of equity or debt securities in Switzerland.

2.2 Disclosure requirements and issuance prospectus
With regard to a public offering of equity or debt securities in Switzerland, the issuer is obliged by law to prepare an issuance prospectus in accordance with the CO (*Emissionsprospekt*). The issuance of certain debt securities, in particular those issued by non-Swiss issuers and denominated in Swiss francs, may also be subject to the Directive on Notes of Foreign Borrowers of May 2001 of the Swiss Bankers Association. Even though, in practice, derivatives are usually offered publicly on the basis of an information memorandum or similar offering document, the disclosure requirements of Swiss law do not per se apply to the issue of derivatives. Since 2007, special

rules apply to the public offering of structured products (see section 6.5).

Unlike other jurisdictions, Swiss law does not contain a clear definition of a public offering of equity or debt securities or of a private placement exemption for the offering of such securities. A public offering of equity or debt securities is generally viewed as an offering made to an indefinite number of investors. An offering is deemed to be private if it is addressed to a limited circle of persons. There is no numerical statutory threshold that must not be exceeded in order to keep the private character of a placement. However, in practice, a safe harbour is often assumed for offerings addressed to not more than 20 selected ('hand-picked') potential investors. The focus in this context is always on the end-investors rather than on the financial intermediaries such as the underwriters.

According to the CO, the following information must be disclosed in an issuance prospectus:

- the content of the entry in the commercial register of the issuer;
- the amount and composition of the issuer's share capital (including number, nominal value and type of shares as well as preferential rights of certain categories of shares, if any);
- provisions in the articles of incorporation concerning the issuer's authorised or conditional share capital;
- the number of profit-sharing certificates and the rights connected therewith;
- the issuer's latest annual statutory financial statements and the consolidated financial statements with the auditors' reports, and, if the closing of the balance sheet dates back more than six months (which is, in practice, extended to nine months), interim statutory and consolidated financial statements (which do not need to be audited);
- dividends paid during the last five years or since the date of incorporation;
- the resolution on the issue of the securities; and
- the terms and conditions of the debt securities (in the case of debt securities only).

It follows from this list that the statutory disclosure requirements for a Swiss issuance prospectus are relatively basic. In recent years, however, issuers have started to include additional information in their issuance prospectuses in order to meet the expectations of investors (who are often used to more comprehensive international standards) and to avoid prospectus liability claims (see sections 2.3 and 2.4).

Although not explicitly stated in Swiss law, the general view is that an issuance prospectus must only be updated until the end of the subscription period when issuing equity or debt securities. In the Swiss market, however, underwriting agreements for equity securities often provide that the updating duty lasts until the closing date.

2.3 Prospectus liability

The applicable Swiss rules on prospectus liability set forth, in essence, that anyone who intentionally or negligently participates in the drafting of an incomplete, incorrect or misleading issuance prospectus is liable for damages, provided that there is a direct causal link between the misstatement or omission in the prospectus and the damage suffered by the investor. A prospectus is incomplete if the statutory disclosure requirements are not met, ie, if there is no prospectus at all where required by law, or if it contains only part of the required information. It is misleading if facts material to the investment decision are omitted.

Potential plaintiffs in prospectus liability suits are all persons, in particular the initial subscribers and subsequent purchasers of the equity or debt securities, who suffered damages as a result of a violation of the disclosure requirements. Potential defendants include the issuer itself, its directors and senior (and potentially other) officers, the auditors, the underwriters and the advisers to any of them.

Swiss law does not detail the specific measures to be taken to ensure that the issuance prospectus is not incomplete, incorrect or misleading. In practice, the due diligence procedure for the issue of straight debt securities is rather simple, contrary to the due diligence procedure for the issue of equity securities (including equity-linked debt securities such as convertibles), which follows international standards. As a general guideline, the issuer must ensure that the process followed in the preparation of the issuance prospectus is a sound one. This includes mechanisms ensuring: (i) that all information is provided which is required by law and which a reasonable investor may expect to be disclosed in the prospectus in light of their potential investment; (ii) the correctness of the information; and (iii) a presentation of the information giving a true and fair view of the situation of the issuer.

In a decision of 2002, the Swiss Supreme Court explicitly accepted a due-diligence defence brought forward by the Swiss lead-manager of a foreign bond issuer who was in default. This means that persons who are potentially subject to a prospectus liability may rely on advice given by experts such as lawyers and accountants.

2.4 Prospectus liability in an international context

Based on the Federal Act on Private International Law (PILA), prospectus liability claims relating to a public offering of equity or debt securities in Switzerland may be filed with the Swiss courts at the place where the issue of the securities took place. This place of jurisdiction is mandatory.

The PILA further provides that claims arising from the public issue of equity or debt securities by means of a prospectus, circular or similar publication are governed by the law applicable to the issuer or by the law of the state where the offering was made (ie, Swiss law when the offering is made in Switzerland). This provision offers a potential plaintiff in a prospectus liability suit the right to choose the more favourable law and has the effect that a prospectus prepared in connection with a cross-border issue of equity or debt securities has to follow the standards of the jurisdiction of the issuer or, if more stringent, of the place where the securities are being offered.

3. SIX LISTING

3.1 General

The SIX, the main stock exchange in Switzerland (see section 1), has six trading segments (called 'standards' since the entry into force of the new listing rules of the SIX): (i) the main standard, used for listing and trading of most exchange-traded products (ie, equity securities, bonds and derivatives); (ii) the domestic standard (the former SIX local caps segment); (iii) the standard for investment companies; (iv) the standard for real estate companies; (v) the standard for collective investment schemes (including exchange-traded funds); and (vi) the standard for global depository receipts. Until 2009, the Swiss blue chip companies comprising the Swiss Market Index (SMI) as well as the companies comprising the Swiss share index with capped weightings (SLI) were listed at the SIX, but traded at the virt-x Exchange Limited (called SWX Europe since 3 May 2008), which was located in London and supervised by the UK Financial Services Authority. In 2009, the SIX took the decision to reunify the share trading on the SIX in Zurich, which led to a 'repatriation' of the trading in the shares of SMI and SLI companies.

The listing of securities at the SIX is governed by the SIX LR and its implementing rules and regulations. On 1 July 2009, a new set of SIX LR came into effect. The primary objective of this revision was to streamline the structure of the previous rules and regulations and to bring them in line with today's capital market practice in order to ensure an easier application in practice. The SIX LR consist of the following three main sets of rules: (i) the Listing Rules (LR) contain general provisions and govern the listing of equity securities at the SIX; (ii) the Additional Rules for the Listing of Bonds supplement the LR with regard to bonds, convertibles, bonds with warrants, asset-backed securities and loan participation notes; and finally (iii) the Additional Rules for the Listing of Derivatives supplement the LR with regard to derivatives.

Until 2009, the SIX LR were administered by the SIX Admission Board, which also decided on the admission of securities and supervised the issuers' compliance with the continuing obligations following listing. In the context of a reorganisation of the SIX at the beginning of 2009, the SIX Admission Board was replaced by two separate bodies, the Regulatory Board and the SIX Exchange Regulation. The Regulatory Board acts as rule-setting body for issuers and participants. The SIX Exchange Regulation is responsible for the listing of securities at the SIX and acts as surveillance and enforcement body in this regard.

3.2 Requirements relating to issuers

In order to be authorised to list its securities at the SIX, an issuer (or, alternatively, a third party acting as guarantor) must have existed as a company for at least three years and presented its annual accounts for the three complete financial years preceding the submission of the listing application. Exemptions from this three-year rule may be granted, *inter alia*, for: (i) mergers, spin-offs and other transactions in which a pre-existing company or portions thereof are continued as commercial entities; (ii) issuers of asset-backed securities; or (iii) so-called young companies, ie, companies that have not yet been able to present financial statements for the indicated period of time but nonetheless wish to tap the capital market in order to finance their strategy for growth.

Furthermore, the SIX LR set forth rules with regard to the appointment of the issuer's auditors. In addition, the issuer's capital resources (*ausgewiesenes Eigenkapital*) must amount to at least CHF 25 million. Special rules apply to issuers of derivative securities and to sovereign issuers.

3.3 Requirements relating to securities

The SIX LR set forth, *inter alia*, requirements regarding tradability, denomination and clearing and settlement of the securities. In addition, the SIX LR contain specific provisions for each of equity, debt and derivative securities. For instance, equity securities must have reached an adequate level of free float by the time of listing, meaning in essence that at least 25 per cent of the issuer's outstanding equity securities (corresponding to at least CHF 25 million) are held by the public. Furthermore, the minimum nominal amount of a bond issuance is CHF 20 million.

Bonds and derivative securities may be listed at the SIX as long as their terms and conditions are subject to the laws of any member state of the Organisation for Economic Cooperation and Development (OECD) (or of any other jurisdiction recognised by the SIX upon request). There is no requirement to provide for a place of jurisdiction in Switzerland in the terms and conditions, provided that a place of jurisdiction has been designated in the country whose legal system is applicable to the issued bonds or derivative securities (for prospectus liability claims, however, see sections 2.3 and 2.4).

3.4 Listing prospectus and listing notice

An issuer intending to have its equity, debt or derivative securities listed at the SIX is required to prepare and publish a listing prospectus in German, French, Italian or English. Such a prospectus must provide sufficient information for knowledgeable investors to reach an informed assessment of the assets and liabilities, financial position, profits and losses and prospects of the issuer, as well as the rights attached to the securities. In addition, any special risks need to be disclosed.

The listing prospectus must contain information on, *inter alia*, the issuer, the guarantor (if any), the securities, and the persons or companies responsible for the contents of the prospectus. The precise scope of the information to be furnished is set out in the prospectus disclosure schemes A to F, which have been drawn up for the different kinds of securities and issuers (ie scheme A for equity securities, scheme B for investment companies, scheme C for real estate companies, scheme D for global depository receipts, scheme E for bonds and scheme F for derivative securities). In the case of equity securities, as a rule, financial information for the three business years prior to the listing must be included, and, if more than nine months have passed since the last balance sheet date, the issuer must also include semi-annual interim financial statements. For the listing of debt securities, financial information for only two previous business years is required, and there is no obligation to provide interim financial statements. As to the accounting standards acceptable to the SIX, see section 4.1.

There are certain relief provisions. For example, no prospectus is required if equity securities are to be listed which lead to an increase of the issuer's share capital of less than 10 per cent over a period of 12 months or which have been issued in connection with an employee stock option plan.

The listing prospectus must be published no later than on the day of the listing.

In the case of debt or derivative securities, the prospectus may take the form of a stand-alone prospectus, or alternatively an issuance programme (ie medium term note (MTN)-programmes subject to Swiss or foreign law). Once such an issuance programme has been approved by the SIX, it remains valid for 12 months; the listing of tranches under such programmes then merely requires the submission of a pricing supplement. Foreign issuance programmes (ie programmes not approved by the SIX) do not qualify for this purpose. Hence, from a SIX perspective, an issuance under a foreign issuance programme is deemed a stand-alone issue.

Since December 2008, the publication of a listing notice is no longer required for the issuance of debt and derivative securities. Thus, there is only an obligation to publish a listing notice in the case of equity securities. Such a listing notice may be published in German, French, Italian or English in either printed or electronic form. The SIX offers the opportunity to post the listing notices on its webpage (*www.six-swiss-exchange.com*).

3.5 Listing procedure

Listing at the SIX requires a listing application to be lodged with the SIX in German, French, Italian or English, normally no later than 20 stock exchange days prior to the date scheduled for listing. In addition, the issuer must, *inter alia*, provide a declaration that the listing prospectus is complete, and that there has been no material deterioration of its financial situation since the publication of the listing prospectus. For first-time SIX issuers of debt securities and derivatives, a new pre-approval system was implemented in 2009. In addition, issuers (and guarantors, if any) must sign a declaration of consent in respect of legal proceedings provided for in the SIX LR, in particular the arbitration clause.

Following submission, the SIX examines the application on the basis of the documents provided, and approves it if the SIX LR are complied with. Its review is merely formal in the sense that it only reviews the completeness, not the correctness, of the information submitted to it.

Debt and derivative securities intended for listing may be admitted provisionally to trading at the SIX. Such provisional trading may begin the day (in the case of derivatives) or three days (in the case of bonds) after the respective application has been lodged via the SIX electronic platform ('internet-based listing'). The formal listing application normally needs to be lodged within two months upon commencement of provisional trading.

3.6 SIX Swiss Exchange – Sponsored Segment
The SIX Swiss Exchange – Sponsored Segment enables SIX participants ('sponsoring securities dealers') to initiate trading in equity securities of domestic or foreign issuers that have a primary listing on a stock exchange recognised by the Regulatory Board. Admission to trading in this segment Switzerland does not constitute a listing, so no listing prospectus is required. Each sponsoring securities dealer may lodge an application for the admission of equity securities to trading in this segment. If and to the extent disclosure and reporting requirements apply, they have to be complied with by the relevant sponsoring securities dealer, and not by the issuer. The rules on ad hoc publicity (see section 4.2) are not applicable.

4. ONGOING COMPLIANCE REQUIREMENTS
4.1 Obligation to lodge financial documents
The most important financial disclosure obligations are set out in the CO and the SIX LR. Further disclosure rules apply to banks and securities dealers.

Under the CO, a company has to prepare an annual report, which includes, *inter alia*, the audited annual consolidated (if required) and the statutory company financial statements (including profit and loss statement, balance sheet and notes). In addition, the CO requires Swiss companies that are listed on a stock exchange to disclose in their financial statements any shareholders whose participation exceeds 5 per cent of the voting rights (see also section 4.4). This financial information is available to the shareholders of Swiss companies but, as a matter of Swiss law, not to the holders of debt securities of Swiss or non-Swiss issuers unless the debt securities are listed. However, this information right is, at least with respect to certain debt securities of non-Swiss issuers, indirectly warranted through the Directive on Notes of Foreign Borrowers of the Swiss Bankers Association.

Further, companies whose securities are listed at the SIX (irrespective of whether they are incorporated in Switzerland or not) have to comply with the financial disclosure obligations of the SIX LR. Swiss issuers whose equity securities are listed at the SIX main standard must use International Financial Reporting Standards (IFRS) or US Generally Accepted Accounting Principles (GAAP). Swiss issuers of securities listed on the domestic standard, the standard for investment companies or the standard for real estate companies and issuers of listed debt or derivative securities continue to be allowed to use Swiss GAAP FER, the Swiss accounting standards. Foreign issuers whose equity, debt or derivative securities are listed at the SIX may use their home country standards, provided that these standards have been recognised by the Regulatory Board (such as IFRS, US GAAP, EU and EEA countries' accounting standards or the accounting principles of Australia, New Zealand, Japan, Canada and South Africa). With regards to foreign issuers of debt securities, standards of additional jurisdictions may be admitted if the respective accounting principles provide for a 'true and fair view' in accordance with the SIX LR and the differences between the applied accounting standards and IFRS or US GAAP are sufficiently explained in the listing prospectus and in the annual reports.

Annual financial statements of listed companies must be submitted to the SIX no later than four months after the close of the respective financial year. Semi-annual financial statements (which must be prepared by issuers of equity securities) have to be submitted to the SIX no later than three months after the close of the respective period. Further special provisions apply to real estate companies, investment companies and to global depository receipts.

4.2 Disclosure of price-sensitive facts

The SIX LR provide for an ad hoc publicity requirement. An issuer must inform the market of any price-sensitive facts within the scope of its activities. Facts qualify as price-sensitive when they are capable of triggering a significant price change.

According to the SIX Exchange Regulation, occurrences which usually require immediate disclosure include:

- mergers, substantial acquisitions or dispositions, or major organisational changes;
- material changes in the issuer's earnings;
- board decisions proposing a suspension of or a drastic reduction in dividend payments, illiquidity or suspension of payments;
- important changes in the normal course of the issuer's business; and
- changes in the board of directors, senior corporate management or auditors.

The issuer has to disclose price-sensitive facts as soon as it becomes aware of their existence. The release may only be deferred if such facts are based on a plan or decision of the issuer, and if disclosure would prejudice the issuer's legitimate interests. In this case, the issuer must make sure that the information is kept confidential.

4.3 Disclosure of corporate governance information and management transactions

The SIX Corporate Governance Directive requires Swiss issuers to disclose important information on the management and control mechanisms at the highest corporate level in their annual report. The Directive also applies to issuers not incorporated in Switzerland but having their securities listed only at the SIX and not in their home country.

Issuers must provide information, *inter alia*, on broad categories of information such as group and capital structure, board of directors, auditors, shareholder participation rights, change of control or defensive measures, information policy etc in accordance with the principle 'comply or explain': if the issuer decides not to disclose certain information, it must state the reason(s) why.

Based on Article 663b bis CO on the disclosure of board and management compensation of listed companies, the compensation packages of each of the members of the board as well as the highest total compensation package among the members of senior management has to be disclosed separately. That information is to be included in the (audited) notes to the financial statements.

Based on Article 56 SIX LR the SIX Directive on the Disclosure of Management Transactions imposes obligations on listed issuers to disclose transactions concluded by the members of the board of directors and senior management in the respective issuer's equity securities, convertible and purchase rights thereon and other financial instruments whose prices are largely affected by the issuer's own equity securities.

Each issuer has to ensure that its members of the board and senior management report such transactions to the issuer within two trading days. If the overall amount of the transactions concluded by an individual in one calendar month exceeds CHF 100,000, the issuer has to notify the SIX, within two trading days, of the name and corporate function of the respective person and the specifics of the sale or purchase transaction. The SIX will then publish the report on its website but without mentioning the individual's name. If the per person threshold amount of CHF 100,000 is not exceeded in a given calendar month, those transactions are solely subject to regular monthly reporting to be filed by the issuer with the SIX. On 1 April 2011, revised SIX regulations will enter into force which include the following two main points: (i) the abolition of the above mentioned minimum threshold of CHF 100,000 for the publication of transaction notices; and (ii) the extension of the publication deadline for issuers from two to three trading days.

4.4 Disclosure of substantial shareholdings

Under the SESTA (as revised per 1 December 2007), a shareholder has to disclose its shareholdings if it acquires or sells shares of a company incorporated and listed in Switzerland and thereby attains, falls below or exceeds the percentages of 3, 5, 10, 15, 20, 25, 33.33, 50 or 66.66 of that company's voting rights. This disclosure obligation also applies to beneficial owners indirectly acquiring or selling stakes in Swiss companies listed in Switzerland, and to shareholders acting in concert or as an organised group. In the case of a group (eg, a group of companies), its holdings can be disclosed in the aggregate and do not need to be specified by each individual group member (black-box-principle). Furthermore, certain derivative transactions such as the acquisition or disposal of financial instruments (i) whose terms provide for or allow physical settlement (eg, call options and conversion rights or put options) or (ii) whose terms provide for or allow cash settlement, as well as other differential transactions (such as contracts for difference and financial futures) must also be disclosed if the holdings of these financial instruments (together with shares) reach, fall below or exceed the statutory thresholds.

The obligation to notify is triggered as soon as the (contractual) commitment to acquire or sell the shares is entered into. Hence, an actual transfer of share ownership is not required. The shareholder must notify the Disclosure Office of the SIX and the relevant company within four trading days following the triggering event. The company in turn has the duty to publish the received information within another two trading days. As recent prominent cases have shown, non-compliance with the requirements is sanctioned and enforced by way of fines. An additional sanction in the event of non-compliance with the disclosure rules may be the suspension of the voting rights of the acquired shares for up to five years.

5. INSIDER TRADING AND PRICE MANIPULATION

5.1 Insider trading

According to the Swiss Federal Criminal Code ('Criminal Code'), the abuse of important confidential information concerning a company listed at a Swiss exchange is a criminal offence if it can be foreseen that the abused information will significantly influence the price of securities traded on a Swiss exchange. This provision only applies to persons having access to such confidential information due to a professional or official function and being aware of the confidential nature of the information ('insider'), or to a tippee who has received such information from an insider. Banks, securities dealers, collective investment schemes and asset managers of collective investment schemes subject to FINMA's supervision have to comply with further obligations as set out in FINMA's Market Behaviour Rules for the Securities Market.

Members of the board of directors, managers and auditors of a company or its controlling company or a company under its control can all qualify as insiders. Shareholders of a company are not deemed to be insiders unless they are de facto board members due to their effective influence on the company. Persons who actually create the confidential information (eg, a person intending to take over another company; a company intending to buy its shares back) do not qualify as insiders with regard to that specific information. Agents of the company such as lawyers, tax consultants, financial advisers and underwriters may also qualify as insiders if they gain access to confidential information by virtue of their mandate. Any person who obtains confidential information from an insider may be punished as a tippee in the case of an abuse of such information.

Insider trading necessarily relates to confidential information regarding certain facts, as opposed to mere speculation, projections or rumours. With the abolition of clause 3 of Article 161 Criminal Code (which restricted the notion of 'facts' to capital increases, mergers and similar events) on 1 October 2008, the scope of application of insider regulation was expanded significantly. It is no longer the nature of the information that is relevant but its confidentiality and whether it can be foreseen that the abused information will significantly influence the price of securities traded on a Swiss stock exchange. The precise scope of application has to be defined by practice and jurisprudence. As a general rule, facts which must be disclosed under the ad hoc publicity provisions (see section 4.2) also qualify as relevant facts under Article 161 Criminal Code. However, since the SIX has adopted a very broad and to some extent even formalistic view of the notion of facts, it is questionable whether the SIX interpretation of facts under the ad hoc publicity and the notion of facts under Article 161 Criminal Code are in all instances congruent. In addition, the information must be confidential and its disclosure must presumably and significantly influence the price of the securities on the exchange.

The offence is completed if the confidential information is abused by the insider or the tippee for a financial profit. However, insider trading is only punishable if the insider and/or the tippee wilfully and knowingly abuse(s) the confidential information with the intention of enriching themselves or another person. Negligent behaviour is not a criminal offence under the respective provision of the Criminal Code.

Insider regulation is in the process of being revised and a draft law shall be presented in spring 2011. The revised law shall substantially expand the scope of insider regulation and introduce a general market supervision. All market manipulation shall thereby be prohibited for all market participants. This shall mean that in future non-supervised entities, such as hedge funds and private investors, shall also be subject to partial supervision by FINMA.

5.2 Price manipulation
Pursuant to the Criminal Code, two types of behaviour are punishable as price manipulation if made with respect to securities traded at a Swiss exchange:
- First, disseminating misleading information with the intent to manipulate the price of listed securities ('market rigging'). If the perpetrator does not actively engage in the manipulative behaviour but omits to act (eg, to inform the authorities of the company's over-indebtedness in order not to influence the securities' price), such omission may only be punished as price manipulation if there is a legal or contractual obligation to act.
- Second, conducting sham transactions, specifically 'wash sales' and matched orders. The Criminal Code defines these transactions as executions of sales and purchases of securities that are directly or indirectly made on account of the same person or a number of persons who are associated for such a purpose ('pool').

Other behaviour by which the price of securities may be influenced, intentionally or unintentionally, does not qualify as price manipulation (eg, price stabilisation measures which do not amount to one of the two criminal offences described above, sham offerings and immobilisation of a certain amount of securities ('parking'). Such behaviour may, however, be prosecuted as fraud.

Any individual may qualify as a price manipulator. Price manipulation is only a criminal offence if the perpetrator acts wilfully and knowingly with intent to both significantly influence the price of securities and make an illegal profit.

5.3 Proposed modification of insider trading and price manipulation rules
In January 2010, the Swiss Federal Council released a consultation paper on a modification of certain provisions related to the trading in securities, including on insider trading and price manipulation. Apart from a new

enforcement regime that shall give FINMA the competence to start an investigation when there is an indication of a violation of insider trading or price manipulation provisions and to take action against offenders even if they are not subject to supervision by FINMA, it seems noteworthy that, under the proposed modifications, shareholders may qualify as insiders and that the scope of the insider regulations shall be extended to OTC products relating to a security listed on a Swiss stock exchange.

6. COLLECTIVE INVESTMENT SCHEMES AND STRUCTURED PRODUCTS

6.1 General

On 31 October 2010, 1,400 Swiss and 5,745 foreign collective investment schemes (including sub-funds of umbrella funds) were approved for distribution by the FINMA in Switzerland. Most of the foreign vehicles approved in Switzerland are domiciled in Luxembourg and have Swiss banks or financial groups as promoters. Furthermore, there is a statistically not evaluated, substantial number of foreign collective investment schemes that are only offered to qualified investors in Switzerland and which, therefore, require no FINMA-authorisation. This makes Switzerland one of the most important markets for the distribution of investment funds and similar products in the world.

6.2 Legal forms

The CISA fundamentally distinguishes between open-ended and closed-ended collective investment schemes, depending on whether or not an investor has the right to have its shares or units redeemed at their net asset value. Although in principle applicable to all types of collective investment schemes, Swiss in-house collective investment portfolios of banks and securities dealers as well as Swiss investment foundations, ie, a specific type of collective investment vehicle for pension funds, remain outside the scope of the CISA. Public advertisement for in-house collective investment portfolios continues to be prohibited.

The vast majority of Swiss collective investment schemes are set up in open-ended contractual form which was, prior to the enactment of the CISA, the only admitted legal form. They can be established for portfolios comprising securities, real estate, other traditional investments and alternative investments.

The alternative open-ended legal form created by the CISA is the *société d'investissement à capital variable* (SICAV). In essence, the Swiss SICAV is based on Swiss stock company law; however, with a number of important exceptions in order to meet the needs of a corporate investment scheme with a variable share capital, such as in particular the provisions on capital increases and decreases. The purpose of the SICAV is confined to the collective management of its own assets. The minimum share capital upon incorporation must amount to CHF 250,000. Shares have no nominal value and need to be fully paid in. The CISA further provides that there are two categories of shares:

promoter shares and investor shares. Each share carries one vote, except that the promoters have the exclusive right to decide upon the SICAV's dissolution. Like in other jurisdictions, Swiss SICAVs are construed either as self-managed or as not self-managed. The Swiss SICAV was treated rather with reserve in practice. Up to 31 October 2010, the FINMA had authorised 19 SICAVs.

The CISA provides two legal forms for closed-ended collective investment schemes, the *société d'investissement à capital fixe* (SICAF) and the limited partnership (LP). SICAFs are, however, not subject to the CISA if they are either listed at a Swiss exchange or reserved for qualified investors. Mainly for tax reasons, the introduction of the SICAF was not a success, and not a single SICAF had been licensed by the FINMA up to 31 October 2010.

The LP is intended for investments in risk capital (private equity) and is reserved for qualified investors. To a large extent, the applicable provisions follow the rules of Swiss company law on the (ordinary) limited partnership. However, while in the ordinary LP the general partner (ie the partner with unlimited liability) needs to be an individual, in an LP for collective investments the general partner must be a stock company incorporated in Switzerland. The FINMA had granted 13 LP licences up to 31 October 2010. A reason for the hesitation in establishing Swiss LPs is that the performance-related components of the fund managers' fees (carried interest) is unclear and – depending upon the structuring – can fully or partially be treated as taxable income in Switzerland. This issue is currently the object of further reflections and discussions both at cantonal and federal levels.

6.3 Foreign collective investment schemes

Foreign collective investment schemes may not be publicly advertised, in or from Switzerland, unless they have been formally approved by the FINMA. Public advertising means advertising addressed to the public and is interpreted by the FINMA very broadly. Such advertising is deemed public regardless of the number of (potential) investors to whom the advertising is directed. Registration with the FINMA requires, among other things, adequate supervision in the fund's home-country, which to date has been acknowledged by the FINMA for collective investment schemes domiciled in EU and EEA member states, Jersey, Guernsey, and the US. Foreign funds qualifying as undertakings for collective investments in transferable securities (UCITS) are subject to simplified registration proceedings.

Under the CISA regime, there is no public advertising, however – and hence no FINMA-authorisation requirement – if collective investment schemes are exclusively offered to qualified investors by methods that are customary for this market (such as personal contacts or road shows). Qualified investors include, among others, regulated financial intermediaries and insurance institutions, public entities and pension funds with professional treasury operations, high net worth individuals with bankable assets of at least CHF 2 million, and investors having concluded a written asset management agreement with a regulated financial intermediary. Independent asset managers and investors who concluded a written asset management agreement are also deemed 'qualified' if certain conditions are fulfilled.

6.4 Regulation of asset managers

The CISA also applies to asset managers of collective investment schemes. However, only asset managers of Swiss collective investment schemes are mandatorily subject to FINMA-authorisation. Swiss asset managers of foreign collective investment schemes may apply for FINMA-authorisation if this is required under foreign legislation, and if the foreign vehicles that they manage are subject to adequate supervision abroad. This right primarily aims at allowing Swiss asset managers to manage UCITS-funds.

Further, a delegation to an asset manager incorporated abroad is only permissible if the foreign asset manager is subject to adequate supervision and is qualified to conduct the asset management properly. As a rule, asset managers with the regulatory status of a bank domiciled in the OECD, Hong Kong or Singapore meet this standard. For other foreign asset managers, the applicant has to actually prove that the foreign asset manager is adequately supervised.

6.5 Regulation of structured products

The CISA also applies to structured products if they are publicly offered in or from Switzerland. Until the beginning of the financial crisis, the market for structured products had experienced a tremendous boom in Switzerland, which was discontinued in 2008 and 2009, especially after the Lehman collapse, but has taken up speed again in 2010.

There is no statutory definition of structured products. However, the CISA provides for a non-exhaustive list of examples, such as capital protected products, capped return products and certificates. Conversely, financial products which serve primarily a financing purpose (such as bonds or convertibles), or a risk transfer (such as collateralised debt obligations or asset-backed securities) do not qualify as structured products subject to the CISA. Equally, forward and option transactions are expressly not within the scope of the CISA.

Unlike in the case of collective investment schemes, the FINMA does not perform a product supervision over structured products. However, if structured products are offered by means of public advertising, their issuer, guarantor or distributor needs to be subject to the supervision of the FINMA as a bank, securities dealer or insurance company, or, alternatively, to the supervision of an equivalent foreign supervisory authority. If none of the issuer, guarantor or distributor is supervised by the FINMA, there needs to be at least a FINMA-supervised affiliate office in Switzerland, unless the structured product is listed at a Swiss stock exchange.

The CISA further provides that a so-called simplified prospectus is mandatory if structured products are offered publicly in or from Switzerland, describing the key features and risks of the product, and containing a disclaimer to the effect that the product is not subject to FINMA-supervision. No simplified prospectus is required if the product is listed at a Swiss stock exchange and, as a consequence, a listing prospectus has to be prepared. In 2007, the Swiss Bankers Association published its Guidelines on the Information of Investors regarding Structured Products which include details about the requisite content of the simplified prospectus.

7. PUBLIC TAKEOVERS

7.1 General

Public takeover offers are governed by the SESTA. The guiding principles are transparency, equality of treatment, the proper functioning of the capital markets and in particular the protection of the minority shareholders. Compliance with the takeover rules set by the SESTA and its implementing ordinances is ensured by the Federal Takeover Board (TOB) and the FINMA.

Whereas before the revision of the law on public takeovers on 1 January 2009 the TOB could only make non-binding recommendations, it is since then empowered to issue and enforce binding decisions. This aims at increasing the authority of the TOB as a first instance and, at the same time, at reducing the number of cases on appeal. Decisions of the TOB can be challenged before FINMA by means of an appeal. Such an appeal has to be filed within five trading days and generally has a suspensive effect.

7.2 Scope of takeover regulation

SESTA only applies to public takeover offers in relation to equity securities in Swiss target companies whose equity securities are listed on an exchange in Switzerland.

The relevant SESTA provisions regulate both public takeover offers (tender offers) by shareholders or third parties, and public offers by a company to repurchase its own shares (buyback offers):

* Public takeovers are offers publicly made to the shareholders of a target company to purchase or to exchange all or part of the equity securities in that company. Creeping tender offers (ie, non-public offers) are not regulated by the takeover rules of the SESTA as long as they do not lead to shareholdings in excess of 33.33 per cent of the voting rights in the target company (see section 7.3). However, due to the rules on the disclosure of substantial shareholdings (see section 4.4) an acquirer's possibilities to build up a major participation secretly are limited. Both friendly and hostile takeovers are subject to the SESTA rules.

* Public offers by a company to repurchase its own equity securities – including the announcement of such an intention – also constitute public takeover offers within the meaning of SESTA if more than 2 per cent of the share capital is repurchased. However, on certain conditions (most importantly, if the buyback relates to not more than 10 per cent of the company's share capital), the buyback offer does not have to comply with the provisions governing public takeover offers but is subject to a separate regime. In particular, a prospectus may not be necessary. Such buyback offers must, nevertheless, be notified to the TOB for an exemption via a reporting procedure. A new circular of the TOB on share buybacks took effect on 1 June 2010.

7.3 Mandatory takeover offers and opting-out clauses

Under the SESTA, anyone who directly, indirectly or acting in concert with third parties acquires shareholdings in a Swiss target company which exceed the threshold of 33.33 per cent of the voting rights is obliged to make a takeover offer to the remaining shareholders in order to acquire all listed equity securities of the company.

However, there is no obligation to make an offer if the threshold of 33.33 per cent is exceeded by the acquirer if and to the extent the articles of association of the target company provide otherwise. Thus, the shareholders' assembly of a company may, by amendment to the articles of association, increase the statutory threshold triggering the obligation to make an offer from 33.33 per cent of the voting rights up to a maximum of 49 per cent ('opting-up'), or even entirely abolish such a threshold ('opting-out'). A selective opting-out, ie, an opting-out in view of a specific offer, has, however, been qualified by TOB and FINMA as a non-permissible circumvention of the mandatory bid rules.

Today, approximately 19 per cent of Swiss companies listed at the SIX (but no SMI companies) make use of opting-out clauses, while approximately 5 per cent (including one SMI company) have chosen an opting-up clause.

7.4   Procedure of a public takeover

The procedure of a public takeover can be summarised as follows:

First, an offeror must prepare a prospectus containing detailed information on its offer (in particular on the offeror, the target company, the price, the type of financing, any (permissible) condition to the offer etc). The offer is then launched by publishing an advance announcement or directly the prospectus or a summary of it (with a reference to the prospectus) in several newspapers and in one of the electronic media specialising in stock market data. After a cooling-off period of 10 trading days, the offer normally remains open for 20 up to 40 trading days. Thereafter, the interim result of the offer has to be published and an additional acceptance period of 10 days starts when the offer is successful. This is followed by the calculation and publication of the result of the offer and of its settlement. If the offeror at that point holds more than 98 per cent of the voting rights of the target company, it may within three months petition the competent court to cancel the remaining outstanding equity securities against consideration ('squeeze-out' procedure). If the offeror has acquired 90 per cent but not 98 per cent of the voting rights of the target company, it may consider initiating a squeeze-out merger according to the Federal Merger Act of 2004.

Before the 2009 revision, only the bidder, persons acting in concert with the bidder, and the target company were granted the status of a party in the public takeover proceedings. The possibilities of other shareholders of the target company to participate in the proceedings were limited. Under the revised takeover law, shareholders holding a stake of at least 2 per cent of the voting rights (qualified shareholders) are granted the right to participate in the proceedings as a formal party. As a result, they enjoy full procedural guarantees, in particular the right to be heard including access to the records at the TOB, and the right to appeal. This also means that the procedure has become more complex and in some cases less predictable for a bidder and the other parties involved.

7.5 Pricing

Consideration can be effected in cash and/or equity securities; the offer may also provide for the shareholders' right to choose the type of consideration. In the case of a mandatory takeover bid (see section 7.3), the mechanism to determine the offer price is defined by mandatory law. It shall at least correspond to the volume-weighted average market price during the 60 trading days preceding the offer (or the advance announcement, as the case may be), and shall not be lower than 25 per cent of the highest price paid by the offeror for equity securities of the target company in the preceding 12 months. Within these statutory limits, an acquirer may pay a premium for the acquisition of a controlling block of shares. Following the publication of the offer, the offeror may still buy equity securities of the target company on the exchange. It is, however, obliged to notify the TOB and the SIX of every buy or sell transaction. Moreover, if the offeror, within a period of six months following the expiration of the additional acceptance period, acquires additional equity securities for a price that is higher than the price offered in its public offer, it is obliged to offer that better price to all shareholders ('best price rule').

7.6 Defensive measures against hostile takeovers

While the implementation of preventive defensive measures is admissible to a large extent prior to the launch of a tender offer, the SESTA prevents the board of directors, but not the shareholders' meeting, of a target company from resolving on new defensive measures thereafter. In addition, from the moment an offer (or its advance announcement) is published until the result is announced, the target company must notify the TOB in advance of any defensive measures it is considering.

As a general principle, the board of directors of the target company may not, during the offer, enter into any transactions having the effect of altering significantly the assets or liabilities of the target company. Consequently, measures such as 'scorched earth' (the sale or acquisition of assets at a value or price of more than 10 per cent of the company's balance sheet total), the sale or pledge of 'crown jewels' (assets that are explicitly designated by the offeror to constitute the main subject matter of the offer), the granting of 'golden parachutes' or a buyback of own shares or related financial instruments by the target company from the offeror against a premium ('greenmail') are not permissible. Defensive measures such as the 'Pac-Man defence' (the launch of an offer by the target company to acquire the attacking offeror) may only be permissible under certain conditions and if these measures do not significantly affect the assets of the target company.

The general assembly of shareholders, however, may still resolve on defensive measures once the offer has been submitted. The board may thus implement the measures authorised by the shareholders' assembly, provided that such authorisation is unambiguous and does not amount to a carte blanche for any defensive measures by the board of directors.

United States of America

Davis Polk & Wardwell John B Meade and Jake S Tyshow

1. INTRODUCTION

Since the adoption of the federal securities laws during the Great Depression, securities regulation in the United States has remained conceptually consistent until the 21st century, with the regulatory framework centred around a disclosure-based system to which lawmakers and regulators added in patches to meet the demands of developments in business and financial practices. The challenges presented by the global expansion of financial markets activity and the development of multiple important centres of liquidity in recent decades have produced two distinct, although not always complementary, trends in US securities regulation. On the one hand, global capital and information flows have prompted greater cooperation among securities regulators, as in the International Organisation of Securities Commissions (IOSCO), bilateral cooperation in enforcement through memoranda of understanding and increasing efforts by companies, exchanges and securities regulators to influence the securities regimes of other countries. On the other hand, the freedoms and technologies on which these trends depend have allowed globally-minded capital seekers to become increasingly selective about where they raise capital, putting US lawmakers and regulators in the position of having to compete for business with other countries while at the same time having to stretch the existing regulatory framework to protect investors by monitoring the globally disperse activities of large, widely held and economically significant corporations. The US, which still has the largest and most liquid capital markets in the world, has been a net exporter of securities regulation, but domestic securities reform has, in recent years, been increasingly informed by international pressures. Consequently, US regulators must now balance domestic political concerns with the ability to facilitate the needs of companies and investors in an increasingly mobile and competitive world. Their success or failure in doing so in the years to come will determine how influential a role the US regulatory framework plays in the global capital markets of the future.

The following chapter seeks to summarise the US securities regime, to place it within its domestic, historic and political context, and to note which features of US securities regulation are unique or unusual. Readers are invited to reach their own conclusions on which elements of US securities regulation should or could be updated and which might be an example or counter-example for the rest of the world.

2. GENERAL DESCRIPTION OF THE CAPITAL MARKETS

As noted, the US stock markets are the largest and most liquid in the world. Of fundamental importance, however, is not the absolute size of the markets but the fact that stock ownership in the United States is a middle-class affair. According to one recent Congressional study, approximately 50 per cent of American households own stock. The participation of the middle classes in the stock market, especially as a means to save for retirement in a world of increasing pension uncertainty, has historically meant that it was not politically or socially acceptable for the stock market game to be rigged. While in American society, more than in almost any other, it has historically been seen as acceptable that there are economic winners and losers, the view that winners are supposed to win through fair play remains strongly entrenched among the public. Therefore, in a world where the rules are not always followed, some are punished and with prison sentences that appear severe to those not accustomed to the American legal culture. A distinctive feature of US securities regulation is its emphasis on enforcement and the ability of multiple players – some political appointees and some private – to enforce the laws.

3. REGULATORY STRUCTURE

There was no federal regulation of securities until the Great Depression. Until then all securities regulation, like most economic regulation, had been left to state judges under common law and various state regulators, of which New York State, as the regulator of Wall Street, was the most powerful. It was only after the crash of 1929, when millions of ordinary people lost their savings and investments, and in the wake of widely followed congressional hearings exposing excessive and destructive Wall Street practices of the day, that Congress decided to regulate the securities markets. In 1933, the Securities Act (the Securities Act) was passed and in 1934 the Securities Exchange Act (the Exchange Act) was passed. At the same time, the Securities and Exchange Commission (SEC) was created to maintain the integrity and stability of the capital markets and protect investors from fraud.

The two Depression era statutes survived largely unchanged until 2002, with only minor modifications to address particular problems. The regulatory emphasis of those two statutes, when it came to securities offering and distribution, was heavily tilted towards disclosure rather than directives to companies on internal governance. Much of that changed with the Sarbanes-Oxley Act of 2002 (SOXA), the first major philosophical change in regulatory theory since the Depression-era statutes. In many ways, the Act was a panicked response by Congress to a middle-class revolt prompted by losses in the stock markets and corporate scandals resulting in mounting evidence that some among the managerial classes, aided by bankers, accountants and lawyers, had not been playing fair. At the same time the SEC, partly due to perceived staffing issues and partly because it was seen to be asleep at the wheel, lost prestige on Capitol Hill. The result was SOXA, a statute which for the first time placed direct regulatory governance requirements on companies. Moreover, Congress did not leave to the SEC the explicit or implicit direction to exempt foreign companies where appropriate. As a result, SOXA, and most especially the costly internal controls provision of section 404, has been under severe criticism from many quarters, not least from some US policymakers who are increasingly concerned over the statute's adverse impact on domestic capital formation and the global competitiveness of the US capital markets.

The legislative reaction to the 2008 credit crisis and the global meltdown in financial markets in the wake of Lehman Brothers' bankruptcy built further on SOXA's legacy. Although the impact of the crisis-induced legislative responses has fallen largely on the banking and financial sector, Congress took the opportunity to weight the securities laws more heavily against other would-be transgressors. Thus, the Dodd-Frank Wall Street Reform and Consumer Protection Act of 2010 (Dodd-Frank) marked not only the greatest legislative change to financial supervision since the 1930s but also tasked the SEC with writing rules that would discourage other types of perceived wrongdoing in areas that were previously viewed as being beyond the SEC's scope of expertise. Dodd-Frank's impact on the basic rules affecting the offering and distribution of most types of securities is likely to be relatively limited, although its impact on the effectiveness and independence of an understaffed SEC, responsible for writing scores of new regulations and carrying out Congressionally-mandated research projects over the next two years, remains to be seen.

The SEC is an 'independent' agency not under the direct control of the President or the executive branch. Its five commissioners, three of the President's party, two not, are nominated by the President for a set term, approved by the Senate, and may not be removed except for 'cause', which essentially means virtually impossible to remove. Of course, it is difficult to believe the SEC or other independent agencies are totally removed from political pressure, a fact reinforced by the post-2008 trend in SEC rules, guidance and enforcement actions being adopted by three-to-two votes of the commissioners along party lines. After all, Congress can hold public hearings and controls the budget, and the executive branch has its ways and means. But the SEC has historically been more distant from such pressure than many other regulators worldwide, a fact crucial to understanding the US system.

The two Depression-era statutes, among the first statutory codes drafted against a common law backdrop, are written broadly and, with the exception of certain provisions added by SOXA and Dodd-Frank, the SEC enjoys extensive powers to grant exemptive relief under each of the statutes it administers. The real power, therefore, lies with the interpreter and primary enforcer – the SEC – which issues rules and regulations implementing these statutes and also issues interpretations of and guidance on compliance with various provisions of the federal securities laws. The

SEC's regulatory rule-making takes place in a very open manner, with proposed rules subject to notice and comment by anyone who cares to participate and SEC open meetings broadcast via webcast. Additionally, the SEC manages the registration and disclosure system mandated by the Securities Act and the Exchange Act, and it regulates the activities of entities engaged in buying and selling securities and in investment management.

The SEC has five divisions, organised along functional lines. The Division of Corporate Finance oversees public disclosure of corporate information by issuers of securities. It reviews disclosure documents that public companies are required to file with the SEC, including registration statements for new securities offerings under the Securities Act, periodic reports under the Exchange Act, proxy materials, and materials required to be delivered to shareholders pursuant to tender offers and mergers and acquisitions. The Division of Trading and Markets regulates broker-dealers, securities exchanges, transfer agents, securities information processors and other major participants in the US securities markets. The Division of Investment Management regulates the mutual fund industry and examines statutory filings by such entities pursuant to the Investment Company Act and the Investment Advisers Act. The Enforcement Division is responsible for seeking consent decrees and fines, collecting investor claims funds and, where necessary, going to trial. Finally, the SEC's Division of Risk, Strategy and Financial Innovation was created in September 2009, largely in response to accusations in the aftermath of the financial crisis that the SEC lacked the expertise to regulate complex financial instruments. It is tasked with providing SEC commissioners with sophisticated analysis of systemic risk and economic issues, strategic research and financial innovation.

A key difference between the US system of securities regulation and that of many other countries is the existence of multiple enforcers of the law. As state law was replaced or pre-empted only where it was in direct conflict with the federal securities laws, the states retained a role in securities laws which created a situation of regulatory competition that continues today. The SEC is an active civil enforcer of the securities laws using broad powers to collect information from potential offenders and to enter into settlements, to collect fines and impose other sanctions, and to create claims funds for investors. The ability of private actors to enforce the law, such as wronged investors relying on the entrepreneurial plaintiff's bar to bring class actions, is also uniquely American. Dodd-Frank went some way to marrying the often incongruous public-private enforcement practices by providing for employees who manage to report evidence of their employers' securities laws breaches to the SEC to be rewarded with significant bounties payable out of the fines levied against those same employers by the SEC. Finally, the presence of state enforcers to act as regulatory competitors to the SEC in the area of enforcement, such as certain New York attorneys general, is also a unique feature of the American system. The enforcement culture is more intense and public than in most other jurisdictions, a fact that has come as an unwelcome surprise to many foreign companies in the last few years.

4. ISSUANCE OF NEW SECURITIES

In regulatory terms, there are two broad categories of securities offers and sales: those to the retail public, which are registered with the SEC, require payment of a filing fee and are, in many cases, subject to review by SEC staff; and private placements to limited numbers of sophisticated investors, which are not registered or subject to review by SEC staff.

4.1 Public offerings registered with the SEC

The general rule is that any public offer or sale of securities must be registered with the SEC unless a specific exemption applies. Once a registration statement is filed, it is typically subject to review by the SEC. A 'security' is defined broadly in legislation and case law. As well as common stock, stock options and debentures, the courts have found it to embrace limited partnerships, real estate syndications, notes issued by commercial and industrial companies, investments in citrus groves and oil drilling leases.

Until the SEC's securities offering reforms, adopted as of 1 December 2005, numerous procedural requirements had to be met prior to making any offering or sale of securities in the United States. Under current regulations, all public companies and underwriters of their securities are allowed to use any written materials once a preliminary prospectus is on file with the SEC, while large companies with a good reporting track record and at least $700 million in common equity float, known as 'well-known seasoned issuers' (WKSIs), can make written offers even before a preliminary prospectus is filed, so long as all such written materials are filed and are consistent with the preliminary prospectus that is ultimately filed (for debt offerings, an issuer will be able to qualify as a WKSI by having issued at least $1 billion in SEC-registered debt within the last three years and having filed its SEC reports on time in the past year). This ability to use what is known as a 'free writing prospectus' (a summary written document that meets the sales needs of the offering) is consistent with the securities offering practices of a number of other developed countries.

Most large issuers can extend written offers without delivering a preliminary prospectus and sales could be confirmed without the delivery of a final prospectus as long as an effective registration statement is on file with the SEC on the theory that 'access equals delivery'. Any correction or supplementary material information required to ensure that the preliminary prospectus is not misleading must now be provided to investors before the time at which a contract for the sale of securities is entered into by some other means, typically in the form of a 'free writing prospectus' that need only be filed after delivery. Under US regulations, initial public offering (IPO) companies and other unseasoned issuers are subject to a physical preliminary prospectus delivery requirement at the time that a written offer is made (a term sheet containing pricing and other material information that was not available at the time of delivery of the preliminary prospectus is typically delivered prior to the time that orders to purchase securities are confirmed). The prospectus, together with any issuer free writing prospectus and/or supplementary information, must contain 'full and fair' disclosure of all material information, ie, information that would allow a reasonable investor to make an informed investment decision about the issuer of a security, the offering and the security itself. The prospectus must not be misleading by omission. Once a company has registered securities with the SEC, it is considered a 'registrant' and becomes subject to the secondary trading rules, corporate governance and periodic reporting requirements under the Exchange Act.

Until recently, the disclosure gap between the United States requirements and the rest of the world was significant. That gap has narrowed considerably, either because local requirements have become substantially similar to US requirements (as in the EU) because of the IOSCO disclosure principles, or because US mutual and pension funds investing internationally have pressured companies to increase disclosure. In addition, major corporations worldwide find themselves operating more and more under a global standard.

All registration statements must disclose all material information and must contain or 'incorporate by reference' among other things: the description of the securities offered and the price at which they are offered; a business description of the company; a discussion of recent operating and financial performance and future prospects; risk factors that may affect the issuer's business, results of operations or financial condition or the value of the securities; exposure to market risk; disclosure of any material legal proceedings; disclosure of executive compensation and related party transactions; the plan of distribution in the offering; and audited financial statements (covering, in most cases, the most recently ended three fiscal years) together with the relevant auditors' reports. With some minor exceptions, the US disclosure requirements are very similar to the IOSCO standards.

In essence, regulation has been catching up with the practices of the securities industry, shifting from one of the review of offerings to the review of companies. The shift in emphasis from the regulation and review of primary offerings to the review and support of large companies with active secondary trading markets led to the creation in 1982 of what are known as 'shelf' registrations: certain companies that are already known to the market can pre-register and put up on the 'shelf' potential offerings of stock, debt and derivatives. Shelf registrations allow for offerings and sales in a 'takedown' at a moment's notice. Shelf registration statements, which are valid for three years after effectiveness, have become increasingly important and substantially all of the US Fortune 500 companies have an active shelf registration. By filing a registration statement including a base prospectus with the SEC and incorporating by reference its Exchange Act filings and other material information as it is released, a company can offer securities on short notice as financing needs and market opportunities present themselves merely by filing a prospectus supplement updating for all material information not included in or incorporated by reference into the base prospectus to the date of the takedown. Following the SEC's 2005 reforms, WKSIs are entitled to automatic shelf effectiveness upon filing, meaning that

WKSI shelf registration statements and shelf takedowns are not subject to review by the SEC. The shelf registration statements of non-WKSI issuers are still subject to SEC review, but once declared effective, shelf takedowns are not subject to SEC review.

In order to qualify for shelf registration of securities to be offered on a continuous or delayed basis or in 'at the market' offerings, a public company must be a 'seasoned issuer', meaning that it must be current in its Exchange Act filings for at least 12 months before filing the shelf registration statement, must not have defaulted on any debt or preferred stock since the end of its last fiscal year and must have securities held worldwide by non-affiliates with an aggregate market value of $75 million or more.

4.2 Exempt offerings

The other major types of securities placements in the United States are those which are 'exempt' from registration, of which the largest category is the private placement to sophisticated investors. It is worth noting that the US system of regulation differs from a number of other countries in that an exemption must exist both for the initial distribution and for any subsequent transfer of the securities. Most securities transactions are exempt from registration because they do not involve an issuer, underwriter or dealer as those terms are defined under the Securities Act, since the buyers and sellers are generally ordinary investors involved in secondary trading.

The statutory exemption for private placements is cryptic in that it contains only a few short words – 'not involving a public offering'. Given the existence of the 'put' (a statutory remedy that allows an investor to sell back a security to a company at the original purchase price for one year following purchase in the event that the company violates the registration requirements), and the very broad definition of underwriter, it is not surprising that market actors sought more specific interpretations from the SEC as modern capital markets developed in the aftermath of World War II. The legal technique that the SEC uses, called a 'safe harbour', is another unusual feature. Essentially, if a securities distribution or subsequent sale meets all of the formal and technical requirements of a safe harbour, the company, seller and buyer can be certain that their boat has reached a port in a storm. However, it does not necessarily follow that attempted compliance or other ways of making a private placement outside the safe harbour will necessarily be a public offering. Therefore, the safe harbour mechanic has left enormous room for market practice and legal judgment which, from time to time over the last 60 years, has been either officially adopted or repudiated by the SEC. The most frequently used safe harbours are those established pursuant to Regulation D, Rule 144A and Regulation S.

Regulation D exempts offerings made to an unlimited number of 'accredited investors', a term that embraces most institutions likely to invest in privately placed securities, and up to 35 other persons. No specific disclosure is required if an offering is only made to accredited investors, but the market practice for large offerings by companies which are not well known in the market is to provide information substantially equivalent to that included in a registered deal. No general solicitation or advertising of the offering is permitted and certain offering restrictions and specific policy on resales of the securities must be imposed. The key requirements to be an accredited investor have not changed for over two decades and what seemed like the kind of money only available to the super-sophisticated at that time (net worth of $1 million, or annual income of $200,000 or more during the last two years and a reasonable expectation of the same in the current year) has, by dint of inflation and increasing prosperity, been acquired by a much wider group.

The most internationally well-known private placement exemption is that provided by Rule 144A for resales to Qualified Institutional Buyers (generally, institutions that have $100 million or more invested in securities of unaffiliated issuers), or QIBs. Indeed, the terms '144A' and 'QIB' have passed into the lexicon of bankers and companies from around the world. As a technical matter, Rule 144A provides a resale exemption that effectively allows private placements to be underwritten and permits secondary trading in unregistered securities between QIBs. Rule 144A provides that an investment bank that immediately or otherwise resells securities acquired from an issuer in a private placement under Rule 144A will not be deemed a dealer or an underwriter under the Securities Act. Further, so long as the reselling institution reasonably believes that the purchasers of a security in a Rule 144A private placement are QIBs, the exemption will be preserved. Thus, in one regulation, both the initial distribution and subsequent transfers are permitted in the closed world of QIBs. Rule 144A contains publicity restrictions substantially identical to those prescribed under Regulation D and requires that the company must agree to provide certain current information to potential investors who request it (without limitation as to time). Although the Rule does not require a prospectus or information document to be delivered in connection with a sale, the market practice is to provide an offering circular to QIBs at the time of offer and the time of sale, in which the disclosure closely parallels the disclosure that would be made if the offering were registered. The SEC's 2005 reforms have lessened the need for Rule 144A transactions by WKSIs within the United States, and Rule 144A has become more and more identified as an international technique over recent years.

Regulation S provides a safe harbour for offshore offerings targeted at non-US persons. Regulation S is actually the successor to a series of market practices that developed in the late 1960s and early 1970s with respect to the Eurodollar bond market, then the key means to recycle petrodollars and the only cross-border securities market in the pre-euro days. The safe harbour was widely demanded by market participants, essentially to create clear rules on how long offshore dollar-denominated bonds needed to stay offshore before they could safely be bought by US investors without calling into question the offshore nature of the transaction. In today's world of global equity offerings, euro-based equity markets and other elements, it has gone far beyond its original purposes. To fall within the safe harbour, the offering must be made in an 'offshore transaction'. No directed selling efforts may be made in the US by the issuer, a distributor of the securities, their respective affiliates or any person acting for them and various restrictions on the manner of offering must be implemented depending on the type of securities offered and the type of issuer involved. Despite the suspicions expressed by some who did not understand the safe harbour technique, Regulation S was never an attempt by the SEC to regulate the world securities markets. Rather, it described clear rules about where the SEC would not regulate.

On the same day in 1991 that Rule 144A came into existence, Regulation S clarified and updated a number of SEC interpretations and market practices. The US private placement market has since grown exponentially. Internationally, the rules provided by Rule 144A and Regulation S, as well as the ability for one offering to be made under both rules at the same time (known as a 'side-by-side' transaction) has created a legal framework that permits foreign companies and US sophisticated investors to take advantage of the increasing depth of the global capital markets, most especially within the Eurozone, secure in the knowledge that they need not bother with US registration rules. One unintended consequence of the Rule 144A/Regulation S regulatory framework has been to create the conditions for international regulatory competition. In a business environment of global investing and the new liquidity and depth of the Euro markets, when US securities regulation creates unattractive conditions (as in Sarbanes-Oxley), the Rule 144A/Regulation S framework provides a way for foreign companies to reach US investors while avoiding the more burdensome elements of US securities regulation.

4.3 Foreign private issuers

The basic philosophy of the US securities laws and the SEC is one of national equivalence, which is to say that foreign companies are treated the same as US companies unless a specific exemption has been made to take account of the situation of the foreign company. This treatment contrasts and often conflicts with the EU principle of mutual recognition where the host country recognises and accepts the regulation by the home country, whatever that might be. The difference between these two principles can be expected to create increasing discord over the next few years unless there is substantial regulatory convergence. The SEC has adopted the IOSCO principles with respect to disclosure by foreign companies issuing securities outside of their home jurisdiction. Rearguard battles are being fought in areas such as the disclosure of executive compensation, but these are second order issues. The remaining area of contention is financial disclosure where, for registered offerings, the SEC still insists upon reconciliation to US Generally Accepted Accounting Principles (GAAP), except in certain limited but important circumstances. Since late 2007, the SEC has recognised International Financial Reporting Standards (IFRS) as issued by the International Accounting Standards Board (IASB) and no longer requires companies that report in IFRS as issued by the IASB, ie, most EU companies, to reconcile to US GAAP. The next major leap in the convergence of developed country disclosure standards is likely to be the adoption by the SEC of IFRS for US issuers, something the SEC is currently considering, albeit with little urgency given the more pressing demands of Dodd-Frank.

4.4 Offering publicity

As a legacy from the 1930s, the US securities laws until recently contained a number of outdated restrictions on publicity intended to limit the conditioning of the market for securities offerings. To the relief of those of us who make a living trying to describe these rules to international bankers and foreign companies, the SEC's 2005 reforms marked one of the first times when US securities regulators have been overt 'importers' of more modern international practices.

Under current regulations, all companies enjoy safe harbours for the publication of a broad range of 'non-prospectus' information including: the level of information that may be disclosed about a company and its business and the offering; the terms of the securities being offered; information about the underwriters; offering schedules; account opening procedures; and procedures for submitting initial indications of interest. In addition, Exchange Act reporting companies are permitted, and indeed encouraged, to regularly publish factual business information and forward-looking information such as earnings forecasts before and during an offering.

Underwriters of securities enjoy relatively broad safe harbours for research published before and during an offering, as long as the research reports are distributed in the regular course of business and research is not initiated on a company immediately prior to or during an offering. Research reports published in reliance on these safe harbours would be subject to Exchange Act liability under Rule 10b-5 (discussed further in section 7), but would not be subject to the heightened 'prospectus' liability under the Securities Act or Exchange Act. In addition, a broker-dealer not acting as an underwriter enjoys a safe harbour for any research that is published on Exchange Act reporting and non-reporting companies alike.

5.   LISTING

In general, in the United States, a company is required to 'register' with the SEC if it is listed on NASDAQ or the NYSE or if it has more than 500 investors. Registration will subject the company to the public disclosure and periodic reporting of the Exchange Act. It will also, pursuant to SOXA, subject it to most of the corporate governance and all auditor independence standards.

In practical terms, any company seeking to broadly access the liquidity of the US public markets must be listed. The initial public listing and registration processes can be (and usually are) done simultaneously. A company contemplating a listing must contact the stock exchange to arrange for the submission of a listing application and the signing of a listing agreement. Copies of these and other documents filed with the stock exchange must also be filed with the SEC. A listing application must contain, among other things, information about the issuer's business, organisation and financial history, a requirement that in most cases is satisfied by attaching a copy of a draft registration statement recently or simultaneously filed with the SEC. A listing agreement will require the company, among other things, to comply with various membership, conduct and corporate governance requirements of the stock exchange, as well as with US securities laws and regulations.

A company need not engage in an offering of securities to register and list shares on a national stock exchange. For example, a number of higher profile foreign private issuers having their primary listing outside of the US have listed on the NYSE or NASDAQ after registering treasury stock and/or stock option plans with the SEC. The requirement that a company become a 'registrant' once it has passed 500 investors was put into the law in 1964 in light of abuses where private companies were selling shares to large numbers of retail investors, and the public policy behind it is the mandate of investor protection, especially that of retail investors. Foreign private issuers not otherwise subject to the Exchange Act's reporting requirements, including those that have previously conducted private placements in the United States, may avoid these registration 'triggers' by maintaining a primary listing in one or more foreign markets and ensuring that English language versions of their home country reports are available on their Web sites or through an electronic information delivery system.

In order to 'deregister', until recently a company must have had fewer than 300 investors, or in the case of most foreign companies, fewer than 300 US investors. This numerical threshold, in the wake of SOXA, came as an unpleasant surprise to certain large foreign companies who decided that the benefits of a US listing no longer justified the increased regulatory expenses of SOXA. Following two years of extensive lobbying by foreign private issuers, industry groups and its European sister regulator, CESR, the SEC adopted reforms in 2007, allowing select foreign private issuers to deregister. Under the new rules, the 300 investor test has been retained as a default, but the conditions under which foreign private issuers could deregister have been significantly broadened. Any foreign private issuer listed on a foreign market that has been registered with the SEC for at least one year may exit the US public markets and the associated burdens of the Exchange Act if the average daily trading volume of its equity securities in the US is five per cent or less of the average daily trading volume of such securities in its primary trading market (defined as up to two foreign primary markets) during a recent 12-month period. Any potential 'deregistrant' must not have conducted a US public offering in the past year and has to undertake to publish English-language copies of its home country reports on the Internet.

6.   SECONDARY TRADING, PERIODIC REPORTING AND CORPORATE GOVERNANCE REQUIREMENTS APPLICABLE TO REGISTRANTS

Once a company has become a 'registrant' pursuant to the Securities Act (ie, by registering securities pursuant to an offering) or the Exchange Act (ie, by registering securities pursuant to a listing of securities on a national stock exchange), it becomes subject to the secondary trading, corporate governance and periodic reporting requirements under the Exchange Act.

6.1 Secondary trading

Like most countries, the US prohibits insider trading, selective disclosure and stock manipulation. These rules, widely accepted internationally, are intended to ensure market efficiency through 'information parity' and protect the investing public from the harm caused by its absence.

Insider trading rules prohibit individuals, whether or not they are affiliated with the company, from selling or buying stock if they are aware of material non-public information at the time of the transaction. The US insider trading laws, though still the subject of evolving judicial doctrine, are broader than those of many countries in that 'tippees' unrelated to the company may, in certain circumstances, be captured by the prohibition. Since insider trading in a stock can damage the company's reputation, especially where company insiders are the culprits, companies usually implement restrictive rules or 'trading plans' which govern when officers or directors may sell company stock. Regulation Fair Disclosure prohibits public companies from disclosing information selectively to analysts or any other market participants. Consequently, compliance departments of all listed companies work closely with management to ensure that material information, such as earnings releases or projections, are released simultaneously to market professionals and investors. Regulation M under the Exchange Act prohibits persons from directly or indirectly fraudulently manipulating the price of shares listed on a national securities exchange through market transactions and thereby misleading public investors as to the actual conditions of the public market for the security being distributed. Regulation M contains exceptions for certain stabilisation transactions effected in conjunction with an offering as long as all material information with respect to the plan of distribution for such securities is disclosed. Limited after-distribution ancillary stabilisation sales (pursuant to 'greenshoe' options) are also an accepted practice in US securities offerings. They are used primarily in initial public offerings and exercised only if the price of the securities in public trading following the offering exceeds the offering price. However, there remain key differences in other stabilisation practices between the US and the rest of the world, with various US disclosure rules essentially eliminating the practice in the US while it remains common and accepted for 30 days in the EU. Convergence of stabilisation practices and rules will be an ongoing challenge.

6.2 Corporate governance

No US securities regulation has created as much international controversy as SOXA, which, for the first time in the history of US securities regulation, switched the focus from disclosure in securities offerings to actual conduct of companies. Congress did not give itself much time to deal with the international consequences and the SEC, weakened by public stigma and leadership issues at a crisis moment, was unable to move the draft legislation or obtain an informal understanding that it could exempt foreign companies. The strength of the international reaction would lead an optimist to hope that the lessons have been learned, although an observer of recent Capitol Hill debates will note that Congressional memories are short. SOXA amended and added significantly to the corporate governance provisions of the Exchange Act, which were minimal before the corporate and accounting fraud scandals leading to SOXA's adoption.

Among other things, SOXA requires CEOs and CFOs of companies with securities registered in the US to certify the accuracy and completeness of information contained in the company's quarterly and annual reports and the maintenance of effective disclosure controls and procedures. The extent to which this certification requirement, largely and quickly accepted by US CEOs and CFOs, has stirred deep anxieties and resentments among executives from more collectivist countries is an interesting cultural study beyond the scope of this chapter. In addition, the SEC adopted rules requiring companies to maintain, evaluate and report on a system of disclosure controls and procedures. SOXA also imposed new restrictions on reporting companies, including requirements on the composition and operation of audit committees and outright prohibitions on the performance of certain non-audit services by external accountants. For listed companies, the NYSE and NASDAQ, as directed by the SEC, have adopted new corporate governance standards addressing a broad range of issues, including a requirement of majority-independent boards of directors and board committees, implementation of objective independence standards, the operation of audit committees and executive compensation. The SEC, which found itself hamstrung by Congress and the political environment, provided several exemptions and changes for foreign companies at the margins. However, many of the changes were deeply resented by foreign companies listed in the United States. Surprisingly, those that seemed most controversial at the outset, such as full independence of the audit committee and auditor independence standards, seemed quickly to lose steam in an international environment which was heading towards convergence in any event. The requirement that auditors attest the internal financial controls (section 404), and one initially underestimated, has become the most controversial and costly. The burdens imposed by some of these requirements, particularly section 404, have caused some foreign private issuers to question the benefits of listing in the United States and, along with the risk of litigation in the US, are widely considered to be the impetus behind the SEC's recent deregistration reforms as well as the main cause of the decline in the US stock exchanges' global competitiveness for new issuers.

To highlight the extent of SOXA's adverse impact on the competitiveness of US capital markets, since its adoption in 2002, the number of new cross-border listings on US exchanges has remained flat, while those on the London, Hong Kong and other developed market exchanges have grown steadily and significantly. For example, in 2005 only one of the world's 25 largest IPOs was listed on a US exchange, while US investments in the equity securities of non-US companies reached a record level that same year. The consequences of SOXA have appeared so quickly and been so severe that a number of congressmen, including those who voted for the law in the first place, have recently supported efforts to reform SOXA's most onerous provisions. Of particular note was an unsuccessful 2007 bill introduced by one US Senator to make section 404 optional for companies with market caps below $700 million (which would capture approximately two-thirds of the companies listed on US exchanges). While meaningful SOXA reform may be difficult in the immediate aftermath of the recent financial crisis, longer term prospects, driven by the need to regain competitiveness, are much brighter.

6.3 Periodic reporting

It now seems strange that the Depression-era makers of the US securities laws started first with the concept of the review of the sale of securities and only looked later at what has become the main event, continuing disclosure and transparency by public companies. The current emphasis on periodic reporting is not unusual internationally, as the EU Transparency Directive illustrates. More unusual is the scope of SEC review and comments on these disclosures. The SEC is extremely active in reviewing and commenting on public company periodic filings, including comments on the financial statements. Even so, there were criticisms that not enough reviews were being done and SOXA now requires that each public company be reviewed at least once every three years. It is apparent that Fortune 500 companies or companies in industries where there have been enforcement issues can expect targeted reviews. This shift in emphasis was part of the policy justification for the SEC 2005 reforms on the theory that reviews of WKSIs at the time of offering should not be necessary in light of the ongoing review cycle.

Under the Exchange Act, all registrants and most issuers must file periodic reports with the SEC. Recent legislation and rules have shifted the reporting requirements towards more real-time disclosure of specified material events. Listed registrants must also provide copies of their SEC-filed reports to the stock exchange. Registered US companies must file annual reports (on Form 10-K) and quarterly reports for the first three fiscal quarters (on Form 10-Q). Each report must contain information expressly required, plus all further material information so as to make the required information 'not misleading' in light of the circumstances under which it is disclosed.

Annual reports filed with the SEC require the disclosure of information that is essentially identical to that required by an initial Securities Act registration statement, including Management's Discussion and Analysis and, for US issuers, audited financial statements in accordance with US GAAP. Most registrants will have to file their annual reports within 60 days of their fiscal year end. Because many registrants prepare annual reports separate from their Forms 10-K and the Exchange Act proxy rules require that the proxy statement delivered to shareholders informing them of the annual meeting for the election of directors must be accompanied or preceded by an annual report including most of the information required by Form 10-K, many registrants incorporate material from the annual report into Form 10-K by reference and the annual report is filed as an exhibit to Form 10-K.

Quarterly reports on Form 10-Q need only be filed by US registrants and are essentially updates of information contained in the annual report. Quarterly reports must contain financial statements, although these do not have to be audited. They are an opportunity for registrants to disclose any other material information necessary to ensure that the quarterly disclosure, when read as an update on the annual report, is not misleading. Currently, most issuers must file quarterly reports on Form 10-Q within 40 days after the end of each of the issuer's first three fiscal quarters.

Additionally, registered US issuers must disclose a broad array of material information on an ongoing basis (8-K reports). A Form 8-K must be filed upon the occurrence of a specified event and may be filed voluntarily to disclose any other information the issuer judges to be material to the market or necessary to ensure compliance with secondary trading rules. In most cases, reports on Form 8-K must be filed within four business days of the occurrence of the specified event.

The system for foreign private issuers was set up over 25 years ago in an attempt to be deliberately inviting to foreign companies. Thus, on an annual basis, they have been required to file their Form 20-F six months after their fiscal year end, although this deadline will be accelerated to 120 days after a foreign private issuer's year-end for fiscal years ending on or after 15 December 2011. Notwithstanding these deadlines, any foreign company with an active shelf registration must now file the financial statements and much of the other information required by Form 20-F by the end of the first quarter to retain the possibility of issuing securities. The extent to which Form 20-F will wither as disclosures converge and as IFRS comes into use is a question that the SEC will have to address over the next few years. Form 20-F reflects the IOSCO principles and requires essentially the same disclosure as a Form 10-K, although there are various exceptions that take account of the registrant's home country disclosure regime, one of the most notable of which is the exemption from the SEC's extensive executive compensation disclosure requirements. As noted above, financial statements must be prepared in accordance with US GAAP, IFRS as issued by the IASB or home country GAAP reconciled to US GAAP.

The other key accommodation made to foreign companies was to exempt them from any US periodic reporting requirements and put in place a system of home country recognition of interim reports. Event-driven disclosure requirements are also more flexible with respect to foreign private issuers. Form 6-K is much more limited than Form 8-K in its event-driven disclosure requirements and requires additionally that a foreign company furnish to the SEC material information that it makes public at home.

7. SECURITIES LAW LIABILITY

The US securities laws impose liability for misstatements or omissions contained in the company's Securities Act registration statements or Exchange Act registration statements and reports, as well as for any manipulative or deceptive practices relating to the purchase or sale of securities. It is well known that class action securities litigation has become a major industry in the US. Consequently, companies and underwriters devote significant resources to factual, legal and accounting due diligence both in the context of an offering and also with respect to their annual and periodic reports.

7.1 Liability upon initial distribution

A unique feature of the US securities laws is that any purchaser of securities, whether in a public offering or in a private placement, has a 'put', ie, the right to sell the security back to the seller at the price it was purchased if there has been a violation of the public offering provisions or if there has been a material misstatement or omission in the offering document. In the case of a violation of the public offering provisions there is no defence, but in the case of a material misstatement or omission, any seller other than the company can escape liability by sustaining the burden of proof that it had conducted a reasonable investigation and could not know about the error. This self-enforcing provision has all the *in terrorem* effect on companies and underwriters that one might expect and has led directly to the custom of 'due diligence' by underwriters (an expression that appears nowhere in the US securities laws), and the delivery of disclosure opinions and comfort letters in initial offerings. Luckily, it also has a very short life as it can typically only be used for one year. It is critical for an understanding of this process, which has been largely and uncritically exported into legal systems with a very different structure of liability, to realise that the point of this investigation in US law is to create a record for a defence so that most players, other than the company, may escape liability.

With regard to public or registered offerings, the Securities Act also allows a buyer to recover damages for a decline in the value of a security for untrue statements of material facts and for omissions to state material facts in the prospectus and registration statement at the time that it becomes effective. The scope of those persons covered by potential liability is much wider in the US than in many other countries. It includes the company, certain officers such as the CEO, the CFO and the chief accounting officer, the company's directors, the underwriters and the company's accountants. Controlling shareholders (and control is a wide concept) can also be held liable. As a practical matter, an issuer has virtually no defence against such 'prospectus liability'. Other offering participants, such as directors, underwriters and controlling shareholders, have a 'due diligence' defence and can avoid liability by establishing that they conducted a reasonable investigation of the information contained in the registration statement and that, based on such investigation, they had reasonable grounds to believe and did believe that the statements were accurate and complete at the time the registration statement became effective. The standard of what is reasonable is that required of 'a prudent man in the management of his own property'. The SEC's 2005 reforms have not substantively changed these liability provisions, although they have rectified the perceived timing mismatch between the time at which a contract for the sale of securities is entered into and the time at which a final prospectus is available.

In connection with its 2005 reforms, the SEC clarified that one appropriate time at which to apply liability for material misstatements or omissions is the moment that a contract of sale is entered into or the 'time of sale', which, based on current investment banking and brokerage practices, typically occurs a substantial amount of time prior to the delivery of a final prospectus. In effect, the SEC made clear that any modifications, corrections or additions that are made available to investors after the time of sale (including updates in a final prospectus or registration statement) should not be taken into account for purposes of determining whether all material information has been made available to the investor. In facilitating the timely delivery of information to prospective investors, the SEC has liberalised the manner in which information could be delivered, providing for 'free writing prospectuses' that are subject to Securities Act liability, whether or not they are filed and irrespective of the time of filing.

7.2   Liability for ordinary trading

As a practical matter, companies have a much greater level of protection under the Exchange Act in their annual and periodic reports, which support secondary trading of their securities. A provision of the Exchange Act and the rule adopted under it – Rule 10b-5 – make unlawful the failure to disclose material facts or the use of false or misleading statements or any other manipulative or deceptive practices in connection with the purchase or sale of any security. Liability under this provision requires a finding of *scienter*, a Latin word not used in any other context in American English, which generally means an intent to deceive, manipulate or defraud, or reckless disregard for the truth. Unfortunately for companies with active shelf registrations, this distinction is not meaningful, as they must keep their shelves current by incorporating their Exchange Act filings by reference, thereby subjecting them to prospectus liability. Trading on inside information would constitute a manipulative or deceptive practice. Notably, because Rule 10b-5 regulates all securities transactions in interstate commerce, it applies to private placements, other exempt offerings and, in some cases, even transactions in foreign securities among non-US residents so long as the appropriate jurisdictional nexus exists. Dodd-Frank specifically extended that jurisdictional nexus, but only with respect to actions by the US or the SEC (as opposed to actions by private plaintiffs). In these actions, Dodd-Frank extends jurisdiction to conduct within the US that constitutes significant steps in furtherance of the violation (even if the securities transaction occurs outside the US and involves only foreign investors) as well as conduct occurring outside the US that has a foreseeable substantial effect within the US. Dodd-Frank also requires the SEC to conduct a study on whether a similar jurisdictional nexus should be extended to private plaintiffs, though few idea leaders are likely to support such a result.

8.   OTHER CONSEQUENCES OF TRANSACTING IN US-REGISTERED OR LISTED SECURITIES

8.1 Proxies

Any solicitation of proxies, consents or authorisations with respect to a security registered pursuant to the Exchange Act must be accompanied by a proxy statement containing certain specified information (the posting of such materials on the Internet is sufficient to satisfy the rule as long as shareholders are notified of such materials' availability). Practically all transactions in a registrant's voting equity securities by its officers, directors and 10 per cent holders must be reported to the SEC and the market. Foreign private issuers are exempt from these proxy and transaction reporting requirements. The acquisition by a registrant of its own equity securities is generally permitted under the Exchange Act as long as no manipulation is involved and all such transactions are disclosed in the registrant's annual report. Further, a person who acquires, directly or indirectly, the beneficial ownership of five per cent or more of a class of equity securities registered under the Exchange Act, including equity securities of a foreign private issuer, must report the acquisition to the company, the exchange where the security is listed and the SEC. Such report, in the form of a prescribed schedule, must be filed within 10 days after acquisition of such beneficial ownership.

8.2 Tender offers

A special system of rules under the Exchange Act governs tender offer practices in the United States. Under these provisions, any person who makes a tender offer to purchase, directly or indirectly, more than five per cent of an Exchange Act reporting company's securities must provide information to the SEC, the company, and, if applicable, the stock exchange. The information that must be included in a tender offer statement depends on whether an issuer or another person is conducting the tender offer, whether the tender offer is full or partial and whether cash or securities are being offered in consideration of the tender, but generally must include at least a summary term sheet, information about the subject company, the terms of the offer and the purposes of the transaction. As in any other securities offering, it is unlawful for any person to make any untrue statement of a material fact or omit to state a material fact or to engage in any fraudulent, deceptive or manipulative acts in connection with a tender offer. Because the SEC takes the position that any tender offer involving contact with the US is subject to its regulation, foreign companies seeking to acquire targets with even a minor US investor base have historically faced a myriad of decisions and regulatory requirements, even if the target company's securities are not registered with the SEC (foreign companies may be exempted from some, but not all, of the applicable rules).

   In an effort to expand the number of transactions made available to US shareholders, in 2008 the SEC reformed the tender offer rules so as to limit the applicability of the most onerous aspects of US regulations to transactions in which the US investor base was relatively significant. Under current rules, a tender offer for a foreign issuer target would be exempt from most (but not all) tender offer rules if less than 10 per cent of the target's shares (excluding shares held by the acquirer or the target) are held by US investors. If the exemption is not met, rules governing the conduct of tender offers often present challenges in coordinating with the applicable rules of other jurisdictions, such as the target's home country or the country of its primary listing. These rules include that a tender offer remain open for at least 20 business days, that consideration be paid within three business days of the close of the tender offer and that the target company publicly declare its position on the tender offer within 10 business days of its commencement. Certain tender offer conduct rules will apply even if the above exemption is met (ie, the requirement that US shareholders be treated equally to shareholders in all other jurisdictions and that no securities that are the subject of a tender offer be purchased outside the tender offer). There are many other complex rules governing the manner in which tender offers may be carried out which are beyond the scope of this brief introduction, although we note that the SEC has made efforts to specifically accommodate companies when it can. In addition, if a sufficient US investor base exists and securities of the acquiring company are to be used in consideration of tender, a specific registration statement for use in business combination transactions (which requires extensive disclosure on the acquirer and the target, including pro forma financial statements) must be filed, whether or not the acquirer and/or the target are SEC US-registered prior to the offering.

9. REGULATION OF MARKET PARTICIPANTS

Long a sleepy backwater in the international context, the regulation of market participants has, over the last few years, developed an increasingly international tone even as, at least in the US, the regulatory framework is yet to undergo a fundamental rethink in light of the increasing globalisation of the world's financial markets.

9.1 Broker-dealers
Brokers and dealers of securities in the US are subject to extensive regulation by the SEC, the Financial Industry Regulatory Authority (FINRA), other self-regulatory organisations and by the states. The global financial crisis has intensified the political scrutiny of the regulation of market participants and may lead to significant legislative and regulatory reform.

The Exchange Act generally requires each securities broker-dealer to register with the SEC, to become a member of the FINRA and the securities exchanges on which it intends to operate, and to register with state securities regulators in the states where it has offices or contact with public customers. Registered broker-dealers are subject to numerous regulations aimed primarily at protecting investors from securities fraud and abusive sales practices, including those relating to their net capital, record-keeping and reporting obligations, dealing with customers, control of securities in custody and marketing and trading practices.

In the world of Internet brokerage and cross-border exchange consolidation, the SEC rules on the interaction of foreign broker-dealers with US investors are in need of a substantial rethink and overhaul. Under current rules, a foreign broker-dealer can approach sophisticated US investors under very limited circumstances and most trades require the assistance of a US-registered 'babysitter' broker-dealer. It is virtually impossible for most retail investors to have direct access to a foreign broker-dealer (and thus enjoy decreased transaction costs), no matter how well regulated or solid. By sharp contrast, any US investor who physically travels abroad to open an account can do so. This regulatory situation is not stable and is most harmful to US retail investors that may not have the contacts or wherewithal to travel frequently abroad. It is to be expected that dealing with the appropriate conditions under which US retail investors may diversify internationally while enjoying the decreased transaction costs enjoyed by large investors should be an increasingly important item on the SEC's agenda, although initial reform efforts in this direction by the SEC have been sidelined as a result of the financial crisis.

9.2 Regulation of exchanges

The US stock exchanges are subject to extensive registration requirements and regulation and include within their functions a mandate to be a self-regulatory organisation. These regulations have been designed purely with the US domestic market in mind and there has been a long controversy about the ability of foreign exchanges or broker-dealers to have trading screens or other electronic access into the US without being subject to the full panoply of US regulation. That controversy is still on-going. In addition, the merger of the NYSE and Euronext generated much controversy, some rational but some irrational, about the extraterritorial impact of the US exchange regulations on a foreign exchange and foreign companies listed on that exchange. Ultimately, the relevant European regulators and the SEC were able to work out a framework for cooperation which required no legal changes but which calmed the controversy. It is certain that we have not seen the last of such incidents nor the need for more regulatory frameworks of cooperation.

9.3 Mutual funds and their investment advisers

Mutual funds and their investment advisers face regulation by the SEC on multiple fronts, including pursuant to two distinct statutory regimes: the Investment Company Act and the Investment Advisers Act.

Under the Investment Company Act, an entity that is in the business of investing, re-investing or trading in securities and owns, or proposes to acquire, investment securities having a value exceeding 40 per cent of its total assets, such as most mutual funds, is an 'investment company' subject to regulation by the SEC. Unless an exemption applies, an investment company must register with the SEC by filing a detailed form describing its investment objectives, policies and restrictions.

The Investment Company Act imposes corporate governance, capital structure and market conduct requirements on registered mutual funds.

Most registered mutual funds are required to have boards of directors, at least two-fifths of whom are independent. The Investment Company Act also generally requires that sales and redemptions of redeemable shares of mutual funds be at a price based on the fund's net asset value, places restrictions on the types of investments that can be made by registered mutual funds and imposes strict limits on mutual fund transactions with affiliates.

The Investment Advisers Act requires that all persons providing investment advice to clients register with the SEC as 'investment advisers', unless they are specifically exempt. If the client is a registered investment company, however, no exemption is available and the adviser must register with the SEC. Whether or not registered, all investment advisers are subject to the anti-fraud provisions of the Investment Adviser's Act and owe their clients a series of fiduciary duties, including, but not limited to, the duty to recommend suitable investments based on the clients' financial situation, investment experience and investment objectives and the duty to allocate investment opportunities amongst clients in a fair and equitable fashion. Registered investment advisers are subjected to further requirements, such as reporting, record-keeping and disclosure requirements, as well as marketing and contractual fee restrictions under the Investment Advisers Act. Moreover, registered investment advisers are subject to examination by the SEC.

9.4 Hedge funds and their investment advisers

Hedge funds and their investment advisers historically operated pursuant to certain exemptions under the Investment Company Act and the Investment Advisers Act, respectively, and thus were commonly perceived to be 'unregulated' by the SEC. Notwithstanding these exemptions, however, the activities of hedge funds and their advisers, like those of mutual funds and their advisers, are subject to a host of additional regulatory regimes, including the Securities Act, the Exchange Act and the Commodity Exchange Act.

Most hedge funds rely on one of two exemptions under the Investment Company Act. The first exemption is for funds sold to fewer than 100 people. The second is for funds sold to certain sophisticated investors called 'qualified purchasers'. Both exemptions require that there be no public offering of the fund. Ensuring compliance with these exemptions is critically important for hedge funds because, among other considerations, being subjected to the Investment Company Act would significantly limit their ability to pursue many of the highly-leveraged investment strategies they tend to favour.

Many advisers to hedge funds currently rely on an exemption from the Investment Advisers Act for advisers with 15 or fewer clients. Dodd-Frank eliminates this exemption as of 21 July 2011, meaning that advisers that are unable to find a different exemption to rely on will have to register with the SEC. The new exemptions adopted pursuant to Dodd-Frank will generally be substantially narrower, applying to a limited group of foreign private fund advisers, advisers that act solely as advisers to venture capital funds, advisers that act solely as advisers to private funds and have less than $150 million in assets under management in the US and certain advisers that manage less than $100 million in assets. Under Dodd-Frank, advisers relying on registration exemptions applicable to venture capital fund advisers or private fund advisers with less than $150 million in assets under management in the US will be subject to reporting requirements, albeit at a more limited level of disclosure than that required of registered advisers, according to proposed SEC rules.

The 'Volcker Rule' enacted under Dodd-Frank, will, subject to a transition period and certain exceptions, restrict the ability of banks and their affiliates, to invest in and sponsor private funds and to engage in prime brokerage and other transactions with funds sponsored or advised by the banks or their affiliates. Private funds designated as systemically important by the Financial Stability Oversight Council (FSOC), a new inter-agency body, will be subject to additional regulation by the Federal Reserve. Such regulation must include, among other provisions, liquidity requirements, resolution plan (aka 'living will') and credit exposure report requirements, stress tests, concentration limits and bank-type capital requirements, and may include contingent capital requirements, short-term debt limits and other requirements as the Federal Reserve deems appropriate. FSOC may also recommend additional regulation for certain risky activities, even if the funds or firms engaging in such activities are not systemically important.

Given the perceived impact of hedge funds on market volatility in the aftermath of the recent financial crisis, it remains to be seen whether hedge funds succeed in preserving their unique characteristics in light of more stringent regulation.

10. CONCLUSION

US securities regulation has long had an extraterritorial component that was at times the subject of controversy abroad. Recently, in part as a result of SOXA, the burdens of the random lottery of US class action litigation and the increasing competitive weight of non-US capital markets, the effects of this extraterritoriality have come under closer scrutiny domestically, especially among public and private sector securities law practitioners. The fact that this scrutiny is being applied at a time when a record number of US investors are choosing to leave the 'investor protections' of US securities regulations behind them is an irony that has not been lost on many domestic or foreign observers.

This chapter is a brief overview of complex and lengthy laws and regulations. Readers are encouraged to read it in that spirit.

Contact details

FOREWORD
Willem J L Calkoen
NautaDutilh NV
Weena 750
3014 DA Rotterdam
The Netherlands
T: +31 10 224 00 00
F: +31 10 414 84 44
E: willem.calkoen@nautadutilh.com
W: www.nautadutilh.com

AUSTRALIA
Robert Hanley
Mallesons Stephen Jaques
3rd Floor
10 Old Broad Street
London, United Kingdom
EC2N 1DW
T: +44 20 7496 1717
F: +44 20 7496 1755
E: robert.hanley@mallesons.com
W: www.mallesons.com

BELGIUM
Benoît Feron, Marie-Laure De Leener
NautaDutilh NV
Chaussée de La Hulpe/
Terhulpsesteenweg 120
B-1000 Brussels
Belgium
T: +32 2 566 80 00
F: +32 2 566 80 01
E: benoit.feron@nautadutilh.com
E: marielaure.deleener@nautadutilh.com
W: www.nautadutilh.com

BRITISH VIRGIN ISLANDS
Jacqueline Daley-Aspinall,
Ross Munro
Harneys
Westlaw Chambers
PO Box 71, Road Town
Tortola, VG1110
British Virgin Islands
T: +1 284 494 2233
F: +1 284 494 3547
E: jacqueline.daley@harneys.com
E: ross.munro@harneys.com
W: www.harneys.com

BULGARIA
Svetlina Kortenska
Borislav Boyanov & Co.
82, Patriarch Evtimii Blvd.
Sofia 1463, Bulgaria
T: +359 2 805 50 55
F: +359 2 805 50 00
E: s.kortenska@boyanov.com
W: www.boyanov.com/

CANADA
Alfred L J Page, David R Surat, Andrew M Bunston
Borden Ladner Gervais LLP
Scotia Plaza, 40 King Street West
Ontario Canada
M5H 3Y4
T: +416-367-6000
F: +416-367-6749
E: apage@blg.com
E: dsurat@blg.com
E: abunston@blg.com
W: www.blg.com

ENGLAND & WALES
Robert Boyle & Mark Slade
Macfarlanes LLP
20 Cursitor Street
London EC4A 1LT
England
T: +44 20 7831 9222
F: +44 20 7831 9607
E: robert.boyle@macfarlanes.com
E: mark.slade@macfarlanes.com
W: www.macfarlanes.com

EU
Petra Zijp, Larissa Silverentand,
Willem Verschuur & Elvira de Jong
NautaDutilh
Strawinskylaan 1999
1077 XV Amsterdam
P.O. BOX 7113
1007 JC Amsterdam
The Netherlands
T: +31 20 717 10 00
F: +31 20 717 11 11
E: petra.zijp@nautadutilh.com
E: larissa.silverentand@nautadutilh.com
E: willem.verschuur@nautadutilh.
com
E: elvira.dejong@nautadutilh.com
W: www. nautadutilh.com

FINLAND
Paula Linna, Elisa Heinonen & Essi
Rimali
Roschier
Keskuskatu 7 A, 00100
Helsinki, Finland
T: +358 20 506 6000
F: +358 20 506 6100
E: paula.linna@roschier.com
E: elisa.heinonen@roschier.com
E: essi.rimali@roschier.com
W: www.roschier.com

FRANCE
Antoine Maffei & Guillaume Touttée
De Pardieu Brocas Maffei
57, avenue d'Iéna
CS 11610
75773 Paris Cedex 16,
 France
T: +33 1 53 57 71 71

F: +33 1 53 57 71 70
E: info@pardieu.net
W: www.de-pardieu.com/

GERMANY
Dr. Wolfgang Groß, Dr. Thomas Paul
Hengeler Mueller
Bockenheimer Landstraße 24
D-60323 Frankfurt am Main,
Germany
T: +49 69 17095-122
F: +49 69 17095-7120
E: thomas.paul@hengeler.com
E: wolfgang.gross@hengeler.com
W: www.hengeler.com/

IRELAND
Stephen Hegarty
Arthur Cox
Earlsfort Centre, Earlsfort Terrace
Dublin 2
Ireland
T: +353 1 618 0000
F: +353 1 618 0618
E: stephen.hegarty@arthurcox.com
W: www.arthurcox.com

ITALY
Marcello Gioscia, Gianluigi Pugliese
Ughi e Nunziante
Via Venti Settembre, 1
00187 Rome, Italy
T: +39 06 474831
F: +39 06 4815912
E: m.gioscia@unlaw.it
E: g.pugliese@unlaw.it
W: www.unlaw.it

JAPAN
Kunihiko Morishita
Anderson Mōri & Tomotsune
Izumi Garden Tower, 6-1
Roppongi 1-chome, Minato-ku
Tokyo 106-6036, Japan
T: +81-3-6888-1040
F: +81-3-6888-3040
E: kunihiko.morishita@amt-law.com
W: www.amt-law.com/

LUXEMBOURG
François Warken & Laurence van
Zuylen
Arendt & Medernach
14, rue Erasme
L-1468 Luxembourg
Luxembourg
T: +352 40 78 78-216
F: +352 40 78 04
E: francois.warken@arendt.com
E: laurence.vanzuylen@arendt.com
W: www.arendt.com/

THE NETHERLANDS
Arjan J J Pors, Fleur S M van Tilburg,
Lotte van de Loo & Pim Heemskerk
NautaDutilh NV
Weena 750
3014 DA Rotterdam
The Netherlands
T: +31 10 224 00 00
F: +31 10 414 84 44
E: fleur.vantilburg@nautadutilh.com
E: lotte.vandeloo@nautadutilh.com
E: arjan.pors@nautadutilh.com
W: www.nautadutilh.com

PORTUGAL
Ricardo Andrade Amaro
& Diana Ribeiro Duarte
Morais Leitão, Galvão Teles, Soares
da Silva & Associados, Sociedade de
Advogados
Rua Castilho, 165
1070-050 Lisboa – Portugal
T: +351 21 381 7400
F: +351 21 381 7499
E: ramaro@mlgts.pt
E: drd@mlgts.pt
W: www.mlgts.pt

RUSSIA
Alexey Andrusenko, Tatyana Boyko,
Nikita Gurin, Daria Izotova, Julia
Kulyamina, Elena Kuznetsova,
Valentin Osipov, Alexander
Rudyakov, Nadezhda Rybinskaya,
Irina Skidan, Alexey Vasilyev &
Uliana Volina
Egorov, Puginsky, Afanasiev &
Partners

Bolshaya Ordynka Street, 40/3
Moscow 119017
Russia
T: +7 495 935 8010
F: +7 495 935 8011
E: irina_skidan@epam.ru
W: www.epam.ru

SOUTH KOREA
Je Won Lee & Mark B Rolfson
Lee & Ko
18th Floor
Hanjin Main Building
118, Namdaemunno 2-Ga, Jung-gu
Seoul, Korea 100-770
T: +82 2 772 4000
F: +82 2 772 4001
E: jwl@leeko.com
E: mbr@leeko.com
W: www.leeko.com

SPAIN
Javier Ybáñez, José Luis Palao
J&A Garrigues, S.L.P.
Hermosilla, 3
28001 Madrid
T: +34 91 514 52 00
F: +34 91 399 24 08
E: javier.ybanez@garrigues.com
E: jose.luis.palao.iturzaeta@garrigues.
com
W: www.garrigues.es

SWEDEN
Ola Åhman, Mattias Friberg &
Malin Karvonen
Roschier
P.O.Box 7358
SE-103 90 Stockholm
Sweden
T: +46 8 553 190 00
F: +46 8 553 190 01
E: mattias.friberg@roschier.com
E: malin.karvonen@roschier.com
E: ola.ahman@roschier.com
W: www.roschier.com

SWITZERLAND
Martin Lanz, Lorenzo Olgiati &
Philippe Borens
Schellenberg Wittmer
Löwenstrasse 19/P.O. Box 1876
8021 Zurich
Switzerland
T: +41 44 215 5252
F: +41 44 215 5200
E: lorenzo.olgiati@swlegal.ch
E: philippe.borens@swlegal.ch
E: martin.lanz@swlegal.ch
W: www.swlegal.ch

USA
John B Meade, Jake S Tyshow
Davis Polk & Wardwell
450 Lexington Avenue
New York, NY 10017
United States of America
T: +1 212 450 4000
F: +1 212 701 5800
E: john.meade@davispolk.com
E: jake.tyshow@davispolk.com
W: www.davispolk.com